Werner Gephart (Ed.)
In the Realm of Corona Normativities

GEFÖRDERT VOM

Bundesministerium
für Bildung
und Forschung

Series of the
Käte Hamburger Center for
Advanced Study in the Humanities
»Law as Culture«

Edited by Werner Gephart

Volume 23

Werner Gephart (Ed.)

In the Realm of Corona Normativities

A Momentary Snapshot of a Dynamic Discourse

VITTORIO KLOSTERMANN
Frankfurt am Main · 2020

recht als kultur
käte hamburger kolleg
law as culture
center for advanced study

Bibliographische Information der Deutschen Nationalbibliothek

Die Deutsche Nationalbibliothek verzeichnet diese Publikation in der Deutschen Nationalbibliographie; detaillierte bibliographische Daten sind im Internet über *http://dnb.dnb.de* abrufbar.

1. Auflage 2020

© Vittorio Klostermann GmbH · Frankfurt am Main · 2020
Alle Rechte vorbehalten, insbesondere die des Nachdrucks und der Übersetzung. Ohne Genehmigung des Verlages ist es nicht gestattet, dieses Werk oder Teile in einem photomechanischen oder sonstigen Reproduktionsverfahren oder unter Verwendung elektronischer Systeme zu verarbeiten, zu vervielfältigen und zu verbreiten.
Gedruckt auf alterungsbeständigem Papier ⊗ ISO 9706
Satz: mittelstadt 21, Vogtsburg-Burkheim
Umschlaggestaltung: Jörgen Rumberg, Bonn
Umschlagabbildung: Werner Gephart, Corona-Leviathan.
A Reverence to Thomas Hobbes (46 × 35,77 cm, digital collage with the assistance of Michelle Chlup), 2020.
Druck und Bindung: docupoint GmbH, Barleben
Printed in Germany
ISSN 2193-2964
ISBN 978-3-465-04531-1

Foreword

The following volume aims to provide a snapshot of the current corona crisis: from gradual astonishment to ironic distancing to total insecurity to latent outrage. From the radical shutdown of social life and its successive abolition to the setbacks and successive recovery of civil liberties, freedom of movement, professional freedom, freedom of religion, freedom of assembly, artistic freedom, etc.

I must extend my gratitude to the wonderful authors who, in the shortest possible time, almost as if by acclamation, magically responded to the invitation to comment on the pandemic from their specific regional and disciplinary experiences with regard to the normative dimension of crises. Without the tireless efforts of Jure Leko, who was responsible of the volume's organization, it would not have been possible to coordinate 50 contributions from all over the world within a few weeks. I would also like to thank Carina-Nora Bockard, Sergio Genovesi, Theresa Hanske, and Felix Leven for their invaluable help researching the topics at hand and adapting submissions to the publisher's stylesheet. Our publisher, Vittorio Klostermann, has supported the project with great enthusiasm in every respect from the start. Lastly, I would like to express appreciation to Candice Kerestan, who lent the language skills of her mother tongue as far as this was possible in a very short period of time.

The extent to which the project might also have fulfilled a self-therapeutic function during lockdown will become clear later. But there is no doubt that swiftly »shutting down« the normative achievements of modernity and replacing them with a new type of normativity represents a civilizational break. The modest aim of this book is thus to bring more clarity into this new realm of the normative and its *Kulturbedeutung* for the human condition.

Werner Gephart   Bonn, June 21, 2020

Contents

WERNER GEPHART
Introduction: The Corona Crisis in the Light of the Law as Culture
Paradigm 11

I. Socio-Juridico Reflections

MARIACARLA GADEBUSCH-BONDIO / MARIA MARLOTH
Clinical Trials in Pandemic Settings: How Corona Unbinds Science 29

THOMAS DREIER
»Law as Culture« in Times of Corona 41

JACQUES COMMAILLE
In a Troubled World: A New System of Knowledge about Law? 61

MAURIZIO FERRARIS
Mobilization 67

MARKUS GABRIEL
We Need a Metaphysical Pandemic 71

LAURENT DE SUTTER
The Logistics of Pandemic 75

JURE LEKO
At the Borders of Europe. On Spatial Mobility during the Covid-19
Crisis 81

DIETER GOSEWINKEL
Corona and the Legal Barriers of National Border Restrictions 95

OLIVIER BEAUD ET CÉCILE GUÉRIN BARGUES
L'état d'urgence sanitaire : était-il judicieux de créer un nouveau régime
d'exception? 103

MARTIN SCHERMAIER
Morals Suspend Law. How the Call for Solidarity Casts a Shadow on Law   119

ANGELA CONDELLO
Immersed in a Normative Laboratory 129

II. Corona Normativities

JAN CHRISTOPH SUNTRUP
Corona: Biopolitical Models and the Hygiene of Tact 137

FRANCESCA CAROCCIA
Searching for a Vaccine. Rethinking the Paradigm of (Private) Law
in Times of Pandemic Crisis 147

GIANMARIA AJANI
Possible Effects of the Pandemic Emergency on the Internal Coherence
of EU Law 159

MATTHIAS HERDEGEN
The Corona Crisis: Challenges for the Socio-Cultural Underpinnings of
Constitutional and EU Law 169

UPENDRA BAXI
International Law and Covid-19 Jurisprudence 179

MATTHIAS LEHMANN
Legal System Reactions to Covid-19: Global Patterns and Cultural Varieties 183

VALENTINO CATTELAN
Sacred Euro: Sovereign Debt(s) and EU's Bare Credit in the Corona Crisis 195

THERESA STROMBACH
Stay (At) Home – A Linguistic View on Imperatives in Times of Crisis ... 209

THERESA HANSKE
Knigge in Times of Corona – Recognition, Attentiveness and Esteem 215

SANJA BOJANIĆ / PETAR BOJANIĆ
The »Vocabulary« of Distance 221

III. In the Global Realm of Normativity

RAJA SAKRANI
Religious Co-narration of Corona 233

SAM WHIMSTER
Discovering Society in a Time of Plague 241

MARTA BUCHOLC
The Corona Crisis as a Test of National Habitus: The Imperative of
Obedience 251

CAROLINE OKUMDI MUOGHALU
Igbo Culture and the Coronavirus Pandemic Social Distancing Order of the
Nigerian Government on a Collision Course: Reflections on Law as Culture   257

HELGA MARIA LELL
»Law as Culture« in Argentina's Emergency Context   267

SERGIO GENOVESI
»Support Your Local«: The Ethics of Consumption and the Coronavirus
Pandemic   281

HAMADI REDISSI ET AL.
La Tunisie face au Covid-19. Penser ensemble, agir de concert   287

MASAHIRO NOGUCHI
Cluster-Based Approach and Self-Restraint: Japan's Response to Covid-19 ..   297

DIANA VILLEGAS
Les mafias en temps de pandémie   301

JOACHIM J. SAVELSBERG
Balancing Rights and Responsibilities during a Pandemic: Individuals,
States, and Views from the United States of America   313

IV. Art and Culture in the Times of Covid-19

VALÉRIE HAYAERT
Shallow Graves and Empty Tombs: The Architecture of Death under the
Chinese Concept of *Tianxia*   325

ENRICO TERRONE
The Death of Art by Covid-19   331

MARTIN PRZYBILSKI
Imagining Infection and Dealing with Diseases in Jewish Law   339

ALEXANDRE VANAUTGAERDEN
The Return of the Corpses. »Nosferatu – Phantom der Nacht«
(Werner Herzog) and Illness as a Metaphor   345

ANNE-MARIE BONNET
Aren't So-Called Conspiracy Theories the Most Influential Art of Our Time?   355

BEATRIZ BARREIRO CARRIL
Challenges to Coronavirus Crisis: A Cultural Rights Approach in the
Spanish Context   369

GRISCHKA PETRI
Masking the Invisible / Segments of Political Space 375

FRODE HELMICH PEDERSEN
A Pandemic of Narratives 409

V. No Lesson on the Lesson? Or: »In the Name of Corona«?

PETER GOODRICH
Zoonoses 421

GRETA OLSON
Being in Uncertainty: Thinking the Coronavirus Pandemic 425

AMEL GRAMI
Trapped: Women and Domestic Violence in »Corona Time« 433

PIERRE BRUNET
Nous sommes la raison du virus 443

YOUSRA ABOURABI
A Global Warning on the Global Warming? The Effects of the Corona
Crisis on the Perception of Environmental Norms 451

CLEMENS ALBRECHT
Viral Coupling – Society's Fight for Survival 465

TIZIANA ANDINA
»It's Just a Flu« – What We Can Learn from Our Mistakes 469

GREGOR ALBERS
Personal Sacrifices for Public Health? Doubts on Interfering with Liberty
to Protect Life 479

ALEXANDER F. FILIPPOV
States, Bodies and Corona-Crisis: Sociological Notes to Pandemic 487

MARTIN ALBROW
Has Covid-19 Brought Globalization to an End? 497

RICHARD MÜNCH
With the Corona Pandemic into the Governmentality of the Present? 503

WERNER GEPHART
Conclusion: »Communal« Dimensions of the Corona Crisis and the Rise
of a New Validity Culture 509

About the Authors 519

Werner Gephart

Introduction: The Corona Crisis in the Light of the Law as Culture Paradigm

The corona crisis is met with reflection from experts – especially noticeable in official statements, TV show debates, and podcasts related to the natural sciences – upon which political decision-makers rely. And, at the same time, the power to »define« events has shifted into the sphere of science. It is becoming increasingly clear, however, that value-based decisions are at stake – decisions which are fundamental in nature and call for ethical and cultural-scientific consideration. A cultural-scientific perspective on this all-encompassing crisis in the light of the Law as Culture paradigm can be found in the following debate, which was sparked by a call for contributions and is being continued by successive texts from the Center's former Fellows and friends. From the outset, it was important that the Center address current issues using a research perspective that is rooted in the fundamentals. As such, the normative requirements and consequences of the Arab Spring gained special attention early on at conferences and in publications,[1] problems of normative pluralism were discussed in the context of circumcision,[2] questions of material justice were raised in debates about the restitution of stolen Jewish property,[3] as were provocative inquiries about a legal aesthetic that is reflected in courthouses, films about courts, and portrayals of Justitia. We also discussed the cultural significance of masks at the Art Museum Bonn when they had masks on exhibit,[4] and we pondered the normative requirements of the *flâneur*,[5] a type of movement that, when done in large numbers, is currently penalized in many places.

---

[1] Cf. Al-Azm: Civil Society and the Arab Spring; Gephart/Sakrani/Hellmann (eds.): Rechtskulturen im Übergang.

[2] Cf. Gephart: Constitution as Culture.

[3] Cf. also the project of the Rose Valland Institute, an artwork by Maria Eichhorn.

[4] Cf. Panel discussion on the exhibition in the Art Museum Bonn: *Maske – Kunst der Verwandlung* (June 2, 2019) – a cooperation between the Art Museum Bonn and the Center »Law as Culture«.

[5] This has been the unexpected outcome of our discussion at the Art Museum Bonn, dramatically proven right during the corona crisis when visitation of museums and the innocent *flâneur* were forbidden! In the general context, cf. Panel discussion on the exhibition in the Art Museum Bonn: *Der Flaneur als soziologische Figur der Moderne* (January 13, 2019) – a cooperation between the Art Museum Bonn and the Center »Law as Culture«.

Modernity has not only established itself in a confrontation with nature and in various forms of communicative self-assurance, but it has come to express itself in its normative dynamics: Revolutions are defined by breaking from given normative orders and replacing them with new ones – the act of which, however, is met by restorative counter-movements. Crises of modernity unfold in the ›realm of normativity‹. And sociology emerges as a science of crisis that, especially in Durkheim's work, analyzes the structural change of modernity as a dynamic of its development from repressive to restitutive normative orders; views ›anomie‹, or ›normlessness‹, as a fundamental ill of misguided modernity; and blames individuals' struggles to bond with others as the cause behind rising suicide rates.[6]

Even though Weber devotes great methodological effort into differentiating between empirical and normative validity, the basis of social order – namely the avoidance of a Hobbesian state of nature »where life is poor, nasty, brutish, and short« – can be found with Weber in the orientation towards an at least collectively imagined normative order. Of course, ›validity cultures‹ vary among societies and civilizations and, to this extent, their crisis scenarios also differ. This is recognizable, for example, in world wars and the ensuing cultures of martial law, as well as in the handling of financial crises. In such normative crises, an *Ausnahmezustand*, or state of emergency, is declared. It is impossible to imagine the realm of normativity without this ›exception‹. On both the left and the right, the protagonist of the state of emergency, Carl Schmitt, is quoted: He still attempts to give a legal form to both the ›a-juridical‹ and the history of validity of the state of emergency,[7] as examined by Giorgio Agamben, which he typologically introduces to the source of charismatic, anti-legal rule *per auctoritas* thoroughly in the sense of Weber.[8] Here, however, neither the ›actual‹ nor the ›fictive‹ nor even the ›intended‹ state of emergency of constitutional theory is meant, but rather the extraordinary ›mode of validity‹ of law, morality, custom, decorum, and lifestyle that is encapsulated in the overarching concept of the *normative complex*. This basic orientation becomes clearer when reminded of the main elements of the Law as Culture paradigm.

---

[6] For this context, cf. Gephart: On Law and Religion; see also Gephart / Witte (eds.) The Sacred and the Law.
[7] Cf. Schmitt: Politische Theologie; see also Schmitt: Der Begriff des Politischen.
[8] Cf. Agamben: Homo Sacer; see also Agamben: Ausnahmezustand.

Some Rules of the Law as Culture Paradigm[9]

FIRST RULE:

Legal facts are to be analytically broken down into a symbolic, normative, ritual, and organizational dimension.
The Center's past work has been shaped by the fruitful and novel insight that a *multidimensional concept of law*[10] – which can steer one away from the constrictions of a purely juridical-occidental self-description as an order of norms by capturing a *symbolic* dimension of representation and an appeal to what is right and just in representative symbols – allows room for effervescent forces like anger and revenge to be tamed in the ritualization of procedures and bundles deontic forces in court organization and legal community. This multidimensional concept of law also guides the inclusion of cultural studies.

The consequences of an expanded concept of law for juridical reception research are dramatic: only those who identify the concept of law with legal text as a linguistically formed normative construct are able to insist on questions of translation adequacy or expect that the nominal insertion of a legal concept or legal institution could easily impact the respective legal culture.[11] As soon as the deontic force is drawn not only from a linguistically bound belief in norms, but a symbolic dimension supporting the *force du droit* (Pierre Bourdieu), and the ritual dynamics and organizational power are added, a dimension of social practice that transcends the literal sense comes into play when understanding the interaction between legal cultures!

SECOND RULE:

Both genetically and structurally, ›law‹ bears a special relationship with ›religion‹ and thus requires constant consideration of the difference between the sacred and the profane.
The presumption that ›law‹, even in modernity, only acquires its concrete form through its opposition to ›religion‹ could only be strengthened in individual research papers[12] and colloquia.[13] Enigmas of the modern constitutional state's

---

[9] Cf. esp. Gephart: Einführung. A brilliant extension of the paradigm, done mainly by introducing a narrative dimension and transferring it into a multidimensional analysis of conflicts of legal cultures by Jan Suntrup: Umkämpftes Recht.

[10] Cf. Suntrup: Das Faktum des Rechtspluralismus.

[11] For translation concerns, cf. Renn: Übersetzungsverhältnisse.

[12] Cf. Al-Azm: Civil Society and the Arab Spring; Gephart/Sakrani/Hellmann (eds.): Rechtskulturen im Übergang; as well as Sakrani: The Law of the Other.

[13] Cf. »Recht und Religion in soziologischer Perspektive« – a Conference of the DGS-Sektionen Rechts- und Religionssoziologie at the the Center »Law as Culture« (June 6–7, 2013) or Philipp Stoellger's presentation »Deutungsmacht und Deutungsmachtkonflikte zwischen Recht und Religion: Ergebnisse eines Forschungsprojektes« as part of the Forum »Law as Culture« (July 10, 2012).

deontic power cannot simply be solved by referring to civil-religious foundations. However, following traces of lost sacrality[14] in law is not only due to religious melancholy, but also contributes to enlightenment about the dangerous illusion of secularism, which supposedly bid farewell to the sacred. Whether as a perspective of alienation, as real reason for validity, or as a structural elective affinity, the religious-sociological view of law (and its environments) leads to important insights.

Here, too, consequences for reception research are undeniable: precisely because our kinship with the religious sphere puts us on the trail of *the identity-forming role of law*, it is evident that the reception of the law of others is subject to a *reservation of identity* from the outset. If too many terms are incorporated, a feeling of normative alienation, of an impending loss of identity, arises and different strategies of asserting identity are mobilized. Finally, an analysis of the religious components of a particular legal culture would also indicate how difficult it is to assess transferal burdens and cultural inertia. Therefore, it seems indispensable to take the religious environment of the respective legal cultures into account for paths of reception and modalities. The adoption of a substitute's legal institution for the adaptation forbidden in Islamic law, namely the Kafela,[15] is a fine example of this.

THIRD RULE:
Only when law is removed from particular and local contexts of validity and is understood as a transnational normative force of movable judicioscapes or arbitrary transnational norm-setting can it also be conceived of as ›global‹.
It is simply naïve to formulate the relatively late historical special product of the *nation-state as a universal production site of law*. The fact that local, national, and transnational normative orders are intertwined, that *judioscapes* are spreading, that they are not hierarchical and are not placed next to each other in the same order, but rather are interwoven in the multi-level model, only proves that we must pay greater attention to the *fact of globality* in legal analysis – not least by cutting through vertical connections of derivation and validity in order to pay greater attention to competitors for validity, which is irritating for the lawyer.

These considerations represent something like the unspoken *premise of unbiased reception research* that does not consider the reception space as closed, but rather as open. And that means that any exchanges, interactions, and cultural contacts always also have a normative side, in which reliability and expectability (between rulers and those ruled, colonizers and those colonized, victors and vanquished, and all the competitors) occur for normatively correct law. Determining who is the bearer of the reception process – whether law professors, lawyers, or

---

14 Cf. Gephart: On Law and Religion.
15 Cf. Gephart/Sakrani: »Recht« und »Geltungskultur«.

imperial powers who prescribe the reception as an octroi – depends on the respective historical circumstances.

FOURTH RULE:
Overlap, mix-ups, clashes, and collisions of normative orders take place both within and beyond the nation-state. These conflicts of legal culture deserve greater attention.

FIFTH RULE:
The law not only has an underlying relationship to religion and politics, but is also closely bound to the aesthetic sphere. Legal analysis as cultural research cannot omit this level without ending up in a dangerous legal aesthetic or even legal kitsch. The aesthetic dimension of legal acts cannot be denied: legal style, the art of abstraction, analytical power, elegant jurisprudence. It is suspect to us as an aestheticization in fascism and totalitarianism that veils power or even glorifies violence. The fact that laws are admittedly in a hidden relationship – with literature in its narrative dimension, with sculpture in its Laconian dimension, with the fine arts in their representational power, with music in its extraordinary ability to detach itself from representation and the representable as a power of abstraction, borrowing its performative power from the theatrical, etc. – makes the spherical relationship of law and art interesting for reception research as well.

Should theater cultures, the rhetoric of law, and differences in ›legal styles‹ caused by legal culture not influence whether and how a legal concept, an institute, a legal illusion, or an idea of truth is framed contradictorily, inquisitorially, narratively or transported by the ›spirit of the laws‹? Wouldn't sensitivity to the role of aesthetics in the respective global relationship be necessary, not only to be able to compare, but also to sensuously grasp the aesthetics inherent in the reception of the ›foreign‹?

SIXTH RULE:
This relatively stable paradigmatic core sums up the epistemological, globalizing, religion-oriented, and aesthetic practice-inclusive perspectives on law. At the same time, it bears unique potential for comparative research.
The idea of an analysis and typification of *validity cultures* that is at odds with legal cultural analysis has been met with great response.[16] The analysis of validity cultures can concern the normative complex's structural characteristics and demands semantics of validity of different validity cultures, their symbolic, ritual forms, and guarantees of order. It investigates the logic of understandings of validity and dissent, fictions of validity, and validity gaps in their normative orders, and it attempts to determine the normative power of a particular validity culture.

[16] Ibid.

The importance of the problem of comparison was formulated not least by Émile Durkheim, who is particularly respected at our Center: »la méthode comparative est la seule qui convienne à la sociologie«.[17]

About the Volume

In the light of this basic orientation, our questioning deals with the specific mode of validity thriving on the pathos of the ›exception‹, which counters the banality of the ›normal‹, an exception that tends to be »normalized« at the risk of smoothening its very specific deontic power! As an extra-judicial decision-making power, it clings to the illusion of normative form in order to place the *totality* of normative orders under a single premise of validity for that which is extraordinary; the decision-making power to suspend normative orders appears as an impersonal institution of war[18] – or the pandemic as we now know it worldwide, including criticism towards unresponsive people who do not understand what ›exception‹ means – in order to frame ›real life‹ as a deadly ritual ›vitalism‹ of wartime propaganda or recommend the remedy of social abstinence by way of physical distancing. Using the coronavirus pandemic as an example, it will be illustrated how the normative dynamics and normative implications of a societal crisis, which I understand as a *Gemeinschaftskrise*, can be analyzed fruitfully from the perspective of the Law as Culture paradigm.[19]

The structure of the volume is oriented as such: it begins with general socio-juridico reflections (I.) before attempting to trace the peculiarities of its proper ›corona-normativity‹ (II.), which unfolds in a global realm of normativity with all its contradictions (III.). Finally, it examines the role of culture and the arts in the pandemic, as a lost place of reflection or new space of critique (IV.), and takes up the much-discussed question of whether we are able to learn something from this crisis or should rather refuse to do so (V.).

I. Socio-Juridico Reflections

Mariacarla Gadebusch-Bondio's and Maria Marloth's contribution begins with a special sensitivity for the relationships between epidemiological and virological knowledge and the lack of knowledge for political decision-making processes from

---

[17] Durkheim: Les règles de la méthode sociologique, p. 153.
[18] It is no wonder that Maurizio Ferraris uses the warrior-like metaphor of ›mobilization‹ in his wonderful essay which bears the same title, Mobilization, in this volume.
[19] Cf. esp. Gephart: Einführung.

the perspective of the medical humanities.[20] While Thomas Dreier has his sights firmly set on the Law as Culture paradigm,[21] the view of a new realism, as shaped by Maurizio Ferraris, illuminates the crisis's potential to mobilize,[22] as we know, for example, from observations of World War I. Markus Gabriel subsequently presents a disputed metaphysical meaning of the crisis[23] – which Slavoj Žižek[24] denies – before Laurent de Sutter unveils the subtle logistics of the pandemic.[25] Jure Leko[26] and Dieter Gosewinkel[27] then shed light on the obvious problematization of the social and political demarcation of an infection that ignores borders. While Angelo Condello reveals that we find ourselves in an enormous laboratory of normativities – which we want to use with this volume –,[28] Olivier Beaud and Cécile Guérin Bargues show the inner logic of an »état d'urgence sanitaire« from the perspective of French constitutional law in an exemplary way.[29] And Martin Schermaier, irritated by the fact that in the eternal question of the relationship between positive law and substantive justice morality seems to gain the upper hand in the context of corona regulation,[30] is met by Jacques Commaille, who sees principal opportunities for a new knowledge of the law.[31]

II. Corona Normativities

How do upper limits, as seen with gatherings of 1,000, 100, or two people (*pas de deux*) or two-meter distances for entry into stores, gain their own self-evident *normative power*, and which roles do the natural sciences play in this? What are the paradoxical effects of the standardization of culturally determined distances, which Argyle analyzed in social psychology and which are now being held responsible for the different speeds at which the illness spreads in the Global North and South? In places where family solidarity does not exist anyway, the occurrence of infection is less dramatic. Comparative family sociology teaches us, of course, how simple and misguided these images of family are, especially if we look at Italy.

Corona normativities span customs, recommendations, normative orders, and severely sanctioned behavior, such as not wearing a mask or coming too close to

---

[20] Cf. in this volume Gadebusch-Bondio / Marloth: Clinical Trials in Pandemic Settings.
[21] Cf. in this volume Dreier: »Law as Culture« in Times of Corona.
[22] Cf. in this volume Ferraris: Mobilization.
[23] Cf. in this volume Gabriel: We Need a Metaphysical Pandemic.
[24] Cf., e.g., Žižek: Pandemic!
[25] Cf. in this volume de Sutter: The Logistics of Pandemic.
[26] Cf. in this volume Leko: At the Borders of Europe.
[27] Cf. in this volume Gosewinkel: Corona and the Legal Barriers of National Border Restrictions.
[28] Cf. in this volume Condello: Immersed in a Normative Laboratory.
[29] Cf. in this volume Beaud / Guérin Bargues: L'état d'urgence sanitaire.
[30] Cf. in this volume Schermaier: Morals Suspend Law.
[31] Cf. in this volume Commaille: In a Troubled World.

someone. The range of possible reactions – from social disapproval to surveillance by the police – indicates a normative pluralism in the realm of normativity and a fascinating interpretation of rules by the subjects to the law: shop owners and others who feel they are victims of such regulation express their discomfort with the rules. Theresa Strombach has thus reserved an explicitly linguistic take on this phenomenon.[32] In his contribution, Gianmaria Ajani raises the question of whether the corona experience will require a new era of European normativity, the time before *and* after the crisis.[33] Upendra Baxi, who is known for founding the human rights complex on the idea of ›suffering‹, is instead focused on whether the obligation to protect people equally from disease, as formulated by different legal documents in international law, will be sufficiently be respected.[34] Can a kind of *Corona-Knigge*,[35] as Theresa Hanske claims in her article, be observed that should be analyzed according to manner books of the 18th century?

At the other end of the spectrum of normativities, we find the normative order of illegal organizations like mafias, masterly studied by Diana Villegas.[36] Contrary to initial judgement, the crisis has increased the space of illegal orders. Though border closures have hindered the trafficking of drugs and other illegal goods, this has opened new opportunities to provide illegal pharmaceutical products, masks, and hydroxycloroquine. In addition, the old-fashioned way of delivering drugs and pizza found new grounds in the imposed nutrition system. And – as we know from other crises and events where the state is inefficient and gangs are the guarantors of protection – the mafia becomes a safeguard of social order. Therefore, the Brazilian Minister of Health emphasized the necessity to collaborate. In this sense, the pandemic crisis has, according to Villegas, not only potentialized spaces of illegal action, but also led to a crystallization of normativities.[37]

Without meaningful explanations, the uncertainty generated by the pandemic can hardly be endured. Which roles do *religious patterns of meaning and justification* play in the process? The financial crisis revealed, for example, how the biblical metaphor of the Great Flood plays a central mythological role.[38] Doesn't economic globalization take on such a role if the coronavirus is interpreted as a punishment for the crimes of globalization? And how do religious systems deal with their greatest strength, namely the ability to create ›community‹ through ritual and communication, when authorities close holy places of worship? (We know that in Arab countries, mosques have been exempted from communications restrictions;

---

[32] Cf. in this volume Strombach: Stay (At) Home.
[33] Cf. in this volume Ajani: Possible Effects of the Pandemic Emergency on the Internal Coherence of EU Law.
[34] Cf. in this volume Baxi: International Law and Covid-19 Jurisprudence.
[35] Cf. in this volume Hanske: Knigge in Times of Corona.
[36] Cf. Villegas: L'ordre juridique mafieux.
[37] Cf. in this volume Villegas: Les mafias en temps de pandémie.
[38] Cf. Gephart: Implosion von Wirtschaft, Politik und Religion.

in the Occident's European societies, funerals were all that remained of religious communitization, and these restrictions are only going to be relaxed very slowly.)

Yet religious communities fight for their re-entry into the public sphere. A comparative analysis of how religious communities are reacting to having this core of religious life, that is ceremonies and rituals, taken away is put forward by Raja Sakrani.[39] She insists on the religious narrative of the corona crisis, while Greta Olson enlarges the narrative component to questions of narrative ethics, namely to resist »the desire for narrative closure«.[40] Olson reminds us of the role of »dystopic post-apocalyptic fictions and games« that prepared a whole generation for the pandemic.[41] Frode Petersen's contribution is particularly interesting in this respect because he explores, by way of a narrato-critical analysis of the narrative, Sweden's response from the perspective of a Norwegian. He also warns of the sequent master narrative of a looming massive global economic repression »resulting in widespread unemployment, increased poverty rates and the real possibility of violent social unrest in many countries«.[42] I would like to add that September 11 had a similar effect on our visual memory: Was it not the movie *Independence Day* that foreshadowed the events and gave a surrealistic touch to the apocalyptic imagery? In the end, I would like to hear a hypothesis that the corona crisis itself has a sacred dimension ... because what is most relevant for the distinction between the sacred and the profane in Durkheim's sense is someone or something becoming taboo, untouchable, not apt to laughter: *nicht-comedian-fähig*.[43] The phrase of the day, as I am writing this introduction, is: »Berühren erlaubt« with regard to elderly people in nursing homes. This means that the inverse process of »opening« – the *Lockerung* of the lockdown, deconfinement – represents a sort of re-profanation of the sacred sphere of untouchability. Peter and Sanja Bojanić have deeply looked into this »vocabulary« of distance by making use of Foucault and Simmel.[44]

III. In the Global Realm of Normativity

But what exactly is meant by *globality* in the event of a pandemic?[45] The discourse, the medialization, the contagion as such, the infection's democratic character that appears to strike royal houses and slums equally? What kind of *global community*

---

[39] Cf. in this volume Sakrani: Religious Co-narration of Corona.
[40] Cf. in this volume Olson: Being in Uncertainty, cit. p. 431.
[41] Ibid., cit. p. 430.
[42] Cf. in this volume Pedersen: A Pandemic of Narratives, cit. p. 416.
[43] Cf. Gephart/Witte: The Social, the Sacred and the Cult of Law.
[44] Cf. in this volume Bojanić/Bojanić: The »Vocabulary« of Distance.
[45] With reference here to the very much adored Mary C. Douglas, cf. in this volume Whimster: Discovering Society in a Time of Plague.

was created when international organizations started refusing any further support from the U.S. government as a kind of punishment? Are slums affected in the same way as gated communities in South America or India? Is the spread of the disease more democratic than its curing? What are the patterns of risk distribution in this crisis? Is status a determining factor in being a victim of the disease as a current research in Germany tells us?[46] And what does it mean for standards and expectations to global health justice? Should we understand the exact similarity of lockdowns in France and Germany or substitutes for teaching like e-learning on campuses from Moscow to New York, Bonn to Marseille as an effect of globality? Is Matthias Lehmann right in saying that the »[n]ation-state is definitely having a come-back. It was never really gone but now forcefully demonstrates again its power«?[47] This corresponds by the way to a former observation by Jürgen Habermas, namely that the nation-state – despite all of globalization's effects – remains the main power for upholding and enforcing human rights![48] Insofar a global risk community is opposed by nation-protecting communities supposedly safeguarding their people from infection by the stranger. Borders gained a new symbolical meaning, denying in a way the Schengen Convention in Europe. Special attention has therefore been cast on legal barriers of national border restrictions by Dieter Gosewinkel,[49] and Jure Leko has focused on spatial mobility in Europe during the corona crisis.[50] But »has Covid-19 brought globalization to an end?« remains the question that one of the founders of globalization theory, namely Martin Albrow, replies to in a negative way: We have to distinguish the categories of »totalization« and »globalization« that allowed the specific event of a »total-global« moment in the world.[51]

Given the considerable tension between normative universalities and particular trends in global societies, it can be asked to what extent social-cultural factors play a role in the different patterns of spread. It also begs the question of whether the respective ways of reacting – the case of Argentina is revealed by Helga Lell[52] in a thorough description – are somehow related to collective patterns of overcoming fear, ›stances on the world‹ based on active involvement, or diverging health economies that are derived from different understandings of social policy. Herd

---

[46] Cf. Deutscher Gewerkschaftsbund: Corona-Krise verstärkt soziale Ungleichheit.
[47] Cf. in this volume Lehmann: Legal System Reactions to Covid-19, cit. p. 186.
[48] Cf., e. g., Habermas: Die Krise der Europäischen Union im Lichte einer Konstitutionalisierung des Völkerrechts, fn. 79; see also Habermas: Die Einbeziehung des Anderen.
[49] Cf. in this volume Gosewinkel: Corona and the Legal Barriers of National Border Restrictions.
[50] Cf. in this volume Leko: At the Borders of Europe.
[51] Cf. in this volume Albrow: Has Covid-19 Brought Globalization to an End?
[52] Cf. in this volume the profound article by Lell: »Law as Culture« in Argentina's Emergency Context.

immunity[53] politics against individual protection or the protection of risk groups, such as the elderly or immunocompromised, or strategies of tracing by way of apps and a perfect registration of contact in restaurants and universities? Not to forget the deep clashes between cultures beyond the religious line of demarcation, which Caroline Okumdi Muoghalu explaines in the context of Nigeria.[54]

Coping with uncertainty and fear, as Raja Sakrani rightly points out, is the basis of religiously-impregnated worldviews.[55] How to absorb uncertainty by way of more or less transparency, or a strategy of hiding, has been a lesson in the German-French dialogue after Tschernobyl that took place exactly 34 years ago. As if the contaminated clouds would have magically stopped at it borders, no danger semantics were expressed in France. Germany, however, excelled in keeping children away from their sandpits; no mushrooms should be collected in the German forest, etc. The newly founded Centre Ernst-Robert Curtius at the University of Bonn is reflecting on scientific study to compare the reactions and perceptions of the current crisis in Germany and France. Jacques Commaille[56] and Olivier Beaud (together with Cécile Guérin Bargues) have opened a wide spectrum of questions with regard to the normative implications and problematic nature of creating a new type of emergency, namely: »L'état d'urgence sanitaire: était-il judicieux de créer un nouveau régime d'exception?«[57] Martin Przybilski's contribution »Imagining Infection in the Babylonian Talmud« is not only a further example of how to conceive this type of crisis in a religious context, but also most revealing and a basis for further comparative analysis.[58] Masahiro Noguchi has shown that Japan's cluster strategy for managing the pandemic can be better understood by looking at the meaning of traditional concepts like *Tatemashi* and *Jishuku*.[59] This seems to be particularly relevant for a new wave of awaited studies on resilience – if we pay more sophisticated attention to the specific cultural context! Even if this cultural context shines through in the contribution by Hamadi Redissi and other representatives of the Observatoire du changement sociale (ODCC) in Tunis – a post-revolutionary situation with a party system that does not accept joint responsibility, religious tensions, or extreme inequality structures that are reinforced by the crisis – systematic analysis is at the same time helpful for understanding one's own situation.[60] Although we recently became aware of Minnesota for quite different reasons – namely the murder of George Floyd and the subsequent un-

---

[53] In his piece, Thomas Dreier also touches upon this complex question; cf. in this volume Dreier: »Law as Culture« in Times of Corona.
[54] Cf. in this volume Muoghalu: Igbo Culture and Corona Virus Pandemic.
[55] Cf. in this volume Sakrani: Religious Co-narration of Corona.
[56] Cf. in this volume Commaille: In a Troubled World.
[57] Cf. in this volume Beaud/Guérin Bargues: L'état d'urgence sanitaire.
[58] Cf. in this volume Przybilski: Imagining Infection and Dealing with Diseases in Jewish Law.
[59] Cf. in this volume Noguchi: Cluster-Based Approach and Self-Restraint.
[60] Cf. in this volume excellent article by Redissi et al.: La Tunisie face au Covid-19.

rest — the analyses by our local cosmopolitan expert, colleague, and friend Joachim Savelsberg about a »peacetime emergency« in Minnesota are illuminating![61] The moral sociologist formulates an urgent appeal for a »careful balancing between different types of rights and between rights and responsibilities«.[62]

IV. Art and Culture in the Times of Covid-19

Camus's plague, Kleist's earthquake, Jünger's wars, and Dante's inferno are represented in the respective media culture's *phantasmagorias*: from theater to sculpture, painted pictures to negative utopias of film. How does an aesthetic reflection of the crisis develop, which, in symbolic representations, can hardly be denied its own *viral aesthetic*?[63] ›Corona kitsch‹ cannot be overlooked when multiples of Beethoven are decorated with colorful face masks. Grischka Petri has taken the challenge by looking deeply into the human history of masking and linking it to the image of the plague doctor, as well as to the symbolic denominator for a virus and a monarch, which gives more plausibility for the choice of the covering image.[64] But convincing and valid artwork will be created sooner or later! While Enrico Terrone pleads for »the death of art by Covid-19«, Anne-Marie Bonnet seems to take the augmented awareness for our way of living, even for the »human condition«, as a kind of aesthetic experience urged by relating to the present, imposing a kind of *présentisme*, and rethinking ›otherness‹. From her analysis, I have learned that the current crisis pushes all of us to become artists, comparable to Joseph Beuys's slogan: »Wir alle sind Künstler«. However, Bonnet not only puts in question the existence of an institutionalized and de-differentiated autonomous art world, but also expects changes in art as a production system of symbolical capital.[65] Beatriz Barreiro Carril rather puts her hope into the legal dynasty of cultural rights, which are enshrined in both the Spanish Constitution and in the respective UN Convention (ESCR).[66] Especially when one pursues a non-conventional concept of ›culture‹ that includes indigenous legal cultures and cultural rights, a wide field of new questions opens up that have not yet been addressed in this volume ...

---

[61] Cf. in this volume Savelsberg: Balancing Rights and Responsibilities during a Pandemic, cit. p. 316.

[62] Ibid., cit. p. 320.

[63] Cf. in this volume the ground-breaking philosophical reflection by Terrone: The Death of Art by Covid-19. On the structural relationship between law and the arts, see Gephart/Leko (eds.): Law and the Arts.

[64] Cf. in this volume Petri: Masking the Invisible / Segments of Political Space.

[65] Cf. in this volume Bonnet: Aren't So-Called Conspiracy Theories the Most Influential Art of Our Time?

[66] Cf. in this volume Barreiro Carril: Challenges to Coronavirus Crisis.

V. No Lesson on the Lesson? Or: »In the Name of Corona«?

The question can be raised whether we – at least for a certain period of time – should review all of our actions in the various spheres of society to ensure that we act in accordance with the demands the pandemic has induced. Put more exaggeratedly: Do politics, law, economics, art, and culture now take place *in the name of corona*? And what logic of action unfolds in the process? How will statistical assessments of the pandemic's suspected development and the protection of risk groups, which are prioritized over other factors such as economic stability, individual security, etc., be acknowledged? How can the once prevailing ›gerontic discourse of justification‹ be characterized more precisely? How can we avoid falling into the trap of ›triage choices‹? How can we preserve fundamental structures of the rule of law without denying the reality of a pandemic threat that also reveals a kind of *effet pervers*, the Anthropocene character of climate change?

Some answers may be found in the following articles that past, present, and future Fellows, friends, supporters, and collaborators have provided for this volume in the spirit of the Law as Culture paradigm. Whether there is a lesson to be learned, however, must be answered very differently: In a linguistic tightrope act, Peter Goodrich evokes a »wild jurisprudence« that breaks free from the fetters of the past and looks to the future, recovering the lost spatiality of law and acknowledging the embedding of *homo juridicus* in a natural cosmos.[67] Yousra Abourabi likewise insists on the unexpected positive impact of anti-corona measures on an endangered environment,[68] and Pierre Brunet searches for new categories for an anthropomorphic worldview of jurists, in which a ›natural law‹ on nature does not yet have space.[69] And Alexander Filippov,[70] as well as Martin Albrow[71] and Richard Münch,[72] each accentuate different consequences of understanding our *condition humaine* as a new future orientation, present-ism, or even a new *Gehäuse der Hörigkeit* (badly translated as »cage of enslavement«), as Max Weber put it.[73] He died of a pandemic, the Spanish flu, exactly 100 years ago.

---

[67] Cf. in this volume Goodrich: Zoonoses, cit. p. 423.
[68] Cf. in this volume Abourabi: A Global Warning on the Global Warming?
[69] Cf. in this volume Brunet: Nous sommes la raison du virus.
[70] Cf. in this volume Filippov: States, Bodies and Corona-Crisis.
[71] Cf. in this volume Albrow: Has Covid-19 Brought Globalization to an End?
[72] Cf. in this volume Münch: With the Corona Pandemic into the Governmentality of the Present?
[73] Cf. Weber: Wirtschaft und Gesellschaft, p. 835.

References

Agamben, Giorgio: Ausnahmezustand, Frankfurt am Main 2004.
Agamben, Giorgio: Homo Sacer: Sovereign Power and Bare Life, Stanford, CA 1998.
Al-Azm, Sadik J.: Civil Society and the Arab Spring, in Werner Gephart / Jan Christoph Suntrup (eds.): Rechtsanalyse als Kulturforschung II. Frankfurt am Main 2015, pp. 243–255.
Deutscher Gewerkschaftsbund: Corona-Krise verstärkt soziale Ungleichheit, 26.05.2020; https://www.dgb.de/themen/++co++6bf77ed6-9f34-11ea-9db2-525400e5a74a; last accessed 22.06.2020.
Durkheim, Émile: Les règles de la méthode sociologique, Paris 1894.
Gephart, Werner: Constitution as Culture. Constitutional Universalism and Pluralism of Legal Culture. Inauguration of the Year's Theme »Law and Politics«, Working Paper, November 2016.
Gephart, Werner: Einführung. Das ›Recht als Kultur‹-Paradigma, in: Werner Gephart / Jan Suntrup (eds.): Recht als Kulturforschung II, Frankfurt am Main 2015, pp. 7–18.
Gephart, Werner: Implosion von Wirtschaft, Politik und Religion. Krisenanalysen, in: Georg Pfleiderer / Alexander Heit (eds.): Sphärendynamik II. Religion in postsäkularen Gesellschaften, Baden-Baden 2012, pp. 75–101.
Gephart, Werner: On Law and Religion: Durkheimian Theoretical Perspectives and Some Applications, Frankfurt am Main 2021 (forthcoming).
Gephart, Werner / Jure Leko (eds.): Law and the Arts. Elective Affinities and Relationships of Tension, Frankfurt am Main 2017.
Gephart, Werner / Raja Sakrani: »Recht« und »Geltungskultur«. Zur Präsenz islamischen Rechts in Deutschland und Frankreich, in: Werner Gephart (ed.): Rechtsanalyse als Kulturforschung, Frankfurt am Main 2012, pp. 103–137.
Gephart Werner / Raja Sakrani / Jenny Hellmann (eds.): Rechtskulturen im Übergang – Legal Cultures in Transition, Frankfurt am Main 2015.
Gephart, Werner / Daniel Witte (eds.): The Sacred and the Law: The Durkheimian Legacy, Frankfurt am Main 2017.
Gephart, Werner / Daniel Witte: The Social, the Sacred and the Cult of Law: Some Introductory Remarks on the Durkheimian Legacy, in: Werner Gephart / Daniel Witte (eds.): The Sacred and the Law: The Durkheimian Legacy, Frankfurt am Main 2017, pp. 7–30.
Habermas, Jürgen: Die Einbeziehung des Anderen: Studien zur politischen Theorie, Frankfurt am Main 1996.
Habermas, Jürgen: Die Krise der Europäischen Union im Lichte einer Konstitutionalisierung des Völkerrechts – Ein Essay zur Verfassung Europas, in: Zeitschrift für ausländisches öffentliches Recht und Völkerrecht (ZaöRV), 72, 2012, pp. 1–44.

Renn, Joachim: Übersetzungsverhältnisse. Perspektiven einer pragmatistischen Gesellschaftstheorie, Weilerswist 2006.

Sakrani, Raja: The Law of the Other. An Unknown Islamic Chapter in the Legal History of Europe, in: Rechtsgeschichte, 22, 2014, pp. 90–119.

Schmitt, Carl: Politische Theologie – Vier Kapitel zur Lehre von der Souveränität, Berlin 2015.

Schmitt, Carl: Der Begriff des Politischen, Berlin 2018.

Suntrup, Jan: Das Faktum des Rechtspluralismus und die Konturen einer mehrdimensionalen kulturwissenschaftlichen Rechtsanalyse, in: Werner Gephart / Jan Christoph Suntrup (eds.): Rechtsanalyse als Kulturforschung II, Frankfurt am Main 2015, pp. 115–141.

Suntrup, Jan: Umkämpftes Recht. Zur mehrdimensionalen Analyse rechtskultureller Konflikte durch die politische Kulturforschung, Frankfurt am Main 2018.

Villegas, Diana: L'ordre juridique mafieux. Étude à partir de l'organisation criminelle colombienne des années 1980 et 1990, Paris 2018.

Weber, Max: Wirtschaft und Gesellschaft, 5th ed., Tübingen 1980.

Žižek, Slavoj: Pandemic! COVID-19 Shakes the World, New York 2020.

I. Socio-Juridico Reflections

Mariacarla Gadebusch-Bondio / Maria Marloth

Clinical Trials in Pandemic Settings: How Corona Unbinds Science*

> »There has never been so much knowledge of our ignorance.«
> Jürgen Habermas[1]

1. The Pandemic Scenario

The speed with which the novel coronavirus SARS-CoV-2,[2] the pathogenic agent of the lung disease Covid-19, is spreading globally has put society and science under enormous pressure. Increasing numbers of people around the world are falling victim to the disease caused by the virus, which is why effective measures to slow its spread require careful consideration, rapid decision-making and implementation. On the one hand, the scientific knowledge is currently fragmentary,[3] on the other hand, on the political level there is a moral imperative to protect life. Action must therefore proceed in the face of relative ignorance.

Very little is known about the pathogen.[4] Evidence of this is provided by the abrupt changes of course by political decision-makers – i.e., from trivializing the virus to accepting the danger, and from the vision of achieving herd immunity by allowing the spread of infection to the lockdown of entire cities. Revisions and corrections of initial assessments have added to the uncertainty among the population. The dystopia of an infection spreading rapidly across the globe with lethal consequences for thousands of people – recalling the thriller Contagion (2011) – now appears to have become a reality.[5] The collective imagination, stirred up by

---

* A short version of this article in German was presented in Gadebusch-Bondio / Marloth: Die »historische Studie« SOLIDARITY als Antwort der Forschung auf die Sars-CoV-2 Pandemie.

1 »So viel Wissen über unser Nichtwissen gab es noch nie«, in: Habermas: Interview by Markus Schwering; transl. by the authors.

2 The family of corona viruses was identified in the mid-1960s. This includes a number of pathogens that usually infect either humans or animals, more rarely both. In the case of SARS-CoV (Severe Acute Respiratory Syndrome), MERS-CoV (Middle East Respiratory Syndrome) and the novel coronavirus (SARS-CoV-2: Severe Acute Respiratory Syndrome-2), coronaviruses previously infected animals and were then transmitted to humans (zoonoses). Cf. German Federal Ministry of Health: Basiswissen zum Corona-Virus.

3 Cf. Ioannidis: In the Coronavirus Pandemic.

4 Cf. Paules et al.: Coronavirus Infections.

5 Films about pandemics belong to the genre of disaster films. While »The Seventh Seal« by

the media, is haunted by the specter of historical epidemics. The Spanish flu of 1918/1919 is readily evoked for comparison.[6] In March 1918, the infection first broke out at Camp Funston in Kansas, USA, and in the following weeks spread across several military facilities in the midwestern and southeastern states. As a result of the transport of American troops to Europe during World War I, the virus was able to spread swiftly through Europe. In July 1918, initial hopes of overcoming this wave of flu were dashed, when in August the first cases of a new form of the disease were detected in Brest, from where it spread by sea around the world and back to North America.[7] This second wave claimed many more lives than the first. It is believed that the virus had meanwhile undergone genetic mutation.[8] The American cities of Philadelphia and St. Louis were also struck by this second wave. The way in which they responded to the danger was markedly different – and it is precisely this which is of particular interest from today's perspective on Covid-19. While Philadelphia downplayed the appearance of the first cases in the city and did not take preventive measures to contain the spread of the disease, opting instead to allow a public parade to take place, St. Louis issued far-reaching restrictions two days after the first cases were recorded. Philadelphia reacted with similar decrees only two weeks after the outbreak of the disease. As a result, the Spanish flu claimed significantly more lives in Philadelphia than in St. Louis.[9]

Of the many societies affected by Covid-19, some have decided to implement measures to slow down the spread of the virus, some have delayed. Regional and national approaches vary widely. The spectrum ranges from calls to reduce social contact to complete curfews. Such measures are intended to give health care systems sufficient time to prepare for the care of the burgeoning numbers of those afflicted by the disease. On top of this is the mounting expectation that researchers will arrive at a scientific breakthrough within the shortest possible time. This places them under extreme moral pressure.

How is the international research community reacting to this historic challenge? What strategies promise to lead quickly to a therapeutic treatment for SARS-Covid-2? What are the epistemic and ethical implications of the medical-political emergency?

We wish to pursue these questions in the following, in which we present the SOLIDARITY study launched by the WHO.

Ingmar Bergman (1957) historically deals with the plague in the Middle Ages, a series of dystopian depictions of pandemic outbreaks have been produced since the 1990s. Examples include: »Outbreak« by Wolfgang Petersen, USA 1995; »Twelve Monkeys« by Terry Gilliam, USA 1995; »The Last Days« by David and Alex Pastor, Spain 2011; »Contagion« by Steven Soderbergh, USA 2011.

[6] See for example Smith: Think Social Distancing for Coronavirus Is Overkill?
[7] Cf. Patterson/Pyle: The Geography and Mortality of the 1918 Influenza Pandemic.
[8] Ibid.
[9] Cf. Hatchett et al.: Public Health Interventions and Epidemic Intensity.

2. Rethinking Research in Outbreak Settings

The pandemic expert, US virologist Anthony S. Fauci and his co-authors understand SARS-CoV2 as:

»a stark reminder of the ongoing challenge of emerging and reemerging infectious pathogens and the need for constant surveillance, prompt diagnosis, and robust research to understand the basic biology of new organisms and our susceptibilities to them, as well as to develop effective countermeasures.«[10]

If medicine is to be clinically effective, it must have reliable data and robust evidence. Equally, society and politics depend on scientific evidence to legitimize the sometimes drastic strategies for mitigation or suppression of virus spread.[11] This state of affairs dynamizes and accelerates research. It also provokes a lively process of critical, interdisciplinary discussion coupled to rapidly circulating scientific information, which is difficult even for experts to evaluate, thus causing further uncertainty.[12] Even science journalists complain about the *breathless* condition in which, paradoxically, they are expected to explain things that cannot yet be explained. Added to this, maintaining critical distance is scarcely possible given their personal involvement.[13] Virologists and epidemiologists are among the main actors not only in the scientific, but also in the socio-political and media arenas. However, their role in the public sphere is deeply ambivalent. They are required to communicate complex knowledge in an accessible way, to deal with gaps in knowledge in a transparent manner, and guard against the deceptive facticity of numbers.

Under these exceptional circumstances, medical research has a dual objective: 1. to understand the properties of the novel SARS-CoV-2 and the mechanisms of the disease triggered by it on a biomolecular, infectiological, and immunological level, and 2. to develop therapeutic approaches, and ultimately a vaccine, on this basis. In the context of the pandemic, however, this is associated with a tension between the demand for high research standards (robust research) and the need for rapid development of an effective therapy that is almost impossible to resolve.

The established evidence regime for the quality assurance of preclinical and clinical studies to test the effect and tolerability of potential therapies is very time consuming. Even in the preclinical phases, numerous active substances fail. The

---

[10] Fauci et al.: Covid-19.
[11] Cf. Ferguson et al.: Report 9.
[12] One example is the transmission simulation model developed by epidemiologists at Imperial College, London, Ferguson et al.'s ›Report 9‹, which was published on 16 March. A critical response to this simulation study came from Shen et al. one day after its release. Shen et al.: Review of Ferguson et al.
[13] Cf. Brost/Pörksen: Angesteckt.

complete development of a new drug would take years. In a situation in which thousands of people the world over are dying of Covid-19, healthcare systems and societies are crashing, and doctors are compelled to use triage models to allocate life-saving resources, this time is simply not available. The urgency of the situation forces us to seek alternative, shorter-term solutions. While in politics this attitude is associated with protective measures that entail more or less restrictive limitations on freedom, the normative constraints have been loosened for scientific quality assurance. To this end, the research community is pursuing two strategies in addition to the efforts to develop a vaccine: on the communication level and on the study design level.

The first strategy is the WHO response to the challenge as *Public Health Emergency of International Concern (PHEIC)*,[14] which was later classified as a *pandemic*. Research is to be supported by *data sharing* and access to relevant research data even before publication. The *International Committee of Medical Journal Editors* endorses this initiative.[15] Many publications will be available even before they have gone through a peer review process. A critical evaluation of the literature must therefore be carried out by the readers, which entails increased personal responsibility. The idea is to provide collective and cooperative access to data and preliminary results. Finally, the unimpeded flow of all this data promises a more comprehensive understanding of the disease itself and allows for the development and adaptation of ongoing research to be accelerated. An integral part of this accelerated, *open* scientific exchange is a willingness to compromise, operating on the basis of ever-changing data sets, and to accept public criticism and correction. Similarly, political and social decision-making processes can be progressively adjusted. Validated evidence is already being made available in well-known databases, such as the Chochrane Library[16] or the Oxford Covid-19 Evidence Service of the Oxford Centre for Evidence-Based Medicine.[17] Many medical journals have special sections on Covid-19 that are updated daily (i.e. NEJM, Lancet, etc.). This acceleration of communication is proving to be increasingly problematic in two domains: at the interface between science and media and between science and politics.[18] Scientists have been thrust into the limelight alongside politicians. Among other things, they report on preliminary results and ongoing studies. This carries with it the risk of a skewed response.

The second strategy is the SOLIDARITY clinical trial. On 27 March 2020, the Director-General of the WHO, Tedros Adhanom Ghebreyesus, announced the start of SOLIDARITY with the following words:

[14] Cf. World Health Organization: R&D Blueprint and COVID-19.
[15] Cf. Moorthy et al.: Data Sharing for Novel Coronavirus (Covid-19).
[16] Cf. Chochrane Library: Coronavirus (COVID-19).
[17] Cf. Centre for Evidence-Based Medicine: Oxford COVID-19 Evidence Service Information.
[18] Cf. Brost/Pörksen: Angesteckt.

»One of the most important areas of international cooperation is research and development. A vaccine is still at least 12 to 18 months away. In the meantime, we recognize that there is an urgent need for therapeutics to treat patients and save lives. Today we are delighted to announce that in Norway and Spain, the first patients will shortly be enrolled in the Solidarity Trial, which will compare the safety and effectiveness of four different drugs or drug combinations against COVID-19. This is a historic trial which will dramatically cut the time needed to generate robust evidence about what drugs work.«[19]

SOLIDARITY has been working on the rapid testing of therapies for Covid-19 The prospect of a *dramatic* reduction in the time required to develop these therapies is, in the eyes of Ghebreyesus, unprecedented and therefore of *historical* significance. The *megatrial* includes 45 countries with a correspondingly large number of patients,[20] where drugs to treat Covid-19 are being tested. These are not new drugs developed specifically for Covid-19, but rather the so-called *repurposing* or *drug repositioning* procedure is used.[21] This means that existing drugs, some of which have been approved for other diseases or are close to approval, are tested for their efficacy against Covid-19. Specifically, the SOLIDARITY trial involves the following drugs or drug combinations: 1. Local Standard of care alone OR local standard of care plus one of 2. The antiviral Remdesivir, which was developed to combat the Ebola virus and is administered intravenously; 3. The antimalarial drugs Chloroquine or Hydroxychloroquine; 4. The HIV combination Lopinavir/Ritonavir – known as Kaletra – and 5. This combination supplemented by beta-interferon.[22]

The method used by SOLIDARITY is not new. A glance at the pandemic history of the last 40 years shows comparable precursors. Particularly impressive is the fact that as early as the mid-1980s, in connection with the HIV/AIDS pandemic, clinical research successfully tested so-called drug repurposing.[23] Even today, drug repurposing is still a good alternative in identifying effective therapies for emerging diseases. The fact is that biomedical research has achieved only modest success in the last three decades in terms of developing new drugs.[24] With a virtually unchanged total of 25–30 novel molecules among the approximately 50 new drugs approved by the FDA each year, only 12 % of drug candidates that make it into Phase I clinical trials receive the final green light. This means that

---

[19] World Health Organization: WHO Director-General's opening remarks at the media briefing on COVID-19.

[20] Cf. Kupferschmidt/Cohen: Who Launches Global Megatrial of the Four Most Promising Coronavirus Treatments.

[21] Cf. Xue et al.: Review of Drug Repositioning Approaches and Resources; Newman: Delivering Drugs to the Lungs.

[22] Cf. WHO: Public Health Emergency SOLIDARITY Trial of Treatments for COVID-19 Infection in Hospitalized Patients.

[23] Cf. Killen: HIV Research.

[24] Cf. Strittmatter: Overcoming Drug Development Bottlenecks with Repurposing.

of 5,000 to 10,000 compounds from traditional drug development, probably only one will be approved. According to Pizzorno et al., the reasons for this include the focus of research on complex diseases, the limitations of experimental models for reproducing biological complexity (*reductionist experimental* models), high regulatory control measures and, of course, the question of tolerability and unexpected side effects.[25] On average, it takes 13–15 years to develop a new drug. This makes drug repurposing all the more attractive as a means of filling the innovation gap. The precondition is an excellent understanding of the active pharmacological mechanism of the respective substances. If it is possible to identify drugs for which a new therapeutic application can be validated, long, risky and cost-intensive preclinical and early clinical phases can be avoided. Pushpakom et al. describe three steps that are needed to identify substances that are suitable for repurposing: 1. the relevant molecules for a given therapeutic application must be identified (hypothesis generating); 2. an assessment and evaluation of the effect in preclinical models must have been carried out; 3. an evaluation of the efficacy in Phase II studies must be carried out. The first step in particular is critical, which is why systematic approaches are increasingly being developed.[26]

For repurposing procedures, *sleeping candidates* may also be considered. These are drugs that have been abandoned during the development process and at advanced stages of clinical trials (Phase II and III) because they have proven to be insufficiently effective for the originally intended medical application or have side effects. A new therapeutic application could potentially revive such candidates.[27] An example of such a *sleeping candidate* is AZT (zidovudine). AZT was initially developed as a potential cancer drug, but proved to be ineffective. However, a placebo-controlled study in 1986 confirmed the assumption that it could be effectively used against AIDS. In 1987, AZT was approved as the first antiretroviral drug.[28] The urgency of a pandemic situation, in which a potentially *deadly plague* – be it HIV/AIDS, Ebola or Covid-19 – confronts scientists with the task of developing a therapy under time pressure, provides a favorable context for testing sleeping candidates or drugs already established for other diseases.[29] The SOLIDARITY study design has been streamlined to allow hospitals overburdened by the pandemic to participate without having to substantially increase their workload. To enroll a patient in the study, clinicians must first check whether the Covid-19 diagnosis has been confirmed and then enter the patient's data on a website, including any

---

[25] Cf. Pizzorno et al.: Drug Repurposing Approaches for the Treatment of Influenza Viral Infection.
[26] Cf. Pushpakom et al: Drug Repurposing: Progress, Challenges and Recommendations.
[27] Cf. Hernandez et al: Giving Drugs a Second Chance.
[28] Cf. Fauci: HIV and AIDS.
[29] Cf. Bai/Hsu: Drug Repurposing for Ebola Virus Disease and Zhou et al.: Network-Based Drug Repurposing for Novel Coronavirus 2019-Ncov/Sars-Cov-2.

previous illnesses such as diabetes or HIV. Once the patient has been informed and has agreed to participate in the study, their consent is transmitted electronically to the WHO, along with details of the drugs available to the hospital. The website then randomizes the patient to one of the drugs and the Standard of Care (SoC) or only SoC for Covid-19. This means that patients included in the study will always receive SoC. Finally, the doctor has to document the day the patient was discharged or died, how long the treatment in hospital lasted and whether oxygen therapy or ventilation was necessary.

From an epistemic perspective, it should be stressed that, due to the urgency and the rapidly increasing number of victims, the WHO has decided not only on a streamlined but also a dynamic study design. Adjustments are possible at any time during the course of the study. This is a randomized controlled trial, but without a blinded and placebo group, which is a limitation. During the course of the study, a committee will monitor the data collected and, if necessary, remove one of the four agents from the test if it is shown to have no effect. There is also the possibility of including further drugs in the course of the study.[30]

The dynamic study design is subordinated to the goal of providing patients with effective therapy as quickly as possible. From an ethical point of view, the orientation towards this goal legitimizes the generation of weaker evidence. The WHO study coordinators are aware of this, as the authors of a report on SOLIDARITY published online in Science underline: »The design is not double-blind, the gold standard in medical research, so there could be placebo effects from patients knowing they received a candidate drug. But WHO says it had to balance scientific rigor against speed.«[31] In addition to accepting the increased risk of systematic bias in the results due to the lack of blinding, the time pressure means that not all possible data are collected as would be usual. For example, parameters such as virus load are not monitored. This allows the study to be conducted in different contexts. The heterogeneity of the study population invalidates an objection that is often raised against randomized controlled trials. In favour of comparability, the selected study participants usually form a very homogeneous group, whose characteristics do not correspond to those of the actual patients who will eventually receive the therapy. For example, study participants show fewer or less severe comorbidities.[32] The focus on male study participants has also led to

---

[30] Cf. Deutsches Ärzteblatt: WHO testet in globaler Studie 4 Therapeutika auf Wirkung bei Covid-19. A similarly designed randomised controlled trial – DISCOVERY – is being conducted in France (INSERM research centre), which is limited to a few European countries but also includes hospitalised patients treated with Covid-19 and tests all the same drugs apart from chloroquine.

[31] Kupferschmidt/Cohen: Who Launches Global Megatrial of the Four Most Promising Coronavirus Treatments.

[32] Cf. Campbell-Scherer: Multimorbidity.

recurring debates in medical practice and medical ethics.³³ The SOLIDARITY study design is not subject to these limitations. Knowledge of the potential side effects of the treatments favors a more liberal practice of inclusion.

3. Science Unbound

Finally, strategies, adaptations and compromise solutions that enable clinical trials to be conducted in the context of a pandemic outbreak represent a field that has been little researched in terms of research ethics. This makes the scientific and ethical criteria for conducting studies on experimental therapies for HIV and Ebola, which Lane and co-authors have formulated on the basis of a previous study by Emanuel, all the more valuable at this point:

1. Attention to careful patient education as the basis for consent to participate in the study; 2. Clear definition of the primary endpoints in the study design; 3. good communication and cooperation between the participating countries; 4. Establishment of a body to monitor the scientific work; 5. Transparency and timely dissemination of data to treating clinicians and affected communities.³⁴

These criteria also provide a valuable ethical framework for the current situation in the context of the pandemic outbreak. However, due to the complexity of these exceptional circumstances, which are historically unprecedented on this scale, additional criteria are indicated, which primarily concern the communication between science, politics and the media. With the global spread of the virus, the rapid, global communication channels are a challenging new departure. Moreover, the relaxation of the usual control mechanisms within research communication due to the urgency of the situation and the media exposure of scientists makes the evaluation and examination of information in circulation more difficult. Rules governing the prudent and fair transfer of data, information and interpretations appropriate to the circumstances of the crisis should be laid down at this point. Clarification of the degree of certainty or uncertainty of what is communicated would go a long way towards enhancing quality assurance. In respect of the ongoing study, it can be said that SOLIDARITY is benefiting from the coordination and support of the WHO. The broad inclusion of patients and the flexible architecture of the study, which allows the rapid withdrawal or replacement of the tested substances, are promising features. The pragmatic trials for the development of urgently needed therapies that preceded SOLIDARITY are historical proof that research designed in this way can yield results faster. If

---

[33] Cf. Gadebusch-Bondio: Mann und Frau, ganz individuell.
[34] Cf. Lane et al: Conducting Trials in Outbreak Settings.

it is possible to make the data obtained and the information extrapolated from it available to clinicians and decision-makers and to release all publications – as planned – in open-access format, the international community stands to benefit. It is also possible that decisions will then be made more quickly and more reliably. In principle, the outbreak of the pandemic should serve, on the one hand, to stimulate those epistemic virtues that would also be desirable in *normal* research contexts: instead of interest-based competition and waste of time and resources, targeted cooperation, solidarity, and transparency and openness in communication now predominate in the research. On the other hand, the loosening of habitual control mechanisms and standardization grids presents a challenge to science. Researching in high-speed mode, evaluating interim results, communicating in a differentiated way with sensation seeking media outlets, and coping with everyday life in exceptional situations – all this must be learned. This demands moral backbone from all those involved.

References

Bai, Jane P. F. / Chia-Wen Hsu: Drug Repurposing for Ebola Virus Disease: Principles of Consideration and the Animal Rule, in: Journal of Pharma Science, 108(2), 2019, pp. 798–806.

Brost, Marc / Bernhard Pörksen: Angesteckt. Warum der Journalismus in der Corona-Krise besonders gebraucht wird – und vor welchen Problemen er steht, in: DIE ZEIT, 07.04.2020, https://www.zeit.de/2020/16/coronavirus-berichterstattung-journalismus-information; last accessed 26.06.2020.

Campbell-Scherer, Denise: Multimorbidity: A Challenge for Evidence-based Medicine, in: BMJ Evidence-Based Medicine, 15(6), 2010, pp. 165–166.

Centre for Evidence-Based Medicine: Oxford COVID-19 Evidence Service Information, https://www.cebm.net/covid-19/; last accessed 26.06.2020.

Chochrane Library: Coronavirus (COVID-19); https://www.cochranelibrary.com/covid-19; last accessed 26.06.2020.

Deutsches Ärzteblatt: WHO testet in globaler Studie 4 Therapeutika auf Wirkung bei Covid-19, 23.03.2020, https://www.aerzteblatt.de/nachrichten/111267/WHO-testet-in-globaler-Studie-4-Therapeutika-auf-Wirkung-bei-COVID-19; last accessed 18.06.2020.

Emanuel, Ezekiel J. / David Wendler / Jack Killen / Christine Grady: What Makes Clinical Research in Developing Countries Ethical? The Benchmarks of Ethical Research, in: The Journal of Infectious Diseases, 189(5), 2004, pp. 930–937.

Fauci, Anthony S.: Covid-19. Navigating the Uncharted, in: The New England Journal of Medicine, 382(13), 2020, pp. 1268–1269.

Fauci, Anthony S.: HIV and AIDS: 20 Years of Science, in: Nature Medicine, 9(7), 2003, pp. 839–843.

Ferguson, Neil et al.: Report 9: Impact of Non-Pharmaceutical Interventions (NPIs) to Reduce COVID-19 Mortality and Healthcare Demand, Report, Imperial College London, 16.03.2020.

Gadebusch-Bondio, Mariacarla: Mann und Frau, ganz individuell. Entwicklung eines neuen medizinischen Denkens, in: Gadebusch-Bondio, Mariacarla / Elpiniki Katsari (eds.): Gendermedizin. Krankheit und Geschlecht in Zeiten der Individualisierten Medizin, Bielefeld 2014, pp. 9–18.

Gadebusch-Bondio, Mariacarla / Maria Marloth: Die »historische Studie« SOLIDARITY als Antwort der Forschung auf die Sars-CoV-2 Pandemie, published online ahead of print, 12.5.2020, in: NTM. Zeitschrift für Geschichte der Wissenschaften, Technik und Medizin 28(2), 2020, pp. 1–7, https://link.springer.com/article/10.1007/s00048-020-00257-5; last accessed 23.06.2020.

German Federal Ministry of Health: Basiswissen zum Corona-Virus, 2020, https://www.zusammengegencorona.de/informieren/basiswissen-coronavirus/; last accessed 18.06.2020.

Habermas, Jürgen: Interview by Markus Schwering, in: Frankfurter Rundschau, 03.04.2020, https://www.fr.de/kultur/gesellschaft/juergen-habermas-coronavirus-krise-covid19-interview-13642491.html; last accessed 18.06.2020.

Hatchett, Richard J. / Carter E. Mecher / Marc Lipsitch: Public Health Interventions and Epidemic Intensity during the 1918 Influenza Pandemic, in: PNAS, 104(18), 2007, pp. 7582–7587.

Hernandez, Javier J. / Michael Pryszlak / Lindsay Smith / Connor Yanchus / Nahid Kurji / Vijay M. Shahani / Steven M. Molinski: Giving Drugs a Second Chance: Overcoming Regulatory and Financial Hurdles in Repurposing Approved Drugs as Cancer Therapeutics, in: Front Oncol, 14.11.2017.

Ioannidis, John P. A.: In the Coronavirus Pandemic, We're Making Decisions without Reliable Data, STAT (blog), 17.03.2020, https://www.statnews.com/2020/03/17/a-fiasco-in-the-making-as-the-coronavirus-pandemic-takes-hold-we-are-making-decisions-without-reliable-data/; last accessed 29.04.2020.

Killen, Jack: HIV Research, in: Emanuel, Ezekiel J. / Christine Grady / Robert A Crouch / Reidar, Lie K. / Franklin G Miller / David D Wendler: The Oxford Textbook of Clinical Research Ethics, Oxford 2008, pp. 97–109.

Kupferschmidt, Kai / John Cohen: Who Launches Global Megatrial of the Four Most Promising Coronavirus Treatments, in: Science, 22.03.2020, https://www.sciencemag.org/news/2020/03/who-launches-global-megatrial-four-most-promising-coronavirus-treatments; last accessed 29.04.2020.

Lane, H. Clifford / Hillary D. Marston / Anthony S. Fauci: Conducting Trials in Outbreak Settings: Points to Consider, in: *Clin Trials,* 13(1), 2016, pp. 92–95, https://www.ncbi.nlm.nih.gov/pmc/articles/PMC4767673/pdf/nihms-738356. pdf; last accessed 29.04.2020.

Moorthy, Vasee / Ana Maria Henao Restrepo / Marie-Pierre Preziosi / Soumya Swaminathan: Data Sharing for Novel Coronavirus (Covid-19), in: Bulletin of the World Health Organization, 98(3), 2020, p. 150.

Newman, Stephen P.: Delivering Drugs to the Lungs: The History of Repurposing in the Treatment of Respiratory Diseases, in: Advanced Drug Delivery Reviews, 133, 2018, pp. 5–18.

Patterson, K. David / Gerald F. Pyle: The Geography and Mortality of the 1918 Influenza Pandemic, in: Bulletin of the History of Medicine, 65(1), 1991, pp. 4–21.

Paules, Catharine I. / Hillary D. Marston / Anthony S. Fauci: Coronavirus Infections. More Than Just the Common Cold, in: Journal of the American Medical Association, 323(8), 2020, pp. 707–708.

Pizzorno, Andrés / Blandine Padey / Olivier Terrier / Manuel Rosa-Caltrava: Drug Repurposing Approaches for the Treatment of Influenza Viral Infection: Reviving Old Drugs to Fight Against a Long-Lived Enemy, in: Front. Immunol, 10, 2019.

Pushpakom Sudeep / Francesco Iorio / Patrick A. Eyers / K. Jane Escott / Shirley Hooper / Andrew Wells / Andrew Doig / Tim Guilliams / Joanna Latimer / Christine McNamee / Alan Norris / Philippe Sanseau / David Cavalla / Munir Pirmohamed: Drug Repurposing: Progress, Challenges and Recommendations in: Nature Reviews, 18(1), 2019, pp. 41–58.

Shen, Chen / Nassim Nicholas Taleb / Yaneer Bar-Yam: Review of Ferguson et al. »Impact of Non-pharmaceutical Interventions ...«, New England Complex Systems Institute, 17.03.2020, https://necsi.edu/review-of-ferguson-et-al-impact-of-non-pharmaceutical-interventions; last accessed 29.04.2020.

Smith, Kiona N.: Think Social Distancing for Coronavirus is Overkill? Here's A Cautionary Tale from 1918, in: Online Edition of Forbes Magazine, 16.03.2020, https://www.forbes.com/sites/kionasmith/2020/03/16/a-cautionary-tale-about-social-distancing-for-st-patricks-day-and-every-day/#20e244cc1d99; last accessed 10.04.2020.

Strittmatter, Stephen M.: Overcoming Drug Development Bottlenecks with Repurposing: Old Drugs Learns New Tricks, in: Nature Medicine. 20(6), 2014, pp. 590–591.

World Health Organization: WHO Director-General's opening remarks at the media briefing on COVID-19, 27.03.2020, https://www.who.int/dg/speeches/detail/who-director-general-s-opening-remarks-at-the-media-briefing-on-covid-19---27-march-2020; last accessed 22.06.2020.

World Health Organization: Public Health Emergency SOLIDARITY Trial of Treatments for COVID-19 Infection in Hospitalized Patients, in: ISRCTN registry, 2020.

World Health Organization: R&D Blueprint and COVD-19, 2020, https://www.who.int/blueprint/priority-diseases/key-action/novel-coronavirus/en/; last accessed 18.06.2020.

Xue, Hanqing / Jie Li / Haozhe Xie / Yadong Wang: Review of Drug Repositioning Approaches and Resources, in: International Journal of Biological, 14(10), 2018, pp. 1232–1244.

Zhou, Yadi / Youan Hou / Jiayu Shen et al.: Network-Based Drug Repurposing for Novel Coronavirus 2019-Ncov/Sars-Cov-2 in: Cell Discovery, 6(14), 2020.

Thomas Dreier

»Law as Culture« in Times of Corona

> »I sometimes don't leave the house in eight days
> and live very happily,
> a house arrest just as long on orders
> would throw me into a disease.
> Where freedom can be thought of,
> one moves in one's circle with ease,
> but where there's thought compulsion,
> even the legitimate ones come out with a shy mine.«
> Georg Christoph Lichtenberg[1]

1. The Limited View

Hardly ever has so much – and so internationally – been written on a topic as is currently the case with the Corona virus. However, the chances of contributing something new with a further article are probably much lower than the risk of infection which is said to be 70 percent. Far greater, however, is the danger of contributing just another commentary, which will merely express opinions and feelings, rather than being based on established facts. Valid insights or even truths cannot be gained from the limited perspective of the home office. True, the view out of the window onto a largely depopulated near-world is complemented by the media kaleidoscope of the Internet and social media. But this technical dispositive which was initially called *tele*vision, thus promising a view into the distance, merely throws us back to the closeness of or our own home environment in times in which direct, lived contact with reality is forbidden by law.

Anyway, the time lag is too short to be able to identify longer-term trends and changes. According to the paradox ascribed to Jaron Lanier, there is a general tendency to extrapolate current trends and thereby overestimate short-term effects and underestimate long-term effects. The reason simply is that a mere extrapola-

---

[1] Lichtenberg: Aus den Sudelbüchern, B 143: »Ich gehe zuweilen in 8 Tagen nicht aus dem Hause und lebe sehr vergnügt, ein eben so langer Hausarrest auf Befehl würde mich in eine Krankheit werfen. Wo Freiheit zu denken ist, da bewegt man sich mit einer Leichtigkeit in seinem Zirkel, wo Gedanken-Zwang ist, da kommen auch die erlaubten mit einer scheuen Miene hervor«; transl. by the author.

tion of current data does not take into account the development of counterforces, feedback loops and changes in the conditions that determined the trend in the past.

In view of all this, the present article is not intended to present a major thesis spanning time and space. Rather, only some observations, assessments and individual perceptions will be made on the topic of *Law as Culture* in times of Corona. In the words of Werner Gephart, it is not a matter of »extracting a frivolous stimulus from the present situation«, but »of addressing a neglected, namely normative, dimension of the pandemic event, which goes beyond the comparison of infection and death rates«.[2] It is worth noting, in this respect, that *Law as Culture* is not interested in the content of legal norms, but rather in the question of how the instrument of law is used as a cultural practice and performance in society and what are its effects in this respect.

2. Law as Culture: Some Corona-Induced Functional Transformations

2.1 On the Agenda of the Law

It could be argued that the law does not pursue an agenda of its own but is merely an instrument for implementing political objectives. Against such an assumption, however, it could be objected that at least fundamental rights as well as procedural rules of the rule of law seek to contain mere political decision making. In addition, as a subsystem of society, law claims to provide security and to stabilize legitimate expectations. It secures fundamental rights, strives to ensure that opportunities and resources are allocated and distributed fairly to those subject to the law, and it ensures fair procedures. Even if one is not prepared to ascribe an independent agent to law in this respect, according to the current understanding of the constitution, it is true that law has at least been used for the purposes mentioned, even if the democratic constitutional state may not — as stated by the well-known dictum of Ernst-Wolfgang Böckenförde — itself guarantee the conditions on which it depends.

This makes it seem reasonable to retrace the functional changes law may have undergone in view of the changed external circumstances of the Corona crisis. The question to be discussed here is aimed at the extent to which law continues to perform its traditional tasks in society as before the crisis, either in the same way or in a modified form. The issue is to find out and describe the shifts in the

---

[2] Private correspondence with Werner Gephart regarding my acceptance of participation in the project of 1 April 2020; transl. by the author.

tectonics of the law, discussing whether the changes result in a strengthening or weakening of law as an instrument for structuring and solving problems of society.

2.2 Methodological Considerations

One methodological way of investigating changes in the function of law would certainly be to examine official and unofficial documents by means of text and data mining in search for the purely statistical occurrence of terms such as *law, justice, restriction of freedom* and the like, which speak for a strengthening of the law, as well as other terms which, like in particular that of *fear*, may be interpreted as a sign for the weakening of the law as a stabilizing factor in society. Applied to text corpora before and after the beginning of the crisis, it would thus be possible to empirically determine time lines which would indicate changes in the functions of the law.

However, in the absence of such studies the only remaining methodological option is to pursue a descriptive and analytical view. As a starting point it can be said that the characteristic feature of any emergency situation is that it makes binding decisions urgent which cannot be made quickly enough by routine procedures. What is needed are rapid solutions that do not provide the same level of detail and in which conflicting rights and interests cannot be weighed against each other with the usual care and differentiation. The question to be addressed here is how this simplification of decision-making affects the law as a means of enforcing the decisions made. This question has both a procedural and a substantive aspect, which will be dealt with in more detail below.

2.3 Fundamental Observations

Before doing so, however, two points should be noted: Firstly, there has undoubtedly been a shift in emphasis from law to politics. More than ever before, it is becoming clear that it is the politicians who make the decisions, usually in cooperation with medical doctors (virologists) and – as in the case of the round table in the Chancellery and the Council of Experts in North Rhine-Westphalia – possibly together with sociologists, ethicists and lawyers. The government clearly has the reins of action in its hands, while the opposition has largely been pushed to the side-lines. Law, it might be concluded, is largely relegated to the role of a mere instrument for implementing political decisions. But this development may also give rise to another, contrary interpretation. After all, it may be said that law is being strengthened to the extent that territory is once again being reclaimed for regulation by state action, which was previously left to the self-regulation of the market as well as to technology configured by private providers, which determines what users can do, regardless of what they are legally allowed to do.

Secondly, as long as a state of emergency has not been declared, which would largely suspend the law, the fundamental role of the law in structuring and procedurally determining the manner in which decisions are taken remains, as well as its claim to set a limiting framework for the contents of decisions transported by way of the law. For the time being, even in Russia, Hungary and Turkey, the politically desired changes have been implemented in accordance with the legal procedural rules in place, even if these changes — as in the case of the Hungarian Enabling Act — may result in their abolition and hence a considerable restriction of the role of the law in securing freedoms.

2.4 Procedural Functional Changes

Turning to the details of functional changes of law in times of Corona, in the first place, procedural shifts come into view, i.e. changes regarding the activity of norm-setting. Unless political action limits itself — as in the initial phase — and probably still in Sweden — to recommendations and appeals, the regulation (Verordnung) is the regulatory instrument of choice. It transfers decision-making powers to the executive, which in times of normality are reserved for Parliament. The instrument as such is already to be found in the police law on danger prevention and, as far as Corona is concerned, it is provided for by law in the German Infection Protection Act (Infektionsschutzgesetz). The constitutional framework for normative activity by way of regulations is provided in Germany by Article 80 of the Basic Law (Grundgesetz). According to this provision, the executive (the Federal Government, a Federal Minister or the governments of the Länder) to which the law-making power is delegated, may be empowered, provided that the content, purpose and scope of such empowerment are defined by law. In the case of laws that require the consent of the German Federal Council (Bundesrat) or that are implemented by the Länder on behalf of the Federal Government, or as a matter of their own, in addition the consent of the German Federal Council is required. The present considerable extension of the Federal Minister of Health's authority to adopt measures to combat Corona even without the consent of the German federal Council is reflected in the amendment to § 5 of the Infection Protection Act passed on 27 March 2020.

Insofar as the amended version of § 28 of the Infection Protection Act now also mentions the freedom of movement (Article 11 (1) of the Basic Law) next to the fundamental rights of freedom of the person (Article 2 (2) sentence 2 of the Basic Law), of assembly (Article 8 of the Basic Law) and of the inviolability of the home (Article 13 (1) of the Basic Law), this is apparently intended to legitimise quarantine orders and curfews against non-troublemakers (*Nicht-Störer*). However, this is no longer a question of procedural changes, but rather a question of the substantive content of the provisions.

Furthermore, governance by means of an increasing number of regulations implies a double loss of confidence. On the one hand, a loss of confidence – justified by experience – in timely decision-making by means of parliamentary deliberations and, on the other hand, a loss of confidence that the norm addressees will behave appropriately in the absence of norm-setting by the state.

Moreover, there is another connection between normative regulation and trust. Where a norm exists, there is no need for trust in the actions of others. Rather, only a residual amount of trust is required, namely that the others will adhere to legal norms, be it on their own volition, be it because the state threatens to enforce compliance by way of harsh fines and penalties.

One thing, however, has not changed. As a rule, the norm addressees still do not consult the legal text of any regulation itself but rather rely on the media for the communication of its content. Press releases, news magazines, daily newspapers and – not to be underestimated – social media act as communicators in this respect. In the results of Google searches, the links to the original texts usually appear further down in the sear result lists. The exact wording of amendments to laws and new regulations, however, remains a matter for lawyers. This leads to contradictions and consequently to uncertainties. For example, when Baden-Württemberg's Prime Minister Kretschmann announced that it is only allowed to meet outside in pairs, this information contradicted the wording of his own decree. The rule decreed is not about *inside* or *outside*, but about *public* and *non-public*, i. e. the public versus the private space. The limitation to two persons applies only to the public sphere, whereas in all other respects – including meetings outside – a maximum of five persons is permitted.

Finally, it should only briefly be pointed out that the discussion of the crisis and the respective legal restrictions has, for the time being, pushed other legal issues into the background, in particular those concerning consumer protection, which were normally dealt with in the media on a large scale.

2.5 Substantive Functional Changes

The fact that the threat of Corona in countries like Germany affects all inhabitants in roughly the same way may be conducive to solidarity. But this is probably different in countries with greater income disparities, where only a minority of rich people has access to medical facilities and where large parts of the population are exposed to the virus with only little, if any protection. In economic terms, not everyone is equally affected by Corona. Even if only a few may be benefiting from the crisis, those who may keep their businesses open are still doing comparatively well. Also, civil servants have less to worry about their salaries than employees who might lose their jobs. Moreover, in many countries, such as the USA, the lack of a Corona-compatible infrastructure over long stretches is taking its toll due to the profit-optimising health care system, the widespread lack of health insurance coverage and the failure to cushion the risk of losing one's job, for example through short-time work compensation schemes.

Furthermore, each regulation in turn creates new inequalities. Since justice considerations are no longer negotiated in a democratic body in a lengthy discourse but are – if at all – determined by the executive alone, there is a shift in material terms towards *rough justice*. At present it is not about transforming subtle ramifications of an increasingly differentiated justice into law, but about regulating a reduced set of facts as clearly as possible. How *rough* and woodcut-like or more finely chiselled justice turns out to be depends not only on the time-pressure of necessity, but to a considerable extent on the cultural characteristics of the individual national societies or the groups entrusted with decision-making.

In Germany, there is a general social tendency to reach a consensus and a practice of balancing conflicting interests and rights. This has to do with a rather far-reaching identification with the state and state action, which may be seen as a remnant of the subservient spirit (Untertanengeist) and the resulting self-discipline. This is symbolically expressed by the German Chancellor when she only addresses her fellow citizens at longer intervals during which the director of the Robert Koch Institute, an institutionalized physician, is presented as making *official* announcements. Already in neighbouring France, where appeals to reason initially remained largely ineffective in view of the widespread critical distance to government measures, there was apparently a need not only for far more frequent appearances of President Macron in the media, but also for a restriction of fundamental freedoms to a much greater extent and in a far more finely granulated way than in Germany. However, it should also be noted that the practical effect of these restrictions is somewhat mitigated by the fact that the pass required by law for leaving one's home can be issued *sur l'honneur*, i.e. by the person concerned himself. Whereas in Germany a prohibition is regularly regarded as a prohibition, it appears to be generally accepted in France that a principle which obviously cannot be fully complied with needs not be fully complied with either.

If one looks at the Corona-induced substantive changes of the law, the focus of interest is primarily on the restrictions of fundamental rights as a consequence of the goal of securing the right to life and health. The debate about their admissibility and justification is still – at least in Germany – entirely within the framework of the dogmatic construction of fundamental rights as developed and applied before by the Federal Constitutional Court (Bundesverfassungsgericht). Described in a somewhat simplified and slightly abridged way, state measures restricting fundamental freedoms not only require a valid justification, but they also must comply with the principle of proportionality. It is only within the confines of the proportionality between the restrictions adopted to serve a justified purpose that the legislature has a certain margin of discretion, which it is authorised to fill out with a politically motivated decision. Of course, in situations of uncertainty this margin of discretion is far greater than usually. In the words of the former constitutional judge Udo di Fabio, situations of uncertainty allow the democratically legitimized bodies »considerable room for manoeuvre in assessing the extent of the risks and in shaping the measures they take to combat infection«.[3]

In each individual case of a decision affecting fundamental rights the decisive question is in which respect it is, beyond moral appeals and recommendations, precisely the legal normative order that is needed to achieve the intended effect. This guarantees an appropriate balance between the state's obligation to provide for health care, on the one hand, and individual restrictions of freedom on the other hand. A balance also has to be struck between the rights to freedom of different individual persons, if the freedom of one person can only be achieved at the expense of restricting the freedom of another. At the same time, restrictions of fundamental rights must be formulated in a sufficiently clear and unambiguous manner. It is above all this point that ignites the current criticism of the latest amendment to the German Infection Protection Act. The criticism is directed at both the lack of certainty regarding the formulation of the prerequisites for the norm to apply and of the legal consequences foreseen in cases of non-compliance, which are said not to meet the constitutional requirements of certainty for freedom-restricting measures.

However, the involvement of technology is likely to have far more far-reaching and long-term consequences. The app technology used in China and other Asian countries to track the locations of citizens may still encounter data protection concerns in Germany. Moreover, to the extent that it proves to be successful, the technology available will not only arouse desire, but will also play an important role when it comes to balancing conflicting fundamental rights. At any rate, the ground for acceptance is already prepared by the fitness apps that many people use not only voluntarily but even enthusiastically. Whereas resistance against the use of tracking apps for reasons of collective health protection still seems to predominate, it might be noted that according to rumors, a draft law which would have allowed the use of tracking apps was already formulated by the Ministry of Health. However, there exists an unmistakable trend away from normative regulations which define how people *should* behave towards a technology that defines in which way people *can* behave and that self-executes the normative command.

Last but not least there is the question, which is taboo in German legal discourse, of how many lives can be accepted as potential collateral damage in order

---

[3] Di Fabio: An den Grenzen der Verfassung; transl. by the author.

to avoid overly far-reaching restrictions on the freedom of others, and to prevent excessively negative effects on the functioning of the economy. This question is taboo in Germany, because in the light of the guarantee of human dignity the Federal Constitutional Court declared it inadmissible to offset human lives against each other. True, the case in which this rule was reaffirmed concerned a law that would have allowed the shooting down under certain circumstances of a passenger plane hijacked by terrorists. The law that was struck down contained the authorisation of a specific act which would certainly lead to the death of a specific number of people, whereas regarding Corona, at the time of making any decision affecting the lives of people, it is not known whether people will die as a consequence of that particular decision and, if so, how many. Nor is there a direct link between a future relaxation of the contact ban and those people who may subsequently be infected and eventually die. Similarly to road deaths – which in the 1960s and 1970s were on the scale of a whole small town a year (!) in Germany alone, and which are still accepted today in order to keep the economy going and to maintain freedom of movement at a socially acceptable and accepted level – we will ultimately respond to the Corona crisis with measures based on decisions taken under conditions of uncertainty, accepting the death of some people with the aim of safeguarding the health, rights and interests of the far greater number of others. Such a decision is facilitated by the fact that it is left to chance who as an individual will have to bear the negative consequences and who will not. Again, Udo di Fabio pointed out that constitutional law is only poorly prepared for dealing with the necessity to make a selection of life chances, be it statistically abstract or individual and concrete. At least, however, it can be said that a *not unjustifiably high* inevitable mortality rate may constitutionally justify measures to achieve herd immunity.

But let's get back to the mechanical internal workings of law. At a level below constitutional law, legal instruments are likely to be reactivated which in times of normal operation tended to have a shadowy existence. For example, in civil law, which is largely concerned with the allocation of risks, the corrective instrument available to react to the fact that the basis of a contractual transaction has ceased to exist (Wegfall der Geschäftsgrundlage) could be reactivated, which already served well in times of high inflation in 1923 as a corrective to shifts in the risk unforeseen by both parties.

This instrument was initially developed by the courts and in 2002 found its way into the German Civil Code (Bürgerliches Gesetzbuch, BGB). Section 313 now states that:

»[i]f circumstances which became the basis of a contract have significantly changed since the contract was entered into and if the parties would not have entered into the contract or would have entered into it with different contents if they had foreseen this change, adaptation of the contract may be demanded to the extent that, taking account of all the circumstances of the specific case, in particular the contractual or statutory distribution of risk, one of the parties cannot reasonably be expected to uphold the contract without alteration.«[4]

Also, if an adaptation of the contract is not possible or one party cannot reasonably be expected to accept it, the disadvantaged party may either revoke or terminated the contract. In this way, unjustified risk distributions resulting from the application of the law in place can be corrected, albeit always retrospectively and usually only by way of litigation. For instance, an answer will have to be found to the question whether, and if so, how much and when rent will have to be paid in cases in which due to Corona and the ensuing regulations the rented property cannot be used as originally assumed by both parties. In a similar way, Corona-related default risks could be distributed retrospectively in a fairer way than if the contractually agreed risk-distribution was applied mechanically. The only question remaining is which solution is to be considered as *fair*. If someone has rented a holiday apartment for a year which he cannot use due to Corona-induced travel restrictions, does he have to pay rent also for this period, or should the landlord bear the risk and the resulting financial loss? Of course, such ex post adjustments cannot only be made by the courts in individual cases but may likewise be effectuated by the legislature in a general way for certain types of fact scenarios. It should be noted, however, that because any such state intervention is affecting constitutionally protected property interests, once again a careful balancing of fundamental rights will be necessary. These issues will have to examined in greater detail once a *re-entry* of the law has occurred.

2.6 Re-Entry *of the Law*

Since, as stated above, the characteristic feature of any emergency is that it calls for decisions which cannot be made quickly enough through the routine procedure, it will take a certain amount of time after the beginning of the emergency for the right to review the legality of the restrictions and temporary suspension of rights, i.e. until there will be a *re-entry* of the law. After all, the action for review of the law against the North Rhine-Westphalian contact ban by the administrative court of appeal in Münster can be seen as a first such step towards a judicial review of the limits of the functional change of law and towards a return to normality. Of course, how long it will take before such a re-entry will be completed depends on the legal instruments available before the beginning of the crisis – means of preliminary legal protection, possibility of an abstract procedure for judicial review

---

[4] § 313 Sec. 1 of the German civil code.

of statutory norms or even popular actions – by means of which the measures in question can be reviewed regarding their legality.

However, every re-entry is confronted with difficulties, if the necessary normative basis for such re-entry has itself been removed by means of the emergency measures. In any case, the re-entry of law presupposes that the constitutional order, including the possibility of a constitutional review of fundamental rights and procedural guarantees – and ultimately of all state measures with an impact on civil liberties – has remained intact. This will be discussed in more detail below after having a closer look at the normative use of metaphors and symbols in connection with the Corona crisis.

3. On the Symbolism in Connection with Functional Changes

Law does not only operate in a functional, but also in a symbolic way. This raises the question of the use of metaphors associated with functional changes of law. A distinction can be made between metaphors that are used to legitimize the entire legal reaction to the spread of the virus and metaphors that are used to justify the contents of an individual legal regulation. This can only be illustrated by a few particularly striking examples.

3.1 »Figures«

Of course, symbols and metaphors are less frequently to be found the more arguments on Corona are made based on facts and figures. Nevertheless, it is not to be overlooked that already the mere use of figures as such has a symbolic value just as much as the individual figures themselves. However, the symbolic message emanating from the figures appears to be rather ambivalent.

On the one hand, insofar as the figures – i.e., those communicated by the John Hopkins University or the ones on the website coronazaehler.de – are not rounded, but ostensibly take into account each individual of the *new cases*, of the *deceased* and the *active cases*, they give the prima facie erroneous, albeit reassuring impression that the events could, if not really be controlled, at least be recorded down to every individual and thus in their entirety. This is reminiscent of the famous Washington Memorial erected to commemorate the Vietnam War, which seeks to banish the monstrosity and chaos of the war by meticulously enumerating all the names of GIs who died far away from their homes.

On the other hand, the total number of names listed in the Vietnam Memorial as well as the figures communicated daily with regard to Corona, likewise send the opposite message: Big numbers frighten. Of course, what is understood by the recipients as a *large* number depends on the mind frame of the respective viewer. Most likely, for those who focus on the individual, a number beyond the size of a group of people that can be precisely grasped at a glance appears to be large, and for those who earn € 30,000 a year, 50,000 cases are a lot. However, for those who, as state leaders, put this number in relation to the total population of their country, this number may seem relatively small.

At the same time, the symbolic use of figures conceals the respective point of reference. Thus, absolute numbers of infected persons etc. do not indicate the percentage they represent of the total population. At present, the number of fatal cases in Germany is less than one tenth of a per thousand of the general population. However, the figure of fatal cases could also be put in relation to the total number of deaths in Germany in 2017 (932,272), of which the statistics show 344,500 deaths from cardiovascular diseases and 227,600 from cancer alone.

Moreover, the mere figure conceals the circumstances of its determination. The number of those infected had increased, it was said. But this finding may have been the result of more people having been tested than during the days before. If the figures indicate that the number of deaths has also risen, it is not always made clear whether this is an absolute number or whether only those who died the day before are counted. Likewise, did those who were included in the statistics of fatalities die *because of* or *with* the virus? And would not a particularly large number of people infected be a positive rather than a negative sign regarding the desired herd immunity? Clearly, the way in which such numbers are being perceived by the audience is due to the reference values chosen but not disclosed. Such is the case when, i.e., the number of infected and fatal cases in the USA is compared with those in Germany or even in smaller European member states, without mentioning that the population of the USA roughly corresponds to that of Europe as a whole. Whether such distortions are ideologically intended or not is, of course, difficult to ascertain.

3.2 »Epidemic« and »Pandemic« versus »War«

Attention should also be paid to the metaphors used to describe the threat and the means used to combat it. Here, a striking difference becomes apparent between the rather factual-rational designation as an epi- or pandemic on the one hand and the rhetoric of war metaphors on the other hand, which French President Macron uses and with which he links up – beyond all cultural and political differences between France and the US of the past – to the numerous metaphorical *wars* to which U.S. presidents had previously called (*war on poverty*/Johnson; *war on drugs*/Nixon; *star wars*/Reagan; *war on terror*/Bush; and, lastly, of course, Trump who simultaneously declared *war* on Covid-19, terrorists and drug cartels).

Whereas *epidemic* and *pandemic* emphasize the impersonality of the virus and focus on the degree of its spread determined by objective facts, the *war* metaphor personalises the counterpart and, in a certain way, gives the enemy a face. Above all, *epidemic* and *pandemic* do not pre-determine the means with which the threat is to be countered and the instruments that appear suitable for combating it. The metaphor of *war*, however, evokes a state of emergency right from the outset, i.e. the suspension of certain rights and legal regulations as well as the use of military force.

It should be noted, however, that the *war* metaphor most likely evokes different associations in individual countries. Thus, in Germany, *war* is consistently perceived as a threat due to the tremendous destructions resulting from World War II, which Germany itself had started. In contrast, in France, *la guerre*, of which the French President Macron never tires of speaking, is rather likely to evoke above all the collective narrative of the *resistance* and with it the possibility of a successful individual as well as collective fighting back. Hence what is called up is the hope that such type of warfare with limited means might once again succeed the country to liberate itself from the hated occupiers. Needless to point out that in the US the *war* metaphor has a totally different meaning, where it evokes the overpowering military machinery, which defeats and annihilates the enemy by the use of superior weapon systems. On the one hand, such an understanding manifests the binary scheme of good and evil which is deeply rooted in US culture, as can be seen in almost every US movie production which invariably ends with a man-to-man fist fight between the representative of the good and the representative of the bad. On the other hand, *war* is part of the powerful narrative of the collective US self-image as a world power that – despite the trauma of Vietnam and the less than successful experiences of military engagement in Afghanistan, Iraq and most recently Syria – still considers itself invincible.

3.3 »Boundary« and »Frontier«

The metaphors of *boundary* (Grenze) and *limitation* (Begrenzung), by which the law defines the scope of permissible exercise of freedom, also deserve attention. Law itself lives from the drawing of boundaries like hardly any other social subsystem. In times of Corona, the drawing of boundaries restricting the rights to freedom returns in the form of *containment* (Eingrenzung) of the spread of the virus as well as *limitation* (Beschränkung) of the exponential growth of case numbers and, last but not least, in the reference to the *capacity limit* of hospitals, which is not to be exceeded.

If these borders remain more in the realm of the symbolic, the normatively ordered closure of national borders is about the containment of very real physical spaces of movement. The renewed lowering of the barriers and the suspension of the freedom to travel within the Schengen area – which its inhabitants had long since accepted as an irreversible acquis – with the aim of restricting the spread of the virus may be rationally understandable and presumably justified. Nevertheless, the metaphor of the *border* recalls old subliminal associations. Borders exclude and they include. The closing of borders to protect the confined population understands the threat as an external one, a rhetoric that was already underlying and justifying the Iron Curtain which – at least in the official reading of the GDR – was erected to defend eastern socialism against the presumed attacks by the capitalist west. Signs in border regions that currently indicate that it is not possible to leave one's own country also promote the idea that beyond the barrier there lurks the dangerous, the dark, the unpredictable and ultimately evil.

3.4 »Herd Immunity«

The metaphor of *herd immunity* proves to be particularly ambivalent. On the one hand, *immunity* sounds positive at first, since it removes medical vulnerability and with it the concrete fear of the abstract danger of infection. The term *herd* refers to the multitude of masses in which the individual is absorbed and finds protection. The immunisation of the many limits the spread of the virus and is intended to ensure the survival of the community. On the other hand, the comparison with a herd of animals, which resonates in the metaphor of *herd immunity*, at the same time evokes the idea that the herd gives up some of its members – according to a Darwinian description its *weakest* – in order to ensure the survival of the group. It is not without reason that *risk group* is a related term used in public discussion which, contrary to the idea of a *herd immunity*, tries to protect the particularly vulnerable members of the community not only in medical but also in symbolic terms, i.e. by trying to isolate them from the rest of the population.

3.5 »Necessity«

Finally, a brief comment shall be made on the concept of *necessity*, which has been talked about so much lately. Just like Angela Merkel's famous *without alternative* (alternativlos), *necessary* seeks to exclude every other possibility and every other procedure right from the outset. What remains unmentioned is the purpose to which the statement that something is necessary refers. In one of the Do-it-yourself stores, which are currently still open in parts of Germany not only to craftsmen but to the general public, an announcement was made that one should not only keep the required distance to fellow customers, but also limit the duration of one's stay in the store to the extent *necessary*. However, the question is: Necessary for what? Until the addressed customer has found what he is looking for? But who then decides what the customer may search? Or does *necessary* mean only those items which are absolutely needed, and if so, according to what criteria are these items to be determined? Are those determinations to be made according to objective or subjective criteria, by typified groups of customers or by individual circumstances?

Regarding the law, two things may be concluded from these observations. Firstly, the fading out of the frame of reference by way of metaphorical *short cuts* in thinking leads to considerable uncertainty about what is and what exactly is not permitted. Secondly, such questions, with which the courts in the pre-Corona era had to deal with on a daily basis, remain unanswered for the time being, i.e. at least as long as the re-entry of the law described above does not occur.

4. Unwanted Functional Changes

To what extent the re-entry of the law will succeed cannot be predicted with certainty. Experience to date with restrictions on fundamental rights introduced in Germany at the time of terrorist threats demonstrates that there will be no complete return to the *status quo ante* once the threat is over. Invariably, there will be a desire to extend the simplified procedure of issuing regulations made possibly in view of the Corona crisis to other areas. Most important, however, the more determined the political will is to prevent the re-entry of the law, the less successful it will be. In Russia, for example, Putin brought the constitutional amendment abolishing the time limit on his presidency through the Duma at a time when the Western media had already largely focused their attention on the incipient Corona crisis. After all, he too was then forced by the pandemic to postpone the associated plebiscite.

In Hungary, President Orbán has, in the shadow of – and with reference to – Corona, eliminated the principles of the rule of law and, by means of a parliamentary enabling act, secured for himself dictatorial powers which in Europe go beyond the Polish measures and which have hitherto been known only from Turkey. However, the explanation for this dramatic development is less to be found in the change of the rule of law, but rather by asking what changes occurred in Hungarian society in recent years. After all, Hungary was the most liberal country within the former Eastern bloc which – in spite of the suppression of the 1956 uprising – had furthest escaped Stalinist influence and had helped democratic freedoms to break through in 1989 by opening its borders with Austria. Likewise, Trump undertakes electoral diversionary tactics when he combines the fight against Corona – as mentioned above – with a simultaneous fight against terrorism and drugs, and to this end threatens the government of Venezuela with real military means.

Finally, it can be described as normative collateral damage of the Corona crisis if different normative standards are applied when it comes to distinguish domestic from foreign measures. To cite just one example: Whereas the admission of postal voting is considered to be in line with democratic traditions in the case of the Bavarian run-off vote of the local elections, the Polish PiS-party has been accused of election manipulation with regard to a comparable measure for their presidential elections on the sole ground that unlike Germany Polish law did not previously provide for a universally applicable postal voting and therefore had to introduce it by law before it could be applied.

5. Return to Normality (*Status Quo Ante*)?

The question of the extent to which there will be a lasting change in the functionalities of law and legal instruments is, of course, only part of the more general question which of the currently suspended behaviours will be resumed once the crisis is over. What will remain, what will be cut back? And what will an exit strategy look like?

There can hardly be any doubt that life will pick up again once the Corona crisis is over. For the time being, the longing for faraway places is likely to be merely postponed. Once the travel restrictions have been lifted, the longing will be lived out more intensely, at least to the extent that the virus does not survive and wait at the envisaged travel destinations. However, it seems not entirely unlikely that the upgrading of digital communication tools will make some of the former business trips and project meetings superfluous. Likewise, the digital offer of educational and cultural institutions will certainly not be reduced again once the closure of schools and museums is lifted. In this respect it can already be said that the crisis has initiated and promoted beneficial effects. Whether the normative expectation of not shaking hands as a sign of personal greeting and beyond that to kiss the cheek – i.e. whether there will be a definitive end to the kissing society – seems uncertain. After all, the close relative of the cheek kiss, the socialist brother kiss, did not survive the fall of the Iron Curtain. A more central question will, of course, be to what extent the discourse on saving the world climate can benefit from the current forced reduction in polluting emissions.

To end on a positive note: Perhaps the most important message of the changes in the functionality of the law is that it is not the economy that is the measure of all things, but the well-being of people. Of course, it cannot be denied that human well-being is at least also dependent on the functioning of the economy, just as, conversely, a prioritization of the economy based on utilitarianism, which has reached a climax in neo-liberal ideas, can serve the well-being of the people. However, even though both approaches look at two sides of the same coin, it makes a decisive difference from which side one looks at the problem. From an economic point of view, the guiding principle is primarily one of maximising profits, whereas from a point of view which takes human beings as its starting point, the issue is primarily one of their physical and psychological well-being. Perhaps at the end of the day, ordo-liberal ideas of a social market economy will regain the upper hand. Then the Corona crisis would have re-opened the chance not only to solve the problem of production, but also the so far inadequately addressed problem of distribution.

6. Addendum

The above text was written in the third week of the Corona restrictions. In order to keep it as authentic as possible, rather than revising the text I decided to add a few additional remarks from the perspective of week 11 or 12.

First, the war metaphor as used by the French president was the first subject to change. In his next speech to his people after I had written my text, President Macron deliberately avoided the war metaphor with its semantic and symbolic reference to the dead, which are the inevitable consequence of any military conflict. Rather, he switched to a rhetoric which presented him as the President of the Republic protecting the well-being of his citizens. The semantic and symbolic proximity to the state of emergency and the dead was thus replaced by a semantic of caring for the living.

In Germany, the easing of the restrictions on freedom appears to have been a rather smooth process. This is also attested to Germany from abroad. Of course, as stated above, any crisis requiring rapid action is the hour of the executive. This applies both to the imposition of measures restricting freedom and to their gradual easing by means of a continuous review of the constantly changing circumstances. In this respect, the time factor is of the essence. A measure which may have appeared proportionate at a point in time X may prove to be no longer proportionate at a later point in time Y, particularly since the forecasts on the basis of which the decision was taken are also subject to change over time.

It is the traditional task of the courts to review the political decisions taken in each individual dispute. As a matter of fact, the courts have already begun to do so, first by way of interim relief and subsequently by way of proceedings on the merits. Thus, for example, the courts in Germany have at least partially lifted the absolute ban on demonstrations and the validity of the absolute quarantine after returning from abroad. They also have permitted Muslim Friday prayers to be held again provided the security measures are maintained. It must also be examined whether the Act Protecting against Infection does indeed provide a proper legal basis for the measures which have been taken. Of course, the work of the courts is not over yet, but all in all, the *re-entry* of the law, as it has been called in the text above, can also be said to have worked out satisfactorily. Since the law continued to exist without interruption, what happened was, of course, not a real *re-entry*, but rather a mere time lag between the legal control and the decisions the executive had to take rather quickly.

Even if the courts declared some of the measures taken as contrary to the law, one need not conclude to a failure of policy as such. Rather, the courts have made it clear that in each individual case it is important to weigh up conflicting civil liberties and their delimitation against each other. No freedom is boundless. The freedom of one person ends where the freedom of another person begins. However, since this rule also applies vice versa, the delimitation of the respective freedoms must be determined in an iterative procedure from the perspective of both sides. There is just no absolute right to freedom of action, as much as there is no absolute right to (health) protection. Neither does Corona allow everything, nor does any freedom-limiting measure as such violate the constitution in times of Corona. Moreover, the principle of equality does not mean that all addressees of the law must be treated equally. Rather, it only means that those who are equal are to be treated equally. What matters is the validity of the reasons given to justify a differentiation or no differentiation. This opens the door to differentiate not only in terms of time, but also in terms of place. Not surprisingly, the political decision-making competence has, in times of relaxation, de facto shifted from the federal to the state governments. Finally, an incorrect ex ante assessment cannot ex post be reproached in principle, but only if it has led to an obviously grossly erroneous assessment of the situation. On the whole, as likewise stated by the outgoing President of the German Federal Constitutional Court, the constitutional state has proved to be well equipped and functioning in the face of the challenges of Corona.

In the meantime, however, in times of Corona the law is confronted with another challenge. It is not only a question of the growing public call for relaxation of Corona-related restrictions, and the increasing influence of this pressure on the political decision-making process. Rather, a fundamental resistance seems to be forming itself, which is increasingly crying out its lack of consent.

In this respect, a distinction must be made. It is, of course, everyone's guaranteed fundamental right to express their opinion, even and especially if this opinion is not in accordance with the restrictions imposed by state authorities. This is all the more true because, in view of the uncertain ex ante assessments on the basis of which decisions had to be taken, it is not always clear whether the state authorities have respected or exceeded the limits of their discretion. The demonstrators also question that the state decisions were adopted in the constitutionally prescribed way. The expression of such opinions contributes to the social debate – which, incidentally, is also repeatedly called for by politicians – on the legality of the restrictive measures imposed. Above all, the demonstrators, like the executive, argue on the basis of fundamental rights they want to see protected. Of course, the voices of the demonstrators may give the impression that they are in possession of the sole truth. However, the fact that they do not mention the judiciary, which is ultimately responsible for judging such issues in a constitutional state, is characteristic of any expression of opinion by way of a demonstration and is therefore not a corona-induced particularity.

However, the situation is different for extremist expressions of opinion, which claim the protection of freedom of expression with the sole aim of abolishing democracy, the constitutional order and the freedoms which they make use of. This, too, is not new. Rather, it runs through the history of the Federal Republic like a red thread from the constitutional ban of the Communist Party (KPD) in 1956 to the decrees banning left-wing radicals from entering public service (Radikalenerlasse) in the 1970s and the proceedings for banning the right-wing German nationalist party (NPD), right up to the monitoring of the völkisch wing of the AfD party by the Office for the Protection of the Constitution (Verfassungsschutz). In contrast, the supporters of conspiracy theories fall into a different category. They adhere to a logic which systematically blocks other approaches. At the same time, the large number of those who disagree with their views even confirms their assumption of a conspiracy. It may not be easy to identify the psychological reasons that lead to such patterns of reaction. It may be possible to identify reasons in the self-perception of those who feel pushed to the margins of society and excluded from the general discourse. This is supported by the fact that the arguments of most, if not all, types of conspiracy theories have a strong reduction of complexity in common. Instead of relying on soft factors such as trust, credibility, probability, estimation and prognosis, conspiracy theories are mostly constructed on the basis of simple binary subdivisions of good and evil, friend and foe, victim and perpetrator, true and false, which are then immunized against any verification by facts and possible correction by way of doubt. From this point of view, the rule of law, the judiciary and the legal system as a whole appear to be in the conspirators' camp, because the law supports and stabilises the state of society which – in the view of adherents to conspiracy theories – is undermined by the conspiracy. However, it may well be that the number of those who generally subscribe to conspiracy theories, or are at least inclined to them, has not increased as a result of Corona, but has merely found its way onto the streets under the present circumstances.

The impression that conspiracy theories were enjoying growing popularity could well be due to the nature of media coverage. While media coverage initially focused on the origins of the epidemic and the details of the restrictions, it subsequently moved on to the discussion of the loosening up, in the course of which the initial consensus began to dissolve both at the political level as in the minds of those affected. Out of this increasingly many-voiced concert of opinions, conspiracy theories stand out as extreme positions which call out for being reported on. In this respect, the scolding of the media by the supporters of conspiracy theories would even seem to be justified to a certain extent. However, the fact that media attention distorts and partly constructs reality is nothing new as is the knowledge of the favourable breeding ground that social media provide for conspiracy theories. Of course, the media are in a quandary. If they report too thoroughly, they exaggerate the phenomenon and fuel conspiracy theories. If they report too little, they expose themselves to the accusation of not reporting neutrally and would thus likewise be water on the mills of those who already consider the media to be ideologically loyal to the government, if not even bought by the villains who, in the opinion of adherents to conspiracy theories, deliberately orchestrated the Corona misery with all its consequences.

Looking at the situation of law in times of Corona as a whole, the dictum of the former constitutional judge Ernst-Wolfgang Böckenförde already referred to in the initial text above still applies: »The liberal, secularized state lives from conditions that it cannot itself guarantee« (»Der freiheitliche, säkularisierte Staat lebt von Voraussetzungen, die er selbst nicht garantieren kann«).[5] Therefore, it is decisive for the rule and the role of law in times of Corona that law can assert itself in the role assigned to it by the constitution even – and especially – in times of crisis.

References

Böckenförde, Ernst-Wolfgang: Die Entstehung des Staates als Vorgang der Säkularisation, in: Buve, Sergius (ed.): Säkularisation und Utopie. Ebracher Studien. Ernst Forsthoff zum 65. Geburtstag. Kohlhammer, Stuttgart et al. 1967, pp. 75–94.

Di Fabio, Udo: An den Grenzen der Verfassung, Frankfurter Allgemeine Zeitung, updated 06.04.2020, https://www.faz.net/aktuell/politik/inland/corona-trifft-liberale-demokratie-grenzen-der-verfassung-16710755.html; last accessed 19.06.2020.

Lichtenberg, Georg Christoph: Aus den Sudelbüchern [1768–1771], Berlin 2013.

---

[5] Böckenförde: Die Entstehung des Staates als Vorgang der Säkularisation.

Jacques Commaille

In a Troubled World:
A New System of Knowledge about Law?

The Covid-19 pandemic has not only turned our daily universe upside down – as intellectuals, it has spurred us to reconceptualize the world, to review the meaning of what we do and the pertinence of the knowledge that we produce. In this way, my current projects thinking about the law have brutally collided with a new reality, that of the world's fragility and our new vulnerability, which global warming had previously announced and the Covid-19 pandemic confirms.

Anchored in both general sociology and political science, I venture, too, in the universe of law, thanks to a collaboration with one of its leading figures, Jean Carbonnier. I have been engaged for a number of years in the question of the law, not as such, but as valuable entry point for study of systems of social and political regulation of contemporary societies. I have also been observing the transformations in scholarship on law, in the ways of thinking about the law. To better understand the meaning of these transformations, I have conducted a comparison with ways of thinking politically and socially about *Nature* and *Culture*. I have come to the realization that the exceptionality of the law in regulating societies fits, too, with the nature of its functions – but not with the ways of thinking. Indeed, from this comparison, I observe a strong convergence between three ways of thinking (*Law, Nature,* and *Culture*) and their transformations in the contemporary period. These three ways of thinking, these three types of knowing have each, following different temporalities, been cognizant of first, the time of certainties – for some it is *modernity*, – and then the time of uncertainties, for some, it is *postmodernity*.

1. A System of Knowledge Blinded by Certainties?

In the time of certainties, the ways of thinking about the *Law* are never far from religious influences. Like the *Nature* and *Culture* universes, the social representation of the law (*Law*), such as it is promoted in the ways one thinks, remains inspired by the idea of transcendence. As Bruno Latour affirms, *Science* claims to represent a »transcendent Certainty«.[1] *Society* is not inscribed in a process of secularization; instead, as considered by Émile Durkheim, it is the object of a displacement of the object of worship, where the Republic is the substitute for God.[2] The law (*Law*) is situated in a similar logic. In the scholarly register that is enjoys, thinking about the law borrows from religion the notion of *dogma*, plainly suggesting that what is set forth cannot be discussed.[3]

The ways of thinking about *Law*, *Science*, and *Society* finally found their legitimacy in the recourse to a mythical rationality, to *Reason*, or *meta-Reason*, for which it is often difficult to distinguish whether it originates from metaphysical considerations or from simple speculation rather than from empirically grounded knowledge following proper exigencies to a veritable reason. Such positioning inscribes the ways of thinking about *Law* in a vision of the world analogous to the one equally integrated by other learning: a pyramidal vision, ranked by the regulation of the world authorizing the recourse to the argument of self-justified authority, as illustrated by a certain theory of law where the reference is made to so-called *anthropological foundations* or when the law is proclaimed to be its own proper explanation.

Such a system of common knowledge promotes the evidence of a binary principle according to which the world is divided into the *knowing* (the *clerics*) and the *profane*. Echoing the invocation of *pure science* attached to the observation of *Nature*, emanating from an immanent production, the claim to a *pure theory of law* undertakes more generally to take into account what comes from the *Social* meanwhile, the necessary purity of knowledge of the law guards itself in the name of preserving of *Law's* specific force, in its reality, and in the ways about which it is thought. Similar to knowledge of *Nature*, it is about distrusting contamination by the *Social* and by the knowledge devoted to it.

One of the strongest features of this general system of knowledge, it is a looming position, incompatible with the idea of contingency, consequently justifying the refusal to be *situated*. Paradoxically, in enunciating macro-theories on the transformations of societies that purport to exhaust the meaning of the social and its transformations, in rejecting any reservations inspired by the observation of the complexity of the world and which weakens the certainty of the inevitable, knowledge of the (social and political) *Culture* is inscribed in the same logic.

---

[1] Latour: An Inquiry Into Modes of Existence, p. 5.
[2] Cf. Durkheim: The Elementary Forms of Religious Life.
[3] Cf. Delmas-Marty/Supiot: L'internationalisation du droit: dégradation ou recomposition?

2. An Evolving System of Knowledge?

Speaking of contemporary societies' future and the challenges they face, the American sociologist Immanuel Wallerstein underscored: »we have reached the end of certainties«.[4] There, too, the ways of thinking about the law, far from being specific, are aligned with the ways of thinking about *Nature* and *Culture*. These ways of thinking are inscribed in a process of disillusionment corresponding to the disappearance or the weakening of everything that conspired to significantly emphasize the transcendental representation of the world. The time has come to contest a dictatorship of *Reason*. Demystified, reason became *relative*. And, yet, it is assumed to be situated, contextual.

In the legal domain as in those of *Nature* or *Culture*, it is now recognized that the legal speech of one who claims to espouse the *Truth* can depend one's location and the values that undergird one's action. The ways of thinking about the law cannot no longer claim to work legislatively as in the case of a *Code civil*, which sought to be the »social Constitution of France«[5] in occupying a position of control from above in relation to the existence of social, cultural, economic, and political contexts that are constitutive, as noted in *Nature*, *Culture*, in its social and political declinations, ensues hence from a self-sufficiently produced global causal explanation, the ways of thinking about the law can decreasingly ignore societal complexities, the multiple strategies that develop from individuals, social groups, and institutions in social, economic, and political spheres from which are increasingly affirmed to be actors in their own destiny. The ways of thinking about the law – or about *Nature* or *Culture* can no longer come from all-encompassing grand theories or from meta-narratives. As noted by Dominique Pestre, historian of science and knowledge, they are obligated to progress »to the study of the complexity of human acts in the situation«.[6]

3. A System of Knowledge to Reform?

The extent of the scholarly mutations is such that it suggests that the challenge is ultimately not an issue of knowledge for knowledge's sake. The awareness of uncertainties about mastering the physical and social world encourages us, more than ever, to ask ourselves how to make society in an uncertain world and how knowledge production can contribute to it. Such an inquiry is particularly well

---

[4] Wallerstein: The Heritage of Sociology, the Promise of Social Science.
[5] An expression taken up during celebrations of the bicentennial of the French Civil Code.
[6] Pestre: Introduction aux Sciences Studies.

worth it in terms of the ways of thinking about the law, this exceptional means at the heart of the social and political regulation of societies.

The easy choice can be made. It would be inspired, for example, by a *declinist* view of the future of societies justifying the consideration that it should return to a utopian time of scientific certainties by restoring a political authoritarianism drawing from a dogmatic law in the most original and narrowest of meaning.

This regression could also take another form: the growing imposition of a bureaucratic and technical normativity that bears the double menace of euphemizing politics up until their apparent obliteration and a dispossession of the social actors, including legal professionals, following the dawn of this managerial and technical normativity inscribed in what Pierre Rosanvallon labels »the process of rationalization« to oppose »the process of democratization«.[7] The increasing domination of technical norms, of actuarial instruments, or even an *algorithmic justice* or *governance by the numbers*. The Michel Foucault's prophecy offered the first signs: »And if the universal legalism of modern society seems to fix the limits on the exercise of power, its widespread panoptism operates basic law, a machine both immense and miniscule that supports, reinforces, multiplies the dissymmetry of forces, and renders meaningless the limits we trace«.[8]

The paths that we have chosen to sketch out the ways of thinking about the law and their future are completely different. One must first pay attention to what comes from society and to what has to do with the law. As illustrations among many, microhistory, ethnography, and legal consciousness studies[9] are approaches that highlight the richness of legal life even at the heart of the political effervescence wherein citizens employ multiple means of appropriating or even mythicizing the law.

Such a *bottom-up* perspective does not counteract the finality of the law that is also constructed from *References* in order to structure societies. On the contrary, it is prone to renew it. The challenge is in effect to think about legality not as instituted *from above*, but *also* as a result of citizen involvement, of conferring to this legality a new universality that would not be western-centric but would take into consideration cultural diversity and different categories of conceiving the world (time, property, land, etc.)[10] for the foundation of legal categories. (We note here how these transformations in thinking about the law demonstrate an extraordinary parallelism with the different ways of thinking about *Nature*, where Sheila Jasanoff, one of the key figures in *Science and Technology Studies,* sees a »co-pro-

---

[7] Rosanvallon: L'État en France de 1789 à nos jours.
[8] Foucault: Surveiller et punir.
[9] See, for example, the dossier dedicated to this current of research coordinated by Commaille/Lacour: After Legal Consciousness Studies.
[10] Cf. de Sousa Santos: Epistemologies of the South.

duction«.[11] The philosopher Cynthia Fleury sees the »sharing of knowledge« in the State of law.[12])

In these new perspectives that we can only sketch here, the question of the new exigence of *making society* is at stake, as in the case in the theory of law in Quebec circles, as evidenced by one of its most eminent representatives, Jean-Guy Belley, who considers it crucial to substitute the relationship »law and society« with »law and community«.[13] Or, the law should be not rethought solely as a function of what society does, but it should be *to rediscover, under new forms, certain virtues that modernity makes us lose.*

In this world turned upside down that we are currently experiencing, rethinking the ways in which we think about the law is, ultimately, to shoulder the exigency of inscribing these ways in a new political vision in the most noble sense. As Étienne Tassin wrote superbly in his work: »The world [...] calls for a cosmopolitics that deploys within each State through the reformulation of the relationships between what the public thing must undertake with the different cultural, religious, ethical, or sexual communities that *compose the political society*«.[14]

References

Belley, Jean-Guy: Ubi communitas, ibi ius: *Communitas*, Collectif «droit et société», Montréal/Québec (forthcoming).
Commaille, Jacques/Stéphanie Lacour: After Legal Consciousness Studies: Transatlantic Dialogues, in: Droit et Société, 100, 2018, pp. 547–780.
de Sousa Santos, Boaventura: Epistemologies of the South. Justice Against Epistemicide, London/New York 2013.
Delmas-Marty, Mireille/Alain Supiot: L'internationalisation du droit: dégradation ou recomposition? Dialogue, in: Esprit, 11, 2012, pp. 35–51.
Durkheim, Émile: The Elementary Forms of Religious Life, Oxford/UK 2001.
Fleury, Cynthia: Construire un comportement collectif respectueux de l'État de droit, in: Le Monde, 27.03.2020, https://www.lemonde.fr/idees/article/2020/03/27/cynthia-fleury-l-un-des-enjeux-de-l-epidemie-est-de-construire-un-comportement-collectif-respectueux-de-l-etat-de-droit_6034577_3232.html; last accessed 07.06.2020.
Foucault, Michel: Surveiller et punir, Paris 1975.

---

[11] Jasanoff: States of Knowledge.
[12] Fleury: Construire un comportement collectif respectueux de l'État de droit.
[13] Belley: Ubi communitas, ibi ius: *Communitas*.
[14] Tassin: Un monde commun, p. 301.

Jasanoff, Sheila (ed.): States of Knowledge. The Co-production of Science and Social Order, London/New York 2006.

Latour, Bruno: An Inquiry into Modes of Existence. An Anthropology of the Moderns, Cambridge/MA 2013.

Pestre, Dominique: Introduction aux Sciences Studies: La Découverte, coll. « Repères », Paris 2006.

Rosanvallon, Pierre: L'État en France de 1789 à nos jours, Paris 1990.

Tassin, Étienne: Un monde commun. Pour une cosmo-politique des conflits, coll. « La couleur des idées », Paris 2003.

Wallerstein, Immanuel: The Heritage of Sociology, the Promise of Social Science. Presidential Address, IVth World Congress of Sociology, Montréal, 26 July 1998, in: Current Sociology, 47(1), 1999, pp. 1–37.

Maurizio Ferraris

Mobilization

These quarantine times are also times of »smart working«, and the question arises as to what is »smart« about it. Let's start from an unquestionable point. As always happens, the current crisis is accelerating an ongoing trend, i.e. the transition from labour to mobilization that has been going on for at least twenty years, which has blurred the distinction between working time and living time (this was initially presented as the possibility of working as if you were on vacation, but of course it has come to signify that you *also* work on vacation). There are two ways to see this phenomenon, and they are not mutually exclusive. However, the first is confined to the past, while the second looks to the future.

1. The first consists in observing that capital is expanding its dominion by not even taking charge of the means and places of production, and this trend is decisively driven by the security requirements imposed by the virus outbreak. There is some truth in this view, as one can easily understand. The problem, though, is that it involves a scheming and plotting supernatural entity, i.e. Capital, or a modern Satan (wasn't it Marx who insisted on the Faustian character of Capital?). But the collapse of the stock markets, the unpreparedness of governments, and the general turmoil in progress should at least raise the legitimate suspicion that Satan was not quite on top of things and has failed to warn his followers in time so that they could take full advantage of the outbreak.

2. The second way, perhaps more complicated and a little longer to explain, does not involve Satan, but the human being. This view can give us not only hopes, but actual solutions for the future – a future that will obviously look very little like the past, since the current crisis is of an epochal character, bringing together the two great components of the world, souls and mechanisms, life and technology. Let's start from a simple observation: if computers could only be used in the office, at certain times and places, would we actually »live« at home, leaving computers behind? Of course not. At work, at home, and on the way between home and work, we always look at our mobile phones, both for work and for other reasons, and this is because mobilization is not a command that comes from outside, but the fundamental characteristic of every soul. In fact, every soul is driven by vital urges, be they the remote consciousness of death or the very near need to have lunch. We humans are particularly maladapted organisms, because we are slow

to grow and poorly endowed by nature, but we have mechanisms to enhance our scarce resources. To put it succinctly, we are organisms, but ones that are related to a series of automata which they cannot do without, and that is why even when we could be inert *à la* Oblomov we tinker with our mobile phones instead.

The difference between organisms and automata is very simple. An organism has only two positions, on or off, dead or alive. An automaton, on the other hand, works serially: on/off, on/off, and so on, until the bulb burns out or the battery deteriorates. An organism has an internal purpose, its end is its end, so to speak, and in between there is life. An automaton has an external purpose: knives are made to cut, books to be read, fines to be paid. This mass of external purposes enrich the life of the soul, giving it a little more meaning (this is why pensioners often get depressed: depression is but the revelation of bare life, of the organism without automata), and this is why the human organism has so much need of automata, from clubs to fire to society to culture. But – and this is the main point – if we remove the organism, the soul, then the automata make no sense. Imagine the British Library or Times Square in a world without a soul (something that we can imagine quite easily today, as all souls are locked indoors).

3. However, let's get back to earth. Remote working is still the offshoot of a vanishing old world, a world where souls produce by using automata. But in the meantime, for about ten years now, automata have become capable of recording the souls' smallest gestures, recording them and replicating them. This is what artificial intelligence is. Instead of thinking that automata will take over (why should they? What would be the point? Despite their misleading name, automata don't run themselves, they need souls), and fearing that they will steal our jobs (that's what they are doing, but not fast enough, as this crisis would be much less serious in a fully automated world), let's try to look at the matter a little more carefully (not smartly – let's be wary of this term that always hides a catch). Big Internet platforms are huge automata that record the souls' smallest gestures in an exchange that seems fair (I give you free information, and you give me free information) but is not (automata can capitalize the information and translate it into automation and distribution, as well as profit, whereas souls cannot).

But automata cannot live and produce wealth (they have never produced as much wealth as they are doing at this very moment, when all souls are on the Internet) without souls. Automata need souls just as souls need food. And if souls die, automata are finished: therefore the survival of souls is indispensable, on pain of the end of all things, the end of time – total apocalypse. Of course, this only applies to the association of souls and automata – the rest of the world will get along great without us, but we won't be there.

4. In conclusion, let me explain what the only kind of »smart working« is: doing nothing, »far niente«, that is, living, cultivating one's hobbies and interests, studying, writing, exercising and eating. Each of our acts, today, is recorded and produces value, precisely because it instructs the automata that live by imitating souls. This value must be redistributed, but first of all it must be acknowledged. Think of the groups that are most exposed today, namely all those who are employed and poorly paid. What can be done for them? Those who fought against automation, in their case, may have done so for the noblest of reasons, but ultimately caused their misfortune. And what will support the souls once they have been replaced by automata? Digital welfare: the taxation of the enormous surplus value that souls, by the mere fact of living, generate in their interaction with automata. I repeat: the great Internet platforms have never earned as much as they do today, and if we think about it, the answer to the questions »who will pay Coronabonds?« and »what is the EU doing?« is very simple: Coronabonds will be paid by the platforms, and the EU will collect the taxation and redistribute it in terms of welfare.

Welfare means freedom from material needs, but also from ignorance and prejudice – therefore, it also means culture, i.e. a resource that seems particularly valuable in these weeks of quarantine. If the virus, as is to be expected, ends up accelerating the ongoing processes, then so much blood will not have been shed for nothing. But for this to happen we need to be able to think of the future not as the projection of the past (that's what »smart working« amounts to) but as a radically new era that is coming forward unceremoniously, but that will really change the world, and change it for the better.

Markus Gabriel

We Need a Metaphysical Pandemic

The global order has been shaken. A virus, invisible to the eye and of yet unknown magnitude, is spreading. How many people have been infected with the coronavirus, how many people might still die and when will we have developed a vaccine — these and many other questions remain unanswered. Just like the question of how the radical action currently taken around Europe will impact our economies and democracies.

The coronavirus is not just another infectious disease but a viral pandemic. The word *pandemic* derives from the Greek words pan (all) and demos (people), and it is indeed all people who are affected by it to the same extent. Yet we seem oblivious to this truth, thinking that a reasonable answer is to restrain people within borders. Why would the virus care that the border between Germany and France has been closed? Why has Spain become something to shun in our efforts to contain the virus? The answer you will get is: because health systems are national matters and each state must take care of its sick within its respective borders. While this is true, it is also the core problem. The pandemic affects all people. It shows that we are all connected by that invisible bond of being human. All people are equal before the virus. Indeed, it is only before the virus that people are once more becoming humans, i.e. members of a certain animal species that happen to be good hosts for the replication of an often deadly virus.

Generally speaking, viruses are an unsolved metaphysical problem. Nobody knows whether they are alive. This is due to the fact that we still lack a clear definition of life. In fact, nobody knows where life really begins. Is it enough to have DNA and RNA or do we need cells with the ability to multiply autonomously? The truth is: we do not know, just like we do not know whether plants, insects or even our own livers are conscious beings. The Earth's ecosystem might still turn out to be one giant living organism. Is the coronavirus a planetary immune response against human hubris leading to the destruction of countless creatures simply out of greed for profit?

The coronavirus is revealing the systemic weaknesses of the 21st century's dominant ideology. These include the misbelief that we can drive human and moral progress through scientific and technological progress alone, which in turn leads us to believe that scientific experts can solve universal social problems. The coronavirus is proving this point, making it plain for all to see. This will, however, turn out to be a dangerous misconception. Yes, we do need to consult virologists.

Only they can help understand and contain the virus and save human lives. But who will listen when they tell us that every year, more than two hundred thousand children die from diarrhea caused by viruses caught from dirty water? Why does nobody care about these children? Sadly, the answer is quite simple: because these children do not live in Germany, Spain, France or Italy. This, of course, is not entirely true either. They live in European refugee camps, after fleeing from unjust situations, for which we as consumers are partly to blame.

There is no real progress without moral progress. This is the lesson the pandemic teaches us, with racist prejudice being revealed everywhere. Trump does his best to paint the virus a Chinese problem; Boris Johnson takes the UK down a social-Darwinist path, trying to solve the problem by building up eugenic herd immunity. Many people in Germany believe their health system to be superior to its Italian counterpart, trusting that Germany will somehow do better in handling the crisis. These are dangerous stereotypes coupled with foolish prejudice.

We are all in the same boat. This is hardly news. The 21st century in itself is a pandemic, the result of globalization. All the virus does is reveal what has already been there: our need for an entirely new understanding of global awareness. Peter Sloterdijk provides us with a suitable term: instead of communism, we need co-immunism. This means that we must vaccinate ourselves against intellectual poison dividing us into national cultures, races, age groups and classes competing with each other. Right now, Europeans are protecting their sick and elderly in an unprecedented effort of solidarity. To achieve this, we are locking in our children, closing our schools and creating a medical state of emergency. We are investing billions to boost our economies. If we continue down the same route we were pursuing before the coronavirus outbreak, we will face even worse crises: more dangerous viruses, impossible to prevent; a continued economic war with the USA, currently fought by the European Union; the spread of racism and nationalism aimed at people who seek refuge after we provided their executioners with weapons and the scientific knowledge to build chemical weapons. And let's not forget about the climate crisis, which is worse than any virus because its result will be the gradual self-extinction of human life. The coronavirus has merely slowed this process down for a limited period of time. Before the coronavirus, the world order was not normal, it was lethal. Why can we not invest billions to change our mobility? Why can we not use the digital transformation to hold business meetings online instead of unnecessarily flying all over the world in private jets? When will we finally understand that compared to our misbelief that we will be able to solve all modern-world problems with science and technology, the coronavirus is actually quite harmless?

This is a call to all of us, all human beings, not just Europeans: we need a new kind of awareness. Every human being must receive ethical training to be able to fully apprehend the enormous danger that lies in blindly following science and technology. Of course, fighting the virus with all means at hand is the right strategy for now. All of a sudden, we live solidarity and experience waves of morality. This is a positive development. But at the same time, we must not forget that, within a few weeks, we have transitioned from a state of populist disdain for scientific expertise to what my friend from New York is calling a *science-obeying North Korea*. We must understand that the chains of infection of global capitalism, destroying our nature and dulling our national citizens' minds so that we become full-time tourists and consumers, will kill more people in the long run than any virus ever could. Why does a medical or virological finding yield solidarity while we widely ignore the philosophical conclusion that the only way out of suicidal globalization is a world order beyond an accumulation of competing national states driven by a mindless and quantitative economic logic? After the viral pandemic, we will need a metaphysical pandemic, a unification of all people under the all-embracing sky from which we will never be able to escape. We are, and will continue to be, part of this Earth. We are, and will continue to be, mortal and fragile. So let us become citizens of this Earth, cosmopolitans in a metaphysical pandemic. Everything else will be the end of us, and no virologist will be able to save us.

Laurent de Sutter

The Logistics of Pandemic

1. Plague

Agent Smith was exasperated. He had been brutally interrogating Morpheus for several hours now, without being able to crack him. Never had he been so close to the goal of his mission: to wrest from a human being who knew him the means of accessing Zion, the last resistant city. He was on the brink, however. But Morpheus was entirely sustained by the conviction that he had just discovered the Chosen One – the one who, precisely, would allow Zion to rise up against the reign of the machines represented by Smith. In an unexpected move, the officer therefore decided to address the rebel captain directly, privately – and disconnected his headset from the Matrix:

»I'd like to share a revelation that I have had during my time here. It came to me when I tried to classify your species. I realized that you're not actually mammals. Every mammal on this planet instinctively develops a natural equilibrium with the surrounding environment, but you humans do not. You move to an area and you multiply and multiply until every natural resource is consumed. The only way you can survive is to spread to another area. There is another organism on this planet that follows the same pattern. Do you know what it is? A virus. Human beings are a disease, a cancer of this planet. You are a plague, and we are the cure.«

His was an aggressive and relentless monologue testifying for a superior form of lucidity – while demoralizing his interlocutor. Of course, it was quite possible to dismiss it with the back of the hand, as one would do with a speech too often heard, a caricature as it is drawn from time to time on the side of the great misanthropes. However, Agent Smith was not entirely wrong. If we put aside the rhetoric of contempt, there was something true in the description of a humanity with more than one trait in common with the modes of operation of a virus. Two points in his speech, in particular, echoed the truth: that which characterizes human beings and viruses by their tendency to move; and that this trend is related to the management of the consequences of their wild multiplication – that is, their quantity. One word synthesizes these two points: the word »logistics«.

2. Cohabitation

In fact, the whole history of epidemics rests on something like a community of destiny: there are viruses only where human beings have organized themselves to live in larger groups than a few individuals. From what we continue to call »Neolithic Revolution« (i. e. around 9–7000 BCE), new techniques for exploiting the most fertile lands surrounding a certain number of hydrological basins, such as the Tiger and Euphrates Delta, indeed authorized the creation of the first sedentary installations. Composed of a few families at the start, these would become bigger over time and eventually form the first villages, the first cities – the first areas of mass cohabitation in history. However, this cohabitation did not only involve humans: it also involved all the creatures that accompanied their sedentarization in the name of the requirements of food, equipment, etc. The Neolithic communities were therefore communities which included as many non-humans, animals and plants, as there were humans – or even more if we add microscopic populations living in symbiosis with them: various insects, micro-organisms, bacteria, etc. The Neolithic organization of communities was the first experiment in large-scale cohabitation between species, and even regimes, which were not necessarily made to live together – or, for that matter, to live together peacefully. Symptomatically, the first epidemics in history also date back to this period; it was as early as the Neolithic that we can witness traces of sudden disappearances of entire cities – disappearances whose only possible explanation is that they were due to brutal attacks of diseases. In fact, close coexistence with non-humans, as well as their parasitic populations, favoured inter-species exchanges, for better or for worse, certain animal diseases discovering an affinity for the human biological environment. Very early, therefore, the fact that humans discovered techniques for ensuring a more stable way of life, and a more efficient exploitation of the environment, paradoxically led to the reinforcement of other types of threats to its survival – the viruses also benefiting from the results of human innovations.

3. Traffic

But that's not all. Besides the establishment of a new ecology, the side effects of which were not mastered by those who wanted to be the main beneficiaries, the techniques of exploiting the world developed since the Neolithic era helped its diffusion. As long as certain resources were present (mostly water), it was possible to acclimatize the technologies and strategies developed in the large fertile basins. It was enough to adapt the logistics networks (that is, at the beginning, the first roads as well as the first irrigation and water piping systems) to the local context.

Humans had always been nomadic: they knew better than anyone the importance of traffic — so that when they decided to settle in a specific place, they contented themselves with reversing its movement. Rather than spending their time traveling, they gradually organized ways to bring things to them — whether it was water, precisely, or, later, grain, livestock, workers, and so on. That is to say, the first human groups quickly transformed into *logistical attractors* — more or less important nodes in a network of circulation of beings and things without which local life would remain limited. The growth of the groups became conditional on the extension of its grip on its environment, and therefore on the capacity implemented by them to seize at a distance what they needed in order to ensure their subsistence — not to mention their development. For them to be able to live *here*, there had to be life *there* as well, and both should be put in communication so as to support each other. As was to be expected, this gradual extension of life management was not without consequences for the way parasitic populations of human beings managed their place, too. With the raw materials, the cattle or the traders themselves, the creatures that had made the Neolithic microcosm their residence also accompanied the meanders of its geographical displacements. If epidemics were born from the interspecies concentration organized by human beings, pandemics, on another hand, appeared with their spread over the entire surface of the planet. They were the mark of success in its colonization.

4. Modernity

The necessary consequence of all that is the following: there is nothing new in contemporary pandemics. They have accompanied human history as its shadow — or rather: as the shadow of the successes, more or less brilliant and more or less oblivious, which it encountered on the way to its own diffusion. It would even be possible to draw a kind of pandemic line, which would serve as a counterpoint to the traditional narration of the stages considered to be the most decisive in the human conquest of the planet. The great plagues that have affected the whole world since the time of Antoninus the Pious, in the 2nd century AD, all bore witness to a specific state of the logistical development of the civilizations that they ravaged. The epidemics of malaria, yellow fever, typhus, etc., which swept across the North American continent after the arrival of Europeans, also marked the fact that it is impossible to think of diseases outside the factory of the human world. By closing the globe on itself, the explorers also helped to complete the path of circulation for the creatures that accompanied them — whether pigs, rabbits and horses, a whole series of plants, like sugar cane, or, of course, bacteria and viruses. Pandemics of the industrial age, from this point of view, did not change much: they were content to unfold in a context where logistical connections were more numerous and where human concentration had reached a point of no return. With modernity, pandemics truly became pandemics, in the sense that there was no longer any corner of the globe that could claim to be outside the network of connections allowing the circulation of things and beings. But, from the point of view of their nature, industrial development and globalization did not transform the conditions of cohabitation between humans and their parasites; pandemics were inscribed in the fact that humans cannot live alone – and that certain forms of life take advantage of this impossibility of solitude to be able to exist too. Wherever logistics allow the multiplication of human beings, there will be creatures likely to profit from it; and the more this logistics will make it possible for a large number of individuals to survive, the more likely they are to harbour the very thing that is best able to destroy them.

5. World

When Martin Heidegger allowed himself his famous remark that animals were »poor in world«, he was therefore twice wrong: not only do animals have a world, but this world, for a large part, is none other than the one we made. This is a great lesson from the discussions about whether we have entered the Anthropocene or not: we have suddenly discovered that a world is never given, but always made. All the activities in which human beings have engaged have no other goal than the constitution of something like a world, a liveable space, on the surface of a planet that it was not acquired that it was habitable. It just so happens that such a world is not built entirely by those who imagine it – for there to be a world, it requires the collaboration of a considerable number of beings, some acting in a more or less invited manner, while others operate behind the scenes. To speak of logistics is therefore to speak of all the conditions in the name of which there is a world, and therefore also of the consequences that the application of these conditions to the life of humans entails in terms of unwanted guests. We are not alone in the world; the very fact that there is a world implies cohabitation with myriads of other beings, from pieces of rock excavated in mines to microorganisms synthesizing oxygen or filtering the rays of the sun in the atmosphere. The exorbitant force of human beings, if there is one, therefore only consists in imposing a dominant note, a rule of order, on the world in which it had embarked the others, not without the latter then adapting it to their sauce. Because it is the fact of all cohabitation to alter what we cohabit with – to contribute to modifying the design of the world made by those with whom we invite ourselves. In the case of pandemics, this alteration can be fatal for a whole series of individuals; for the others, it is rather a way of drawing the ultimate consequences from the facilities offered — until, by a defence reaction, these are closed. It would be foolish to believe that we could prevent it — that we would be able to decide access to the world as we pretend to decide access of such and such a category of person on the territory of such or such nation. In a world, closing a door is always like opening a window.

6. Fault

An essential conclusion must be drawn from all of this — a conclusion radically opposed to the one Agent Smith wanted Morpheus to understand in order to demoralize him. This conclusion would be that in the history of pandemics, and in particular in its contemporary aspect, it is not possible to designate the culprits, those responsible, the individuals to blame. There are many candidates, however: from industrial capitalism to neoliberal management of populations, including the colonizing West and the anthropocentric psyche of humans, they have not failed to receive the attention of critics from all walks of life. But there is nothing more ridiculous, more absurd, than this critical reflex. In the same way that a virus has no moral reason to blame the person it kills, no one is responsible for the state of the world that we all help to build — for our greatest benefit, and that of a series of other species. In reality, the very fact that the world is manufactured, the result of our care as jealous as incompetent, should arouse in us a paradoxical reflex of solidarity with the stowaways of the life we have organized. In the world as we have designed it, it has indeed become difficult to distinguish what is virus and what is not, what is parasitic and what is not, which world our logistics infrastructure is support of or not. While it is undeniable that a large number of parameters relating to the concentration and logistical extension of humanity on planet Earth could be better managed, this management is not a question of political or economic project. It is a question of a cosmological project — even a *cosmologistical* one. The roads, canals, bridges, rails, tunnels, cables, pipes, conduits, pipelines, which cover the planet with their networks, are by definition traffic systems without which there would be no life at all — to properly speaking: they are life, because they are the world. The whole issue, for those who would like to have more control over the flow of undesirable, therefore consists in starting by measuring to what extent, more than any form of discourse or ideology, it is from these systems that, all together, we depend. We can never get rid of this blurry border set — but at least we can learn the reason for it.

Jure Leko

At the Borders of Europe.
On Spatial Mobility during the
Covid-19 Crisis

The border is back! That was the headline of numerous media reports when, in response to the Covid-19 crisis, European states introduced various forms of border closings in a publicly visible way, thereby performatively showcasing evidence of their sovereignty. The kilometer-long traffic jams of trucks and passenger vehicles at German-Polish border crossings, the grounding of entire airplane fleets, the entry bans for non-EU citizens, and the closing of ports in Italy and Malta for civil sea rescues bear testament to this. For »sovereignty apostles«, to use a term coined by Maurizio Ferraris,[1] the border closings had a signaling effect: The state is capable of action after all – something that had been sorely missed in the huge migration movement of 2015.

The border restrictions have moved Ivan Krastev to reaffirm his thesis of a »comeback of the state«, which will once again strengthen states' individual roles within the European Union and thereby save the community of states from its downfall.[2] Coming from the opposite argumentative direction, Wendy Brown concludes that the raising of borders in general (e.g. in form of walls, fences, or by means of digital technology) is merely the desperate expression of dwindling statal power and that the new trend of ›walling-off‹ represents waning sovereignty.[3] Beyond all differences between these two standpoints, they both share the initial observation according to which the end of the East-West conflict thrived: accelerated globalization, accompanied with de-territorialization of the political, and a loss of state sovereignty in terms of migration control. They also operate on the assumption that the construction of borders outlines an attempt to reestablish self-determination. In this larger context, border closings during the Covid-19 crisis could be interpreted as approaching a climax of a long-standing development, namely the re-territorialization of political and legal spaces accompanied by de-globalization.[4]

---

[1] Ferraris: Liebe Leute, wollt ihr denn ewig leben?
[2] Krastev: Seven Early Lessons from the Coronavirus.
[3] Brown: Walled States, Waning Sovereignty.
[4] On the thesis of de-globalization, cf. Glorius: »De-Globalisierung findet auch im Kopf statt«.

In the following contribution, I will demonstrate, however, that merely viewing border closings as re-territorialization and de-globalization falls short. Rather, with the concept of the ›simultaneity of the non-simultaneous‹, I wish to render useful an old figure of thought in order to analyze ambivalent configurations of the ›social‹ during the Covid-19 crisis. The overarching question is what power of validity corona normativities have on the configuration of border relations and which political and legal developments from the past decades they encompass. In the context of spatial mobility, a simultaneity of de-globalization and globalization of the political; a de- and re-territorialization of law; and, yes, a multiplication of diverse border practices can be observed — which is why, following Martin Albrow, I hypothesize that: »The virus has brought the total moment [of the border practices] to global society.«[5]

(1.) To answer this question in connection with Europe, particularly from a historical viewpoint, I will begin by sketching the reconfiguration of European borders that first manifests itself in an extra-territorial extension (›externalization‹) as well as in a shift within nation-states' state territory (›internalization‹), and for some time now also in increased digitalization. Accordingly, the border can be viewed not only as a political line (e. g. as a fence or green border), but also as a de-territorialized, dynamic ›borderscape‹ — in the sense of transnational, governmental techniques — that in practice re-territorialize themselves ad hoc and legally encase the political body of migrants.[6] At the (preliminary) climax of the Covid-19 crisis, both border phenomena have become visible: While the sudden closing of inner-European borders led to a renaissance of the border line, borderscapes remain.

(2.) I will further raise an objection against a dominant interpretation within migration research, according to which the securitization of the border during a state of exception primarily affects the most vulnerable groups in its exclusionary effects, i. e. those who do not have access to fundamental rights. While the disenfranchisement of refuge seekers is a fact (one need only look at the dead in the Mediterranean), the empirical reality does not end with such a victimizing viewpoint. In Italy and Portugal, the normative dynamics during the Covid-19 crisis provoked the inclusion of migrants in the sense of social bonding and legal communitization (*Rechtsvergemeinschaftung*). I make use of this observation to introduce the concept of differential inclusion, with the aim to analytically grasp the *modi operandi* of border demarcation more precisely. Its relational approach also makes it possible to weaken assumptions about the binary coding of border demarcation, to introduce context-bound analysis, and to thereby utilize sliding-scaled and nested modes of recognition.

---

[5] Cf. in this volume Albrow: Has Covid-19 Brought Globalization to an End? Ins. J. L.
[6] Hess et al.: Regime ist nicht Regime ist nicht Regime.

1. The Reconfiguration of the Border

The Covid-19 pandemic struck at a time during which the EU was, and still is, in a normative crisis as Krastev described it – a phase of disintegration in which the migration of segments of the European populace is felt as a threat and in which populists, conservatives, and the new right are demanding to reclaim national sovereignty.[7] From this perspective, the extensive closure of nation-states' territorial borders in reaction to the spread of the virus represents the temporary climax of this development. Such closings not only mark a setback for the human right to free movement for European citizens, but also a (provisional) suspension of the central symbol of the European integration process – the Schengen Agreement.

Nevertheless, the reintroduction of border controls at (state) borders within Europe merely represents the visible part of a massive securitization of European border practices that set in after the end of the East-West conflict. While inter-state borders may have been taken down in the form of walls and barbed wire fences, a process has since taken place through which the relationship between visibility and invisibility of the border, as well as the regulation of migratory movements, has been transformed. While classical state theory views the European nation-state as a triad of state territory, state people, and state force in which nation-state territoriality and the validity of law coincide and the border is therefore primarily conceived as a line running between two political systems of order,[8] accelerated globalization has provoked a »de-territorialization of the political«,[9] a »re-territorialization of the political and the invention of new political spaces«.[10] The political lines were joined by extra-territorialized and dynamic borderscapes which, according to Julia Schulze Wessel, are, in their validity, more effective than any wall or fence.[11]

The central driver of this development in Europe has been and remains the Federal Republic of Germany, which has successively established a governmental and network-like system of migration control since the 1990s, thereby solidifying its hegemonial position within the European border regime. In reaction to the introduction of the Schengen Agreement, an increasing number of asylum and refuge seekers, and a shift to the political right within society, the German government considered itself forced to change its migration policy via a constitutional amendment, the ›Asylum Compromise of 1993‹. A central goal was keeping asylum seekers away from German state territory and thus avoiding territorial jurisdiction

---

[7] Krastev: Seven Early Lessons from the Coronavirus.
[8] Turner: Biopolitics and Bare Life in a Refugee Camp.
[9] Schroer: Räume, Orte, Grenzen.
[10] Schroer: Räume, Orte, Grenzen. In the global context and that of the corona pandemic, cf. Mau: Die Corona-Pandemie aus der Perspektive der Grenzforschung.
[11] Schulze Wessel: Grenzfigur Flüchtling.

over them, which is connected to the non-refoulement prohibition. Towards this end, it invented various legal instruments: The ›provision on third countries‹ and the concept of ›safe countries of origin‹, in particular, resulted in Germany establishing a legally secured *cordon sanitaire* around its territory, thereby factually relocating migration control to the EU's external borders — a process that was further reinforced with the EU (South-)East expansion in the 2000s.[12]

Whereas the German federal government — in coordination with other EU states — translated national (migration) law into EU law, shifting responsibility structures in the process, the EU possesses a further instrument to regulate migration dynamics in the form of the EU accession process. From a migration policy perspective, accession procedures serve to create various circulation spaces of leveled mobility, thus embedding migration dynamics more effectively within the EU's political economy. In this process, (potential) accession candidates are actively tied into the EU's migration policy and, in the name of good governance, receive specific consideration, e. g. in form of visa-free entry to the Schengen Area.[13] Recently, this externalization strategy has been combined with a relocation of legal and administrative structures into the territory of (potential) accession candidates. For instance, Frontex, the European border and coast guard agency, took up activities for the first time in Albania in 2019, enjoying immunity that protected it from criminal liability towards the Albanian state. Possible activities in other West Balkan countries have already been decided on and were, or are being, translated into national law by the respective countries, including North Macedonia, Serbia, and Bosnia and Herzegovina.[14]

In face of the Covid-19 pandemic, Frontex did suspend its operations outside the EU (in Albania) to protect its personnel.[15] At the same time, extra-territorialized border practices persist in African countries — practices that are directly linked to the EU's externalization strategy. In this respect, African countries serve as border guardians for the EU and assist in limiting migration via the central Mediterranean route. In return, they receive several billion euros in development aid or are promised that bureaucratic measures for obtaining visas will be eased.[16] While African countries have suspended border traffic in reaction to the spread of Covid-19, this did not apply to the deportation of persons migrating from West and East Africa towards North Africa to reach the EU via the Mediterranean Sea.

---

[12] Holert/Terkessidis: Fliehkraft; Transit Migration Forschungsgruppe (ed.): Turbulente Ränder. On the history of the German migration regime in the context of Europe, cf. Comte: The History of the European Migration.

[13] Kacarska: Europeanisation through mobility. On the technique of leveled mobility, cf. Tsianos/Karakayali: Die Regierung der Migration in Europa.

[14] Deutscher Bundestag: Erste Frontex-Operation in einem Drittstaat (Albanien).

[15] Deutscher Bundestag: Umsetzung der neuen Frontex-Verordnung.

[16] Brocza: Aus den Augen, aus dem Sinn.

NGOs and journalists have registered thousands of arrests in North African states, particularly in Libya, where migrants are interned in ›reception facilities‹ as they await their deportation or have already been deported to their respective countries of origin by the hundreds.[17] Even during the Covid-19 crisis, it is not the Mediterranean Sea, but North, West, and East Africa that represent the actual Southern border, viz. borderscape, of the EU. While border activities at the Greek-Turkish border and in the Mediterranean have moved to the back burner of critical public discourse during the times of corona – albeit remaining present[18] – migration policy measures in the Sahel and neighboring countries completely slipped off the political radar.

If the image of Europe is deconstructed and provincialized against this backdrop, then Europe extends far into the African (and also Asian) continent and represents a cross-continental entangled borderscape.[19] These externalization strategies make it possible to regulate migration dynamics far outside the EU, depending on the extent to which it is a political issue, without European states needing to abandon their self-commitment to human rights (Geneva Refugee Convention (GRC), European Convention on Human Rights (ECHR)). Since the extra-territorial borderscape is inserted between (potential) asylum or refuge seekers and the territorially anchored European human rights norms, the former often never receive the possibility to plead for asylum on European territory. In face of the deprivation of rights, as Schulze Wessel asserts, refugees cannot be described as ›figures of exclusion‹, as Hannah Arendt suggested, but rather as ›border figures‹.[20]

The flexibility of border practices are observed not only in extra-territorial space, but over the past two decades, border practices within the state have also become established as a firm part of the repertoire of migration control,[21] giving rise to the creation of new borderscapes of securitization. While police controls of personal identity take place at airports, train stations, in trains, at rest stops, at river crossings, on main downtown streets, and at cultural events, law enforcement officers apparently focus on the appearance or ethnic origins of migrants. This practice, also described as racial profiling, may contradict national, European, and international human rights norms, but nonetheless occurs habitually. Apart from France, Germany is also considered a trailblazer when it comes to the securitiza-

---

17   Ikade: Illegal Migrants Are More Vulnerable; Naceur: EU-Abschottung – Abschiebungen trotz Corona; Ben Hamad: Migrants in Niger. For symbolic demarcations (colonial view) and racisms in times of Corona towards persons from African states cf., e. g. Sarr: »Wir sprechen uns nach der Krise!«.
18   Cf. e. g. #LeaveNoOneBehind.
19   De Genova: Introduction, pp. 18 ff.
20   Schulze Wessel: Grenzfiguren.
21   On the establishment of inner-state borders during the Covid-19 crisis, cf. in this volume the illuminating and detailed contribution by Gosewinkel: Corona and the Legal Barriers of National Border Restrictions.

tion of the inner territory,[22] for instance, with its enactment of laws on the determination of identity in 1998. These allow for German federal agencies to perform so-called ›suspicion-independent controls‹ in areas located dozens of kilometers from the actual state border. It is thus unsurprising that the overwhelming majority of occupants of ›near-border‹ deportation facilities are asylum and refuge seekers that have been registered during identity controls.[23] If talk of a return of internal European borders surfaces during the Covid-19 crisis, then this is the view of the legally privileged.[24] Further, the use of the concept of internal European borders reveals a methodological nationalism, or EU-Europeanism, that is well practiced in the social and cultural sciences. This additionally equates the term with the Schengen Agreement or reduces it to territorial state borders, thereby omitting inner-state border controls to determine identity from the scheme of perception, interpretation, and evaluation.

With the digitalization of border controls, one can identify, following Ayelet Shachar, a third form of metamorphosis of the border that has also become visible to the larger public during the Covid-19 crisis. Her central thesis is that the border is, or is being, digitally inscribed into political bodies and that every migrant carries a quasi-stigma rendering them traceable on their routes. In the case of Israel, the government, without consulting parliament and under the guise of health aspects (hygiene discourse), exploited the Covid-19 emergency situation to justify infringements of privacy that are troubling from a human rights perspective, for example introducing corresponding measures such as a corona tracking app that can also later be used for the surveillance of spatial mobility.[25] The European population is approaching a similar scenario – and not just with the introduction of a corona tracking app. Rather, the digitalization of mobility surveillance was already in full swing before the Covid-19 crisis. For example, in the context of migration policy, the EU is financing the Horizon 2020 Project: iBorderCtrl (Intelligent Portable Control System), which utilizes a comprehensive instrument to monitor the mobility and border control of non-EU citizens. Concretely, the software is intended to determine the identity of migrants with the aid of biometric data, track bureaucratic procedural steps for migration control, and capture mobility dynamics in real time, with each of these measures being analyzed and optimized through AI technology. Although this digitalization measure for mobility surveillance has not gone beyond the test phase yet, it does point towards a likely future reality.[26]

---

[22] From a comparative perspective, cf. Glaeßner/Lorenz: Europäisierung der inneren Sicherheit.
[23] Oulios: Deutschlands Grenzen, pp. 12 ff. On racial profiling cf. also European Commission against Racism and Intolerance: Bericht über Deutschland; Hunold: Polizei im Revier.
[24] See also Mau: Die Corona-Pandemie aus der Perspektive der Grenzforschung.
[25] Shachar: Borders in the Time of COVID-19.
[26] iBorderCtrl: Project Summary.

In this overall context, Shachar paints the picture of an Orwellian dystopia – a development that has become further reinforced through corona normativities.[27] While the evidence of this dystopian image cannot be downplayed, history also shows that wherever power is exercised, a counter-power can arise, i.e. digital technologies can also be used by the surveilled for their means or be regulated by state or non-state institutions. In the context of spatial mobility, for instance, the migration dynamics of 2015 have revealed that numerous migrants from Asia, Africa, or the Balkans would not have made it to Western Europe without appropriating digital technology (smartphones, communication platforms, GPS, online payment services, document editing software). Particularly against this backdrop, the power of migrants to act or the deontic power of migration (as a social movement and ordering force) – or to put it more generally, the contingency of future developments – should not be interpreted in a determined manner. This leads me to the second substantive part.

2. Differential Inclusion

It is important, however, to not only make the exclusion of migrants during the Covid-19 crisis visible, but also bring the diversity of migrant realities into perspective. For with the aid of the concept of differential inclusion, it becomes apparent that according possibilities for social participation does not simply follow a binary logic (inside/outside), but can also be applied in a sliding-scaled and nested manner. Such an approach opens itself up to methodological relationalism[28] and not only views relationships of inclusion from a statal perspective, but also observes how, from the perspective of differentiation theory, inclusion can be conceived both within and beyond positivized law. Relationships of inclusion can be seen in the mirror of an ›as well as‹ logic, and as a result of actor-specific embedment in socially differentiated contexts, which in turn represents a prerequisite for a critical stance towards classical integration paradigms and inherent methodological nationalism.[29] Based on examples from Italy and Portugal, I would now like to outline how acts of recognition towards (irregularized) migrants can

---

[27] Shachar: Borders in the Time of COVID-19.
[28] A good overview of the status and perspectives of relational sociology is offered by Witte et al. (eds.): Geordnete Verhältnisse?
[29] Bojadžijev/Römhild: Was kommt nach dem »transnational turn«?, p. 21. On the concept of differential inclusion, cf. especially Mezzadra/Neilson: Border as Method, esp. pp. 159 ff. On the critique of the binary logic of processes of inclusion and exclusion, cf. also Gephart/Sakrani: »Recht« und »Geltungskultur«.

be analyzed initially in a binary way, and then, with the help of the concept of differential inclusion, as sliding-scaled and nested modes.

When the lockdown prompted a shutdown of the economy in almost all European states, the primary economic sector, agriculture, was noticeably exempt. In order to counter possible food shortages for the European population under quarantine during the climax of the pandemic, seasonal workers and the illegalized workforce notably became the focus of population policy measures. Whereas Germany escorted tens of thousands of highly flexible temporary workers from Romania and Bulgaria via chartered flights, thereby attempting to maintain the inter-state pendulum migration established in the past also during the Covid-19 crisis,[30] Italy and Portugal followed a different path: With the Relaunch Decree, Italy enabled the (temporary) legalization of residence for migrants who had previously worked irregularly either in the primary sector or in the service sector (care work).[31] The Portuguese government, meanwhile, went one step further and announced a temporary right of residence for all migrants who applied for a residence permit at the Aliens and Borders Office (SEF) before 18 March 2020. This way, they would be placed in a similar position as Portuguese citizens in terms of right of residence, which in practice entails legal access to healthcare, work, and housing.[32]

All differences between the Italian and Portuguese cases aside, they both share the trait that, besides their utilitarian considerations,[33] the states especially used human rights semantics as a justification narrative for the inclusion of migrants. It was declared imperative in a state of emergency to accord elementary human rights to migrants with an uncertain residence status, particularly ›persons without papers‹ and/or asylum seekers, as well as to protect them. Thereby, the »validity culture of the ›state of emergency‹«[34] by virtue of its symbolic power of naming transformed the biological existence (*bios*) of asylum seekers by including them in the state's legal community and thus making them a political being (*zoé*). Rights reinstated during the state of emergency therefore appear as a new normality and a possible permanent state. The Covid-19 crisis's power of validity thus also lies in how it weaves a social bond between citizens and non-citizens and provokes acts of legal communitization (*Rechtsvergemeinschaftung*).

From the perspective of refugee theory, Giorgio Agamben's classic theory[35] – according to which the state of exception signifies the power in which legal va-

---

[30] Weisskircher et al.: The Only Frequent Flyers Left.
[31] European Commission: Italian Government Adopts Targeted Regularisation for Migrant Workers.
[32] European Commission: Portuguese Government Gives Temporary Residence.
[33] Palumbo/Corrado: Keeping the Italian Agri-Food System Alive.
[34] Cf. in this volume Gephart: Conclusion, p. 513.
[35] Agamben: Homo Sacer.

lidity is suspended and the figure of the refugee represents the symbol of lawlessness – is turned upside down. What remains of this thesis, which follows a statist perspective, is the fact that the sovereign (the state) is the entity capable of effectively drawing the symbolic difference between biological and political life. In the Italian and Portuguese cases, the difference between biological and political life remains in the sense that the legalization of the right of residence is conditional and therefore does not include all persons, leaving a ›rest‹ which in turn represents the basis for reproducing the relation of *bios* and *zoé*.

As mentioned, the *modi operandi* of recognition of access and participation rights cannot be reduced to a binary coding. The concept of differential inclusion is helpful to first understand how inclusion can be viewed as a sliding-scale of validity (*Geltungsgefälle*).[36] Succinctly put: While migrants who meet the political requirements for a right of residence receive far-reaching rights, they are not absolutely in an equal position as citizens, and migrants who do not fulfill the political requirements are tolerated or deported.

When viewing irregularized migrants with the help of a differentiation theoretical perspective, the multiple migrant statuses can also be described as nested relationships of inclusion, which can be exemplified particularly with the case of irregularized field workers in southern Italy. Irregularized migrants are thus initially included in the field of the global economy despite lacking state-approved rights of affiliation and consequently experiencing significant disenfranchisement. Usually coming from African countries, they are often recruited by the mafia as harvesters and snuck into global production chains under exploitative conditions. The functionality of irregularity lies in how the mafia, farmers, and discount supermarkets, as well as consumers, profit from the exploitation of field workers who harvest at low production costs and without workers' rights.[37]

The recognition of positive rights for field workers would likely not have occurred, however, if in previous years there had not been legal struggles for recognition that made the situation of irregularized migrants visible. Besides labor unions, churches (the Vatican and church associations), NGOs, artists, and not least irregularized migrants themselves contributed to raising public awareness and thus exercising normative pressure.[38] For example, Swiss artist Milo Rau, together with irregularized field workers from African countries, organized a demonstration that gained the public's attention in the form of »symbolic-ritu-

---

[36] The term *Geltungsgefälle* is taken from Gephart/Sakrani: »Recht« und »Geltungskultur«.
[37] International Institute of Political Murder: Die Revolte der Würde & Das Neue Evangelium. On the mafia in times of Covid-19, cf. in this volume Villegas: Les mafias en temps de pandémie.
[38] Ironically, human rights NGOs, cultural scientists, and artists also profit from irregularized migrants, as they work with them, write about them, or do art projects with them, thereby earning money and professional recognition.

alistic tribunalization«[39] in the southern Italian city of Matera and integrated the performance of the ›bloody‹ destruction of illegally produced tomatoes into his new Jesus Christ film *The New Gospel*. What would Jesus the Messiah do today if he saw the current human rights situation of irregularized migrants in Italy? This represents the departing question and motivation of his piece *border act (Grenzakt)*.[40] With the film performance, he created a third space, a space of translation in the sense of a process of mediation between refugees, the city, and the wider political public. From the perspective of differentiation theory, the mix of protest and film in turn represents an attempt to artistically adjoin economic, political, and religious order to materialize, and thereby make visible, the negotiation of human rights at a staged place of justice – the tribunal in Materia. The list of ways in which various differentiation contexts are interwoven, that render visible the multiplicity of migration statuses, could be continued with numerous further empirical examples. What has become clear, however, is that the »disambiguation«[41] of relationships of inclusion and exclusion, which is popular particularly in crisis situations, should be sacrificed for a differential and ambiguous, and thereby more relational, perspective.

Conclusion

The present contribution illustrated how corona normativities affect the configuration of border relationships and can provoke forms of border delineation and opening – an ambivalent state which I described at the outset with the expression ›simultaneity of the non-simultaneous‹. In this context, I sketched the simultaneity of re-nationalization and governmental transnationalization of border practices. While the closure of state borders underlines the narrative of re-nationalization, the externalization of border controls persisted in extra-territorial Europe at the same time. Towards this end – not to put too fine of a point on it – describing the Covid-19 crisis as the end of globalization falls short. Rather, the Covid-19 crisis epitomizes the reconfiguration of the political-legal space, in which new and old border practices are reconciled. For this reason – following Albrow – I identified in the crisis a totalization of the border in global society.[42] Subsequently, I alluded to how border practices are not only targeted at exclusion and socio-cultural distancing towards migrants. With the aid of differential inclusion, I rather high-

---

[39] Gephart: Law as Culture, p. 27.
[40] International Institute of Political Murder: Die Revolte der Würde & Das Neue Evangelium. See also Zahn: Am Filmset von Milo Rau.
[41] Bauer: Die Vereindeutigung der Welt.
[42] Cf. in this volume Albrow: Has Covid-19 Brought Globalization to an End?

lighted empirical realities and described the border as a filter, or more generally as a social relationship.

Admittedly, in this contribution I concentrated on a statal perspective and overly simplified border practices as a dualistic juxtaposition of state and migration, thereby merely implying the network-like character of governmentality (the role of NGOs, the United Nations, churches, the media, and, last but not least, discourses). Nevertheless, state sovereignty or power cannot be downplayed when it comes to regulating migration. Of course, apologists for sovereignty might protest that the migration dynamics of 2015 reflect the impotence of the state or of the EU. While the normative dynamics have made clear »[w]hy our refugee policy harms all«,[43] one nevertheless too quickly forgets – particularly from a German perspective – that the border opening of 2015 was itself an act of sovereign power. But that is another story.

References

Agamben, Giorgio: Homo Sacer: Sovereign Power and Bare Life, Stanford, Calif. 1998.
Bauer, Thomas: Die Vereindeutigung der Welt. Über den Verlust an Mehrdeutigkeit und Vielfalt, Stuttgart 2018.
Ben Hamad, Fatma: Migrants in Niger Protest Seemingly Endless Quarantine, 28.04.2020, https://observers.france24.com/en/20200428-migrants-niger-protest-quarantine-without-end-covid19; last accessed 08.06.2020.
Betts, Alexander / Paul Collier: Gestrandet. Warum unsere Flüchtlingspolitik allen schadet – und was jetzt zu tun ist, Munich 2017.
Bojadžijev, Manuela / Regina Römhild: Was kommt nach dem »transnational turn«? Perspektiven für eine kritische Migrationsforschung, in: Labor Migration (eds.): Vom Rand ins Zentrum Perspektiven einer kritischen Migrationsforschung, Berlin 2014.
iBorderCtrl: Project Summary, https://www.iborderctrl.eu/; last accessed 09.06.2020.
Brocza, Stefan: Aus den Augen, aus dem Sinn. Die zunehmende Auslagerung des EU-Grenzregimes, in: ÖGfE Policy Brief 13'2018.
Brown, Wendy: Walled States, Waning Sovereignty, New York 2010.
Comte, Emmanuel: The History of the European Migration. Germany's Strategic Hegemony, London / New York 2018.

---

[43] Translation from the subtitle of the volume by Betts / Collier: Gestrandet. Warum unsere Flüchtlingspolitik allen schadet – und was jetzt zu tun ist (German edition).

De Genova, Nicolas: Introduction, in: Nicholas De Genova (ed.): The Borders of Europe. Autonomy of Migration, Tactics of Bordering, Durham and London 2017, pp. 1–36.

Deutscher Bundestag: Erste Frontex-Operation in einem Drittstaat (Albanien). Antwort der Bundesregierung auf die Kleine Anfrage, Drucksache19/11678, 20.12.2020.

Deutscher Bundestag: Umsetzung der neuen Frontex-Verordnung. Antwort der Bundesregierung auf die Kleine Anfrage, Drucksache 19/19456, 22.04.2020.

European Commission: Italian Government Adopts Targeted Regularisation for Migrant Workers, 18.05.2020, https://ec.europa.eu/migrant-integration/news/italian-government-adopts-targeted-regularisation-for-migrant-workers; last accessed 11.06.2020.

European Commission: Portuguese Government Gives Temporary Residence to Immigrants with Pending Applications, 28.03.2020, https://ec.europa.eu/migrant-integration/news/portuguese-government-gives-temporary-residence-to-immigrants-with-pending-applications?lang=de; last accessed 11.06.2020.

European Commission against Racism and Intolerance: Bericht über Deutschland (Sechste Prüfungsrunde), 17.03.2020, https://rm.coe.int/ecri-report-on-germany-sixth-monitoring-cycle-german-translation-/16809ce4c0; last accessed 10.06.2020.

Ferraris, Maurizio: Liebe Leute, wollt ihr denn ewig leben?, in: Neue Züricher Zeitung, 19.03.2020, https://www.nzz.ch/feuilleton/wir-werden-das-coronavirus-ueberleben-notizen-aus-der-quarantaene-ld.1547125; last accessed 07.06.2020.

Gephart, Werner: Law as Culture. For a Study of Law in the Process of Globalization from the Perspective of the Humanities, Frankfurt am Main 2010.

Gephart, Werner / Raja Sakrani: »Recht« und »Geltungskultur«. Zur Präsenz islamischen Rechts in Deutschland und Frankreich, in: Werner Gephart (ed.): Rechtsanalyse als Kulturforschung, Frankfurt am Main 2012, pp. 103–137.

Glaeßner, Gert-Joachim / Lorenz, Astrid (eds.): Europäisierung der inneren Sicherheit. Eine vergleichende Untersuchung am Beispiel von organisierter Kriminalität und Terrorismus, Wiesbaden 2005.

Glorius, Birgit: »De-Globalisierung findet auch im Kopf statt«, 13.05.2020, https://www.forschung-und-lehre.de/zeitfragen/de-globalisierung-findet-auch-im-kopf-statt-2761/; last accessed 07.06.2020.

Hess, Sabine / Bernd Kasparek / Maria Schwertl: Regime ist nicht Regime ist nicht Regime. Zum theoriepolitischen Einsatz der ethnographischen (Grenz-)Regimeanalyse, in: Andreas Pott et al. (eds.): Migration Regimes: Interdisciplinary Approaches to a Key Concept, Wiesbaden 2018, pp. 257–284.

Holert, Tom / Mark Terkessidis: Fliehkraft: Gesellschaft in Bewegung – von Migranten und Touristen, Cologne 2006.

Hunold, Daniela: Polizei im Revier. Polizeiliche Handlungspraxis gegenüber Jugendlichen in der multiethnischen Stadt, Berlin/Freiburg 2016.

Ikade, Faith: Illegal Migrants Are More Vulnerable in Face of COVID-19 Pandemic, 05.05.2020, http://venturesafrica.com/illegal-migrants-are-more-vulnerable-in-face-of-covid-19-pandemic/; last accessed 08.06.2020.

International Institute of Political Murder: Die Revolte der Würde & Das Neue Evangelium, http://international-institute.de/das-neue-evangelium/; last accessed 11.06.2020.

Kacarska, Simonida: Europeanisation through Mobility. Visa Liberalisation and Citizenship Regimes in the Western Balkans, CITSEE Working Paper Series, No. 21, 2012.

Krastev, Ivan: Seven Early Lessons from the Coronavirus, 18.03.2020, https://www.ecfr.eu/article/commentary_seven_early_lessons_from_the_coronavirus; last accessed 08.06.2020.

Mau, Steffen: Die Corona-Pandemie aus der Perspektive der Grenzforschung, 10.06.2020, https://coronasoziologie.blog.wzb.eu/podcast/steffen-mau-die-coronapandemie-aus-der-perspektive-der-grenzforschung/; last accessed 13.06.2020.

Mezzadra, Sandro / Brett Neilson: Border as Method: Or, the Multiplication of Labor, Durham 2013.

Naceur, Sofian Philip: EU-Abschottung – Abschiebungen trotz Corona, 24.04.2020, http://www.sofiannaceur.de/2020/04/eu-abschottung-abschiebungen-trotz-corona/; last accessed 08.06.2020.

Oulios, Miltadis: Deutschlands Grenzen: Tauziehen um das Recht auf Bewegungsfreiheit, in: A-PuZ: Europas Grenzen – Grenzenloses Europa – Migration, Flucht, Asyl, 63(47), 2013, pp. 7–13.

Palumbo, Letizia / Alessandra Corrado: Keeping the Italian Agri-Food System Alive: Migrant Farmworkers Wanted!, 29.04.2020, https://www.opendemocracy.net/en/pandemic-border/keeping-italian-agri-food-system-alive-migrant-farmworkers-wanted/; last accessed 11.06.2020.

Sarr, Felwine: »Wir sprechen uns nach der Krise!«, 07.04.2020, https://www.sueddeutsche.de/kultur/coronavirus-senegal-gesellschaft-1.4869649; last accessed 08.06.2020.

Schroer, Markus: Räume, Orte, Grenzen – Auf dem Weg zu einer Soziologie des Raums, Frankfurt am Main 2006.

Schulze Wessel, Julia: Grenzfigur Flüchtling. Nationale Grenzziehungen und neue Räume des Politischen, in: Mittelweg 36 27(3), 2018, pp. 43–60.

Schulze Wessel, Julia: Grenzfiguren, in: ZPTh 3(2), 2012, pp. 151–166.

Shachar, Ayelet: Borders in the Time of COVID-19, 04.04.2020, https://www.mpg.de/14650555/borders-in-the-time-of-covid-19; last accessed 10.06.2020.

Transit Migration Forschungsgruppe (ed.): Turbulente Ränder. Neue Perspektiven auf Migration an den Grenzen Europas, Bielefeld 2007.

Tsianos, Vassilis / Serhat Karakayali: Die Regierung der Migration in Europa. Jenseits von Inklusion und Exklusion, in: Soziale Systeme 14 (2), 2008, pp. 329–348.

Turner, Simon: Biopolitics and Bare Life in a Refugee Camp. Some Conceptual Reflections, in: Katharina Inhetveen (ed.): Flucht als Politik: Berichte von Fünf Kontinenten, Köln 2006, pp. 39–62.

Weisskircher, Manès / Julia Rone / Mariana S. Mendes: The Only Frequent Flyers Left: Migrant Workers in the EU in Times of COVID-19, 20.04.2020, https://www.opendemocracy.net/en/can-europe-make-it/only-frequent-flyers-left-migrant-workers-eu-times-covid-19/; last accessed 11.06.2020.

Witte, Daniel / Andreas Schmitz / Christian Schmidt-Wellenburg (eds.): Geordnete Verhältnisse? Vielfalt und Einheit relationalen Denkens in der Soziologie, Berliner Journal für Soziologie 27 (3–4), 2018.

Zahn, Philipp: Am Filmset von Milo Rau. »Was Jesus zu den Priestern sagt, fordern auch wir heute«, 08.10.2020, https://www.srf.ch/kultur/film-serien/am-filmset-von-milo-rau-was-jesus-zu-den-priestern-sagt-fordern-auch-wir-heute; last accessed 11.06.2020.

Dieter Gosewinkel

Corona and the Legal Barriers of National Border Restrictions

»Viruses do not have a passport«, declared French President Macron on 12 March 2020 in a major television address to the French people.¹ He was particularly interested in the measures taken by neighboring Germany which had declared the French region of *Grand Est* a *risk area* the day before. This meant that people who crossed the German border from eastern France were high-risk migrants who could be subjected to restrictive measures on German soil. Four days later, the German federal police subjected the borders with neighboring countries, including France, to strict entry restrictions – without prior consultation with the French government, as the French side claimed.² One day later, on 17 March, the French government imposed a curfew (*confinement*), which was continuously tightened in the following weeks. From then on, foreigners were only allowed to enter both France and Germany for *valid reasons*. Evidently, potential virus carriers with foreign passports were different and more dangerous than those of their own people.

In the weeks that followed, France, like almost all of Europe, went through a painful and sacrificial process of pandemic infection. The country sealed itself off from people outside its borders. Only goods could pass unhindered. But even this no longer happened as a matter of course. The French Minister of Agriculture recalled the quality of local products and began to promote the consumption of French cheese and wine from Bordeaux.³

Within three weeks, a pandemic had turned the idea of a Europe united in openness upside down. The most European of European leaders rediscovered the national economic and commercial state. The two leading European states, Germany and France, sealed themselves off from each other by restricting their borders to a degree not seen since the post-war period.

The return to borders is the sign of the times. There is talk of *renationalization* in science and, time and again, in politics. But this word describes only a part of the development. In Europe, at the beginning of the 21st century, within a few

---

1   Macron: Adresse aux Français. The Prime Minister of North Rhine-Westphalia, Armin Laschet, took this idea up (»The virus has no nationality«), Altenbockum/Burger: Laschet zur Corona-Krise.
2   Cf. Soldt/Wiegel: Virus kennt keine Grenzen.
3   Cf. Wiegel: Leben von Bordeaux und Camembert.

weeks a turnaround took place to concepts and positions which historically in the 19th century had experienced their theoretical and institutional formulation: from supranationality to nation; from open free trade zone to economic intervention state; from democratic parliamentarism to the primacy of the executive. All these shifts have one thing in common: they are reflected in terms of the law and are enforced by means of the law. In the legal forms of a constitutional state of the 21st century, the decline to 19th-century ideas of political order, which preceded the democratic constitutional state, is taking place. However, according to the thesis, it is precisely the law that not only enables a turn to the 19th century, but also forces a return to the parliamentary constitutional state of the 21st century.

According to the World Health Organization, within four months of the outbreak of the corona crisis in China, 194 countries in the world had closed all or most of their national borders. The first signs of easing, especially in Europe, did not come up until mid-May. As a matter of principle, only the country's own nationals, and in very limited exceptional cases foreign nationals with *valid reasons* were allowed to enter the country. This also applied between the vast majority of EU member states. The EU Commission's hope that the closure of the EU's external borders would quickly reopen Europe's internal borders had not been fulfilled. Under the pressure of the pandemic wave in mid-March, half of the more than 20 Member States closed their own borders. Some also failed to comply with the obligations contained in the Schengen Borders Code to notify the European Commission and other Member States in good time.[4] The free movement of persons was thus more restricted than at any time since the creation of the Schengen area, indeed of the European Community as a whole. One of the four fundamental freedoms of European contract law was suspended. While goods freely crossed the borders and Union citizens willing to travel were jammed at the crossings, the Union fell back into the market community of its beginnings. »The borders are doing very well right now,« diagnosed the Polish Nobel Prize winner Olga Tokarczuk, who lived in her home country under curfew.[5] The container nation-state was closed because the governments of the states hoped to reap quick benefits: psychologically, to give their own citizens a feeling of stability and controllability in their own space in the face of the globally borderless danger; pragmatically, to use the available closing mechanism at the old, traditional state borders.

The crisis thus ideally exposed the basic elements of the nation state as it had developed in the 19th century: a state that determines and protects its own territory and its own people; a state whose power takes precedence over any other,

---

[4] Regulation (EU) 2016/399 of the European Parliament and of the Council of 9 March 2016 establishing a Community Code on the rules governing the movement of persons across borders (Schengen Borders Code), Articles 25 and 28.
[5] Tokarczuk: Neue Zeiten.

external political power and therefore conveys trust.[6] This retreat to familiar structures was combined with the historically common endeavor to protect, even immunize, the well-defined structure of one's own state against strangers and foreigners, against intruders and invaders. The perception and keeping away of immigrants as potential carriers of epidemics is a historical defense pattern that unfolds its strongest effect with the unfolding of the nation-state, producing technical systems of border control and a comprehensive set of legal rules for the selection and keeping away of *intruders*.[7] Thus, in March and April there was a wave of decrees and orders in the European states, which confirmed legal border regimes and established new ones. The recourse to traditional institutions and — often unconscious — collective defense patterns created confidence in a global crisis. It was legitimized by law, which sanctioned unauthorized intrusion into the nation-state space.

The deeply insecure population was to be reassured and perhaps temporarily allowed to calm down. But to what extent do the reassuring mechanisms of closure in the nation-state tempt people into self-delusion? As the crisis lasted, it became clear that danger zones did not coincide with national boundaries. On the contrary, it became clear that within the nation-state borders, individual regions (such as Lombardy, eastern France, Bavaria and the Heinsberg district in Germany) were the most virulent crisis areas. Conversely, border regions between states are often not particularly at risk. Rather, their closure cuts off economic and cultural ties that have grown over generations and destroys political trust. This is demonstrated by the joint, coordinated reactions of politicians from eastern French departments, Saarland and North Rhine-Westphalia.[8] Data from the Robert Koch Institute from the phase surrounding the border closures in mid-March indicate that the spread of the virus was introduced at least as much by the return of the country's own citizens as by the border crossings of foreigners.[9]

A global debate, led by natural scientists, economists, social scientists, and gradually also lawyers, is underway.[10] It revolves around the question of the extent to which, beyond the closure of national borders, other and more differentiated measures can contain the spread of the virus at least as effectively, if not more effectively.[11] There are indications that this is the case. So do the gains in health

---

[6] On the classical model of the modern state, which underlies the construction of the nation state cf. Jellinek: Allgemeine Staatslehre, pp. 394–434.
[7] Cf. Gosewinkel: Schutz und Freiheit?, pp. 253–262.
[8] Cf. Hans/Rottner: Mehr Zusammenarbeit.
[9] Cf. Robert Koch-Institut: Täglicher Lagebericht.
[10] To give an impression of the recent, global discussion: cf. Linka et al.: Outbreak Dynamics of COVID-19; Lee et al.: Global Coordination on Cross-Border Travel and Travel Measures; Kraemer et al.: Effect of Human Mobility; Alemanno: European Dream.
[11] See the remarkable study on the (lack of) effectiveness of national border closures in the face of the AIDS crisis in the 1980s by the biomathematician Antoine Flahault: Flahault/Valleron: HIV and

care justify the deep border police intervention in the freedom of citizens? This is where contemporary law shows the full ambivalence of its importance: it does not just provide traditional forms of state, police security from the 19th century. It also justifies and, conversely, enables effective judicial control and repeal of these measures in the service of individual freedom. The law of the European Union and the national law – which it has helped to shape – provide the means to check the nature, extent and duration of border control measures in a legally effective manner. The legal foundations are the fundamental right of Union citizens to freedom of movement (Article 21 of the Treaty on the Functioning of the European Union), which is enshrined in the constitutional law of the European Union, and the right to general freedom of action (Article 2(1) of the Basic Law), which is also enjoyed by foreigners, especially Union citizens. These fundamental freedoms certainly allow restrictions for the purpose of health care and disease control.

But these possibilities for restriction in turn come up against barriers. In particular, the fundamental prohibition of discrimination under European law applies, namely that no stricter rules may be applied to EU foreigners and EU nationals than to their own nationals.[12] In addition, the principle of proportionality, which is demanded by both the European Court of Justice and the Federal Constitutional Court for all restrictions of civil liberties, must be observed.[13] This means, for example, that complete border closures, if the virus has already spread in the country, are illegal. Also, the Federal Police cannot carry out border controls at their discretion, but must give comprehensible reasons for their decisions and observe EU law, which guarantees the free movement of goods, persons, services and capital.[14] In addition, as the pandemic progresses, the knowledge of the virulence of the virus and thus the type and speed of its spread in social and physical space changes. There are plausible reasons why differentiated, flexible restrictions on freedom of movement for certain regions within the nation states that are significantly affected or threatened by the virus (i.e. in tourist areas and urban agglomerations) are more suitable for containing it than sharp restrictions at national borders that are applied across the board. These are then increasingly less necessary to maintain public health in a country. In view of this, persistent border restrictions justify less and less the resulting threats to cross-border economic existence and production chains as well as family and cultural relations. The purpose of collective health care is then no longer in a legally justifiable relationship

---

Travel. On 25 February Flahault publicly took up his theses in the Corona Crisis, cf. Vasak/Chaverou: Fermer les frontières; On the Relatively Limited Effect of National Border Closures in the Corona Crisis, see Chinazzi et al.: The Effect of Travel Restrictions on the Spread of the 2019 Novel Coronavirus (COVID-19) Outbreak.

[12] Cf. Article 18 of the Treaty on the Functioning of the European Union.
[13] Explicitly regulated in Article 26 of the Schengen Borders Code.
[14] Cf. Thym: Grenzkontrollen wegen Coronavirus.

with the restriction of individual freedom of movement. National border closures could then prove to be what they predominantly were: a historical recourse to the familiar surgical instruments of the national military hospital.

However, the effective combating of this extremely dangerous, globally active virus requires other, new instruments. The spontaneous solidarity of German clinics with overburdened, seriously suffering Italian and French hospitals pointed the way.[15] Here, for the purpose of forward-looking, cross-border cooperation and effective civil protection, the law is able to provide a framework that makes agreements and planning possible.[16]

The crisis is the *hour of the executive*, one hears everywhere – the *national* executive, one might add.[17] This is not empirically incorrect, if one looks at the legal instruments that are available to the executive power to act quickly and decisively in a crisis. And yet the sentence contains less than half the truth. It contains, especially in Germany, a kind of trust that ties in with political attitudes of an earlier epoch: faith in the authorities, reinforced by the longing for the charisma of a leader who undoubtedly embodies authority, whether monarchical or otherwise *directly* legitimized, i.e. through acclamation or opinion polling. The liberal constitutional state of the 21st century, on the other hand, presupposes a different kind of trust: trust in the uninterrupted mutual control of the powers and thus in institutionalized mistrust. The national powers are also bound by supranational law. In a parliamentary republic, the parliament remains the democratic governing body even in a crisis. And finally, all executive action, without exception, is subject to constitutional binding and control by the courts. In a crisis, the executive and the nation draw confidence in themselves. But as organizational forms of state power and political order, they do not stand outside but within the constitutional order and are bound by its limits.

But the law must be enforced. The Commission of the European Union, which is called upon to watch over the free movement of people in Europe, was conspicuously reticent towards the member states from the beginning of the crisis. It only admonishes the restoration of intra-European border openings in a *graduated and coordinated procedure.* No EU citizen has yet challenged national border controls in court. A successful appeal would bring about a clarification of principle for the future: with regard to the right to freedom of movement and to future border closures. After all, even if the borders are currently being relaxed, recent experi-

---

[15] Cf. Crossey: Corona.

[16] Cf. Landfried: Virus kennt keine Schlagbäume; cf. Alemanno: Europe Doesn't Have to Be So Helpless.

[17] On the origin of the formulation of the state of emergency as the »Hour of the Executive« used in the debate on an emergency constitution by the Federal Minister of the Interior Gerhard Schröder in 1960 from an etatist, parliament-sceptical constitutional tradition, see Diebel: Die Stunde der Exekutive, pp. 28–35, 63–120.

ence shows that, in the event of a second wave of the pandemic, there would be a return to national borders.

References

Alemanno, Alberto: Europe Doesn't Have to Be So Helpless in This Crisis, in: The Guardian, 26.03.2020, https://www.theguardian.com/world/2020/mar/26/europe-doesnt-have-to-be-so-helpless-in-this-crisis; last accessed 05.06.2020.

Alemanno, Alberto: We Lived the European Dream. Will Any Politician Stand up for Open Borders?, in: The Guardian, 22.05.2020, https://www.theguardian.com/world/commentisfree/2020/may/22/european-dream-politician-stand-up-for-free-movement; last accessed 05.06.2020.

Altenbockum, Jasper von / Reiner Burger: Laschet zur Corona-Krise. »Ihr seid nicht alleine!«, in: FAZ.net, 21.04.2020, https://www.faz.net/aktuell/politik/inland/nrw-ministerpraesident-armin-laschet-zur-corona-krise-16735390.html; last accessed 05.06.2020.

Chinazzi, Matteo / Jessica T. Davis / Marco Ajelli / Corrado Gioannini / Maria Litvinova / Stefano Merler / Ana Pastore y Piontti / Kunpeng Mu / Luca Rossi / Kaiyuan Sun / Cécile Viboud / Xinyue Xiong / Hongjie Yu / M. Elizabeth Halloran / Ira M. Longini Jr. / Alessandro Vespignani: The Effect of Travel Restrictions on the Spread of the 2019 Novel Coronavirus (COVID-19) Outbreak, in: Science, 368(6489), 2020, pp. 395–400.

Crossey, Nora: Corona – neue Herausforderungen und Perspektiven für Grenzraumpolitiken und grenzüberschreitende Governance, in: Christian Wille / Rebekka Kanesu: Bordering in Pandemic Times: Insights into the COVID-19 Lockdown, pp. 69–73.

Diebel, Martin: »Die Stunde der Exekutive«. Das Bundesinnenministerium im Konflikt um die Notstandsgesetzgebung 1949–1968, Göttingen 2019.

Flahault, Antoine / Alain-Jacques Valleron: HIV and Travel, No Rationale for Restrictions. The Lancet, 336(8724), 1990, pp. 1197–1198.

Gosewinkel, Dieter: Schutz und Freiheit? Staatsbürgerschaft in Europa im 20. und 21. Jahrhundert, Berlin 2016.

Hans, Tobias / Jean Rottner: Deutsch-französische Grenze. Wir brauchen mehr Zusammenarbeit!, in: FAZ.net, 14.04.2020, https://www.faz.net/aktuell/politik/inland/gastbeitrag-mehr-zusammenarbeit-an-der-grenze-16725182.html; last accessed 05.06.2020.

Jellinek, Georg: Allgemeine Staatslehre, 3rd edition, Berlin 1914.

Kraemer, Moritz U. G. / Chia-Hung Yang / Bernardo Gutierrez / Chieh-Hsi Wu / Brennan Klein / David M. Pigott / Open COVID-19 Data Working Group /

Louis du Plessis / Nuno R. Faria / Ruoran Li / William p. Hanage / John S. Brownstein / Maylis Layan / Alessandro Vespignani / Huaiyu Tian / Christopher Dye / Oliver G. Pybus / Samuel V. Scarpino: The Effect of Human Mobility and Control Measures on the COVID-19 Epidemic in China, in: Science, 368(6490), 2020, pp. 493–497.

Landfried, Christine: Das Virus kennt keine Schlagbäume. Wo bleibt die Europäische Union in der Corona-Krise?, in: FAZ, 03.04.2020, 80, p. 12.

Lee, Kelley / Catherine Z. Worsnop / Karen A. Grépin / Adam Kamradt-Scott: Global Coordination on Cross-Border Travel and Trade Measures Crucial to COVID-19 Response, in: The Lancet, 395(10237), 2020, pp. 1593–1595.

Linka, Kevin / Mathias Peirlinck / Francisco Sahli Costabal / Ellen Kuhl: Outbreak Dynamics of COVID-19 in Europe and the Effect of Travel Restrictions, in: Computer Methods in Biomechanics and Biomedical Engineering, 05.05.2020, https://www.tandfonline.com/doi/full/10.1080/10255842.2020.1759560; last accessed 19.06.2020.

Macron, Emmanuel: Adresse aux Français, 12.3.2020, https://www.elysee.fr/emmanuel-macron/2020/03/12/adresse-aux-francais; last accessed 05.06.2020.

Robert Koch-Institut: Täglicher Lagebericht des RKI zur Coronavirus-Krankheit-2019 (COVID-19), 27.03.2020, https://www.rki.de/DE/Content/InfAZ/N/Neuartiges_Coronavirus/Situationsberichte/2020-03-27-de.pdf?__blob=publicationFile; last accessed 05.06.2020.

Soldt, Rüdiger / Michaela Wiegel: Das Virus kennt keine Grenzen, in: FAZ, 14.03.2020, 63, p. 2.

Thym, Daniel: Grenzkontrollen wegen Coronavirus. Wer noch reisen darf, und warum, in: Legal Tribune Online, 16.3.2020, https://www.lto.de/recht/hintergruende/h/corona-grenzkontrollen-keine-schliessung-triftige-gruende-wer-noch-reisen-darf/; last accessed 05.06.2020.

Tokarczuk, Olga: Jetzt kommen neue Zeiten! in: FAZ, 31.03.2020, 77, p. 9.

Vasak, Stanislas / Eric Chaverou: Coronavirus: »Fermer les frontières n'est pas efficace, les virus n'ont pas de passeport«, in: France Culture, 25.02.2020, https://www.franceculture.fr/sciences/coronavirus-fermer-les-frontieres-nest-pas-efficace-les-virus-nont-pas-de-passeport; last accessed 05.06.2020.

Wiegel, Michaela: Patrioten leben jetzt von Bordeaux und Camembert, in: FAZ.net, 02.04.2020, https://www.faz.net/aktuell/gesellschaft/gesundheit/coronavirus/macron-frankreich-soll-unabhaengiger-vom-ausland-werden-16709081.html; last accessed 05.06.2020.

Olivier Beaud et Cécile Guérin Bargues

L'état d'urgence sanitaire : était-il judicieux de créer un nouveau régime d'exception ?

Entré en vigueur le 24 mars 2020, l'état d'urgence sanitaire est venu ajouter un nouvel état d'exception à un ordre juridique français qui en était déjà généreusement pourvu. Cet état d'urgence est prévu par le premier titre de la loi du 23 mars 2020 dite « loi d'urgence pour faire face à l'épidémie du covid19 » qui a été adoptée dimanche 22 mars au sein d'un hémicycle, par la force des choses, largement déserté.[1] En réalité la loi, comme son nom l'indique, ne se contente pas de régir les seules mesures relevant du droit sanitaire, mais s'avère beaucoup plus vaste. Elle prévoit des mesures d'urgence d'ordre économique en un titre II très dense, puis des mesures politiques : disposition électorales variées en titre III et contrôle parlementaire dans un bref titre IV. Le point commun à toutes ces dispositions disparates est double : il s'agit d'un coté de prendre en compte l'urgence de la situation – urgence sanitaire résultant de l'existence d'une pandémie – et de l'autre, d'énoncer les diverses mesures destinées à lutter efficacement contre la propagation du Covid-19 qui bouleverse la vie quotidienne et paralyse le pays. Cette loi vient compléter un ensemble de mesures déjà prises. Le gouvernement a en effet commencé par prendre, dès le 16 mars, un décret sur le confinement[2] tandis que le ministre de la santé signait un arrêté pour fermer la majeure partie des commerces et interdire les rassemblements. La loi du 23 mars permet quant à elle de prendre de nouvelles mesures et parfois de régulariser celles qui avaient été prises.

Il ne s'agira pas ici de commenter l'ensemble de la loi et des problèmes qu'elle soulève. Diverses études ont déjà permis d'éclairer certains points délicats,[3] tandis que le tout récent rapport de la « mission de suivi » du Sénat offre un premier bilan de l'application de l'état d'urgence sanitaire.[4] Nous nous efforcerons plus modestement d'interpréter cette innovation qu'est la création d'un nouveau régime d'excep-

---

[1] Sur la question du bon fonctionnement d'une assemblée travaillant en « comité restreint », voir Lemaire: Le Parlement.
[2] Décret n° 2020-260 du 16 mars 2020.
[3] Voir notamment les divers billets publiés depuis le début du confinement sur le Blog de Jus Politicum.
[4] « Dix premiers jours d'état d'urgence sanitaire : premiers constats », Rapport de la mission de suivi du projet de loi d'urgence pour faire face à l'épidémie du Covid-19.

tion. La situation française se distingue en effet par la multiplicité et la diversité des états d'exception. Deux d'entre eux figurent dans la constitution : d'un côté, l'article 16, sorte de « super état d'exception »[5] et de l'autre, l'état de siège prévu à l'article 36 mais qui n'a jamais été appliqué. Deux autres sont désormais prévus par la loi ordinaire : l'état d'urgence et l'état d'urgence sanitaire.

Il n'est pas difficile de démontrer que ces deux régimes législatifs sont différents même si le plus récent, l'état d'urgence sanitaire, est « inspiré » de l'état d'urgence pour reprendre la formule utilisée incidemment par le Conseil d'Etat.[6] Leur différence provient évidemment d'une différence de source : deux lois régissent la matière, d'ailleurs codifiées dans des emplacements distincts. L'état d'urgence sanitaire figure dans *le Code de santé publique* et notamment le titre III du livre Ier de ce code, alors que l'état d'urgence de 1955 se trouve dans le *Code de la sécurité intérieure.*[7] Plus encore, l'objet de ces deux lois diffère. Tandis que l'état d'urgence de la loi de 1955 est essentiellement ce que l'on pourrait appeler un état d'urgence « sécuritaire », les dispositions de l'état d'urgence sanitaire touchent, comme son nom l'indique, principalement à la santé, même si elles portent elles aussi atteinte à des droits et libertés fondamentaux. L'analogie entre les deux régimes n'en demeure pas moins frappante (1.), même si l'état d'urgence sanitaire semble assortir de davantage de garanties les mesures susceptibles d'être prises sous son égide (2.). Sa création vient donc ajouter un nouvel état d'exception à l'ordre juridique français, alors même que celui-ci comprenait déjà l'état d'urgence de 1955, qui fut utilisé à plusieurs reprises sous la Ve République.[8] On peut dès lors se demander pourquoi le gouvernement ne s'est pas contenté de réactiver ce dernier, quitte à en compléter le régime pour prendre en considération la dimension « sanitaire » (3.).

1. Le pendant sanitaire de l'état d'urgence sécuritaire

La première parenté entre ces deux régimes juridiques profondément dérogatoires au droit commun réside dans leur nature profonde d'état d'exception. Ce sont des régimes qui, l'un comme l'autre, permettent de déroger à des droits et des libertés constitutionnelles. Concernant l'état d'urgence sanitaire, le nombre de droits

---

[5] Qui a d'ailleurs été évoqué, à tort selon nous, au début de la crise du Covid-19. Cf. Beaud : La suprenante invocation.

[6] Le Conseil d'Etat : Avis sur un projet de loi d'urgence pour faire face à l'épidémie de Covid-19, séance du 18 mars 2020, p. 4.

[7] Voir notamment les articles 15 et s. de la loi n° 2016-987 du 21 juillet 2016 prorogeant l'application de la loi n° 55-385 du 3 avril 1955 relative à l'état d'urgence et portant mesures de renforcement de la lutte antiterroriste qui viennent modifier le code de la sécurité intérieure.

[8] Qu'il nous soit permis de renvoyer à notre ouvrage Beaud/Guérin Bargues : L'Etat d'urgence.

et libertés annihilé ou paralysé, est tout bonnement impressionnant. L'essentiel des dispositions en la matière figure dans l'article 2 de la loi du 23 mars, qui vient modifier divers alinéas de l'article L. 3131-15 du code de la santé publique, afin de permettre au Premier ministre, par décret réglementaire, de prendre une multitude de mesures destinées à protéger la santé publique. On songe évidemment à la privation de la liberté d'aller et venir – ou liberté de circulation – imposée tant aux véhicules qu'aux citoyens obligés de rester confinés chez eux. Ce n'est que par exceptions dûment prévues et encadrées que ces derniers peuvent sortir pour effectuer les seuls déplacements « strictement indispensables aux besoins familiaux ou de santé ».[9] L'analogie est frappante avec l'état d'urgence sécuritaire dont la principale mesure restrictive était l'assignation à résidence pour des individus susceptibles de commettre des attentats. La privation peut aller plus loin encore dans le cadre de l'état d'urgence sanitaire avec la mise en quarantaine des personnes « susceptible d'être affectées »[10] ou « le maintien en isolement [...] des personnes affectées »[11] par le virus. On peut ajouter à cette liste l'absence de liberté de réunion – puisque les rassemblements sont interdits[12] – et les limites apportées à la liberté d'expression. Celle-ci est en effet nécessairement affaiblie par l'interdiction d'ouvrir les établissements recevant du public,[13] catégorie qui comprend cinémas, théâtres et autres lieux de spectacles. Quant aux droits et libertés d'ordre économique, le tableau est presque aussi impressionnant en raison de l'atteinte portée à la liberté du commerce et d'industrie, à la liberté d'entreprendre ou au droit de propriété par la fermeture administrative de la plupart des lieux recevant du public,[14] la mise en place de mesures de réquisition[15] ou de mesures temporaires de contrôle des prix.[16]

L'autre cousinage marquant est que cette dérogation à l'état normal s'effectue sans aucune habilitation constitutionnelle. On retrouve ici la figure étonnante d'un régime d'état d'exception qui déroge à des libertés constitutionnelles en vertu d'une simple loi. Au regard de l'ampleur des dérogations, la loi du 23 mars 2020 peut-elle être considérée comme étant conforme à la Constitution alors même que l'état d'urgence, qu'il soit sanitaire ou sécuritaire, n'est pas prévu par le texte

---

[9] Article 2 de la loi du 23 mars 2020 précitée, modifiant l'article L. 3131-15 (2°) du code de la santé publique.
[10] Ibid. : L. 3131-15 (3°).
[11] Ibid. : L. 3131-15 (4°).
[12] Ibid. : L. 3131-15 (6°).
[13] Ibid. : L. 3131-15 (5°).
[14] Les catégories d'établissements concernés figurent à l'article 1er de l'arrêté du 14 mars 2020, complété par l'arrêté du 15 mars 2020 portant diverses mesures relatives à la lutte contre la propagation du virus Covid-19.
[15] Article 2 de la loi du 23 mars 2020 précitée, modifiant l'article L. 3131-15 (7°) du code de la santé publique.
[16] Ibid. : L. 3131-15 (8°).

constitutionnel ? On sait comment en 1985,[17] puis en 2015,[18] le Conseil constitutionnel a légitimé une telle entorse à la légalité via un *obiter dictum* récurrent, qui a consisté, par une interprétation audacieuse de l'article 34, à interpréter le silence de la Constitution comme formant une habilitation implicite du législateur.[19] L'article 34 fut ainsi considéré comme conférant au Parlement non seulement la compétence de « définir de nouvelles libertés », mais aussi de « restreindre l'exercice des libertés » au nom de la sauvegarde de l'ordre public. Ce raisonnement avait d'ailleurs contraint le Conseil constitutionnel à constitutionnaliser le principe de sauvegarde de l'ordre public, afin de disposer de l'indispensable symétrique à la garantie des libertés publiques.[20] Le Conseil constitutionnel sera-t-il amené à en faire autant au regard de la santé publique, si d'aventure il devait être interrogé, par voie de QPC sur la conformité de telle ou telle disposition de la loi du 23 mars, aux droits et libertés que la constitution garantit ? Par ailleurs, le Conseil constitutionnel, en mars 2020, ne fut pas plus saisi *a priori* de la loi d'urgence Covid-19 qu'il ne fut saisi jadis de la loi du 20 novembre 2015 sur l'état d'urgence ou de ses six prorogations. Il en résulte qu'une loi de moindre envergure comme la loi organique d'urgence relative à la suspension des délais en matière de QPC a été contrôlée par le Conseil constitutionnel[21] alors que celle qui la rend en réalité nécessaire – la loi créant l'état d'urgence sanitaire – ne fut pas soumise à un tel contrôle, faute de saisine du Conseil. Explicable du point de vue formel – les lois organiques étant obligatoirement soumises au contrôle obligatoire du Conseil constitutionnel avant leur promulgation – le résultat n'en est pas moins surprenant du point de vue matériel : ce sont les dispositions les plus fondamentales du régime juridique de l'état d'urgence sanitaire qui ne sont pas contrôlées *a priori* !

De plus, on retrouve au sein de l'état d'urgence sanitaire la complexe distinction entre déclaration et application de l'état d'urgence prévue par la loi du 3 avril 1955. L'état d'urgence sécuritaire, du seul fait du décret déclaratif, autorise un nombre limité de mesures d'exception immédiatement applicables (possibilité pour le préfet d'interdire la circulation des personnes ou des véhicules par exemple). Toutefois, l'extension des mesures de police (aux assignations à résidence notamment) exige un décret « appliquant » l'état d'urgence.[22] Ce double mécanisme décrétal figure également au sein de l'état d'urgence sanitaire, conformément à la procédure dorénavant prévue par l'article 3131-13 du code de la santé publique : un pre-

---

[17] Décision n° 85-187 DC du 25 janvier 1985 : Loi relative à la Nouvelle-Calédonie et ses dépendances. Pour une analyse de cette décision, cf. Beaud/Guérin Bargues : L'Etat d'urgence, p. 98 et s.

[18] Décision n° 2015-527 QPC du 22 décembre 2015, M. Cédric. D.

[19] Cf. Beaud/Guérin Bargues : L'Etat d'urgence, p. 100.

[20] Cf. Wachsmann : Note sous, p. 364.

[21] Décision n° 2020-799 DC du 26 mars 2020 : Loi organique d'urgence pour faire face à l'épidémie de Covid-19.

[22] Cf. Beaud/Guérin Bargues : L'Etat d'urgence, p. 25–26.

mier décret en conseil des ministres, pris sur le rapport du ministre chargé de la santé, est nécessaire pour déclarer l'état d'urgence sanitaire et déterminer les circonscriptions territoriales d'application.[23] Un second texte – cette fois un décret réglementaire du Premier ministre pris sur le rapport du ministre chargé de la santé – vient ensuite s'ajouter au décret déclaratif pour préciser les mesures prises dans le cadre de l'état d'urgence sanitaire. Ce décret d'application a bien été pris le 23 mars 2020[24] : il reprend et précise les mesures d'interdiction déjà édictées par le décret précité du 16 mars. Nulle trace en revanche du décret déclaratif car, en réalité, l'état d'urgence sanitaire est entré en vigueur non par décret, mais par la loi. C'est en effet la loi précitée du 23 mars qui, en même temps qu'elle crée dans son article 2 le régime juridique de l'état d'urgence sanitaire, déroge immédiatement aux dispositions qu'elle vient de créer – et notamment au caractère décrétal de la déclaration d'état d'urgence sanitaire – en précisant en son article 4 que « par dérogation aux dispositions de l'article L. 3131-13 du code de la santé publique, l'état d'urgence sanitaire est déclaré pour une durée de deux mois à compter de l'entrée en vigueur de la présente loi. ». L'alinéa 2 du même article en tire la conséquence : « L'état d'urgence sanitaire entre en vigueur sur l'ensemble du territoire national. »

Cette curieuse entrée en vigueur appelle deux remarques. On notera tout d'abord un surprenant retour, à l'occasion cet état d'urgence sanitaire, à la pratique de la IVè République puisque la lourde responsabilité de déclarer l'état d'urgence revenait alors au Parlement, tandis que le gouvernement avait pour charge les décrets d'application. Toutefois, cette résurgence de la compétence législative n'est que temporaire, circonscrite au cas de 2020 et par ailleurs très relative : en l'espèce, la mise en œuvre de l'état d'urgence sanitaire a précédé sa déclaration, le Premier ministre ayant pris, on l'a vu, dès le 16 mars 2020 et en vertu de l'article 21 de la Constitution, un décret qui interdisait, sauf exception, tout déplacement hors du domicile.[25] Plus fondamentalement, cette déconcertante manière de procéder – un législateur qui déroge immédiatement et à son profit au principe qu'il vient de poser – témoigne du caractère hybride de la loi du 23 mars 2020. Cette dernière apparait à cet égard au moins aussi baroque que celle du 3 avril 1955 : non contente de créer un nouvel état d'exception, elle en déclare la mise en œuvre immédiate. Elle mêle donc allégrement, au sens d'un même instrument, deux actes juridiques différents : une loi générale – qui crée un nouveau régime juridique – et une loi

---

[23] Article 2 de la loi du 23 mars 2020 précitée, modifiant l'article L. 3131-13 du code de la santé publique.

[24] Il s'agit du décret n° 2020-293 du 23 mars 2020 prescrivant les mesures générales nécessaires pour faire face à l'épidémie de Covid-19 dans le cadre de l'état d'urgence sanitaire qui reprend et renforce les dispositions du décret n° 2020-260 du 16 mars 2020 et de l'arrêté du ministre de la santé du 15 mars 2020.

[25] Décret n° 2020-260 du 16 mars 2020 portant réglementation des déplacements dans le cadre de la lutte contre la propagation du virus Covid-19.

spéciale qui en prévoit l'application. Signe que la malfaçon législative accompagne décidément l'état d'urgence, la dualité matérielle de la loi du 23 mars 2020 aboutit, comme la loi du 3 avril 1955 avant elle, à combiner acte-règle et acte-condition.[26]

On notera par ailleurs que l'état d'urgence sanitaire peut, comme son cousin sécuritaire avoir un champ d'application variable. L'article 2 de la loi du 23 mars prévoit en effet la possibilité d'en limiter l'application à certaines circonscriptions territoriales.[27] On sait que tel ne fut pas le choix du législateur, l'article 4 précisant que « l'état d'urgence sanitaire entre en vigueur sur l'ensemble du territoire national ». Une possibilité similaire est prévue par la loi de 1955, même si les précédents témoignent plutôt d'une tendance à l'extension géographique de l'état d'urgence sécuritaire, que ce soit entre 1955 et 1958 ou en 2015.[28]

Enfin, la dernière parenté frappante entre les deux états d'urgence concerne les règles relatives à l'aménagement temporel de cet état d'exception. Comme on le sait, l'état d'urgence est un état nécessairement temporaire de sorte que l'aménagement de sa durée est l'une des questions fondamentales de son régime juridique. Cela ressort ici de la double règle selon laquelle d'une part, le gouvernement peut interrompre avant son terme l'état d'urgence et, d'autre part, les mesures décidées en application de cet état cessent avec lui.[29] Ici encore, il s'agit d'une pure copie de l'état d'urgence « sécuritaire ». Plus complexes sont les règles sur la durée et la prorogation qui sont d'ailleurs celles à propos desquelles s'est exprimée l'opposition parlementaire. De ce point de vue, la loi du 23 mars créant l'état d'urgence sanitaire ne se distingue guère par sa clarté. L'article 2 de la loi, qui vient modifier l'article L. 3131-14 du Code de santé publique précise en effet que « la loi autorisant la prorogation au-delà d'un mois de l'état d'urgence sanitaire fixe sa durée ».

La lecture de cette formule sibylline incite à un triple commentaire. D'abord, le législateur a presque intégralement recopié la formule de l'Ordonnance du 15 avril 1960 qui modifiait la loi du 3 avril 1955 selon laquelle la « loi autorisation sa prorogation [de l'état d'urgence] (…) fixe sa durée définitive » sans qu'on sache ce que cela signifie, une telle équivoque ayant permis les six prorogations de l'état d'urgence de 2015 à 2017. Ensuite, l'état d'urgence sanitaire devrait être initialement déclaré pour une durée d'un mois, durée qui excède déjà largement celle de douze jours prévue dans le cadre de l'état d'urgence sécuritaire. Enfin, comme dans le cadre de ce dernier, la prorogation de l'état d'urgence sanitaire relève du domaine de la loi.[30] Mais là encore, les conséquences de la dualité matérielle de la loi du 23 mars se font sentir. L'article 4 de la loi, qui met en œuvre immédiatement cet

---

[26] Pour une démonstration similaire en ce qui concerne la loi du 3 avril 1955, cf. Beaud/Guérin Bargues: L'Etat d'urgence, p. 37–39.

[27] Précision qui figure dorénavant à l'article 3131-13 du code de la santé publique.

[28] Pour les détails, cf. Beaud/Guérin Bargues: L'Etat d'urgence, p. 21 (note 10) et p. 73.

[29] Art. L. 3131-14.

[30] Sa prorogation au-delà de 12 jours par la loi est prévue par l'ordonnance du 15 avril 1960.

état d'urgence sanitaire à peine créé, vient à nouveau déroger à la règle posée par l'article 2. Sur suggestion du Conseil d'Etat, il dispose en effet que l'état d'urgence sanitaire est déclaré pour une durée non pas d'un mais de « deux mois à compter de l'entrée en vigueur de la présente loi » (soit jusqu'au 24 mai 2020). Par ailleurs, signe d'une rédaction hâtive, il précise ici déroger « aux dispositions de l'article L. 3131-13 du code de la santé publique » sans curieusement faire mention de l'article L 3131-14, pourtant exclusivement consacré à la durée de l'état d'urgence. Certes, l'époque n'est pas au juridisme pointilleux, mais décidemment, qui légifère vite, légifère mal.

Si l'on peut bien entendu comprendre que le gouvernement et la majorité parlementaire, ne sachant pas très bien dans quelle mesure il serait possible au Parlement de voter une éventuelle prorogation au bout d'un mois de mise en œuvre de l'état d'urgence sanitaire, aient opté dès le début pour une durée de deux mois, le procédé n'en est pas moins gênant. L'exigence d'une loi de prorogation a en effet vocation à permettre à la représentation nationale de s'assurer de la nécessité du maintien de cette légalité extraordinaire que porte en elle tout état d'exception. Dans cette perspective, on ne peut que se féliciter de voir que les parlementaires ont réussi à mieux encadrer les mesures susceptibles d'être prises en période d'état d'urgence sanitaire et à maintenir un embryon de contrôle.

2. La mise en place de mesures proportionnées et contrôlées?

Une contradiction majeure semble en réalité dominer, sinon saturer, le débat autour de cet état d'urgence dans lequel deux camps s'opposent de façon frontale. D'un côté, les partisans des droits de l'homme et des libertés publiques clament, comme en 2015, leur inquiétude devant les atteintes majeures portées aux droits et libertés que la loi du 23 mars 2020 impose à l'immense majorité de la population. Ils s'émeuvent notamment du faible contrôle exercé par le Conseil constitutionnel, ce qui contraste avec la situation de 2015 où un mois après le déclenchement de l'état d'urgence, le Conseil dût statuer sur la première QPC.[31] Force est de reconnaitre que l'adoption de la loi organique du 30 mars 2020[32] ne peut que conforter de telles inquiétudes. Jugée conforme à la Constitution alors même qu'elle a été adoptée en violation de l'article 46 de la Constitution – qui prévoit un délai de 15 jours entre le dépôt de la loi organique et son examen par le Parlement, délai

---

[31] Décision n° 2015-527 QPC du 22 décembre 2015 – M. Cédric D. [Assignations à résidence dans le cadre de l'état d'urgence].

[32] Loi organique n° 2020-365 du 30 mars 2020 d'urgence pour faire face à l'épidémie de Covid-19.

réduit en l'espèce à 24 h compte tenu des « circonstances particulières »[33] – cette loi organique suspend de surcroit, jusqu'au 30 juin 2020, les délais trimestriels d'examen des QPC,[34] afin d'éviter une transmission de plein droit au Conseil et un risque, réel ou supposé, d'engorgement de la haute juridiction.[35] On peut craindre dès lors que les QPC, sans contrainte de délais, perdent une partie de leur intérêt. On pourrait également citer au nombre de ces sujets d'inquiétude pour les défenseurs des libertés le rejet quasi systématique, depuis le début du confinement, des référés liberté et ce parfois même sans débat.[36] D'un autre côté, les représentants des personnels soignants et médicaux multiplient les référés libertés devant le Conseil d'Etat afin d'enjoindre le gouvernement à aller plus loin encore dans les mesures restrictives de liberté.[37] Au nom du droit au respect de la vie, rappelé notamment par l'article 2 de la convention européenne de sauvegarde des droits de l'homme et des libertés fondamentales, l'Etat devrait imposer des contraintes plus drastiques encore aux citoyens, certains rêvant d'une sorte de « modèle » chinois.

L'état d'urgence sanitaire pose ainsi, du point de vue des principes, le même problème que l'état d'urgence sécuritaire : la délicate conciliation entre la liberté et la sécurité largement entendue. Le droit à la santé, ou plus particulièrement droit à la vie, a en effet remplacé le droit à la sûreté. Le gouvernement secondé par le Parlement dans un premier temps, puis le juge dans un second temps, sont chargés de trouver ce délicat équilibre ... qui n'en est jamais vraiment un tant il est évident que face à la peur, terroriste hier, sanitaire aujourd'hui, l'impératif sécuritaire lato sensu l'emporte sur les libertés fondamentales. Pour remettre en cause cet édifice, il faut adopter un point de vue radical, comme celui du philosophe italien Giorgio Agamben qui critique cette vision consistant à privilégier ce qu'il appelle « la vie nue »[38] (la vie biologique) sur toute autre considération. Nul doute que sa voix est peu audible de nos jours, la morale kantienne l'ayant emporté si l'on peut dire.

Une fois relevé cet éternel dilemme, il reste à noter que l'état d'urgence sanitaire contient une série de dispositions venant encadrer le pouvoir exécutif. Affectant l'ensemble de la population et non une petite partie d'entre elle comme sa version sécuritaire, ce régime d'exception comprend des atteintes considérables à

---

[33] Formule qui ne saurait être assimilée à la théorie séculaire des circonstances exceptionnelles. Voir en ce sens le billet de M. Carpentier, cf. Carpentier : L'arrêt.

[34] En vertu de l'ordonnance n° 58-1067 portant loi organique sur le Conseil constitutionnel, Conseil d'État et Cour de cassation ont trois mois pour transmettre, après examen, une question prioritaire de constitutionnalité au Conseil constitutionnel. Ce dernier dispose d'un délai identique pour se prononcer sur la question transmise.

[35] Pour une vision critique et convaincante de la LO suspendant les délais d'examen des QPC, voir Benzina : La curieuse suspension.

[36] Voir à titre d'illustration le sort réservé par le Conseil d'Etat le 3 avril 2020 aux multiples contestations de l'ordonnance du 25 mars allongeant les délais de détention provisoire. Cf. Jacquin : Coronavirus : le Conseil d'Etat valide la prolongation.

[37] Voir par ex, l'ordonnance du 22 mars 2020 – Confinement total de la population.

[38] Entretien avec N. Truong, Le Monde du 24 mars 2020, cf. Truong : Giorgio Agamben.

plusieurs droits et libertés. En raison de cette circonstance, il a fallu prévoir symétriquement une série de limites objectives dans la même loi. La contestation du projet de loi gouvernemental fut avant tout l'œuvre du Sénat qui, à la création d'un régime pérenne, aurait préféré un dispositif d'application temporaire, destiné à gérer la seule épidémie du Covid-19. Seule l'hypothèse – au demeurant plutôt anxiogène – de voir survenir une nouvelle dégradation de la situation sanitaire dans plusieurs mois semble avoir convaincu la commission des lois d'admettre la création d'un régime de longue durée.[39] Les sénateurs ont néanmoins voulu éviter que l'exécutif disposât d'un blanc-seing en matière de mesures à prendre. Alors que le gouvernement souhaitait bénéficier d'une sorte de clause générale de compétence, les parlementaires ont heureusement obtenu que les dix domaines dans lesquels le gouvernement peut user de son pouvoir réglementaire soient énumérés dans l'article 3131-15 du Code de la Santé.

En outre, le Parlement a obtenu que les mesures que peuvent prendre le Premier ministre et le ministre de la Santé répondent à un objectif clair et précis – garantir la santé publique – comme à un impératif de proportionnalité. Le critère finaliste apparaît déterminant dans les dispositions qui autorisent le gouvernement à prendre les mesures qui s'imposent. On retrouve ici la logique instrumentale de rapport entre moyen et fin qui est d'ailleurs au cœur de l'article 16 de la constitution.[40] Le Premier ministre est habilité par la loi à prendre un nombre conséquent de mesures attentatoires à la liberté mais « aux seules fins de garantir la santé publique » (art. L 3131-15). La formule a remplacé celle contenu dans le projet de loi initial, qui prévoyait « des mesures générales (…) afin de lutter contre la catastrophe sanitaire ». De plus, le ministre de la Santé peut « prescrire, par arrêté motivé, toute mesure réglementaire relative à l'organisation et au fonctionnement du dispositif de santé, à l'exception des mesures prévues à l'article L. 3131-15, visant à mettre fin à la catastrophe sanitaire » (art. L. 3131-16.). Le fil directeur de toutes ces dispositions est « la lutte », « la disparition » ou encore « l'éradication » de la « catastrophe sanitaire ».

Par ailleurs, la loi contient plusieurs dispositions soulignant l'impératif de proportionnalité qui doit guider les acteurs lorsqu'ils déterminent les mesures à prendre. Ces dernières doivent en effet être « strictement proportionnées aux risques sanitaires encourus et appropriées aux circonstances de temps et de lieu ». Cette contrainte vaut tant pour les décisions du Premier ministre (art. L3131-15)

---

[39] Rapport Sénat n° 381, Commission des Lois, 19 mars 2020, p. 25. Dans le même genre d'idée, un amendement de la commission, finalement rejeté, proposait de limiter à une année la durée de validité (ie. jusqu'au 1er avril 2021), les dispositions introduite à charge pour le Parlement de pérenniser, si nécessaire et par la suite le dispositif.

[40] L'article 16 al. 1 évoque des « mesures exigées par les circonstances » et l'alinéa 3 précise que ces « mesures » doivent être « inspirées » par l'idée de rétablir les moyens d'agir aux pouvoirs publics constitutionnels.

que du ministre de la Santé (art. L3131-16). La formule est presque la même pour « les mesures nécessaires et proportionnées » prises par les préfets (art L3131-17). Or, l'équivalent de telles dispositions ne figurait pas dans l'état d'urgence sécuritaire, le législateur de 2015–2016 n'ayant pas fait le choix, lorsqu'il modifia la loi de 1955, d'inscrire la lutte contre le terrorisme comme finalité de cet état d'exception. Cela lui permit notamment d'interdire les manifestations des écologistes lors de la COP 21 ou d'assigner à résidence des militants écologistes connus pour leur activisme radical.[41] L'équivalent d'une interprétation aussi extensive nous semble difficile dans le cadre d'un état d'urgence sanitaire qui parait donc plus contraignant en ce qui concerne la nature et la portée des mesures susceptibles d'être prises.

Enfin, la commission des lois du Sénat s'est attachée à renforcer le contrôle du Parlement, initialement prévu dans le texte du gouvernement mais dont le Conseil d'Etat avait préconisé la suppression[42] au motif, pour le moins curieux, que « la disposition imposant au Gouvernement la transmission d'informations relatives à la mise en œuvre de l'état d'urgence sanitaire (…) constitue une injonction du Parlement au Gouvernement et ne relève pas du domaine de la loi ».[43] La notion d'injonction – qui dissimule mal une référence au principe commode, car éminemment plastique, de séparation des pouvoirs – est censée ici servir de repoussoir.[44] Pourtant, elle ne parvient, pas plus que la référence à l'article 34 de la Constitution, à emporter la conviction.[45] Comment en effet concevoir la possibilité même d'un contrôle parlementaire dans le cadre d'un état d'exception sans contraindre d'une manière ou d'une autre le gouvernement à fournir les informations sur lequel il porte ? Toujours est-il que, s'inspirant là encore d'un mécanisme issu de l'état d'urgence sécuritaire et plus précisément du dispositif mis en œuvre pour le suivi de la loi SILT[46] – loi qui avait introduit dans le droit commun nombre de dispositions issues de la loi du 3 avril 1955 modifiée – la commission des lois du Sénat, arrive de haute lutte à obtenir la réintégration du contrôle. Toutefois, celle-ci se fait après réunion de la commission mixte paritaire et sur le modèle de la disposition qui avait été adoptée par l'assemblée nationale en première lecture, sur amendement du gouvernement.[47] L'article L. 3131-12 dispose en conséquence que « l'Assemblée

---

[41] Sur cet épisode, cf. Beaud/Guérin Bargues : L'Etat d'urgence, p. 152.

[42] Sénat, p. 44.

[43] Avis du Conseil d'Etat sur la loi d'urgence pour faire face à l'épidémie du Covid-19, Conseil d'Etat, 18 mars 2020, avis n° 399873, cons. 18.

[44] L'argument est repris lors de débats par la majorité parlementaire et notamment par Alain Richard lors des débats en commission devant le Sénat afin de limiter la portée du contrôle parlementaire. Rapport Sénat n° 38, précité, p. 64.

[45] Voir sur cette question l'analyse très critique et convaincante de M. Altwegg-Boussac que nous remercions d'avoir bien voulu nous transmettre son article: « La fin des apparences. A propos du contrôle parlementaire en état d'urgence sanitaire » (Altwegg-Boussac : La fin de apparences).

[46] Loi n° 2017-1510 du 30 octobre 2017 renforçant la sécurité intérieure et la lutte contre le terrorisme. Sur cette source d'inspiration, cf. Rapport Sénat n° 38, précité, p. 37.

[47] Cf. tableau comparatif, Rapport CMP du 22 mars 2020, p. 51.

nationale et le Sénat sont informés sans délai des mesures prises par le Gouvernement au titre de l'état d'urgence sanitaire. L'Assemblée nationale et le Sénat peuvent requérir toute information complémentaire dans le cadre du contrôle et de l'évaluation de ces mesures ». Il en résulte un net recul non seulement par rapport au contrôle initialement envisagé par le Sénat mais aussi au regard de celui qui existe dans le cadre de l'état d'urgence sécuritaire.[48]

Figurant dorénavant sous le titre I de la loi consacré à l'état d'urgence sanitaire, le contrôle parlementaire ne concerne en conséquence que ce dernier et non, comme le souhaitaient les sénateurs, l'ensemble des mesures découlant des quarante-trois ordonnances prévues par la loi du 23 mars 2020. Toutefois, le Sénat dans le premier rapport de sa « mission de suivi » est allé bien au-delà du texte en examinant les ordonnances prises dans le domaine économique et social,[49] ce qui prouve que la distinction entre mesures d'urgence sanitaire et mesures d'urgence économique n'était pas tenable.[50] Par ailleurs si, comme dans l'article 4-1 de la loi de 1955 modifiée, les chambres disposent d'un droit d'information sans délai des mesures prises par le gouvernement au titre de l'état d'urgence, il n'est plus question d'imposer plus largement aux autorités administratives de leur transmettre copie de tous les actes qu'elles prennent en application de la loi de la loi du 23 mars. L'utilité d'un tel contrôle relève pourtant de l'évidence à la lecture du premier rapport de la mission de suivi sénatoriale. Elle s'inquiète en effet des dérives déjà constatées dans l'application de l'état d'urgence sanitaire, notamment lorsque des maires décident de couvre-feux sans fondement légal assuré et demande au gouvernement de lui adresser tous les actes de « réglementation locale ».[51] Un tel contrôle parlementaire apparaît indispensable tant on sait que les abus en période d'état d'urgence peuvent être commis aussi bien par l'Administration que par les élus locaux. On peut donc être non pas soulagé, mais au moins satisfait, que le Parlement soit compétent pour effectuer ce contrôle, que le Conseil d'Etat a pourtant voulu lui ôter.

3. La contestable création d'un nouvel état d'exception

En dépit de ces différences de régimes juridiques, la parenté est donc frappante entre les deux types d'état d'urgence. Dès lors, il est surprenant de constater que le gouvernement n'ait pas envisagé de réactiver l'état d'urgence de 1955, pourtant largement renouvelé lors des attentats terroristes de 2015–2016. Que cette hypothèse,

---

48 En ce sens, Altwegg-Boussac: La fin de apparences.
49 Rapport précité (note 2), pp. 31 et suiv.
50 Comme l'observe M. Altwegg-Boussac, cf. Altwegg-Boussac: La fin de apparences.
51 Rapport précité, pp. 25–26.

sauf erreur de notre part, n'ait jamais été soulevée lors des débats parlementaires de mars 2020, alors qu'elle semble s'imposer d'évidence, en dit long sur l'influence du Conseil d'Etat. Comme toujours en France, son opinion donne le « la » et aucun pouvoir public n'ose s'en écarter. Or, le Conseil d'Etat, dans son avis sur le projet de loi, n'a rien trouvé à redire à la création d'un nouveau type d'état d'urgence, estimant que « l'existence d'une catastrophe sanitaire rend utile un régime particulier de l'état d'urgence pour disposer d'un cadre organisé et clair d'intervention en pareille hypothèse ». Utile peut-être, mais était-il judicieux, compte-tenu de l'existence d'un régime déjà existant ? En effet, selon l'article 1er de la loi de 1955, l'état d'urgence peut être déclaré non seulement « en cas de péril imminent résultant d'atteintes graves à l'ordre public » mais aussi « en cas d'événements présentant, par leur nature et leur gravité, le caractère de calamité publique ». En évoquant des faits avérés, cette seconde hypothèse est d'ailleurs plus exigeante que la première qui se contente d'une simple menace. Elle avait à l'époque été ajoutée par le gouvernement, qui avait présent à l'esprit le terrible tremblement de terre d'Orléans-Ville,[52] pour dissimuler le fait que la raison profonde de la loi de 1955 était la lutte contre la rébellion algérienne.

Quoi qu'il en soit, il n'est pas difficile de soutenir qu'une « catastrophe sanitaire » constitue bien un cas possible de « calamité publique ». Dès lors, on pouvait estimer que seconde condition d'application de l'état d'urgence était remplie par l'existence de la pandémie. Certains de nos partenaires européens y ont d'ailleurs eu recours, à l'instar du Portugal qui a déclaré un état d'urgence assimilable à celui prévu par la loi française du 3 avril 1955, tel qu'il est prévu par la Constitution de 1976.[53] En France, il aurait suffi au président de la République de prendre un décret en conseil des ministres afin de « déclarer » l'état d'urgence et à son gouvernement de proposer dans la foulée une loi de prorogation qui aurait ajouté à la loi de 1955 le contenu les dispositions sur l'état d'urgence sanitaire figurant au titre 1er de l'actuelle loi du 23 mars. Certes, une telle solution avait pour inconvénient légistique la nécessité d'adopter, en plus de cette loi sur l'état d'urgence renforcée d'une dimension sanitaire, une autre loi comprenant l'équivalent des dispositions d'ordre économique et politique de la loi du 23 mars 2020. Il aurait donc fallu deux lois au lieu d'une, alors que le temps pressait. Mais cet inconvénient aurait été effacé par l'avantage qu'il y aurait eu à disposer à propos de l'état d'urgence d'une norme unitaire épousant les deux conditions de déclenchement de ce régime d'exception dorénavant modernisé : ordre public, d'une part, calamité publique de l'autre. Bref, on aurait eu un genre, l'état d'urgence, avec deux espèces, sécuritaire et sanitaire, prévues dans deux titres formellement différents d'une même loi.

---

[52] Septembre. Aujourd'hui Chlef en Algérie.
[53] Sur le cas du Portugal, voir le billet d'A. de Moura, cf. de Moura : La « solidarité institutionnelle ».

L'intérêt d'une telle solution eut été de rendre sans doute plus difficile le cumul des deux états d'exception, en raison de la nature alternative des deux hypothèses de déclenchement ou plus précisément, du lien entre la satisfaction d'une condition (*atteintes graves à l'ordre public / calamité publique*) et le déclenchement d'un régime juridique spécifique. Le risque du choix qui a été fait d'ajouter un nouveau type d'état d'urgence au droit positif français réside en effet dans l'éventuel cumul de l'état d'urgence sécuritaire et de l'état d'urgence sanitaire.[54] Un tel cumul est interdit par le code de défense entre état de siège et état d'urgence, ce qui peut se comprendre car les autorités, militaires dans le premier cas et civiles dans le second, ne peuvent pas exercer les mêmes compétences. Dans le silence de la loi, l'hypothèse d'un cumul des deux états d'urgence (loi de 1955 et loi de 2020) pourrait en revanche être envisagée. Il suffirait que la condition relative à l'ordre public soit remplie, par exemple par le soulèvement d'une partie de la population qui ne supporterait plus les mesures de confinement. On aurait alors deux régimes d'état d'urgence qui coexisteraient, ce qui ferait beaucoup.

En réalité, un seul argument vraiment sérieux, en plus de l'urgence à agir, pouvait justifier la création de l'état d'urgence sanitaire. L'application de la loi de 1955 à la situation actuelle aurait rendu applicables de plein droit les mesures prévues par l'état d'urgence sécuritaire. Certes, certaines d'entre elles ont été transférées dans le droit ordinaire, via la loi SILT du 21 octobre 2017, mais toutes ne l'ont pas été. On aurait alors reproché au gouvernement d'être gravement liberticide, profitant de la « catastrophe sanitaire » pour rouvrir un état d'urgence « sécuritaire » dont on était difficilement sorti en 2017 après six lois de prorogation. C'est probablement pour prévenir cette objection que le gouvernement a opté pour un régime *ad hoc*. Pourtant, ce risque d'instrumentalisation de la situation pouvait facilement être écarté. Puisque l'entrée en vigueur de la loi de 1955 aurait nécessairement entraîné qu'elle soit complétée, on aurait parfaitement pu imaginer une disposition précisant que seules les dispositions sanitaires de l'état d'urgence entraient en vigueur.

Bref, il y avait mieux à faire du point de vue de la technique législative. Sans doute dira-t-on qu'il est facile aux universitaires de critiquer ceux qui agissent, ce dont on veut bien convenir tant nous paraissent déplacées les objections de tous ceux qui ont la solution une fois que les faits sont établis. Toutefois, cette concession faite, il n'est pas inconvenant d'observer qu'on aurait pu espérer des « bureaux » des ministères comme du Parlement davantage d'imagination et de rigueur juridiques. On avait déjà dressé ce constat à propos de l'état d'urgence de 2015. Décidément, on légifère bien mal en France, ce qui en dit assez long sur le déficit juridique grandissant dans notre pays, jadis considéré comme étant celui des légistes. On osera

---

[54] Nous empruntons cette idée à Lecatelier : L'état d'urgence sanitaire.

avancer qu'un tel constat n'est pas sans rapport avec l'état de notre enseignement supérieur, dès lors que nos élites juridiques sortent des grandes écoles et fuient les universités où elles auraient pourtant pu faire un peu de « vrai » droit.

Références

Altwegg-Boussac, Manon : La fin des apparences, in : La Revue des droits de l'homme, Acualités Droits-Libertés, mis en ligne le 12.04.2020, http://journals.openedition.org/revdh/9022.

Beaud, Olivier : La surprenante invocation de l'article 16 dans le débat sur le report du second tour des élections municipales, 23.03.2020, http://blog.juspoliticum.com/2020/03/23/la-surprenante-invocation-de-larticle-16-dans-le-debat-sur-le-report-du-second-tour-des-elections-municipales-par-olivier-beaud; dernier accès 10.06.2020.

Beaud, Olivier / Cécile Guérin-Bargues : L'Etat d'urgence. Une histoire constitutionnelle, historique et critique, 2nde édition, Paris 2018.

Benzina, Samy : La curieuse suspension des délais d'examen des questions prioritaires de constitutionnalité, 30.04.2020, http://blog.juspoliticum.com/2020/04/03/la-curieuse-suspension-des-delais-dexamen-des-questions-prioritaires-de-constitutionnalite-par-samy-benzina%e2%80%a8/; dernier accès 10.06.2020.

Carpentier, Mathieu : l'arrêt Heyriès du Conseil constitutionnel ?, 04.04.2020, http://blog.juspoliticum.com/2020/04/04/larret-heyries-du-conseil-constitutionnel-par-mathieu-carpentier; dernier accès 17.06.2020.

de Moura, Annette : La « solidarité institutionnelle » dans l'état d'urgence : la réponse portugaise au Covid-19, 10.04.2020, http://blog.juspoliticum.com/2020/04/10/la-solidarite-institutionnelle-dans-letat-durgence-la-reponse-portugaise-au-covid-19-par-annette-de-moura/; dernier accès 17.06.2020.

Jacquin, Jean-Baptiste : Coronavirus : le Conseil d'Etat valide la prolongation de la détention provisoire sans juge, in : Le Monde, 04.04.2020, https://www.lemonde.fr/societe/article/2020/04/04/coronavirus-le-conseil-d-etat-valide-la-prolongation-de-la-detention-provisoire-sans-juge_6035548_3224.html; dernier accès 17.06.2020.

Lecatelier, Alexis : L'état d'urgence sanitaire: une innovation qui pose question, 19.03.2020, https://theconversation.com/letat-durgence-sanitaire-une-innovation-qui-pose-question-134078; dernier accès 17.06.2020.

Lemaire, Elina : Le Parlement face à la crise du Covid-19 (1/2), 04.02.2020, http://blog.juspoliticum.com/2020/04/02/le-parlement-face-a-la-crise-du-covid-19-1-2-par-elina-lemaire; dernier accès 17.06.2020.

Mission de suivi du projet de loi d'urgence pour faire face à l'épidémie du Covid-19 : Dix premiers jours d'état d'urgence sanitaire : premiers constats, 02.04.2020, http://www.senat.fr/fileadmin/Fichiers/Images/commission/lois/MI_Covid19/Mission_suivi_urgence_Covid-19_Premiers_constats.pdf; dernier accès 17.06.2020.

Truong, Nicolas : Giorgio Agamben : « L'épidémie montre clairement que l'état d'exception est devenu la condition normale », in : Le Monde, 24.03.2020, https://www.lemonde.fr/idees/article/2020/03/24/giorgio-agamben-l-epidemie-montre-clairement-que-l-etat-d-exception-est-devenu-la-condition-normale_6034245_3232.html; dernier accès 17.06.2020.

Wachsmann, Patrick : Note sous CC n° 85-187 du 25 janvier 1985, État d'urgence en Nouvelle-Calédonie, AJDA, 1985

Martin Schermaier

Morals Suspend Law.
How the Call for Solidarity Casts a Shadow on Law

1. Morals and the Rule of Law

We live in a secular constitutional state. All state action is based on laws. The state's officials can act only within the realm of their legal capacity, and in doing so, they are completely subjected to judicial control – even where they have been afforded legal discretion. Judicial control is also founded on a legal basis, i.e. on laws whose content is continuously concretized by jurisdiction and academia. This legal state is not only *secular* because of its denominational neutrality, but also because neither its law nor its actions are rooted in a specific ideology. Only in this way can it equally represent Catholics, Protestants, Muslims and Jews, atheists and agnostics, and people of every other possible creed or mindset. There is no doubt, though, that many areas of the German legal system are shaped by western (meaning generally: Christian) values. But the law itself is by all means secular, as its acceptance does not require adherence to a certain ideology.

This radical neutrality of the state is sometimes challenging, especially when it comes to balancing individual freedom against the common good. This is primarily the function of public law, which is rooted in the *Grundgesetz* (GG), the German constitution. But private law, balancing the interests of private subjects, also aims at the trouble-free coexistence and cooperation of all private actors – in its basic principles as well as in its countless individual rules. In the past years, though, there has been a tendency in both fields to, instead of just applying the given law, call upon the *good* or *useful* in order to realize certain aims in the interest of the common good. This is questionable not only because such appeals elude critical discourse; who would opt for something *evil* or *harmful*? These appeals are also problematic in regards to the rule of law as they often include implicit instructions which either leave the realm of given law or even intend to modify it. Some already suspect a transgression of given law when appeals are made to support given law, because the moral component becomes the center of attention: When someone demands morality, they lack the legal basis to achieve their aim. In a crisis like the one we are facing right now, these incidents increase.

2. An (Imaginary) Catastrophe?

Stress tests reveal a system's weaknesses. In social systems, it does not even matter whether the strain is real or imagined. Instead of perceiving the world objectively, we always interpret it as a precondition for the realization of our ideas of life. Therefore, it does not take concrete threats or real limitations to our way of life, neither famine, disease nor poverty, to trigger our flight instinct: All it takes is the mere fear that our life might develop in a different direction than anticipated. As such fears do not only arise from our individual experience, but also from that of millions other individuals, shared only within seconds, we constantly live in fear and always consider ourselves close to the abyss. The virtual world does not distinguish between real and imagined threats. A threat is what the majority perceives as such. That is the reason why the Corona crisis bears the potential of a social and economic catastrophe, regardless of how much the virus increases the risk of major or lethal individual illness.

In any case, the »most severe challenge since World War Two«[1] exceeds all epidemics, wars and crises that have occurred since then, it even overshadows climate change. Climate change and Coronavirus are comparable in so far as both threats are real, but their potential damage is hard to quantify. In situations like individual fates become our point of orientation as they make the threat more tangible. Images shared millions of times increase the fear beyond imagination. They dominate the discourse about the pandemic, the media coverage and the measures of political actors. And those actors seem to mistrust their own legal system when while adopting measures head over heels they still feel the need to appeal to the good in people.

3. The System Functions

In fact, the legal system itself seems to be a haven of tranquillity and calm: Ministries issue regulations, courts give judgements (voiding parts of those regulations), one can conclude contracts (if one desires to do so, given the circumstances), get married or divorced, draw up a will and rely on it being respected. Some procedures take more time than usual due to Corona: Whoever applies for a building permit will wait for the permission even longer than usual, registering or deregistering a car requires proof that one is systemically important, marriage ceremonies take place without any attendees, whoever wants to take his state examina-

---

[1] Merkel: Fernsehansprache der Bundeskanzlerin; transl. by the author.

tion has to wait until hygiene measures have been realized for the exam hall. But, after all, anyone will confirm that state and law are still functioning.

This also applies to the norms of our legal system. Most of them have developed over centuries, have been tested in and purified through many crises. Why should they not be able to deal with this new threat? But the system is crumbling. This is seen where mean and deem are taken as sources for action guidelines, supposedly without any alternative, and ascribed a normativity which in a legal state should only be ascribed to laws. This has not just happened in the past few weeks but has been going on for years. The Corona crisis only reveals the signs of erosion just like other weaknesses of our society: law is replaced by what is deemed right.

One might argue that our legal system was not prepared for Covid-19 and that it is therefore necessary to leave the legal realm and act according to the best of one's knowledge and belief. That is equally true and false. It is true, for instance, that the *Infektionsschutzgesetz* (*infection-protection-statute*) had to be equipped with additional provisions affording state authorities more competence and powers of intervention[2] to create a legal basis for the many limitations of fundamental rights. Nonetheless, that objection is faulty at least regarding the area of private law. Private law does not attend to the state's right to intervene but balances private interests. And it has always been capable to distribute risks across private actors in cases of unforeseen circumstances posing an economic threat to one of them.

4. Solidarity Replaces Balancing: Corona and Private Law

Therefore, a look into tenancy law is appropriate. In Roman law, the decision if and to what extent the tenant should be unburdened of the obligation to pay the rent was decided based on the kind of catastrophe and the function of the object of tenancy. Whoever rented out farm land which had become impossible to cultivate due to storms or enemy invasions had to waive their right to the rent.[3] This idea can be transferred to renting out spaces which are used as hotels or restaurants: When these are unusable due to Corona-related regulations, the landlord loses the right to collect rent. Since they do not just rent out any kind of space but a hotel or restaurant, the primary goal of the contract is unattainable. If the tenant's business is only partially impaired, the rent can be reduced. Under Roman-European law this is called *remissio mercedis*, the *waiver of payment*, for the use.[4] If the rented space can be used in another way for the time being, the situation is

---

[2] Cf. Bundesgesetzblatt (BGBl) 2020 I Nr. 14, pp. 587 ff.
[3] Cf. for example D. 19,2,15,2 (Ulpianus libro 32 ad edictum).
[4] Cf. for example du Plessis: A History of Remissio Mercedis.

different. In that case, the tenant bears the sole risk of usage: They must pay the rent in full even though they could not use the rental object in the intended way. The cornucopia distributed by the state to business owners ignores these principles. They hand out money without even asking whether the rent has had to be paid while the space could not be used due to Corona.

Admittedly, none of this is dictated by morals, even though the attitude of a uniformly well-meaning authority fits a government that demands morals. Sure enough, all regulations passed in late March 2020, but also tenancy law in general, are influenced by morals. According to currently applicable law, a landlord may terminate their contract with the tenant if they are in arrears with the payment of two whole months' rent (cf. § 543 II nr. 3 BGB[5]). This provision was already part of the German Civil Code in 1900 (then § 554 BGB). Its core is also rooted in the Roman law tradition: If one party is behind schedule for paying what is due, the other may terminate the contract. Rent arrears occurring between 1st April and 30th June are exempt from this rule according to the new Art. 240 s. 3 EGBGB.[6] This statute was introduced by the »Law for mitigating the consequences of the Covid-19 pandemic in private, insolvency and criminal procedural law«[7] from March 27th 2020. In the explanatory statement for this law provided by the ministry of justice (from March 3rd 2020) landlords are appealed to that this is a necessary act of solidarity in view of the enormous challenge posed by the virus.[8] With less pathos, this translates to: Dear landlord, be a nice person and temporarily waive your right to claim for sake of the common good.

This justification isn't only strange because of the morally loaded demand. It is also strange because the possibility to terminate the contract in § 543 II nr. 3 BGB necessitates the tenant to be *in arrear* (*im Verzug*) with the payment. And this is only the case if they can be held legally responsible for not paying the rent in a timely manner, for example by mismanagement or wasting the money. While, generally, any party is expected to have money and the inability to pay, called *difficultas dandi* by the Romans,[9] does not release anyone from their obligation. But an unforeseen event, like a near-complete standstill of the whole economy and its consequences, like the widespread loss of salaries, is pretty much the definition of a circumstance outside of the debtor's control (§ 286 IV BGB). Therefore, the tenant is not *in arrear* in the legal sense and the landlord may not terminate the tenancy agreement. A similar idea with even more far-reaching consequences can be found in § 313 I BGB. It states that existing obligations must be renegotiated

---

[5] BGB = Bürgerliches Gesetzbuch (German Civil Code).
[6] EGBGB = Einführungsgesetz zum BGB (introductory statute to the German Civil Code).
[7] »Gesetz zur Abmilderung der Folgen der COVID-19-Pandemie im Zivil-, Insolvenz- und Strafverfahrensrecht« (transl. by the author), BGBl. 2020 I Nr. 14, pp. 569 ff.
[8] The relevant link was deleted after 11th June 2020.
[9] Cf. for example D. 45,1,137,4 (Venuleius libro 1 institutionum).

or cancelled if there is a change of circumstances relevant to the contract. Either the ministry of justice was unaware of these provisions, or the new statute was introduced simply to make a political statement. Either way, the outcome stays the same: The landlord isn't partaking in the usual distribution of risks as usually dictated by tenancy law, but is requested to practice solidarity – not only with his tenants, but with society as a whole.

5. »Gemeinnutz geht vor Eigennutz«?

Burdening private contracts with public concerns has been the aim of authoritarian regimes in Germany's past.[10] Tenant and landlord, debtor and creditor in general, should enter a contract not solely to satisfy their personal interests, but also to serve the public weal. Large parts of legal academia, though, missed that the Corona pandemic is not the first time the German legislator introduced the demand that everyone should make some personal sacrifice for sake of the common good: A similar thought could already be found in the statute that modernized the law of obligations in 2002. An example for this is the (then introduced) § 275 II BGB which states that the debtor must make additional efforts to fulfil their obligation – even to a greater extent than originally promised in the contract. Only where their financial burden would exceed the other party's interest in specific performance, the debtor can refuse to perform. This has been interpreted that a performance can always be demanded where this would be economically beneficial for society.[11]

Statutes like this place private law in service of the common good. That, though, is contradictory to our liberal economic and societal model, which presupposes autonomously acting individuals, free of collectivist regulations. This model person is not only allowed to be egoistic they are supposed to be. The primary task of private law is balancing out the selfish interests of the market participants, distributing risks, assigning disadvantages, and securing advantages. It is alarming when the private law is not trusted to fulfil this task anymore. There were times when it was considered appropriate to instruct or even force people to act *correctly* in order to achieve public benefits. We all remember those times as dreadful ones.

---

[10] Pt. 24 of the party program of the NSDAP (National Socialist German Workers' Party, 1920): »Gemeinnutz geht vor Eigennutz« (»Common interest outstrips self-interest«; transl. by the author), § 44 ZGB (of the GDR, 1976): »Bei der Vorbereitung, dem Abschluß, der inhaltlichen Ausgestaltung und der Erfüllung von Verträgen haben die Bürger und Betriebe als Vertragspartner vertrauensvoll zusammenzuwirken und sich von den Grundsätzen der sozialistischen Moral leiten zu lassen.«

[11] For details on that context see Schermaier: Was schuldet der Schuldner, pp. 409, 412 ff.

6. Solidarity Trumps Constitutional Rights: Corona and Public Law

But the Corona-politics do not only demand consideration of the common good in the field of private law. In the area of public law, which has been committed to *utilitas publica* since Ulpian D. 1,1,1,3, moral appeals are often preferred to judicial arguments, too. This has been discussed more frequently in the last couple of weeks than the moral turn in private law. This may be because lawyers familiar with constitutional law are a bit more keen-eared since the restriction of individual rights in favor of the general public is only permitted when based on a solid legal foundation. At the end of March, just after the so-called *contact ban*[12] was imposed, a brief discussion flared up whether such a restriction and other precautionary measures should be enforced upon all people or just upon the members of the *high risk group*. Quickly the argument was brought forward that it would be wrong to treat people differently at all. Why should young people be allowed to wander around freely while the older part of the population suffers in their rooms? Solidarity means: everyone stays home.

There it was again, the call for solidarity, uttered frequently in these times. Hardly anyone, though, discussed that solidarity can only be demanded where it is useful for others. It remained uncertain what advantage there is for old people if the youth does not get infected.[13] An assessment of the necessity and adequacy of the contact ban was omitted not just because the evidence was ambiguous. It was also suppressed because no one wanted to risk waiting for and evaluating the effect of decided measures, such as the ban on major events and the closure of schools. That way, the call for solidarity transformed into a »normative incantation«[14] and a fill-in for all neglected, but legally necessary, considerations about the proportionality of the intended confinements of constitutional rights.

The replacement of law by morals recurs in the discussion about when and how the return to the constitutionally protected *everyday life* will be possible. One proposal by the Minister of Health is to restore the rights of those who have developed antibodies due to surviving an infection. To accomplish this, the draft of the »Second law for the protection of the public in an epidemic situation of national proportions«[15] originally included that an *immunity certificate* will be issued in analogy or in combination with the *vaccination certificate*. This led to a storm of protests from both political opponents and constitutional lawyers. One

---

[12] §§ 1–2 CoronaSchVO NRW = Verordnung zum Schutz vor Neuinfizierungen mit dem Coronavirus SARS-CoV-2 (Coronaschutzverordnung).

[13] Cf. Bublitz: Es gibt keine Freiheit.

[14] Ibid.: »Normative Zauberformel«; transl. by the author.

[15] Zweites Gesetz zum Schutz der Bevölkerung bei einer epidemischen Lage von nationaler Tragweite, final version of 19th May 2020, BGBl. 2020 I Nr. 23, pp. 1018 ff.; transl. by the author.

cannot treat people differently in such a crushing situation! From those who have recovered from a Corona infection – and thus most likely immune – one can expect the same solidarity.

7. No Equality in Injustice

These and similar reservations are surprising because the Bundestag had passed the so-called »Masernschutzgesetz« (*Measles Protection Act*)[16] only a few weeks earlier, on 10 February 2020, which contains a remarkably similar differentiation. The *mandatory vaccination* laid down in this statute is not an *obligation* in the literal sense. Instead, people who are not vaccinated are denied admission or employment in community facilities – including daycare centers, schools, care facilities and hospitals (cf. § 20 VIII–XIV InfektionsschutzG). Those who cannot be vaccinated for health reasons or who have already overcome measles and are now immune to it are exempt from these restrictions. The *Measles Protection Act* does not restrict fundamental rights (such as the so-called »freedom of occupation«, Art. 12 GG) for persons who have already been immunized, however, it does so for those who are not. Therefore, both groups are treated differently. This does not need further justification because there is no equality in injustice: the restriction of the fundamental right is the exception; it is the state of injustice which requires justification.

The highly controversial *immunity certificate* would not be any different: the restrictions on fundamental rights imposed by government would not apply to those who are already immune. Again, the point is not to treat someone better than others, but to restrict those who can still spread the infection. But even constitutional lawyers are tempted to call the immunity certificate »unconstitutional and inhumane«[17] on the basis of their moral reflex that everyone should be treated equally. However, the simple formula of formal justice should point the way for overeager equalizers: it is just to treat the identical equally. When it comes to facing the challenges of the epidemic, which alone can justify the curtailment of fundamental rights, those who are not (yet) infected and those who have already recovered are not equal. Therefore, it would be unjust to treat them equally when referring to moral criteria. A completely different and undoubtedly valid argument against the introduction of *immunity certificates* is that it is not yet clear how long the immunity acquired through a Sars CoV II infection lasts.

---

[16] Gesetz für den Schutz vor Masern und zur Stärkung der Impfprävention, BGBl. 2020 I, Nr. 6, S. 148 ff.
[17] Boehme-Nessler: Inhuman und verfassungswidrig; transl. by the author.

8. Weak Law, Strong Morals?

However, why are morals so important in the public debate? Why does it often overlap or even outweigh the argument derived from current law? Why does the defense of fundamental rights suddenly need to be justified? There may be various reasons for this. One could be based on the vague intuition of the stakeholders, that the value structure of the modern legal system lacks the necessary persuasiveness. One might think of Böckenförde's dictum that the liberal, secular state thrives from normative requirements that it cannot guarantee.[18] If one takes this dictum seriously, the state today creates a secular morality because it believes that it has to reconstruct the prerequisites that support our understanding of state and society. The evocation of *solidarity* and *public spirit* could then be interpreted as an attempt to absorb the perceived or actual distrust of the state and its institutions. Böckenförde had already warned against this consequence.

However, maybe one does not have to reach that far. Perhaps the upturn of moralism is related to the imagined catastrophes we are tumbling into, one by one. Life in a state of exception, in constant exaggeration, has blunted the sword of law. Instead of analyzing the facts rationally, we see the *casus perplexus* in every new event, which current law cannot grasp and certainly not solve. We see the law as being overwhelmed because we imagine that which it is supposed to regulate as overpowering.

A parallel to this can be seen in what constitutional theory calls *inflation of fundamental rights*. Because it is expected that the state will protect every interest, no matter how particular, the scope of application of fundamental rights established in the *Grundgesetz* has been expanded ever further. For example, begging is seen as protected by the fundamental right to freedom of expression (Art. 5 I GG) and street music by artistic freedom (Art. 5 III GG). There is also discussion about whether prohibited activities are also protected by the fundamental right to freedom of occupation (Art. 12 I GG). Such marginal problems reduce the impact of the addressed fundamental rights. The dough pulled out at the ends thins out in the middle. The law looks pale and flimsy, the really difficult cases seem to be unregulated and therefore unsolvable. One therefore feels the need to fall back on principles laying beyond law, which are nothing but ideas of *correct behaviour* negotiated in political discourse.

Both developments, social alarmism, and the inflation of fundamental rights, start at opposite points: the latter on the trivialization of fundamental rights, the former on the overestimation of real challenges. However, they are similar in the fact that the public discourse seems to mistrust that the legal order is able to solve deep conflicts and crises satisfactorily. With moral appeals to do the right

---

[18] Cf. Böckenförde: Die Entstehung des Staates, p. 93.

thing, practice charity or at least *show solidarity*, one underpins the law or – as some examples in everyday political life during Corona have shown – even undermines it.

9. The Value of Secularity and the Silence of Lawyers

The fact that morality suspends law has been observed in legislation, jurisprudence, but above all in political discourse for a longer period of time. The Corona crisis is accelerating this process or at least making it more visible. But even more alarming than the process itself is the silence of the lawyers. Today's lawyers grew up in a constitutional state and were educated in the laws of a liberal democracy. They should be the first to protest when they are asked to judge, advise and to draft statutes not according to the law, but according to moral criteria. The fact that modern western legal systems have become secular orders, free from religious shackles as well as from the moral demands of absolutist or collectivist systems, was a lengthy and painful process for which countless people (including lawyers) risked their economic and social existence, their health and even their lives. Today one seems to be ready to give away part of these achievements.

Secularity is not a value in itself. But it is the hallmark of a free society and a state that perceives its primary purpose in guaranteeing the freedom of its citizens and defending them against external and internal enemies. Secularity is also a necessary requirement for a legal system that distinguishes and balances these freedoms within the community – regardless of ideological or political orientation. Of course, one desires citizens who think and act morally. And one will also accept that politicians claim to be moral. However, by demanding morals publicly, one wants to please. In the mildest case one is a populist, in the worst case, one is overriding law.

References

Böckenförde, Ernst-Wolfgang: Die Entstehung des Staates als Vorgang der Säkularisation, in: Sergius Buve (ed.): Säkularisation und Utopie. Ebracher Studien. Ernst Forsthoff zum 65. Geburtstag, Stuttgart 1967, pp. 75–94.
Boehme-Nessler, Volker: Der Corona-Pass ist inhuman und verfassungswidrig, in: Die Zeit, 05.05.2020, https://www.zeit.de/gesellschaft/2020-05/immunitaetsausweis-coronavirus-antikoerpertest-grundrechte-verfassungsrechtler-volker-boehme-nessler; last accessed 22.06.2020.

Bublitz, Christoph: Es gibt keine Freiheit, Teil einer Infektionskette zu sein: Solidarität und Pflicht in der Pandemie, in: praefaktisch.de – Ein Philosophieblog, 09.04.2020, https://www.praefaktisch.de/covid-19/es-gibt-keine-freiheit-teil-einer-infektionskette-zu-sein-solidaritaet-und-pflicht-in-der-pandemie/; last accessed 22.06.2020.

du Plessis, Paul J.: A History of Remissio Mercedis and Related Legal Institutions, Rotterdam / Deventer 2003.

Merkel, Angela: Fernsehansprache der Bundeskanzlerin, 18.03.2020, https://www.tagesschau.de/multimedia/video/video-676493.html; last accessed 22.06.2020.

Schermaier, Martin: Was schuldet der Schuldner? Die »Pflicht zur Anstrengung« im modernisierten Schuldrecht, in: Friedrich Harrer / Heinrich Honsell / Peter Mader (eds.): Gedächtnisschrift für Theo Mayer-Maly, Wien 2011, pp. 409–422.

Angela Condello
Immersed in a Normative Laboratory

1. Immersion

»Deliberation is expressed *subjunctively*; which is a speech proper to signify suppositions, with their consequences; as, *if this be done, then this will follow*; and differs not from the language of reasoning, save that reasoning is in general words; but deliberation for the most part is of particulars. The language of desire, and aversion, is *imperative*; as *do this, forbear that*; which when the party is obliged to do, or forbear, is *command*; otherwise *prayer*; or else *counsel*. The language of vain-glory, of indignation, pity and revengefulness, *optative*: but of the desire to know, there is a peculiar expression, called *interrogative*; as, *what is it, when shall it, how is it done, and why so?* Other language of the passions I find none: for cursing, swearing, reviling, and the like, do not signify as speech; but as the actions of a tongue accustomed.«[1]

The Covid-19 pandemic has progressively caused, on top of the sanitary emergency, an economic and a political one: the latter, in particular, has often been interpreted through the philosophical-juridical paradigm of the state of exception, i.e. in terms of a suspension of the democratic communicative regime in favor of decisionism. Hungary and some other cases apart, the risk of such interpretation of the recent events should be avoided: indeed, and quite on the contrary, there is nothing exceptional, from the juridical point of view, in the moment we are undergoing. The situation is, rather, such that we experienced an exaggeration of (some) peculiar aspects of legal normativity that we usually neglect.

Indeed, we have suddenly discovered ourselves *immersed* in a normative lab, in which we lived a *total* experience, embracing diverse instants of our daily lives and choices. Not only did we understand, but we perceived in depth what it means to have our existence regulated by legal norms. Legal instruments like the necessity and urgency decrees or the derogation are foreseen, for instance, both in the Italian Constitution (Art. 77) and by the EU Convention on human rights (Art. 15). Against this background, the emergency laws which have increasingly had an impact into our daily rhythms have progressively compressed (and, later on, de-compressed) the fundamental rights of us all, without exceptions, because of the need to balance the freedom of *each individual* with the collective right to

---

[1] Hobbes: Leviathan, p. 41.

health and security, that are fundamental goods of *everyone*. In order to do so, the legal operations during the emergency could intervene only under certain circumstances: in a state of necessity; always in respect of a proportional logic; and in respect of the condition that these could be the only measures left and, nevertheless, without these measures undermining the essential nucleus of fundamental rights.

Thus, beginning some months ago, we have been experiencing, especially in Italy, something that before could have been foreseen only through a mental experiment: following (some more, some less) the emergential norms that have made our days similar to the life inside a normative lab, we made direct experience of *what is the law*, of its impact and of its *hold on life*. We acted, in other words, like test animals inside a model which would have been useful to a normativist like Hans Kelsen.

We witnessed changes and reductions, following singular and very general normative sources (urgency decrees), of our personal freedom, freedom of movement, freedom on economic initiative, etc. – among others. At the same time and symmetrically, we exposed and circulated (more or less voluntarily) data that profiled ourselves and that are extremely useful to subjects we can't even imagine.

For decades now, especially among legal anthropologists, there have been interesting studies on the concept of legal consciousness, i. e. on how we perceive and understand an intangible artifice like the law, which (almost always) vinculates us without our complete perception of its bonds. This seems to be instead the moment in which legal consciousness emerges in each one of us: it is penetrating into our imaginary more than when – automatically, like in the example reported by Max Weber – we stop in front of a red light before crossing on the white stripes, or when we pay our taxes. By now, we expect that that law is imperceptible to our daily experience, because we are used to its invisible presence.

Inside the normative lab, each one of us (re-)lives the feeling of a three years old to which we tell that he *cannot* eat that candy he absolutely *wants* to eat (and now!): we are going back to feel the chains. We are, thus, capable to see the bonds instituted by the law to contain our pulsions and our needs, from the morning till the evening, because we are having a direct, prolonged and continuous experience of such bonds. Just as if we were inside a laboratory, the current condition allows us to look with a magnifying glass inside the nucleus of the concept of law, revealing the conundrum on which the connection between individuals and the law is based. In the first place, the *privileged* perspective in which we are immersed shows an interesting fold in the relationship between law and force – a theme that has crossed the history of juridical thought since antiquity and that we find in Montaigne, Pascal and (lastly) in the beautiful pages of Derrida on the mystical foundation of juridical authority. In light of the experience that we are living, the aspect that seems to be emerging is that in the relationship between law and force the element of cooperation should not be disregarded. Such element makes possible the *grip* of the norms on our life. In other terms: these decrees have often been characterized by a general and abstract language more than it is usual for legal norms, and in the first decrees promulgated one could even find expressions like ›it is suggested‹ or ›it would be preferable‹. Nonetheless, some exceptions apart, it seems that these norms are widely respected. Why? In which way and for what reasons the level of legal consciousness is variating in the current situation? When we stop in front of the red lights, we adequate to a practical normativity we are used to, taking for granted the legitimacy of the normative source: in such case, habit makes us perceive the act of following the norm as a fulfillment of our own will, in the form of the *respect* for a daily legality that we *owe* to the society. In the case of the decrees, we likewise perceive the heteronomous nature of the source of the obligation to do or do not; what makes these decrees particularly effective, more than the fear of the sanction, is the content or *end* which those norms intend to realize (more security and health for each one). Beyond this, to conclude on the first aspect, there is certainly also the individual dread for the potential consequences that the contagion could have on us and our families. In other terms, on top of the normative force deriving from their content, these decrees are effective because the current situation has (re)awakened a fear, a Hobbesian *metus*, that brings us back to a new *state of nature*.

2. Repression

»Fear of death, and wounds, disposeth to the same; and for the same reason. On the contrary, needy men, and hardy, not contented with their present condition; as also, all men that are ambitious of military command, are inclined to continue the causes of war; and to stir up trouble and sedition: for there is no honor military but by war; nor any such hope to mend an ill game, as by causing a new shuffle.«[2]

On the second point. While we assist to the resurgence of categories, like the state of exception, that erroneously seem to fit all seasons, we have (instead) the chance to understand what it means, for each one of us and for everyone, to obey the law in order to witness, unhappily, to the *sacrificial* advantages of civilization or *Kultur*, following Freud. The tension between our pulsions and the regulatory force of the (almost) daily decrees, is showing – almost a century after the societal psychoanalysis by Sigmund Freud – how human relations can be productive only if they entail repressions. In the Freudian project, the primordial man was feeling better than us because he had no repressions. Yet, his condition was only apparently better, because he could not fully enjoy his freedom: without *deprivations*

[2] Ibid., p. 66.

for *each one*, *distress* and *discomfort* grow for *everyone*, in the forms of insecurity, prevarication, and death. Freud's theory of societal rules and repressions, with all its consequences, is lumped into a tradition of occidental myth in which civilized society can, as well, relapse into the dissipating savagery whence it came.³ In other words, order entails partial repression: the discontent is a necessary disease,⁴ in psychoanalytical terms, which is ineradicable and which ever attends the ordered norm. Intersubjective recognition and social organization are based on a renunciation of instinctual gratifications which are typical, instead, of the primal condition.

The immersive perspective we have entered, therefore, reveals the trading foundations on which modernity is constructed: liberty, as Hobbes phrases it, is »the absence of external impediments: which impediments, may oft take away part of a man's power to do what he would«. Yet, the impediments »cannot hinder him from using the power left him, according as his judgement, and reason shall dictate to him«.⁵ The passage through a direct perception of the value proper of the exchange between liberty and repression unveils, thus, how the search for the *just* at a specific time entails individual and collective responsibility:

»And as the last appetite in deliberation, is called the will; so the last opinion in search of the truth of past, and future, is called the *judgment*, or resolute and final sentence of him that discourseth. And as the whole chain of appetites alternate, in the question of good, or bad, is called deliberation; so the whole chain of opinions alternate, in the question of true, or false, is called *doubt*.«⁶

3. Judgment

Thirdly, and conclusively, the mediation between individual freedom and the highest wealth for the largest number of people has shown its *critical* attitude together with its fragility: as reasonable as the sacrifices we are asked to face can be, emergency laws intensify the vulnerability of everyone. Consequently, these sacrifices radicalize the situation of those who are ordinarily vulnerable: not only as it is obvious, of women, children and old people, but also (among others) of migrants, inmates, single mothers, illegal workers. The normative lab in which we are immersed reveals, thus, the ambivalent capacities of legal norms: on the one hand, by clarifying characters of social regulation otherwise imperceptible; on the other hand, strengthening the *raison d'être* but also the precariousness of the

---

3 Cf. Fitzpatrick: Modernism and the Grounds of Law, p. 3.
4 Cf. Freud: Civilization and Its Discontents, infra.
5 Hobbes: Leviathan, p. 86.
6 Ibid., p. 42.

normative structure forming our social regulation. The laws, in other words, are artifices functional to realize a precise task: in the short run, they aim at conducting us outside the hobbesian state of nature and they should prevent the risks of the conflict of everyone against everyone else. In the long run, and through the historical crises, they should however work like the tendons inside a body: compensating, slowing down, and pushing where necessary.

The precise task that legal orders are aimed at realizing is at stake especially in times of crises: the unforeseen, what emerges suddenly, calls for what Hannah Arendt has named the »wind of thought«. In times of crisis, Arendt writes, »thinking ceases to be a marginal affair in political matters« because those who possess the capacity for critical thought are not swept away unthinkingly. Crises and moments of transition liberate (or *should* liberate) the most human of all faculties: the faculty of judgment, the most political of man's mental abilities:

»the most political of man's mental abilities. It is the faculty to judge particulars without subsuming them under those general rules which can be taught and learned until they grow into habits that can be replaced by other habits and rules. The faculty of judging particulars (as Kant discovered it), the ability to say, ›this is wrong‹, ›this is beautiful‹, etc., is not the same as the faculty of thinking. Thinking deals with invisibles, with representations of things that are absent; judging always concerns particulars and things close at hand. But the two are interrelated in a way similar to the way consciousness and conscience are interconnected. If thinking, the two-in-one of the soundless dialogue, actualizes the difference within our identity as given in consciousness and thereby results in conscience as its by-product, then judging, the by-product of the liberating effect of thinking, realizes thinking, makes it manifest in the world of appearances, where I am never alone and always much too busy to be able to think. The manifestation of the wind of thought is no knowledge; it is the ability to tell right from wrong, beautiful from ugly.«[7]

The exchange between *repression* and *relation* must, thus, always aim at something. Therefore, if on the one hand it seems plausible to claim that, in the future, as incredible as it may sound, theorizing the law will correspond again, almost four centuries after the *Leviathan*, to find solutions for the survival of the species; on the other hand, the immersive experience – not at all virtual – that we have undergone and that we are to some extent still undergoing, outside all philanthropic rhetoric, should lead us to reflect on the insufficiency of our legal and institutional instruments. Immersed in a normative lab, just like scientists and therefore observing, inducing and deducing *why* and *how* the social objects that we name ›norms‹ work, we have the chance to look at the law through the values that the normative orders should realize. Among these, undoubtedly, equality and freedom: values that have always been complicit and rival, and among which lays down the opportunity – better: the hope – for the realization of a *just* society.

[7] Arendt: Thinking and Moral Considerations, pp. 445 f.

References

Arendt, Hannah: Thinking and Moral Considerations, in: Social Research 38(3), 1971, pp. 417–446.
Fitzpatrick, Peter: Modernism and the Grounds of Law, Cambridge/UK 2001.
Freud, Sigmund: Civilization and Its Discontents, New York 1961.
Hobbes, Thomas: Leviathan, Oxford 1996.

II. Corona Normativities

Jan Christoph Suntrup

Corona: Biopolitical Models and the Hygiene of Tact

The corona crisis reveals the ambivalence of the human condition in the 21st century. The number of victims, the shutdown of public life, the pragmatic and sometimes worrisome adjustment of political procedures, and the revolution of the rules of social behavior, which constitute a dramatic restriction of basic rights, provoke a shared feeling that we are living in exceptional times. As justified as that impression may be, given that for most people affected by the crisis its implications are indeed unprecedented, this does not seem to be the whole picture. Terrorist attacks, financial crises, war-induced streams of refugees, and the devastating effects of climate change have fostered a widely spread emergency mentality that receives claims to and experiences of exceptionality with a certain routine – at least on the part of privileged persons who are not entirely absorbed, sometimes in an existential fashion, by trying to cope with the effects of the current pandemic. Academic discourse is undoubtedly part of this emergency routine, sometimes recalling Blumenberg's observation in *Work on Myth* according to which »stories are told in order to kill (*vertreiben*) something. In the most harmless, but not least important case: to kill time. In another and more serious case: to kill fear«,[1] fear of the unknown, or rather, with some observers, the fear of revising their analytical categories. Unfortunately, not all commentators currently show the Socratic wisdom of Jürgen Habermas who recently stated that »there has never been so much knowledge about our ignorance and the compulsion to act and live under uncertainty«.[2]

Most incidences that are quick to be labelled exceptional trigger routines and coping rituals. Politicians speaking of urgency and necessity and the swift changing of procedural rules is something citizens worldwide are experiencing on a more or less regular basis. This bears important consequences: The more frequently the »pathos of the ›exception‹«[3] and the symbolic framing and setting of the extraordinary[4] are resorted to, the more easily we can observe the *Veralltägli-*

---

[1] Blumenberg: Work on Myth, p. 34.
[2] Habermas: »So viel Wissen über unser Nichtwissen gab es noch nie.«
[3] Cf. Gephart: Introduction, p 16; Conclusion, p. 514, in this volume.
[4] Suntrup: The Symbolic Politics of the State of Exception.

chung, or routinization, of such charismatic moments. Thus, the iterative suspension of certain basic rights and democratic procedures (seldom the suspension of the complete legal order as in Carl Schmitt's exceptionally pathetic exception, in which »life breaks through the crust of a mechanism that has become torpid by repetition«[5]) might either be harder to justify, inciting the protest of a heterogenous multitude whose members vary from liberal right activists to resentful conspiracy theorists, or foster an increasingly indifferent and fatalist view on legal certainty.

Generally, the expectation of crises and catastrophes is part of the specific temporality of risk societies. The idea of risk is intrinsically connected with the »aspiration to control and particularly with the idea of controlling the future«,[6] thus emphasizing the power of human action over the fatalist belief in the inescapable forces of nature, god, or history. While the perspective of risk includes the belief that decisions matter, the prospect of controlling the future is nevertheless bound to fail, as in many social domains »the future becomes ever more absorbing, but at the same time opaque. There are few direct lines to it, only a plurality of ›future scenarios‹«.[7] For Ulrich Beck, one of the pioneers of risk sociology, modern »risk societies« are characterized by the self-observation that »we live in a world that has to make decisions concerning its future under the conditions of manufactured, self-inflicted insecurity«, while renouncing the conviction that these unintended effects of (successful) modernization can be fully mastered.[8]

The plurality of current crisis narratives certainly shows that the awareness of *self-inflicted* insecurity is not commonly shared. While some voices stress the likelihood of mutated and dispersed viruses in the Anthropocene, there is no lack of political leaders (and other commentators) who deny the very existence of a crisis, nourish conspiracy theories (the »Chinese virus«), or try to shift the debate on common ground (»we are at war with the virus«). While in general the validity of legal orders and political decisions is to a large extent based on comprehensive narratives,[9] states of emergencies are no exception to this rule, never appearing as a pure and uncontested natural »given« (regardless of their concrete causation). Schmitt's famous opening to *Political Theology* – »sovereign is he who decides on the exception«[10] – should be understood in this regard, as »to decide on« can mean much more than the formal declaration of a state of exception by extending to the authoritative interpretation of its causation and the procedural steps and political measures during a state of emergency.

---

5   Schmitt: Political Theology, p. 15.
6   Giddens: Risk and Responsibility, p. 3.
7   Ibid., p. 4.
8   Beck: World at Risk, p. 8.
9   Suntrup: Umkämpftes Recht, pp. 145–231.
10 Schmitt: Political Theology, p. 6.

Hence, a general anticipation of future catastrophes (and hence *states of exception*) is rather common, while the search for causation and scapegoats follows a different path. Politically, this specific perspective on the future has been translated into different strategies and objectives of prevention. While an ex-post evaluation of decisions taken under conditions of uncertainty always runs the risk of being cheap, there is some evidence that in most countries the main focus was on the »war on terror«, sometimes culminating in a medicine of hyper-prevention with »autoimmune« consequences (as observed by Derrida[11] and others), i.e. the gradual self-destruction of the democratic and legal body by the same measures (of surveillance and restrictions of basic rights) which were purported to protect it. On the contrary, and despite multiple warnings and crisis simulations, which have for many years stressed the high probability of an imminent pandemic, the public health sector has suffered from a policy of under-prevention, often having fallen prey to privatization, austerity, and the mismanagement of public revenue.

Evidently, the corona pandemic raises the question of its biopolitical implications. Michel Foucault introduced the term »bio-power« in the 1970s to refer to a

»number of phenomena that seem to me to be quite significant, namely, the set of mechanisms through which the basic biological features of the human species became the object of a political strategy, of a general strategy of power, or, in other words, how, starting from the eighteenth century, modern Western societies took on board the fundamental biological fact that human beings are a species.«[12]

This strategy effected modern population management based on new analytic means such as statistics and the comprehensive collection of data. Bruno Latour, apparently exasperated by the very strict restrictions on circulation in France, commented »that by remaining trapped at home while outside there is only the extension of police powers and the din of ambulances, we are collectively playing a caricatured form of the figure of biopolitics that seems to have come straight out of a Michel Foucault lecture«[13] instead of launching the necessary ecological reforms for a revised 21st century biopolitics. When Latour, however, feels he has been sent back to the state of the 19th century, a closer look at Foucault's lectures might be rewarding and allow for a better understanding of different models of pandemic management that can be observed at the moment. Although Foucault officially dedicated a whole lecture series to the topic of biopolitics in 1978/79, he never developed this concept in a satisfactory way. At the same time, his work is marked with biopolitical observations in a wider sense and proves especially re-

---

[11] Derrida: Autoimmunity.
[12] Foucault: Security, Territory, Population, p. 1.
[13] Latour: Is This a Dress Rehearsal?

vealing when illustrating the historical transformation of power models by focusing on the fight against infectious diseases.

In the Middle Ages, the spread of leprosy was countered by a strict model of exclusion, involving

>»first of all a rigorous division, a distancing, a rule of no contact between one individual (or group of individuals) and another. Second, it involved casting these individuals out into a vague, external world beyond the town's walls, beyond the limits of the community. As a result, two masses were constituted, each foreign to the other. And those cast out were cast out in the strict sense into outer darkness. Third, and finally, the exclusion of lepers implied the disqualification – which was perhaps not exactly moral, but in any case juridical and political – of individuals thus excluded and driven out«.[14]

According to Foucault, this exclusionary power model had more or less disappeared by the end of the 17th century, replaced incrementally by the disciplinary model, whose strategy was expressed in plague regulations that utilized means other than exclusion, »literally imposing a partitioning grid on the regions and town struck by plague, with regulations indicating when people can go out, how, at what times, what they must do at home, what type of food they must have, prohibiting certain types of contact, requiring them to present themselves to inspectors, and to open their homes to inspectors«.[15] This disciplinary model was linked to a specific politics of space, replacing physical and juridical exclusion from the community by the technique of quarantine, the meticulous assignment of places, and the constant surveillance of every individual.[16]

Finally, the fight against small pox serves as an illustration for the rise of security technologies; disciplinary techniques are not suspended in this process, but strict surveillance of every individual is less important than precise statistical data about the population and specific parts of it, providing knowledge about »how many people are infected with smallpox, at what age, with what effects, with what mortality rate, lesions or after-effects, the risks of inoculation, the probability of an individual dying or being infected by smallpox despite inoculation, and the statistical effects on the population in general«.[17] The more that is known about the statistically »normal« processes of the disease, the more the fight against it may transcend a general order discipline. Furthermore, in the case of inoculation and vaccination, the disease is no longer banned, but biologically included by making it part of the solution. Thereby, these security technologies enable a form of refined

---

[14] Foucault: Abnormal, p. 43.
[15] Foucault: Security, Territory, Population, p. 10.
[16] Foucault: Abnormal, p. 46.
[17] Foucault: Security, Territory, Population, p. 10.

risk assessment, which is much more compatible with the rights and liberties in liberal societies than the disciplinary model.

For Foucault, these medical strategies serve as illustrations of comprehensive power models far beyond the narrowly biopolitical sphere. Nevertheless, they may serve the present observers of the corona pandemic as useful ideal types.[18] An authoritarian system like that in China, which turns more and more into a totalitarian system of complete digital surveillance of its citizens, is able to resort to the harsh plague model (implemented in Wuhan), while liberal democracies principally rely on the small pox model, which allows for the proportionate restriction of rights by limiting risks and granting freedom as much as possible. At the same time, the developments in Europe and elsewhere in March 2020 have amply evidenced the model's limits, as under-equipped healthcare systems and ignorance of the virus's concrete effects and impact prompted many national governments to take refuge in the disciplinary model. To my mind, a return to the leprosy model, the possibility of which Philipp Sarasin discusses,[19] is not very likely. Recurrent ideas, such as getting rid of restrictions of movement, including denying the elderly special protection, in order to return to business as usual as soon as possible, does not imply a return to the binary model of leprosy suppression by deliberate exclusion, but rather makes it clear that the protection of life as such is not prioritized at all costs.

The metaphor of »herd immunity«, which has been used by many politicians who – at least initially – opted against restrictively handling the crisis, is ambivalent, as Thomas Dreier has underlined in a commentary:[20] It conveys the impression of protection by the community on the one hand, while featuring a Darwinian touch by implying the idea that some members of the herd might be dispensable for the sake of the many. Anyone acquainted with Foucault's governmentality lectures cannot fail to notice at this point the blatant contradiction between the image of herd immunity and Foucault's analysis of Christian pastoral power, a model in which the pastor (the shepherd) was obliged to care for the salvation of the whole congregation (the fold) without sacrificing just one sheep – *omnes et singulatim* …[21]

This idea of pastoral power should be kept in the back of our minds when turning to who is likely the most famous contemporary theoretician of biopolitics, Giorgio Agamben. Unlike Foucault, Agamben does not regard biopolitics as a modern phenomenon, having instead become known for his statement that Western politics is from the start inextricably bound to mastering life in a biopolitical way:

---

[18] Sarasin: Mit Foucault die Pandemie verstehen?
[19] Ibid.
[20] Cf. in this volume Dreier: »Law as Culture« in Times of Corona, p. 53.
[21] Foucault: Security, Territory, Population, lecture 5.

»Western politics first constitutes itself through an exclusion (which is simultaneously an inclusion) of bare life«.[22] The *homo sacer*, which could be killed without punishment, but not sacrificed, was simultaneously expelled – banned – from legal and religious order but included (by being an obscure figure of Roman law) into law. In Agamben's eyes, this production of bare life is the main signature of sovereignty, which is situated in a topologically analogous position by concurrently standing outside and inside of the law. Thus, both *homo sacer* and the sovereign are in this sense exceptional personae, »limit figures«,[23] which leads Agamben to the bold thesis that »at once excluding bare life from and capturing it within the political order, the state of exception actually constituted, in its very separateness, the hidden foundation on which the entire political system rested«.[24] In the course of Agamben's grand narration, the *homo sacer* still haunts Western societies in the different shapes of refugees, over-comatose patients, or victims of ethnic wars, up to the point that he declares all citizens to be virtually *homines sacri* in our times.[25]

As successful as this conceptual apparatus has become in the humanities and social sciences, it lacks analytical sharpness and faculty of judgment, which can also be conceived in Agamben's multiple commentaries on the corona crisis. He started with comparing the »alleged epidemic of coronavirus« against all established evidence to a normal flu[26] before bemoaning the failure of priests to embrace the sick and comparing the justification of rights restrictions on the base of overriding moral principles to Adolf Eichmann's invocation of Kantian ethics as self-defense.[27] Agamben does not seem to see any remarkable difference between Eichmann, who sent millions of victims into the gas chambers, and his infamous distortion of the Kantian concept of duty on the one hand,[28] and the impetus of saving, while in Italy masses of corpses were carried away by military trucks, as many lives as possible on the other hand. For Agamben, however, the key point is as follows: »A norm that affirms that it is necessary to renounce what is good in order to save what is good is as false as the norm that, in order to protect liberty, forces one to renounce it«.[29] Even though a general suspicion against political restrictions of rights and liberties can be credited as civic virtue – especially given that emergencies have often been used (look at Poland, Hungary, or Israel) to infringe on basic rights in an enduring way, sometimes even transforming »commissary dictators« (Carl Schmitt) into permanent ones – to reject, as Agamben does,

---

[22] Agamben: Homo Sacer, p. 7.
[23] Ibid., p. 27.
[24] Ibid., p. 9.
[25] Ibid., p. 111.
[26] Agamben: The Invention of a Pandemic.
[27] Agamben: Ich hätte da eine Frage.
[28] Arendt: Eichmann in Jerusalem, chap. 8.
[29] Agamben: Ich hätte da eine Frage.

this argument and the possibility of a balancing of goods altogether, betrays an ethics of purity, which misfits the complexity and demands of political decisions.

Beyond all these aberrations, however, there is a fundamental thesis that deserves scrutiny:

»The first thing the wave of panic that's paralysed the country has clearly shown is that our society no longer believes in anything but naked life. It is evident that Italians are prepared to sacrifice practically everything – normal living conditions, social relations, work, even friendships and religious or political beliefs – to avoid the danger of falling ill. The naked life, and the fear of losing it, is not something that brings men and women together, but something that blinds and separates them. [...] Men have become so used to living in conditions of permanent crisis and emergency that they don't seem to notice that their lives have been reduced to a purely biological condition, one that has lost not only any social and political dimension, but even any compassionate and emotional one«.[30]

This is the well-known *homo sacer*, sound with an insignificant variation of the *nuda vita* theme. I will restrict myself to just a few comments. First of all, critics of the *homo sacer* narrative have rightly argued that human beings, as miserable as their condition might be, can never be reduced to their biophysical condition, as they are always constituted by social and cultural processes (and not only in a passively subjected form, but with real agency, usually including the possibility of resistance). »Every way of life is biocultural and biopolitical«.[31] And what is the alleged »fear of losing naked life« if not a social (and very emotional) process? Furthermore, is the act of caring for the health of the most vulnerable just a matter of the sacralization of naked life as such and not – at least occasionally – a very emotional and compassionate act? Agamben is right that social life is fundamentally reproduced by common rituals, which is why the restriction on funerals, by which many friends and relatives of the deceased were precluded from taking leave of them, is indeed dramatic. This is why a permanent reflection on the balancing of health security concerns and other human needs is necessary. At the same time, Agamben has no sense for »distant socializing« (beyond the virtues and vices of online communication), which can be expressed in the norm of so-called »social distancing«.

Perhaps this is the right time, at the conclusion of this concededly indecisive essay, to consult a classic text that has nothing to do with viral infections, but nevertheless tells us a lot about the civilizing and socializing force of distance-keeping: Helmuth Plessner's *Limits of Community*, published in 1924, when it was directed against radical models of community from the right and the left in the fragile Weimar Republic. One of the most important chapters of this essay is tellingly

[30] Agamben: Clarifications.
[31] Connolly: The Complexities of Sovereignty, p. 29.

entitled »The Hygiene of Tact«, in which Plessner describes a form of sociability (*Geselligkeit*) between the distant interaction of business life and forms of transgressive social bonding. While Norbert Elias has depicted the process of civilization as complexly interrelated dynamics of sociogenesis and psychogenesis, the concept of tact relies on an entire anthropological theory, as for Plessner by »a culture of restraint, the mature person first demonstrates his full competency. The animal is ultimately direct and honest in expression; if it depended on nothing more than expression, nature would remain better off with elementary forms of beings and spare itself the fractured being of humans«.[32] Again, this is not a commentary on a widespread infectious disease – but the current crisis might give us the occasion to recall the human »art of not coming too close«[33] (*die Kunst des Nichtzunahetretens*) as an important socializing and not anti-social force.

References

Agamben, Giorgio: Clarifications, 17.03.2020, https://www.journal-psychoanalysis.eu/coronavirus-and-philosophers/; last accessed 16.06.2020.

Agamben, Giorgio: Giorgio Agamben zum Umgang der liberalen Demokratien mit dem Coronavirus: Ich hätte da eine Frage, in NZZ, 15.04.2020, https://www.msn.com/de-ch/nachrichten/politik/giorgio-agamben-zum-umgang-der-liberalen-demokratien-mit-dem-coronavirus-ich-h%C3%A4tte-da-eine-frage/ar-BB12GHS1; last accessed 16.06.2020.

Agamben, Giorgio: Homo Sacer. Sovereign Power and Bare Life, Stanford 1998.

Agamben, Giorgio: The Invention of an Epidemic, 26.02.2020, https://www.journal-psychoanalysis.eu/coronavirus-and-philosophers/; last accessed 16.06.2020.

Arendt, Hannah: Eichmann in Jerusalem. A Report on the Banality of Evil, New York 2006.

Beck, Ulrich: World at Risk, Cambridge/UK 2009.

Blumenberg, Hans: Work on Myth, Cambridge/MA 1985.

Connolly, William E.: The Complexities of Sovereignty, in: Matthew Calarco / Steven DeCaroli (eds.): Giorgio Agamben: Sovereignty and Life, Stanford 2007, pp. 23–42.

Derrida, Jacques: Autoimmunity: Real and Symbolic Suicides. A Dialogue with Jacques Derrida, in: Giovanna Borradori (ed.): Philosophy in a Time of Terror: Dialogues with Jürgen Habermas and Jacques Derrida, Chicago 2003, pp. 85–136.

---

[32] Plessner: The Limits of Community, p. 162.
[33] Ibid.

Foucault, Michel: Abnormal. Lectures at the Collège de France, 1974–75, London 2003.
Foucault, Michel: Security, Territory, Population. Lectures at the Collège de France, 1977–78, Basingstoke 2009.
Giddens, Anthony: Risk and Responsibility, in: The Modern Law Review 62(1), 1999, pp. 1–10.
Habermas, Jürgen: »So viel Wissen über unser Nichtwissen gab es noch nie«, Kölner Stadtanzeiger, 03.04.2020, p. 3.
Latour, Bruno: Is This a Dress Rehearsal?, 26.03.2020, https://critinq.wordpress.com/2020/03/26/is-this-a-dress-rehearsal/; last accessed 16.06.2020.
Plessner, Helmuth: The Limits of Community. A Critique of Social Radicalism, Amherst 1999.
Sarasin, Philipp: Mit Foucault die Pandemie verstehen?, 25.03.2020, https://geschichtedergegenwart.ch/mit-foucault-die-pandemie-verstehen/; last accessed 16.06.2020.
Schmitt, Carl: Political Theology. Four Chapters on the Concept of Sovereignty, Chicago 2005.
Suntrup, Jan Christoph: The Symbolic Politics of the State of Exception: Images and Performances, in: Zeitschrift für Politikwissenschaft 28(4), 2018, pp. 565–580.
Suntrup, Jan Christoph: Umkämpftes Recht. Zur mehrdimensionalen Analyse rechtskultureller Konflikte durch die politische Kulturforschung, Frankfurt am Main 2018.

Francesca Caroccia

Searching for a Vaccine.
Rethinking the Paradigm of (Private) Law in Times of Pandemic Crisis

1. The epidemic emergency brings a period of extraordinary circumstances affecting social, economic, juridical contexts. These are truly unimaginable times. On a daily basis, we are challenged in ways most of us have never experienced before. To preserve itself, the world, as we used to know it, is trying to react, to rethink, to absorb unknown situations: revolutions are »defined by breaking from given normative orders and replacing them with new ones«.[1] But, we are very attached to the given normative order. Faced with such a threat of a pandemic crisis, which means the threat of a normative crisis, the big family of jurists closes ranks and comes back to the origins. In doing so, legal scholars largely use the cultural argument in different ways:[2] as it was clearly resumed,[3] they hold culture as an independent variable to explain variations in law (legal culture and even individual judicial decisions are heavily conditioned by values and behavior of the society: the Durkheimian assumption that real structures serve as determinants of social phenomena);[4] they take law as an independent variable to explain culture (legality influences the construction of cultural schemas: the Durkheimian assumption that law plays a central role in *coercively* regulating social practices);[5] they consider law *as* culture (law as a legitimate object of cultural analysis and interpretative cultural framework through which individuals can understand – maybe change – the reality, as Werner Gephart suggests).[6]

This last methodology is useful both to prevent risks of tautological reasoning and to verify the tightness of the current normative order, faced with the pandemic crisis. On these premises, my research hypothesis is that the cultural

---

[1] Cf. Gephart: Introduction, p. 12, in this volume.
[2] On different meanings of the expression »Legal culture«, cf. Michaels: Legal Culture, pp. 1060 ff.
[3] Cf. Saguy/Stuart: Culture and Law, p. 149 f.
[4] Cf. Durkheim: The Division of Labor in Society; Friedman: The Legal System; Friedman: On The Interpretation of Laws, pp. 252 f. It is interesting to recall the doctrine of legal realism: a dated, but good bibliography was resumed by Llewellyn: Some Realism about Realism, pp. 1222, 1257–1259. More recently: Karl Llewellyn and the Origins, pp. 12 ff.
[5] Cf. Durkheim: The Division of Labor In Society.
[6] Gephart: Introduction, in this volume.

ground, on which the western legal paradigm is funded, still offers acceptable answers to public law, whereas it is completely insufficient to manage challenges posed to private law. Once again, the emergency perspective shows that the constitutionalization of private law is effective at a *regulatory* level, while it has not yet been assimilated at a *cultural* level.

2. The current western legal culture is basically grounded on the idea of the law, as a tool that allows individuals to live in common. Such a sense of community is what distinguishes our modern democracies. It is not a case if this term sees a successful revival in these difficult times, during which »various levels of community will become visible, ranging from the figure of the ›legal community‹ to the ›European community‹ to family and neighborhoods as primordial communities«.[7]

»*Communitas*« originates from *cum-munus*, that is, it reminds us of the idea of »obligation« (*onus, officium*) and, at the same time, of the notion of »gift« (*donum*), but a particular kind of gift, »distinguished by its obligatory character«.[8] The root of the word »*munus*« (*mei-*), as its suffix (*-ties*), has a strong social connotation: *communitas* is an aggregation of individuals sharing duties toward each other,[9] as much as law is an institutionalized body of pre-existing collective moral agreements.[10] The authentic dimension of the community is such a sense of mutual compulsoriness; in modern constitutional democracies, the deep meaning of social relationships belongs to the respect of reciprocal obligations, especially of the fundamental duties of solidarity. Such a cohesive side does not affect only a purely legal aspect:

»the *communalization* of social relationships occurs if and insofar as the orientation of social behavior [...] is based on a sense of solidarity: the result of emotional or traditional attachments of participants.«[11]

By this way, solidarity is affirmed as a second pilaster, on which normative modernity is built. Since the end of the XIX century, legal orders underlined its (first) social, (then) political dimension, promoting solidarity to the rank of a fundamental principle.[12] However, the authentic origins of this concept lie in the juridical background. In ancient Roman law, »*in solidum*« is a form of reciprocal liability whereby each member of a community bore the sum of all existing debt and, vice

---

[7] Ibid.
[8] Esposito: Communitas, p. 4. The concept of »communitas«, with particular reference to private law, has also recently recalled by Di Marzio: Editoriale, p. 1.
[9] Cf. Esposito: Communitas, p. 4.
[10] Cf. Durkheim: The Division of Labor In Society.
[11] Weber: Basic Concepts in Sociology, p. 91.
[12] Cf. Supiot: La solidarité.

versa, the community bore the liabilities of each individual;[13] in modern private law, *solidary obligation* refers to a legal relationship where one or more of several debtors are each liable to pay the total debt, which expires for all if it is paid by one, or one or more of several creditors are each able to collect the whole.[14] The conceptual core remains the same. Solidarity denotes 1) a reciprocal obligation, 2) applied to situations of need, danger or emergency, 3) within closed groups. As it was clearly resumed, »communities of solidarity are communities of danger and emergency, to which the proverb ›we are all in the same boat‹ applies«. More precisely, »[s]olidarity is required whenever suffering is neither self-inflicted nor caused by others, when one must speak of fate«.[15]

Thus, shared value-commitments, reciprocal obligations and duties of solidarity are identified as key elements of the modern *normative* order, operating to secure *social* order.

3. In such a perspective, *shared* and *effective* rules are the last defense against the Virus. By this way, it is possible to obtain two results, at least:

— to recall the founding pact of our societies, that is, the respect of *common* rules
— to present the rule itself as the condition for the survival of humanity.
Within this framework, even a not so careful observer can easily retrace the broad outlines of the social contract theories.[16]

Hobbes is widely invoked: the normative order at the societal level contains a solution to the problem of preventing human relations from degenerating into a »war of all against all«. It is not surprising if the »state of war« is the most often invoked analogy to justify drastic economic or political choices, as much as emergency governmental powers. The acceptance of rules is fundamentally based on the fear of death and this fear ensures that rules will be obeyed, since what men have in common, what makes them more like each other than anything else, »is their generalized capacity to be killed«.[17]

The main consequence is known. In order to escape a »solitary, poor, nasty, brutish, and short« life, a common power must be established by a mutual trans-

---

[13] Inst. Iust.: I. 3.16 (*De duobus reis stipulandi et promittendi*); Dig. 45.2 (*De duobus reis constituendis*); Cod. Iust. C.8.39 (*De duobus reis stipulandi et duobus reis promittendi*).
[14] See, e.g, art. 1292 It. Civil Code.
[15] Höffe: Democracy in an Age of Globalization, p. 57. Such shared need and/or emergency is essential, to correctly understand the meaning of this expression, as if the suffering is caused by others, »then those others are obliged to assist for reasons of justice«; if the suffering is self-inflicted, »then help is required by charity«.
[16] See Hobbes: Leviathan, and, after him, obviously Locke: Two Treatises of Government; Rousseau: Il contratto sociale; and finally Rawls: A Theory of Justice.
[17] Esposito: Communitas, p. 13.

ference of (natural) right, to protect the individuals not only from foreign invaders, but also from each other. Political authority is thereby funded and delimited on the grounds of individual self-interest and rational consent, supposing that all those entering into a political arrangement are free and equal. Such a »mutual transferring of right« builds modern societies and justifies political power and, to some extent, ensures (or should ensure) the effectiveness of norms.

4. Public law scholars can easily move within such a perimeter.[18] Faced with the coronavirus pandemic, they are called to answer essentially three questions:[19]

- hierarchy of norms, that is, the problem of an effective and efficient structure of sources of law. The crisis in the already endemically compromised system of legal sources is further aggravated.[20] The issue involves the relationship between State and different levels of Local institutions,[21] as much as the relationship between Government and Parliament.[22] The ambiguous definition of competences and powers becomes a way to contrast strategic and political choices of the central Government; the law-making process seems complex and confused, thus entailing serious consequences for legal certainty;
- constitutional democracy and state of exception, that is, the long debate on the constitutionalization of the emergency. To be effective, emergency legislation would need to empower the Government. As a study of the European Parliamentary Research Service notes:

»crucial aspects of the exercise of public powers under a pandemic threat include not only the extent of the measures adopted, but also their legitimacy, raising the question of their duration and of the degree of the parliamentary oversight.«[23]

In such a situation, democracy is openly challenged, above all in legal systems that do not contain specific rules governing the »state of emergency«. This is the case of the Italian constitution, which notably do not provide for the »state of exception«, by reason of the historical moment, in which it was approved (art. 78 of the Italian Constitution disciplines the »state of war«, but it is ques-

---

[18] In order to have an idea of the current debate, it is sufficient to take a look at the discussion among public law scholars in Italy. See Giurcost: Consulta Online (see in particular vol. 1/2020 and 2/2020).

[19] Cf. Groppi: Le sfide del coronavirus alla democrazia costituzionale; Ruggeri: La garanzia dei diritti costituzionali.

[20] Cf. Ruggeri: Il coronavirus.

[21] Haffajee/Mello: Thinking Globally, Acting Locally: »The coronavirus is exactly the type of infectious disease for which federal public health powers and emergencies were conceived: it is highly transmissible, crosses borders efficiently, and threatens our national infrastructure and economy«; Bennet: Legal Rights during Pandemics, pp. 232 ff.

[22] As noted Ruggeri: La forma di governo nel tempo dell'emergenza.

[23] EPRS: States of Emergency in Response to the Coronavirus Crisis.

tioned if it can be applied to the current situation). However, constitutional democracies have legal tools to prevent risks of authoritarianism: temporariness, proportionality, transparency and respect of procedural safeguards ensure the respect of the rule of law;[24]
- balancing political power and individual rights, and comparing individual rights and public health, that is, the new dimension of the relationship between public power and subjective rights.[25] The pandemic affects people's daily life, posing a collective challenge not only to the right to life and health, but also to other fundamental rights, as freedom of movement, civil rights and liberties, right of property. We come back to first-generation rights, to the primary need to protect individuals *against* the excesses of the State. The answer could be to understand that human rights and public health are not an »either/or« choice. In this case also, public responses need to be assessed in terms of their necessity, proportionality and respect for the principle of non-discrimination.

All the above-mentioned questions are not simple to solve, but can be easily inserted in the well-known conceptual frame, which I rapidly described before. The sense of *munus*, the network of reciprocal duties funding democracies, is well interpreted in modern Constitutions, conceived to guarantee the ordinary life of citizens and institutions, but written or consolidated in exceptional circumstances, often as a reaction against excesses of political power (after a war, after a dictatorship, after a declaration of independence). As such, on the one side modern Constitutions fix a set of fundamental and not negotiable values, which guide the interpreter in establishing a necessary hierarchy and translating principles in reciprocal duties/rights; on the other side they contain a number of clauses, which request to adapt principles to concrete circumstances.[26] The three pilasters of modern legal order – shared value-commitments, reciprocal obligations and duties of solidarity – are concretized in both written and oral constitutional rules. Within the juridical paradigm of modernity, public law scholars rediscover the same *cultural* background of their own discipline. They have scientific tools to respond to unexpected situations. Against pandemic, they are vaccinated.

5. Could we say the same about private law? Since the XIX century, the civilian law theory centered on two main assumptions: the »technical« and apolitical nature of private rules and the egoistic/individualistic approach.

---

[24] See the interview to Marta Cartabia, President of the Italian Constitutional Court, with Giovanni Bianconi: Coronavirus, intervista a Marta Cartabia.
[25] Cf. Gatta: I diritti fondamentali alla prova del coronavirus.
[26] »We could say that constitutional principles are always open windows into reality«, in: Bianconi: Coronavirus, intervista a Marta Cartabia.

The first assumption highlighted the Savignyian idea that private law existed prior to the ›intervention of the State‹ (thus, it could be distinguished from public law). The cultural background of private law denies the idea of ›living *in common*‹, the idea of community in itself (although it would be interesting to reflect upon the improperly affirmed identity between *communitas* and *res publica*).

The second assumption promoted individual freedom through the rule of law and the concept of equality of opportunity, up to its extreme consequences. The individualistic approach proposes an atomistic view of social reality, as far as to state that the idea of solidarity is completely extraneous to a market-based society.[27]

As it is known, at the *foundational* level, the *cultural* paradigm of propertied male bourgeoisie resumed these assumptions and deeply influenced civil rules. Property right is affirmed *erga omnes* and *contra omnes*: toward the other and against the other. The private contractual logic requires antagonistic relationship, presupposes conflictual interests and assumes the illusion of an (inexistent) equal bargaining power. There is no reason why individuals should have universal legal duties toward each other. The only universal duty, *nemo neminem laedere*, gives way to the possibility to counterbalance potential damages with money, though.

It is perfectly opposite to the idea of *munus*, to the sense of reciprocal duties, which funds the community: the idea of emphasizing duties rather than, or in a manner complementary to, rights is familiar to private law, but in the sense of an obligation, not of a gift.[28]

6. Within such a cultural heritage, private law scholars are called to find solutions to pandemic emergency.[29] However, they discover that private law offers neither efficient tools nor a valid theoretical frame:

– The Covid-19 emergency forces us to recognize that our populations are not homogeneous. The fiction of the equality is definitively unveiled. Certain individuals and groups are particularly vulnerable, because of their health, their age, or their socio-economic situation (employment, gender, actual conditions where confinement takes place, access to digital communication and so forth). New types of *de facto* discrimination appear. Faced with that all, civil law remedies reveal their complete inadequacy. Incapacitation is not a sufficient tool, as it focuses almost exclusively on the patrimonial side of private relationships.

---

[27] It is obvious to mention Hayek, especially: Individualism and Ecnomic Order and The Mirage of Social Justice. For commentaries, see, *ex multis*, Barry: Hayek's Theory of Social Order; Galeotti: Individualism, Social Rules, Tradition.

[28] Cf. Di Marzio: Comunità, pp. VII ff.

[29] For a general view of problems and solutions in privatistic area, see the special issues of giustiziacivile.com (1/2020 and 2/2020).

Private law offers neither sustain nor assistance, leaving individuals alone with their own weakness.
– The pandemic has forced couples and families into close quarters, disrupting routines and, in the case of some separated or divorced spouses, custody arrangements. Family law has no answer for such cases. We discover that even the definition of »family«, or »immediate family«, is not obvious. Parents are asked to cooperate and »to be reasonable and stay calm«, trying to ensure, for example, a close relationship with the child. However, the impression is that, now more than ever, judicial decisions are driven by common sense, more than technical issues.
– The epidemic state also means a period of extraordinary circumstances affecting many contractual relationships. The effort of private law scholars is mainly direct to analyze legal tools offered to parties facing difficulties in enforcing private law contracts. Two proposals have been essentially tabled. The first solution deals with renegotiating the terms of the agreement on the grounds of the unforeseen change of circumstances at the time of the conclusion of the contract. Civil law provides for certain constructs that will enhance the content of contracts in exceptional circumstances, but only to a limited extent. However, faced with the pandemic, many contractual obligations do not qualify for the use of technical mechanisms such as *rebus sic stantibus* or *force majeure* or *imprévision*. And yet it seems axiologically inappropriate to be indifferent to such cases. Thus, legal scholars turn to judges, asking them to resuscitate principles and general clauses (history surely offers some examples in this sense).[30]
Among general clauses, good faith is the most invoked, filled with a healthy dose of solidarity. The consequence is well known: judges are called to make contracts for the parties, in spite of private autonomy and freedom of contract, that is, in spite of the entire cultural background of private law. The second solution invokes the intervention of the legislator, to suspend the effect of the contractual default mechanisms: the Covid-19 suspends contractual obligations, as it suspends human life.[31] The legislative measure is preferred, as it allows to define the balance between social interest and private autonomy and to clearly locate political responsibility for such a choice, guarantees organic, non-episodic and non-jeopardized measures, avoids the construction of an alternative and disruptive discipline of private contracts.[32] In this case also, however, a retraction of private law occurred, leaving space to a different logic. The widely invoked value of solidarity is called to replace, not to reinforce private law.

---

[30] Cf. Benedetti: Il »rapporto« obbligatorio al tempo dell'isolamento, pp. 143 ff.; Bendetti: Sospensione del contratto e »immunità« emergenziale.
[31] Cf. Cicero: Introducing.
[32] As suggested by Grondona: Il contratto concluso durante l'emergenza.

— In the area of torts, the existence of a pandemic event is not, *per se*, a reliable legal basis for avoiding liability. Moreover, during the last 40/50 years tort law had been inspired by EAL logics of efficiency, forgetting both cultural contexts and social consequences of legal and jurisprudential solutions. The risk is concrete, of an unsustainable increase of litigations for compensation. The question of how to measure the impact of illegal conducts on environment, economy and human health has long been posed by prominent scholars. However, the liability system is structurally based on a patrimonialistic dimension, and the monetization of damages still is the most widely spread solution. Thus, the most invoked (sometimes, applied) solution to avoid a social disaster is to create an area of exemption from liability for certain categories and, at the same time, compensation systems for victims contaminated by the Virus. A purely privatistic logic reveals as inadequate and the governmental intervention seems to be necessary.[33]

7. The current pandemic is showing the structural weakness of the traditional privatistic cultural background. All of the solutions, which have been pointed out, claimed withdrawal or suspension of purely individualistic approaches. Does a vaccine exist to save private law? As it was underlined:

»substantive and formal conflict in private law cannot be reduced to disagreement about how to apply some neutral calculus that will ›maximize the total satisfactions of valid human wants‹«.[34]

At a deeper level, private law scholars are divided »between irreconcilable visions of humanity and society, and between radically different aspirations for our common future«. [35] The way is suggested by the constitution itself. The emergency perspective shows that the constitutionalization of private law is effective at a *regulatory level*, while it has not yet been assimilated at a *cultural level*. Thus, it should be useful to open property to its *social* function (see, for example, art. 42 it. Cost.), to emphasize the communitarian and solidaristic dimension of individual relationships, to address economic initiative to social utility (see art. 41 it. Const.) and to the respect of human dignity (see art.1 German Const.).[36] Such a reading, however, should be done in a context of well-defined political responsibilities and

---

[33] Cf. Izzo: Responsabilità sanitaria e Covid-19; Maggiolo: Una autentica solidarietà sociale, pp. 39 ff.

[35] Ibid.

[36] It seems to be, however, a purely European suggestion: cf. Micklitz: Constitutionalization of European Private Law; Collins: Private Law, Fundamental Rights, and the Rule of Law. In Italy, at least, Perlingieri: Il diritto civile nella legalità costituzionale; Alpa: The Constitutionalization of Private Law in Italy.

appropriate legislative action: the entry of private law in a communitarian dimension cannot merely signify to delegate judges to find emergency solutions.[37]

Put to the pandemic test, we discover that legal paradigm, which funds modern democratic societies, can resist. But the condition for its survival is the constitutionalization of the given normative order.

References

Alpa, Guido: The Constitutionalization of Private Law in Italy, in: Oregon Review of International Law, 2, 2000, pp. 83–107.
Barry, Norman P.: Hayek's Theory of Social Order, in: Il Politico, 4, 1995, pp. 557–581.
Benedetti, Alberto Maria: Il »rapporto« obbligatorio al tempo dell'isolamento: una causa (transitoria) di giustificazione?, in: Giustiziacivile.com, Emergenza COVID-19 Speciale, 2/2020, Uniti per l'Italia, pp. 143–149.
Benedetti, Alberto Maria: Sospensione del contratto e »immunità« emergenziale del debitore, Webinar »I rapporti giuridici al tempo del COVID-19«, Cagliari, 29.05.2020, https://www.unica.it/unica/page/it/webinar__i_rapporti_giuridici_al_tempo_del_covid19__cagliari_29_maggio_2020?contentId=AVS222718; last accessed 01.07.2020.
Bennet, B.: Legal Rights During Pandemics: Federalism, Rights and Public Health Laws – A View from Australia, in: Public Health, 123(3), 2009, pp. 232–236.
Bianconi, Giovanni: Coronavirus, intervista a Marta Cartabia: »Nella Costituzione le vie per uscire dalla crisi«, in: Corriere della Sera, 29.04.2020, https://www.corriere.it/esteri/20_aprile_29/coronavirus-intervista-marta-cartabia-nella-costituzione-vie-uscire-crisi-c1893622-8982-11ea-8073-abbb9eae2ee6.shtml; last accessed 01.07.2020.
Cicero, Cristiano: Introducing, Webinar »I rapporti giuridici al tempo del COVID-19«, Cagliari, 29.05.2020, https://www.unica.it/unica/page/it/webinar__i_rapporti_giuridici_al_tempo_del_covid19__cagliari_29_maggio_2020?contentId=AVS222718; last accessed 01.07.2020.
Collins, Hugh: Private Law, Fundamental Rights, and the Rule of Law, in: West Virginia Law Review, 121, 2018.
Di Marzio, Fabrizio: Editoriale. Comunità. Affrontiamo la nostra prova, in: Giustiziacivile.com, Emergenza COVID-19 Speciale, 1/2020. Uniti per l'Italia, pp. VII–IX.

---

[37] This risk is particularly visible in the process of an European Private Law building: see, *ex multis*, Niglia: The Struggle for European Private Law.

Durkheim, Emile: The Division of Labor in Society, transl. G. Simpson, New York 1933.
European Parliamentary Research Service (EPRS): States of Emergency in Response to the Coronavirus Crisis: Situation in Certain Member States, Bruxelles 2020.
Esposito, Roberto: Communitas. The Origin and Destiny of Community, Stanford 2010.
Friedman, Lawrence M.: The Legal System: A Social Science Perspective, Englewood Cliffs, NY 1975.
Friedman, Lawrence M.: On the Interpretation of Laws, in: Ratio Juris, 1(3), 1988, pp. 252–262.
Galeotti, Anna Elisabetta: Individualism, Social Rules, Tradition. The Case of Friedrich A. Hayek, in: Political Theory, XV, 1987, pp. 163–181.
Gatta, Gian Luigi: I diritti fondamentali alla prova del coronavirus. Perché è necessaria una legge sulla quarantena, in: Consultaonline, 2020/I, http://www.giurcost.org/studi/gatta.pdf; last accessed 17.06.2020.
Grondona, Mauro: Il contratto concluso durante l'emergenza sanitaria, Webinar »I rapporti giuridici al tempo del COVID-19«, Cagliari, 29.05.2020, https://www.unica.it/unica/page/it/webinar__i_rapporti_giuridici_al_tempo_del_covid19__cagliari_29_maggio_2020?contentId=AVS222718; last accessed 01.07.2020.
Groppi, Tania: Le sfide del coronavirus alla democrazia costituzionale, in: Consultaonline, 2020/I, http://www.giurcost.org/studi/groppi3.pdf; last accessed 17.06.2020.
Haffajee, Rebecca L. / Michelle Mello: Thinking Globally, Acting Locally – The U.S. Response to Covid-19, in: New England Journal of Medicine, 02.04.2020.
Hayek, Friedrich: Individualism and Economic Order, London 1944.
Hayek, Friedrich: The Mirage of Social Justice, London 1976.
Hobbes, Thomas: Leviathan, New York 1962.
Höffe, Otfried: Democracy in an Age of Globalization, Dordrecht 2007.
Izzo, Umberto: Responsabilità sanitaria e Covid-19: prime riflessioni sui rischi di una pandemia giudiziaria, Webinar »I rapporti giuridici al tempo del COVID-19«, Cagliari, 29.05.2020, https://www.unica.it/unica/page/it/webinar__i_rapporti_giuridici_al_tempo_del_covid19__cagliari_29_maggio_2020?contentId=AVS222718; last accessed 01.07.2020.
Kennedy, Duncan: Form and Substance in Private Law Adjudication, in: Harvard Law Review, 89(8), 1976, pp. 1685–1778.
Llewellyn, Karl N.: Some Realism about Realism – Responding to Dean Pound, in: Harvard Law Review, 44(8), 1931, pp. 1222–1264.
Locke, John: Two Treatises of Government, New York 1963.

Maggiolo, Marcello: Una autentica solidarietà sociale come eredità del coronavirus: per una diversa destinazione dei risarcimenti del danno alla salute, in: Giustiziacivile.com, Emergenza COVID-19 Speciale, 1/2020. Uniti per l'Italia, pp. 39–44.

Michaels, Ralf: Legal Culture, in: Jürgen Basedow / Klaus J. Hopt / Reinhard Zimmermann (eds.): The Oxford Handbook of European Private Law, Oxford 2006.

Micklitz, Hans: Constitutionalization of European Private Law, Oxford 2014.

Niglia, Leone: The Struggle for European Private Law: A Critique of Codification, Oxford 2015.

Perlingieri, Pietro: Il diritto civile nella legalità costituzionale secondo il sistema italo-comunitario delle fonti, Napoli 2006.

Rawls, John: A Theory of Justice, Cambridge/MA 1971.

Rousseau, Jean-Jacques: Il contratto sociale, Milano 2005.

Ruggeri, Antonio: Il coronavirus, la sofferta tenuta dell'assetto istituzionale e la crisi palese, ormai endemica, del sistema delle fonti, in: Consultaonline, 2020/I, http://www.giurcost.org/studi/ruggeri107.pdf.; last accessed 25.06.2020.

Ruggeri, Antonio: La forma di governo nel tempo dell'emergenza, in Consultaonline, 2020/II, http://www.astrid-online.it/static/upload/rugg/ruggeri109.pdf; last accessed 25.06.2020.

Ruggeri, Antonio: La garanzia dei diritti costituzionali tra certezze e incertezze del diritto, in: Consultaonline, 2020/I, http://www.giurcost.org/studi/ruggeri106.pdf; last accessed 17.06.2020.

Saguy, Abigail C. / Forrest Stuart: Culture and Law: Beyond a Paradigm of Cause and Effect, in: The Annals of the American Academy of Political and Social Science, 619(1), 2008, pp. 149–164.

Schwartz, Alan: Karl Llewellyn and the Origins of Contract Theory, Faculty Scholarship Series, Yale Law School, Paper 4862, 2000, http://digitalcommons.law.yale.edu/fss_papers/4862; last accessed 17.06.2020.

Supiot, Alain: La solidarité. Enquête sur un principe juridique, Paris 2015.

Weber, Max: Basic Concepts in Sociology, trans. H. P. Secher, New York 1962.

Gianmaria Ajani

Possible Effects of the Pandemic Emergency on the Internal Coherence of EU Law

1. The Relevance of Law in the Building of the European Union

Within a span of less than three months the coronavirus (Covid-19) pandemic has challenged health security, social habits and (an already unstable) economic development globally. Quite paradoxically, a time of slowness, due to the confinement of half of humanity, turned out to be a tremendous accelerator of some problems: an already fragile global equilibrium has been severely challenged. No country in the world has been immune, and even where the virus spread only marginally, immediate economic damages have been caused by the disruption of global chains of supply and distribution. It is well true that social lock down speeded up the recourse to digital communications, to smart work practices, and reduced the recourse to unnecessary humans' commuting. At the same time, however, governmental management of special regulatory powers has injected in some of our democracies a dangerous appetite for massive social control, solicited by the need to contain the infection.

At the time of writing this paper the pandemic impact has affected all continents and countries in the globe, causing more than 5.800.000 ascertained cases and 370.000 certified deaths.[1] The fast spread of this transmissible disease has immediately overwhelmed health care structures and prospectively threatened economic growth worldwide. In reaction to this exceptional situation and to prevent the spread to become unbearable, most governments have established confinement, social distancing, school closures, borders controls and moved to impose shutdowns and travel restrictions, affecting various aspects of social, political, and economic lives.

These actions did not occur simultaneously: somehow imitating the pandemic wave and its moving from East to West, governments have taken measures only at the moment the disease began to display its deathly effects within national borders (from 1 to 3 weeks of scaled delay). These belated reactions had an impact

---

[1] ECDC: COVID-19 Situation Update Worldwide.

on the affected population, causing thousands of (otherwise avoidable) casualties in a short span of time.

We are told Covid-19 provokes not only a respiratory, but a *systemic* disease;[2] a kind of metaphor for the risk of systemic challenge to partition of powers, to the hierarchy of the sources of law[3] and to the functioning of parliamentary democratic institutions some of the Western democracies have been exposed to during the first months of the year 2020.

As a direct effect of the global lock down an actual, and huge, damage stroke free trade practices and policies. A damage which could last far more than the (not yet known, but anyhow due to an end) expected duration of the disease.

In fact, national reactions to the pandemic have defied some established narratives of our times. The »global village« chronicles of a world where news, capitals, trade decisions and (to a lesser degree) people, were moving rapidly, have been disproved by a lack of smart and effective communication among the governments, and also between the international (WHO) and the national layers of administration. As soon as the pandemic revealed its force, national governments limited interstate trade, confiscated medical equipment intended for export, to support national health care, and started to allocate investments in possible therapies »for domestic use only«. A global economy based on international markets and supported by porous borders and delocalization[4] has been urged, without a warning alert, to reconsider its *modus operandi*. The European »Demos«, having been waiting silently to find its space, has been unexpectedly hit by the pandemic; in a very short span of time the Nation State revealed itself as the only ›safe space‹, the only community[5] able to provide a reassuring answer to millions of scared citizens.

Some observers found those deficiencies in governments' coordination to be nothing but another proof of the deteriorating spirit of globalization.[6] Others contend that the pandemic wave has triggered an irreversible countdown on the dissolving of the EU.

These opinions are quite often biased by political agendas. Nevertheless, the current crisis is surely a real test for Europe. As Guy Verhofstadt, member of the European Parliament has lucidly pointed out:

---

[2] Cf. Zhao et al.: Lymphopenia Is Associated with Severe Coronavirus Disease 2019 (Covid-19) Infections.

[3] For example, in France, the Law of March 20, 2020 has set stringent limits to constitutional freedoms on the premise of a state of emergency that are not foreseen by the same French Constitution.

[4] When we look back at 2003, at the Sars epidemic, PR of China accounted for 4% of global output. Now it accounts for 16%.

[5] Cf. Gephart: Conclusion, in this volume.

[6] Cf. Rapoza: The Post-Coronavirus World May Be the End of Globalization.

»From the Gulf War to 9/11, SARS to the financial crisis and the Eyjafjallajökull ash cloud, Covid-19 is not just another crisis in a long list of disasters. Covid-19 is more than that. It is an existential crisis that has the potential to break countries and continents alike, and maybe even humanity. Will European Union survive it?«[7]

The pandemic strikes against the backdrop of existing tensions, such as: doubts about internal European solidarity, further doubts on external solidarity (towards asylum seekers), increased uncertainty in global trade – due to discretionary custom duties imposed by some countries – North-South divide on sovereign debt, growing relevance of populism. It provides an unexpected chance to authoritarian political leaders, like the Hungarian Prime Minister, and reopens unresolved fundamental debates about fiscal solidarity.[8] It favors increased national activism in the People's Republic of China (included the proposed new and harsh Law on Security in Hong Kong) and stimulates disinformation and new forms of isolationism.[9]

Shortly, the most threatening consequence of the Covid-19 crisis is that citizens' only shield turns out to be, in spite of decades of active globalization policies, the *nation-state*. As a result, the coronavirus threatens not only human beings, but also international unification projects, including the European Union, which was established and assembled to end centuries of conflicts among major nations of the continent.[10]

Having all this in mind, I believe it is time to observe how the current state of international affairs can incite our professional cultures (I refer in particular to international and comparative lawyers) to measure whether and how the mentioned lack of coordination within Europe has an impact on the destiny of European Law and on its role for European integration. Rather than pointing at financial and legal instruments announced by the EU institutions to support economic recovery from economic shock, I am here focusing on the role of the Law on political dynamics emerging within the EU in times of Covid-19.

These notes, therefore, are a first attempt to identify how the situation caused by the pandemic is changing the dynamics of European Law. More research will be, obviously, needed, over time, to verify these suppositions and to understand whether there will be good reasons to consider Spring 2020 as the divide between two different ages in the life of the European construction.

The European project has been, and remains, a *political* undertaking, originated from an innovative political vision on the economic future of a continent that had been devastated by innumerable national wars. Its territorial progression,

---

7 Cf. Verhofstadt: The Union and COVID-19.
8 Washington Post: Coronavirus Reopens Europe's Angry Divide.
9 Atlantic Council: Is China Winning the Coronavirus Response Narrative in the EU?
10 Cf. Gabriel: The Lethal Threat of COVID-19 Isolationism.

however – particularly for the case of enlargements towards Central and Eastern European Countries[11] (2004–2013) – and the consolidation of the Single Market, occurred having the Law as a main instrument for policy making. As a mandatory pre-requisite for accession, between 1995 and 2007 all Central Eastern Countries aiming to join the EU had to reframe their legal systems, to make them consistent with the European *Acquis*.[12] Also, demise of some national prerogatives in the management of the single EU market has been affirmed by a pro-active European Court of Justice. Law, then, has been central, even beyond limits originally designed by national representatives, to the making of what we have called until now as a European *Union*.

As it is well known, the largest enlargement the EU ever had in the course of its existence, namely the accession to the Union of most Central and Eastern European countries, occurred at the end of a long process of adaptation and harmonization of national legal orders to the main traits of the »European *Acquis Communautaire*«. Unlike the case of Spain and Portugal, in the year 1985 and, even earlier (1972), of UK and Ireland, consistency of national legal orders with the EU law was considered to be a necessary requirement.[13] Why such a difference in the procedures of accession, and why *law* had become so central to the process of enlargement of the EU? Answers must be found in the origins of globalization, and in the process that led free trade to become a new paradigm for economic growth.

In fact, the construction of European Union occurred at times when national economies were, all over the world, the main champions for production and consumption of goods and services. It is well known that recovery after II World War, as well as economic support to new countries emerging from the end of colonization (5oies and 6oies of last century) were based on a simple economic model, called: Import Substitution Industrialization (I.S.I.). Within the I.S.I. model (extensively promoted from the International Monetary Fund and the World Bank until mid-7oies), governments led economic development through nationalization, subsidization of core industries and services providers (like agriculture, power generation, railways, banks and insurance companies), significant taxation, currency control and highly protectionist trade policies. That model, essentially a Keynesian one, proved to be quite efficient in supporting development and growth in several newly independent national economies in Asian and Africa. Basically, it

---

[11] The EU enlargement was grounded on the principles agreed among the States representatives at the Copenhagen European Council in 2003. Those principles and criteria concern: 1.) stability of institutions guaranteeing democracy, the rule of law, human rights and respect for and protection of minorities; 2.) existence of a functioning market economy as well as the capacity to cope with competitive pressure and market forces within the European Union; 3.) ability to take on the obligations of membership including adherence to the aims of political, economic and monetary union.

[12] The body of rights and obligations that are binding on all EU countries.

[13] Cf. Schulze/Ajani: Gemeinsame Prinzipien des Europäischen Privatrechts.

was also considered by some highly industrialized countries, like UK, Italy, where public funding played an essential role in the reconstruction of post-war economies. At the moment the European Community was established, many countries in the world, with the relevant exception of United States, had experienced the I.S.I. paradigm as a fruitful one. The Europe Community, therefore, was born on the foundations of Keynesianism and its very beginning, namely the establishment of a common market for coal and steel among the six founding states, meant to deactivate competition within European nations over natural resources, maintained the role of robust governmental control on market activities.

The sudden demise of I.S.I. as a recipe for development, and its radical substitution with the Free Global Trade paradigm was undoubtedly caused by the oil-shock crisis (1973–1975)[14] and the correlated weakening of an essential supposition of that model: low cost of energy. I.S.I. was a top-down policy pattern based on an economic idea, implemented by (national) political decisions. Law was not central; in particular, legal diversity among the many countries of the world was not supposed to be an impediment. Everything changed, however, when Free Global Trade paradigm and neo-liberal policies took the lead: globalization needed harmonization among nation legal orders. It also required predictable and fair systems of adjudication, judicial review of the administration, protection of property rights and of foreign direct investments. Law became the center[15] of the new paradigm. On its top: discontinuation of governmental subsidies, demonopolization and privatization of all productive assets in public hands.

Within this landscape, it was quite consequential that new accession of Central and Eastern European Countries to the EU had to be governed by a preliminary process of adaptation of incoming national legal orders.[16] Today, the acceleration triggered by the Covid-19 crisis is questioning what had been considered to be an irrevocable occurrence, i.e. the estrangement of the State from the functioning of the economy. It is true that the 2008 financial crisis had already called back some *ad hoc* interventions by national governments, to rescue national financial institutions, or (more rarely) to mitigate citizens' economic losses caused by the break. These mediations, however, had been received by the media and citizens as an exception to the general rule rather than a comprehensive change of paradigm.

---

[14] Cf. Braithwaite/Drahos: Global Business Regulation, pp. 256–296.
[15] Cf. Kennedy: A World of Struggle, pp. 23–53.
[16] Cf. Ajani: Ruling by Indicators.

2. A Diachronic Test

Having all this in mind, we can now try to assess the possible effects of the pandemic emergency on the internal coherence of EU Law. To establish a comparative test *between the pre-2020 period and the current time of emergency*, I propose to identify as a first component of our *tableau comparatif* the following traits, dating from the pre-Corona virus crisis:

a) During the 1990ies, particularly before the accession of Central and Eastern European Countries, an enlarged European Law (meant as EU law, and also as national legal orders changed by EU law) has been built upon the idea that policy-makers can recognize the ›good‹, or, comparatively speaking, ›better‹ state of social and economic conditions in a given space (i. e., a Country).
b) This has provided legitimacy to promote, as a prerequisite for accession, the imitation of wide set of rules, such as statutes, codes. Constitutions are also part of the game: fundamental principles such as multipartitism, parliamentary democracy, protection of fundamental rights, to say, the classical themes addressed by constitutional charters, have been perceived as key factors for the proper functioning of the internal market.
c) Following a *functionalist* approach, prominent legal researchers, together with neoliberal scholars in law & economics, have eroded from legal theory the concept of »law as a value« and traded it for the understanding of law as a set of »technical tools and principles *needed for a purpose*«. This approach bestowed new legitimacy to the law at the same historical moment when the law was losing grip within the local (national, or sub-national) communities. This new kind of legitimacy, however, has a different nature from the one we were used to recognize in a traditional parliamentary State: it is based on a comparative assessment of the »best practices« and on the assumption that a certain regulation has direct effect on economic performance.
d) Spread of functionalist theories has supported the recognition of law (namely, but not only, private law) as inherently indifferent to the social context, while law & economics has reinforced, since the popularization of the Coase theorem, the idea of »indifference« of the law from local contexts.

Moreover, a wide recourse to functionalist arguments, has:

a) Affected the value-contents of the Rule of Law principle, slightly transforming this standard in a vague, multi-tasked concept, conditioned by economic/commercial considerations of efficiency;[17]

---

[17] Cf. Micklitz: The Visible Hand of European Regulatory Private Law.

b) Reaffirmed a positivist understanding of the law (law as a tool rather than law as a value);
c) Favoured the use of *vagueness* and indeterminacy[18] in normative terminology (indeterminacy opens the way to legal reforms without irritating local cultures), to overcome national resistances in the name of sovereignty;
d) Advantaged the status of the »citizen as consumer«;
e) Made individuals' freedom of movement conditional on economic basis.

As a *second set for comparison* I propose to consider, looking at the current state of the EU in Spring 2020, the following points. All of them signal, in different ways, a sliding from established normative choices adopted by EU law before the Covid-19 emergency:

a) Administrative Law plays an essential role in overcoming pandemics. It determines the institutional structures and the processes that provide the best protection to individuals and communities during epidemics and sets time limits and modes for the exercise of extraordinary powers over natural and legal persons. This has also been the case in the Spring 2020. Restrictions are lawful when imposed proportionately with the aim of protecting public health. To this end, they should not be discriminatory, indefinite, or give room for arbitrary controls by authorities;
b) Article 12 of the International Covenant on Economic, Social and Cultural Rights and Article 35 of the EU Charter of Fundamental Rights recognize the fundamental right to obtain preventive health care and to benefit from medical treatment. However, the high number of people hit by Covid-19 has, in some Countries, overwhelmed medical services. As a result, patients have been turned away for treatment, or replaced in secondary unfit institutions. Country and their governments have the competence and the obligation to respect, protect, and satisfy fundamental right to health. When needs cannot be met due to a breakdown in undertaking these commitments, many people are deprived from the enjoyment of this right.
c) An unprecedented massive quarantine falls over individuals with differentiated effects. This depends on the nature of the employment, on the actual conditions where confinement takes place, on the access to digital communication and so forth. New types of *de facto* discrimination appear and must be added to the ones already present before 2020 (such as, i.e. the right to health in prisons or

---

[18] The recourse to vague terminology (i.e. »good governance«, »due process«, »transparency«) detached as it is from specific social and cultural contexts, is instrumental to finding a multi-governmental agreement on some issues without confronting the details of regulation, where lack of consensus could resurge.

in refugees and migrants hotspots). As several countries have suspended refugee status determination processes and resettlement programs, asylum seekers also face unsettling and uncertain situations.

d) Emergency, any kind of it, goes along with urgency in adopting regulations. This favors a wide recourse to governmental powers to enact decrees and other administrative measures (remembering that in many countries administrative enactments are not under supervision from constitutional courts).

More elements can be itemized on both sides of the *tableau comparative*. The ones I have listed here already show the methodology we can follow by crossing the different elements in the perspective of a forthcoming post-Covid-19 phase.

A matrix could therefore be developed, based on comparative contrasts, highlighting diversities in the functioning of the law before and during\after the crisis, or showing similarities in the instrumental recourse to the law. The matrix could provide answers to questions like:

a) How is the status of »individuals as consumers« modified by a sanitary crisis that has mortified consumption?
b) Is the instrumental recourse to concepts like »good governance«, »rule of law« subject to a reconsideration, in terms of refilling it with different fundamental values (first of all, right to health)?
c) Is the trend from *formal* towards *actual* consideration of anti-discrimination policies positively affected by discrimination in healthcare experienced during the pandemic?
d) Has the Covid-19 emergency hyperactivated national trepidations towards »citizens as nationals« already winding before the crisis?
e) Is the meandering sentiment of national competition, already activated as a response to the 2008 financial crisis, fortified by the health emergency situation (cases are the ban to export within the EU market pharmaceuticals and other devices considered to be vital for nationals)?

Over the course of next months EU and national institutions will have made clear the nature and size of normative responses to the dramatic fall-out of the Covid-19 emergency, namely the prospected EU-wide economic distress. The comparative methodology proposal I have here sketched out represents a first exercise on the attempt to understand how EU law will be transformed in a way to support the emerged distress, and whether it will deviate from its original course, based on the *ordoliberalismus*.

References

Ajani, Gianmaria: Ruling by Indicators: How the Use of Vague Notions and Quantitative Indicators Facilitates Legal Change, in: Cardozo Electronic Law Bulletin, 23(1), 2017, pp. 3–25.

Atlantic Council: Is China Winning the Coronavirus Response Narrative in the EU?, in: www.atlanticcouncil.org, 25.03.2020, https://www.atlanticcouncil.org/blogs/new-atlanticist/is-china-winning-the-coronavirus-response-narrative-in-the-eu/; last accessed 23.06.2020.

Braithwaite, John / Peter Drahos: Global Business Regulation, Cambridge 2001.

European Centre for Disease Prevention and Control (ECDC): COVID-19 Situation Update Worldwide, www.ecdc.europa.eu/en/geographical-distribution-2019-ncov-cases; last accessed 29.05.2020.

Gabriel, Sigmar: The Lethal Threat of COVID-19 Isolationism, in: Project Syndicate, https://www.project-syndicate.org/commentary/covid19-protectionism-undermines-europe-global-role-by-sigmar-gabriel-2020-04; last accessed 16.06.2020.

Kennedy, David: A World of Struggle, Princeton 2016.

Rapoza, Kenneth: The Post-Coronavirus World May Be the End of Globalization, in: Forbes, 03.04.2020, https://www.forbes.com/sites/kenrapoza/2020/04/03/the-post-coronavirus-world-may-be-the-end-of-globalization/#259eec2a7e66; last accessed 16.06.2020.

Micklitz, Hans-Wolfgang: The Visible Hand of European Regulatory Private Law. The Transformation of European Private Law from Autonomy to Functionalism in Competition and Regulation, in: 28 Yearbook of European Law, Oxford, 2009, pp. 3–59.

Schulze, Reiner / Gianmaria Ajani (eds.): Gemeinsame Prinzipien des Europäischen Privatrechts, Baden-Baden 2003.

Verhofstadt, Guy: The Union and COVID-19: Is There a Future after Failure?, in: European Policy Centre, 25.03.2020, http://www.epc.eu/en/publications/The-Union-and-COVID-19-Is-there-a-future-after-failure~30ef58; last accessed 16.06.2020.

Washington Post: Coronavirus Reopens Europe's Angry Divide, 31.03.2020, https://www.washingtonpost.com/world/2020/04/01/coronavirus-reopens-europes-angry-divide/; last accessed 23.06.2020.

Zhao, Qianwen / Meng Meng / Rahul Kumar / Yinlian Wu / Jiaofeng Huang / Yunlei Deng / Zhiyuan Weng / Li Yang: Lymphopenia Is Associated with Severe Coronavirus Disease 2019 (Covid-19) Infections: A Systemic Review and Meta-Analysis, in: Int. J. Infect. Dis., 96, 2020, pp. 131–135.

Matthias Herdegen

The Corona Crisis: Challenges for the Socio-Cultural Underpinnings of Constitutional and EU Law

1. The Corona Measures as Test for the Socio-Cultural Foundations of Law

The invasive legislative and executive measures adopted in the Corona crisis stand in a complex, ambivalent interrelation with the socio-cultural underpinnings of our legal orders. On one hand, these measures respond to fundamental legal values which are also deeply anchored in societal perceptions and legal culture. On the other hand, the design of the State's interference with individual rights, as a political choice putting certain interests over others, triggers concerns of even traumata equally entrenched in societal perceptions. This holds particularly true in context of the constitutional order of Germany. On European level, discussions over the legitimate and desirable scope of solidarity between EU member States reflect a sharp dissent in the understanding of the finality of the European Union and the meaning of treaty rules as a normative order.

2. The Spectre of Executive Overreach

According to a long-established view, times of crisis enhance the standing and authority of the executive branch of government. A number of western constitutions vest the executive with broad special powers in times of civil crisis (»state of siege«, »state of alarm«, »state of necessity«). The French constitution of 1958 (art. 16) is a model of very extensive empowerment of the President, triggered by a grave threat for the institutions of the French Republic, the independence of the nation, the integrity of its territory or the fulfilment of its international obligations.

Still, in some countries the government did not rely on exceptional powers under the constitution, but sought legislative authorisation confined to large-scale risks for public health. Thus, in France, Parliament adopted a special framework for the »state of health urgency« (»état d'urgence sanitaire«) in March 2020.¹ This legislation empowers the Government to take far-reaching measures including confinement of persons at their home or price-regulations. In Germany, the Infection Protection Act (*Infektionsschutzgesetz*) as amended in March and May 2020 places vasive regulatory powers at the hands of the Federal Government (Ministry of Health) and the governments of the home states (*Länder*).² This almost instantly activated quasi-Pavlowian reflexes among constitutional lawyers. In this context, critical voices drew parallels to the Prussian constitutional conflict (with the government led by Bismarck violating the power of Parliament to authorize increased expenditure for the army in 1862) or even the infamous »Empowerment Act« (*Ermächtigungsgesetz*) of 1933 which dismantled the Republic of Weimar's constitutional order and laid the foundation of the Third Reich's totalitariansm. However, the evocation of these and similar traumata was confined to a very sensitive sector of constitutional doctrine.

From a normative perspective, it is important that the empowerment of governments on federal and State's level depends on the formal declaration of »an epidemic situation of national reach« by the Federal Parliament.³ Thus, it is Parliament which opens the door for intervention by the Executive. The alignment of Federal government with the Governments of the *Länder* and the multi-party consensus in the initial stages of the crisis were other factors in easing concerns about the separation of powers and an overstretch of executive authority. In addition, the German society had witnessed not only the alarming spread of the virus in Northern Italy and in Spain, but also the harsh measures adopted by the Italian and Spanish Governments. Both governments, in the post-fascist period, never were suspect of regulatory overreach.

The regulatory management of the Corona pandemic within constitutional »normality«, i.e. outside a framework or special powers in a state of exception seems to collaborate the resilience of the constitutional order in times of crisis and the »inclusive« operational capability of the Basic Law.⁴ This conclusion seems to hold true at least in context of threats to large sectors of the population or even the nation's life which are not orchestrated by human actors, but stem from natural sources. The fight against threats and risks which are not man-made does not trigger the same concerns about a shift in the balance of powers and abuse of executive competences which are typically associated with the confrontation of external and internal »enemies«.

---

1   Cf. Beaud / Guérin Bargues: L'état d'urgence sanitaire, in this volume.
2   Gesetz zur Verhütung und Bekämpfung von Infektionskrankheiten beim Menschen, §§ 5, 32 in conjunction with §§ 28–31.
3   Gesetz zur Verhütung und Bekämpfung von Infektionskrankheiten beim Menschen, § 5(1).
4   Cf. Kaiser: Ausnahmeverfassungsrecht, pp. 85 ff., 122 ff.

3. Protection of Human Life v. Individual Liberties

The restrictions on the freedom of movement, the lock-down of businesses and public institutions as well as the ban of cultural, religious and other events marked a political option which places the protection of human life and health over individual autonomy and civil liberties. Although the prolonged maintenance of lock-down measures has provoked increasing criticism in the course of time, the initial containment measures met with broad societal consensus, despite their invasive nature. The reasons for this strong public support are manifold. In Germany (and in neighbouring countries) the restrictions met with a very high degree of risk-aversion which seems more deeply rooted in the materially »saturated«, prosperous societies of continental Europe than in other regions of the globe. This risk aversion is, at least as a rule, coupled with a high level of sensitivity for scientific and empiric indications of risks to health and the environment.

In the tradition of western constitutionalism not only the respect for, but also the protection of human life has been firmly established as a constitutional objective of the highest rank. In Germany the trauma of the Holocaust and the Nazi program of euthanasia has left its socio-cultural imprint. In post-war Germany, the discussion of human life in different stages and context and emblematic rulings of the Federal Constitutional Court the State's duty of protection of human life (in the cases of abortion,[5] persons held as hostages,[6] and protection against the risks flowing from nuclear energy)[7] had a strong impact on the socio-juridical DNA of German society. Scope and degree of required measures of protection are governed by the principle of proportionality which is the most potent instrument of rationality in our legal system. The relation between the objective of a restrictive measure and its impact on civil liberties call for an empiric scrutiny of risks, the effectiveness of protective measures and less invasive alternatives in light of available empiric knowledge in the state of science.

Proportionality allows for a considerable dose of executive discretion and administrative appreciation of complex scenarios wherever the state of science and available knowledge leave us with uncertainty as to chains of causation and the scope of identified risks. In such a situation of scientific uncertainty, precaution justifies and even requires protective measures within a »reasonable« risk management.[8]

Members of government painstakingly tried to justify invasive measures with support of ever-present scientists, in particular of representatives of the Federal

---

[5] BVerfGE 39: 1 (41).
[6] BVerfGE 46: 160 (164).
[7] BVerfGE 49: 89 (140 ff.).
[8] BVerfGE 49: 89 (143).

Agency for Infections and Other Diseases (Robert Koch Institute). Some constitutional lawyers criticized the lock-down of public life and restrictions on the freedom of movement as an excessive encroachment of personal autonomy and therefore also of human dignity which covers the core of self-determination. It may not be unfair to resume that some of this criticism targets a regulatory regime preferring protection of the life of few (elderly and weak) persons over self-determination of many (young and healthy) citizens. In the argumentation in favour of self-determination, human dignity thus appears as a constitutional value trumping »mere« human life. Similar confrontations can be seen in the ethical discourse in Italy and other European countries.

In the end, the confrontation of human life and its regulatory protection with human dignity leads to an impasse. The respect for human dignity cannot abstract from human life. For decades, German jurisprudence has anchored the State's duty of protection towards human life in human dignity.[9] It therefore seems futile to oppose the sacredness of the individual with the sacredness of human life. In the sense of Emile Durkheim's sacrality of the human being encompasses both, individual self-determination and human life. Human dignity, as a legacy of Judaeo-Christian thinking, of the renaissance and the enlightenment extends both to the human being as *imago dei* and to the individual as self-determined and creative *plastes et fictor*.

4. Triage: Regulating What Escapes Regulation?

The socio-cultural heritage of European constitutionalism, in Germany more than elsewhere, harbours a strong yearning for a maximum of normative density which, as far as possible, captures different scenarios wherever individual interests conflict with each other in a concrete case. The anticipated shortage of life-saving medical equipment fuelled a debate in France, Germany and elsewhere on whether specific legislation should establish parameters for preferential treatment (›triage‹).

These issues clearly show that certain choices are not beyond the reach of the law, but escape detailed regulatory determination. It is impossible for legislation to capture all possible elements relevant for a decision and place them in a sort of hierarchical order. Age or preceding diseases may be indicators for life expectancy, but other factors may be contra-indicative for prognostic purposes. Nor is it clear whether it is desirable that social criteria (such as responsibility for children, partners and parents) should govern preferences. Any kind of triage-legislation

[9] BVerfGE 39: 1 (41).

transcends the limits not of the law, but of reliable regulatory guidance. Sometimes normativity simply refers to the standards of responsible decision-making in light of the circumstances of the individual case, based on experienced practical reasoning and »human« balancing of interests by the person in charge (be it the responsible medical person in charge of limited resources or the »reasonable commander« in international humanitarian law).

5. Solidarity v. Normativity?

In the European Union, Mediterranean member states particularly effected by the Corona crisis have been calling for massive financial support by the European Union and other members. This support encompasses a broad range of measures: purchase programmes of the European central Bank (ECB), »Coronabonds«, loans granted by the European Stability Mechanism (ESM) or funds directly flowing from the EU budget. A keyword in the debate on support for indebted Euro countries is »solidarity« which is a »weasel word« (Friedrich von Hayek) par excellence. The current discussion in the Euro zone and the whole European Union suggests that many interested actors use the term as a kind of magic word to soften the fabric of well-established normativity under the European Treaties; »Solidarity« as a kind of overarching value which trumps the rules on fiscal discipline, conditionality for borrowing from intra-State organisms like the ESM, the limits of the monetary powers of the ECB and the budgetary restraints of the European Union itself. As part of the argumentative arsenal, »solidarity« is mounted against »austerity«, legal formalism and avaricious inflexibility. In the end, all this debate is not about whether other member States or the European Union should provide generous support for the countries particularly affect by the economic disruption caused by the Corona pandemic. It is only about the proper scope and design of financial assistance.

A particular problem in defining solidarity is its possible interrelation with previous (non-) compliance with fundamental rules which the actors previously mutually agreed upon. The addressees of solidarity claims are countries which a relatively high degree of fiscal discipline has placed in a position to provide financial assistance to ailing EU partners, be it via contributions to the EU budget and the ESM, or good standing on the capital markets. In good and in bad times, the countries claiming solidarity have heaped up public debts. The corona crisis hit the heavily indebted countries hardest. Many disruptive effects lie entirely beyond the responsibility of governments, whilst other adverse impacts stand in relation with budgetary restraints and public debt. For some countries, the accumulated debt, even before the corona crisis, has passed the limits of sustainability.

In some cases, this liability could be anticipated already at the moment when the country was admitted to the Euro zone. In the case of Italy, economic and financial concerns about the »convergence« necessary for admission competed with a widely held view that the cradle of Roman civilisation and the *rinascimiento*, by birth right, belongs to the inner circle of European integration. It may be submitted that admission to the Euro zone once granted (be it for economic or other, socio-cultural considerations) imposes solidarity on all members of the club. Some politicians plead against granting fresh money for solving old problems. However, it is difficult to disentangle the new, Corona-related problems from pre-existing liabilities. The extent in which solidarity should stand in relation with norm-conforming policies in the past or entirely focus on present needs is an issue which escapes reliable guidance by legal rules. The power of the European Union to assist countries in an emergency[10] is not limited to situations beyond government's responsibility or control.

A delicate, probably politically incorrect question relates to the preliminary issue of wealth distribution with the European Union or the Euro zone. Comparative analysis seems to suggest the aggregated private wealth *per capita* in Italy is superior to private wealth in Germany (results vary according to the inclusion of real property). Can solidarity require the citizens (and other tax-payers) of one country to grant financial assistance to a country whose private wealth surpasses their own? In the long run, the consideration of such criteria may determine the acceptance of solidarity measures as legitimate and even the affinity of Europeans to integration. This being said, there is a range of economic reasons, even coupled with self-interest, which support generous financial solidarity to weaker countries, e. g. the reactivation of purchasing power in favour of exported domestic goods and the interest of domestic banks engaged on foreign capital markets.

At an early stage of the Corona crisis, the ESM established a loans program of 500 Billion Euros with rather flexible conditions. In support of the Euro countries heavily affected by the Corona crisis though the purchase of government bonds, the European Central Bank initiated its gigantic *Pandemic Emergency Purchase Programme*, now expanded to 1.35 billion €. This ECB operation, even more than previous purchase programmes, dramatically increases the money supply and redistributes wealth and economic benefits not only among the Euro countries, but also with the society of each country. These redistribution effects lie at the heart of the widespread concerns that the ECB is overstepping the confines of its monetary powers in favour of overindebted countries like Italy, France and Spain. The German Constitutional Court recently responded to these concerns. In its *PPSP* judgment of May 2020, it held that the ECB, in order to comply with the proportionality of its measure, must demonstrate an adequate balancing of interests and

---

[10] Art. 122(2) of the TFEU.

that the all too lax scrutiny by the European Court of Justice rendered the Court's confirmation of the ECB operations *ultra vires*.[11]

In addition, the »Mediterranean« sector of the European Union pushed for so-called »Corona Bonds«. This is a version of Euro Bonds limited by all Euro countries, with a joint liability for the full sum owed to creditors. This form of raising money on the capital market means that the financially stronger member states like Germany or the Netherlands share their creditworthiness (superior rating) on the capital markets with their highly indebted partner countries. Such common responsibility for debt would violate the founding principle of the European Monetary Union that each member State is fully and exclusively responsible for its own debt. Under European law it is controversial whether such joint debt instruments would violate the »no bail-out« rule of the Treaty on the Functioning of the European Union (art. 127 of the TFEU). Under the German Basic Law, the Constitutional Court clearly stated that Germany (and her citizens) may not be held liable for debts flowing from the operations of a government in whose election the German people did not have a say (»*fremde Willensentscheidungen*«).[12] This constitutional ban of joint liabilities recalls the old maxim »no taxation without representation«. Still, the countries opposing Eurobonds (Austria, Finland, Germany, and the Netherlands) have been stigmatized as the »avaricious four«. This indicates alarming conflict lines between the heavily indebted southern member States, on the one hand, and the financially rather stable and relatively prosperous North of the EU, on the other.

As in the handling the ever-growing public debt in countries like France, Italy or Spain, the clash of national postures in context of an »European solidarity« reveals fundamental divisions both in the understanding of normativity enshrined in treaty rules and on the perception of monetary stability or fiscal discipline as a value in itself.[13] In Germany (and, to some extent, in other »northern« member states) the normative character of treaty rules is understood as unconditional. From this perspective, the European Union is, first and foremost, not only a community of values and interests, but also a community based on law (*Rechtsgemeinschaft*). The opposing view held by large sectors of the political class in France or Italy takes a more instrumental view of legal rules and allows them to be trumped by overriding national interests, at least if shared by other countries. This applies in particular to the treaty rules governing the European Monetary Union. The relevant treaty framework is the most ambitious attempt in human history to

---

[11] Bundesverfassungsgericht: 2 BvR 859/15 et al., judgment of 5 May, 2020, ECLI:DE:BVerfG:2020: rs2002505, 2bvr085915.

[12] BVerfGE 153: 317 (402) paras 16–17.

[13] Cf. Ajani: Possible Effects of the Pandemic Emergency, in this volume.

translate economic wisdom into normative standards which govern the very essence of State sovereignty, such as the power to raise and spend money.¹⁴

In Germany and some neighbouring countries, the understanding of the treaty rules on the European Monetary Union as a strictly binding regime in the interest of monetary stability corresponds to a widely shared expectation in society (although some years ago Germany, together with France, openly violated standards for fiscal discipline of the »Stability and Growth Pact«). From this perspective, the so-called »stability culture« has not only legal foundations, but also forms part of the socio-cultural legacy. This fosters an understanding of monetary stability and fiscal discipline as a condition for individual planning and of personal freedom. Criticism prevailing in, but not confined to »southern« countries of the European Union challenges this posture as an adoration of the golden calf. By contrast, in its *Maastricht* judgment, the German Federal Constitutional Court repeated Fjodor Dostoevsky's dictum that money is coined freedom.¹⁵ Of course, in Dostoevsky's times, the *beati possidentes* did not have to worry about monetary stability: The gold standard adopted in the major economies granted monetary stability, fixed exchange rates placed effective restraints on excessive public spending.

In all this debate an intriguing question emerges: Why do ethical moral and socio-cultural postures so often coincide with what is commonly perceived as national interest of the home country of the author (this may even apply to these lines)? We may recall Benjamin Cardozo's statement: »We may try to see things as objectively as we please. None the less, we can never see them with any eyes except our own.«¹⁶ This particularly applies to the »*Kulturwissenschaften*«. Still, the relapse of scientific analysis to more or less bounded subjectivity remains a matter of concern.

Beyond the discussion on the joint liability of European States, the Corona crisis highlights also the different understandings of solidarity with respect to the role of the European Union itself. Countries like France or Italy call for financial support from the European Union in the form of grants financed by the EU budgets via loans. The European treaties do not empower the European Union to borrow money on the capital markets to finance grants. On the contrary, they require a balanced budget.¹⁷ In a radical turn-around, the German Government took sides with the French President, adopting the Macron-Merkel Plan for a European reconstruction fund of the European Union financed by loans. The European Commission now follows the same line, only enlarging the proposed reconstruc-

---

14 Cf. Herdegen: Price Stability and Budgetary Restraints.
15 BVerfGE 89: 155 (199).
16 Cardozo: The Nature of the Judicial Process, p. 13.
17 Art. 310(1) of the TFEU.

tion budget by an additional loan programme. The necessary expansion of the EU budget and the increase of the European Union's own funds require a simplified modification of the Treaty on the Functioning of the European Union by all member States. In Germany, the necessary assent required a 2/3 majority in both legislative bodies. Insisting on strictly playing by the Treaty rules, four countries (Austria, Denmark, Finland and the Netherlands) are sharply opposed to finance EU grants with borrowing, In a way, borrowing money on the capital markets for rescuing highly indebted member States with grants goes well beyond joint liability for Eurobonds which does not affect the liability of overindebted member States and thus places restraints on fiscal policy.

In light of all these developments we might ask whether the Corona crisis catalyses a constitutional moment for the European Union. The German Finance Minister already referred to a »Hamilton moment«. In 1790, Alexander Hamilton, as US Secretary of the Treasury pushed for the Federation taking over the debts of the States (debt assumption), thus increasing the standing of Federal Government in the early stages of the United States of America. These and other historical analogies are misplaced. In the European Union, there is no constitutional basis for a »Federal Government«. Nor is there a »European people« to which the governments in the member States are accountable. Furthermore, the US constitution no way obliges the Federation to rescue heavily indebted States from insolvency.

The crucial issue is whether in times of severe crisis we should allow tectonic changes in the foundations of the European Union and the common monetary system without changing the treaties, thus dispensing with the democratic legitimacy claimed by the existing constitutional framework. Such a step might satisfy those who demand more or less unrestrained solidarity within the European Union, at the cost of the more austere countries. It might strengthen the identification of the French, Italian or Spanish people with the European Union, which would then gradually replace the national State as the guarantor of stability of the last resort. On the other hand, such a tectonic shift in the functions of the European Union might alienate large sectors of the population in other countries from European integration.

At the beginning of the European Monetary Union two decades ago, like many others, I applauded this ambitious attempt from a rather »northern« and »austere« perspective – with the reservation that there may be developments where other interests may trump monetary stability and fiscal discipline as the overarching and overriding objective. At that time nobody would have foreseen the disruption of economic life by the Corona pandemic which affects all EU member states, but not all of them equally, as an asymmetric shock. In the end, any change, whether bending or breaking the existing treaty rules, requires consensus among all member States. This need to work for consensual solutions may be the key for strengthening European integration in the long run. Consensus might also be the key to heading the interests of those who have political standing but will be the most strongly affected: the future generations whose shoulders will have to carry a huge financial burden.

References

Cardozo, Benjamin: The Nature of the Judicial Process, New York 2009.
Herdegen, Matthias: Price Stability and Budgetary Restraints in the Economic and Monetary Union: The Law as Guardian of Economic Wisdom, in: Common Market Review, 35, 1998, pp. 9–32.
Kaiser, Anna-Bettina: Ausnahmeverfassungsrecht, Tübingen 2020.

Upendra Baxi

International Law and Covid-19 Jurisprudence

The deadly Covid-19 virus has now enveloped the globe and generated new forms of governmentality and bio-legitimation practises in its wake. But only new forms of human compassion and solidarity can help us overcome this lethal and formidably grim challenge. Even amidst the disease and death caused by the pandemic, theoretical discourse rages: on the one hand, our focus rests on the intensification of state of exception in combatting Covid-19. On the other, we explore the projection of the crisis as an opportunity for building a new future for global politics, one that is marked by empathy, fraternity, justice, and rights as fidelity to establish novel forms of sources of self in society.

Here, we engage only one facet of the new developments: How can international law discourse be read as we step into the future? Respect for norms and standards of international law is among the paramount constitutional duties of the Indian State under Article 51 of the Constitution, regardless of the quibbles of whether the language only refers to treaty-obligations or also to customary international law. It is an egregious error to think that international norms, standards, and doctrines are irrelevant to making policy and law regarding disasters or pandemics.

A threshold distinction of the United Nations, as a site of normative discursivity and of exercising global power politics, is sadly manifest even during this ever-accelerating pandemic. President Donald Trump's insistence on calling Covid-19 the ›Chinese virus‹ renders it extremely unlikely that the pandemic will be discussed during China's current monthly presidency of the Council. And the threat of veto, both by China and Russia, will always loom large whenever the matter is raised for discussion.

But the UN also illustrates systems of norm enunciation. Responsible for the progressive codification of law (along with the International Law Commission, ILC), the UN system has developed a web of lawmaking and framework treaties as well as provided auspices for systems of ›soft‹ law that may eventually become binding. Some robust norms, standards, and doctrines have emerged. For example, the peremptory *jus cogens* – a few fundamental, overriding principles of international law, such as crimes against humanity, genocide, and human trafficking – apply to all states. And Article 53 of the Vienna Convention on the Law of Treaties goes so far as to declare that a »treaty is void if, at the time of its conclusion, it conflicts with a peremptory norm of general international law«. And even when ingredients of genocide remain difficult to prove, the International Court of Justice has held, for example in 2007, that states have a duty to prevent and punish acts and omissions that eventually furnish elements for committing the crime of genocide.

There also exists an *erga omens* rule prescribing specifically determined obligations that states owe to the international community as a whole. This was enunciated by the World Court in 1970 when it enumerated four ›situations‹ of obligations: the outlawing of acts of aggression, the outlawing of genocide, protection from slavery, and protection from racial discrimination. A great significance of this judicial dictum is that it imposes obligations which transcend consensual relations among states. Justice Prasana Varale (of the Aurangabad Bench of the Bombay High Court) suggested on April 8, 2020, that the administration can create several centres across districts to avoid large gatherings, thereby recognizing the need of vegetables, medicines, and other essential goods as well as the emphasized role of the fundamental duties of all Indian citizens under Article 51-A of the Constitution. He admirably stated that »while it expects effective measures from the state government for migrants and health workers«, the Covid-19 pandemic requires citizens, who are »always protective about their fundamental rights« to »remind themselves and discharge the fundamental duties«. In doing so, he invoked Article 51-A of the Indian Constitution, which calls on all citizens to »promote harmony and the spirit of common brotherhood amongst all the people of India« and transcend »religious, linguistic and regional to renounce practices derogatory to the dignity of women«.

In this context, we should also remember the American Declaration of the Rights and Duties of Man, also known as the Bogota Declaration, the inaugural international human rights instrument that preceded the Universal Declaration of Human Rights (UDHR) by less than a year. And on December 9, 1998, the eve of the 70th anniversary of the UDHR, the UN General Assembly adopted a resolution declaring the Right and Responsibility of Individuals, Groups and Organs of Society to Promote and Protect Universally Recognized Human Rights and Fundamental Freedoms. It asserts in Article 18, Section 1 that: »Everyone has duties towards and within the community, in which alone the free and full development of his or her personality is possible«. And Article 18, Section 3 states that:

»Individuals, groups, institutions and non-governmental organizations also have an important role and a responsibility in contributing, as appropriate, to the promotion of the right of everyone to a social and international order in which the rights and freedoms set forth in the Universal Declaration of Human Rights and other human rights instruments can be fully realized.«

It is eminently arguable to maintain that this Declaration has become an aspect of customary international law binding on all states – and further that it remains particularly relevant to the global Covid-19 situation, which unites the state and civil society actors to care for the concrete suffering of others. In this connection, the »morality of aspiration« (to recall the phrase of lamented Professor Lon Fuller) is crucial because, as Professor John Finnis reminds us, »universalist and agent-neutral« duties make moral sense even if these »moral duties regarding people's well-being are not impartial, and if they are agent-relative«.

In addition, there are three other sets of international law obligations. These are primarily derived from the no-harm principles crystallized in the ILC 2001 Draft Articles on the Prevention of Transboundary Harm (DAPTH) and the 2015 Paris Framework Agreement on Climate Change. DAPTH has carefully developed norms of due diligence, stressing entirely that these may be adapted to contextual exigencies. But due diligence obligations may not be gainsaid altogether when the environmental invasions have a transboundary impact. Each state is obliged to observe these standards in the fight against Covid-19 as a matter of international law.

The second set of obligations relate to other core human rights measures: no law or policy to combat epidemics or pandemics can go against the rights of migrant workers, internally displaced peoples, refugees, and asylum seekers. In combating Covid-19, respect is owed to the inherent dignity of individuals, the rights of equal health for all, and the duties of non-discrimination. And the norms of human dignity further reinforce the accountability and transparency of the state and other social actors. Panicky and sadist policing endeavours to maintain lockdown regimes and shoot at sight orders in collective migrant labour exodus situations – and militaristic responses to food riots instantly de-justify public health lockouts and curfews.

The third set of obligations arise out of international humanitarian law. The Biological and Toxin Weapons Convention (BTWC) must be mentioned in this context. Without joining any conspiracy or racist theory about the origins of Covid-19, the Foreign Minister of India rightly affirmed the BTWC obligations on March 26, 2020, the 40th anniversary of that Convention. Surely, this first global and non-discriminatory disarmament convention is worthy of applause because it outlawed a range of weapons of mass destruction. India rightly again called for a »high priority« to enable »full and effective implementation by all states parties«.

Moreover, multinational and domestic corporations are also liable before an increasing number of domestic courts. In an illustration of this, the Canadian Supreme Court ruled on February 28, 2020, in *Nevsun Resources Ltd. v Araya et al.*, 2020 SCC 5, that customary international law can give rise to a direct claim in Canada if obligations of avoiding and eliminating forced labour, slavery, cruel, inhumane and degrading treatment, and crimes against humanity are violated.

The metaphor of ›war‹ is often invoked in a determined fight against Covid-19; even when there are some pacific conscientious objections to the starting point, this has to be based on a full-throated repudiation of an ancient Latin maxim *Inter arma enim silent lēgēs* (popularly rendered as »In times of war, the law falls silent.«) Combating this fierce and fearsome pandemic calls for a re-dedication to existing international law obligations and frameworks, not in their violation or denial.

What illustrious thinkers of the pre-Covid-19 era, such as Sir Wilfred Jenks, called the »common law of Mankind«, and what Professor John Rawls later christened the »Law of Peoples«, is a code of summoning and sustainability nested obligations for all states and peoples that must now be fully upheld. Put differently, the innate morality of post-Westphalian international law provides the necessary conditions of the »cultural validity« (as Professor Werner Gephart develops this notion)[1] governing anti-Covid-19 platforms of action.

---

[1] Cf. in this volume Gephart: Introduction; Conclusion.

Matthias Lehmann

Legal System Reactions to Covid-19: Global Patterns and Cultural Varieties

Most countries were unprepared for the spread of Covid-19. Governments around the world are still scrambling to respond to the pandemic. Through different measures, they strive to curtail its worst effects. These interventions, however, raise many questions. They can be seen as proof of the Nation-State's continued importance as the ultimate holder of power. But one can also fear they sound the death-knell for the process of globalisation, which had already been suffering as a result of trade wars and a reawakened taste for national sovereignty. In the midst of the pandemic, it is at present still way too early to predict the long-term effects of the measures taken by governments on the legal system. At this moment, the only reasonable analysis is limited to an overview of the measures currently taken. How does the law react to such an unexpected and far-reaching crisis?

In this respect, some interesting patterns are emerging all over the globe, which form the subject of the first part of this contribution. The second part will focus on the considerable divergences at the level of individual States and examine whether and to what extent they can be traced back to different legal, social and economic »cultures«. The third, concluding part assesses these responses.

1. Global Patterns: The Three Level Model of Crisis Intervention

In the wake of the Covid-19 pandemic, the State has taken a strong role. Around the world, legislators and governments have actively responded to the crisis. They have intervened on different levels.

Level 1: Fighting the Virus

At the first level, the State can be seen as acting as the guardian of order and protector of life and health. It imposes proscriptions and prohibitions, such as curfews, social distancing, the closure of shops or restaurants, and travel restrictions. As a result, social life is grinding to a halt. In this context, the risks to both public and private interests need to be carefully weighed. Questions that must be decided include: Which services are »essential« and need to continue, despite the crisis? Supermarkets? Bakers? Leisure clothing shops? Which parts of the economy can be excluded from the shutdown because they pose no or little risk? For instance: manufacturing? Or construction?

Level 2: Mothballing the Economy

At the second level, States try to limit the negative economic effects of the measures taken the first level. In effect, they attempt to »mothball« companies and business relationships for the duration of the crisis, so that they can continue thereafter as if the past months have not happened. The idea is to put the economy into deep-freeze.

To illustrate, the following techniques have been used for mothballing. The rules on insolvency have been relaxed, like the liability for wrongful trading or the duty of the directors to apply for the opening of an insolvency procedure. Companies have been allowed to postpone the dates for shareholder meetings and for mandatory audits. Sanctions for not meeting contractual obligations have been mitigated or excluded, for instance by banning the eviction of tenants for failure to pay rent. Curiously, the most effective mothballing has been achieved by very simple measures, as illustrated by China's extension of the New Year by a couple of days. In all of these cases, the legislator acts as a regulator by intervening in the functioning of the market. In this context, difficult decisions need to be made, involving many conflicting private interests. These include: Which obligations or duties are suspended, and which are not? For instance, do rents need to be paid or not? Must debt be serviced or not? Who bears the risk of any suspension – the creditor or the debtor?

There is one remarkable exception from mothballing: the financial markets continue to operate in most countries. Financial markets operate as gauges of the future. They constantly evaluate the economic impact of the crisis, adjust prices, and reallocate capital. That is why they have so far been spared from hibernation.

Level 3: Giving the Economy a Lift

Not everything lends itself to »mothballing«. Life goes on, despite the deep freeze of the economy. Employees need to be paid, food must be bought, children's mouths need to be fed. Deep-freeze legislation cannot change or satisfy these basic necessities. As a result, the State intervenes on yet another level, this time as a substitute for the market. It bails out companies, distributes subsidies, gives loans or guarantees, or pays cash directly to those in need. In other words, what the market used to deliver is now provided by the State. The bill for the taxpayer will be huge, but there is no other chance: The State provides the ultimate insurance for every part of the economy and society.

In this context as well, important decisions need to be made. Which industries or companies are to be bailed out, and on what terms? Airlines? Car manufacturers? Banks? Who is to benefit from a subsidy, and how much should that subsidy be? Who is eligible for a loan or a direct payment? The answers are intimately connected to the decisions taken on the first two levels. For instance, it only makes sense to grant subsidies to the industries where continued economic activity was disallowed. And it is not sensible to pay support to individuals who continue to get salaries. The three levels of intervention can be summarised in the following table:[1]

	Level 1	Level 2	Level 3
Function of the state	Guardian of order	Market regulator	Ultimate insurance
Type of intervention	Freezing social activity through: – bans – curfews – closures – social distancing	»Mothballing« the economy through: – alleviation of duties under insolvency law – postponement of corporate events – suspension of reporting and other regulatory duties – moratorium on contractual obligations	Substituting the market through: – bail-outs – subsidies – loans – guarantees – salary payments – direct cash hand-outs
Interests at stake	life & health continuity of economic activity	business existence income of shareholders and bondholders interests of creditors	business existence individual subsistence

Fig. 1: Three levels of intervention.

All three types of measures, the freezing of social activity, the mothballing of the economy and the substitution for the market, are decided on the national level. There is no global authority to steer them. Not even the European Union has

---

[1] Cf. Lehmann: Mothballing the Economy, pp. 155–157.

achieved uniformity in this regard. The Nation-State is definitely having a comeback. It was never really gone but now forcefully demonstrates again its power. The crisis is also a reminder that the market and the State are two complementary forces. The latter not only sets the conditions for the functioning of the former, but also acts like an emergency power generator where the market fails.

Strong state intervention at all three levels simultaneously is unprecedented, at least in the Western hemisphere. There have been previous emergencies, such as the oil crisis, the 9/11 terrorist attacks or the global financial crisis, but these were triggered by a single event and limited in time. In their aftermath, there was enough time to adapt the economy to the new conditions. The difference with the Coronavirus crisis is that it is both extremely urgent and extremely long in duration. It completely paralyses societal life for an unforeseeable period of time. Perhaps the closest analogy is with war time, but even then, economic activity continued and was merely shifted to the production of arms and other war goods.

The need for »hibernation« through »mothballing« is a rather new phenomenon. It demonstrates an urgent need for quick reactions to unexpected events. The pandemic has led to the realization that is not enough for business law to be efficient. It is equally important that legal systems are resilient to exogenous shocks. This upends the existing paradigms of values. Despite the strive towards precise, economically sound and legally certain solutions, the law needs to also be flexible, adaptable and changeable depending on the circumstances.

2. Cultural Varieties: Differences in National Covid Responses

Despite similar patterns around the globe, there are a number of deviations in the way in which countries have reacted to the crisis. These concern all of the three levels outlined above.

Comparison of Reactions at Level 1

For starters, not all countries have engaged in the same type of lockdown, bans and freezes of social activities. Rather, one can find considerable variety in their attempts to stop the spread of the virus. The Asian countries responded most rapidly, stringently and comprehensively. Social distancing was imposed very early on; testing and tracing subsequently followed; masks were ubiquitous. To be sure, there were national differences. The People's Republic of China, for instance, imposed strict lockdowns, for instance in the province of Hubei, with an iron fist, while Taiwan managed the crisis without such draconian measures. Japan had comparatively few cases, while South Korea suffered considerably. But overall, the reaction has been swift and effective across the Asian continent. This becomes especially clear when one compares it to responses seen elsewhere.

In Continental Europe, the reactions were quite different. Masks were first shunned, then accepted, before their use finally became mandatory. Public gatherings were still allowed in most parts of Europe as late as early March, then increasingly restricted. Lockdowns were imposed, often of longer duration than those in Asia, despite the serious limitations they set to the exercise of freedoms by citizens.

The Anglo-Saxon countries were the slowest to react to the crisis. The US and the UK governments in particular ignored and actively denied the threat posed by the virus for a long time. With a few exceptions, in particular an early ban on flights from China to America, measures were taken half-heartedly, very late on, and in an uncoordinated way. The exit from the lockdown looks to be similar. Despite recording the highest number of fatalities in the world, the US is already opening up its economy again.

The picture emerging is thus one of the restrictions gradually declining in stringency from Asia, to the European continent, and then ultimately to the Anglo-Saxon countries. This seems in line with cultural values of common weal and individual freedoms.[2] Asian countries typically rank the collective very high, and emphasize the interest of the community and the common weal over that of the individual. At the other end of the spectrum are the very liberal Anglo-Saxon countries, which tend to strike the balance between collectivist and individual interests in favor of the latter. Continental Europe occupies somewhat of a middle-ground between the two. Divergent attitudes have also been shown to exist with regard to risk. In Asia and Europe, aversion to risk is considerably higher than it is in Anglo-Saxon countries.[3] The latter are generally more optimistic. In their hope for success, they are also more willing to embrace the danger of negative outcomes.

Given this background, the divergent reactions to the crisis do not seem to be a coincidence. On the contrary, they can be seen as a direct result of different attitudes, value systems and perspectives that underpin different cultures. Collectivist, risk-averse countries are more likely to act decisively and stringently to the outbreak of a pandemic than individualistic, risk-tolerant countries. The variety of reactions to the Covid-19 virus should thus not be a surprise; they were, from this perspective, entirely predictable.

---

[2] Cf. Heine: Cultural Psychology, pp. 217–221 (distinguishing between individualistic and collectivistic societies); Gorodnichenko / Roland: Culture (examining the relationship between the individualistic/collectivist dichotomy and the propensity to innovation).

[3] Cf. Foellimi et al.: Loss Aversion (testing loss aversion for 31 OECD countries and the EU). For a comparison of attitudes towards different types of risks in the EU and the US on the basis of regulatory rules, cf. Wiener et al. (eds.): The Reality of Precaution.

There are of course exceptions and counter-indications. An example is Sweden, which despite being a Continental European country, adopted a very relaxed attitude to the virus. The same is true, to a lesser extent, for the Netherlands. Yet both countries are very liberal countries and value individual freedoms very highly. Within the community of Continental legal systems, they are in this regard culturally closest to the Anglo-Saxon countries. Another counterargument is the role played by individual politicians. Rather than general cultural factors, the particular personalities of those currently leading the governments in the US and the UK may be responsible for the incoherent response to the pandemic in those countries. On the other hand, it may be asked whether it is truly a coincidence that the people of these countries have elected the particular leaders currently in office. Perhaps an argument could be made that these personalities embody to some extent the values, attitudes and mind-set that is prevalent in these countries — liberalism, self-confidence and an appetite for risk.

A further alternative explanation — other than culture — for the differences in the reactions to Covid-19 may lie in the divergent historical experience. Because of prior outbreaks such as SARS, Asian countries there had prior exposure to epidemics; they knew what to expect and already had at their disposal the necessary equipment and techniques to fight the spread of a highly infectious disease. This factor has certainly played a role in the velocity and efficiency with which the virus was fought in these countries. At the same time, it cannot alone account for the swift and coordinated reaction seen in the Asian countries. Of at least equal importance is the highly disciplined way of behaving and the respect for official commands that is characteristic of Asian societies. Moreover, prior experiences also shape culture: the massive pandemics may have played their role in the current form of behavior that can be seen in Asia.

Comparison of Reactions at Level 2

Divergences can also be seen on Level 2, albeit for different reasons. For instance, Continental European countries have been quick to adopt legislation to help »mothballing« the economy.[4] Germany and Austria for instance have adopted far-reaching »payment holidays« for consumer loans.[5] Italy has introduced legislation for the reimbursement of booked holiday trips.[6] Virtually all European countries have suspended the right of landlords to evict their tenants for non-pay-

---

[4] For an overview, cf. the comparative contributions in Revista de Derecho Civil 7(2).
[5] Cf. Lehmann: Las medidas legislativas alemanes; Mateo y Villa: Medidas en materia de Derecho civil en Austria.
[6] Cf. Barba: Las intervenciones del Legislador italiano.

ment of rent. For the duration of the pandemic, companies may not dismiss their employees. Some European countries even have stymied parts of the financial market by prohibiting short selling, in order to avoid speculators benefitting from the pandemic.[7]

Although data is scarce and the reactions probably different from country to country, it seems that most Asian countries have also adopted measures to protect households and employees. Special aid has been granted to small- to medium-sized companies. The vulnerable members of society have been protected. The reaction could not have been more different in the US. No restrictions have been placed on the capacity of companies to hire and fire. The number of jobless people has climbed to new records; the highest since the global economic crisis of the 1930s. While unemployment benefits have been increased, they do not reach the self-employed, who make up a large part of the US economy. As compensation, one-time payments of US$ 1.200 have been made to every adult (US$ 500 to every child). Moreover, gigantic programs have been enacted by Congress to stimulate the economy. The UK has adopted a middle-position. It has not introduced formal payment holidays, but the Financial Conduct Authority (FCA) has requested banks to grant them in case of need. Tenants are still obliged to pay their rents, yet evictions will not be enforced. Firing employees is not banned, but companies that »furlough« their staff are granted a state subsidy.

It seems that once again each part of the world follows its own cultural assumptions and preferences. In their fear of the economic consequences of Covid-19, continental European countries have turned to the State. They use legislation to protect borrowers, tenants and employees. This is in line with their traditional concern for the protection of the most vulnerable members of society, and a cultural belief in the power of the State as a problem solver. The Anglo-Saxon countries, in turn, decline to interfere with the sanctity of contracts. They trust in private actors and the markets to sort out the consequences of the pandemic. Although they may find it regrettable, they accept considerable individual hardship and suffering. Their hope is that the considerable downturn will soon turn into a quick (»V-shaped«) recovery. Underlying this attitude is an unshakable belief in the dynamism of the economy, which they take as a constant alternation of boom and bust.

Again, the picture is far from uniform. Switzerland, for instance, has also been very reluctant to change its legislation, despite its location at the heart of Continental Europe. Swiss contract law has been left untouched; the enforcement of evictions of tenants merely has been temporarily suspended.[8] This, however, falls into line with the rather individualistic attitude of the Swiss people in comparison to their European neighbors.

---

[7] Cf. ESMA: ESMA Issues Positive Opinions.
[8] Cf. Lein: Las medidas legislativas suizas.

Comparison of Reactions at Level 3

Finally, there are also noticeable differences at the third level of governmental intervention. Continental European countries were relatively quick to hand out generous subsidies, loans and grants to the most affected enterprises in the economy. They also have not shied away from outright bail-outs of companies, such as airlines, train companies or car manufacturers. The State will take a substantial part in these companies. Strong conditions have been set for their future governance, such as bans on dividends and bonuses caps for management.

The US and the UK both adopt quite a different attitude. They are generally much more hesitant to directly intervene in the economic playing field. Where money is granted to individual enterprises, it is often in the form of a mere guarantee. This secures that a commercial bank needs to make the final decision over the creditworthiness of the company. The Anglo-Saxon countries also adopt a very conservative attitude to nationalisations. Where the State takes a share in a company, it is often very passive, shying away from exercising its shareholder rights to influence corporate governance or receive dividends. That does not mean that the Anglo-Saxon countries are indifferent to their economies. The contrary is true: the growth of their GDP is of special concern for them as they know their well-being depends on it. Yet instead of directly interfering with the economy, their prefer to stimulate it in an indirect way. At the center of their action is the provision of monetary liquidity through the central bank. To illustrate, the Federal Reserve of the US has now lowered the standard of its bond buying program to the point where it is willing to buy below investment grade (so-called »junk bonds«). The Bank of England has agreed to buy »gilts«, i. e. sovereign bonds, directly from the British government. This is direct State financing by the central bank.

This variety of reactions is the result of different cultural attitudes to debt. Largely for historical and religious reasons, Continental European countries see debt as negative. This can be witnessed, for instance, from the German homonym »Schuld«, which means both »debt« and »culpability«. The limits EU law places on the debt burden of States (one of the so-called »Maastricht criteria« are another consequence of this strained relation to debt. Anglo-Saxon countries see debt much more neutrally. They are rarely afraid of it. In their eyes, borrowing money is just a means to enable investments at the appropriate time. No wonder therefore that they do not worry issuing additional sovereign and private debt.

3. Which Culture is Most Adapted?

The crisis will undoubtedly have a long-lasting effect on countries across the globe. It will test their legal, social and economic setup to breaking point. Those societies that are most resilient and efficient will ultimately prevail. Seen from this perspective, the crisis may be a factor contributing to more global uniformity rather than deglobalisation. Some authors welcome the Darwinian outlook of the survival of the fittest. For instance, Horst Eidenmüller strongly favors competition between regulators in devising the best solution to the challenges of the pandemic.[9] He does not believe in worldwide solutions, which he considers to be both illusory and harmful. He views rapid learning from the experience of others and coordination through imitation to be the best way to combat the virus and contain the associated economic fallout.[10] The question remains which approach is the most likely to prevail. Again, it is necessary to distinguish between the three levels outlined above.

It has been shown that the Asian countries benefitted from their cultural values and attitudes, which allowed them a swift, coherent and decisive response to the pandemic. This may imply a superiority of collectivist attitudes over individualistic ones. However, it must not be forgotten that the belief in authority and the failure to take individual responsibility caused considerable delay in discovering the pandemic at its inception. The high degree of discipline exhibited in Asian countries may also be a double-edged sword because it does not allow a rational debate about the measures that are best adapted. The deliberative, individualistic culture prevailing in the Western hemisphere certainly leads to longer reaction times, yet it may ultimately yield a reaction that is better suited than that chosen by other systems. The same goes for the measures on the second level. At first sight, it seems that those countries which opted for a high degree of state intervention were victorious in their attempt to »mothball« the economy. Yet preventing the demise of companies implies certain costs. Some of the bailed-out companies may have been inefficiently managed and therefore should have been allowed to become insolvent. Those countries where companies have currently gone bankrupt may still benefit in the future from the new start-ups that have replaced the incumbents.

Finally, no one can presently foresee what long-term effects the different measures on Level 3 will have. It is entirely possible that countries with an extremely high debt burden will pay the price in the form of inflation and economic decline. But one can as well imagine that these countries may leap-frog others thanks to

---

[9] Cf. Eidenmüller: The Race to Fight COVID-19, p. 33.
[10] Cf. ibid.

the enormous liquidity they have injected into their economies. Again, it is too early to make predictions of any sort.

The competition between different cultures will therefore go on for the time foreseeable, without any definite conclusion as to which system will ultimately prevail. The virus has added just another parameter, that of resilience, to this competition, which vies with the parameter of efficiency that was so far considered predominant. Which culture is the most resilient is by no means certain. What can, however, be observed right now is that cultures to some extent adapt to crises. The way in which face masks have become common in Continental Europe, for instance, is testimony to the adaptability of societies. But then again, the ability to learn from each other has also always been a feature of culture.

References

Barba, Vincenzo: Las intervenciones del Legislador italiano en relación con los aspectos de Derecho civil para hacer frente a la emergencia del COVID-19, in: Revista del Derecho Civil, 7(2), 2020, pp. 75–87.

Eidenmüller, Horst: The Race to Fight COVID-19: On the Desirability of Regulatory Competition, in: Gert-Jan Boon et al., The COVID-19 Pandemic and Business Law: A Series of Posts from the Oxford Business Law Blog, Oxford Legal Studies Research Paper 2020, pp. 30–34.

European Securities and Markets Authority (ESMA): ESMA Issues Positive Opinions on Short-Selling Bans by Five Jurisdictions, https://www.esma.europa.eu/press-news/esma-news/esma-issues-positive-opinions-short-selling-bans-austrian-fma-belgian-fsma; last accessed 27.04.2020.

Foellimi, Reto / Adrian Jaeggi / Rina, Rosenblatt-Wisch: Loss Aversion at the Aggregate Level across Countries and Its Relation to Economic Fundamentals, https://ideas.repec.org/p/snb/snbwpa/2018-01.html; last accessed 02.06.2020.

Gorodnichenko, Yuriy / Gerard Roland: Culture, Institutions, and the Wealth of Nations, in: The Review of Economics and Statistics, 99(3), 2017, pp. 402–416.

Heine, Steven J.: Cultural Psychology. Third Edition. New York / London 2016.

Lehmann, Matthias: Las medidas legislativas alemanas relacionadas con la crisis del COVID-19 en el ámbito del Derecho civil, in: Revista del Derecho Civil, 7(2), 2020, pp. 3–7.

Lehmann, Matthias: Mothballing the Economy and the Effects on Banks, in: Christos V. Gortsos / Wolf-Georg Ringe (eds): Pandemic Crisis and Financial Stability, European Banking Institute Working Paper Series, 2020, pp. 155–171, https://ssrn.com/abstract=3607930; last accessed 02.06.2020.

Lein, Eva: Las medidas legislativas suizas relacionadas con la crisis del COVID-19 en el ámbito del Derecho civil, in: Revista del Derecho Civil, 7(2), 2020, pp. 129–133.

Mateo y Villa, Íñigo: Medidas en materia de Derecho Civil por el COVID-19 en Austria, Revista del Derecho Civil, 7(2), 2020, pp. 9–14.

Revista de Derecho Civil, 7(2), especial (mayo 2020), 2020.

Wiener, Jonathan B. / Michael D. Rogers / James K. Hammitt / Peter Sand (eds.): The Reality of Precaution: Comparing Risk Regulation in the United States and Europe, Washington 2010.

Valentino Cattelan

Sacred Euro: Sovereign Debt(s) and EU's Bare Credit in the Corona Crisis

Introduction: Money, *Nomisma* and *Nomos*

Far from being a neutral medium of exchange, money affects the daily practice of our economic dealings while being intrinsically connected to the whole of legal, social, and political interactions of the community to which we belong. In this light money enjoys its own morality, where voluntary customary usage (›moral‹ from the Latin *mos*, ›manner, custom‹) is backed by the subsistence of a normative order, a *nomos*: the former and the latter being collectively practiced, shared and endorsed in a certain social group. Hence, sovereign power (the beholder of the law) can hardly posit the use of ›fiat money‹ by decree when mechanisms of inflation, mistrust, recession or even depression are in action. Here ›positive money‹ (money imposed by the state) contrasts ›monetary *nomos*‹ and, then, it is soon replaced by alternative ›natural money‹ that can better work as store of value (for instance, commodities such as precious metals, gold or silver), unit of account and means of exchange (the rise of cryptocurrencies, e.g. bitcoins, represents the most recent example in this direction). It is indeed the criterion of public trust that fosters the morality of positive money by its convergence with natural money: the public *gives* political credit to the sovereign to the extent to which through its *nomisma* (currency as ›monetary *nomos*‹) people can trust *receiving* economic credit in the reciprocity of their dealings. In doing so they use money as something that represents (as store of value, unit of account and means of exchange) their shared/mutual needs in/for participating in the same community. A conceptual equivalence with the jurisprudential couple ›positive law‹/›natural law‹ (that kind of sovereign law whose legitimacy derives from providing ›what is right‹, to wit, ›rights‹) can be easily implied from the previous reflection, a point on which I will come back later.

Aristotle, in his *Nicomachean Ethics*, underlines the deep intersection between monetary practice and normative/social order (what the elision ›monetary *nomos*‹ actually describes) by noting the etymological correspondence in Greek language between ›currency‹ (*nomisma*) and ›law‹ (*nomos*), both related to the need for the subsistence in any given community of a standard for exchanges and social relations established by common agreement:

»There must [...] be one standard by which all commodities are measured [...] money has become by convention a sort of representative of common need (demand); and this is why it has the name ›money‹ [*nomisma*, customary currency] – since it exists not by nature [*physis*] but by ›law‹ [*nomos*, ›custom, usage, law as natural/social order‹, distinct from *lex posita* or *ius positum*]«.[1]

Moving from these preliminary considerations this paper aims to shed some light over the Corona crisis by applying a law-as-culture paradigm to the European Union and its money. To this specific objective it interprets the impact of the emergency by depicting the EU as a polity whose ›positive money‹, the Euro, seems still unable today to function as ›natural money‹: that is to say, a polity still lacking in a full monetary *nomos*. In particular, this contribution argues that the current pandemic has revealed the persistently contradictory nature of the Euro as a kind of *sacred money* (*nummus sacer*)[2] that may be borrowed by member states via sovereign debt(s), but whose credit is not backed (yet) by the EU polity as a whole (§ 2): a condition of *sacertas* that the recovery plan proposed by the EU Commission at the end of May 2020 may actually overcome, in a sort of ›return to *Life*‹ (if not a resurrection) for the EU political project as grounded on solidarity (§ 4).

Besides drawing from the scholarship by Giorgio Agamben,[3] valuable hints for some conclusive remarks will be found in George Simmel and Marcel Mauss. More precisely, by locating the discussion of the ›sacred Euro‹ (§ 2) in-between the chronicle of the first version of the EU Coronavirus relief deal (as agreed on by the Eurogroup on Thursday 9th April 2020) and the final proposal of its contents by the EU Commission, the paper will move from a critique to the bailout system embedded in the ESM loans model (as a signal of the political failure of the Euro as monetary *nomos*: § 1) to an appraisal of the recovery plan in terms of an embryonic full *nomisma* for the EU polity (§ 3). Accordingly, while by highlighting the failure of the European *nomos/nomisma* the ›bare credit‹ of the EU will be related to an inescapable revival of nationalism and of the sovereign power in the member states, the resurgence of the EU political project will be linked, on the contrary, to the re-discovery of solidarity as its founding value (§ 4). This ›return to *Life*‹ will be conceived in connection to more ambitious actions to be taken, so to fully transform the *nomos* of the EU market into that of the EU polity: a radical transformation that may be actually ignited, as we will see, by the Corona-crisis recovery plan.

---

[1] Aristotle: Nicomachean Ethics, Book V, 1133a 29–30.
[2] The etymology of the Latin word *nummus*, ›coin‹, relates to the Greek *nomisma* too.
[3] To which the title of this paper clearly refers by paraphrasing his »Homo Sacer: Sovereign Power and Bare Life«.

1. The First EU Coronavirus Relief Deal: A Failure to Get Credit, a Sentence to Death?

»Europe suffered a historic defeat on Thursday night« (*The Guardian*, Saturday 11th April 2020).[4] The first line of an article written by Yanis Varoufakis, former finance minister of Greece, immediately after the meeting of the Eurogroup on Thursday 9th April 2020, gave voice to the hope, ambition and regret coming from the EU member states devastated by the impact of Covid-19 crisis. A shattered hope in a more supportive EU; a broken ambition for an »ever closer union among the peoples of Europe«;[5] a regret about the dramatic lack of »awareness of a common destiny«[6] that not only did the pandemic make clearer for European peoples, but for the humanity as a whole. The EU's Coronavirus relief deal, Varoufakis argued, »[b]esides constituting an epic dereliction of duty, [...] dealt a decisive blow to the foundations of the European union – much to the delight of Europe's critics and enemies«.[7]

Writing amid the general lockdown affecting continental Europe at the pick of the Corona crisis,[8] Varoufakis pointed at the cowardice of many EU actors in (not) taking action in a decisive moment of history. The reasons underpinning this vital necessity to act, I believe, can be better understood by embracing a law-as-culture paradigm looking at the circulation of money (which by convention represents common needs and demand: Aristotle) not only as a crucial factor to protect the economy, but also to foster the legal, social and political values of community *Life* (see § 4).

In this light one may raise the question if some contradictions are still affecting or not the *life* of the Euro as currency of the EU market (polity?). In fact, if any lockdown »do[es] not care what currency we use«[9] and polities like the US, Japan and the UK did already increase their public expenditures to counterbalance the falls in private incomes, the 19 countries of the eurozone were paradoxically hampered in their need for a massive boost in public debt by their arrangement of sharing a »(European) central bank that [...] has no common treasure to lean against and [...] is banned from backing directly the 19 treasuries that must borrow in euros to fight the crisis«.[10] Accordingly, a conundrum was actually faced by the weakest and most indebted Euro countries, such as Italy, Spain and Greece

---

[4] Varoufakis: The EU's New Coronavirus Relief Deal.
[5] As declared in the Preamble of the founding Treaty of Rome of 1957.
[6] European Council: Solemn Declaration on EU.
[7] Varoufakis: The EU's New Coronavirus Relief Deal.
[8] With the real economy of goods and services hibernated by the lack of consumption and production, previsions of fall in GDPs and the highest rates of unemployment since WWII.
[9] Varoufakis: The EU's New Coronavirus Relief Deal.
[10] Ibid.

after the EU Coronavirus relief deal, as proposed on Thursday 9th April 2020: they could issue new sovereign debt(s) to finance their economies (so to save their peoples from the depression of the Covid-19 crisis as only possible action to be undertaken), but with the fate not be able to repay their debt(s) (as a likely corollary for the action to be taken). Sovereign debt(s) that would have pushed these states into further austerity, depression or even default. Hence, what was presented as a triumphant agreement about an impressive sum of € 500bn to rescue Europe masked, in fact, the enchanting voices of Sirens luring EU states by the promise of salvation just to shipwreck their boats on the rocky coasts of the myth of the eurozone financial stability. In the middle of the Coronavirus perfect storm, the extension of »credit lines to countries such as Italy, via Europe's bailout fund (the European Stability Mechanism, ESM), to the tune of 2 % of a recipient country's national income ... [plus] more loans, of about € 100bn, to the social security systems«[11] had the (cruel) effect of reviving the spectrum of financial disintegration for weaker EU states. But, above all, it sounded to some ears as a death sentence by the Eurogroup to the greatest creation of international politics of the last century in Europe: the EU itself.

Indeed, the failure of an appropriate politics about *giving* credit to EU states[12] sentenced, implicitly, the factual EU incapability to *receive* credit by its peoples – and so the end of an »even closer union« sustained (only) by a market *nomos* (as validity culture of its own normativity) that has imperfectly backed the last 20 years of the EU polity by means of its *nomisma*, the Euro.

In a condition where »debt-sharing is banned by the treaties that created the Eurozone, at the insistence of the northern European countries running a trade surplus with the rest«, the eurozone itself, as Varoufakis argued, »will remain an iron cage of austerity for most and a source of economic stagnation for everyone«.[13] In this situation, the demand for money (*nomisma*) through the issuance of so-called euro-bonds[14] was killed by the EU *nomos* in a two-faced Janus's failure to *get* credit.[15] The inherent paradox of a *nomos* sentencing to death its own *nomisma* (and vice-versa)[16] requires at this point further critique to shed light over what could have been the destiny of the EU without a radical change of the contents of the recovery deal at the end of May 2020 (see § 3). An interpretation

---

[11] Ibid.
[12] Despite a plurality of mechanisms being certainly advanced: from the ESM to the role of the EIB, the European Investment Bank; from the SURE, Support to mitigate Unemployment Risks in an Emergency, to the promise of a Recovery Fund.
[13] Varoufakis: The EU's New Coronavirus Relief Deal.
[14] Common debt instruments that allow long-term risk to shrink by transferring a portion of it from weaker to stronger member states via risk-sharing.
[15] (*Not*) giving *economic* credit to member states so (*not*) to receive *political* credit from European citizens.
[16] Causing, in the end, the self-defeat (suicide?) of the EU polity itself.

that the next section will advance in relation to the Roman figure of *homo sacer* as conceptualized by Giorgio Agamben.

2. *Homo Sacer*, Sacred Euro

When examined more carefully, the metaphor of the death sentence released by the Eurogroup on 9th April looks less adequate than intended: in fact no trial was held; no judgement was enacted; no intention was formally addressed to declare the end of the Euro (the *nomisma* of EU economic order) nor of EU law (the *nomos* of Europe's legal, social and political order). More correctly, one could ascribe these consequences to the two sides of the same coin: the failure of the EU polity and its currency (its monetary *nomos*) derived from breaking the ›oath‹ of its origin as grounded on the pursuit of »an ever closer union among the peoples of Europe«.[17]

Significantly, an ancient figure, that of the *homo sacer* in Roman law, may offer valuable hints to interpret what would have been the destiny of the EU in the Corona crisis (without a radical revision of the recovery plan: § 3). Literally »sacred man«, in antiquity the meaning of *homo sacer* was actually closer to the idea of »accursed man«: being the oath essentially an act of conditional self-cursing by invoking one or more deities, the oath-breaker condemned himself to punishment without any emitted sentence. It was the act of oath-breaking itself to imply his *sacertas*, his status of outlaw deprived of civic rights. Self-responsible for the breaking of the *pax deorum* (the fundamental harmony between humans and gods in Roman ancient religion), the *homo sacer* was banned from the *civitas*, put outside the law (better, beyond it): hence, not only could he be killed by anybody without the killer being regarded as a murderer, but he neither could be sacrificed according to religious rituals (having lost the protection of the gods, he did not belong to human society anymore, nor he could be consecrated to a deity). In summary, the action of the *homo sacer* jeopardized the *pax deorum*, the harmony between men and gods, to the extent that the survival of the entire community of Rome was put in danger: his status of outlaw immediately related to his *sacertas*.

As well-known this obscure figure of ancient Roman law constitutes the starting point of the main work by Italian philosopher Giorgio Agamben's *Homo Sacer: Sovereign Power and Bare Life*.[18] In positing fundamental questions about the nature of law and power in general, Agamben highlights the intrinsic paradox of the man ›under the spell‹ of the law by being *excluded* from it while being *included* in it at the same time (the *homo sacer* was within the juridical order only by being

---

[17] Treaty of Rome.
[18] Cf. Agamben: Homo Sacer.

outside it, to wit, by its capacity to be killed by anybody) – the exact mirror of the ›spell‹ of the power for the sovereign, who stands *within* the law by being *outside* the law (through his political force to suspend law in a state of emergency). It is by qualifying human political life (in form of *bios*, hence the concepts of biopower and biopolitics in Agamben) that law operates via a simultaneous inclusion and exclusion of ›bare life‹ (the Greek *zoe*): by actively constructing the lives of political beings (citizens), while positing cases ›beyond the law‹ (the *homo sacer* and the sovereign) to re-affirm the nature of its ultimate power. Sovereignty, in the end, incorporates citizens in the *bios* of the political body by an original exclusion of the ›bare life‹, as much it embodies the power of the sovereign to suspend the law in the state of emergency (a concept expanded by Agamben in his *State of Exception*).[19]

It does not come as a surprise that the interpretive strength of Agamben's *homo sacer* contextualized in the emergency of the Corona crisis can shed light on the contradictory nature (and possible destiny) of the Euro when a parallelism is drawn from the category of law (*nomos*) to that of money (*nomisma*). Betraying its own raison d'être (the pursuit of »an ever closer union among the peoples of Europe«), the EU has posited in the original version of the Coronacrisis recovery deal its *nomisma* ›outlaw‹ (beyond its own *nomos*) by allowing the Euro to be borrowed by member states via sovereign debt(s), but without being expendable through the (economic, political, but also moral) credit of a unified polity as a whole. The myth of the EU shared sovereignty, dignified in hundreds of academic articles and books, has revealed itself as the enchanting singing of Sirens, since deprived of a mechanism of shared risk grounded on the monetary *nomos* of an (inexistent) unified EU sovereign debt (logical prerequisite for the issuance of euro-bonds in the form of ›corona-bonds‹, so to face the ongoing crisis). The substantial impact of the paradoxical *nomos* of the EU (allowing member states to deny the value of its own *nomisma*) can be deemed equivalent to a condition of *sacertas* where financial markets[20] can attack the finances of weaker EU member states, while more stable EU members may protect (or even reinforce) their economies.

If the criticism about the economic implications of risk premium among financial instruments of EU member states (e.g. the spread between 10-year Italian bond and the benchmark of 10-year German *Bund*) has often been raised in the persistence of the validity the EU *nomos*, the emergency of the Corona crisis could have brought about the end of the *pax deorum*, i.e. the harmony between the ›gods‹ of the EU polity and the ›men‹ of EU citizens, rendering the Euro a kind

---

[19] Cf. Agamben: State of Exception.
[20] I.e. the collective ›anybody‹ of capitalism deprived of immediate responsibility for ›killing‹ economic actors by bankruptcy.

of »sacred, accursed money«. A *nummus sacer* that the global financial markets could have killed[21] while not being *expendable*[22] according to the shared rules of the EU budgetary policies (the ›rituals‹ at law).

The *sacertas* of the Euro in the Covid-19 recovery deal of 9th April, in the end, has revealed the persistent contradictions of the EU *nomos*, whose ›positive money/law‹, while being ›ruled‹ by the sovereignty of founding treaties and an operating European Central Bank, is undermined by the ›natural money/law‹ still ›ruled‹ as store of value at the level of member states' sovereignty.[23] Locating itself beyond the categories of positive/natural *nomisma*, the ›accursed destiny‹ of the Euro as *sacred money* could have found its death in the demolition of the EU polity and the new rise of nationalisms unless urgent action taken. In the end, what the Covid-19 emergency plan disclosed in its original version was how the EU *Life* still suffers from a *bare credit* (a sort of financial *zoe*) dependent (in terms of the political inexistence of the EU/Euro as a comprehensive *nomos*/*nomisma*) on the primacy of member states' sovereign (*debts*).[24]

3. The Euro In-Between Rigor Mortis, Legal Order and Economic/Political Resurrection

If the ›sacred money‹ paradigm may shed light over the ›death sentence‹ for the Euro in the original version of the Coronavirus relief deal, the bimester April–May 2020 (at the middle of which the European summit in charge for discussing the deal proposal took place on 23rd April 2020)[25] witnessed a turmoil in the Euro(/EU)'s struggle to survive: a turmoil from which some hope for a return to *Life* can be foreseen (§ 4). The race to save the EU from the pandemic has seen some courageous actors debating against more conservative member states in a wake of the EU *nomisma* to become a vehicle for a re-generated EU *nomos*. Thus, in the middle of the negotiations not only did the rescue package become a factor of economy recovery, but also a fundamental opportunity of renovated political action, so to boost the transformation of the EU market (a Europe of traders) into the EU polity (a Europe of peoples).

---

[21] By killing the economies of weaker EU member states borrowing in Euro via their own sovereign debts.

[22] ›The expendables‹ of the EU budget as precise mirror of the ›one that can be sacrificed‹.

[23] With stronger states maintaining an advantage over weaker states, and even reinforcing it in the crisis.

[24] Hence the *bios* of their own political/economic powers, witnessed by the spread in risk premiums, where stronger states are fated to overrule the economies of weaker states.

[25] Actually, the fourth virtual summit in seven-week time from the beginning of the crisis.

On the one side of the Euro(/EU)'s struggle Pedro Sánchez (Spanish Prime Minister) called on Europe to produce a Marshall Plan to recover the continent's economies (5th April 2020), echoed by Giuseppe Conte (Italian Prime Minister), as well as by Emmanuel Macron (President of France), who remarked how »[w]e are at a moment of truth, which is to decide whether the EU is a political project or just a market project. I think it's a political project [...] We need financial transfers and solidarity, if only so that Europe holds on« (16th April 2020). On the other side those who the chronicle re-named »the Frugal Four« in their attempt to keep a rigorous eye over the EU spending system[26] were led by Mark Rutte (Dutch Prime Minister) in their strong resistance to any plan for euro-bonds or for sharing the costs of the pandemic. Next to the pressure from France, Spain and Italy to pledge solidarity, Paolo Gentiloni (former Italian Prime Minister and now the EU's Economy Commissioner) stressed how the Coronavirus crisis posed an »existential threat to the building of the Union« (13th May 2020). For the good luck of the EU, the austerity backed by the Frugal Four (some sort of ›rigor mortis‹ played over the body of the Euro, keeping the metaphor of the ›sentence to death‹: see § 1) was strongly opposed by the German Chancellor, Angela Merkel, sustaining a common initiative with her French counterpart Emmanuel Macron (18th May 2020) for a recovery plan of € 500bn to collectively finance the EU response to the Coronavirus crisis by instruments of joint debt, direct grants (not debt, as in the original idea linked to the EMS) and an increased budget to sustain the weakest member states.

The principle of austerity was then rapidly replaced by the re-discovery of a solidarity principle in a recall of the distant founding text of the EU, the Schuman Declaration of 9th May 1950, urging after WWII that »Europe will not be made all at once [...] [but] through concrete achievements which first create a de facto solidarity«.[27]

Significantly for the intersection between the *nomisma* and the *nomos* in the eurozone, this re-emergence of solidarity as core value backing the EU polity found at the beginning of May 2020 an obstacle precisely in the EU legal order. At that time the German constitutional court expressed concerns about the European Central Bank's plan (as announced by its President Christine Lagarde) to support the recovery with a credit line at the lowest interest rate by a quantitative easing strategy – as it could breach German law. The lack of a common EU debt (as background for the stability of the Euro) re-emerged as the reason for the *sacertas* of the Euro, with the European Commission President, Ursula von der Leyen, obliged to issue immediately an official statement warning of possible EU legal action against Berlin (so to protect the EU common market), and Angela

---

[26] Namely Austria, Denmark, Sweden and the Netherlands.
[27] Schuman: The Schuman Declaration.

Merkel promptly stepping in to try to find a way out of a bilateral damaging clash between Germany and Brussels.

In the peril of a debt shipwreck (see before, § 1), the outcome of the negotiations led to a final proposal by the European Commission of a total of € 750 bn recovery plan, split into € 500 bn of grants for EU member states and € 250 bn of loans at the end of May. As Ursula von der Leyen remarked, if the EU was facing against the pandemic a crisis that it had never seen before in 70 years, the recovery plan itself could be seen as a ›defining moment‹ in the EU history. In fact, although the term ›euro-bonds‹ was not mentioned, the extra EU debt was going to be serviced by new EU taxes,[28] so defining a nascent economic/political resurgence[29] linking the ›return to *Life*‹ of the Euro to the intersection between money, taxes and debt as backbone for a renewed EU polity (see § 4). While the European Central Bank agreed to inject an additional € 600 bn of emergency financial support into the EU market, it is precisely within the background of the € 750 bn rescue program by the EU Commission that a historical change can actually be foreseen for the EU polity through the coherent integration of its *nomisma* and *nomos*.

4. Conclusions. Back to Solidarity? Life, *Gift* and a Historic Opportunity for the EU Polity

The turmoil that the Euro has experienced in the negotiations for the Coronavirus recovery plan has been summarized in this paper as a ›threat to death‹ (§ 1) that the EU *nomisma* has faced *because of* the EU *nomos*. In this regard, the metaphor of the ›sacred Euro‹ as economic/political counterparty of Agamben's *homo sacer* (§ 2) has been functionally oriented to depict this destiny, but also to highlight a potential resurgence of the EU polity by a new system of grants, shared debt and loans that seems to pave the way for the future of the eurozone (§ 3).

In this light, we can better understand at this point not only Varoufakis's words[30] (§ 1) but also the warning launched at the end of April 2020 (immediately after the EU summit of 23rd April) by Shahin Vallée, French economist and former adviser to Emmanuel Macron:

»The European summit last week was hailed as a moment of truth. […] The leaders agreed on an economy recovery plan that is incomplete and unbalanced, and is planting the seed of profound divergence between member states. […] [E]ach government's ability to support

---

[28] Such as corporate levies, a plastics tax or charges on imported goods with a high carbon footprint.
[29] Or even resurrection from death.
[30] Varoufakis: The EU's New Coronavirus Relief Deal.

economy recovery will be highly constrained by their level of debt [...] [with a] long-term unsustainable debt burden that the crisis will create. In the absence of true mutualisation [...] and real monetisation, European countries will either spend the next generation in austerity and depression [...], or they will go through the socially and politically destructive restructuring of some of it. [...] The eurozone needs to move towards a true form of fiscal federalism under the democratic control of the European parliament with taxing, borrowing and spending powers, wich the current EU budget doesn't permit. Short of that, the EU will carry on on its crutches, medically assisted by the drip-feed of a central bank that is forced to provide the vital energy to a political project that has lost its soul.«[31]

It is by elaborating on these reflections in the light of the nature of money as the ›life of goods‹ by circulation that the risk for the EU to lose its soul (as a sort of Mozart's *Don Giovanni* devastated by the *sacertas* of its *nomisma*) can be providentially translated into an opportunity for a historic change. A radical transformation of the rationale of its *nomos*, from the EU market to the EU polity, where the Coronacrisis recovery plan[32] can work as a ›return to *Life*‹ through the re-appearance of solidarity as founding value of the EU polity.

In an essay originally published in 1976 under the title *Geld oder Leben: Eine metaphorologische Studie zur Konsistenz der Philosophie Georg Simmels*,[33] the influential post-war German cultural theorist Hans Blumenberg highlights how money stands as Simmel's ›proto-metaphor‹ for *Life* in the latter's nascent *Lebensphilosophie*. Accordingly, as noted by Robert Savage, precisely like money, in Simmel's scholarship *Life* itself »turns out to be pure circulation, sociation, and interactivity, an endless cycle of extensions and intensifications of value emerging through processes of social exchange«.[34] So, in Blumenberg's interpretation »the two key concepts in Simmel's intellectual development – first *value*, then *life* – [...] [are] mediated by the theme of money [through the publication of his famous *Philosophie des Geldes*],[35] which was meant originally to provide access to the concept of value and ended up forcing a path to the concept of life«.[36] In a period where collective *Life* is put at stake by a global pandemic and shadows of death may obscure the legitimacy of the sovereign power (as claimed in the noteworthy book *Necropolitics* by Achille Mbembe),[37] looking for the re-emergence (or even resurrection) of *Life* »through processes of social exchange«, circulation, sociation and interactivity, requires to re-think (better, to re-affirm) the role of money in

---

[31] Vallée: Coronavirus has Revealed the EU's Fatal Flaw.
[32] By means of the provision of € 500 bn of grants for the most affected EU member states: under the Commission's blueprint, Italy will get € 82 bn, Spain € 77 bn, France € 39 bn, Poland € 37 bn and Germany € 29 bn.
[33] And later translated into English by Robert Savage, cf. Blumenberg: Money or Life.
[34] Ibid., p. 249.
[35] Cf. Simmel: The Philosophy of Money.
[36] Blumenberg: Money or Life, p. 249.
[37] Cf. Mbembe: Necropolitics.

shaping the normative order of a community and how EU money exercises a fundamental function in maintaining the stability of the EU order.

The impasse by the Eurogroup decision of Thursday 9th April in taking more ambitious choices for the future of the EU polity (by *not* conceiving the Euro as core metaphor of the political *Life* of the EU) may have caused a destiny of *sacertas* that is inherently connected to the oath-breaking of its pursuit of »an ever closer union among the peoples of Europe«. Left *within* the realm of ›positive money‹ (as a currency dependent on the ›positive laws‹ of member states' treaties) only by *excluding* its nature of ›natural money‹ (since the implications of excessive sovereign debts for weaker member states would have implied a reality of recession contrary to the function of any monetary *nomos*), the euro zone, as the place of *sacred money*, would have suffered from intrinsic instability due to the attacks by speculators in the global financial market. Precisely, the metaphor of the life of the *homo sacer* equals here the *Life* of the Euro as *nummus sacer*: money not *expendable* by the EU polity, whose collective *bare credit* is specular to the individuality of member states' *sovereign (debts)*.

With a pandemic bringing mass death and economic catastrophe, while the draft of the recovery plan (9th April) was utterly disappointing (§ 1),[38] the deep meaning of the radical innovations embodied in its final version (§ 3) can be better understood through another masterpiece of economic anthropology, namely Marcel Mauss's *Essai sur le Don*.[39] In some fortunate ways, in fact, the rationales of *The Gift* as ›form and reason for exchange‹ illuminated the European summit of 23rd April 2020, shaping the future of the eurozone and of the EU polity as a whole.

The European Council faced at that precise moment the responsibility to free the EU still jailed in nationalistic *sovereign debts* (each confirming the sovereign power, the ›positive laws‹ of the states) towards the transformation of its *bare credit* into the qualified *Life* (in terms of ›natural law‹ and political *bios*) of an »ever closer union among the peoples of Europe«.[40] That moment was a historic choice between a destiny of *sacertas* for the Euro or of resurrection for the EU.

Then, the correspondence between *giving* (economic) credit and *receiving* (political) credit suggested that braver actions were necessary for the survival of the EU *nomos* by means of its *nomisma*. And to this aim, the exchange of ›gifts‹ (i.e. the acceptance of mechanisms of shared risk connected with the shared sovereignty of which the EU is entitled), with the obligation to reciprocate beyond the strict rules of financial capitalism (on which the logic of the *sovereign debt*

---

[38] The »EU's response to the pandemic has been depressingly slow, hesitant, stingy and unsupportive« wrote Javier Cercas in The Guardian, 15.04.2020; cf. Cercas: The EU was Created to Keep Nationalism in Check.
[39] Cf. Mauss: The Gift.
[40] Treaty of Rome.

is grounded), became the only possibility for the extension of the *Life* of the EU system beyond the necro-politics of the Corona crisis.

It is by reading Mary Douglas's *Foreword* to Mauss's *The Gift*, I believe, that the paradigm of law-as-culture can offer further support to interpret the future of the EU polity beyond its ›sacred Euro‹. By commenting Mauss's work, Mary Douglas remarks how in any functioning community *there are no free gifts*, as only by means of reciprocity and counter-exchanges (i.e. by returning the gift) mutuality can be promoted among the members of the society: exempting the recipient from any return, »puts the act of giving outside any mutual ties. […] A gift that does nothing to enhance solidarity is a contradiction«.[41] If a striking parallelism can be drawn between the gift's mechanism of giving and returning and the nature of currency (*nomisma*) as ›monetary *nomos*‹ (in the bilateral correspondence of people *giving* political credit to the sovereign so they *receive* economic credit through money: see Introduction), it is again in the idea of reciprocity that a great lesson can be drawn from the Coronavirus recovery plan, and a great opportunity for a historic change for the EU polity may be carried out as well.

In this regard, Ferdinando Giugliano, Bloomberg Opinion Editor and former member of the editorial board of the Financial Times, has significantly written that the rescue fund »would break many taboos, possible paving the way for EU taxes and EU treasury«.[42] The final deal that followed Ursula von der Leyen's proposal, in fact, could mark a radical transformation (a new *Life*) for Europe:

»The fund breaks a number of EU taboos. First, it raises significantly the amount the Commission can borrow on the financial markets. These are not »euro bonds« in the classic sense of the word […]. However, it will be a very useful blueprint if the euro zone chooses to move closer to a much-needed fiscal union. The second big change is that two-thirds of the money would [be] given away as grants. This is the most controversial part of the plan, and it risks being watered down in the forthcoming negotiations between member states. […] But the generous provision of grants is a step change from the European Stability Mechanism, the euro area's rescue fund, which only offers loans. The final taboo to be possibly broken is on EU-wide taxation.«[43]

Waiting for the rescue of the sacred Euro and an economic resurrection of the EU from the Coronavirus pandemic, a political metamorphosis may actually take place, where the provision of grants may settle the solidarity of Schuman Declaration ›back to the future‹ of the EU by strengthening mutual ties (EU taxation, EU shared debt, EU fiscal union) on the grounds that gifts that do not enhance solidarity are, indeed, a contradiction (see Douglas, above).

---

[41] Douglas: Foreword, pp. x f.
[42] Giugliano: The European Union Is on the Brick of Historic Change.
[43] Ibid.

Hence, in challenging the *sacertas* of the Euro and in the wake for a common response to a global threat, for once »political stars may be aligned. If so, 2020 might be remembered in Europe as more than just the year of the pandemic«.[44] As stars can lead sailors in their common journey, saving them from the perils of the sea and the danger of shipwrecking, this might be, indeed, a historical opportunity for the EU to move from the EU market to a coherent EU polity by a new *nomos* backing its *nomisma*. After 70 years from WWII, the common destiny of European citizens will depend, once again, on how the stars of the EU flag will direct their path.

Afterword

Ironically enough, the final proofreading of this paper before publication occurred in the precise days (17–19 July 2020) in which the EU summit in charge of negotiating/approving the recovery plan proposed by the EU Commission (see § 3) was taking place. I trust that the reader will find in the text good points to make his/her own evaluation about the summit development and final outcomes.

References

Agamben, Giorgio: Homo Sacer. Sovereign Power and Bare Life, Stanford 1998.
Agamben, Giorgio: State of Exception, Chicago 2005.
Aristotle: The Nicomachean Ethics, London 2004.
Blumenberg, Hans: Money or Life: Metaphors of Georg Simmel's Philosophy, in: Theory, Culture & Society, 29(7/8), 2012, pp. 249–262.
Cercas, Javier: The EU was Created to Keep Nationalism in Check. Coronavirus is a Dangerous Test, in: The Guardian, 15.04.2020, https://www.theguardian.com/books/2020/apr/15/the-eu-was-created-to-keep-nationalism-in-check-coronavirus-is-a-dangerous-test; last accessed 12.05.2020.
Douglas, Mary: Foreword. No Free Gifts, in: Mauss, Marcel: The Gift. The Form and Reason for Exchange in Archaic Societies, London/New York 1990, pp. ix–xxiii.
European Council: Solemn Declaration on European Union, Stuttgart 19.06.1983, in: Bulletin of the European Communities, No. 6/1983, aei.pitt.edu/1788/1/stuttgart_declaration_1983.pdf; last accessed 01.06.2020.

[44] Ibid.

Giugliano, Ferdinando: The European Union Is on the Brick of Historic Change, in: Bloomberg 31.05.2020, https://www.bloomberg.com/opinion/articles/2020-05-27/eu-pandemic-recovery-fund-puts-europe-on-brink-of-historic-change; last accessed 05.06.2020.

Mauss, Marcel: The Gift. Forms and Functions of Exchange in Archaic Societies, London 1954.

Mbembe, Achille: Necropolitics, Durham/NC 2019.

Schuman, Robert: The Schuman Declaration, 09.05.1950, https://europa.eu/european-union/about-eu/symbols/europe-day/schuman-declaration_en; last accessed 03.06.2020.

Simmel, George: The Philosophy of Money, London 1978.

Treaty of Rome – Treaty Establishing the European Economic Community (EEC Treaty), https://eur-lex.europa.eu/legal-content/EN/TXT/?uri=LEGISSUM%3Axy0023; last accessed 03.06.2020.

Vallée, Shain: Coronavirus has Revealed the EU's Fatal Flaw: The Lack of Solidarity, in: The Guardian, 28.04.2020, https://www.theguardian.com/commentisfree/2020/apr/28/eu-coronavirus-fund-share-crisis-soul-european-parliament-fiscal; last accessed 25.05.2020.

Varoufakis, Yanis: The EU's New Coronavirus Relief Deal is a Gift to Europe's Enemies, in: The Guardian, 11.04.2020, https://www.theguardian.com/world/commentisfree/2020/apr/11/eu-coronavirus-relief-deal-enemies-debt-eurozone, last accessed 20.05.2020.

Theresa Strombach

Stay (At) Home – A Linguistic View on Imperatives in Times of Crisis

When being confronted with borders and restrictions, problems and obstacles, fears and worries to an unprecedented extent, it might be the least of these worries to care about things like grammar. But surprisingly: It is not. It is, of course, not the first, but it is neither the least. People seem to suddenly care about an (oh so inappropriate) compound like *Öffnungsdiskussionsorgien* (which already ranks as a top candidate for the *Unwort des Jahres* 2020[1]). They seem to care if a newscaster or a journalist is talking about *den Virus*, instead of *das Virus*. They seem to even care whether it has to be either #stayhome or #stayathome.

Fig.1: Grizelda, Grammar Police.

Are we thus playing grammar police, when caring about language in times of corona? Maybe. But we are particularly observing linguistic developments and habits of a society in crisis. According to a corpus analysis of the language of Covid-19 by *Oxford English Dictionary* the word *coronavirus* has – when it comes to frequency – not only overwhelmed »[...] words referring to other major news topics in recent times [...]«[2] like *climate*, *Brexit*, and *impeachment* by far, but it does also exceed »[...] one of the most frequently-used nouns in the English language [...]«[3], namely: *time*. Moreover, there is a huge number of new expressions which are not only appearing, but spreading (quite pandemically) in official as well as private life, among them obviously lots of (more or less complex) terms with ›restrictive‹ character, such as *self-isolation* or *social distancing*, and some kind of ›protective‹ imperatives[4] like *keep distance*, *flatten the curve* or *stay (at)*

---

[1] Cf. Neuhann: Ein Unwort, das nachhallen wird.
[2] Cf. Oxford English Dictionary: Corpus Analysis of the Language of Covid-19.
[3] Ibid.
[4] Some imperatives like *Bleib gesund!* or *Bleiben Sie gesund!* (= *Stay healthy!*) even advance to new leave-taking expressions, both in spoken and written communication.

home. So let's have a look at imperatives as linguistic products[5] in times of crisis — or (at least for that matter): let's even play grammar police!

The imperative is a grammatical mood that is used to express commands, requests or suggestions. If we try to abstract the intended purpose of somehow ›corona-specific‹ imperatives like the above mentioned, this might lead to a public call for self-discipline for the good (or in fact: the health) of society as a whole. However, a closer look reveals that these imperatives are not as utilitarian as one might suppose: They rather emphasize that it's up to each and every person to literally behave as ordered in order to protect individuals at risk.

Places, where people from more than one household tend to meet (in particular: supermarkets, stores, restaurants etc.) have to communicate these orders, not only in the spirit of solidarity, but in order to implement the newest ordinance. That is why posters and notices concerning infection-preventive measures might be especially suitable to analyze imperatives and their normativity in everyday life. The following pilot analysis will focus on such posters and notices spotted in the city of Bonn.[6]

In general, we can observe two main types of imperatives:[7]

(1) prototypic imperative sentences, which are introduced[8] by a finite verb, either a genuine imperative form[9] (e. g. *Halte Abstand*), an indicative form (e. g. *Haltet Abstand*, see Fig. 2a) or a distance form with the pronoun *Sie* (e. g. *Halten Sie Abstand*, see Fig. 2b), and (2) elliptic sentences with imperative meaning, including an infinitive (stem + *-en*) without *zu* (e. g. *Abstand halten*, see Fig. 3). Although they are combined with an explicit politeness particle like *bitte*, infinite imperatives, which are mainly used in asymmetrical contexts, seem to be rather functional than polite.[10]

Furthermore, people obviously tend to verbalize imperatives by using simple declarative sentences,[11] in particular with a verb in the first person plural (e. g. *Wir halten Abstand*, see Fig. 4). Such expressions[12] remind very much of the so-called

---

[5] Regarding the sovereignty of an (seemingly) alternativeless »virological imperative« cf. Gabriel: Warum der virologische Imperativ auch gefährlich ist.

[6] My warmest thanks go to Philine Schramek for taking and providing significant photographs from all of Bonn and of course to Professor Werner Gephart for inspiring me to have a look at this collection of material from a linguistic perspective.

[7] Cf. Duden: Die Grammatik, marginal no. 785 ff.

[8] There are two more types of so-called verb-first-clauses (cf. Duden: Die Grammatik, marginal no. 1343): yes-no-questions and unintroduced subordinate clauses with (usually) conditional meaning.

[9] A specific imperative form is only existent in the singular. It comes from the 1. Stammform (stem) of the verb, supplemented by *-e*, but the final schwa can mostly be apocopated. In the plural we use indicative forms, more precise: second person plural indicative in the present tense (cf. Duden: Die Grammatik, marginal no. 609 f.).

[10] Cf. Duden: Die Grammatik, marginal no. 794.

[11] Cf. Duden: Die Grammatik, marginal no. 793.

[12] See also the following writing, which embellishs a bank branch in exposed location in the city center of Bonn: »Auch wir halten die Anordnungen der Bundesrepublik ein.«

Fig. 2a & 2b: Imperatives with finite verbs.   Fig. 3: Imperatives with infinite verbs.

Fig: 4: Declarative sentences with imperative meaning.

adhortative, but differ with regard to topological criteria: The adhortative is not only characterized by a certain intonation structure, but also by a defined placement of verb and pronoun, technically: by verb-first positioning. On the contrary, sentences like the above show verb-second word order, which is characteristic of declaratives. Therefore, the imperative meaning has to result either from other features, like punctuation techniques (i. e. exclamation marks) or modal particles (see Fn. 12), or it has to be non-compositional, that is to say: The possibility of an imperative interpretation might arise from the overall construction.

Altogether, it is hardly surprising, that a verbal phrase like *Abstand halten* ranks among the most common constituents of imperative sentences in times of Covid-19. The same applies to several predicatives with the copula *bleiben*, especially *zuhause* (or without univerbation: *zu Hause*) *bleiben* and *gesund bleiben* (see Fig. 5). Of course, it might not be too much to ask someone to *keep distance*

Fig. 5: Imperative sentence with copula and predicative expression.

or to *stay at home*. But how to *stay healthy*? Easier said than done! In principle, imperatives can only occur, if the required operation can be controlled by the subject: »Von manchen Verben sind Imperativformen unüblich oder überhaupt nicht zu erwarten. Das ist der Fall, wenn das Verb einen Vorgang beschreibt, der nicht unter der Kontrolle des Subjektaktanten steht.«[13]

Nevertheless, even the Federal State Government of North Rhine-Westphalia[14] asks us not only to *stay healthy*, but also to *stay informed* (*Bleiben Sie gesund – Bleiben Sie informiert*), which – at first glance – can be managed more easily. But when staying informed does also mean to keep track of all those innumerable ordinances, both imperatives seem to be equally illusive. Moreover, premises tend to change every day: Restrictions are imposed and abolished again, measures are taken and eased up, and *Verbote* (›prohibitions‹) shall be gradually replaced by *Gebote* (›requirements‹).[15]

It is at least questionable, how such a replacement becomes apparent on a linguistic level: Maybe things are no longer *untersagt* (›prohibited‹), but people are *angehalten* (›obliged, required‹) to refrain from them (which would still conflict with the original definition of *Gebot*, but so what) – or maybe it might initiate

---

[13] Cf. Duden: Die Grammatik, marginal no. 792.
[14] Cf. Landesregierung NRW: Coronavirus in Nordrhein-Westfalen.
[15] See the linked initiative of Thuringia's Prime Minister Ramelow, cf. Jaeger: Gebote statt Verbote.

some kind of *imperative turn*, introducing imperative sentences (as a recent feature of legal texts) to a completely new genre: ordinances and laws. With that in mind: Let's *stay at home*, *healthy* and – above all – *law-abiding*.

References

Duden: Die Grammatik, ninth, completely revised and updated edition, edited by Angelika Wöllstein, Berlin 2016.

Gabriel, Markus: Warum der virologische Imperativ auch gefährlich ist, in: NZZ, 26.03.2020, https://www.nzz.ch/feuilleton/coronavirus-warum-der-virologische-imperativ-auch-gefaehrlich-ist-ld.1548594; last accessed 16.06.2020.

Jaeger, Mona: Gebote statt Verbote, in: FAZ, 24.05.2020, https://www.faz.net/aktuell/politik/inland/ramelow-macht-tempo-gib-es-bald-gebote-statt-verbote-16783935.html; last accessed 16.06.2020.

Landesregierung NRW: Coronavirus in Nordrhein-Westfalen, https://www.land.nrw/corona; last accessed 16.06.2020.

Neuhann, Florian: Ein Unwort, das nachhallen wird, in: ZDF.de, 20.04.2020, https://www.zdf.de/nachrichten/politik/coronavirus-oeffnungsdiskussionsorgien-merkel-kommentar-100.html; last accessed 16.06.2020.

Oxford English Dictionary: Corpus Analysis of the Language of Covid-19, https://public.oed.com/blog/corpus-analysis-of-the-language-of-covid-19/; last accessed 16.06.2020.

List of Figures

Fig. 1: Grizelda, Grammar Police. Reproduced with the permission of the copyright owner The Spectator.

Fig. 2a & 2b: Imperatives with finite verbs. Reproduced with the permission of the photographer Philine Schramek.

Fig. 3: Imperatives with infinite verbs. Reproduced with the permission of the photographer Philine Schramek.

Fig. 4: Declarative sentences with imperative meaning. Reproduced with the permission of the photographer Philine Schramek.

Fig. 5: Imperative sentence with copula and predicative expression. Reproduced with the permission of the photographer Philine Schramek.

Theresa Hanske

Knigge in Times of Corona – Recognition, Attentiveness and Esteem

We are all by now familiar with the distancing and hygiene regulations that came into effect several weeks ago in order to contain the coronavirus epidemic. When such measures were tightened from recommendations to regulations, the reasoning behind them and their justification moved from protecting oneself to protecting oneself and others. Numerous placards, loudspeaker announcements, and other actions in public areas document the efforts to render the measures plausible by appealing to a sense of responsibility and community. They are primarily calls to thoughtfully include others more than usual – to treat each other respectfully, show consideration, and protect each other.

In the beginning, it was very popular, especially in the media, to call these rules »Coronavirus-Knigge«[1] and then also have behavioral coaches express their views on this matter. They were expected to reconcile the measures with common expectations of courtesy. This seemed to be a suitable way of making the rules of conduct known and, at the same time, facilitating compliance by anticipating possible uncertainties and thinking« them through. The experts on »correct« behavior hardly ever failed to refer to the ratio of courtesy in general, which involves mutual respect and meeting on an equal footing – one may well see this as a somewhat trivialized formulation of recognition of the other as a free and equal person.

Conduct books from the last 250 years are full of regulations, demands, and explanations which suggest that recognizing the other is the moral foundation of courtesy in general. Although this initially seems to be quite obvious, from a historical point of view, the usual caution about anachronism is appropriate. Undoubtedly, this moral maxim was only able to develop as a result of the creation of the modern concepts of tolerance and identity. And yet in conduct books – between the classical demands of unconditional attention, de-centering oneself, and avoidance of talking about religion – education in recognition of the other seems to have its origin.[2]

---

[1]   In Germany »Knigge« is the collective term for conduct books and social manners. It is a metonymical development of meaning derived from Adolph Freiherr von Knigge, author of *Über den Umgang mit Menschen* [On Human Relations] (first edition 1788, Hannover: Schmidt; with countless new editions up to today). Though Knigge's book is not considered to be an etiquette book in the stricter sense, it was influential for naming this genre.

[2]   For an extensive bibliography of conduct books published in Germany between the 16th and

1. Recognition as Esteem

Recognition is known to be a multifaceted term. Depending on its context and theoretical or ideological orientation, it can range from a mere attribution of dignity or respect to an interpretation of esteem. Its ambiguity between a moral category and an ordinary, material interpretation, viz. rights or perhaps money, is responsible for its notorious vagueness in discourse.

With regard to the moral category, the question is what sort of recognition – respect or esteem – does society, politics, and the public in general owe the individual. Opting for esteem, the question obviously arises on how to measure it, and in capitalism »achievement« is infamously considered to be the most promising benchmark. Although it should be considered whether an attribute – however defined – should be decisive for systemic relevance in a crisis situation. But there are also other reasons for having reservations about generalizing esteem as a normative basis. In this sense, recognition really seems to be too precarious of an issue, which all too easily can be withdrawn or become an empty phrase. Therefore, quite a few points indicate that esteem should be reserved as a normative basis for familial bonds, intimate relationships, and friendship, while leaving it at recognition in the sense of respect within the public domain and regarding all government actions.

There is no doubt that we need esteem for our mental wellbeing. It seems doubtful, however, that it has to evenly penetrate all aspects of our lives. From this perspective, the generalization of esteem seems to largely arise from a longing to organize society as a whole, as well as our lives within it, from the private area of life, and thus overcome alienation and fragmentation.

Those who interpret labor disputes, feminist struggles, anti-colonial liberation efforts, and fights against racism as struggles for recognition do not realize that they were and are about the dissolution of a certain social relationship – and largely not about a basic mental need. There can be no disagreement that exploitative relationships also have mental correlates. But to analytically reduce them to claims of disregard or recognition rather conceals the materialistic and sometimes violent foundations that maintain them.

20th centuries, cf. Montandon: Bibliographie; additionally, for 1870 to 1970, cf. the appendix in Krumrey: Entwicklungsstrukturen von Verhaltensstandarden. A good overview of the history of the ideals of behavior in theories of propriety can be found in Döcker: Zur Konstruktion des ›bürgerlichen Menschen‹. For good manners as a connection between a moral and an aesthetical lifestyle under special consideration of Knigge's *Über den Umgang mit Menschen*, cf. Pompe: In der Welt zu Hause. Concerning the question of parallel development of terms of tolerance and courtesy, cf. Thomas: In Pursuit of Civility.

2. Recognition by Reserved Attentiveness

On the one hand, conduct books, with their »intent to educate«, keep in mind the recognition of the other. On the other, it is probably unsurprising to find that they rarely go as far as comprehending or even demanding recognition in the sense of esteem. They create a different ideal, namely that of reserved attentiveness. As a rule, they recommend an attentiveness which is nevertheless coupled with a certain restraint, but without turning it into indifference. To the authors of conduct books this attitude seems to be best suited for maintaining the autonomy of the other as well as of the self. This is often substantiated by a warning not to get carried away and accept the other's position with no questions asked; or by the assurance that not contradicting is not the same as agreeing. Advice to maintain an inner distance is often linked with a warning of being too close. This is done with the intention of preventing claims from being derived from courteous and quite friendly interaction.

In a strict sense, conduct books only cover certain sections of life and thereby define their own field of application. Their point is not to say what behavior with family, friends, or intimate partners is or should be like. For a long time, they mainly tended to the half-public area of conviviality. Nowadays, of course, the workplace takes up a prominent amount of room. No matter how much etiquette books call for authenticity and naturalness, they explicitly do not propagate carrying needs and behaviors from close range into other areas of life. In them, not only is society functionally differentiated, but everyday life also differentiates itself. Etiquette manuals are not always clear on this, but it is their basic tendency to maintain the borders between private and half-public life – even when (and where) these borders are in danger of being weakened, such as with working from home due to the coronavirus. Such demarcations are, for instance, recommendations to wear clothing suitable for the office and have a neutral background when joining an online meeting from home.

3. »Thank You to All Helpers for Their Efforts during the Corona Pandemic«: Esteem Discourse in Times of Crisis

Over the past weeks, aides in hospitals and nursing homes, employees in supermarkets, and workers in postal service, logistics, public transportation, and refuse collection received much acclaim. They were applauded from balconies and thanked by posters all across town. The Cologne public transit system put »Thank you to all helpers« as the moving text on their display screens. The media praised everybody who kept the supply chain intact during the pandemic. This discourse about esteem, celebrated as an example of solidarity by some yet warily scrutinized by others, is even now a solid point of reference in comments, interviews, and articles.

The corona crisis has revealed the structural flaws in healthcare and nursing, and raised the question of working conditions and protection of employees, especially in jobs considered essential. High levels of sickness (mostly not due to corona infection) in businesses where people are still working make the situation even tenser. As the esteem discourse itself demonstrates, the crisis seems to have reversed the struggles for recognition as discussed in recognition theories. Recognition came from »the top« – from politics and even private balconies – before it had been demanded by anybody. In view of bad equipment, poor pay, and unfit working conditions, all determined by the system, not corona, these cheap acknowledgements leave a nasty taste in many people's mouths. Under the slogan, »Applause is not enough!«, demands are being articulated for better pay and special premiums, as well as for the cost-effective financing and abolition of flat rates for hospital stays.

The »granted« esteem is not only stale. It is also contradictory, as it accompanies political measures which are actually the opposite of what it pretends to be. The hollowing out of work time regulations and discussions about a reduction of minimum wage must be mentioned here. In the end, the promised corona one-off payments also only became a reality for a couple of sectors (goods trade and nursing).

The esteem discourse is ambivalent. Because of the corona crisis, the condition of health and nursing systems, as well as the precarious situation of many employees with low wages, has become evident. In this context, the esteem discourse itself has also brought such employees into the center of attention and thereby, as it initially seemed, opened possibilities to make their long overdue demands be taken up by politics and employers. But it turns out that in the end, the willingness of employers and politics did not go that far. In an interview in the weekend edition of *Neues Deutschland* from May 30/31, 2020, Frank Werneke, head of the services union Ver.di, made clear that he does not expect an improvement of the employees' situation to automatically follow from esteem:

»[ND:] At the moment everybody is talking about esteem of retail employees, nurses, and educators. Does that help the unions to argue for better working conditions?

[FW:] I would like to be convinced of something different, maybe I am too pessimistic: But my guess is that everything that right now is under the magnifying glass – financing of hospitals, working conditions in nursing care, often no union wages in the retail trade, the mini-jobbers who are now without protection as well as the solo self-employed with low income – very soon will be forgotten again. Furthermore, this feeling of esteem at the moment is declining with employees.«[3]

---

[3] Wallrodt: »Aus Dankbarkeit passiert nichts«, p. 4; transl. by the author.

One may well be surprised that Frank Werneke accepts the in fact already disqualified term »esteem« at all. By granting esteem, a framework for the whole discourse has been created from which, as it seems, none of the parties involved can really escape. As already hinted at above, with regard to their implicatures (in the Gricean sense), terms like »recognition« and »esteem« create ambiguous structures of discourse. It is no longer clear whether they are to be understood as moral categories, or if other things, like better pay or special premiums, will be their outcome. This allows one side to cancel certain implicatures: not having included a certain intention and thus representing claims as illegitimate. Reversely, the other side can insist on implicatures only when it is clear from what term they usually, and under other circumstances, result. Therefore, it is difficult to give up the term »esteem« completely in such a debate without risking that in its course, the demands will again stand isolated and unconnected in the discursive sphere.

References

Döcker, Ulrike: Zur Konstruktion des ›bürgerlichen Menschen‹. Verhaltensideale und Lebenspraxis im Prozeß der ›Verbürgerlichung‹, in: Österreichische Zeitschrift für Geschichtswissenschaft, 1(3), 1990, pp. 7–47.

Knigge, Adolph Freiherr von: Über den Umgang mit Menschen, Hannover 1788.

Krumrey, Horst-Volker: Entwicklungsstrukturen von Verhaltensstandarden. Eine soziologische Prozeßanalyse auf der Grundlage deutscher Anstands- und Manierenbücher von 1870 bis 1970, Frankfurt am Main 1984.

Montandon, Alain: Bibliographie des traités de savoir-vivre de langue allemande, Clermont-Ferrand 1989.

Pompe, Hedwig: In der Welt zu Hause: Der gute Ton, in: Anna Ananieva / Dorothea Böck / Hedwig Pompe (eds.): Geselliges Vergnügen: kulturelle Praxis von Unterhaltung im langen 19. Jahrhundert. Bielefeld 2011, pp. 253–282.

Thomas, Keith: In Pursuit of Civility. Manners and Civilization in Early Modern England, Waltham 2018.

Wallrodt, Ines: »Aus Dankbarkeit passiert nichts«. Verdi-Chef Frank Werneke über Wertschätzung und niedrige Gehälter, Streiks in der Altenpflege, Staatsverschuldung und Vermögensabgabe, in: Neues Deutschland, 30./31.05.2020, pp. 4–5.

Sanja Bojanić / Petar Bojanić

The »Vocabulary« of Distance

How has ›distance‹ come about? Has there been a transformation of thinking distance? Does its normalization and subsequent normativization announce a paradigmatic shift ›about‹ distance? An important note about the present thematization of ›distance‹ is that it has emerged from observations of sanitary processes, as well as political and institutional decisions made during the 2020 pandemic, including the coercions and restrictions it caused.

We begin thinking distance physically or geographically through the arbitrary 1.5- or 2-meters gap, as physical or geographic space, space between, understanding displacement and occupation of empty spaces in any world that could – but does not have to – have points of overlap. We think distance through circles, nuclei that do not touch or intersect, designed to fit persons in their rooms and physical houses, hospital wings, quarantined neighborhoods, cities, regions, states, even islands, and continents. Assigned inter-space are thus marked in concentric circles, while AI algorithms process carefully inputted values to produce models, short-term or long-term predictions of sundry scientific and social responses, in order to both prevent the disease spread, reduce its negative effects, but also construct several scenarios that span the transition towards still unknown novel social relations. Hence, the measurement of distance in the present moment should be conducted through the coordinate system and equations with variables consisting of general biological processes like life, contamination, infection, transmission, as well as immunity and autoimmunity. These elements of course belong to the same thesaurus and can be visually represented through multidimensional value sets.

In the next step, however, it is important to think distance as an epistemological process (people in the world think the world, but also themselves within that world) that (1.) connects various elements of reality or the same elements of various realities; (2.) with their conspicuous mixing, these elements become unavoidably interactive; (3.) in that interaction they find their naming reason; and (4.) they might cause an (albeit not necessarily causal) chain of events that turn the phenomenon and revived concept of ›distance‹ into necessity for any thematization of social relations.

Nevertheless, the first step in delineating the ›vocabulary‹ of distance is not testing and processing the word itself, but rather in seeking those elements due to which thinking distance turns into the word ›distance‹, and then the concept in which ›distancing‹ is an operative vector.

We have embarked on this adventure following Michel Foucault and his phrase *vocabulaire de la distance*, used in a 1963 manifesto-text, commenting on the status of ›fiction‹ in relation to reality. His intention was to scrub the use of words and contradictions that sustain fiction (so easily ›dialecticalizing‹ it); seeking, instead, the confrontation or abolition of the [opposition] of the subjective and objective, the interior and exterior, the real and imaginary. Indeed, Foucault wanted to substitute »a mixed lexicography« (*lexique du mélange*)[1] with *le vocabulaire de la distance*, in order to show that the fictional is by its nature the distance of language in relation to things.

Historically, the methods used in ethnography, sociology, anthropology, social psychology applied to describe, map, measure, analyze distance and construct models of social distancing, *distanciation sociale*, and social distance, have, especially with the introduction of new techniques and technologies, varied in their degrees of pragmatism. Rarely have they been unequivocal, reaching for economic, political, ideological input from neighboring disciplines. They included increasingly complex terms to describe newly-observed factors and develop first diagrammatic and then parametric structure of social relations. The human world gradually lost its one-dimensionality, becoming the world of all living beings and things; the old, human coordinate system became more inclusive. Consider the great expansion in use of microscopes and telescopes in the seventeenth century, rendering visible the infinitesimally small and apparent the unfathomably distant. By simply shifting the scale of what was perceivable, the human relationship to distance became more complex: the tiny world of bacteria and cells was brought closer in vision, but further away in otherness. From its very first explorations by Robert Hooke[2] and Antoni van Leeuwenhoek[3] to the present moment and our grappling with the nature of Covid-19, humans have had to open up room – set themselves at a distance – for the otherness it sought to include.

Recall that for Georg Simmel's operationalization of distance manifested in problematizing the stranger. He introduces the notion of spatial sociology, thus categorizing distance in social world differentiating »the wanderer«, »the outsider«, and »the stranger« – and the last must never be classified as complete reject: »the stranger« is so close yet far, loosely connected to the community, while the reject is so very far away.[4] Simmel connects the idea of the stranger and concept of social distance with the category of humanity. More important still for the present understanding of transformation of social distance, the category of humanity is considered through a three-dimensional Euclidean coordinate system. Social dis-

---

[1] Cf. Tel Quel: Théorie d'Ensemble.
[2] Cf. Hooke: Micrographia.
[3] Cf. Leeuwenhoek: Alle de Brieven van Antoni van Leeuwenhoek.
[4] Cf. Simmel: The Sociology of Georg Simmel.

tance is defined as a social gap between social groups, with a clear effort to delimit definite categorizations of race, ethnicity, gender, and other divisions that would become the clichés of the twentieth century. (After all, the stranger too becomes a versatile figure imputed with myriad biases.) In the univalence of such a coordinate system, having never belonged to a group, but precisely in his non-belonging, the stranger was always the factor of its consolidation. In the course of the nineteenth and twentieth centuries, social distancing solidified into a process in which acceptance and separation, assimilation and rejection served the purpose of well-known binary opposite models: urban/rural, young/old, white/color, individual/community. The consequences have been complex and lasting, as they expressed themselves through different systems of values when it comes to describing social distancing in various disciplines. Lest we forget, in the history of emancipatory movements, the struggle against segregation began first in the abolition of various *de jure* segregations, only later taking up the far more difficult task of rooting out *de facto* segregation.

In sharpening the struggle against binaries, we must certainly mention Adolf Reinach. Namely, in the early twentieth century, using the phenomenology of binaries, Reinach identified the existence of certain negative social acts (*negative soziale Akte*).[5] He indicated the imaginary difference between negative social acts and simple negative acts, which fits into the image of social distance as distinct from physical distance. The effort Reinach deployed to think the construction of social distance and negative social acts is inversely proportional to the present moment necessitating the opposite process of thinking. What remains of social relations if they are shaped in a situation in which distance, the elementary, separates two bodies that have no contact? How can we determine the gap that still assumes or implies partial or imaginary belonging to a social group? What is taking place between two bodies that do not touch or approach one another, even if they are able to move closer or towards others?

Although social distance indicates a clear presence and existence of another – in contrast with Simmel, this other is similar to us, standing at a commensurable and sufficient length from us – it would appear that such a concept of the other has certain unusual characteristics: the other not one who can determine us and upon whom we depend; the other cannot be assimilated or reduced its difference to us; the speech of the other is not my speech; with the other, one cannot work or conduct joint work; with the other, one cannot walk together, eat together, shake hands, nor can the other either be guest or host. All the basic forms of closeness and intimacy implemented and regulated through social distance could be further defined and reconstructed more precisely for the purpose of seeking its opposite: the meaning of ›social‹ in the phrase ›social distance‹. The other at a distance is

---

5   Cf. Reinach: Die sozialen Akte; and Reinach: Nichtsoziale und soziale Akte.

one to whom we are necessarily different (which difference or differentiation produces distance), and this other is substantively unlike us.

Further, the »pathos of distance« as formulated by Nietzsche is not different to Levinas' insistence on the existence on the otherness of the other, the absolute other (so other that they are God or enemy, and therefore not at all close or intimate, which brings us back to Simmel). Nietzsche's formulation was at some point interesting, as it described a specific effort characteristic of certain epochs for distance or differentiation to be aggressively produced in relation to the other or another body. Thus, a basic feature of distance is its auto-referential dimension or imperative. And it is entirely current today, when we hear the speech act: »keep your distance!« or »*faire de la distance!*«[6]

It is important here to mention one further reference: Aby Warburg, upon whom many twentieth-century semioticians have drawn, laments monumental art, contrasting »bourgeois ›primitive‹ desire to grasp things and to demand ›palpable‹ detailed and concrete art with a more civilized attitude,« thus actually introducing a critical perspective on taste that ought to be the first test in distance-practicing. Warburg writes: »there is no more distance!« [es gibt keine Entfernung mehr!], adding immediately: »*Du lebst und thust mir nichts!*« (You live and do me no harm!).[7] Even the misunderstood Warburg considered distancing a recipe and desirable form of acting and thinking.

What does this speech act really say? Does it now carry a new meaning, sure to transform our vocabulary of distance? What do the slogans ›keep clear,‹ ›do not touch (me)‹ or else ›I have nothing to do with you‹ (even though I am aware of you and your proximity), but also, ›I do not wish to be hurt or contaminated by you,‹ ›I do not wish to be mortal like you, to be given your mortality,‹ ›I do not wish to receive that of which you too should be free or clear‹ (that which is alien – virus, corruptibility, or mortality). Such resistance to the other, in reality producing distance, almost certainly gives an illusion that some simple, separated life (or one's one bare life) or life that is not communal or in a group, is even possible.

Is it really a matter of mere or bare life (*bloßes Leben*), that is, a life that seems to precede everything not itself (and thus also law, i.e. norm)? What is this bare life? Recall that Walter Benjamin uses the phrase »*bloßes Leben,*« four times in *Zur Kritik der Gewalt,* while Giorgio Agamben unjustifiably turns into »bare life« (*nuda vita*),[8] *nacktes Leben* in *Homo sacer.* The same happens in *Nudità*, where the phrase *nuda corporeità* makes an appearance.[9] For the sake of accuracy and for the sake of later repercussions in this brief dictionary of distance, it should be

6 Cf. Lütticken: Keep Your Distance.
7 Cf. Warburg: Fragments sur l'expression.
8 Agamben: Homo sacer, p. 75.
9 Cf. Agamben: Nudità, p. 89.

added that Benjamin uses this phrase in order to oppose Kurt Hiller and his position that existence as such is more important than happiness and a just existence or life (»*Falsch und niedrig ist der Satz, dass Dasein höher als gerechtes Dasein stehe, wenn Dasein nichts als bloßes Leben bedeutet soll – und in dieser Bedeutung steht er in der genannten Überlegung*«).[10]

But let us go step by step, for when it comes to semiotic constraints of life, it is particularly important to move through the first two decades of the twentieth century: What, in the first place, is life? Specifically, what is the life of one living (*la vie d'un vivant*)?[11] At the beginning of his lecture *La nouvelle connaissance de la vie* from 1966, Canguilhem is clear: »By life, we mean the present participle or the past participle of the verb to live, the living and the lived«.[12] Positivist and functional, the definition from the beginning of the nineteenth century is sufficiently convincing: »Life is a set of functions that resists death«.[13] A variation of this position is also put forward by Claude Bernard in *Définition de la vie*, published 1875 in *La Revue de deux mondes*. »A surgeon at the school in Paris, Pelletan, teaches that life is the resistance offered by organized matter to causes that seek ceaselessly to destroy it«.[14] This definition incorporates a negation into itself: the negation and end of life, but it also implies a concept of organization or plurality of functions that life ought to possess in order to resist and withstand its own end. Thus, this definition that implies that life is a complex and complicated order still defies the fiction of »mere or bare life« (*bloßes Lebens*). In 1930, Georg Misch used the phrase »bloß menschliches Leben«.[15] The idea that life can be determined without the help of other terms, that life can be directly experienced is indeed empty banter. Heinrich Rickert assigns this fantasy to intuitive vitalism in the book *Die Philosophie des Lebens* with the claim: *Das bloße Leben halte ich für sinnlos*, because it is of no value and because it is naught but vegetating.[16] Bruno Bauch repeats this argument seven years later in *Philosophie des Lebens und Philosophie der Werte*. A little later, in the foreword of the second edition, Rickert writes: »I consider bare life meaningless. Only a philosophy of a meaningful life, which is always more than mere life, would seem to me to be a goal worthy of striving, and only based on the theory of non-living valid values that give meaning to life can promise that a goal will be achieved«.[17] Explaining over the course of a hundred places that *die Philosophie des bloßen Lebens* has no future whatsoever,

---

10 Benjamin: Zur Kritik der Gewalt, p. 62.
11 Cf. Canguilhem: Études d'histoire et de philosophie des sciences, p. 764.
12 Canguilhem: Vie, p. 335.
13 Bichat: Recherches physiologiques sur la vie et la mort, p. 57.
14 Bernard: Définition de la vie, p. 23.
15 Misch: Lebensphilosophie und Phänomenologie, p. 24.
16 Rickert: Philosophie des Lebens, p. 129.
17 Ibid. XI.

Rickert in a counterintuitive way and in opposition to his own constructive efforts, opens a clear path for thinking this very dimension of non/accountability of bare or mere life, and does so precisely through a construct and new concept of social distance that would come to be discussed nearly a century later.

In this confusion and *lexical mélange* – lest we forget Foucault – ruled on the one hand by polyvalent meanings of social distancing grounded in a functional differentiation of various social systems, while on the other, we find a very important biological dimension of life in general, and human life in particular – it is necessary to overcome the classical and standard understanding of social distancing. We will not find either Marx nor Polany, or else Norbert Elias or Helmuth Plessner helpful, nor even Bourdieu, since, as mentioned, the coordinate system and factors analyzed through measurement or forecasting of effects of distancing cannot display the complexity of the contemporary model of distance. In an endeavor to include this biological dimension of the life of humans (noting that biopolitical variations are also not satisfactory), what is needed is to indicate the very insufficiency of our natural language and a lack of a conceptual corpus with which to analyze this new form of social distance.

How come the descriptions, recommended laws, temporary measure of protection are all dominated by expert languages of biology, epidemiology, infectiology, and related disciplines? Do these expert fields have a firm grasp on the terminological *differentia specifica* among the key words of contagiousness, contamination, infection, transmission, hygiene, as well as immunity and autoimmunity, allowing them to no longer carry equivocation and confusion into the domain of lay and mass use? It would be useful to vectorize this use, that is, follow the various iterations in order to recognize factors presentable in a multidimensional coordinate system, in which the concept of distance would be pragmatic, but also have an unequivocal performative value. Perhaps it is not sufficient to be merely performative, but in its performativity to also not sow the negative emotions of fear and panic or animosity, but rather unreserved values of care. Let us not forget, however, the cultural backlash experienced by those doctors who pursued changes in habits and conventions: not even so long ago, in the mid-nineteenth century, the man to whom we owe the basic act of hand-washing, Ignaz Semmelweiss, perished, aged only fifty, isolated in a sanatorium for the insane, completely ignored.

Here are the questions from the beginning of the text, once again: How has ›distance‹ come about? Has there been a transformation of thinking distance? Does its normalization and subsequent normativization announce a paradigmatic shift ›about‹ distance? Seeking to formulate a problem through which these questions could be more easily answered, we will cite a recent marketing scheme at a California presentation of a new driverless car. The market had been primed; all the preconditions of production were completed when the pandemic struck. The CEO of The Steer Tech start-up, Anuja Sonalker, launched a PR campaign with the slogan »Humans are biohazards, machines are not«.[18] Leaving aside the benchmark analysis of intentions or motives, or the language coming to the rescue of finances, and indeed the market patterns of any start-up, the slogan provides a perfect chiasmus for pause and warning.

Humans – as living – are potentially detrimental to the lives of other humans. Much as other particularly mobile animals, mosquitos, rats, or other less widespread rodents, people are a biological danger, as they are vectors of disease spread to themselves and others. In opposition to previous preventive and hygienic discourses on epidemics, infections, pestilences, etc., the development of AI in conjunction with other processes of automation, allow for the formation of ethical, emotional, and ontologically neutral models that will in the near future allow humans to be thought of exclusively as a biological vector.

It is no longer merely matter of Warburg's noble formulation, »You live and do me no harm!«[19] that could not only aestheticize, but humanize Anuja Sonalker's statement; rather, by reconstructing ›the vocabulary of distance,‹ we could also closer establish the values that follow the determining vector of degree of protection to simultaneously preserve one's humanity and one's selfish need for self-preservation.

To employ the language of epidemiology, we are seeking two values of equal importance. The first is R *number* or the R_0 representing ›the basic reproduction number,‹ used to measure the transmission potential of any disease. It is the number of persons that an infect individual will, on average, pass the virus on to. R_0 is influenced by characteristics of the specific disease, i.e. how easily it passes from person to person. Our behavior largely impacts the R number. It is important to keep the R number value bellow 1, which means that the documented number of cases is shrinking. Anything above 1 suggests new cases and subsequent infections, or the situation of contagiousness. Still, the R number is not sufficient as it only shows the increase or decrease of an epidemic, but not how large it is. »R should always be considered alongside the number of people currently infected,« as explained on the UK government website,[20] continuing »If R equals 1 with 100,000 people currently infected, it is a very different situation to R equals 1 with 1,000 people currently infected«. In order to complete the picture, there is also the K number, or K value, as a metric used to shed light on the variations of the R number now in the context of all UK Covid-19 cases. It provides scientists with a more nuanced view of how the disease is spreading, rather than simply tracking whether it is spreading. While R number represents the average number of people a single infected person will go on to infect, K number highlights that not all

---

[18] Cf. Lekach: »It Took a Coronavirus Outbreak for Self-Driving Cars to Become More Appealing«.
[19] Warburg: Fragments sur l'expression.
[20] Government Office for Science: The Latest R Number Range for the UK.

infected people will go on to infect the same number. When K value is less than one, this indicates a high variation in spreading patterns. Dr Adam Kucharski, an expert at the London School of Hygiene and Tropical Medicine explained that: »The general rule is that the smaller the K value is, the more transmission comes from a smaller number of infectious people, Once K is below one, you have got the potential for super-spreading.«[21]

Why, then, would it be helpful to follow Warburg's advice to *keep the distance*, while rationalizing it with some scientific knowledge?[22] Let us resume that alongside R number, K number may determine how, when, and at what rate it will be possible to continue with life, revive quotidian habits without at any point endangering social relations or discriminating against anyone.

References

Agamben, Giorgio: Homo sacer. Il potere sovrano e la nuda vita, Torino 1995.
Agamben, Giorgio: Nudità, Roma 2009.
Benjamin, Walter: Zur Kritik der Gewalt und andere Aufsätze, Frankfurt 1965.
Bernard, Claude: Définition de la vie, Paris 2016.
Bichat, Xavier: Recherches physiologiques sur la vie et la mort, Paris 1800.
Canguilhem, Georges: Études d'histoire et de philosophie des sciences, Paris 2016.
Canguilhem, Georges: Vie, in: Encyclopædia Universalis S.A. Vol. 16, 1977, pp. 764–769.
Centre for the Mathematical Modelling of Infectious Diseases (CMMID) at the London School of Hygiene & Tropical Medicine, https://www.lshtm.ac.uk/research/centres/centre-mathematical-modelling-infectious-diseases; last accessed 26.06.2020.
Davis, Nicola: K Number. What Is the Coronavirus Metric That Could Be Crucial as Lockdown Eases?, in: The Guardian, 01.06.2020, https://www.theguardian.com/world/2020/jun/01/k-number-what-is-coronavirus-metric-crucial-lockdown-eases; last accessed 07.06.2020.
Government Office for Science: The Latest R Number Range for the UK, 15.05.2020; https://www.gov.uk/government/news/government-publishes-latest-r-number; last accessed 07.06.2020.
Hooke, Robert: Micrographia. The Project Gutenberg eBook 2005, http://www.gutenberg.org/ebooks/15491; last accessed 07.06.2020.

---

[21] Kurcharski cited by Davis: K Number.
[22] Cf. Centre for the Mathematical Modelling of Infectious Diseases.

Leeuwenhoek, Antoni van: Alle de brieven van Antoni van Leeuwenhoek, Deel 3, pp. 1679–1683, digitale bibliotheek voor de Nederlandse letteren, https://www.dbnl.org/tekst/leeu027alle03_01/leeu027alle03_01_0002.php#b0043 2005; last accessed 07.06.2020.

Lekach, Sasha: »It Took a Coronavirus Outbreak for Self-Driving Cars to Become More Appealing«, https://mashable.com/article/autonomous-vehicle-perception-coronavirus/?europe=true; last accessed 24.06.2020.

Lütticke, Sven: ›Keep Your Distance‹: Aby Warburg on Myth and Modern Art, in: Oxford Art Journal, 28(1), 2005, pp. 45–59.

Misch, Georg: Lebensphilosophie und Phänomenologie, Darmstadt 1975.

Reinach, Adolf: Die sozialen Akte (1913), in: Karl Schumann / Barry Smith (eds.): Sämtliche Werke, München 1989, pp. 158–169.

Reinach, Adolf: Nichtsoziale und soziale Akte (1911), in: Karl Schumann / Barry Smith (eds.): Sämtliche Werke, München 1989, pp. 355–360.

Rickert, Heinrich: Philosophie des Lebens, Tübingen 1922.

Simmel, Georg: The Sociology of Georg Simmel, New York 1908/1950.

Tel Quel: Théorie d'Ensemble: The Manifest of the de Tel Quel Collectif with Roland Barthes, Jacques Derrida and Michel Foucault followed by Jean-Louis Baudry, Jean-Joseph Goux, Jean-Louis Houdebine, Julia Kristeva, Philippe Sollers, and Jean Thibaudeau, Paris 1968.

Warburg, Aby: Fragments sur l'expression, Paris 2015.

III. In the Global Realm of Normativity

Raja Sakrani

Religious Co-narration of Corona

At the dawn of 2020, everyone was continuing their race: men of power and powerless citizens, economic giants and penniless little people, warriors and refugees, destroyers of the planet and defenders of colors and smells, of everything that still moves in the universe of the living. While the machines and machinists were roaring all over the world, some vague stories started emanating from China. An unknown virus presented itself as mysterious, elusive and *perhaps* dangerous. Then suddenly, as soon as the new protagonist took on a global dimension and spread at lightning speed, everything came to a sudden halt. We thought we couldn't brake, couldn't stop the installed mechanisms and turntables without respite. Individuals, families, institutions, and states suddenly came to a standstill, as if by magic unimaginable. The end of the Second World War lies far in the past, and *Homo sapiens* believe themselves to be invincible, as masters in control of land and sky, of the dead and the living.

Only, here, however, they are dethroned by a virulent virus that strikes hard until death – and, beyond damaging the human body and its vital functions, attacks the social body as a whole. A phenomenal malfunction has occurred. The relationship between the *self* and the *other* becomes challenged more than ever. And institutions that »think«,[1] communicate, organize, and coordinate are disorganized, overwhelmed, and catastrophic. From hospitals to schools, universities to courts, ministries to factories, airports to military bases … everything, absolutely everything, is now destabilized and affected.

An unbelievable situation? Not quite, and the history of medicine proves it. The work of globalization carried out by viruses has been known since humans were first hit by epidemics. Nevertheless, a major difference has emerged with the novel coronavirus. We have seen that the reaction of each state – of each society according to its economy, healthcare system and culture – varies significantly. From Trump and his constituents who blame media hysteria and the Democrats' and China's *viral* conspiracy, to Macron who activates his lexicon of war, to religious orthodoxies – of all tendencies – who sell off containment measures and implore divine intervention to eradicate the diabolical virus. Everywhere, the psycho-social effervescence seems to be at its height, and the coronavirus's ability to thwart national or global narratives is quite astounding.

[1] Douglas: How Institutions Think.

Ironically, after only a few weeks, doctors, nurses, and orderlies who were demonstrating or resigning *en masse* to fight against the application of market laws to healthcare, and the unworthy conditions of their work, were transformed into national heroes. Politics are now forced to change the discourse – to justify to lawyers and guardians of constitutions the questioning of fundamental rights, as well as military and police intervention, to enforce the limits imposed on freedoms. Moreover, the legitimacy of the political narrative sometimes seems to be lost between epidemiologists and science professionals.

Are we faced with an exploding narrative mode? And if so, which new narrative mode? In the midst of discussion about a post-corona era on normality, which will certainly not be the same conversion as before, as well as the return to normalcy, or even the formula for the *neue Normalität* that kept repeatedly being uttered by certain German political figures, what will become of our individual and collective narrative? Of our cultural identity according to Covid-19? Will we be more selfish or more supportive? Will we be more consumerist or more protective of nature and life? Will we narrate the story by ourselves more or will we be more attached to new communication giants that contrive stories and shape minds?

Albert Camus already knew this in 1941 – in the middle of World War II, European fascism, and the brutal colonization of Arab African countries – when he wrote: »But once the doors were closed, they realized that they were all, and the narrator himself, caught in the same bag and had to be dealt with«.[2] »The plague had swallowed up everything. No longer were there individual destinies but a collective destiny which was the plague and emotions shared by all«.[3] For an epidemic does not only lock individuals in their homes, it forces them to suspend the communicational experience of feeling together, tasting together, looking at each other, touching each other, and, above all, talking with each other. The coronavirus strikes bodies *and* words. The collective narrative is thus forced to stop, or metamorphose.

In the midst of the confinement that has spread throughout the world, the fight against the new virus has been forced to leave medical facilities and take on another color: that of spiritual warfare.

Holy April! All the big monotheistic parties were there: Easter for Catholic, Protestant, and Orthodox Christians; Jewish Passover; and Ramadan, which was scheduled for the last week of April. Due to the coronavirus and containment measures, masses, celebrations, and prayers were cancelled and generally replaced by other forms of digital communication. The image of the Pope walking alone to the Church of San Marcello, in the center of Rome and transmitted to the whole world, touched souls and left a lasting impression that was never before seen. Two

---

[2] Camus: La peste, p. 1273.
[3] Camus: The Plague, p. 138.

weeks later, he prays alone, in the middle of St. Peter's Square, deserted and desolate. In Jerusalem, for the first time in more than a century, the Holy Sepulchre is closed during Easter weekend. The communal history of a religion, of believing groups or individuals, is thus taking shape, from private rooms and spaces to fragmented and disparate narratives that come together to weave a collective co-narration. Co-narration, or almost. For these limitations and deprivations of *normal* religious sociability have not been to the liking of more fundamentalist currents, such as Christian and Jewish ultra-Orthodox, evangelicals, and Muslim extremists. And a counter-narrative emerged. During Easter weekend, the priest for the Saint-Nicolas-du-Chardonnet parish in Paris organized an open night mass. On the parish's website, a message encouraging physical presence was addressed to the faithful: »The video transmission of Sunday Mass does not replace or dispense those who are able to do so from the obligation to attend Mass in person.« For Orthodox Christians, apart from a majority who followed the services at home, resistance from some religious and political authorities was observed in Belarus, Georgia, and Ukraine. In March, *Le Monde* had already reported that the head of the Kiev Cave Laureate called on the faithful to »rush to the churches«.[4] No wonder that this place of worship has become one of the virus's major epicenters, with almost a fifth of all contamination in Kiev traced back to it.

A similar pattern was observed with Jewish festivities. In Israel, where all places of worship for the three monotheistic religions are closed, a controversy has arisen over the division of rabbis. The Durkheimian debate on the profane and the sacred has rightfully regained its place here. The problem is none other than whether the use of a videoconferencing application, which is intended to allow families to meet in a different way, could replace collective communions. Some rabbis have not found it difficult to adapt to an emergency situation by accepting the use of this medium to celebrate the feast. The Chief Rabbinate of Israel, however, opposed it. According to him, it was out of question to *desecrate* a sacred day. Needless to say, the confinement imposed in Israel has been significantly difficult to implement among the ultra-Orthodox. They account for 50 % of the patients with Covid-19, while only representing about 10 % of the Israeli population.

Some of them are also very religious and highly distrustful of the State of Israel. The only authority they refer to is their rabbi. On March 17, an ultra-Orthodox wedding brought together more than 120 people in the Beth Shemesh neighborhood of Jerusalem, defying the rules of confinement. A few days later in Bnei Brak, near Tel Aviv, hundreds of people gathered for a rabbi's funeral.

Of course, such attitudes are not always justified on strictly religious grounds. British Prime Minister Boris Johnson also became ill from Covid-19 after dis-

---

[4] See also the article by: Vitkine: La pandémie de coronavirus met du sel sur les plaies de l'Ukraine, confinée et fragile.

playing denialist behavior at the beginning of the pandemic, refusing to accept containment measures and advocating a narrative of strengthening the immune system through exposure to the virus. This policy was shattered by the rapidly increasing infection and death rates. Nevertheless, it is the narrative framework and arguments deployed that make the difference. Israeli health minister Yaakov Litzman, an ultra-Orthodox Jew, said the following in an interview on March 19: »We are praying and hoping that the Messiah will arrive before Passover, the time of our redemption. I am sure that the Messiah will come and bring us out as [God] brought us out of Egypt. Soon we will go out in freedom and the Messiah will come and redeem us from all the troubles of the world.«[5]

The Jewish messianic argument takes another detour elsewhere. Among the evangelists, as among many Muslims, it is rather a question of diabolical forces which must be combated by means other than medicine. Let us note in passing that if one of the major specificities of Islam is the absence of a clergy capable of taking in hand the normative regulation of worship, evangelism in turn ignores all regulation: each pastor practically has his own »deontic power«.[6]

In the United States, where evangelists are indispensable supporters of Donald Trump, there is no shortage of examples. In Florida, the evangelical pastor Ronald Howard-Browne was arrested for having celebrated several masses with hundreds of faithful while ignoring confinement measures. He accused the media of stirring up »religious hatred and intolerance« at a time when churches, he said, were a vital means of fighting the evil powers of the coronavirus.[7] From the devil to the charlatan, the gap is not far off. This is how the extremely wealthy Kenneth Copeland, one of the richest televangelists, promised on his television channel that he could cure the coronavirus through the screen ... all he had to do was put his hand on the television set!

A political and evangelist friend, the country of Brazil is not lacking in anti-diabolic narrative either. Jair Bolsonaro, president of the extreme right, supported by evangelists during his election, did not even hesitate to issue a decree to include evangelical churches in the list of essential sectors that cannot be affected by containment measures. At the beginning of April, he proposed to set up a day of religious fasting to »deliver Brazil from the evil« of the coronavirus. Silas Malafaia, head of one of the most important churches in the country, first declared: »My friends, do not worry about the coronavirus. It is a tactic of Satan. It feeds on fear.« An on his narration too, by the way.

---

[5] Health Minister Yaakov Litzman, also head of the ultra-Orthodox United Torah Judaism party, at a press conference in Jerusalem, March 19, 2020. See also Ahituv: Israeli Health Minister's Cure for COVID-19?

[6] As reference to John Searle's work on deontic power.

[7] Lush/O'Meara: Pastor Arrested for Violating Rules Amid Virus Outbreak.

Outside of places of worship, some Muslims in Egypt (Alexandria), Morocco, and Tunisia, although an abortive attempt in the latter, took to the streets, invoking the greatness of the Almighty (*Allah aqbar*) to eradicate the virus by using a formula drawn from the theological lexicon: *li-raf 'i balā al-corona*. A young Egyptian civil society activist had commented with dark humor on the nonsense of the night demonstration in Alexandria, stressing the irrationality and ignorance of men holding hands instead of keeping the recommended distance and staying home. »Do you think – he asked – that the virus will be afraid of you? That it will spare you when you hold hands because it will stop spreading in the evening, for example?«

The total scramble in the minds of many Muslims throughout the Arab world and the non-differentiation between the political, religious, economic, sanitary, etc., reduces their narrative account of the coronavirus to a kind of macabre caricature and bears witness to a deep collective trauma linked not only to epidemics of the past centuries, but to any irruption of the external enemy. The young activist aptly calls out to them through social networks: »Do you think it's Napoleon's French companion or the British occupation? All you have to do is shout, ›*yasqut, yasqut hukm al-vayrus!*‹ (»down, down with the power of the virus!«),[8] a slogan that Egyptian demonstrators have used and abused since the popular uprising against Mubarak, Mursi, and even President al-Sisi. Strange normative ambiguity exists in this Islamic narrative. But the political is not the only one to identify with the religious. Or vice versa. The scientist, too. Let us recall that in Iran, the Muslim country most affected by the epidemic so far, the debate did not take long to agitate religious authorities. Some religious leaders have not hesitated to place the religious above all normativity, even that of medical science. The academic and theologian of the holy city of Qom, Moshen Alviri, said that this »historical debate between Muslim jurists goes back to the early days of Islam«.[9] He is obviously right. Except he did not address one fascinating question: Why do normative interferences and ambiguities in spheres that are viscerally different from each other continue to be so active today? Why must a religious narrative impose its logic on political or medical narratives, for example? In the wake of this questioning, an ayatollah from Qom had already been calling pilgrims since the month of February to go to the mosque which he called a house of healing. No wonder then that on March 17, confrontations arose between Iranian police and worshippers who were desperate to visit two holy mausoleums, or that Shiites in Iraq were visiting the *al-qādhim* mausoleum despite government measures banning gatherings.

---

8   Direct Interview on France 24, March 31, 2020.
9   On this debate see for example: Quantara.de: COVID-19 Re-Opens Religion vs. Science Debate in Iran.

In this, Shia Islam is not isolated. Sunni Islam, too, invents its own narrative. Generally speaking, religious authorities have complied with political decisions in the fight against the pandemic. One symbol of this: the mosque in Mecca, which has already been closed since the beginning of March. The pilgrimage planned for the end of July will probably not take place this year. *Fatawa* from here and there are calling on Muslims to pray and celebrate the holy month of Ramadan at home. This is emotionally and symbolically very delicate, since Ramadan is the perfect occasion to strengthen family and social ties, as well as share meals, night vigils, parties, and prayers. While for Muslims in Europe and in several Arab-Islamic countries the measures are generally respected, other countries are already ticking like a time bomb. In Pakistan, a country of 200 million inhabitants, mosques and places of worship have been open since the beginning of April and are packed with worshippers. From March 10–12 in Lahore, authorities found themselves unarmed in front of monster gatherings of more than 100,000 people from 70 countries, despite the fact that the fundamentalist organization *al-tabligh* had not obtained the required permission. Cases of contamination linked to participants were subsequently recorded not only in Pakistan, but also in India, Turkey, and elsewhere.

Surfing on anguish and collective ignorance often bears fruit. The Algerian Imam Shems-eddine Aljazairi did not hide his zeal when he wrote on Facebook that he is »afraid that God sent us this virus to make us come back to him and when he sees that we have closed the mosques, he will send us another more virulent virus«.[10] His macabre prophecy strangely rhymes with a famous formula that circulates throughout the Arab world from Morocco to Yemen: »whoever will not be killed by war, will be killed by the Coronavirus!«

Is fear the essential framework of the Arab co-narration during the times of corona? Fear of death? Death by war, by the pandemic, by Daech, by failed revolutions, by an enlightened Islam that struggles to find a different, freer, and more humane narrative path?

Surfing on anguish is, however, not the only lot of Arab-Muslims, nor is it the only lot of religious Orthodox. It is even more serious because it has become the driving force of a global narrative. The crisis of the virus is, at its roots, only a test of the machine that was in full swing. Since the 1990s, and the change in the history of the media, communication, marketing, and management giants have been able to recover the academic momentum of narrative techniques to format minds. The objective: to tell *stories* for the benefit of the gurus of capitalism who are greedy for endless consumption, as well as for elected officials eager to turn citizens into electoral puppets. And then, an even more formidable element was added to the dictatorship of media narration: social dictatorship. Michel Foucault

---

[10] On the polemic between this Imam and health authorities in Algeria: Schahrazed: Algérie: Cheikh Chemseddine critique la fermeture des mosquées.

had already identified it well in his writings on surveillance societies. But if surveillance is a virus, it feeds on fear.

Every civilization, every culture cultivates the art of telling stories, tales, and myths. Religious co-narration is at the very heart of social dynamism, of the *effervescence* that requires the co-presence of the other, of what makes us human. This dynamism has been greatly destabilized by the pandemic, and researchers are already observing a growing trend of radicalization among both religious extremists and supporters of extreme right-wing policies.

Anxiety is exploding everywhere. The fear of contracting the virus and dying from it, of never seeing one's dying loved ones again or burying them with dignity. The fear of losing one's job, of being homeless, voiceless, and disenfranchised. Fear of violence that explodes in homes against women and children, the extent and consequences of which we do not yet know. World organizations are uttering cries of anguish of famine and impoverishment that will affect millions of human beings. The coronavirus hides behind it many others, and if the anguish explodes, we still have the hope that the current ordeal we are all going through will serve as a warning signal and invite us to rethink our values and systems for a more stable and peaceful existence on this planet.

References

Ahituv, Netta: Israeli Health Minister's Cure for COVID-19? The Messiah, Opinion, in: Haaretz, 26.03.2020, https://www.haaretz.com/israel-news/.premium-israel-coronavirus-health-cure-1.8703719; last accessed 18.06.2020.

Camus, Albert: La peste, in: Théâtre, récits, nouvelles, Paris 1962.

Camus, Albert: The Plague, translated by Stuart Gilbert, New York 1948.

Douglas, Mary: How Institutions Think, New York 1986.

Lush, Tamara / Chris O'Meara: Pastor Arrested for Violating Rules Amid Virus Outbreak, in: AP News, 31.03.2020, https://apnews.com/6c8068e57e6d7fe80445f9f04bbd65ff; last accessed 18.06.2020.

Qantara.de: COVID-19 Re-Opens Religion vs. Science Debate in Iran, 04.03.2020, https://en.qantara.de/content/covid-19-re-opens-religion-vs-science-debate-in-iran; last accessed 18.06.2020.

Schahrazed Ikour: Algérie: Cheikh Chemseddine critique la fermeture des mosquées, in: Dzair Daily, 18.03.2020, https://www.dzairdaily.com/algerie-cheikh-chemseddine-critique-fermeture-mosquee-coronavirus-covid-19/; last accessed 18.06.2020.

Vitkine, Benoît: La pandémie de coronavirus met du sel sur les plaies de l'Ukraine, confinée et fragile, in: Le Monde, 04.04.2020.

Sam Whimster

Discovering Society in a Time of Plague

The pandemic that is the virus Covid-19 can be considered sociology's greatest natural experiment to date. The methodology of the experiment is to divide two alike populations, one becoming the control group the other the experimental group, with the latter having something assumed to be causative introduced by scientific design. The testing procedure involves close monitoring of the results and the assessment of the results according in the first instance to whether the differences between the groups are random or not. A natural experiment is not designed. A large event impacts the population studied, in this case as a whole; this gives the opportunity to observe and assess changes in that population. Such large events are obviously not planned for, or wanted, and they override normal scientific protocols and ethics. To give a small example, there is a debate, aired on UK television, among epidemiologists on the efficacy of face masks. Those adhering to normal experimental method demand evidence based on data from carefully constructed samples of the population; those favoring the natural experiment say try out face masks immediately and then assess the results. The pandemic overrides normal scientific procedure which, as its critics have it, fails to grasp the huge opportunity that nature has unkindly delivered. At the time of *die Wende* c. 1990, the Heidelberg sociologist Rainer Lepsius argued (in conversation with the author) that sociology was missing an opportunity to study a given stable society undergoing dissolution. It was a suggestion that if taken up seriously by social scientists would demand a research design that selected which aspects of change it would investigate and with what empirical methods. The natural experiment arrives, so to speak, by accident and the scientific question is how to capitalize on the manifold changes that appear immediately and how those changes modulate in the future.

It is a characteristic of a pandemic that it affects the whole of society – there is no comparator group that continues blithely on its way unaffected. New Zealand could perhaps be the control group since it has not been badly hit by Covid-19 in terms of death and infections rates. While it might seem to be an antipodean island outside the course of world events, its government and especially its prime minister Jacinda Adern were highly effective in communicating to New Zealand citizens what counter-measures had to be observed. So, the natural experiment in respect to Covid-19 is a matter of comparing before and after. Peter Hennessy the British contemporary historian opined, on the radio, that we would divide history up between the pre- and post-corona virus eras.[1] He is arguing for a big effect, even epochal. For the social scientist, the issue is how would we investigate such a large hypothesis.

A preliminary starting point is to consider the sociological effects of previous pandemics, or plagues as they were biblically referred to. The word quarantine comes down to us from the European middle ages where a plague victim was coercively isolated often outside the city walls for forty days. As the plague passed, life went on as normal. In the Seven Year War epidemics of cholera and typhus were a result of the devastation of invading armies on the civilian population, just as a medieval siege tactic catapulted a diseased body into a city in order to decimate its population. Epidemics, one could say, were embedded into the conventions of a hostile human environment.

The Spanish flu of 1918 killed somewhere between 20 and 50 million people and the figure for Americans was reckoned at 675,000. Although certain American cities imposed strict rules – social distancing and face masks – others were far laxer. Because it occurred during the last year of the Great War, it was overshadowed by the seemingly far greater carnage of that war. Although in sheer number of deaths the flu was more significant, that is a retrospective judgment. Wartime censorship and a refusal to acknowledge the existence of the flu lead to its downgrading and minimization. Postwar societies, especially the main combatant countries grieved and memorialized only those who *fell* in the conflict. The war had made a visible gap in the young male population, a generation lost to the slaughter. Whereas the no less devastating flu was absorbed as a more diffuse phenomenon.

At this point in the Covid-19 pandemic, it is premature to opine whether it changes everything in the way Peter Hennessy predicts. It is also predicted that hyper-modernity will be dialled down: less foreign travel, more localism, the shrinking of economic value chains, home-working not office working, and fundamental changes in attitudes towards the environment. The expansion of the Simmel's metropolitan life on a global scale is predicted to have reached its zenith, now to decline to the less dynamic networks of *Gemeinschaft*. However, how will we know whether there is occurring or will have occurred – a move from *Vergesellschaftung* to *Vergemeinschaftung*, to use Weber's sociological categories? If sociologists are going to investigate the issue, they need to set up a research design. A generalization that everything will change is too nebulous to investigate. The *Problemstellung*, what is the research question, or the problematic has to be defined.

For example, the economic sociology could be far more important than the disruption of everyday behaviour, the latter being of obvious immediate impact – but not necessarily long lasting. The Black Death of the 14th century reduced the population by a third. In terms of everyday life, as described by Braudel, life was

---

[1] Hennessy during the broadcast at BBC Radio 4, World at One, 17 March 2020.

much reduced but not structurally changed. But for the economic historian over a longer time scale it caused a structural change in feudal political economy. There was a permanent shortage of labor which led to a loosening in feudal personal *Herrschaft* and to outright rebellion by serfs against their manorial lords. This led to a rise in wages and resources going to the laborer whose status upgraded to freeman. In a further step of the argument labor shortages led to increased agricultural productivity, and all these factors moved the European economy out of the stasis of the middle ages onto the growth path of early modernity. This was an epochal change.[2]

This is the *Problemstellung* for economists, who at the moment – unlike sociologists and other commentators – are predicting a bounce back to normality, the so-called V curve. Economists, recently though, have come up with the metaphor of scarring. Rising unemployment, bankrupt businesses, reduced income, huge indebtedness at person, corporate and state levels indicate a deep depression as a possibility. The point of comparison then becomes the New Deal of 1930s America under President Roosevelt and Treasury Secretary Henry Morgenthau. This shaped the post-1945 economies of advanced capitalist economies, the social market economy and welfare state. At the time of writing the European Union out of economic necessity is putting in plans to increase economic coordination at the federal level, with a proposed fiscal authority and fiscal union; something that the Great Depression forced upon the Jeffersonian tradition of individual state autonomy in the United States.[3] Economics, which is still just about a policy science despite its more doctrinaire aspects, is being forced into a paradigm change in its thinking.

Sociologists, especially in their current descriptivist and experiential mode, have become very excited about everything changing. But, as noted, pandemics historically do not of themselves force change, and if they did, research methods would have to be put in place to give a reliable account of the changes that do happen. The phrase »the new normal« (introduced by Christine Lagarde in 2014 as head of the IMF)[4] to which we are supposed to have become accustomed can equally be a talisman that induces people to adapt to whatever are the prevailiing conditions. We are geared, so it might seem, to conformity, and post pandemic we might revert to the »old normal«. This strikes me as a plausible hypothesis, especially if we consider the media of persuasion that at one point frighten us with our imminent death and at another point command us back to work.

The interesting part of the natural experiment I think is the immediate and, by its nature, *temporary* dislocation. The surface cover of society has been ripped

---

[2] Cf. Braudel: Civilization and Capitalism, p. 87.
[3] Cf. Whimster: What Is a Hamilton Moment?
[4] Lagarde: Navigating Monetary Policy in the New Normal.

away and we can see in plain view what is underneath, how it works and how it malfunctions. Sociology has an opportunity to look through a window, previously opaque, which is now fully opened. In policy studies they refer to the »Overton window«, which occurs when a disruptive event changes public attitudes so much that new policies, previously unacceptable, are considered feasible.[5] Sociological theory is not led by policy debate, but a near equivalent is ethnomethodology. Harold Garfinkel argued that only by disrupting the surface of normality that the underlying structuring of the normative can be seen and understood. Famously, he instructed his students to act as a stranger to their own parents, and to record their reactions.[6] Covid-19 is one of those disruptive events. Garfinkel was not doing this for the fun of it, although enormous; instead he was disputing the Parsonian version of the normative. Talcott Parson used »norms« as a constitutive part of social cohesion without explaining their controlling effects on the ground. Norms held such an important place in his sociology because his theory of action and social system stipulated that they were constitutive by definition — a kind of extra-cathedra explanation taking over the place of Christian morality in a secular society.[7]

So, if sociology is to use its Overton window it will be to assess the validity of core theories and consider their possible modification. For example it would be interesting to play Garfinkel to Niklas Luhmann. In a crisis do Luhmann's interfaces of subsystems swing into action to stabilize the overall social system? That is a somewhat daunting challenge and instead I will pursue the present disruption through a Durkheimian lens. Mary Douglas stands in the Durkheimian tradition. She analysed the anthropology of danger in *Purity and Danger* (1966) and in a later work with Aaron Wildavsky she examined *Risk and Blame* in modern societies. The difference between attitudes is that »moderns follow a line of reasoning from effects back to material causes« and »primitives a line from misfortune to spiritual beings«.[8] In advanced societies we have lost the habit of acculturating ourselves to what nature throws at us, and we are still living according to the maxim of world mastery — the ambivalent inheritance of modernity as Max Weber saw it. Unlike small group and tribal societies we can no longer distinguish between purity and danger and the necessary rituals that develop to culturally contain these. We do have handwashing, the guarantee of purity, but the danger is invisible and unknowable. We lack an adequate cultural representation of danger.

While making these distinctions between primitive and modern, Douglas herself substitutes the term »risk« for »danger«.[9] The Covid-19 virus signals danger

---

[5] Cf. Conceptually: What Is an Overton Window?
[6] Cf. Garfinkel: Studies of the Routine Grounds of Everyday Activity, p. 232.
[7] Cf. Garfinkel: Parsons Primer, pp. 284–292.
[8] Douglas: Risk and Blame, p. 3.
[9] »The language of danger, now turned into the language of risk, often makes a spurious claim to be scientific«, in: ibid., p. 14.

and the possibility of death from seemingly nowhere. It is perceived and publicly handled as risk. The risk of infection, the rate of infection, the probabilities of infection per 100,000 head of population and so on. The quantification of risk and its obsessive scrutiny rises with the death rate. Death itself goes ritually unmourned. Moderns cannot handle or face up to uncontrollable risk, i.e. uncertainty and danger. Another of Douglas's insights was to note that we are bad at recognizing risks. We invest our subjective agency with the ability to discount and dodge oncoming risks, minimizing their extent and approach. The perception of subjective risk, though, is sociologically determined. Speaking over the recent period to self-employed trades people as I have – builders, craftspersons, and labourers – they tend to play down the risks. Their livelihood is under threat, and their line of work anyway involve dangers which cannot always be avoided.

Political leaders have been notable in how high they pitch the risk to their citizens. President Trump speaks to a libertarian base who don't want to be told how they ought to behave. The wider social consequences – the dangers of exponential growth of infections – is ignored. Trump for months consistently ignored the dangers of the virus, insisting that it would go away, as if by magic as he recommended chemical potions that do more harm than good. The President of the United States has taken on the mantle of a witch-doctor. This is an extreme example of where the denial of modern science leads to regression. Somewhat attenuated, Prime Minister Johnson in the UK refused for weeks to acknowledge the danger, shaking hands with hospital patients, not wearing a face mask, and admitting his attraction to the mayor in the film Jaws, »who kept the town open«. Sweden tried to blend science with citizen individual responsibility, whereas neighbouring Denmark followed a stricter lockdown strategy.

Douglas also argued that natural dangers and lethal risks tends to be politicised: »we moderns have every bit as much scope as they, the primitives, for politicized readings of danger«.[10] In the UK, many blame Boris Johnson's government for adopting an initial strategy of so-called »herd-immunity«. In America, President Trump tries to shift the blame onto the Chinese and away from himself. The anthropological point, universalised, is that where there is risk there is blame – or rather, the attribution of blame as providing a material cause.

The Durkheimian point in this is the reaction to risk, here in the substance of novel danger, can be explained in terms of the social organization of the society. Douglas criticised the social psychology literature for individualising the perception of risk; for example, heuristic bias is the malfunctioning of human intelligence that has to be corrected. Douglas was aiming higher for a general cultural theory.

---

[10] Ibid., p. 8.

It may be feasible to treat the mortality statistics from Covid-19 in the same way as Durkheim analysed suicide statistics. Durkheim in *Le Suicide: étude de sociologie* (1897) established the societal forces at work that determined the quantum of suicides – that most individual of acts – in any given society.[11] His investigation was dependent on mortality statistics and recorded deaths, and his explanation was rooted in a new sociology. He divided social bonds along two axes: one was egoism and altruism, the other anomie and fatalism. Different sorts of societies, say Catholic, Protestant, Shia, atheist, can be placed within this orthogonal space and the suicide rate explained. Falling into poverty does not raise the suicide rate (because of resilient upbringing), acquiring unimaginable wealth does raise the rate, the anomie of affluence.[12]

There are emerging striking differences in the mortality rates with Singapore and Taiwan achieving a very low fatality rate while Lombardy has been overwhelmed by – initially – an unrecognised danger. In the UK the prime minister warned of high rates of fatality, almost as an inevitability. As with suicidogenetic currents, there is a social determination at work. The UK government's attitude is determined by a deeper utilitarian philosophy that lives can be traded in terms of outcomes – however those might be assessed. Asian governments influenced by a neo-Confucian philosophy see it as an ethical failure not to have saved lives, whatever is happening. South Korea, evidenced by their impressive Foreign Minister, sees the epidemic as a challenge to their highly prized civil society – and openness, transparency and high tech are prioritised. Television pictures of pilgrims protesting at the closure of the holy shrines of Qom in Iran testify to a religiosity that abnegates the body. Worldviews are different and determinative.

As a first step different societies can be placed within the space of the two axes. Traditional Islamic societies can be placed towards the fatalism pole, advanced public health systems towards the altruistic, Republican America on the egoistic pole, and those societies that fall apart in the face of the pandemic towards the anomie pole, from which the USA is not far distant. Theorizing society's structural divides according to solidarity and the division of labour does not, however, capture the complexity and further differentiation of 21st century societies. Mary Douglas and colleagues in the 1980s brought forward the theoretical design of grids and groups. Group is the substance and degree of solidarity, and grid is the salience of the imposition of rules and regulations. This gives a 2x2 table and four types of society:

1. Low group sense and few regulations producing a risk-taking market environment. Neo-cons have aggressively expanded this form of society especially in

---

[11] Durkheim: Le Suicide.
[12] Cf. Simon/Gagnon: Anomie of Affluence, pp. 356–378.

the Anglosphere – to a degree that would have shocked Douglas. Individuals have to take risks as a lifestyle necessity and in the absence of society-based insurance schemes they also have to bear the risk of failure. Trump's view of America follows this script. Eliot Weinberger reporting from America writes, »Libertarian Republicans don't want the ›nanny state‹ telling us what to do. Precautionary measures such as face masks are seen as typical liberal weakness. A poll shows that far more Democrats wear masks when leaving home than Republicans.« Protests against the lockdown include »Fake Crisis, Covid-19 is a Lie, Jesus is my Vaccine, *Arbeit macht Frei*«.[13]

2. High group sense with rejection of rules. This is the world of sects and elective communities closed against the wider world and its rules and norms. These societies are risk averse in the sense that they desire stable security. Inward looking religious sects are greatly at risk to virus contagion, unless they make a collective decision to disband temporarily.

3. High group sense and high grid salience. Germany's combination of corporatist groups and Ordoliberalism is an exemplar. Citizens make their own choices in an environment which is stabilised, ideally on a permanent basis. Public administration is prized, as is occupational expertise and career. Government, at all levels, is not denigrated, as is the neo-conservative version of New Public Management that seeks market solutions for everything. The People's Republic of China also belongs in this box, though presuming a similarity to Germany completely fails to take account of a different political system. Douglas labelled this box »hierarchical« which is valid for China where power is vested in the Chinese Communist Party and reaches its apex in the Chairman of the Party, President Xi. If German society is re-described as segmental rather than hierarchical, this would be an improvement, but one that introduces a third axis. Strong hierarchy and strong collective consciousness would seem to fit China. Long Ling reporting in May on lock down in Beijing describes a literal grid management of lockdown:

> »Viewed on a computer the grid is like a map, with each building assigned to a zone. Technicians randomly clicked on a building and selected a household. The ›household information‹ popped up immediately, including the names, ages, jobs and contacts details of everyone living there. [...] Managing the epidemic requires exactly the sort of community supervision made possible by the grid.«[14]

4. Low group sense and high grid salience. This is a society of anomic individuals with no strong social bonds living a fatalistic existence, often in hierarchical societies. These would include theocracies, communities of faith closely regulated.

---

[13] Weinberger: The American Virus, p. 3.
[14] Ling: Inside Beijing, p. 14.

Douglas's group/grid schema requires further work to become a more valid research framework. Her main point, to note, was to address the *societal* determination of risk attitudes. Also Douglas admitted that it is a static analysis and that she was not a theorist of societal change. In that sense it is not an analysis of before and after the pandemic. Instead it presumes that the societal organization and its collective representations determine how a pandemic will be handled; and when the pandemic passes societies will revert to the state they were in before. The theoretical advantage of Douglas's approach is that we can now see the mechanisms of cohesion, solidarity, hierarchy and segmentation at work. A final modification of the Douglas schema would be to introduce cleavages and the structural divides. American society remains fractured broadly speaking between big city Democrats and inland Republicans. The pandemic has simply intensified that divide. Douglas did, however, allow for »surprise« as an agent of change.

Martin Albrow would remind us the pandemic will also drive the furtherance of global society as a new consciousness forms in the face of common danger.[15] What is striking is that Covid-19 is the first global pandemic at the level of an awakening global consciousness. All economies have been stopped which has never ever happened in human history – and as argued above the economic consequences will be more profound than the sociological ones. Preventing the spread of the novel corona virus, while varying in effectiveness and degree, has been *universal* and is altruistic in Durkheim's sense. It brings a new normativity to the global consciousness. Societies will compare how they handled the pandemic; so China is congratulating itself on its effective reaction – despite its lethal failure of Wuhan officials to report the initial outbreak of Covid-19. International responses to pandemics will be strengthened despite President Trump's politically infantile withdrawal of US funding from the WHO.

At the time of writing this chapter the Black Lives Matter movement has risen to international prominence following the the police killing of George Floyd on 25 May 2020 in Minneapolis – and relayed around the world on social media. The Nigerian writer Ben Okri writes of this event:

»Never in my lifetime has the case of such visible injustice moved white and black people, moved them as human beings. There have been protests all across America. But there have been huge protests in Britain, in Spain, in Nigeria, in fact all across the world. Why has the killing of George Floyd struck such a profound chord in us? Maybe it was that phrase: ›I can't breathe.‹ The consonance of the phrase with the very root of our pandemic fears is uncanny. The phrase linked the coronavirus with the ubiquitous and implacable nature of institutional racism. ›I can't breathe‹ – yet people were prepared to risk being afflicted with coronavirus just so they could express their protest at the chokehold killing of a black man […]. ›I can't breathe‹: we need a new language to express the fundamental clarity of

---

[15] Cf. Albrow: Has Covid-19 Brought Globalization to an End?, in this volume.

what happens when people are demonised, excluded, deprived, oppressed, and killed because of the colour of their skin. We need a new language, a phrase for that condition.«[16]

One normativity begets another, each on a global scale. Is this a ›surprise‹ moment in Douglas's sense, or does the ›unheimlich‹ in public gaze trigger a new cultural representation in the time of plague?

References

Braudel, Fernand: Civilization and Capitalism. 15th–18th Century. The Perspective of the World, London 1984.
Conceptually: What Is an Overton Window?, https://conceptually.org/concepts/overton-window; last accessed 08.06.2020.
Douglas, Mary: Risk and Blame. Essays in Cultural Theory, London 1994.
Durkheim, Émile: Le Suicide: étude de sociologie, Paris 1897.
Garfinkel, Harold: Studies of the Routine Grounds of Everyday Activity, in: Social Problems 11(3), 1964, pp. 225–250.
Garfinkel, Harold: The Parsons Primer, Berlin 2019.
Hennessy, Peter: Broadcast at BBC Radio 4, World at One, 17.03.2020, https://www.bbc.co.uk/programmes/m000gd09; last accessed 08.06.2020.
Lagarde, Christine: Navigating Monetary Policy in the New Normal, Monetary Policy in a Changing Financial Landscape, Speech by Christine Lagarde at the ECB Forum on Central Banking May 2014, https://www.imf.org/en/News/Articles/2015/09/28/04/53/sp052514; last accessed 08.06.2020.
Ling, Long: Inside Beijing, in: London Review of Books, 04.06.2020, p. 14.
Okri, Ben: »I Can't Breathe«: Why George Floyd's Words Reverberate around the World, in: The Guardian, 08.06.2020, https://www.theguardian.com/commentisfree/2020/jun/08/i-cant-breathe-george-floyds-words-reverberate-oppression; last accessed 10.06.2020.
Simon, William / John Gagnon: The Anomie of Affluence a Post-mertonian Conception, in: American Journal of Sociology, 82, 1976, pp. 356–378.
Weinberger, Eliot: The American Virus, in: London Review of Books, 04.06.2020, pp. 3–8.
Whimster, Sam: What Is a Hamilton Moment?, https://gpilondon.com/publications/opinion/what-is-a-hamilton-moment; last accessed 08.06.2020.

---

[16] Okri: »I Can't Breathe«.

Marta Bucholc

The Corona Crisis as a Test of National Habitus: The Imperative of Obedience*

The Coronavirus pandemic has caused many human tragedies, and this will be the primary basis on which its consequences will be debated. Not only out of respect for human suffering, without the consideration of which law is but an inhumane cutting edge of abstract formal normativity. But also because of the effect that human suffering and human tragedy – or, in most cases, the threat thereof – has on people's thoughts, words and actions. From the socio-legal point of view, the Corona crisis has triggered a wave of phenomena about whose exact weight we will long be pondering, and the gravity of which cannot be doubted.

Direct existential threat understandably dominated the public Corona debate in early 2020, with hectic discussions about the number of intensive medical care stations, hospital beds, masks and respirators – in addition to the gruesome counting of deaths and infections and the indefatigable curve-drawing in all possible media. Accusations of indolence, negligence and carelessness filled television shows and newspapers, in some countries more than in others. Interestingly enough, it was the great revival of the intercountry comparison that struck the eye in the pandemic's first weeks. All the discredited national stereotypes were suddenly in play again, used as handy *post hoc, ergo propter hoc* heuristics: the lighthearted and nonchalant Italians, the stubborn Britons, the independent Swedes, the all-too-well-prepared Germans, the disciplined Chinese, Koreans and Taiwanese.

Gradually, it was the latter point that dominated the image of the pandemic: the discipline. When it became clear that the long-term goal of every single society on Earth was to stop or limit the spread of the disease, almost all states applied some or all of the range of extraordinary measures: compulsory medical testing, quarantines, school closures, prohibitions to move in public spaces, banning gatherings of people, closures of public spaces, shutting down shops, businesses, cultural institutions and public facilities. Some countries applied a near-total lockdown, which was, for all practical purposes, a house arrest order that was imposed on every single person in the country – not by an individual court decision issued by an independent judiciary preceded by a due process of law, but by a universal

---

* The author acknowledges the support of Polish National Science Centre in Kraków (»National Habitus Formation and the Process of Civilization in Poland after 1989: A Figurational Approach«, 2019/34/E/HS6/00295).

and general decree of the executive. And, statistically speaking, all around the world, people obeyed.

1. Where Have All the Non-Conformists Gone?

Of course, not literally everyone around the world responded with obedience, and media reports were filled with tales of desperados who simply had to »get out there« for a number of reasons, ranging from very serious existential ones up to no less serious and probably no less existential like the bad need to get a drink while under quarantine. However, the sheer fact that in all countries, the lockdowns and limitations seem to have taken effect as of the end of April 2020 serves as *indirect* proof of compliance by a majority of the population.

Why do people everywhere obey, despite all the differences between them? A socio-legal scholar presented a year ago with a moot question of how the world would react to an extraordinary situation like this would probably have come up with a number of hypotheses, such as these: In the countries where the belief in legitimacy of law is strong, and trust in public institutions is solid, the extraordinary measures would be effective, and the people would by and large obey. However, in the countries where the authorities are despised and the power of law is demonstrably inefficient, the laws made in order to fight the epidemiological crisis would not work, simply because people would not comply with them. If people disregard tax laws, park their cars wherever they like and litter in public, why would they obey lockdown rules introduced to fight an epidemic?

Of course, there is a lot to be said against this line of argument. It is based on an idea that law is in fact a homogenous concept and that its validity is based in a homogenous validity culture. In this simplistic variant, the study of the validity of law would work in a »broken windows« paradigm: if rules in one sphere of social life are adhered to, it increases the probability that the rules would also be applied in other spheres, and vice versa. People who »cheat« on the water ban to sprinkle their lawns during a hot summer would also cheat on the quarantine rules, simply because they do not, as a rule, follow the rules.

True, the laws made to counter the epidemic are based on some values which seem to have made quite a career in many of our societies: long life, health and security. Water and littering bans do not work that well as a comparison; people may disregard the rules which they perceive as mere fastidious overregulation, but still comply with those which are legitimized by their important goal. Health and security are important for us, for a number of historical and structural reasons to the understanding of which many students of human societies have contributed substantially, including in particular Thomas Hobbes, Michel Foucault and Ulrich

Beck. People can be governed efficiently by an authority whose legitimacy claim relies on human longing for health and security, especially in its late-modern biopolitical rendition based on the steel-hard logic of populational risk assessment.

2. Habitual Sources of Law-Abiding Behavior

However, the laws against an epidemic are not by the same token the only biopolitical governance measures in place. If long life, health and security cause a leap in obeying the law, a good proxy measure of expected compliance with anti-epidemic measures could be other laws and regulations made to safeguard these exact same values: traffic regulations (in particular speed limits), smoking restraints, vaccination schedules, rules on the sale and consumption of alcoholic beverages, control of other psychoactive substance use and trafficking, anti-smog policies, etc. However, we observe not only deep-running differences within societies in respect to compliance with all these and many other rules, but also intersocietal differences. Norbert Elias once suggested that street and traffic behavior would be an excellent comparative indicator of the state of the process of civilization in a society: it would also be an excellent measure of general attitude towards the law. Some drive carefully, stick to the speed limit and never park out of place, even though nobody is watching. Others, however, are more than happy to break the rules, especially when no one is there to tell them off. And, apart from various other differences in this respect, there is also a national pattern behind it.

Raymond Fisman and Edward Miguel documented this pattern in 2007 in their research of United Nations officials' parking habits. They found that diplomats from high-corruption countries, who until 2002 were protected by diplomatic immunity, accumulated significantly more unpaid parking violations than those coming from low-corruption countries. Clearly, finding a parking place can be a nuisance in New York ... However, in 2002, the rules changed. From now on, those caught violating parking rules would need to surrender their diplomatic license plates to law enforcement. Suddenly, someone was watching, ready to tell the easy-rider off. The result was a sudden drop in the number of unpaid violations.[1] Fisman and Miguel conclude that »cultural norms and (particularly in this context) legal enforcement are both important determinants of corruption«.[2] But one could also reason the other way around. The state of corruption and the cultural norms interplay constantly, one of them conditioning the other. While some cultures simply do not seem to support high corruption levels, the societies

---

[1] Cf. Fisman/Miguel: Corruption, Norms, and Legal Enforcement.
[2] Ibid., p. 1020.

dominated by these cultures also tend to have stronger and more stable public institutions and more equitable, predictable legal systems that are, on the whole, better at watching citizens and telling them off. However, they fortunately do not need to do this because the societies are watching themselves, by way of internalized self-constraints.

The Eliasian concept of a national habitus, as a part of human second nature formed by the participation in the figuration of a nation-state-society, links these two aspects of law-abiding behavior: the institutional framework created in a historical process of social change translates into a pattern of self-constraints which can more poetically be called habits of the heart, mind and body, prevailing in what Elias called a state-society. However, this benign scheme of culture and state institutionalization going hand in hand should not make us blind to the reality of individual freedom and social deviance. Humans are able to act against their habits if somebody is watching to tell them off, and they are also capable of changing their habits, especially in the face of a strong external constraint, such as one coming from effective law enforcement. But some of them are harder to change than the others, and not all of them can be changed at once. That is what Elias described as »drag-effects« of habitus; while circumstances change, some habitual layers that are harder to change just linger, sometimes despite their blatant counter-adaptiveness in the new environment.

3. Global-Scale Social Experiment: National Habitus-Testing in Times of Corona

In recent world history, we have never had such an opportunity to observe the national habitus being tested comparatively in conditions verging on a global social experiment. The same primary factor (the virus) caused essentially similar reactions, implemented by way of law. It is not an accident that Max Weber, defining legal order, explained that there must be a chance of obedience, and that the obedience cannot in fact be a straightforward consequence of the prevailing moral rules or suchlike, not to mention other automatism of non-normative nature. The law is a law because it is not 100 % effective *per se*. Differences in measures taken against the virus are, of course, matters of immense importance for the quality of life of the affected populations, but in Europe they can in fact be reduced to a kind of narcissism of minor differences in most cases (How long do we have to stay at home? When will the schools open? What size stores can open when? How many people can talk to each other in public from what distance? How many people can pray together? Are children allowed to go out, too, or only the dogs?). True, in some countries, the measures applied verge on the extravagant: a prohibition of people under 18 moving outside on their own for any reason whatsoever, a prohibition of more than two people being together in a car, irrespective of whether they live in the same household or not, etc. But, on the whole, with an important legal exception of the approach to using personal data and relaxing the regime of data protection for infection prevention, the measures applied aggregated to a state of exception everywhere, and the side-effect research question of the global Corona experiment was: how do various national habitus react to this state?

Some national habitus are not only less trustful towards their rulers than others, but they are also better at circumventing the law – any law. Let's return to Weber, who insisted that the existence of the legal order depends on the chance that people will obey and not on the effective possibility of the authorities to punish the violators: nobody can control, much less punish, a whole society. And practice is everything in matters of lawbreaking. Some societies are more skilled at it than others thanks to their historical paths, which do not necessarily need to go back a long time. Even in Europe, especially in the East and in the South, there are many societies with very recent stories of successful long-lasting anti-systemic partisanship. The memory of such experience and the layer of national habitus corresponding to it is a cultural resource which could be mobilized against the Corona-prevention regime. However, it seems that it was not.

The result of the global Corona experiment is, in all probability, that the states differ more than societies do, a painful conclusion for a social researcher. The legal, political and institutional setup of states, as well as the good old factors like geographic conditions, population sizes and economic status, seem to matter in the epidemic, whereas societies just conform to the rules. The universal global imperative of obedience prevails over particularities of validity cultures and intricacies of national habitus. While the Corona pandemic certainly did not translate into a global regime of unified biopolitics, but rather unfolded into a series of state-delimited nationalized epidemics, the societal reactions in all these state-determined units seem to be surprisingly conformist. Everybody reacts to the state of exception much in the same manner, unless these are some really minor differences we are after.

Of course, this conclusion only holds for the time being. As weeks and months pass, the inevitable habituation to new conditions will take place, and the old habits will die hard. Moreover, there are non-habitual, existential reasons for people to rebel. Especially the people whose precarious employment situation and thin financial reserves make them particularly economically vulnerable are now as we speak redefining their situation as a struggle for survival against the measures applied by their governments. Not even Hobbes believed that a human being is bound to sacrifice their own life following an order of the ruler, which is why he allowed a soldier in the battlefield to desert out of fear for his life ... But this much exaggerated parable does not erase the question of sources of the obedience to anti-Corona measures, or, to rephrase it now, of the powerful uniformizing and conformizing effect of the state of exception.

4. Habitual Effects of the Pathos of Exception?

The Corona crisis supports the insight that the ›state of emergency‹ has its own validity culture, which is not coextensive with the validity culture on which law of the normal state relies. In societies which have as little in common as possible in the global age, people obey their local Leviathans. The basis of their obedience, apart from health and security concerns, is the logic of the state of exception as such. The suspension of normal rules of social life, of many of the dearest civic rights and liberties, is in fact effective by virtue of a formal operation of removing the epidemic from the sphere of the normal. Normally, people would behave according to their well-embedded cultural models, but they fail to do so because the whole situation is moved beyond the area of the normal by a legal performative. The pathos of exception is literally related to experiencing and enduring the abnormal; the trouble is that there are no habitual instruments in our toolboxes for the abnormal. That is why we all behave more or less alike: we are being deprived by the state of exception of all that makes a difference.

Of course, this is a philosophical exaggeration. The state of exception is never exceptionless, and some people are allowed to retain more normality than others, which does constitute a difference in the uniformity. In the recent crisis, for example, people with dogs were somewhat privileged in comparison to those without them. Nevertheless, the mechanism of uniformization by abandoning differences creates a minefield of habitual effects of the pathos of exception. Will the validity culture of the state of exception withdraw and cede its place to the idiosyncratic validity cultures of the law for the normal times? And, to extrapolate on this, will the legitimacy of normal norms, the normativity of parking tickets, income taxes and trash bins, benefit or lose as a result of the unprecedented globalization of exception with its uniformizing effects? Will it become people's universal habit, a constituent of their global second nature, to just obey with no questions asked?

References

Fisman, Raymond / Edward Miguel: Corruption, Norms, and Legal Enforcement: Evidence from Diplomatic Parking Tickets, in: Journal of Political Economy, 115(6), 2007, pp. 1020–1048.

Caroline Okumdi Muoghalu

Igbo Culture and the Coronavirus Pandemic Social Distancing Order of the Nigerian Government on a Collision Course: Reflections on Law as Culture

Abstract

Recently, the coronavirus pandemic has been devastating the world. At the time of this writing, more than a million people have been infected and more than 100,000 have died. In Nigeria, the coronavirus pandemic has resulted in the federal government issuing orders on social distancing, staying at home, visitation, and social gatherings such as weddings and burial ceremonies. This new way of living, which stands in contrast to the Igbo people's (South East Nigeria) culture, has made it difficult for them to comply with the directives.

This paper examines the collision between Igbo culture and the new approved ways of living due to the coronavirus, which I termed the ›coronavirus culture‹, especially as it relates to social distancing directives. The paper elucidates the different aspects of social distancing, such as keeping two meters apart; sheltering in place; and limiting social activities, including the closure of markets. In particular, it is shown how these directives sharply differ from the Igbo people's culture. The Igbo people's non-compliance with federal directives is also explored, revealing that the government's efforts are largely ineffective. This implies that if the coronavirus was to come to the area, its containment would prove difficult. The paper concludes that government measures to curb the coronavirus pandemic in Igbo land are not effective because the new lifestyle demanded by the pandemic stand in contrast to Igbo culture. It is ultimately recommended that the Igbo people should be sensitized before receiving such directive in the future.

1. Introduction

The recent coronavirus pandemic is giving governments and people around the world great concern. First identified by scientists in 1931, coronaviruses, particularly the HCoV-229E strain, was later isolated from humans in 1965.[1] In the United States, coronaviruses were first recognized in turkeys in 1951 and were associated with various disease syndromes. The disease can now be found everywhere in the world, especially where turkeys are raised.[2] However, the most recent coronavirus outbreak becomes highly topical and problematic due to its global character: Modern globalization, accelerated by developments in communication and transportation, has made it possible for people to be in Britain in the morning and in the United States by the evening.

The current pandemic has devastated the world and not spared countries that are better versed in modern science and medical technology. For instance, the United States, China, the United Kingdom, and many other countries recorded many deaths within a short frame. As of today (April 14, 2020), China had more than 7,000 confirmed cases and more than 3,000 deaths; the United States just hit 400,000 cases and recorded 20,000 deaths. In the same vein, Italy, the United Kingdom, and Spain are having their own share of infections and fatalities. Africa has also recorded sizeable number of coronavirus infections and deaths. Globally, the total number of confirmed cases stands at 1,915,148, and the number of deaths at 118,684 (Worldometer, April 13, 2020). Indeed, one can comfortably say that the world and its leaders are frightened. This is especially true for those in Africa given the continent's fragile healthcare systems and economies.

In Nigeria, 323 cases have been confirmed, 10 of which have resulted in death (Nigeria Centre for Disease Control (NCDC), April 13, 2020). These figures come from 16 of the country's 36 states. Importantly, the nature of the infection in Nigeria somehow defies the disease's democratic nature: Elsewhere, the virus infects the rich and the poor alike, but in Nigeria, most of the infected people, at least at first, were political leaders, the wealthy, and the elites who returned from abroad. I use ›defy‹ above with every sense of seriousness because, in Nigeria, the political class does not experience disease like the rest of the citizens. In fact, diseases here are mainly for the poor. As such, the nature of the coronavirus came as a surprise to many Nigerians, and the federal government is at its wits end. Now, the virus has entered the general population through the political class.

As a precautionary measure, the Nigerian federal government has instructed people to keep at least a two-meter distance from each other (NCDC, 2020). The government also ordered all markets to close (except those selling groceries, drugs,

---

[1] Cf. Korsman et al.: Virology, p. 94 f.
[2] Cf. Maclachlan et al.: Fenner's Veterinary Virology, pp. 435–461.

and other essential items), and it introduced stay-at-home orders, restrictions on visitation, and guidelines for social interaction that limit hugging, kissing, and standing close to others. People are told to greet one another with their elbows and feet instead. This is where the new coronavirus culture has a head-on collision with Igbo culture, and indeed, it is a running battle.

The Igbo – a cultural group that lives east of the Niger River in southeast Nigeria – are a very vibrant people who are always on the move. The new coronavirus culture of social distancing has come as a contravention of the Igbo culture, and state governments are finding it difficult to explain and control people's behavior in this regard. The Igbo people are known for their close-knit relationships in an extended family structure in which everyone is one another's keeper.

As a cultural group, the Igbo were and still are republicans who were governed by elders in stateless societies without any central government structure. This communal orientation continues even after colonialism instituted a centralized form of governance in the area.

With view to the Law as Culture paradigm, it can be said that in this context, the Igbo people's culture represents a law to which they strictly adhere, evidenced in their lived experiences daily. This cultural orientation also represents law in that anybody who fails to conform is punished with ostracism, stigma, or banishment depending on the seriousness of the cultural violation. As this piece will do, exploring the problems associated with a cultural group trying to follow directives – in this case, ones that are meant to save their lives – will go a long way in generating knowledge about people's reactions to such issues and help create effective intervention programs in the future. This paper will therefore add insights into the role of culture in infectious disease prevention in Igboland and in Nigeria. This contribution is significant as not much research has been done on culture and adherence to new rules in regard to infectious diseases.

This paper is premised on the Igbo philosophy and worldview, as well as how these made it difficult for the Igbo people to begin to live a different kind of life due to the coronavirus. I therefore argue that the Igbo people's difficulty adjusting stems from the Igbo worldview, which has always been deeply embedded in everyday life and is thus hard to change overnight, even in the face of a deadly virus. In this paper, I attempt to examine the Igbo people's reaction to the Nigerian federal government's orders on social distancing, staying at home, and interacting with one another. The paper will first discuss the overall context before looking at government directives and how they collided with the Igbo culture.

2. The Context

This paper concerns the Igbo of southeast Nigeria. Five states can be found in this geographic area: Abia, Anambra, Ebonyi, Enugu, and Imo. The Igbo people speak the Igbo language, and they are traditionally traders, farmers, and fishermen. In recent times, however, many work as artisans, bankers, doctors, and professionals.

Since the Igbo people are vibrant group filled with versatile business people and travelers, it is not uncommon to run into them in any corner of the globe. Indeed, Asikaogu described the Igbo people (natively called ›NDI IGBO‹) as the third largest and the most dispersed ethnic group in Nigeria.[3]

Despite this dynamic nature of the Igbo, they still hold their cultural heritage close, a part of which is the practice of embracing extended family and brotherhood. The Igbo uphold the principle of brotherhood, as noted by Asikaogu,[4] and Nyerere, in his Ujamaa declaration, described African socialism as an attitude where everybody cares for one another. Asikaogu maintained that this principle manifests in a strong sense of community, good relation, sacredness of life, and respect for elders and authority.[5] Indeed, Davidson summed up the Igbo sense of community as such: an Igbo proverb says »go the way people go, if you go alone, you will have reason to lament«.[6] This shows how important community is to the Igbo, and this explains why there is network of Igbo people in every country, or as I call them, the ethnic villagers in urban areas. In these faraway lands, the Igbo people still celebrate new yam festivals and other cultural events. In these networks away from home, they continue to practice their culture and teach their children; this is how cultural heritage is transferred from one generation to another, irrespective of where the children are growing up.

Politically, the Igbo people are organized along patriarchal lines in which the eldest man is the head of the family and community leadership is in the hands of the elders. Igbo society is built along the principle of egalitarianism in which everybody is equal. This is why it is said that the Igbo taught the world the republican form of governance. As such, they lived in stateless communities, and communal life is a daily routine and experience, even after colonialism instituted a central governance system in the area. Igbo are always in close proximity to one another, and this is where the culture clashes with the new culture brought about by the coronavirus. This is because in the Igbo worldview, philosophy, and cosmology, a human being is not an individual. A human being is an entity who

---

[3] Cf. Asikaogu: Igbo Cultural Values and the Effect of Globalization.
[4] Cf. ibid.
[5] Cf. ibid.
[6] Cf. Davidson: The African Genius.

is connected to other human beings, the dead, children yet unborn, and the universe – and all of them form one body and a person cannot live a normal life without these others.

3. The Igbo Culture as It Relates to Social Distancing

I deem it necessary to discuss the meaning of culture before delving into the Igbo culture, as it relates to social distancing orders given in response to the pandemic. This will provide the reader with background information about the Igbo culture. Culture has several definitions, and many scholars find it difficult to have a unified definition. Tylor defined culture as a complex whole which includes belief, knowledge, arts, morals, law, custom, and any other capabilities and habits acquired by man as a member of the society.[7] In a same manner, Keesing defined culture as systems of shared ideas, systems of concepts and rules, and meanings that underlie and are expressed in the ways that humans live.[8] These definitions indicate that culture emanates from the reality of humans living together in particular environments. This prompted Helman to posit that culture is a set of guidelines which individuals inherit as members of a particular society and which tells them how to view the world; how to experience it emotionally; and how to behave in it in relation to other people, supernatural forces, and the environment.[9] To me, culture represents ways through which members of a society adapt to and survive in their environment. As such, over the years, the Igbo people have developed and evolved a cultural orientation, and these norms and values have been handed down from generation to generation. The Igbo culture stems from the Igbo philosophy and cosmology – the entire Igbo worldview. It is argued by Asikaogu that culture characterizes a particular group of people and their very ways of life, which differentiates them from other people.[10]

As mentioned earlier, the Igbo people live communal lives with chains of connections. In this area, family is the closest knit unit for every human being, and the family here means father, mother, children, uncles, nephews, nieces, cousins, grandparents, great grandparents, the dead, and children yet unborn. Asikaogu noted that Igbo, as a nation, regard the family and its name, sacredness of life, chastity, respect for elders and parents, marriage, honesty, and hospitality as particularly important. These values are inscribed in the spirit of the people and their

---

[7] Cf. Tylor: Primitive Cultures.
[8] Cf. Keesing: Cultural Anthropology, pp. 459–462.
[9] Cf. Helman: Culture, Health and Illness.
[10] Cf. Asikaogu: Igbo Cultural Values and the Effect of Globalization.

history.[11] This goes to show that the family is cherished and held in high esteem by the Igbo. Importantly, several families form a community which represents a group of people who are related largely by blood and marriage in a very complex body with chains of relationships. Also noteworthy is that the Igbo community is made up of so many people at different realms of existence in terms of the living, the dead, and posterity. In fact, Abraham captured this when he said that in Western culture, the community is conceived of as a mere circular institution while in Africa, a community is conceived of as having sacral unity which comprises its living members, its dead (those who live at less substantial form), and its unborn children.[12] This indicates that the community means so much to the Igbo. Indeed, Agulanna posited that Africans see community as supreme over the individual.[13] This is not different from the Igbo concept of community – no wonder this value system stood the test of time despite onslaughts from formal education, Westernization, and globalization.

As such, one person is related to so many people and must try as much as possible to maintain the relationships. As noted by Agulanna, for the African, no one can live successfully outside of the human community. For the Igbo, from the time a person is born to the time he/she dies, the person is made aware of the value and importance of the communal group, or her/his dependence on the kin group. The community is thus the Igbo's base of the life, and Agulanna further affirms that a person is judged either as good or bad depending on the community's (dis-)approval.[14] This fosters close-knit relationships among the Igbo and could explain why they cling tenaciously to this age-old tradition.

This close-knit relationship also shows in greetings among the Igbo. When an Igbo person encounters another, they usually stand in close proximity to one another (about a foot or two, depending on their relationship) and say to each other *ututu oma* (good morning), *ehihe oma* (good afternoon), or *ugbede oma* (good evening). If the person is a titled man or woman, he/she will be greeted by using the title name *ozo*. As they greet each other, they tend to stand for a long time asking about the welfare of each other, all the people in their families, and their friends.

Apart from this exchange, most Igbo people hug when they encounter each other. In my particular culture, which is Idemmili in Anambra State, we hug each other whenever we encounter one another especially if we are friends, relatives, a relative of a husband or wife, or an acquaintance. It is important to point out here that the people a person regards as being related to are many because in

---

[11] Cf. ibid.
[12] Cf. Abraham: Crises in African Culture.
[13] Cf. Agulanna: Ezigbo Mmadu.
[14] Cf. ibid.

this culture, a friend of my blood relative is also my friend, and the circle goes on almost to infinity. This is because everything is communally owned, including friendship and even shame. If any family member is involved in a shameful act, the shame is corporate in nature in the sense that every member of the clan will share in the shame. With this chain of relationships, one person in this culture ends up hugging so many people in one day. It is also important to note that this way of living has been embedded in each person from childhood to adulthood, which makes it particularly difficult to change.

Moreover, the bonding does not stop there. Every morning, neighbors visit each other, especially if the neighbor is elderly. The younger person will visit to inquire how the neighbor slept last night. Sometimes, many people may be in one person's house, and in the process, they will break kola nuts and use it to pray for everybody. In the study area, the kola nut is a prayer symbol used to communicate with ancestors. After this, they will eat the kola nuts and disperse to their various homes to face the day's activities. In the evening, they repeat the same ritual.

The people are also usually involved in festivals, rituals, naming ceremonies, weddings, and burials – and all these bring people together on a daily basis. This is why ostracism is one of the biggest and most effective tools of social control in the area.

Another important issue is that the Igbo people are very dynamic and always on the move. This is why they are great travelers and can go to any part of the world. Indeed, Macebuh observed that the Igbo are noted for their enterprise, creativity, and their intellect.[15] They are notorious for their refusal to admit the constraint of geography and boundaries of language and religion.

4. Directive of the Nigerian Federal Government in Regard the Coronavirus Pandemic

In response to the coronavirus pandemic, the Nigerian federal government introduced social distancing measures, stay-at-home orders, visitation restrictions (including for burials and weddings), and limited social interactions. To show their seriousness, the Lagos state government recently sentenced a popular actress and her husband to three months of community service and fined them 100,000 Naira each for holding a birthday party in their house. This collectively represents the ›new coronavirus culture‹ which I referred to earlier.

---

[15] Cf. Macebuh: Humanism in Chains.

5. The Collision of Two Cultures

The two cultures in this collision are that of the Igbo and that of the coronavirus. In terms of greetings, the Igbo people hug and shake hands, but the coronavirus culture in Nigeria stipulates that people should not touch each other besides with their legs or elbows. To the Igbo people, this is absurd, and they are resisting it. My personal observation shows that the Igbo people continued to hug one another and shake hands despite the fact that it has become risky to do so. In fact, many of them do it unconsciously. Many will finish hugging and shaking hands before they remember that they are told not to do so. Their reaction generally is that they will begin to laugh heartily and tell one another that they have forgotten that they told us not to hug, as if the government is joking.

When I ponder this, it is not easy to untangle why a people will be adamant in the face of a threat to their own lives. However, when looking critically at the issue, one notes that Igbo children have been socialized to imbibe these values. As noted by Uchenna, community spirit is very strong among the Igbo almost from birth; the individual is aware of his/her dependence, and he/she also realizes the necessity of making his/her own contribution to a group to which he/she owes so much.[16] He/she seldom, if ever, becomes really detached from the group wherever he/she may live. This close-knit relationship is part of the reason for the difficulty encountered by Igbo in obeying this new order. Sometimes, I wonder if it will ever be possible for the Igbo people to change and embrace this new way, even if only temporary. The major problem here is that as observed by Asikaogu, this way of living (in this case greeting) has been inscribed in the Igbo person from childhood.[17] This reminds me of an Igbo adage which says that »an individual cannot learn to use left hand in old age«. This means that it is not easy to change an adult to stop what he/she has been doing since childhood.

On the issue of greeting and standing/staying for a long time while greeting, the Igbo people still stay for long time when they ask each other about their loved ones. The people still even go further to discuss issues and recent events in society, including the coronavirus. As such, nothing has changed about the way Igbo greet one another and how long they stay during greeting. This also goes for visiting neighbors. People still visit their neighbors as usual, despite the government's directive. The government is somehow incapacitated to enforce the order because most Igbo people live in rural areas where police patrols are infrequent.

Also, the two-meter social distancing order sounds absurd to people, and they find it difficult to come to terms with such a directive. They usually ask themselves »how can one distance himself from one's brother?«. Therefore, they still

---

[16] Cf. Uchenna: The Igbo of South East Nigeria.
[17] Cf. Asikaogu: Igbo Cultural Values and the Effect of Globalization.

stand or sit in close proximity to one another. This particular directive is the most difficult because in Igbo culture, the individual's personal space/distance from another person is usually short, and this is still the practice. People do not want to know whether there is coronavirus or not.

Furthermore, the Igbo have been directed not to gather in groups larger than 30. As a result, some have suspended burial ceremonies in their families, but others have gone ahead and held them despite all warnings. In fact, in one particular community, the state governor had to send soldiers and police to stop an ongoing burial ceremony and use force to disperse the crowd. Many of the people involved in that burial ceremony were grumbling that the governor does not have any right to stop the burial of their brother.

This same resistance goes for the government's stay-at-home order. The Igbo people hardly stay at home by themselves. Therefore, this order was not well received, especially in rural areas. They still go to their farms, markets, and churches as if nothing is happening.

All these have exposed the resilience of culture in the life of a people. I wish to note that the Igbo people find it difficult to adapt to the new way of living occasioned by the coronavirus pandemic because all governmental directives stand in opposition to the Igbo people's way of life. This means that the people will have to change quickly and completely to a lifestyle regarded by them as abominable. This adaptation is particularly difficult due to the fact that it must be done instantly, something many found and still find strange. It is true that culture is dynamic, but cultural change is typically gradual and happens in a discreet way.

The implication is that the preventative measures put in place by the government are not effective in Igbo land. If the coronavirus enters such a place, it will be very catastrophic, and this goes for other infectious diseases, too. As such, this behavior/cultural trait may need to be critically examined to find a way forward. It is also a lesson to government that they should not stay in Abuja to dish out orders, but rather be sensitive to the people and culture and endeavor to design intervention programs that would allow their policies to be effective. This is why the government should not keep quiet. The lives of many are at stake.

6. Conclusion

The paper concludes that governmental measures to curb the coronavirus pandemic in Igboland have not been effective because the new lifestyle demanded to combat the coronavirus contrasts Igbo culture. People therefore are unable to adapt to this new way of living despite the fact that it is for their own good. This piece recommends that before such orders are given in Igboland, the people should be sensitized about the specific problem and its consequences. They should also be told that it is not to abolish their culture but to safeguard their lives – and that they will go back to their normal lives after the crisis. The collision of two cultures was thus an attempt to bring to the fore the problem encountered by the Igbo people in adapting to the new way of living due to the coronavirus.

References

Abraham, W. Emmanuel: Crisis in African Cultures, in: Kwasi Wiredu / Kwame Gyekye (eds.): Person and Community: Ghanaian Philosophical Studies, Washington D.C. 1992, pp. 13–35.

Agulanna, Christopher: Ezigbo Mmadu: An Exploration of the Igbo Concept of a Good Person, in: Journal of Pan African studies, 4(5), 2011, pp. 139–161.

Asikaogu, Joannes: Igbo Cultural Values and the Effect of Globalization: A Critical Analysis, in: International Journal of Social Sciences and Humanities, 12(2), 2018, pp. 42–51.

Davidson, Basil: The African Genius, Boston 1969.

Helman, Cecil G.: Culture, Health and Illness: An Introduction for Health Professionals, London / Boston 1990.

Keesing, Roger M.: Cultural Anthropology: A Contemporary Perspective, New York 1971.

Korsman, Stephen N. J. / Gert U. van Zyl / Louise Nutt / Monique I. Andersson / Wolfgang Preiser: Virology: An Illustrated Colour Text, Amsterdam 2012.

Macebuh, N. Stanley: Humanism in Chains: An Applied Example. 17th Alumni Annual Lecture University of Ibadan, 08.11.2002.

Maclachlan, N. James / Edward J. Dubovi / Stephen W. Barthold / David E. Swayne / James R. Winton (eds.): Fenne's Veterinary Virology, Amsterdam 2017.

Nigeria Centre for Disease Control (NCDC): Update on Corona Virus Pandemic, http//www.ncdc.nig.org; last accessed 17.06.2020.

Tylor, Edward Burnett: Primitive Cultures: Researches into the Development of Mythology, Philosophy, Religion, Arts and Custom, London 1981.

Uchenna, Victor C.: The Igbo of Southeast Nigeria, New York, 1965.

Helga Maria Lell

»Law as Culture« in Argentina's Emergency Context

1. The »Emergency« as a Non-Novel Concept in Argentina

The last months of 2019 and the first ones of 2020 were not peaceful times in South America. With different levels of manifestation, social movements took the streets for multiple reasons, mainly to protest against governments (both left-wing and right-wing, according to the State), inequality and corruption in many countries: Venezuela, Peru, Ecuador, Colombia, Chile and Bolivia. In the same semester, in Argentina, elections were held to choose a new President and to partially renew the Congress. Between the Primary Elections (PASO) in August and the General Elections in October, an economic disaster happened that is complex to describe. The (at that time) President and candidate Mauricio Macri came in second and with a great difference below the opposition's candidate, Alberto Fernández. Popular discontent was evident in the vote and the results created uncertainty about the future. The main consequences were the devaluation of the national currency (»Peso«) in a drastic way (almost 100 % of its value) and the return of the exchange clamp (inability to buy more than US $ 200 per month). The rumor of a possible »corralito«[1] reminded the crisis of 2001. Inflation, which was already increasing, was intensified to be around 53,8 % per annum.

When the international crisis caused by the Coronavirus reached Argentina, the idea of a state of emergency that could justify an alteration of institutional power over citizenship was not new. It was not even recent. The mere idea of a law of emergency or in emergency did not scandalized anyone. The country has a long political and legislative tradition which, as a result of successive moments of economic and social emergencies, from the 1920s to the present, has continuously granted special powers to the Executive Branch so that it could take extraordinary decisions in economic and tax realms. These include affecting rights in order to overcome a crisis. The right to property has been the most recurrently affected one to fulfill what has been called by doctrinaires a »social function« which justifies different taxes.

---

[1] A regulatory measure that prevents taking savings out from the bank in cash.

On December 10, 2019, the new President, the deputies and senators took office. One of the first actions was the enactment of the Law 27541, on December 20, which declared, once again, the economic, fiscal, sanitary, administrative, retirement and energy emergency in the country. This rule established a large number of measures that raised a controversy that it is not possible to describe here. The most important one was to give the President more power of action for six months to review the legal conditions in those emergency areas and to regulate some issues. In this context, it must be added that the period of ordinary sessions of the Congress had ended on November 30. It began again on March 1 but shortly after that, the Congress meetings were suspended because of the pandemic. Therefore, any urgent decision that would require treatment by the Legislative Branch could be made by the President through a Decree of Necessity and Urgency (DNU), which has the force of law. In other words, the Executive Power can legislate to replace Congress (this institution, later, will review the actions).[2] If we add to this context that the Argentine government system is presidential and, as some authors describe »hyper-presidential«,[3] granting special powers to the Executive Power in an abnormal and exceptional instance does not seem like a measure that draws attention at all.[4]

In Argentina, normality is the emergency, although the phrase might seem paradoxical. Despite what has been said, the emergency that was unleashed by Coronavirus was different, not in relation to politics, or to the regulatory powers of the Executive Branch over the citizens' rights, but because of the major impact it had in daily life. This time, the crisis hit the economy, but also life itself in several dimensions: life in the biological sense is at tangible risk, life as a way of social and cultural relations changed. Words like *positive case, testing, authorization to circulate, face mask, alcohol in gel, imported cases, community circulation, recovered, stranded, flattening the curve*, among other, have been incorporated into daily use to provide meanings to these new surroundings. Nowadays, we work and study at home, we can no longer visit family, we won't share *mate* or *asado* on Sundays. There are no open churches, there is no football, there are no open banks. Going to the supermarket or to a pharmacy involves making long queues. Circulating in the streets without a very valid motive, far from being part of individual freedom, can be a crime against a collective good. A face mask is a mandatory clothing; there is an appropriate method for sneezing; face should not be touched; exercising

---

[2] After a consult to the Supreme Court, the Congress began its sessions again by mid-May.
[3] Cf. Nino: El hiperpresidencialismo argentino.
[4] The political configuration of the constitutional distribution of power is attached to historical struggles. The Presidential system (and non-Parliamentarian) comes from a long tradition of »caudillos« (a sort of warlords) that had a clear leadership and responsibility. Concentration of authority was the key for expectations but also for blaming. Cf. Tau Anzoátegui / Martiré: Manual de Historia de las Instituciones Argentinas, pp. 366–367; Chiaramonte: Usos Políticos de la Historia, p. 99.

in a park is a crime against public health and one should learn how to wash hands properly. All those expected actions configure a new normativity.

The first positive case of Coronavirus, in Argentina, was confirmed on March 3, 2020. It was a national citizen arriving from Europe. After that, the cases increased. By April 12, the majority of cases were »imported«, this is, it was about cases that belonged to people that have come from abroad recently (37,3 %) or to people directly related to them (34,8 %). However, there was also community circulation – the own/national Coronavirus – (14 %).[5] One month later, by May 13, the »imported« cases, are 14,2 % and those directly related to them are 45,3 %. Community circulation, the one that has not come from abroad but that has been produced inside the Argentinean borders, is 29,3 % and increasing fast. Lethality rate is 4,9 %, which produces deep fear. The President made a comparison with other countries in a way that it could show that if quarantine would not have been done, mortality could have been way much more serious.[6] »Fear« and »salvation« are criteria that are constantly interpreting statistics. The Law as Culture paradigm helps to understand how feelings and social emotions are involved in order to legitimate the authority of legal and political decisions, especially when they are as exceptional as the nowadays restrictions.

Since March 12, among other measures, the mandatory quarantine in some cases, the suspension of shows, the closure of public spaces and the prohibition of flights from Europe, the US, China, Japan, South Korea and Iran were established. A few days later, on March 19, social, preventive and compulsory isolation (hereinafter, ASPO) was decreed for all citizens (with the exception of those that work in the considered as essential services) and the complete closure of the borders. Now the risk was also in the countries of the South American region (the »patria grande« or the »big homeland«). Since then, the emergency is not the same as always. The effects over citizens' rights are much more noticeable. The principle of legality, formally, is intact: everything that is not forbidden is allowed; materially, it seems to have been reversed: outside from home, permission is the exception. The emergence of Covid-19, even in a country accustomed to crisis, has had a strong impact on various spheres of life.

---

5   The rest of the cases remain under investigation.
6   Conferencia de prensa del presidente de la Nación, 09.05.2020.

2. Argentine Anomie and Compulsory Isolation

One of the most remarkable effects of the Corona-crisis in Argentina is that Law is quite well complied and respected. Most people are obeying legal rules that involve social distance and isolation despite it is hard. This is not the usual behavior. The Corona Argentinean culture is different to the normal one when it comes to respect law. Carlos Nino linked what he called the *Argentine anomie* or *dumb anomie* to the underdevelopment of the country. He explains that this kind of anomie, unlike the one described by Durkheim, is actually a trend to illegality that involves a general violation of a rule, not because there is a lack of rules, because rules are not clear, because normative realms are contradictory to each other or because rules do not satisfy interests, but it is violated just in order to obtain an advantage for one's own, with the expectation that other citizens do comply.[7]

In a context in which public and individual health require collective abstention from circulation, respecting distances and changing social habits, the cultural factor that tends to systematic non-compliance can relativize the emergency rules. Let's see an example: a few days after the first official announcements on the suspension of events that would agglomerate people and the emphatic recommendation not to circulate except for extreme needs, that is, when there was no mandatory quarantine, news was published about the massive turnout of families to tourist destinations in such a way that there were delays in the access to cities and beaches. These events derived in the ruling of compulsory isolation with strong control by the security forces (police and military) and interpreting its violation as a crime against public health in the terms of the Penal Code.

In discourse and in practice, measures taken by national authorities demand constant justification grounded in emergency, health and the possible risk of death of population since they affect fundamental rights that have been the result of historical struggles. For example, the restriction of the freedom to circulate without being able to invoke a specific and allowed cause, the prohibition to work in cases of non-essential services, the prohibition of entry to the country for nationals who were stranded abroad unless they are rescued by the State, the restriction of seeing children in cases of divorced parents, the prohibition of practicing sports in common places or attending public events, the restriction of religious freedom which was completely relegated to the private sphere, are measures that were accepted by citizens. Even when a state of exception is not formally declared in constitutional terms, these measures show how formal Law yields to an informal form of social interpretation during the emergency.

On the other hand, the surveillance carried out by the security forces of the quarantine compliance has been one of the concerns that required an explana-

---

[7] Cf. Nino: Un país al margen de la ley, pp. 17–42.

tion by the President. He clarified that everything that is done is done within the framework of what democracy allows.[8] This is due to the fact that the intervention of the armed forces in cases of restriction of civil rights has been a sensitive issue in the country since the last military dictatorship.

3. The Dilemma between Health and Economy

In a speech, the President said that there is no dilemma between health and economy. He explained a series of actions that were taken in order to take care of the economic aspects, but he also stressed that the government's priority is health. To do this, he made an analogy: in 2003, he was part of the government of the then president Néstor Kirchner. Back then, the country was going through a deep economic, political and social crisis that can be symbolized in the succession of five presidents in eleven days in December 2001. However, there was a recovery. »An economy that falls always rises again, but a life that ends cannot be arisen anymore« were the president's words in his speech.[9] The phrase seeks for legitimacy showing the President's expertise in situations of economic crisis and invoking the probability of the most extreme consequence of the pandemic: death. It can be seen that, deep down, there is a message about the relationship between the State, citizen obedience and biological control: The State can overcome an economic crisis and the latter is not as serious as death. The State cannot solve a death, but obedience to the State can prevent death by Coronavirus. Disobedience, on the contrary, can generate an irreparable risk and collective damage.

It is interesting in this combination between the biological realm and obedience to the rules that the greatest citizen contribution to combat the pandemic is staying at home, that is, avoiding physical proximity to others. The collective good is cared for from the separation of individuals. The message is that individuality is what saves the community. Isolation is the legal response to a biological threaten.

---

[8] Palabras del presidente de la Nación, 20.03.2020.
[9] Palabras del Presidente de la Nación, 30.03.2020.

4. Changes in Communicative Acts

In general terms, the culture of Latin America is usually characterized as collectivist in the sense of the relevance of interactions between individuals and socialization groups, among them, family, friends and communities nucleated around some interest (neighborhood, sports, etc.).[10] Physical contact between people is something common in the framework of communicative acts in Argentina as a way of showing the bond.[11] Greeting each other with a kiss (not only with very close friends or family, but with colleagues or even someone who one has just met), touching the shoulder or arm of another person during a conversation, hugging for a few seconds at a farewell are part of daily life and that, as codes, their non-practice may seem impolite. Physical closeness is not an invasion but a sign of comfort. Since the emergence of the Coronavirus, the greeting has become an elbow bump and the distance of two meters between person and person is a new rule. The violation of these new emergency social rules might be considered as a way of putting others at risk. How will the safety and hygiene rules be designed for public spaces, for example, a university classroom, during this pandemic? A space that previously could be considered safe and adequate, can now be unsafe if it does not have space to maintain the same authorized capacity of people with the respective space of 2 meters. The regulations may not have formally changed, but their »reasonable« interpretation in light of the pandemic invalidates it and changes its meaning. A transitory culture for a transitory law is born and developing.

A practice that is extremely widespread in the country is drinking *mate*. *Matear* alone when there are other people around can be understood as a rude and a lack of consideration for others. Integrating a round of *mate* is not an obligation, although not doing so is a way of distancing. *Mate* in meeting should be shared, since this drink is actually an excuse for social interaction. In a context of great potential for contagion, this practice has been suspended at least in public, probably, not in the majority of homes. Sharing a *mate*, since the emergence of Covid-19, is a symbol of unconsciousness and contempt for the health of others. A renowned case in this regard was the death of an infected woman who would have shared the *mate* with the considered patient o from the province of Chaco (one of the most affected provinces of the country and certainly the most surprising one because it has not so much population and no international frontiers). Now then, could someone make a criminal complaint against others for drinking *mate*? Would this, in the Coronavirus times, be a penal typical behavior?

Another relevant change has occurred in the framework of the funeral ritual. There are no longer gathering of friends, family and relatives for hours at a wake.

---

[10] Cf. Hofstede: Culturas y organizaciones, pp. 221–222.
[11] Cf. Cerda-Hegerl: Dimensiones centrales de la cultura, pp. 328–343.

The regulations indicate that there are no open rooms for this purpose. The farewell must be done briefly and only with the immediate direct family of the deceased. If the person has died of Coronavirus, then their relatives must be quarantined and cannot attend to see the body for the last time.

Regarding religious practices, there are no open temples and they have been relegated to the private sphere. Masses and preaches are transmitted on line and, for example, Catholics are invited to spiritual contemplation as a way of communion. Only religious services for spiritual assistance in extreme cases are considered an essential service (for example, extreme unction of the sick). However, a priest could not attend to pray for a deceased at his funeral.

5. Coronavirus and the Political Crack

A particularity that Covid-19 disease took in Argentina during the first month is that it seemed to mainly affect the upper and middle social classes. This is because the vast majority of those affected were people who had been abroad (mainly in Europe and the United States) during the summer vacation period,[12] that is, they had enough money to pay for tickets and stays abroad. It is important to consider that paying services abroad after the devaluation of the national currency that occurred in 2019 and plus a 30 % tax, is very expensive. Coronavirus is associated with purchasing power.

In the last two decades, in the country, a political phenomenon has occurred that the contrast between liberal and populist ideologies, has generated a great social division. Explained in very simplistic terms, this division has implied whether supporting the Kirchner party (originally, *Frente para la Victoria*, today, *Frente de Todos*), with a center-left tendency, or supporting the party of *Cambiemos* (today, *Juntos por el Cambio*), with a center-right orientation. This phenomenon has been metaphorically called *the crack* (*la grieta*) since one is on one side or the other; in the middle, there is only an irreconcilable break. In this framework, the role of the State vis-à-vis the poor and tax policies have been discussed endlessly. Should the State grant subsidies for the most vulnerable sectors at the cost of increasing taxes for the middle and upper social strata? This was one of the central questions. In another group of ideas, also under the focus of the disputes was the national airline: Aerolíneas Argentinas which, for the Kirchner government, was a relevant part of the country's connection system and got many subsidies; and, for the liberal opposition, it was an icon of corruption.

[12] In the Argentine summer (December–March).

The appearance of the Covid-19, as a disease that has mainly affected those who have been abroad and their relatives, has made the crack vivid again. After national borders were closed, many Argentineans were stranded abroad. Their repatriation could only be made through Aerolineas Argentinas since other companies are not allowed to enter to the country. So, it was pointed out that those who once criticized the company (the supposed upper classes) now depended on it for their return.

It should be noted that these are the discourses that can be found in the framework of the media and social networks as a form of expression of the crack and what has been generated during the pandemic times. There are inconsistencies between the premises: who is abroad does not necessarily belong to a high class (many were with scholarships or for work reasons), not everyone who was abroad criticized Aerolineas Argentinas, not every member of middle or upper class is liberal, etc. However, in symbolic terms, the Coronavirus was associated with upper classes and the oppression of capitalism and economic liberalism over the poor.

In these examples it can be seen how the growing role of the State is considered as essential to save collective goods such as health, also to care for merchandise prices against excessive increases, to ensure rental contracts (prices are cannot be raised, contracts are extended and eviction is prohibited) and loan interests, and to repatriate the stranded. The National State is the one that can *flatten the curve*. As the collective becomes important, individuals are configured as reciprocal risks (each one can infect another person and each one can be infected be another one) that can only save the common realm by separating and isolating. Before, the political motto to invoke solidarity was *homeland is the other (la patria es el otro)*;[13] in times of pandemic, *the risk is the other*. What is shared is separation, paradoxically. Coronavirus has changed the way of creating the public sphere and of bonding.

6. Football Suspension

Football is the most famous sport in Argentina. It is not only a sport or a spectacle, but it is a means of building citizenship since its massive transmission by television or other media considers everyone under the same category: the one of *fans*,[14] it does not matter if someone is rich or poor, it is about following teams and games. Watching the games of the most important clubs is a ritual that many Argentineans enjoy. Not only that, but during the week, friends often get together to play

---

[13] This phrase was used in a speech in 2013 by the then President and current Vice President, Cristina Fernández de Kirchner. It became very popular and is a motto of populist groups.

[14] Cf. Alabarces: Fútbol y patria, p. 29.

a *picadito* (an improvised and informal soccer game). Quarantine has changed habits in this regard. However, in some places, citizens could not hold their desires. For example, in Chaco, a group of 11 women was arrested for violating the quarantine.[15]

In his speech of March 12, when requesting social distancing (still without quarantine) and suspending public shows, the President pointed out that the matches of the first league could be played behind closed doors. He asked television companies to show the football games for free so that all Argentineans could enjoy them (typically people must pay to watch the games).[16] A day later, the River Plate Club decided not to show up to play a game since a player had symptoms compatible with Coronavirus. Thus, the club denounced the risk for the health of the players of continuing with the Super League Cup. Finally, the Argentinean Football Association decided to suspend the activity.

The President's request for the continuity of the show and for the free broadcasting of the entertainment has a strategic background. The lack of soccer on television and on the fields eliminates one of the most relevant distractions that Argentine society has had in recent decades. Through the homogeneous mass media transmission, without paying, everybody can attend the same games. This erases on an imaginary level other barriers that in reality remain.[17] So, the continuity of football would have been a sort of a gate to avoid the isolation of the quarantine.

7. Asphalt Law and Poverty in Times of Pandemic

Poverty is one of the deepest stigmas of Argentina. Year 2019 ended with 35.5 % of poor according to official data.[18] Poverty not only implies measuring a per capita income as low, but also encompasses observing its effects: poor housing conditions, overcrowding, unhealthiness, little or no access to basic services, bad nutrition, informal jobs, contexts that facilitate domestic violence, etc. In the context of the pandemic, the first recommended sanitary measures have been social isolation and hygiene habits such as washing hands. These have certainly been difficult to fulfill in deprived neighborhoods where there is no access to water or where large families live in small rooms. Income is usually barely enough to live one day at a time and not being able to look for jobs makes it impossible to buy basic food. The government has taken economic measures to lessen the problems. Con-

---

[15] Cf. La Nación: Coronavirus en la Argentina.
[16] Mensaje por Cadena Nacional del presidente, 12.03.2020.
[17] Cf. Sebreli: La era del fútbol.
[18] Cf. INDEC: Informes técnicos.

tagion was slow in coming to poor neighborhoods. The first confirmed case took place on April 21. After that, the spread turned to be catastrophic. The speed of the spread is very high and marks a clear contrast with the speed of contagion in the rest of the country. Two weeks after the first case, every three tested people, two are positive. The risks over there are huge and health and sanitary devices and institutions are scarce.

A case that should be highlighted is that of the slums (*villas miseria*). A characteristic phenomenon of the city of Buenos Aires is the existence of these extremely poor neighborhoods, generally usurped, with precarious housing and little degree of urbanization. The *villas* have their own logic, they are redoubts with different codes, the State is absent there. In the framework of the pandemic, the interference of the armed forces is seen with fear since their entry and surveillance now have extra legitimacy: they are there to care for the inhabitants. Priests (*curas villeros*) have become key actors in this framework since they are interlocutors between the poor and the government and have offered the churches as refuges to house the most vulnerable.

The *Law of the asphalt*, as Boaventura de Sousa Santos named it while showing the contrast of state regulations against those of the Pasárgada favela,[19] it is not the natural one for the villas. How can a mandatory quarantine be imposed from the State where the State does not arrive or is not always welcomed? Until contagion arrived to the *villas* the quarantine could be done, in facts (not by legal permission), in a neighborhood way, this is, without crossing the limits of the neighborhood. Inside, life continues in an almost normal way, that is, people circulate, go to common places, etc.[20] However, »almost« is due to the fact that the income has decreased: the national economy outside the villas is paralyzed the effects are felt everywhere. After contagion arrived, danger is inside and outside the houses.

8. Adapted Rituals

The quarantine brought changes in social dynamics. Those with artistic gifts go out onto the balconies to sing, for example. At 9:00 p.m., every night since the isolation began, the doctors, nurses, security personnel, garbage collectors, licensed shop workers, etc. are applauded. These are new forms of expression, a way to participate in collective practices despite isolation. Some facts were particularly interesting. The first of these occurred on March 24. This is a significant date for Argentineans as it commemorates the starting date of the last and bloodiest dictatorship.

---

[19] Cf. de Sousa Santos: Sociología Jurídica Crítica.
[20] Cf. Centenera: El hambre se ensaña con las villas miseria de Argentina.

Every year, on this day, events take place in the Plaza de Mayo (Autonomous City of Buenos Aires), a symbolic place since the mothers of the *disappeared* (people kidnapped, tortured and killed by the non-democratic government in 1976–1983) marched during the dictatorship, demanding information of their children. To identify themselves, they wore a white headscarf. This year the congregation in that special place was impossible. The commemoration of that milestone is not merely a formality, but is a ritual of collective memory that shows the social commitment to not forget what happened and thus avoid that something similar occur again (*Never again* is the slogan) in addition to an invocation to human rights against state terrorism. During the quarantine, the rite was changed: no act was attended, but a white handkerchief was placed in windows and doors as a symbol. This was the new way of showing that, despite difficulties, the spirit remains alive.

Another interesting event occurred in relation to the deepening of the economic crisis. Because many sectors are paralyzed, revenues have decreased, but costs remain. The financial crisis is growing and the confrontation between the government and the business sector increases. In this framework, citizens began to demand politicians to reduce their salaries. On March 30, an ancient form of expression against politicians was revived, albeit in a different way: the *cacerolazo*. The *cacerolazo* is a peaceful practice of the middle classes, in which the citizens march against the government with the noise produced by hitting saucepans or any other metal device than can be easily found at home. The calls are not partisan and are a sample of the low representativeness of government decisions.[21] That night in quarantine, there was no march. Citizens protested from their balconies, but with pans in hand.

9. Some Reflections

1. Law in and of emergency is not new in Argentina. Neither are the extraordinary powers of the Executive Power. Some restrictions on rights, mainly those on property, are not new. Others, the most extreme, are novel.
2. The State is configured as a guardian of collective goods and is present in every space outside the domestic. Only home is exempt from State's interference.
3. When it comes to fighting for health as a human right, even in a sort of global war against a common invisible enemy, strategies are to be taken with closed frontiers. The pandemic has shown that despite the international markets and communities that countries may integrate, decisions are to be taken by National States.

---

[21] Cf. Kammerer/Sánchez Roncero: El cacerolazo como nueva forma de expresión popular.

4. In the pandemic, the collective is built from the individual as isolation. Not contacting physically is the way to take care of the health of others. However, there are many ways to build relationships and renew participation in social fields: Masses on line, hanging on pots on balconies, applauses at night, etc.
5. The state of exception is shown beyond what is formally declared. Democracy is still in force and guards the tensions created by Law in emergency. Health and emergency justify that Law changes. It is a transitory Law, which suddenly breaks in and is also legitimized by an emergency culture that enables it. Regardless of the legitimacy of the measures, the restriction of rights exists.
6. Until now, there has been no contagion among indigenous peoples. If there were, how will communal habits, forms of housing, family relationships, non-traditional medicine and even mortuary rituals be regulated by the State? How can the State intervene in communities responding to other normative conceptions and customary in a world that is imposing global protocols of safety?
7. What will happen to law when the state of emergency of the Coronavirus is reduced? What will happen to the penal causes initiated for circulating? Will there be lawsuits for damages to those who, allegedly ill, put others' health at risk?
8. How will the relationship between the social uses of greeting, physical contact sharing beyond the domestic and legal regulations be conceived?
9. Will there be changes in family law that, during the emergency, has reminded the responsibilities of the youngest of taking care of the older adults? How will the best interests of the child and the parenting regime be interpreted in isolation? Should the parents who did not live with the minors financially compensate the one who did live despite not being guilty for the breakdown of the parental responsibility regime? How can the State take care of people shut at homes where there is domestic violence?
10. What is the conception of the elderly adults in normality and which will be the relation of it after de pandemic? The Corona-crisis has developed a special speech on what can elderly adults do or not (for example, prohibitions of going out from their homes) and about the paternalism that daughters and sons should exercise over their own parents. Adult residences have been under the scopes as dangerous places. Are these the only risky ones?
11. Argentina has a very high rate of contagion between health professionals. What is the relationship between the recognition of them as heroes but, at the same time, as the unprotected ones?
12. What criteria will be taken for prisons where there is prison overlap and where prisoners have requested house arrest? If in Corona-era health is a motivation for house arrest, will this criterion remain for granting such a measure in the future?

13. Under criminal law, the alleged criminals who would have violated the quarantine by circulating without justification, in case of being judged post-emergency, will they fall under the emergency Law or will the most benign law be applied to them, that is, the non-emergency one?
14. What is the reason for closing borders in a globalized and interconnected world where a virus cannot distinguish between nationalities? What is actually protected: human health, the national's health, the virus non-circulation, the prevention of resources (human resources, health system buildings, artificial respirators, Covid-19 tests) not to scarce?

References

Alabarces, Pablo: Fútbol y patria: el fútbol y las narrativas de la nación en la Argentina, Buenos Aires 2002.
Centenera, Mar: El hambre se ensaña con las villas miseria de Argentina por la pandemia, in: El País, 03.04.2020, https://elpais.com/sociedad/2020-04-03/el-hambre-se-ensana-con-las-villas-miseria-de-argentina-por-la-pandemia.html; last accessed 12.05.2020.
Cerda-Hegerl, Patricia: Dimensiones centrales de la cultura y la comunicación en América Latina hoy, in: Instituto Cervantes Múnich (ed): Actas del Programa de Formación para el profesorado de Español como Lengua Extranjera del Instituto Cervantes de Múnich (2005–2006), Múnich 2006, pp. 328–343.
Chiaramonte, José Carlos: Usos políticos de la historia. Lenguaje de clases y revisionismo histórico, Buenos Aires 2013.
Conferencia de prensa del presidente de la Nación, Alberto Fernández; del Jefe de Gobierno de la Ciudad de Buenos Aires, Horacio Rodríguez Larreta y el Gobernador de la provincia de Buenos Aires, Axel Kicillof, acerca de la extensión de la cuarentena, 09.05.2020, https://www.casarosada.gob.ar/informacion/discursos/46863-conferencia-de-prensa-del-presidente-de-la-nacion-alberto-fernandez-del-jefe-de-gobierno-de-la-ciudad-de-buenos-aires-horacio-rodriguez-larreta-y-el-gobernador-de-la-provincia-de-buenos-aires-axel-kicillof-acerca-de-la-extension-de-la-cuarentena-por-el-co; last accessed 13.05.2020.
de Sousa Santos, Boaventura: Sociología Jurídica Crítica, Madrid 2009.
Hofstede, Geert: Culturas y organizaciones. El software mental: La cooperación internacional y su importancia para la supervivencia, Madrid 1999.
Instituto Nacional de Estadística y Censos de la República Argentina (INDEC): Informes técnicos. Vol. 4, n° 59. Condiciones de vida. Vol. 4. N° 4. De la pobreza y la indigencia en 31 aglomerados urbanos. Segundo semestre de 2019. Minis-

terio de Economía, INDEC, Argentina, 2019, https://www.indec.gob.ar/indec/web/Nivel4-Tema-4-46-152; last accessed 03.07.2020.

Kammerer, María Luján / María Victoria Sánchez Roncero: El cacerolazo como nueva forma de expresión popular, in: Question, 1(6), 2010.

La Nación: Coronavirus en la Argentina: detienen a 11 mujeres por violar la cuarentena para jugar al fútbol en Chaco, https://www.lanacion.com.ar/sociedad/coronavirus-argentina-detienen-11-mujeres-violar-cuarentena-nid2350802; last accessed 12.05.2020.

Mensaje por Cadena Nacional del presidente Alberto Fernández ante la emergencia por coronavirus, 12.03.2020, https://www.casarosada.gob.ar/informacion/discursos/46767-mensaje-por-cadena-nacional-del-presidente-alberto-fernandez-ante-la-emergencia-por-coronavirus; last accessed 12.05.2020.

Nino, Carlos Santiago: El hiperpresidencialismo argentino y las concepciones de la democracia, in: Carlos Santiago Nino: El presidencialismo puesto a prueba: con especial referencia al sistema presidencialista latinoamericano, Madrid 1992, pp. 37–77.

Nino, Carlos Santiago: Un país al margen de la ley. Estudio de la anomia como componente del subdesarrollo argentino, Buenos Aires 1992.

Palabras del Presidente de la Nación, Alberto Fernández, acerca de la pandemia del coronavirus COVID-19, desde Olivos, 30.03.2020, https://www.casarosada.gob.ar/informacion/discursos/46803-palabras-del-presidente-de-la-nacion-alberto-fernandez-acerca-de-la-pandemia-del-coronavirus-covid-19-desde-olivos; last accessed 12.05.2020.

Palabras del presidente de la Nación, Alberto Fernández, luego de su reunión con los Gobernadores, para analizar la pandemia del coronavirus, COVID-19, desde Olivos, 20.03.2020, https://www.casarosada.gob.ar/informacion/discursos/46783-palabras-del-presidente-de-la-nacion-alberto-fernandez-luego-de-su-reunion-con-los-gobernadores-para-analizar-la-pandemia-del-coronavirus-covid-19-desde-olivos; last accessed 12.05.2020.

Sebreli, Juan José: La era del fútbol, Buenos Aires 2011.

Tau Anzoátegui, Víctor / Eduardo Martiré: Manual de Historia de las Instituciones Argentinas, Buenos Aires 2005.

Sergio Genovesi

»Support Your Local«: The Ethics of Consumption and the Coronavirus Pandemic

»Support your local«. We all already knew this sentence from our local bakeries, breweries and clothing shops, reminding us that if we want to keep having nice small businesses in our town we should avoid buying everything we need from big malls, online shops and multinational chains. This imperative concerning our ethics of consumption started spreading more than ever during the first lockdown phase of the Coronavirus crisis, supported by new and more persuasive evidence that our purchasing choices do have a tremendous impact on other people's lives.

There are two main facts showing the ethical charge of every single purchase we do:

1.) Without customers, small businesses are witnessing a hard crisis that may lead them to quickly go bankrupt, even though states are trying to provide financial aid. Purchasing their products is not just a matter of shopping preferences. It has become an act of solidarity. Without our support, our neighbors and friends selling local products will literally go under, while big businesses have much greater chances of surviving the crisis. Buying a takeaway meal from a small restaurant at the corner instead of from a big fast-food chain or ordering a book from a small bookstore instead of from Amazon might make the difference between keeping a rich diversity of local businesses in your neighborhood and seeing them replaced by another big mall.

2.) Many products, whose production is outsourced in other countries for a cheaper price, were no more available on the shelves of our shops. On the one hand, the supply of many goods went slower or even stopped in reason of the restrictions in crossing national borders. On the other hand, people started panic-buying the last stocks. This undeniable evidence of our dependence from the countries where the production is outsourced clearly shows the ethical responsibility behind the outsourcing choice: in order to get cheap products, we foster producers who care less about workers' rights and the environment. Every cheap buy is done at the cost of someone else's rights.

So what? These facts were known as well before the pandemics. However, the average consumer did not take them seriously or just ignored them. What is different now is their urgency: they cannot be ignored anymore since Covid-19 made it a matter of life or death. In times of crisis, people seemed to be finally ready to pay more for a not outsourced and made-by-locals product. That's not all: every purchase by a local store is celebrated as a good action by the whole community, showing a connection between a change in our normativity and the target-switch of our social approval and disapproval.[1]

The post-Corona scenarios might therefore be a kind of accelerationist promised land, where capitalism, brought to its extreme consequences, causes by itself a system collapse and an anti-capitalistic reconfiguration of norms and values.[2] In the present case, the Coronavirus would be the catalyst. Indeed, a certain kind of blind trust in the capitalist logic of consumption looks to have been undermined during the spread of the virus. Reporting the failure of a globalized economy in times of a pandemic, the media have increasingly shown the negative consequences of our consumerism on a world scale, from the climate crisis to the human rights violations, raising awareness among viewers. Thus, a new moral imperative has established itself: support your local, be good, respect workers' rights, do not pollute. Yet, we still live in a globalized society and we still want to go to Hawaii on holiday and eat avocados.

The Coronavirus offered to us a useful metaphor to describe the complex implications of our actions as consumers. During a pandemic in a globalized society, every person might inadvertently infect hundreds of people and be one of the rings of a causal chain that leads to the death of thousands of individuals on the other side of the earth. The most common immediate solution adopted to face this problem was breaking the chain of infection by imposing home quarantine and forbidding traveling (in Europe every country closed its borders, in Italy people weren't even allowed to leave their town). In the same way, in a globalized capitalistic economy, through every single purchase the consumer might unknowingly be a ring of a causal chain that leads, among other things, to work exploitation of children and adults. In this case, breaking the unfair production chains by planning every step of the production on a local level in a fair and environment-friendly way does not look like a possible scenario. Nowhere in the world there is a place with enough resources and skilled workers to produce a made-by-a-local Smartphone or laptop.

If we really want to stick to the »support your local« imperative in times of revision of our economical rules, we should then first ask ourselves who our locals are. Assuming that they are just our immediate neighbors, our friends or our fellow citizens would imply being ready to take responsibility only for the first immediate consequences of our behavior, rejecting all further implications. In this

---

[1] The direct connection between social disapproval and a new Corona-normativity has been highlighted by Gephart: Introduction, in this volume.
[2] Cf. Shaviro: No Speed Limits.

scenario, we would discharge accountability for buying goods whose production process harms people and the environment outside our local sphere since we are at least being nice to »our locals«. This is exactly the pre-corona scenario (and, of course, the pre-Fridays for Future, etc.).

After the pandemic, we are all witnesses of the fact that pausing globalization – together with its harmful production chains – has as a concrete result the scarcity of many goods that we buy on a daily basis. In this scenario, the question about »our locals« needs to be generalized and extended to all the people who are really affected by our consumeristic behavior. As Markus Gabriel suggested, this generalization is of such magnitude, that the moral question about the impact of our actions on our fellow human beings should get metaphysical,[3] becoming a general matter of principle. If our consumption habits make *de facto* the global scale the smallest scale possible to satisfy our demand for goods, every human being should be considered as a local. »Our local« would so become a more and more abstract character, getting even further than the Levinassian concept of The Other (*L'Autre*)[4] or to the Christian idea of Neighbor (*thou shalt love thy neighbor as thyself*, Mattew 22:39): »our local« is not only whoever we might meet in person, but everybody that might be concerned by the effects of our economic behavior – that is everybody.[5]

How is it possible to support everybody? If we see ourselves as the constitutive bricks of a bigger moral whole called society and we just equally share among us the moral responsibility imputable to our capitalistic system, no one of us will come out with a clean conscience. Being »supportive« would be basically made impossible by the fact that in a holistic system of interactions between consumers and producers we cannot independently determine the extent of the moral implications that derive from our actions as individuals. Indeed, these implications are always affected by the choices of other people and their impact on the market. Also the Thoureauan choice of quitting society and living in the woods – that is, the choice of having no locals to support or harm – would not redeem us. First of all, it is not a moral choice because it implies to stop undertaking moral actions rather than trying to do good – and that despite the awareness of the harm that society is causing to many people. Moreover, it is hardly imaginable that this choice can be generalized.

In a globalized market and society like the one we are living in, where the moral charge of an individual economical behavior is built through the inter-

---

[3] Cf. Gabriel: We Need a Metaphysical Pandemic, in this volume.
[4] Levinas: Totalité et infini.
[5] The moral problem of the universalization of a »local« ethics is tackled by Gephart: Conclusion, in this volume. As particularly relevant for the discussion, he mentions Benjamin Nelson's work on the concept of »brotherhood« (The Idea of Usury. From Tribal Brotherhood to Universal Otherhood) and Georg Simmel's essay on the »stranger« (»Exkurs über den Fremden«).

action with many actors (let's call that »moral pandemic scenario«), supporting our fellow human beings is a complex task. Of course, our individual behavior alone cannot directly determine alone its *Wirkungsgeschichte*. However, every purchasing choice can indirectly affect many other chains of production and the sum of many purchasing choice which attempt to minimize their harmfulness may effect a change in the economic system, in society and in its norms and values.

In a moral pandemic scenario, we should look for general ethical guidelines that can be applied to our behavior towards our locals in the global village. Even though they were developed in a not globalized time, two Kantian imperatives may work for us. The first goes »*Sapere Aude*« (dare to know) and is advised in the essay *Was ist Aufklärung*.[6] In current German the word *Aufklärung* means both the cultural movement of Enlightenment and the act of clarifying and raising awareness. Considering this double meaning of the word, Markus Gabriel claimed that we need nowadays a new *Aufklärung*. Indeed, by identifying fake news, collecting true information and pondering the different moral weight of our purchasing choices, it is possible to make informed decisions and avoid buying goods that are particularly harmful to the globalized society.

The second imperative that should guide our decisions is the well-known second formulation of the categorical imperative: »Act in such a way that you treat humanity, whether in your own person or in the person of any other, never merely as a means to an end, but always at the same time as an end«.[7] In other words, we should consider workers not only as rings of a productive chain but always as persons whose human rights and dignity should come first. Although our idea of human rights and human flourishing might change from time to time according to our knowledge about the world and our nature, the fact that by definition human rights are the same for all human beings — irrespective of their position in the production chain — still remains a constant that should constitute the foundation of our attitude toward the others.

The Coronavirus pandemic has shown to us in new ways how complex the *Wirkungsgeschichte* of our actions in a globalized society can be and how far away our behavior can affect other people. Our moral responsibility toward our fellow human beings cannot just be hidden from our sight outside our allegedly »local« bubble anymore since the consequences of our actions, which may well go round the world, manifestly affect us and our loved ones back home. Self-care and support for the locals can only be achieved by caring for everybody and leaving no one behind. This should not only happen in reason of egoistic self-preservation and production-aimed environmental safeguard, but rather for a moral reason, that is the recognition of the value of other individuals for their own sake.

---

[6] Kant: Beantwortung der Frage: Was ist Aufklärung?
[7] Kant: Grundlegung zur Metaphysik der Sitten [1781], p. 36.

References

Kant, Immanuel: Beantwortung der Frage: Was ist Aufklärung?, in: Berlinische Monatsschrift, 1784, H. 12, pp. 481–494.

Kant, Immanuel: Grundlegung zur Metaphysik der Sitten [1781], English translation by J. Ellington: Grounding for the Metaphysics of Morals, Indianapolis 1993.

Levinas, Emmanuel: Totalité et infini, Den Haag 1961.

Nelson, Benjamin: The Idea of Usury. From Tribal Brotherhood to Universal Otherhood, Chicago 1969.

Shaviro, Steven: No Speed Limits. Three Essays on Accelerationism, Minneapolis 2015.

Simmel, Georg: Exkurs über den Fremden, in: Soziologie, Untersuchungen über die Formen der Vergesellschaftung, Berlin 1983.

Hamadi Redissi et al.*

La Tunisie face au Covid-19. Penser ensemble, agir de concert

Avec un nombre réduit de personnes décédées ou déclarées positives à ce jour, la Tunisie, et relativement à d'autres pays, présente un tableau « satisfaisant » dans la gestion de la crise du Covid-19 (acronyme de *Coronavirus Infectious Disease 2019*, pouvant se décliner en français au féminin comme au masculin). Les mesures assez strictes prises presque à temps (couvre-feu décrété à partir du 18 mars et confinement général imposé à partir du 22 mars, même si ce dernier ne semble pas s'appliquer partout avec autant d'efficacité et de discipline) parviennent pour le moment à contenir la propagation du virus. Comme partout ailleurs, la pandémie a suscité des débats aussi serrés qu'animés sur ses multiples aspects et répercussions. Tout en saluant les prises de positions provenant essentiellement d'instituts et de cercles de réflexion ayant apporté des réponses économico-sociales à la crise, L'Observatoire Tunisien de la Transition Démocratique estime que la pandémie est un « fait social total » au sens durkheimien appelant forcément une réflexion globale. Même si la Tunisie reste en marge de la réflexion sur le covid-19, puisque les médias nationaux sont généralement pris dans le feu de l'actualité entre données statistiques, annonces politiques et information sur le terrain, on peut estimer qu'il est appauvrissant d'entreprendre une analyse de la situation tunisienne, en dehors des grandes lignes thématiques, ou problématiques qui sont en train de s'imposer comme tendances lourdes dans l'appréhension de cette crise sanitaire. Un suivi des débats autour de cette « situation de guerre » met en lumière quelques problématiques phares. Elles se posent aussi bien durant le confinement qu'après le déconfinement, à ne pas confondre avec l'après-Covid-19. Nous les synthétisons en cinq axes, chacun posant une question appropriée : la vie ou l'économie ? (1.), la mondialisation ou la souveraineté ? (2.), l'état d'exception ou l'État de droit ? (3.), est-ce une crise politique ou une crise du politique ? (4.), enfin la solidarité ou l'égoïsme ? (5.).

* The following authors have contributed to the writing of this article: Asma Nouira, Hafedh Chekir, Chafiq Sarsar, Hafidha Chekir, Sonia Mbarek, Tarek ben Chaabane, Abdelkrim Allagui, Sahbi Khakfaoui, Fatma Ellafi, Cheyma M'barki, Cyrine Ben Said, Hatem Chakroun.

1. Préserver la vie ou assurer la continuité de la vie économique

Le premier dilemme auquel est confronté la Tunisie est de concilier entre la préservation de la vie et la sauvegarde de l'économie. A l'instar de tous les pays du monde, elle a fait le choix de protéger la vie des Tunisiens et des Tunisiennes. D'où la décision du confinement général prise début mars 2020, certes après quelques tergiversations un peu comme partout. Peut-être la Tunisie l'a-t-elle fait par mimétisme, mais bien d'indices montrent qu'à l'évidence l'État avait peur d'être en situation de compter les morts, de les ensevelir et de les pleurer, en l'absence manifeste de moyens sanitaires à même d'affronter la pandémie et de prendre soin des contaminés. Cet affolement (critiqué par ailleurs) exprime la conscience universelle et inédite d'être le « gouvernement des vies ». Après tout, le bilan des décès n'est lourd ni en Tunisie (une quarantaine de morts) ni dans le monde (près de 200 milles), comparé à celui des pandémies du passé (citons l'exemple de la « grippe asiatique » des années soixante du XXe siècle ayant fait au moins un million de morts ou un à quatre millions de morts selon l'OMS).

1.1 La primauté de la vie

En effet, outre sa capacité à se propager par-delà les frontières, ce qui différencie l'actuelle pandémie des maladies contagieuses antérieures est la primauté accordée à la vie, au sens biologique, un peu ce que les Grecs appellent le *bios Politkon*, la vie humaine, par rapport à la vie animale et dont on peut trouver un analogue dans la « préservation de la vie » (« hifdh al nafs »), l'une des finalités de la politique dans la culture islamique. Pour la première fois dans l'histoire de l'humanité, la vie, la survie même physique dans son expression la plus élémentaire à savoir la peur de mourir s'arroge la priorité sur les autres finalités de la politique : la liberté, l'égalité, le bonheur et l'utilité, pour nous en tenir aux quatre grandes valeurs qui structurent toutes les doctrines politiques.

1.2 Inégaux dans le confinement

Le choix du confinement a été judicieux. Seulement, nous sommes inégaux dans le confinement. Nous le savions déjà mais le confinement rend plus inacceptables les inégalités entre les riches et les pauvres, les nantis et les démunis, les classes supérieures et les classes subalternes, les régions côtières et l'arrière-pays, le nord et le sud. Mais encore entre ceux qui ont une source de revenus et ceux qui n'en ont pas. Le confinement n'est pas vécu de la même façon, non plus par les travailleurs manuels et intellectuels. Les récits poignants sur le confinement de familles entières dans des espaces exigus et le spectacle affligeant des attroupements devant les sièges de gouvernorats et des délégations montrent que le devoir de se confiner ordonné par le gouvernement ne peut être respecté, non par défiance mais pas impossibilité matérielle de le mettre en oeuvre. A cela s'ajoute le manque de précautions, de distanciation sociale ou de mesures d'hygiènes. L'inégalité s'étend aux nombreux aspects psychosociaux, de lésions psychologiques et d'aggravation des souffrances post-traumatiques dues à une solitude imposée ; et elle s'est accompagnée d'une recrudescence de la violence contre les femmes au sein de la famille et dans l'espace public (elle est de 7 % que d'habitude). Il est encore tôt de faire le bilan du confinement, mais pour le moment le gouvernement par le nombre qui veut en l'occurrence épargner des vies humaines se trouve décalé par rapport à la vie réelle des Tunisiens et des Tunisiennes. Il a certes choisi d'être le gouvernement des vies, et de toutes les vies. Seulement, il ne dispose pas des moyens de les préserver toutes et dignement. Des pans entiers échappent même à ses recensements (il suffit de penser à l'économie parallèle). La biopolitique de la crise sanitaire s'est trouvée ainsi face à un autre pays qui n'est pas forcément considéré par les politiques publiques. D'où cette contradiction : un confinement inégal s'est révélé être plus préjudiciable pour la survie que le risque de contracter la maladie en menant librement une vie sociale, en travaillant, en luttant quotidiennement pour gagner sa vie.

1.3 Le contrepoint économique

Aussi inestimable soit-elle la vie a un coût calculé par les économistes (il ne s'agit pas du coût global du confinement, mais de la vie par habitant). En Tunisie, nous disposons du coût d'une journée Covid-19 (à peu près 200 millions de dinars selon les calculs de l'économiste Azzedine Saïdane). Le gouvernement n'a pas fourni d'évaluation chiffrée. Nous disposons également du coût global du confinement, évalué à près de 150.000 chômeurs de plus (faisant passer le taux de près de 15 % à plus de 18 %) et une contraction du taux de croissance de près de 4 %, (selon une étude des économistes Hakim Ben Hammouda et Hédi Bchir). La stratégie du gouvernement a été de compenser d'un bout à l'autre de la chaîne, les plus vulnérables et les entreprises. Or, le spectre de ceux qui subissent les effets délétères du confinement est beaucoup plus large. Mais encore, les mesures prises par le gouvernement pour en atténuer les effets sur les couches les plus fragiles sont des expédients (150 MD pour les personnes vulnérables à faible revenu ou à besoins spécifiques et 300 MD pour les travailleurs en chômage technique) et le montant individuel de 200 dinars est dérisoire. Quant aux aides accordées aux entreprises, elles sont insuffisantes. D'où la tentation de transformer le confinement en opportunité pour collecter des ressources par tous les moyens, les dons, les ponctions sur les salaires, les mesures fiscales. Le ciblage des catégories sociales et l'équité dans la distribution des charges suscitent également une polémique. Une mobilisation de ressources à long terme est annoncée début mai.

2. Mondialisation ou autosuffisance

La pandémie Covid-19 marque indéniablement un tournant sur la scène internationale et ses implications politiques et économiques ont déjà ébranlé les équilibres internationaux (financiers, économiques institutionnels et géopolitiques). Il faut reconnaître que la portée de ces changements n'est pas encore certaine. La récession économique mondiale, la chute vertigineuse des prix du pétrole, la paralysie du transport aérien et les nouvelles vagues de chômage ne sont que quelques manifestations de ces changements profonds auxquels la Tunisie doit se préparer à y faire face. Le Covid-19 confirme les critiques adressées à une mondialisation néolibérale et inégalitaire, un modèle qui a sacrifié les valeurs humanistes sur l'autel de la croissance ne profitant qu'à une minorité. Mais en même temps, la réponse souverainiste toute faite est une recette inappropriée à un virus véritablement mondial qu'aucune frontière nationale n'est à même d'arrêter. La démondialisation est une chimère. Le virus n'est pas confiné. Une nation ne se confine pas. Pour ce qui est de la Tunisie :

2.1 Autonomie stratégique.

La pandémie révèle l'importance vitale des secteurs alimentaire, de la santé, de l'éducation et du transport qui ne peuvent pas être livrés à la loi du marché. D'où la nécessité de rompre notre dépendance, d'impulser une nouvelle politique industrielle tendant à mobiliser les ressources budgétaires et à réorienter les investissements publics et privés vers ces secteurs déclarés prioritaires et de les protéger de la concurrence internationale. Il appartient à l'État de fixer les priorités, en concertation avec les parties concernées.

2.2 Discrédit du libéralisme et du souverainisme

Le Covid-19 a délégitimé le discours néo-libéral qui demande instamment le démantèlement des entreprises publiques les plus stratégiques et les plus performantes et de réduire l'État à ses fonctions régaliennes. Par la même, la crise montre l'inanité du discours souverainiste primaire, démagogique et électoraliste selon lequel la Tunisie regorge de ressources naturelles (pétrole, or, sel) détenues par des puissances étrangères. Aucune voix ne s'est élevée dans ce sens. Bien au contraire, les appels les plus pressants demandent à ce que les autorités acquièrent de l'étranger les médicaments et les dispositifs sanitaires pour affronter la pandémie.

3. État d'exception, État de droit

La pandémie déclenche une grande polémique autour de ce qu'on appelle « l'état d'exception ». Il a deux acceptions, philosophique et juridique.

3.1 L'état d'exception et biopouvoir numérique

Du point de vue philosophique, « l'état d'exception » désigne ce statut inhérent au Souverain qui consiste à légiférer, tout en se situant en dehors du droit, d'énoncer la norme juridique sans y être soumis. Ce concept est inventé par le philosophe allemand Carl Schmitt à la deuxième décade du XXe siècle. Dans sa formulation initiale, « l'état d'exception » est le régime juridique de droit commun : tout État (légiférant) est dans l'Exception (hors droit). Il est repris récemment par le philosophe italien Giorgio Agamben et le philosophe slovène Slavoj Zizek. Ils l'ont appliqué d'une manière opportuniste au cas d'espèce, un état d'exception temporaire. Ce concept est articulé au « biopouvoir », un néologisme inventé par Michel Foucault pour désigner le pouvoir de l'État moderne sur la vie des gens. Ce qui est inédit avec la prévention de la maladie c'est la « biopolitique numérique », sur le modèle chinois important le consentement des citoyens (tracking biométrique des contaminés et autres mesures attentatoires aux libertés). Cet « état d'exception » qui suspend l'exercice de la démocratie ne nous concerne pas dans la mesure où la numérisation en Tunisie est élémentaire. Elle est même une aspiration nationale. La crise a montré que faute de digitalisation suffisante de notre administration et de nos entreprises, le travail à domicile n'a pas été possible pour assurer la continuité en temps de crise. Toutefois, des efforts sont accomplis, par exemple pour le payement des aides sociales. Ils montrent que le pays a des potentialités pour la digitalisation.

3.2 L'état d'exception provisoire

La deuxième acception de l'exception est juridique. Elle nous concerne à travers le mécanisme constitutionnel de l'article 80 activé par le Chef de l'État. Pour sa part, le Chef du gouvernement a activé l'article 70 l'habilitant à légiférer par ordonnance, afin de pouvoir prendre les mesures nécessaires pour limiter la propagation du virus et ceci pour une durée de deux mois. Il appartient aux juristes de répondre à la question de leur compatibilité. Sur la base de l'habilitation, seize décrets-lois ont été pris pour mettre en oeuvre les mesures d'urgence, qui n'ont soulevé aucune protestation des juristes, sous bénéfice d'inventaire. En tous cas, le gouvernement s'est engagé à respecter les mécanismes constitutionnels et juridiques. Cependant, il existe des craintes justifiées de voir les droits humains sacrifiés à des fins de sécurité, d'inscrire le transitoire dans la durée et de faire du régime dérogatoire l'ordre naturel des choses. Un indice : l'utilisation d'un langage musclé par le Chef du gouvernement dans l'affaire dite des « bavettes » pour défendre son ministre de l'industrie ayant commandé par téléphone à un industriel qui se trouve être un député deux millions de bavettes, alors que la loi interdit au dit député de conclure des marchés à caractère commercial avec l'État, les collectivités locales et les organismes publics (article 25 du règlement intérieur de l'ARP). Pourtant, nous savons tous que c'est précisément lors des crises que le respect des droits humains est encore plus important notamment les droits et libertés individuelles, le droit à la santé, le droit à la protection de l'intégrité de la personne, les droits des femmes, les droits des migrants, les droits reproductifs et sexuels ; et qu'on ne peut aliéner ou limiter ces droits au titre de l'urgence sanitaire et de l'état d'exception.

4. Politique de la crise, crise du politique

La crise a mis à nu le délitement du système de santé, de l'éducation nationale notamment de l'école publique et républicaine en déclin et des mécanismes de la solidarité (passée d'un clientélisme étatique durant l'ère Ben Ali à un clientélisme privatisé). Mais encore, elle a exposé au grand jour les travers du système politique. Cette crise a-t-elle été appréhendée à sa juste mesure par les acteurs politiques et sociaux ?

4.1 Une gestion improvisée

Contrairement à un Chef d'État complètement décalé par rapport à une situation qui ne cadre pas avec le populisme épique qu'il s'est imposé d'un côté et des partis impotents de l'autre, le gouvernement gère la crise certes de manière rationnelle avec le peu de moyens dont il dispose, cependant au jour le jour, de façon improvisée, confuse et non prospective. Cette gestion s'appuie sur une pluralité de structures aux attributions concurrentes : l'Instance nationale de lutte contre le Coronavirus, instituée le 25 mars (qui regroupe de hauts cadres des ministères de l'Intérieur, de la Santé et des Affaires sociales), le Comité de lutte contre les catastrophes naturelles (créé en 1993) ayant des ramifications régionales (en état de veille permanente depuis le 21 mars), la Commission permanente pour le suivi du Covid-19 auprès du ministère de la santé et le Conseil de sécurité nationale présidé par le Chef de l'État. A cette concurrence horizontale, le conflit est ouvert entre un pouvoir central d'allure jacobine et des collectivités locales élues jalouses de leurs attributions, le Président de la république et le Chef de gouvernement ayant déclaré la prééminence du pouvoir central (respectivement les 20 et 26 mars 2020).

4.2 La résilience de l'État et l'impotence des partis politiques.

Malgré sa déliquescence l'État résiste. La crise a jusque-là resserré les liens entre l'État et la population. On redécouvre le rôle social de l'État à travers ses instances malgré toutes leurs insuffisances. La montée du ministre de la santé et du premier ministre dans les sondages et la popularité dont jouissent les responsables sanitaires de la lutte contre la pandémie expriment à la fois une culture de sujétion à l'État et une reconnaissance aux efforts fournis par les cadres de la République, indépendamment de ce qu'on peut penser de la qualité de la réponse ou de la crédibilité de ces mêmes responsables. On s'aperçoit aussi des limites de l'État face au non-respect du confinement ou dans la lutte contre le détournement des marchandises subventionnées. En revanche, les partis politiques apparaissent comme tétanisés. Aucun débat, aucune déclaration solennelle, aucune alerte sur tel ou tel aspect de la crise, aucune proposition concrète sur la sortie de la crise ; bref les partis se sont illustrés par une absence sidérale de vision. Voire. La plupart d'entre eux continuent à s'invectiver les uns aux autres, de manière frivole et vulgaire. L'indigence de la classe politique apparaît aussi dans ce qui s'apparente à du populisme en porte-à-faux par rapport à la responsabilité morale en période de crise. Sur cela se greffe le manque de confiance flagrant entre l'exécutif et le législatif et entre les différents acteurs politiques. Ceci est la conséquence de la non reproduction de la noblesse d'État depuis la révolution.

4.3 La valorisation du Médecin de la santé publique

Dans un paysage marqué par la défiance à l'égard des élites, une figure typique émerge : le Médecin qui travaille dans le service public de la santé. Il tire sa légitimité de la science, en tant que technique. Celle-ci a une valeur pour ceux qui lui donnent de la valeur, ceux qui se méfient de la médecine « traditionnelle » et des charlatans religieux qui prospèrent dans de pareilles circonstances, quand le mal est mystérieux, invisible et terrible. Mais, contrairement à ce qui se passe ailleurs, cette légitimité ne semble pas s'étendre au personnel paramédical pour des raisons qu'il s'agit d'explorer. Le Médecin participe à réduire la séduction de la théorie du complot (selon laquelle le virus est une conspiration ourdie par des forces occultes). En prenant la parole, il concurrence sur le plan de l'expertise technique le Juriste omniprésent durant la première phase de la transition (2011–2014) et l'Économiste détenteur du secret de la crise sociale durant la seconde période (2014–…). Le Médecin profite enfin du discrédit qui frappe les deux figures du Religieux mystificateur et du Politicien chicaneur.

5. Solidarité, repli sur soi

La pandémie a ébranlé le vivre-ensemble. Elle déclenche un mouvement contradictoire d'altruisme et d'égoïsme : une solidarité active contrebalancée par un repli sur soi.

5.1 Une solidarité active

Elle se manifeste à travers de nombreuses actions, qu'elles prennent la forme de dévouement du personnel médical et paramédical, les dons collectés par les instances publiques, les prélèvements sur les salaires, les innombrables actions des structures locales et citoyennes. L'accord signé entre l'UGTT et le patronat sur le paiement des salaires du mois d'avril dénote d'un sens louable des responsabilités.

5.2 Un repli sur soi

A l'inverse, l'hystérie de la survie a poussé au repli sur soi et à l'égoïsme forcené, voire à des incivilités. Elle menace même la société de désintégration. Des acteurs économiques notamment dans le patronat ont fait preuve d'une grande crispation. La plus indigne des manifestations de cet instinct grégaire a été indiscutablement le refus d'enterrement de victimes du Covid-19 dans certaines régions, en dépit des précautions sanitaires appropriées fixées par un protocole mis en place par les autorités.

5.3 Un même monde

La crise a mis à nu la même antinomie (solidarité versus égoïsme) entre nations et continents. L'une des thèses fortes consiste à ramener l'origine du mal à notre rapport à la nature. Tels sont les termes de l'équation. Perceptibles bien avant, il est vrai dans le cadre de cercles contestataires, de lanceurs d'alertes qui vont des « décroissionnistes » (contre l'obsession de la croissance) aux « collapsologues » (nous allons à notre perte), mais qui deviennent avec la pandémie l'horizon de toute réflexion sur notre actualité. En Tunisie, les acteurs politiques n'ont pratiquement pas de sensibilité à l'égard de l'environnement. En même temps, le pays n'a fort heureusement pas d'industries prédatrices à grande échelle et émettrices de gaz à effets de serre ; ce qui est une chance pour une économie écologique à construire.

6. Conclusion

Ces cinq axes de réflexion nous interpellent pour agir de concert. Mais les recommandations ne sont pas les mêmes pour affronter la crise, agir durant le confinement ou après le déconfinement. Elles deviennent pratiquement sans effets à plus long terme si jamais on ne découvrait pas un vaccin ou un traitement médical contre le Covid-19 dans un délai raisonnable. Aussi, est-il des plus grandes urgences de penser ensemble et d'agir de concert et ce, afin de (1.) continuer à donner la primauté à la vie, tout en agissant sur les effets du confinement conformément à la théorie de la justice, c'est-à-dire en compensant graduellement en premier lieu les plus désavantagés socialement (les sans-emplois, les personnes aux besoins spécifiques et les travailleurs intermittents et les familles nécessiteuses) en montant dans l'échelle jusqu'à compenser les dommages subis par les entreprises, dans l'ordre des plus petites firmes aux grands cartels (2.) encourager par des incitations l'autonomie industrielle dans les secteurs stratégiques (alimentaire, de la santé, de l'éducation, du transport...), protéger l'économie nationale de la concurrence internationale déloyale, promouvoir les domaines à « forte valeur ajoutée », notamment la science, l'éducation et le numérique et mener une réflexion stratégique sur les systèmes de santé, de l'éducation et des transferts sociaux (3.), utiliser à bon escient « l'état d'exception » dans le respect des droits humains et des libertés publiques et privées sans aucune discrimination, (4.) préserver le lien social du délitement, développer la solidarité, se départir de l'égoïsme et oeuvrer pour l'intégration sociale et enfin (5.) concevoir une vision stratégique de l'après Covid-19 en préparant les scénarii de sortie de la crise à mettre en place éventuellement en créant un institut multidisciplinaire du suivi des pandémies.

Masahiro Noguchi

Cluster-Based Approach and Self-Restraint: Japan's Response to Covid-19

Covid-19 is raging worldwide. This can be called a pandemic. However, national government responses to the new coronavirus have been quite different. Japan is said to have taken a »unique path«, with two distinct features marking its reaction: First, Japan adopted a cluster-based approach, rather than conducting large-scale polymerise chain reaction (PCR) tests, to counter Covid-19. Second, the government asked its people to refrain from going out without using lockdown or other compulsory measures. In this context, the Japanese word Jishuku (自粛) was used, which means to voluntarily refrain from actions and attitudes and literally translates into English as »self-restraint«. In this paper, I would like to consider these two measures, characteristic to Japan's response, in light of the Law as Culture paradigm.

1. Cluster-Based Approach

South Korea established a system for PCR testing at an early stage, succeeded in reducing the number infected, and largely contained the spread of the virus. A similar sequence has been also observed in Germany. On the contrary, the Japanese government's team of experts has focused on »clusters«. As soon as an infected person is discovered, the people with whom he/she has been in contact with are analyzed. Each infection cluster is traced to its origin, and all people in it are considered infected and immediately isolated. The cluster-based approach is not uncontroversial. This approach has repeatedly been pitted against South Korea's choice of carrying out large-scale PCR testing. Especially in April, when the number of infected people increased, such criticism intensified. However, we can say that this approach has yielded some positive results: Japan has the lowest number of Covid-19 cases and deaths per million people among G7 countries. Prime Minister Shinzo Abe lifted a nationwide state of emergency and declared that the unique approach succeeded in containing Covid-19's spread in just six weeks. Moreover, German virologist Christian Drosten referred to Japan as a model for suppressing a possible second wave.[1]

---

[1] Cf. Wedekind: Japan bestes Beispiel.

As I am not an infectious disease expert, I cannot medically discuss the pros and cons of the cluster-based approach. I would, however, like to point out that the cluster strategy is connected with the thinking style of »additional building«, which was once discussed by Shuichi Kato. Kato is a postwar Japanese intellectual who played an important role in comparative studies on literature and culture between European countries and Japan. He used the Japanese word *Tatemashi* (建増し), which can be translated as »additional building« in English. According to Kato, European architecture fills in the details starting from the whole, whereas Japanese architecture combines discrete parts that ultimately result in the whole. Therefore, in Japanese architecture, an asymmetric structure is added as needed.[2]

This tendency is also a characteristic of the Japanese language. Kato uses the Japanese version of Max Weber's *Ancient Judaism* as an example.[3] In Weber's text, sentences are generally long and complicated. Yoshiaki Uchida, the Japanese translator of *Ancient Judaism*, translated the long sentences written by Weber into several shorter sentences. The Japanese language is less suitable for writing long sentences with complicated structures than German. In regard to this, Kato offers the following: »It is easier to understand by translating a long sentence in the European language into shorter Japanese sentences, but the structural relationship between short propositions is more or less sacrificed.«[4] We can say that the cluster-based approach to Covid-19 corresponds to the pattern of »additional building«.

2. *Jishuku*, or Self-Restraint

The Japanese government also declared a nationwide state of emergency when the number of people infected with Covid-19 expanded dramatically, which heavily interrupted economic activity. However, this declaration of emergency was not legally binding and was much weaker than that of other countries. Again, the Japanese word for self-restraint, *Jishuku*, was used in these situations. The term refers to people who follow certain norms voluntarily rather than by force. Self-restraint is linked to »weak leadership«. Political leaders in European countries called for stay-at-home orders in times of crisis, often in a strong tone, sometimes even using

---

[2] If you are familiar with Japanese animated films, imagine Hayao Miyazaki's Howl's Moving Castle.

[3] Yoshiaki Uchida won the 1999 Lessing Translation Award (Lessing-Übersetzerpreis) for his translation of Max Weber's *Das antike Judentum*. The award was given by the German Embassy Tokyo for excellent translations from German into Japanese from 1998 to 2009. The recommender of Uchida's translation was Shuichi Kato.

[4] Kato: Nihonbunka niokeru Jikan to Kūkan, p. 46. See also Kato: A History of Japanese Literature; Kato: Der Mischcharakter der japanischen Kultur.

the word »war«. Various types of leader persuasion techniques exist. In the case of Japan, politicians simply asked the people to stay at home, without using force. The citizens understood their government's ask and honored it. Japan's response to the crisis can be characterized by a combination of strong self-restraint and weak leadership. Masao Maruyama, a political scientist and researcher of Japanese political thought, called the wartime Japanese regime a »system of irresponsibility«. Maruyama used the term to question the idea that responsibility for the war is extremely unclear.[5]

Maruyama's thesis of a »system of irresponsibility« would also be valid for the Japanese government's response to Covid-19. The government makes soft and vague requests, and the people proactively comply with them. At the same time, they also voluntarily strengthen the surveillance of neighborhood residents who do not restrain themselves. The Abe cabinet has largely avoided using powerful instruments during the corona crisis, so it is difficult for liberal opposition parties to criticize the government. In these situations, it must remain unclear who is responsible for the outcomes. However, it does not mean that we simply need »strong leadership«. Maruyama criticized »irresponsibility« by saying that Japanese war criminals had a »weaker spirit« than German war criminals.[6] However, no matter how irresponsible Japanese war leaders may have been, there is no reason to praise Nazi officials. Some local Japanese governors have gained popularity by asserting the need for powerful legislation, severe penalties, and strong leadership. Political leaders who gain popularity by criticizing the »weaknesses« of powers will inevitably have authoritarian characteristics.

Carl Schmitt argues in *Political Theology* that »all key concepts of the modern doctrine of the state are secularized theological concepts«.[7] According to this thesis, we can say that different responses to the new coronavirus correlate with different pre-political or pre-legal order ideas. To examine this background, I discussed governance that relies on »additional building« and »self-restraint«. Political leaders are generally »weak« in this cultural context. However, that does not mean that they will not explode. As seen with one character in George Orwell's novel, a weak subject can be pushed by the public's expectations and shoot an elephant that he doesn't want to shoot.[8]

Will such political management characterized by a cluster-based approach and self-restraint continue, or will opposition to it be followed by public support for constitutional amendments and authoritarian leadership? Faced with the corona crisis, Japanese society is at a crossroads.

---

5   Cf. Maruyama: Thought and Behaviour in Modern Japanese Politics, p. 128.
6   Ibid., p. 96.
7   Schmitt: Political Theology, p. 36.
8   Orwell: Shooting an Elephant, pp. 31–40.

References

Kato, Shuichi: A History of Japanese Literature. From the Manyoshu to Modern Times, Richmond 1997.
Kato, Shuichi: Nihonbunka niokeru Jikan to Kūkan [Time and Space in Japanese Culture], Tokyo 2007.
Kato, Shuichi: Der Mischcharakter der japanischen Kultur, in: Ken'ichi Mishima / Wolfgang Schwentker (eds.): Geschichtsdenken im modernen Japan. Eine kommentierte Quellensammlung, München 2015, pp. 75–80.
Maruyama, Masao: Thought and Behaviour in Modern Japanese Politics, London et al. 1963.
Orwell, George: Shooting an Elephant and Other Essays, London / New York 2009.
Schmitt, Carl: Political Theology, Cambridge / MA 1985.
Wedekind, Klaus: Japan bestes Beispiel. Drosten jagt die Superspreader, 29.05.2020, https://www.n-tv.de/wissen/Zweite-Corona-Welle-vermeiden-Drosten-nimmt-Superspreader-ins-Visier-article21811320.html; last accessed 16.06.2020.

Diana Villegas

Les mafias en temps de pandémie

> « *Estremecido por la certidumbre de la presencia física de Dios, el doctor Juvenal Urbino pensó que una casa como aquella era inmune a la peste.* »
> Gabriel García Márquez[1]

Durant cette période marquée par des décrets d'état d'urgence, de confinement, de fermeture des frontières, de limitation accrue de la liberté d'aller et venir, d'arrêt quasi total de la circulation mondiale de marchandises ; le premier réflexe serait de penser que les mafias se trouvent affectées par ces différentes mesures prises pour contenir le coronavirus, mais en réalité il faut plus qu'une pandémie pour anéantir une mafia.

Paradoxalement, les crises et catastrophes s'avèrent extrêmement favorables pour l'ordre socio-économique que ces organisations représentent. Auparavant, les mafias ont fait face aux tremblements de terre, aux inondations, aux catastrophes nucléaires sans souffrir de perturbations majeures.[2] Aujourd'hui, la crise sanitaire a pour spécificité le statisme, alors que les mafias sont dynamiques par nature ; et, le fait de devoir jongler avec un tel degré d'immobilité introduit une variable non négligeable dans l'équation. Malgré cela, les mafias semblent indéracinables.

L'analyse des organisations mafieuses durant cette pandémie permet cependant une lecture plus complexe de ces phénomènes, car s'il y a bien un enseignement à tirer de ces derniers mois c'est que l'impact du coronavirus sur les mafias amène à potentialiser les illégalismes (1.) et à cristalliser les normativités (2.).

---

[1] « Bouleversé par la certitude de la présence physique de Dieu, le docteur Juvenal Urbino pensa qu'une maison comme celle-ci était à l'abri de toute maladie » (Garcia Marquez : L'amour aux temps du choléra, p. 151).

[2] La mafia japonaise, les yakuzas, pendant le tremblement de terre de Kobe en 1995 et le tsunami de Fukushima en 2011, avait envoyé de l'aide à la population lorsque l'intervention étatique se faisait attendre. Sur ce point, cf. Kessler : Japon : l'influence persistante des yakuzas se vérifie à l'occasion de la crise sanitaire.

1. Potentialiser les illégalismes

Ceux qui attendaient l'apparition d'une épidémie pour éradiquer la criminalité seront déçus, car l'extinction des organisations mafieuses ne semble pas être à l'ordre du jour de cette crise. Au contraire, elle paraît potentialiser les illégalismes au point de créer également une épidémie de criminalité.

À en juger par les données encore très approximatives qui nous parviennent du terrain, certaines organisations mafieuses, face au virus, sont plutôt obligées de changer de méthodes tandis que d'autres réinventent leurs vielles pratiques. Le coronavirus n'agit pas de la même manière sur chacune des organisations mafieuses.[3] Ainsi, face à la grande diversité des organisations et de leurs *modus operandi*, le virus peut produire des effets amenant à la mutation, au renouvellement, à la réaffirmation, au simple maintien de l'organisation, mais aussi à la création de nouvelles formes mafieuses, mais certainement pas à leur disparition. Pour le moment, la mutation et l'adaptation représentent les *réponses immunitaires* les plus visibles face au virus, à l'aide desquelles certains groupes mafieux ne connaîtront pas de véritable crise.

Au fil du temps, les organisations mafieuses de divers horizons ont démontré être très actives : elles ont appris à combattre leurs ennemis, à agir dans la clandestinité et à s'infiltrer dans les activités légales. Pour ce faire, en vue de leur objectif de profit, elles ont toujours été disposées aux grandes mutations. Cette crise n'est point l'exception. En très peu de temps, elles ont réussi à se reconfigurer pour mieux répondre à une situation inédite. Certaines se sont initiées dans de nouvelles activités illégales en s'emparant des territoires habituellement contrôlés par d'autres groupes et en diversifiant leur portfolio d'activités. Le plus représentatif de cette crise est la façon dont le crime organisé s'est initié dans la contrebande de produits pharmaceutiques comme l'hydroxychloroquine, les masques, le gel hydro-alcoolique et toute sorte de matériels médicaux en capitalisant sur les réseaux criminels déjà actifs et les routes de commerce illégal.[4] On voit également des organisations s'immiscer dans l'espace virtuel : les jeux en ligne illégaux viennent remplacer les casinos fermés par les mesures de quarantaine. Les activités illégales n'ayant plus leur place dans le monde réel basculent ainsi dans le *darknet* et

---

[3] Il faut souligner que les organisations mafieuses englobent une grande diversité de phénomènes dont la mafia italienne n'est qu'un référent : « On peut donc dire que la Mafia sert depuis longtemps comme modèle d'organisation à la criminalité internationale. Cela autorise à parler de mafia en un sens large, pour désigner toutes les associations criminelles qui recourent à un tel type d'organisation intégrée. » (Falcone : Qu'est-ce que la Mafia ?, p. 118).

[4] L'opération Pangea XIII menée par Interpol entre le 3 et 10 mars a permis d'établir l'augmentation de la criminalité organisée suite au coronavirus : 37 groupes ont été démantelés, 34 000 masques chirurgicaux contrefaits ont été saisis, plus de 2000 liens internet menant vers des produits liés au Covid-19 ont été identifiés. Cf. Interpol : Global operation sees a rise in fake medical products related to COVID-19.

certaines organisations profitant de l'essor du télétravail s'improvisent également hackers en multipliant des actes de *phishing*, « arnaques au président » (notamment en lien avec des commandes de médicaments et de produits d'hygiène) et *ransomwares*. Serait-ce l'émergence d'un cyber ordre mafieux, d'une mafia 2.0 ? Pour le moment, il est difficile d'affirmer s'il s'agit d'une nouvelle forme d'organisation ou d'une diversification temporaire des activités de l'organisation mafieuse qui s'ajoutent à la réalité virtuelle propre aux hackers et aux cybermalfaiteurs. En tout cas, ce basculement d'un espace vers un autre fait penser au phénomène de *balloon effect*, déjà bien connu en matière de trafic de drogues.[5]

Puisque les membres de la mafia réfléchissent toujours en termes de profit, à quoi bon changer une formule qui gagne ? Ainsi, d'anciennes pratiques mafieuses se sont adaptées au contexte et se sont avérées très efficaces pour garantir la survie de l'organisation. Par exemple, la captation des fonds étatiques est une pratique répandue au sein de la mafia qui a trouvé un terrain favorable grâce à la crise du Covid-19 puisqu'il est désormais établi que des mafieux italiens ont détourné des aides d'État.[6] Les malfaiteurs sont également prêts à recycler de vieilles pratiques en les enrobant de modernité : le service à domicile et les *drives* en sont un bon exemple. La livraison de drogue chez les particuliers dans une boîte à pizza est l'une des pratiques les plus utilisées pendant cette crise prenant le nom d' « ubérisation » du trafic de drogue,[7] mais sa généralisation fait faussement penser à une mutation de l'organisation. Elle est simplement l'une des manifestations de la capacité des organisations mafieuses pour profiter des ressources qu'elle possède à portée de main.

Par ailleurs, les organisations mafieuses ont démontré une capacité d'anticipation inouïe. Les trafiquants de drogue colombiens ont vu juste lorsqu'ils ont depuis le mois de janvier inondé le marché européen avec des convois de conteneurs de drogue arrivant aux ports de Rotterdam et de la Belgique. Les mafias dites « classiques » ont, pour leur part, également compris les avantages de l'anticipation. Les mafias italiennes, grâce à la diversification de leurs activités au sein de la sphère légale, peuvent faire face aux futures conséquences de la crise à travers leurs

---

[5] Le phénomène de *balloon effect*, ou *efecto cucaracha*, permet d'expliquer que la production change d'emplacement géographique sans pour autant disparaître réellement. Sur ce point, cf. Uprimny Yepes : El laboratorio colombiano, p. 410.

[6] L'organisation *Transparency International* met en garde par rapport à ces pratiques et élabore une série de recommandations afin de renforcer le contrôle des marchés publics et pour garantir l'éthique et la probité dans l'octroi des fonds et des aides financières débloquées suite à la crise du coronavirus. Sur le sujet, cf. Transparency International France : Marchés publics et plans de relances en temps de crise.

[7] Le 15 mai 2020, lors d'une conférence de presse au siège du tout nouvel Office antistupéfiants (OFAST), le ministre de l'Intérieur français, Christophe Castaner, présente un bilan de la situation du trafic de drogue en France suite aux effets du Covid-19 et expose le développement de la cannabiculture, l'ubérisation du trafic et l'usage des réseaux sociaux comme de nouvelles pratiques sur le territoire français. Cf. vidéo disponible sur AFP : Castaner.

entreprises de services, du transport ou de l'agroalimentaire.[8] En s'emparant de ces secteurs d'activités légales afin d'en faire des espaces de blanchiment d'argent, les mafias ont surtout souscrit à une assurance pour les mauvais jours.

L'exemple plus représentatif des illégalismes se constate au sein de la mafia du trafic de drogue. Face à un système de trafic complètement mondialisé, la fermeture des frontières et les restrictions à la circulation de personnes bouleversent indéniablement les chaînes d'approvisionnement. Pour cette raison, l'ONUDC s'est empressée de rédiger un rapport à ce sujet. D'après cette institution, le virus a rendu le marché international de drogue complètement instable et une lecture homogène de la situation mondiale s'avère actuellement impossible.[9] En effet, la fermeture de frontières a transformé les canaux d'approvisionnement des matériaux de base de production. En Colombie, il a été constaté une pénurie de gasoil, matière première pour la production de cocaïne provenant essentiellement du Venezuela ; au Mexique, des produits essentiels pour la fabrication de méthamphétamine et de fentanyl ne parviennent pas à être livrés depuis la Chine.

Les chaînes de distribution se sont également vues affectées, car elles n'ont pu utiliser les routes d'acheminement classiques (c'est le cas du commerce d'héroïne et d'ecstasy) et cela a provoqué une altération des prix de certaines drogues, voire leur pénurie.[10] En outre, les régions productrices de drogue souffrent des restrictions de circulation de personnes : c'est le cas des cultivateurs d'opium en Afghanistan et des mules venant de Guyane qui n'arrivent pas à traverser les frontières. Malgré toutes ces difficultés, le commerce de drogues ne s'est pas arrêté, loin de là.[11]

Certes, les effets négatifs du virus sur les mafias sont importants, notamment pour celles dédiées au trafic de drogue, car elles sont aujourd'hui intimement liées à l'essor de la mondialisation. Cependant, les mafias sont loin d'être les organisations les plus affectées par les ravages du coronavirus. Du Mexique au Japon, de l'Italie à la Colombie, des Balkans à l'Afrique de l'Ouest, de la Chine à l'Afghanistan, les différents réseaux mafieux tirent un grand profit de la crise mondiale.

---

[8] Cf. Saviano : La faiblesse, c'est de se croire invincible.

[9] ONUDC : Covid-19 and the Drug Supply Chain, p. 37.

[10] Au Pérou, le prix de la cocaïne s'est effondré. En revanche, il a augmenté aux États-Unis et au Brésil (Ibid., p. 30). Au niveau local, selon l'Office antistupéfiants (OFAST), le trafic de drogue en France a diminué de 30 à 40 % suite aux difficultés d'approvisionnement durant le confinement. Cela a provoqué une augmentation des prix de 30 à 60 % environ. Un autre facteur s'ajoute à ce panorama : les habitudes de consommation ont changé durant le confinement provoquant une variation dans le prix des drogues. Par exemple, le prix du cannabis a été majoré de 56 % suite à l'augmentation de sa demande (OFAST : Note de situation sur l'impact du coronavirus sur la criminalité liée au trafic de stupéfiants).

[11] Les saisis, suite aux contrôles de douanes, sont aujourd'hui plus fréquents dus au faible flux de circulation de marchandise mondiale, mais les chiffres démontrent la grande activité du trafic mondial de drogues. Cf. ONUDC : COVID-19 and the Drug Supply Chain, p. 30.

L'impact du Covid-19 sur la mafia et la façon dont celle-ci a réagi à la crise mondiale s'avère être finalement un bon indicateur de l'état de santé de ces organisations en révélant également une multiplicité de normativités qui jaillissent.

2. Cristalliser les normativités

La mafia, elle, ne reste pas confinée. En effet, les membres de ces organisations n'ont pas respecté de quarantaine. Au contraire, n'y a-t-il pas un meilleur moment pour sortir de l'ombre et asseoir son pouvoir, étendre ses racines, ficeler ses réseaux si ce n'est celui où les États portent leurs regards ailleurs? À titre d'exemple, en plein mois d'avril, le cortège funéraire du frère d'un grand patron de Cosa Nostra a traversé la ville de Messina en Sicile.[12]

Cette pandémie ne fait ainsi qu'accentuer les normes de l'ordre social et économique de la mafia.[13] D'une part, les règles de contrôle social du pouvoir mafieux sont cette fois-ci affirmées à travers l'application du couvre-feu. En effet, celui-ci s'avère être une façon de consolider la présence et le contrôle des organisations mafieuses sur les territoires. En Colombie, par exemple, des groupes armés distribuent des tracts menaçant de mort celui qui ose méconnaître le confinement imposé par le gouvernement;[14] drôle de mécanisme de collaboration alors qu'il est habituel de retrouver ces mêmes groupes opposés à l'ordre étatique en temps de « normalité ». Les Maras en Amérique centrale et les gangs dans les favelas brésiliennes font de même : elles se présentent en tant que garantes de la protection de la population locale suite à l'inefficacité du gouvernement. Mais le respect du confinement est instrumentalisé aux fins des activités de l'organisation (trafic de drogues, armes, etc.) tout en assurant la stratégie du contrôle de territoire et de la circulation de la population. D'autre part, lorsque tout s'arrête, la mafia, en revanche, reste active. Cette période de confinement a permis de constater ses influences, qui seront élargies davantage avec la future crise économique. Sans aucun doute, cette crise laissera libre cours à la spéculation mafieuse. Il faut ainsi s'attendre à ce que la mafia soit un acteur présent sur la scène de la restructuration économique mondiale comme ce fut le cas à l'époque de la grande dépression ou lors de la crise des *subprimes*, lorsque les réseaux mafieux ont porté à bout de bras l'économie mondiale, étant l'un des rares à pouvoir injecter de grandes sommes de capitaux.

---

12 Cf. Tondo : Mafia linked funeral investigated amid coronavirus lockdown.
13 Pour un développement approfondi du système normatif d'un ordre mafieux, cf. Villegas : L'ordre juridique mafieux, not. p. 79 et s.
14 Cf. AFP : Colombie.

Les groupes mafieux proposent également des prêts d'argent aux petits commerçants et aux citoyens qui n'arrivent pas à faire face à la crise.[15] Contrairement à ce que peuvent penser ses bénéficiaires, la mafia impose ses règles économiques en le faisant très souvent payer au prix fort, très fort même. La mafia entretient un système complexe de prêt d'argent et d'échange de faveurs.[16] Le premier est un système de prêt usurier que l'organisation se réserve le droit d'effacer ou d'augmenter de façon aléatoire et de manière injustifiée, en étant souvent accompagnée de mesures d'extorsion. Le but de ces contrats de prêt est *in fine* de phagocyter les petits commerçants qui, face aux problèmes de maintenir leurs commerces à flot et pour obtenir un prêt auprès des banques, se tournent vers la mafia en laissant un bien en garantie ; une fois que les intérêts deviennent insoutenables, ils sont dans l'obligation de remettre leur propriété à l'organisation mafieuse.[17] Avec la crise du coronavirus, il est possible que cette pratique de prêt d'usure soit généralisée au sein d'une population de plus en plus fragilisée.[18] Le second est un système d'échange de faveurs, c'est-à-dire de « petit service » contre « petit service » : la mafia propose des services à la personne (livraison de courses, surveillance du quartier) pour lesquels le bénéficiaire lui sera redevable et devra payer en retour avec un autre « petit service » (obtention d'informations, assassinat). Ce système de prêt d'argent et d'échange de services garantit la cohésion, l'observance des normes et la fidélité à l'organisation. À long terme, il consolide un système normatif facilitant la corruption, la délation et, finalement, la pénétration de la mafia dans la société.

Par ailleurs, les organisations mafieuses de tous les horizons ne passent pas à côté de l'occasion de s'ériger en bienfaitrices de la population en lui procurant des services que l'État ne peut pas ou ne peut plus fournir. Avec la crise sanitaire, il n'est donc pas rare de voir les membres de ces organisations en train de distribuer des paniers, des denrées et produits médicaux. Au Mexique, les cartons des « *chapodespensas* »[19] distribués par la fille de « El Chapo » Guzman sont imprimés avec le visage du renommé ex-chef du cartel de Sinaloa. Les dealers n'hésitent pas à proposer à leurs clients un kit sanitaire contenant des masques et du gel hydroalcoolique pour chaque achat de drogue. Finalement, toutes les méthodes sont bonnes pour maintenir le *business as usual* !

[15] « Per ogni imprenditore sano che sta rischiando di chiudere il proprio ristorante o il proprio negozio, c'è un clan che è pronto a intervenire per strozzare o rilevare. Se lo Stato non agisce sin d'ora sulle aziende in crisi, se attenderà una fase di minore allarme, sarà tardi, tardissimo. Dove il coronavirus non arriverà, arriveranno le mafie. » (Saviano : La mafia del coronavirus).

[16] Sur ce sujet, cf. Villegas : L'ordre juridique mafieux, not. p. 97 et s.

[17] D'après un rapport de Confcommercio Italie, ce phénomène est devenu très présent pendant la crise. Cf. CONFCOMMERCIO : Esposizione delle micro e piccole imprese del terziario di mercato alla criminalità durante e dopo il lockdown.

[18] Les déclarations d'Enza Rando de l'association italienne Libera sont assez illustratives du phénomène actuel. Cf. Libera : Coronavirus.

[19] Ce sont des paniers contenant de la nourriture et des masques en tissu destinés à être distribués à la population à faible revenu.

En s'érigeant bienfaiteur, la mafia noyaute la communauté et établit un consensus social au sein de la société locale. Cela lui permet de renforcer sa légitimité auprès de la population en lui garantissant un lien de subordination et en se substituant à l'État.[20] Ce phénomène devient encore plus frappant lorsque l'État lui-même lui fait grâce : en Italie, 500 membres de la criminalité organisée sont libérés sous l'argument de prévenir une contamination au sein de la prison, tout en sachant que certains d'entre eux étaient des chefs mafieux placés à l'isolement en quartier de haute sécurité ;[21] au Mexique, le président du pays arrête son parcours lors de sa visite à l'inauguration d'une œuvre publique à Baridaguato, territoire du Cartel du Sinaloa, pour saluer la mère de « El Chapo Guzman »[22] et sans respecter les gestes barrières ! Ou encore, au Brésil, le ministre de la Santé avoue la nécessité de collaborer avec les gangs afin de pouvoir combattre la crise sanitaire.[23]

Ces éléments ne font que démontrer la puissance et l'enracinement d'un véritable ordre paraétatique : un *ordre de fait*, et sans doute un *ordre de jure*, préexiste au coronavirus, mais il est renforcé par celui-ci. La crise du Covid-19 est donc un terrain et un moment inédit pour constater l'existence d'un pluralisme juridique issue des mafias.[24] Il est en soi un véritable espace-temps[25] où les normativités convergent, car les mesures prises en temps de pandémie favorisent ce que l'on

---

[20] Max Weber l'avait déjà évoqué lorsqu'il fait allusion au système de racket en le qualifiant de prélèvement de «‹discontinu› parce qu'[il] se fond [e] sur des pratiques ‹illégales›» ; en réalité, elles prennent souvent le caractère d'un ‹abonnement›, en échange duquel l'association offre quelques contreparties, en premier lieu de sécurité », et donne un exemple : « Un fabricant napolitain me répondit, il y a une vingtaine d'années, comme je l'interrogeais sur l'incidence de la Camorra sur la sécurité des entreprises : ‹ Monsieur, la Camorra me prend X lires par mois et elle me garantit de sa protection ; l'État me prend dix fois plus et ne garantit rien du tout. › » Le texte original étant : « Signore, la Camorra mi prende X lire al mese, ma garantisce la sicurezza ; lo Stato me ne prende dieci volte tanto e garantisce niente » (Weber : Économie et société, p. 271).

[21] Une circulaire du ministre de la Justice, Alfonso Bonafede (Mouvement Cinq Étoiles), est à l'origine de cette mesure. Le ministre invitait les juges d'application des peines à prendre des mesures pour éviter la contamination des personnes détenues. Face au tollé et les critiques venant des magistrats antimafia, le ministre de justice revient sur sa demande et sollicite la remise en prison de grands chefs mafieux pour les placer finalement dans des centres hospitaliers. Cette demande lui coûtera une motion de censure. Sur le sujet, cf. Milella / Palazzolo : Mafiosi e trafficanti.

[22] Beauregard : López Obrador desata una tormenta política con su saludo a la madre de El Chapo.

[23] « Aujourd'hui, nous avons commencé le premier plan de gestion, et je ne dirai pas dans quelle communauté, car là il faut comprendre la culture, la dynamique. Comprenez que ce sont des zones où l'État est souvent absent, où le trafic, les milices sont en charge... Comment construire ce pont au nom de la vie ? Les dialogues sur la santé, oui, avec la circulation, avec les milices, car ce sont aussi des êtres humains et ont aussi besoin de collaborer, d'aider, de participer. Donc, en ce moment, quand nous faisons ce type de placement, nous précisons que tout le monde va aider, faire sa part. » Propos traduits et disponibles sur O Globo : « Saúde dialoga com tráfico e milícia », diz Mandetta.

[24] Pour une étude du pluralisme juridique et l'ordre mafieux, cf. Villegas : L'ordre juridique mafieux.

[25] Pour la notion d'espace-temps, cf. Gurvitch : La multiplicité des temps sociaux et de Sousa Santos : Vers un nouveau sens commun juridique, p. 144.

peut appeler un *Far West* normatif.[26] Par ailleurs, la pandémie reconfigure aussi l'espace-temps de la société, de la mafia ainsi que de tous les autres ordres normatifs. La crise oblige les mafias, mais aussi l'État à modifier leurs terrains d'actions et à adapter leurs réactivités. Pour ce qui est de la mafia, on l'a vu, elle réaffirme sa place comme un ordre normatif et juridique en faisant appel à ses normes de contrôle social et en élargissant son pouvoir économique à tel point qu'elle se présente comme un substitut et un collaborateur très efficace de l'ordre étatique.[27] En outre, l'espace laissé par le *lockdown* de la justice des tribunaux contribue également à cette cristallisation des normativités.

Aujourd'hui, il est difficile de constater complètement l'étendue des illégalismes et des normativités qui ont réussi à exploser et à se diversifier pendant la crise sanitaire. L'impact du Covid-19 sur les mafias et la façon dont elles réagissent est ainsi un véritable chantier de recherche qui s'ouvre aux chercheurs en sciences sociales, mais son ampleur est pour le moment approximatif, car le *tempo* de la pandémie n'est pas le même de celui de la recherche. Il est cependant possible de faire des projections pour un agenda de recherche sur les organisations mafieuses du « monde d'après ». Pour cela, il faut, tout d'abord, penser les scénarios dans lesquels s'inscrivent ces organisations comme des espaces-temps placés dans un *continuum*. La rupture entre un « monde d'avant » et un « monde d'après » est une tentation trompeuse. Un *continuum* entre la sphère illégale et légale est également utile, car il impose l'étude transversale des activités de ces organisations sans privilégier la traditionnelle perspective économique et criminologique. Ensuite, il est essentiel d'attirer l'attention sur les relations d'internormativité entre l'ordre mafieux et les autres ordres (notamment l'ordre étatique, mais aussi et pourquoi pas, l'ordre numérique, l'ordre scientifique, l'ordre économique et financier), ainsi que les interactions entre les différentes échelles (local, national et transnational) sur lesquelles les organisations mafieuses agissent.[28] Dans ce sens, il est possible d'analyser de nouveaux territoires vers lesquels ces organisations s'orientent et les espaces qu'elles rendent plus tangibles comme c'est le cas du *darknet* et du cybercrime, ou les possibilités d'un basculement vers la criminalité pharmaceutique (falsification de médicaments, etc.). Enfin, la relation *droit et culture* se présente comme un paradigme d'ouverture fécond permettant notamment d'exploiter les questionnements d'une évolution normative piégée entre une culture juridique de l'exceptionnalité étatique et une possible culture juridique mafieuse. Une forte ef-

---

[26] Molfessis : Les risques du Far West, p. 734.
[27] Comme l'exprime Saviano : « La pandemia è il luogo ideale per il mafie e il motivo è semplice : se hai fame, cerchi pane, non ti importa da quale forno abbia origine e chi lo stia distribuendo ; se hai necessità di un farmaco, paghi, non ti domandi chi te lo stia vendendo, lo vuoi e basta. È solo nei tempi di pace e benessere che la scelta è possibile » (Saviano : La mafia del coronavirus).
[28] Pour une cartographie des relations entre les ordres, cf. Twining : Normative and Legal Pluralism.

ficacité symbolique du droit étatique, des pratiques issues d'une culture *borderline* au sein de la population et des concertations entre le droit étatique et l'illégalité sont des situations déjà visibles dans d'autres contextes où les mafias opèrent. Un regard comparé sur les spécificités de la relation *droit et culture* dans ce moment inédit par rapport à d'autres contextes n'est pas à négliger.

Même si de nombreuses questions restent à aborder, pour établir un agenda de recherche sur les mafias en période de pandémie, il serait surtout pertinent de commencer par considérer l'hypothèse que l'organisation mafieuse constitue un véritable ordre socio-économique semi-autonome et endémique devenu aujourd'hui systémique et d'une puissance telle que cela le rend immun à presque tout, même au Covid-19.

Références

Agence France-Presse (AFP) : Castaner : « Le trafic de drogue a baissé de 30 à 40 % pendant le confinement », in : Le Parisien, le 15.05.2020, https://www.leparisien.fr/video/castaner-le-trafic-de-drogue-a-baisse-de-30-a-40-pendant-le-confinement-15-05-2020-8317845.php; dernier accès 27.06.2020.

Agence France-Presse (AFP) : Colombie : le confinement, un prétexte à la terreur dans les zones rouges, le 21.05.2020.

Beauregard, Luis Pablo : López Obrador desata una tormenta política con su saludo a la madre de El Chapo, in : El País, le 31.03.2020, https://elpais.com/internacional/2020-03-31/lopez-obrador-desata-una-tormenta-politica-con-su-saludo-a-la-madre-de-el-chapo.html; dernier accès 17.06.2020.

CONFCOMMERCIO : Esposizione delle micro e piccole imprese del terziario di mercato alla criminalità durante e dopo il lockdown. Nota dell'Ufficio Studi Confcommercio sui risultati dell'indagine di Format research, le 07.06.2020, https://www.confcommercio.it/documents/20126/216697/Indagine+Format+Research+nota+integrale+Uffcio+Studi+Confcommercio.pdf/c65a9449-6832-73e2-1468-1e1e5d0f1e6d?version=1.0&t=1591511992397; dernier accès 17.06.2020.

de Sousa Santos, Boaventura : Vers un nouveau sens commun juridique. Droit, science et politique dans la transition paradigmatique, Paris 2004.

Falcone, Giovanni : Qu'est-ce que la Mafia ?, in : Revue Esprit, 10, 1992, pp. 111–118.

García Márquez, Gabriel : L'amour aux temps du choléra, Paris 1987.

Gurvitch, Georges : La multiplicité des temps sociaux, Paris 1958.

Kessler, Christian : Japon : l'influence persistante des yakuzas se vérifie à l'occasion de la crise sanitaire, in : Le Figaro, le 20.05.2020, https://www.lefigaro.fr/vox/monde/japon-l-influence-persistante-des-yakuzas-se-verifie-a-l-occasion-de-la-crise-sanitaire-20200520; dernier accès 27.06.2020.

Interpol: Global Operation Sees a Rise in Fake Medical Products Related to COVID-19 le 19.03.2020, https://www.interpol.int/News-and-Events/News/2020/Global-operation-sees-a-rise-in-fake-medical-products-related-to-COVID-19; dernier accès 27.06.2020.

Libera: Coronavirus: »Allarme Libera, molti imprenditori cercano aiuto da usurai, denunce in calo«, https://www.libera.it/schede-1277-coronavirus_allarme_libera_molti_imprenditori_cercano_aiuto_da_usurai_denunce_in_calo; dernier accès 17.06.2020

Milella, Liana / Salvo Palazzolo: Mafiosi e trafficanti, in 376 fuori dal carcere per l'emergenza virus, in: La Repubblica, le 03.05.2020, https://www.repubblica.it/cronaca/2020/05/03/news/mafiosi_e_trafficanti_in_376_fuori_dal_carcere_per_l_emergenza_virus-255528216/; dernier accès 17.06.2020.

Molfessis, Nicolas: Les risques du Far West, in: JCP G., 15, 2020.

O Globo: «Saúde dialoga com tráfico e milícia», diz Mandetta, in: O Globo, le 08.04.2020, https://oglobo.globo.com/rio/saude-dialoga-com-trafico-milicia-diz-mandetta-24361014; dernier accès le 17.06.2020.

Office Antistupéfiants (OFAST): Note de situation sur l'impact du coronavirus sur la criminalité liée au trafic de stupéfiants, Paris, 2020 cité par Piel, Simon: L'effet du confinement sur le trafic de drogue: fin des »mules« des »go fast« cannabis bloqué en Espagne, in: Le Monde, le 07.04.2020, https://www.lemonde.fr/societe/article/2020/04/07/le-trafic-de-drogue-en-temps-de-crise-sanitaire-au-scanner-de-l-office-antistupefiants_6035860_3224.html; dernier accès 17.06.2020.

United Nations Office on Drugs and Crime (ONUDC): COVID-19 and the Drug Supply Chain: From Production and Trafficking to Use, COVID-19 and the Drug Supply Chain: From Production and Trafficking to Use, Vienne, le 7.05.2020, http://www.unodc.org/documents/data-and-analysis/covid/Covid-19-and-drug-supply-chain-Mai2020.pdf; dernier accès le 17.06.2020.

Saviano, Roberto: La mafia del coronavirus. Dalla droga alla sanità, la pandemia aiuta l'economia criminale, in: La Repubblica, le 23.03.2020, https://www.repubblica.it/cronaca/2020/03/23/news/la_mafia_del_virus_dalla_droga_alla_sanita_la_pandemia_aiuta_l_economia_criminale-252023708/, dernier accès le 17.06.2020.

Saviano, Roberto: La faiblesse, c'est de se croire invincible, in: Le Monde, le 12.04.2020, https://www.lemonde.fr/idees/article/2020/04/12/roberto-saviano-la-faiblesse-c-est-de-se-croire-invincible_6036361_3232.html; dernier accès le 17.06.2020.

Tondo, Lorenzo: Mafia-Linked Funeral Investigated Amid Coronavirus Lockdown, in: The Guardian, le 14.04.2020, https://www.theguardian.com/world/2020/apr/14/mafia-linked-funeral-investigated-amid-coronavirus-lockdown; dernier accès le 17.06.2020.

Transparency International France: Marchés publics et plans de relances en temps de crise: la transparence au défi de l'urgence sanitaire, https://transpar

ency-france.org/actu/covid-19-marches-publics-et-plans-de-relances-en-temps-de-crise-la-transparence-au-defi-de-lurgence-sanitaire/#. Xtyr6y_pPOQ; dernier accès le 17.06.2020.

Twining, William: Normative and Legal Pluralism: A Global Perspective, in: Duke Journal of Comparative and International Law, 20, 2010, pp. 473–517.

Uprimny Yepes, Rodrigo: El laboratorio colombiano: narcotráfico, poder y administración, in: Boaventura de Sousa Santos / Mauricio García Villegas (eds.): El caleidoscopio de las justicias en Colombia, Bogotá 2004, pp. 261–315.

Villegas, Diana: L'ordre juridique mafieux. Étude à partir de l'organisation criminelle colombienne des années 1980 et 1990, Paris 2018.

Weber, Max: Économie et société. Les catégories de la sociologie, Paris 1995.

Joachim J. Savelsberg

Balancing Rights and Responsibilities during a Pandemic: Individuals, States, and Views from the United States of America*

In a recent book, political scientist Kathryn Sikkink demands that we, scholars, activists and citizens, pay greater attention to the fact that rights are associated with responsibilities.[1] Her demand gains validity in times of crisis, as experiences and observations around the Covid-19 outbreak show. Basic rights can only be secured if those who claim rights also live up to responsibilities. When governments take rights away from citizens (or citizens delegate them to governments), then the rights Leviathan appropriates are accompanied by substantial responsibilities as well. I propose three theses, which I explicate in three sections of this essay: First, individuals must and do take responsibility if basic rights are to be secured. Second, the state must take responsibility toward the same goal. Third, the delegation of rights to the state, especially in times of emergency, must be counter-balanced by individual and civil society engagement.

1. Individuals – Rights and Responsibilities

The realization of individual rights indeed is at risk during a pandemic, most obviously the right to life and health, but also the right to dignity in times of strict government restrictions, as well as social and economic rights, especially the right to work and to appropriate nutrition. A pandemic also impresses on us with particular clarity what always applies: that rights are interdependent. Under its reign, the right to life and health especially depends on the realization of basic social and economic rights. Lives lived in tight quarters, in prisons and refugee camps,

---

* This essay is based on the author's comments at a webinar on »Rights and Responsibilities during a Pandemic and Beyond.« The session is part of a series on »Envisioning the Future: Advancing Human Rights in a Time of Crisis,« organized by the Human Rights Lab and the Center for Global Health & Social Responsibility, co-sponsored by the Institute for Global Studies, University of Minnesota. The session also included Ranit Mishori (Georgetown), Shailey Prasad (Minnesota) and Kathryn Sikkink (Harvard). Cf. Human Rights Program-University of Minnesota – YouTube-Channel: Envisioning the Future: Balancing Rights and Responsibilities.

[1] Sikkink: The Hidden Face of Rights.

in overcrowded housing for migrant workers, and insecure work places, especially in the absence of health insurance and health care, are at particular risk. A pandemic shows further that rights, despite such interdependency, may be in partial conflict with each other, in need of careful balancing. Conflicts between the right to work and to operate businesses versus the right to life and health become most visible during a pandemic. Yet, this is not a zero-sum conflict as the realization of the right to work also contributes to securing lives and livelihood. Policy makers struggle to find the right balance.

The Covid-19 pandemic shows – and this is the core point of this essay – that rights can only be realized if they are accompanied by responsibilities. Consider individual actors who must and do accept responsibilities to contribute to the collective good of public health for at least two reasons.

First, humans are moral beings, animals able to want to do what they are obliged to do. They have internalized normative expectations. They live by a code of ethics, and during a pandemic, they take responsibility for others beyond the normal call to duty. We learn about parents teaching children at home during school closures, even while simultaneously doing *home office* work. Occasionally we learn about young people delivering groceries to elderly and vulnerable neighbors. We receive news about nurses who move to hot spots of the pandemic such as New York City, fully aware of the risk to their health and lives, but committed to delivering their professional service where the need is most desperate. Many around us wear masks, knowing that doing so primarily protects others, not themselves from infection.

Not just moral codes, but also the law obliges us to take responsibility. In social democracies especially, many rights are coupled with obligations. The German Constitution (*Grundgesetz*), for example, secures the right to the ownership of private property, but it follows up immediately with the responsibility claim of *Sozialpflichtigkeit*, the duty to live up to obligations toward society that grow out of such ownership. Further, the duty to help others in situations of emergency is written into tort law in some countries (e. g., United States) and into criminal codes in others (e. g., Germany). Legal norms thus back up moral codes, even if conflicts between law and informal norms may become virulent during crises as well. Antigone's family and religious commitments overrode King Creon's order in times of war, and the kinds of dilemmas Antigone faced abound during a pandemic.

Humans, while moral beings, are also capable of self-interested rational action, at least in the sense of bounded rationality. This too becomes visible during a pandemic. If people *shelter in place*, as ordered by the governors in many US states, they do not just do so because of the perceived legitimacy of executive orders, but also because they are aware that staying at home and keeping *social distance* reduces the risk of them contracting Codid-19. When they avoid shopping trips to a grocery store and instead have food delivered to their doorsteps, they again do so to reduce their individual risk of infection – while simultaneously contributing to public health. There is an element of Adam Smith's »invisible hand« at work: self-interested action serves a public good: the public health goal of keeping the number of infections low or at least *flattening the curve*, assuring that not too many infections occur in a limited period to overwhelm the capacities of hospitals and intensive care units.

In short, human actors are obliged to take responsibility, and they often live up to that responsibility. They do so because they are moral beings and legal subjects, which is not to deny potential conflicts between law and morality and between various sets of norms to which different clusters of actors subscribe in pluralist societies. Human actors also engage in rational action. They may contribute to public health in both ways.

2. The State – Rights and Responsibilities

Citizens may give up rights during a pandemic, delegating them to the state. In the alternative, Leviathan may simply seize rights at the expense of individuals. Different from individuals though, states are not moral actors. Only legal norms might link their acquisition of rights with responsibilities, but such laws require enforcement, which is more difficult to secure in times of crisis.

Normative theory suggests that states bear special responsibility during crises, first because states are principle suppliers of public goods. While individuals' rational action in part contributes to the public good (staying at home and thereby slowing the spread of the virus), individual rational action may also exploit the efforts of others. Actors may be tempted to take free rider positions: Let others practice caution and secure public health; I will take my liberty and benefit without sacrificing. Here the state needs to enforce rules, which in the United States, during the Covid-19 crisis, included protecting state capitals against occupiers equipped with military-style weapons or intervening when businesses open against instructions by public health authorities, often also under armed *protection*.

Law enforcement, securing public goods by force or the threat of force, of course is not the only way to secure public health. States may provide public services, testing sites and protective gear that markets do not sufficiently supply in time of crisis. They fund research toward the development of medications and vaccines. They coordinate public health efforts through specialized agencies such as the US Centers for Disease Control. They support international efforts through funding contributions to the World Health Organization – but note the recent withdrawal of such funding by the US administration under President Trump.

State and local branches of government play special roles. In the State of Minnesota, for example, where the governor *(Ministerpräsident)* issued *shelter in place* orders, his office also sends daily emails to all residents of his state to inform them of new executive actions, lately of the easing of restrictions, to provide information on sources of support and to practice moral suasion to back up moral commitments. Consider the following example from April 13, 2020:

»Today, Governor Tim Walz extended Minnesota's peacetime emergency in Minnesota for 30 days. A peacetime emergency allows Minnesota to continue many of the public health and economic relief measures it has implemented to help Minnesotans weather the COVID-19 pandemic.«

»Minnesota's actions have saved lives, but the threat of COVID-19 remains,« said Governor Walz. »The next stages of this pandemic are going to challenge us – an extension of Minnesota's peacetime emergency will allow us to protect Minnesotans' health and wellbeing and continue to respond effectively to this rapidly-evolving situation.«

Minnesota's peacetime emergency has allowed Minnesota to take strong steps to combat Covid-19, including:

- »Enhanced protections for veterans in our veterans homes
- Activation of the National Guard to assist in relief efforts
- Measures to preserve personal protective equipment
- Efforts to provide economic relief and stability to those impacted by the pandemic
- Regulatory changes allowing our state agencies and licensing boards to ensure fast relief to Minnesotans
- And an order directing Minnesotans to stay at home to slow the spread of the virus«.

The message was accompanied by information about access to public health and to unemployment benefits. Information about resources and appropriate action during a pandemic are a regular part of such daily updates:

»Everyone can work to reduce the spread of Covid-19:
- Cover your coughs and sneezes with your elbow or sleeve, or a tissue and then throw the tissue in the trash and wash your hands afterwards.
- Washing your hands often with soap and water for 20 seconds, especially after going to the bathroom or before eating. If soap and water are not readily available, use an alcohol-based hand sanitizer that contains at least 60 % alcohol.
- Avoid touching your face – especially your eyes, nose and mouth – with unwashed hands.
- Stay home if you have cold- or flu-like symptoms, for seven days after your illness onset or three days after your fever resolves without fever reducing medicine, and avoid close contact with people who are sick.
- Up-to-date guidance from the Department of Health on recommended community mitigation strategies can be found here.«

Elsewhere, heads of executive branches of government chose, for daily updates, forms of communication that resembled public rituals. Well-known examples are

New York Governor Andrew Cuomo and President Donald Trump's daily briefings. Flanked by epidemiologists and public health officials they entered the stage each night for public pronouncements, often in the form of press conferences, televised to broad audiences.

These events fulfilled the criteria of rituals as spelled out, for example, in the neo-Durkheimian work of Randall Collins:[2] Two or more people physically assembled in the same place, affect each other by their bodily presence; participants focus their attention upon a common object or activity, and by communicating this focus to each other become mutually aware of each other's focus of attention; and they share a common mood or emotional experience. Only boundaries to the outside world, distinguishing between participants and outsiders, are missing. Today, in our mass mediated societies, however, physical co-presence – still highly effective – may no longer be a necessary precondition for the mobilization of emotional energy. In fact, concrete, embodied rituals themselves become enduring symbols that carry the ritual charge through time. Film depictions or televised transmissions of ritual events, today stored in electronic repositories, are one mechanism.[3]

Rituals are especially powerful in times of crisis as Kai Erikson showed in his famous study on punishment in the Massachusetts Bay Colony.[4] Describing three »crime waves«, Erikson demonstrates how these periods, not actually marked by increased criminal behavior, experience a perceived threat to the unity of the colony. Perceptions of threat resulted from the arrival of new, less religiously dogmatic immigrants, a loss of political autonomy, and internal discord. They advanced three waves of ritual punishment, of which the Salem witch-hunt is best known. Erikson interprets the outcome of these penal campaigns as the redrawing of boundaries around the community and the strengthening of its inner coherence and normative commitment. This benefit came at a price, however, and that price had to be paid by those defined as responsible for social crises and insecurity. In today's United States, in the context of the Covid-19 crisis, some state actors – in control of rituals – use the occasion to attribute responsibility to external enemies, seeking to strengthen in-group solidarity – and their political power base. President Trump's attribution of guilt to China (*Chinese Virus*) and to the World Health Organization are but examples, in part aimed to deflect from his administration's failures, especially its late response to the pandemic. Such attributions, many uttered in the context of public rituals, had substantial effects, including growing resentment and aggression against Asian-Americans.

Simultaneously, the current situation provides us with a fascinating natural experiment, teaching lessons about the effectiveness of rituals. Approval of Gover-

---

[2] Collins: Interaction Ritual Chains.
[3] Cf. Dayan / Katz: Media Events.
[4] Erikson: Wayward Puritans.

nor Cuomo (and of many other governors), measured through public opinion surveys, increased significantly during the pandemic crisis. Instead, the President's approval initially did not change noticeably and dropped substantially when another crisis, prompted by the police killing of George Floyd, an unarmed African American man, joined the public health crisis, furthering an intense sense of insecurity in the American population. It seems that those who perform public rituals achieve the desired effects only if their performance reveals or successfully displays empathy with the targeted audiences, and – in times of crisis – competency.

The situation also teaches lessons about the technocratization of law and its special weight in times of crisis.[5] Technocratic expertise legitimizes legal (and executive) intervention, and it enhances the steering capacity of states.[6] The approval of public health experts at the national level, especially Anthony Fauci, Director of the National Institute of Allergy and Infectious Diseases, a regular presence in nationally televised crisis updates, increased and far exceeded that of the President.

In addition to providing public goods, the constitution of welfare states (*sozialer Rechtsstaat*, according to the German *Grundgesetz*) demands that states take responsibility where the protection of vulnerable populations is a recognized goal. During a pandemic, states then need to secure the safety and health of those who cannot themselves take protective steps. These are the elderly, especially those in assisted living and nursing homes. In the state of Minnesota, for example, six out of seven Corona-19 related deaths occurred in such institutions. Other groups at special risk are people in detention, in prisons or asylum and refugee homes, especially children and juveniles, and those at the low end of the stratification system. Crowded conditions in densely settled immigrant neighborhoods, and in migrant worker facilities, are but extreme examples. They are often accompanied by unhealthy working conditions as horrendous stories about waves of infections in the meat packing industry demonstrate, in both Europe and the United States, and on both continents primarily among migrant workers.

Responsibilities of the state include short-term support, such as the supply of medical testing, unemployment benefits for those who lost work because of government-imposed prohibitions to keep businesses open, and help for businesses to survive. The pandemic also had devastating effects on those without medical insurance or care, especially in the United States, where insurance is often tied to employment, and where 40 Million employees lost their jobs during the novel Corona virus pandemic. In addition, those at the low end of the stratification system became dependent on food banks in order to avoid starvation. Securing a universal medical insurance and a minimum government-provided income may be appropriate solutions.

---

[5] Cf. Stryker: Limits on Technocratization of Law.
[6] Cf. Habermas: Legitimation Crisis; Skocpol: Political Response to Capitalist Crisis.

3. Dangers of Leviathan – and the Role of Civil Society and Social Movements

Historically, the buildup of central states, with their institutions of law and its enforcement, has been associated with benefits, including a substantial reduction of civil society violence.[7] Thomas Hobbes, trusting Leviathan to whom we delegate rights for him to keep us from hurting each other (man as man's wolf), may thus have had a point. Yet, modern states also developed mechanisms to keep Leviathan in check: election systems and division of government powers (checks and balances) and, in some countries, regional decentralization (federalism). Whenever these internal checks failed, Leviathan has abused the delegated authority to cause excessive harm compared to harm in civil society.[8] More recently, external mechanisms have thus become important supplements: international conventions, treaties, and enforcement tools such as international courts of human rights and the International Criminal Court.

Caution is warranted thus when in crises, for example during pandemics, governments declare states of emergency and when rule by decree becomes the order of the day, weakening the checks and balances that normally support individual rights and protect against state violence. Again, weaker members of society, minorities, immigrants and asylum seekers, are especially at risk. Governments justify their actions as serving the public good. Werner Gephart summarizes it well when he writes:

»The validity culture of the ›state of emergency‹, that is of the ›corona emergency‹, is determined by the unlimited power to suspend the *entire* existing normative order and align it with the extraordinariness of a war, plague, or natural disaster. Symbols and rituals of validity, as well as the organizational validity of the commissioners, censors, and norm-bound agents of the state of emergency, are fixed on this one basis for validity, which superimposes traditional narratives of validity.«[9]

The rise of National Socialism in Germany was an extreme case, and – within its system of terror – medicine *for the collective good*, manifested in eugenics programs, brutally endangered and took the health and lives of uncounted individuals. Tragically, professional experts, including major parts of the medical profession, supported this approach to medicine.[10] *Volkswohl* trumped individual dignity, and eventually the *Volk* paid dearly. Also in democracies, rights delegated to Leviathan during crises are not easily returned. In the United States, for ex-

---

[7] Cf. Johnson/Monkkonen: The Civilization of Crime.
[8] Cf. Savelsberg: Crime and Human Rights.
[9] Cf. in this volume Gephart: Conclusion, cit. p. 513.
[10] Cf. Marrus: The Nuremberg Doctor's Trial and the Limitations of Context.

ample, the Patriot Act of 2001, passed in response to the September 11 terrorist attacks and cutting substantially into civil liberties, has still not been repealed.

It is thus imperative that states be kept in check, especially during crises when the delegation of rights seems appropriate. Civil society, that part of organized social life that mediates between individuals and the state, is best suited to intervene. Non-government organizations play crucial roles, especially human rights NGOs with their range of strategies,[11] but also NGOs working in the field of medicine. Doctors without Borders, for example, ties its medical mission with the command to bear witness against government abuses of human rights.[12] In addition, individuals who contribute, as moral actors, to social movements provide safeguards against government overreach during these situations. It is conceivable that the massive movement in response to the police killing of George Floyd in Minneapolis on May 25, 2020, was at least partly motivated by the restrictions on civil liberties imposed during the public health crisis of Covid-19. While causality is hard to prove, the fact that many comparable killings of black men at the hands of police did not evoke similar movements provides at least plausibility.

In short, times of crisis, evoked by a pandemic such as Covid-19, demand a careful balancing between different types of rights and between rights and responsibilities, on the part of individuals, the state, and civil society. Great risks ensue when this balancing act fails.

References

Collins, Randall: Interaction Ritual Chains, Princeton/NJ 2005.
Dayan, Daniel/Elihu Katz: Media Events: The Live Broadcasting of History, Cambridge/MA 1992.
Erikson, Kai T.: Wayward Puritans: A Study in the Sociology of Deviance, Boston 2004.
Habermas, Jürgen: Legitimation Crisis, Boston 1975.
Johnson, Eric A./Eric H. Monkkonen: The Civilization of Crime, Urbana/IL 1996.
Keck, Margaret E./Kathryn Sikkink: Activists without Borders, Ithaca/NY 1998.
Human Rights Program – University of Minnesota – YouTube-Channel: Envisioning the Future: Balancing Rights and Responsibilities, 22.05.2020, https://www.youtube.com/watch?v=pTNYnBo1j_I; last accessed 23.06.2020.
Marrus, Michael: The Nuremberg Doctor's Trial and the Limitations of Context, in: Patricia Heberer/Jürgen Matthäus (eds.): Atrocities on Trial: Historical

---

[11] Cf. Keck/Sikkink: Activists without Borders.
[12] Cf. Weissman: Silence Heals.

Perspectives on the Politics of Prosecuting War Crimes, Lincoln/NE 2008, pp. 103–122.

Savelsberg, Joachim J.: Crime and Human Rights: Criminology of Genocide and Atrocities, London 2010.

Sikkink, Kathryn: The Hidden Face of Rights: Toward a Politics of Responsibilities, New Haven/CT 2020.

Skocpol, Theda: Political Response to Capitalist Crisis: Neo-Marxist Theories of the State and the Case of the New Deal, in: Politics and Society 10, 1980, pp. 155–201.

Stryker, Robin: Limits on Technocratization of Law, in: American Sociological Review 54, 1989, pp. 341–358.

Weissman, Fabrice: Silence Heals … From the Cold War to the War on Terror, MSF Speaks Out: A Brief History, in: Claire Magone / Michael Neuman / Fabrice Weissman (eds.): Humanitarian Negotiations Revealed: The MSF Experience, New York 2011, pp. 177–198.

IV. Art and Culture in the Times of Covid-19

Valérie Hayaert

Shallow Graves and Empty Tombs: The Architecture of Death under the Chinese Concept of *Tianxia*

The disruptive situation caused by the Corona virus we are currently experiencing reveals various narratives of self-isolation, levels of catastrophe and an acute sense of our vulnerability. The ubiquitous masks, surreal outfits, health care gowns as well as the many graveyard scenes pose questions regarding our representations of death. An elegiac pathos of distance has developed, unbelievable fights over stocks of masks on European airports tarmacs have occurred: from savagery to humanitarianism, this pandemic has revealed the burning scars of our modern societies. As a reminder of mortality, the ongoing disaster becomes the occasion for a philosophical reflection, challenging the founding assumptions of secular democracy with an urgent need to rethink the relationship between nature and culture.

Just as many science fiction stories have explored the mythical significance of the encounter between new forms of living in dystopian universes, the events surrounding us today are placed in suspension of the usual narratives of economic cycles, by counterposing various ways of isolating new sequences, unforeseeable periods and a longue-durée epoch with its terrifying agonistic nature. The pathos if not tragedy of the Corona virus outbreak we are now observing with dismay gives a historical resonance to past episodes of human vulnerability. Such events are also vulnerable to misrepresentation, ideologies and the rewriting of history.

The Chinese government has constantly monitored the media coverage and the treatment of the Corona crisis since its early stages when priority was given to tame and conceal the virus behind the untouched image of an ultra-modern state, an emblem of empowerment. When the Chinese Communist party finally admitted, though with a deadly delay, its spread across China, figures were systematically underestimated. The ridiculously low number of alleged deaths in China (at the time of writing, the official publicized count amounts to circa 4000) strikingly contrasts with the much higher number of funeral urns given to Wuhan families mourning their deceased. Imperceptible and shapeless, Covid-19 death is not acknowledged neither at the individual nor at the societal level. Mourners were left with nothing to visualize, but an obvious discrepancy, where lost individuals have died in a no-go zone, in an indistinct space of anonym gravediggers, skulls without lower jaws, unable to testify. If the concept of testament is (as the Bishop Isidore of Seville punned once) *testa – mentis*, these dead bodies are left without testaments, they cannot prompt the living to speak for the dead. There is no horizon, no community for the dead, no time allowed for the sorrow of bereavement.

The Faustian pact made with Wuhan mourners by Chinese officials seems to equate the following: keep silent about your dead and we will instead give you a material object (a funerary urn) binding together individuals who stand both inside and outside the enclosure. Akin to the curse of death without gravestone, mourners are left with unofficial deaths without burial rites. Not only is their bereavement contained inside the private sphere, but the rites of the community of bonds between the living and the dead are not even performed. Instead of acknowledging the necessary remembrance of death within life, official media focus on the vain glory of human's industrious fight to build gigantic hospitals, out of prefabricated cubes.

Philippe Ariès once taught us that mourning apparatuses appeared between the thirteenth and the fourteenth century in Europe and this was an important shift in our mentalities as the symbolical apparatus of the catafalque led to the concealment of the corpse.[1] This monument is meant to be an extreme representation offered by those who remain alive to the memory of the deceased, it becomes *muta eloquentia* as it gives voices to the corpses. Throughout the early modern period in Europe, the *castrum doloris* (»castle of sorrow«) was a common iconography, applied in Baroque exequies to catafalques in order to accompany the prestigious rites offered to the famous deceased (emperors, kings, queens, cardinals and bishops).[2] European emblems of death would draw on biblical roots to offer mourners Christian solace.

While the death toll has now reached more than one hundred and sixty thousand victims across the world, the situation in China is now presented as if normality had come back. In one of a series of propagandist translations of the Chinese dominant order, the pompous reopening of Wuhan's key spots has dramatized the fable of the omnipotent Chinese apparatus chasing the devilish virus as the Virtuous Republic bringing light to the world.

A recent article by Anne Cheng[3] has highlighted the misrepresentations of Chinese official discourses about the so called »Chinese model« playing off the virtues of auto-discipline and the spirit of sacrifice, an inheritance from the revolutionary military warfare »made in China« which would have overcome, thanks

---

[1] Ariès: L'homme et la mort. Ariès has extended his survey into contemporary practices and he analyses the ways in which death has now sunken into total oblivion and has now become more savage than before. See especially, Ariès: L'homme devant la mort.

[2] Cf. the collective volume Calabritto / Daly (eds.): Emblems of Death, and especially, Knapp / Tüskés: The Motif of Death, pp. 149–198 and Richard Dimler's essay on Jesuit Emblems, pp. 269–286.

[3] Cheng: De la Chine-monde.

to its civic heroism, the overwhelming outbreak in the record time of two months. Anne Cheng adds in conclusion that she had planned to bring her contrastive thoughts to a conference held in Beijing about a much-debated concept, called in Chinese »tianxia« meaning literally »all that exists under heaven«. The conventional translation of *tianxia* simply means »the Chinese world«, or perhaps, more precisely, »China as the world«.

Contrary to other civilizations, China hasn't only represented itself as the center of the world, but simply as *the world* i.e. the whole known geographic space. The Chinese Emperor, appointed by heaven (*tian*), held his mandate from heaven. This concept of political legitimation (a Chinese concept comparable to the European notion of *imperium*) was combined with a moral ideal as the Emperor would represent the highest level of virtue. Anne Cheng has shown persuasively how this authority, which is not constrained by territorial boundaries, is the exact embodiment of the archetypal totalitarian state.

The cosmological worldview located in the »center« of the Communist party has now turned global and aims at preserving a powerful control through cyber sovereignty at home. Over the past decades, the meaning of the geopolitical term *tianxia* has led to highly controversial debates. The variegated meanings of *tianxia*, a highly flexible and nomadic concept, may serve to question the effects of the dramatic rise of Chinese power over the world. Since its recent reemergence in the writings of Chinese mainland scholars, the ultimately utopian concept of *tianxia* seems to presents a new hegemony where the idea of Chinese empire has simply been adapted and revamped for the twenty-first century. Many Chinese thinkers have used this notion to fight the Eurocentric concept of international order and Western norms which have prevailed for several centuries.

What is left to Wuhan mourners is only shallow graves and empty tombs, the disconnected marbles hinting at the absence of the disappeared. The celebratory kind of fable crafted by the Chinese government reasserts the totalitarian violence of its domination. Perhaps the clearest illustration of this escalation of technological warfare is the image of the construction of virus hospitals in record time (8 to 10 days). These temporary and seemingly substandard hospitals were given names reflecting the power to cure: »Huoshenshan« meaning the »Moutain of the God of Fire« and »Leishenshan« meaning »Mountain of the God of Thunder«. Their aesthetic form is akin to a construction kit but with an attempt to reaffirm some kind of Colossian aptitude to build immense purpose-built spaces rearming the government capacity to tackle evil. These prompt constructions were hailed as a political triumph and they were carefully staged as a victory over time by many state newspapers. In order to hide the evident failures of a belated response to the outbreak, state newspapers published day-by-day accounts of crews assembling prefabricated rooms overnight. The website *Economy Net* reported that the Leishenshan building had been equipped with infrared scanners able to detect signs of the disease's distinctive fever. The pictures showing units of these prefabricated containment structure never show any sign of empathy or humanity.

Patterns of fluxes, rules for segregated corridors and ultra-modern scanning technology are put before the public eye, in such a mechanical way that these bricks echo the iced words of militant ideologies. During his travel to China in April and May 1974, Roland Barthes had depicted in his notebooks his disgust towards the cemented doxa of all the ideological stereotypes he had collected from Chinese official discourse: »faire une liste des X Stéréotypes (briques) que j'ai recueillis«.[4] He used the metaphor »brick« to describe how clichés would consolidate, until their nauseous replication would have brought insomnia and physical distress.

The media coverage of these building designs has brought to the fore another type of »brick«, the visual stereotypes of productivism and efficiency, associated with an oppressive state surveillance regime. The Chinese idiom of emergency construction reflects images conveying a zeal for feverish constructivism, rewriting the ongoing disaster by claiming themselves successful at controlling the virus. The architectural idiom of Chinese government is central to its hegemonical power: it offers visual proofs of its mechanisms for isolation and, at the same time, it transfers a voyeuristic control to all confined viewers watching from a distance.

The extension of the Covid-19 outbreak has profoundly disrupted our ways of understanding what is the world. The ways in which an unknown transitory micro-organism, in need of a living body to multiply, has imposed itself as a geopolitical global operator[5] beyond knowingness in such a short time span continues to challenge us. The unintended consequences of confinement measures have inspired movement toward a utopian future, not a return to an imagined Eurocentric past. This pandemic revolution has also triggered new ways of figuring, spatializing and apprehending such cardinal notions as space, time, life and death.

References

Ariès, Philippe: L'homme devant la mort. Le temps des gisants, Paris 1985.
Ariès, Philippe: L'homme et la mort, Paris 1977.
Barthes, Roland: Carnets du voyage en Chine, Paris 2009.
Calabritto, Monica / Peter Daly (eds.): Emblems of Death in the Early Modern Period. Cahiers d'Humanisme et de Renaissance, Vol. 120, Geneva 2014.

---

[4] Barthes: Carnets du voyage.
[5] Lussault: Le monde du virus.

Cheng, Anne: De la Chine-monde à la mondialistation du »virus chinois«, https://www.fondation-cdf.fr/2020/04/10/de-la-chine-monde-a-la-mondialisation-du-virus-chinois/; last accessed 10.04.2020.

Dimler, Richard: Jesuit Emblems of Death, in: Monica Calbritto / Peter Daly (eds.): Emblems of Death in the Early Modern Period. Cahiers d'Humanisme et de Renaissance, Vol. 120, Geneva 2014, pp. 269–286.

Knapp, Eva / Gàbor Tüskés: The Motif of Death in Literary Emblematics, in: Monica Calbritto / Peter Daly (eds.): Emblems of Death in the Early Modern Period. Cahiers d'Humanisme et de Renaissance, Vol. 120, Geneva 2014, pp. 149–198.

Lussault, Michel: Le monde du virus – une performance géographique, in: AOC, 14.04.2020, https://aoc.media/analyse/2020/04/13/le-monde-du-virus-une-performance-geographique/; last accessed 10.05.2020.

Enrico Terrone

The Death of Art by Covid-19

1. How Art Has Represented What We Are Living

Initially, I thought of setting this article as a reflection on the most suitable works of art to represent the situation that we are experiencing because of Covid-19. I considered four options:

First, those works that directly portray an epidemic, in a range that goes from classic works of literature such as Lucretius' *De rerum natura*, Alessandro Manzoni's *I promessi sposi*, Albert Camus' *La Peste* up to Hollywood films such as Wolfgang Petersen's *Outbreak* (1995) and Steven Soderbergh's *Contagion* (2011). The latter belong to disaster movie as a film genre whose hallmark is a narrative structure in which the very existence of community is threatened by an external unexpected element such as a monster, an impact event or a virus.[1]

Secondly, one might consider those narratives that focus on how the virus attack a particular person rather than a community as a whole. A peculiar member of this category is Farrelly Brothers' *Osmosis Jones* (2001), which tells how a virus named Thrax threatens the life of zookeeper Frank Detorri. The peculiarity of *Osmosis Jones* is that Frank's battle for survival is mainly told from within his body, where the brave white blood cell Osmosis Jones fights Thrax the villain. The fight is portrayed through an animation (directed by Tim Sito & Piet Kroon) that alternates with live action scenes in which Frank Detorri is played by Bill Murray. Indeed, this is one of Murray's last great performances as a comedian, just before Sofia Coppola's *Lost in Translation* (2003) turned him into an icon of art house films. The achievement of the film, in my opinion, lies in its capacity to show that even the humblest and roughest person, namely, Frank Detorri as portrayed by Murray, can be a wonderful being if we consider him from the inside. In its attempt to use animation to represent inner life, *Osmosis Jones* anticipates the Pixar Studios' *Inside Out* (2015), yet in the former film the inner life is not that of the mind but rather that of the body as a whole. While *Inside Out* depicts the soul as a sort of ghost in the machine, thereby presupposing a sort of dualistic Cartesian approach to the mind-body problem, *Osmosis Jones* conceives of the person as nothing but a living body. Blood cells, from this perspective, are more important than mental states, especially when a person is under the attack

[1] Cf. Sontag: The Imagination of Disaster.

of a virus. *Osmosis Jones*, just as Covid-19, reminds us that a person is, first of all, a fragile body that has to struggle at any moment against the biological threats that might destroy it.

Thirdly, one might consider works of art that that do not literally represent the effected produced by viruses and pandemics but rather metaphorically extend the mechanism whereby a biological virus threatens the integrity of a living body to the social level. *Parasite* by Bong Joon-Ho (2019), whose surprising triumph at the Academy Awards took place just some weeks before the pandemics, is an exemplary case of such a peculiar genre, of which *Ossessione* (L. Visconti, 1943) and *Teorema* (P. p. Pasolini, 1968) can be seen as forerunners.[2] The basic idea is that some individuals can destroy a social entity, typically a family, in the same way as biological parasites can destroy a biological entity.

2. Welcome Back to the Desert of the Real

In addition to narratives on viruses and contagion, both in the literal and in the metaphoric mode, one might consider a fourth category, constituted by those science fiction narratives such as *The Matrix* (1999), which contrast a desertified real space with an artificial space in which life seems to flourish. They are relevant to the Covid-19 situation inasmuch as our society responded to the pandemic by moving many activities and practices to the artificial space supplied by the internet.

In *The Matrix*, this duality of spaces leads to the well-known choice between the blue pill and the red pill. However, for us, now, this choice is different from that on which Morpheus and Neo were reasoning. For Neo, the blue pill means remaining in the digital dream whereas the red pill means facing the truth of »the desert of the real«. For us, on the other hand, the desert of the real is the given: Covid-19 dramatically brings us back to it, frustrating any strategy one might contrive to obliterate it. We are back in the desert of the real, whether we like it or not.

In this situation, choosing the red pill would mean venturing into the deserted streets, jeopardizing our and others' health. Thus, the choice of the blue pill seems more sensible. We are keen to favor the artificial space in which we have transferred activities and practices that we previously carried out in the real space not yet desertified.

In this sense, one might say that the Covid-19 pandemic has provided us with the occasion to fully exploit the capacity of the internet that had remained so far underused, as if the inertia of the pre-digital way of life were still affecting

[2] Cf. Botz-Bornstein/Stamatellos: Parasite: A Philosophical Exploration.

the beginning of the digital era. The pandemic, from this perspective, can be seen as the catastrophic event that has finally enabled the true beginning of the digital era. Virtual reality might be the next step in this direction. Just as face masks protect us when we walk in the dangerous and desertified real streets, virtual reality headsets will allow us to walk in the much safer and more appealing digital streets.

3. Locking Art Down

So far I considered four ways in which representational arts can help us to think to the dramatic situation we are facing. Focusing on cinematic representations, I have considered films such as *Contagion* that directly portray epidemics, films such as *Osmosis Jones* that portray the attack of a virus to a particular individual, films such as *Parasite* that use the virus as a biological metaphor of a social conflict, and finally films such *The Matrix* that helps us to figure out the technological response to the pandemic through the shift of human activities from the real physical space to the virtual digital space.

The latter category of films, however, leads us to consider another way in which arts and Covid-19 can be related. It is not just a matter of how art can represent a pandemic but also how the latter affects the former. Art, indeed, just as many other cultural activities, in these days seems to have been locked down and moved from the real space to the artificial one. The duplicity of the term *lockdown*, which expresses both social isolation and production block, allows us to clearly formulate the quite paradoxical condition that art is undergoing. On the one hand, the lockdown, understood as a production block, has reduced artistic production to a minimum. On the other hand, the lockdown, understood as confinement, has increased the time available for experiences of appreciation of art, especially music, literature and film.

I am aware that this statement is somehow unfair to several categories; sick people first of all, but also, just to mention the most evident cases, nurses, doctors, parents of young children, business owners who are risking bankrupt. The pandemic, in this sense, makes us aware that enjoying art is not necessarily a feature of human life. It is rather a sort of privilege. However, I do not think that this is a specific feature of the pandemic. Art is a privilege at any time of human history. We when reflect on art, we should always remember that we are speculating about an activity that many, if not most, human beings are not in the proper condition to enjoy. That said, my point is just that, during the lockdown, the privileged people who normally are in the condition to enjoy art seem to have more time at their disposal for such a rewarding activity. We lived in a society where arguably art was more produced than consumed, but in the last few months art has been consumed more than ever and, at the same time, it has been produced less than ever.

In this unprecedented situation, as a very little compensation of the moral anguish concerning the unjust suffering and death of many innocent people, one can feel a sense of aesthetic relief in not having to chase the latest news in any artistic domain, in not having to keep up with the times anymore. In the void created by the collapse of the artistic production, I can start reading novels that I had never found the time to read, listen to records I had not listened to for too much time, and I can finally see those films whose vision I had always postponed. It is a fact that a whole life is not enough to appreciate all the works of art that one would like to appreciate and that would deserve appreciation. But then, why should we continue to create new works of art? Wouldn't it be better to focus our limited energies on that endless amount of works that is already available? Is the lockdown revealing to us a less anxious, more rewarding, more appropriate way to live our relationship with art?

4. Art Resurrection

One might be tempted to positively assess the lockdown of art but, on closer inspection, there is something unbearably dismal in this perspective. First of all, there is something unbearable from a moral and political point of view. Art is not only a privilege that makes our lives more enjoyable and meaningful. Art is also an industry on which the subsistence of many people and families depend. It would be deeply unjust to favor the end of artistic production just because one would like to focus on the already existent masterpieces without being distracted by new works of art.

In sum, there are good reasons for keeping art alive that have nothing to do with aesthetic preferences. However, in what follows, I would like to focus on *aesthetic* reasons to keep art alive. Let us imagine that we live in a much richer society that can easily find a rewarding new job for all the people whose subsistence depended on artistic production. Even in that society, I will argue, production of art is worth preserving. We should prevent art from dying even if there were no longer moral and political reasons for keeping it alive.

Hegel spoke of the death of art in the sense of an overcoming of artistic activity in the direction of higher forms of knowledge such as religion and philosophy. Arthur Danto offered a twentieth-century variation on the Hegelian theme speaking of an overcoming of art in the direction of a reflection on art itself. For Hegel, we might let art die when religion and philosophy are mature enough to represent our spiritual nature in more effective ways than those that art makes available. Likewise, for Danto, art dies when artists become sorts of philosophers for whom understanding art itself is more important than simply making it: »All there *is* at the end, is theory, art having finally become vaporized in a dazzle of pure thought about itself, and remaining, as it were, solely as the object of its own theoretical consciousness«.[3]

The death of art by Covid-19 is not exactly what Hegel or Danto had in mind, but the idea remains of an overcoming of art, understood as the creation of works, in the direction of a new cognitive attitude, which now is the exploration of an immense repertoire of works, finally removed from the flow of becoming. Yet, this repertoire resembles a cemetery, and this makes the expression »the death of art« especially salient. Or, if you prefer, this repertoire resembles a paradise, which is however the lugubrious and inhospitable one sung by the Talking Heads: »Heaven / Heaven is a place / A place where nothing / Nothing ever happens«. The recent TV series *Upload* provides us with an insightful variation on the theme of how miserable life in Heaven – a digital Heaven, in that case – might be.

The point is that art cannot be reduced to the dimension, albeit gratifying, of the experience of beautiful things. Art is above all a historical phenomenon; paraphrasing another famous Hegelian phrase, art is one's own time apprehended in images. Thus, the art paradise that the lockdown seems to offer us, however tempting it may seem, is no longer art, since it has lost its essential connection with history. To keep existing as such, art must continuously produce new works, keeping pace with historical events.

Maurizio Ferraris aptly pointed out that works of art are »things that look like persons«, that is, they elicit mental attitudes such as emotions and feelings that are usually elicited by persons.[4] Moreover, a work of art looks like a person in the sense that it appears to have its own individuality; the work is presented as an individual to which we are inclined to attribute not only material properties (small, colored ...) but also mental ones (intelligent, brilliant, melancholic, passionate).

Ferraris' conception of the work of art as a sort of person helps us to notice that, in times of lockdown, our relationship with works of art changes just like that with persons. There are no more opportunities for new meetings and new friends, and yet the overabundance of time and technological resources, provided that we are among the happy few who do not have to care about more urgent issues, offer us long conversations in video-conference with the friends of a lifetime, even those that we have not been able to contact since months if not since years. Fair enough, but, even if one leaved moral and political issues aside, one should feel something excessively artificial and ultimately mournful in this option. Friendship, like art,

---

[3] Danto: The Philosophical Disenfranchisement of Art, p. 111.
[4] Ferraris: La fidanzata automatica.

cannot be conjugated only in the past tense: it needs present and future tenses as well, it needs to keep up with history.

When history will have overcome the lockdown, we should stay aware that we had too often chased the ephemeral news of the art world, letting ourselves be guided by curiosity, gossip and the fear of appearing unfashionable. The lockdown rightly reminded us that art is not just the foam of the present; indeed, its most precious treasures lie in the depths of the past. But without present and without future, without the continuous historical change that takes place in the desert of the real, there cannot be art. The red pill remains the right one to take, possibly after carefully washing one's hands.

5. How Art Will Represent What We Are Living

Among the challenges that art shall face in order to keep its connection to history, one seems to be especially significant. At the beginning of this paper I considered how art, in the past, has represented situations similar to the one we are living. However, when it comes to representing life rebooting after Covid-19, art faces an unprecedented challenge. Assuming that we will wear face masks and we will keep social distancing for quite a longtime, the way in which art will tell stories after the lockdown is meant to be sharply different from before.

As pointed out by scholars such as Kendall Walton and Stacie Friend, storytelling relies on a »Reality principle« or »Reality assumption« such that the audience assumes the the fictional world is just like the real world unless differences are stated by storytelling itself.[5] Thus, if we will live in a world in which wearing face masks and keeping social distance will be the norm, we will expect that also fictional characters do so. Of course, representational arts might face this issue by setting stories in the past, or in a science fiction future, or in some fantasy world, thereby providing the audience with clear reasons why the characters are not wearing masks and keeping social distances. Yet, genres such as comedy and drama, which are aimed at representing the present, can hardly escape the challenge of representing a world in which people wear masks and keep social distancing. These features thus will become signs of the times, that is, features that allow us to individuate the historical period in which a story is set without the need of explicit indication.

Cars, clothes, phones, televisions, computers are typical signs of the times since they often help us to individuate the historical period of a story. Currencies also can do so, for example if we see a French film in which characters use the franc to

---

[5] Walton: Mimesis as Make-Believe; Friend: The Real Foundation of Fictional Worlds.

pay we are warranted that the story takes place before 2002. Yet, the signs of the times related to Covid-19 surely will have a stronger impact on storytelling since they do not concern artifacts that characters use but rather the way in which people act and behave. It is not just a matter of representing new objects, but rather a matter of representing new ways of being a subject in the social domain.

Even though the new works of representational art will not be as aesthetically good as the masterpieces that we already have at our disposal, the former have something important that latter lack, that is, they deal with our current historical situation in the attempt to represent if and reflect on it. Doing so is as crucial to art as is pursuing an aesthetic achievement.[6]

References

Botz-Bornstein, Thorsten / Giannis Stamatellos (eds.): Parasite: A Philosophical Exploration, Leiden [forthcoming].
Danto, Arthur: The Philosophical Disenfranchisement of Art, New York 1986.
Ferraris, Maurizio: La fidanzata automatica, Milano 2007.
Friend, Stacie: The Real Foundation of Fictional Worlds, in: Australasian Journal of Philosophy 95(1), 2017, pp. 29–42.
Sontag, Susan: The Imagination of Disaster, in: Commentary, 40(4), 1965, pp. 42–48.
Walton, Kendall: Mimesis as Make-Believe, Cambridge/MA 1990.

---

[6] I would like to thank Sara Guindani for precious insights concerning the sections »Locking art down« and »How art will represent what we are living«, as well as Jacopo Domenicucci for a helpful suggestion concerning the section »Art resurrection«.

Martin Przybilski

Imagining Infection and Dealing with Diseases in Jewish Law

The danger of contaminating infection of a cultural, ritual or medical nature is an important topic of normative Jewish tradition. The historical reality of late ancient, medieval and early modern Judaism unfolded under the condition of constant challenges by differing cultural systems, and since being Jewish as a diasporic experience always included one's own existence as an interdependent category in relation to non-Jewish groups, large parts of the Talmudic and post-Talmudic legal discussion are dedicated to mark the demarcation between one's own and the others.[1] Quite essentially the means of rhetorical polemics are used to draw these demarcation lines as clearly as possible.

Of equal importance are ways of avoiding these forms of infection. The Babylonian Talmud lists a number of ways in which the sages would avoid infection with and the spreading of contagious and pandemic diseases. Especially famous is the case of an infectious disease called *ra'atan* that is discussed at length in tractate *Ketubot* 77b:

»It is taught: Rabbi Yosei said: ›A certain elder from among the residents of Jerusalem told me, there are twenty-four types of patients afflicted with boils, and the sages said that to all of them sexual relations are harmful, and those afflicted with *ra'atan* are harmed more than all of the others.‹ From where does this disease come about? It is taught: One who let blood and afterwards engaged in sexual relations will have weak children. If both of them let blood and engaged in sexual relations, he will have children afflicted with *ra'atan*. Rav Pappa answered: We said this only if he did not eat anything between bloodletting and intercourse, but if he ate something we have no problem with it. What are the symptoms? His eyes water, his nose runs, drool comes out of his mouth, and flies rest upon him. [...] Rabbi Yochanan announced: ›Be careful of the flies on those afflicted with *ra'atan*.‹ Rabbi Zeira would not sit in a spot where the wind blew from the direction of the afflicted. Rabbi Eleazar would not enter the tent of the afflicted. Rabbi Ami and Rabbi Asi would not eat eggs from an alley in which the afflicted lived. Rabbi Yehoshua ben Levi attached himself to the afflicted and studied Torah with them, saying: ›The Torah is a loving hind and a graceful doe. [Proverbs 5:19]. If it bestows grace on those who learn it, does it not protect them from illness?‹«

---

[1] Cf. Fraade: Navigating the Anomalous.

The disease mentioned in this and other Jewish sources from late antiquity has not been definitively identified, and there exist several theories as to its nature.[2] Among other things, the medical-historical research literature has suggested that pneumonia[3] or nasal myiasis[4] could be behind the description of this disease. However, yet another and possibly the most likely explanation is that it refers to Hansen's disease because its modern, nosological catalogue of symptoms most closely matches the description in the Talmud.[5] Apart from a severe toughening of the skin, this disease also causes a great deal of nasal mucus. It is infectious, but it requires close, prolonged contact for contagion to occur. But perhaps this question, which emanates from the modern perspective of a symptomatically oriented medicine, also completely misses the ancient ideas of illness and health, since it cannot be ruled out that today's medical science with its nosological concept of illness classifies conditions as different, which ancient medical science understood as belonging together.

Everything that is known about *ra'atan* in the Talmud is declared to be expert knowledge that in addition, in the attribution to a certain elder from Jerusalem, is moved into the realm of unquestionable knowledge secured by far-reaching tradition. Translated into modern terms this would mean that the knowledge about this specific disease had been secured by long-lasting, empirical test series. With regard to the disease's origin, its generational transmission and its general ways of spreading, the sages of the Talmud emphasize that physical proximity, whether to the diseased person himself or to secondary carriers of the disease who have been in contact with the diseased person (insects, food, dwellings, even the air itself), plays the decisive role. The most intimate form of human closeness, sexual intercourse, is considered particularly dangerous in the Talmudic ›thought collective‹;[6] a most perilous time in which the normative rules of everyday life seem to be suspended and the intoxication of ecstasy can open doors to all forms of negativity and abjection that can become haunting realities. Thus, active social distancing is declared the method of choice to prevent infection with *ra'atan* – not only from the primary carriers of the disease, but also from all conceivable forms of possible secondary infection. At the same time, the sages are aware of the resulting serious problem of social stigmatization and exclusion of the sick – reflected in the Talmudic narrative in the behavior of Rabbi Yehoshua ben Levi, which is diametrically opposed to the behavioral maxims of the other rabbis. It is remarkable that this position is put into the mouth of just this sage, because Yehoshua ben Levi is generally regarded by the Talmud as the personification of character

[2] Cf. Preuss: Biblical and Talmudic Medicine, pp. 347–350.
[3] Cf. Ostrer: *Ra'atan* Disease.
[4] Cf. Rosner: Medicine in the Bible and the Talmud, pp. 74–78.
[5] Cf. Koren Talmud Bavli, Vol. 17: Ketubot, p. 77.
[6] Cf. Fleck: Genesis and Development.

integrity and personal piety, but also as the most important authority on questions of Jewish law in the generation of the sages of the first half of the third century of the Common Era. Thus, it is not just any, marginal or apocryphal voice that speaks here and formulates its position against a radical social exclusion of those suffering from *ra'atan* or, as can be concluded from the generality of the words of Yehoshua ben Levi, any other disease considered highly infectious. It is hardly surprising that his preferred spiritual remedy, the study of the Torah, was a tried and tested medicine in the sense of ancient normative Judaism, as another passage from the Biblical collection of aphorisms attributed to king Solomon, which is still repeated various times in synagogue worship today, is an almost classical Jewish definition of the living essence of the Torah: »She is a tree of life to them that lay hold upon her« (Proverbs 3:18).

Thus, from the perspective of the Babylonian Talmud, it seems reasonable, in times of increased danger of infection with pandemic diseases, to ask for the knowledge of experts – literally, the nowadays severely deconstructed ›old men‹ – based on experience and testing and to orient one's behavior by it. At the same time, despite all the necessary orientation on supposedly assured factual knowledge, the dignity of the individual, based on the awareness of the humanity of all, whether (still) healthy, (already) sick, or healed (again), must not be sacrificed on the altar of an excluding community of hygienically sound people. Even in the face of a highly infectious disease that endangers a whole society, Judaism does not allow for the total abrogation of the rights of the individual in favor of the demands of the community – the coexistence of all does not weigh heavier than the existence of the individual, and the latter can therefore not be sacrificed to the former. Indeed, also in this context Judaism proves itself to be a »living alternative to empires, because imperialism and its latter-day successors, totalitarianism and fundamentalism, are attempts to impose a single regime on a plural world«.[7] From the perspective of the Talmud, what happens to me does not define who I am. Reality is not seen as a ceaseless war of the elements to be worshipped as gods nor is history perceived as a battle in which might is right and power is to be appeased. The individual may never be sacrificed for the mass, although the individual nevertheless has obligations to his group, or in our case obligations to other individuals, because the Talmudic discussion on *ra'atan* is part of a larger legal context: the *Mishnah*, to which the *Gemara* in *Ketubot* 77b refers, counts Jewish men who are afflicted with boils among those – like people who suffer from polyps or work as gatherers of dog excrement or melders of copper or tanners – from whom the rabbinical court can demand that they agree to divorce their wives if they make it clear that a continuation of the marriage is no longer bearable for them due to the condition of the respective husbands.

[7] Sacks: The Dignity of Difference, p. 60.

However, the propriety of visiting people stricken with contagious diseases is discussed in the main early modern codifications of Jewish law such as the *Shulkhan Arukh* by Joseph Karo (1488–1575) and Moses Isserles (around 1525–1572). Some Jewish legal authorities hold that there can be no distinction, in respect of this religious duty expressly mentioned in the Babylonian Talmud as an act of emulation of the Divine (*Sotah* 14a), between ordinary and infectious diseases, with the sole exception of leprosy. Others maintain that nobody can be expected to endanger his own life for the fulfilling of this precept.[8] In practice, the latter view prevailed, and approval is expressed for the custom not to assign visitations of plague-stricken patients to anyone except persons specially appointed to this task by the town's Jewish community. From the point of view of Judaism, dealing with diseases and the sick is therefore also a question of the all-encompassing life-shaping program which is Jewish religious law – *halakha* in Hebrew, literally the »way« –, because obedience to normative Judaism lends to every act the quality of ritual and makes it seem a direct link between man and his Maker,[9] and textual exegesis has been its classic mode of expression from the onset until recent times: »Halakhic man's relationship to existence is not only ontological but also normative in nature.«[10]

At the same time, we can see from the conflicting attitudes of the Talmudic sages that positions that shape our discussions and our handling of worldwide pandemics in globalized modernity were already held in the, in its own way, hardly less networked Antiquity of the Mediterranean region. From this it becomes evident once again that supposedly new ideas or ideological patterns often consist not in the invention of new categories or new figures of thought, but rather in a surprising employment of existing ones. As a consequence, the transition from an old to a new theory often is a case of radicalization of already present possibilities of interpretation.[11]

The fundamental applicability of this insight to the discussion process within Jewish law, to the halakhic decision-making process, is also demonstrated by a look at more recent developments and questions in the face of pandemics. Based on our knowledge of the transmission routes of contagious diseases and their acceleration, for example through air travel, the question arises whether someone without acute symptoms should be allowed to board an aircraft to flee his place of residence, where the pandemic has already gained a foothold, although he could be a possible ›silent spreader‹? In the light of a well-known Talmudic dictum found in tractate *Pessachim* 25b, nobody knows whose »blood is redder«, whose life more valuable

---

[8] Cf. Jakobovits: Jewish Medical Ethics, pp. 106–109.
[9] Cf. Steinsaltz: The Thirteen Petalled Rose, p. 95.
[10] Soloveitchik: Halakhic Man, p. 63.
[11] Cf. Funkenstein: Theology and the Scientific Imagination, pp. 14–18.

than the life of any other person. Thus, committing murder or accessory to murder to save one's own life is strictly forbidden from normative Judaism's point of view – only in the case of somebody attacking with the intent on killing is it an obligation to reject any form of passive tolerance and, in the sense of yet another Talmudic saying, to choose active action: »If anyone comes to kill you, get up early and kill him first« (*Sanhedrin* 72 b). But what is the take of *halakha* on our case of the potential silent spreader? As the only possibly contagious person would not be actively and directly killing other people, but only indirectly and potentially, it may be halakhically permissible to board a plane and to flee a place stricken with disease according to the opinion of Yitzchok Zilberstein, a contemporary expert in questions regarding medical issues and Jewish law.[12] Whether such behavior would be justifiable from a practical-moral point of view, from the perspective of what is called *hashkafa* (literally »outlook«) in normative Judaism, remains nevertheless questionable. In addition, the special restrictions resulting from the rhetorical question of »whose blood is redder« only apply in cases of forced murder, while doctors, for example, should also be entitled from a halakhic point of view to make decisions about salvageable and unsalvageable patients – especially in the face of a highly contagious disease spreading pandemically.[13]

Thus, also with regard to questions of life and death, of the individual and society, of hygiene and contagion, Jewish law undertakes the »objectification of religion in clear and determinate forms, in precise and authoritative laws, and in definite principles«[14] that are ultimately grounded in Divine revelation, but nevertheless a purely worldly affair, left for man to apply and re-apply over and over again:

»Since man has no way of deciphering the ultimate purpose, from his perspective all existence is absurd. He is asked only to deal with this absurdity and be aware that there *is* purpose, which only makes sense to God. The fact that man is asked to do so is in itself completely absurd. It means that man deals with radical absurdity from the moment he is born until the day he dies. [...] We cannot, then, escape the fact that Halacha is the art of dealing with existential absurdity. Its function, after all, is to guide man how to live his life. And since life is absurd, Halacha, by definition, is absurd as well. In other words, its function is to help man deal with an absurdity in a way that gives meaning to this absurdity, although from the perspective of man, the meaning itself is ultimately absurd.«[15]

---

[12] Cf. Zilberstein: Aleinu L'Shabeiach, pp. 171–173.
[13] Cf. Etengoff: Triage in Halacha.
[14] Soloveitchik: Halakhic Man, p. 59.
[15] Cardozo: Jewish Law as Rebellion, p. 305.

References

Cardozo, Nathan Lopes: Jewish Law as Rebellion. A Plea for Religious Authenticity and Halachic Courage, Jerusalem / New York 2018.

Etengoff, David: Triage in Halacha. The Threat of an Avian Flu Pandemic, in: Journal of Halacha and Contemporary Society 55, 2008, pp. 74–90.

Fleck, Ludwik: Genesis and Development of a Scientific Fact, translated by Frederick Bradley and Thaddeus J. Trenn, Chicago 1979.

Fraade, Steven D.: Navigating the Anomalous. Non-Jews at the Intersection of Early Rabbinic Law and Narrative, in: Laurence J. Silberstein / Robert L. Cohn (eds.): The Other in Jewish Thought and History. Constructions of Jewish Culture and Identity (New Perspectives on Jewish Studies), New York / London 1994, pp. 145–165.

Funkenstein, Amos: Theology and the Scientific Imagination, Princeton 1986.

Jakobovits, Immanuel: Jewish Medical Ethics. A Comparative and Historical Study of the Jewish Religious Attitude to Medicine and its Practice, New York 1967.

Koren Talmud Bavli, Vol. 17: Ketubot, Part Two, commentary by Adin Even-Israel Steinsaltz, Jerusalem 2015.

Ostrer, Boris S.: *Ra'atan* Disease in the Context of Greek Medicine, in: Review of Rabbinic Judaism 4, 2001, pp. 234–248.

Preuss, Julius: Biblical and Talmudic Medicine, translated by Fred Rosner, New York 1978.

Rosner, Fred: Medicine in the Bible and the Talmud. Selections from Classical Jewish Sources, augmented edition, The Library of Jewish Law and Ethics 5, Hoboken 1995.

Sacks, Jonathan: The Dignity of Difference. How to Avoid the Clash of Civilizations, London et al. 2003.

Steinsaltz, Adin: The Thirteen Petalled Rose. A Discourse on the Essence of Jewish Existence and Belief, translated by Yehuda Hanegbi, New York 1980.

Soloveitchik, Joseph B.: Halakhic Man, translated by Lawrence Kaplan, Philadelphia 1983.

Zilberstein, Yitzchok: Aleinu L'Shabeiach – Vayikra. Wisdom, Stories, and Inspiration, translated by Moshe Zoren, New York 2010.

Alexandre Vanautgaerden

The Return of the Corpses.
»Nosferatu – Phantom der Nacht« (Werner Herzog) and Illness as a Metaphor

It's hard to be sententious or a preacher while people are dying. Dead people, who we don't see. In Wuhan, the epicenter of the pandemic, the real surprise was the thousands of funeral urns that appeared after the deconfinement. The corpses, reduced to ashes, came to unmask the lie of Chinese power about the real number of deaths.[1] On Good Friday, we heard a singular St. John Passion by Johann Sebastian Bach. In the empty St. Thomas Church in Leipzig, a tenor sang alone, accompanied by a harpsichordist and a xylophonist.[2] Turning away from the nave, without any congregation or music lovers, Benedikt Kristjánsson sings the first chorus (*Herr, unser Herrscher*) in front of the church choir. He is filmed from behind, his long hair falling over his shoulders. The slow gestures of the singer, his movements that seem choreographed, resonate with the portrait of Christ transmitted by Renaissance and Baroque painting.

In two months, from March to April 2020, thousands of texts have been written about coronavirus all over the world. Our Western society largely rejects the idea of God. The virus crept into the center a deserted sanctuary. Thousands of texts are now converging on it. Biologists, virologists, sociologists, politicians, journalists, all write and express themselves, with as much passion as the theologians of the past. Faced with the arbitrariness of death, everyone tries to make up for the absence of meaning by looking for a historical or literary referent. References to Albert Camus' novel *The Plague* (1947), Boccaccio's *Decameron* (1349–1353), or science fiction works such as Richard Mathesen's *I am legend* (1954) are often made.

I would like to draw attention to a film: *Nosferatu – Phantom der Nacht* (1979), a tribute by the great German filmmaker Werner Herzog[3] to the *Nosferatu – Eine*

---

[1] Deconfinement took place in Wuhan on 8 April 2020 at midnight, after 77 days of containment. On 17 April, in the face of worldwide disbelief, the Chinese government decided to add 50 % more deaths to the statistics. See Barnes: C.I.A. Hunts for Authentic Virus Totals in China.

[2] Johannes-Passion, BWV 245, adapted for solo tenor, harpsichord and xylophone after a concept by tenor Benedikt Kristjánsson. Performed by Elina Albach on harpsichord and Philip Lamprecht on xylophone, conducted by Gotthold Schwarz. Remote choirs were performed, via video conference, by the Ottawa Bach Choir, J. S. Bach-Stiftung St. Gallen, members of the Thomanerchors Leipzig, Bachfest Family Chor, and Malaysia Bach Festival Singers and Orchestra.

[3] Werner Herzog's official website offers an excellent introduction of his multiple talents (film-

Symphonie des Grauens (A Symphony of Terror) filmed by Friedrich Wilhelm Murnau in 1922.[4] Herzog doesn't hesitate to show in the first scene what is hidden from us today under the abundance of statistical tables or maps produced by the Center for Systems Science and Engineering (CSSE) at Johns Hopkins University:[5] corpses deformed by an infectious disease. Werner Herzog films at length the mummified bodies of victims of a cholera epidemic in 1833.[6] The filmmaker had filmed the mummies himself by taking them out of the display cases and placing them against a wall, after taking care to classify them by age. This panorama renews the well-known theme of the dances of death by presenting the ages of life. Herzog doesn't insist on the path that leads every human being to death, but on the capacity of death to strike people simultaneously regardless of their age. The mummies all have their mouths open, they seem to be shouting, singing a painful chorale.[7] The end of the scene is marked by the flight, in slow motion, of a bat that comes to haunt the heroine's sleep (Isabelle Adjani) who wakes up with a cry of fear. This bat, which heralds the upcoming illness (here, the plague), replaces the microscopic views featured in the 1922 film. Werner Herzog shows us during the beginning credits two kittens playing in a china cabinet. Then, like a never-ending story, he will show us them again at the end of the film, to underline that the story will start again, like the one that touches us today.

maker, writer, opera director). See the bibliography about Herzog on his official website and Eldrige: Werner Herzog. Filmmaker and Philosopher, pp. 210–216. About Nosferatu, see the script published in German: Herzog: Stroszek-Nosferatu; and, in English, in the volume: Scenarios III. See also Prodolliet: Nosferatu, pp. 79 ff.; Prawer: Nosferatu; and Ervig: Werner Herzog.

[4] Werner Herzog's film is not a remake of Murnau's film. He is reweaving the thread that had been cut because of Nazism. It gives Werner Herzog's film a historical depth that German cinema had lost. With his contemporaries (Fassbinder, Schlondorff), he creates a new German school. Werner Herzog develops several projects to redraw the imaginary map of Germany, including a walking tour of the country. In 1978, he stated in an interview: »My hope is that the film will one day become a link to the great film of German Expressionism. Our films are legitimate German culture, but we lack the historical context, the continuity, which in film only in our country is so completely broken off. However, real continuity can never really be established, it is irrevocably lost, and so the search will remain«; transl. by the author.

[5] Center for Systems Science and Engineering (CSSE) at Johns Hopkins University: COVID-19 Dashboard. See, for example, New York Times: Coronavirus-Maps.

[6] These mummies are kept in the Museo de las Momias de Guanajuato in Mexico. The images are magnified by the musical composition of the rock band Popol Vuh created by the pianist Florian Fricke. See the album in 1978: Brüder des Schattens, Söhne des Lichts – Nosferatu.

[7] Werner Herzog writes in his screenplay: »Mummies are lined up on the two walls, and all of them, with their mouths wide open, form a powerful chorale. To the left and right, mummified corpses lean against the wall, like boarders who have been shot. It's a scary sight. Many of the mummies are in corroded clothing, some are completely naked. A young woman has only small shoes on her feet. Her skin is brownish, like parchment. Some bodies are half decomposed, but their posture and expression are still very clear. There are men and women and many, many children. They stand inside and don't bring any signs. The most horrible thing is their open mouths. They stand like a chorus of ghosts from which no sound ever comes« (Herzog: Stroszek, pp. 158 ff.; transl. by the author).

The threat of a new coronavirus was known and expected.[8] This makes the slow reaction of western governments all the more disturbing, as the rhetoric of war to declare a state of emergency later unfolds, insisting on the idea of »being at war« to better designate an external enemy. But the enemy is not at all alien. A virus can only exist and reproduce inside our bodies. As we observe every day, the geographical dimension exceeds any local political discourse. As the geographer Michel Lussault wrote: »We are still a little incredulous that a transitory microorganism, unknown to the battalion, which needs a living body to perpetuate itself by multiplying, has been able to impose itself as a global geopolitical operator«.[9] Let us observe how Werner Herzog's film initiates the propagation of infection as a global operator, acting at the level of myth magnitude. During the Biedermeier period in Wismar, in the middle of the 19th century, Jonathan Harker (Bruno Ganz) is entrusted with a delicate mission by his superior, the real estate agent Renfield (Roland Topor): he has to go to Transylvania to sell a house to Count Dracula.

Ironically, the hero exclaims: »It will do me good to escape from this city, to leave these canals that lead nowhere and come back to themselves«. It's a metaphor for the world we're living in today: we live in an all-encompassing geographical system. His wife, Lucy (Isabelle Adjani), is opposed to his departure because she has a terrible premonition, she knows that he is going to face danger. He doesn't listen to her. As a child of the Enlightenment, Jonathan Harker doesn't care about superstition or what our dreams teach us.

After a four-week riding trip on horseback, Jonathan Harker arrives at Count Dracula's castle. He discovers a disturbing but affable man, who speaks with gentle courtesy. He moves with the same slowness as we found in the tenor of the Johannespassion. The singer announces the death of Christ, Nosferatu, literally, the »undead« in the interpretation of the novelist Bram Stocker, author of *Dracula* (1897),[10] is struck with great weariness because death does not come. The character played by Klaus Kinski is deeply tragic, he suffers from not being able to die, and not being able to love, and be loved. Count Dracula only appears on the screen

---

[8] See Diamond/Wolfe: How We Can Stop the Next New Virus. Jared Diamond, a geographer and biologist at UCLA, is the author of Guns, Germs and Steel. Nathan Wolfe is a virologist. See also the documentary film Ansteckungsgefahr! Epidemien auf dem Vormarsch (»Epidemics: the invisible threat«) by Anne Poiret and Raphaël Hitier, filmed in 2014 on the coronavirus.

[9] See geographer Lussault: Le monde du virus. The quote goes on and on: »A microorganism which acts well beyond its order of magnitude, which is that of the individuals it contaminates, and also well beyond its sphere of action, which is that of infected organisms, and not that of mobility, production activities and world markets, nor that of the monetary policies of central banks«; transl. by the author. See also the very interesting article by another geographer, Jacques Lévy: L'humanité habite le Covid-19.

[10] The Irish writer Bram Stocker repeated a mistake by one of his sources, Emily Gerard (1885), who thought that Nosferatu meant »vampire« or »not dead« in Romanian. Nosferatu, whose correct form is »nesuferitu«, means the offensive, the embarrassing, the unspeakable, and then, the devil.

just a few minutes, while the movie lasts 107. These 17 minutes are pregnant with metaphysics and pain.

On that first night, Count Dracula bites the neck of his sleeping guest. We don't see the scene. The next day, intrigued by this mosquito bite (»Ein Mückenstich«, says the script), Jonathan Harker realizes that he is infected. He doesn't want to admit it, but he is infected. Slowly, the disease will spread inside him.

Count Dracula returns to haunt him the next night. Many times in the film, Werner Herzog asks his actor, Klaus Kinski, to meticulously repeat the gestures of Max Schreck, who played the Count in Murnau's film. The frames are identical, and in 1979 the filmmaker reproduces scenes already shot by Murnau in 1922. The vampire and the disease cross the ages. The images are superimposed. The imaginary deepens.

The infection has occurred. When the Count infected Jonathan Harker, Lucy, his wife, with a dreadful foreboding, awoke in the night. Count Dracula hears this call ... He forsakes the rigid body of the husband and joins forces with the wife. A journey begins, he takes a boat hidden in a coffin to reach the Baltic through the Black Sea. An unlikely route. To reach Wismar, the Hanseatic city of Mecklenburg-Vorpommern in northeastern Germany, one had to cross the lands of the Austro-Hungarian Empire (today Hungary, Slovakia, the Czech Republic), then from Dresden, go to Berlin, turn away from Hamburg and head north to reach the Baltic. But it doesn't matter. The important thing is to remember the image of the ship, of the sea: disease travels.

During Count Dracula's voyage, Renfield, the real estate agent who had sent Jonathan Harker to Transylvania, was locked up. He seems to have gone mad. He tries to bite the neck of one of the guards. He stops: »[H]e hears sails rustling«. The evil does not come from elsewhere. It is he who attracts Count Dracula to Wismar. At each stopover, the Count spreads the plague and becomes satiated. He finally lands in a ghost ship filled with thousands of rats ready to perform their duties. Reading the captain's logbook, the word plague is pronounced. Dr. Van Helsing (Walter Landengast), the town's physician, urges everyone to go home and confine themselves. Considerably weakened, Jonathan Harker is pursuing the Count. He arrives too late at Wismar. Apathetic, he no longer recognizes his wife. The disease is at work. He's slowly metamorphosing. Already he can no longer tolerate the sun.

As the evil spreads through Jonathan Harker's body, Dracula spreads the plague. Werner Herzog had brought 11,000 rats from Hungary to invade the city of Wismar (Herzog chooses the town of Delft for the shooting). When Herzog announced to the mayor of Delft, his plan was to release thousands of rats into the city, the director faced a categorical refusal. The sequence of the boat arrival, bringing Nosferatu to town, was shot in a more accommodating city, Schiedam, a few miles away. If we think of today's policies in favor of animal rights, Herzog's intention of letting loose laboratory rats raised in Hungary, painted in grey as he had only been able to obtain white ones (the rats in the Murnau's film were black), appears not only cruel or insane, but also unaware of potential risks of igniting infectious diseases. Maarten 't Hart,[11] a Dutch expert of laboratory rats Herzog had added to his crew, he witnessed that rats had been starved during their travel from Hungary and began to eat each other upon their arrival in the Netherlands. The insanity of dyeing snow-white rats grey for a pure aesthetic motive led to a 50 percent death toll as the process entailed dipping caged animals in a boiling dye liquid. Maarten 't Hart subsequently decided to withdraw from the filming. Although Herzog utterly denies the words of his »rat consultant« by treating them as false allegations,[12] what is left to us is the porous side of fiction when what first appears as a sublime film is transform into a horrible reality.

Many things can prevent us from accepting and interpreting what we observe. Dr. Van Helsing, an heir to the Enlightenment, nevertheless refuses to analyze what he sees and to hear what Lucy understood when she read the diary of her husband's stay in Dracula's castle. Nosferatu comes to visit her in her room. She extinguishes the fear in her and, clearing her chest to better discover the cross she carries around her neck, she declares to the vampire: »Salvation can only come from us alone. You can hold on to ensure that even the inconceivable will not disconcert me.« In an atmosphere of »Apocalypse joyeuse«, the inhabitants of Wismar, who survived the plague, get together on the Grand'place to dance and get drunk, in a last banquet among the rats. Lucy keeps telling passers-by, »I know the reason for all this evil. Why won't you listen to me? I know the reason.« Dr. Van Helsing, meanwhile, said, »These are enlightened times. Science has long since disproved the superstitions of which you speak.« Lucy understands that she must act alone. She sacrifices herself because she knows that if a woman with a pure soul can make the vampire forget the rooster crowing, the first rays of the day will get the better of him. She kisses her husband one last time. Her husband, who is no longer himself. Then she offers herself to the vampire. Just as he infects her, just as he bites her, the slow flight of the bat reappears: *Illness as a metaphor.* While Werner Herzog was filming *Nosferatu,* Susan Sontag was writing her inspiring book, in which she taught us that disease can only be fatal if we allow ourselves to be convinced of its inevitability and of our inability to change the world around us.[13]

This problem (the representation of the disease) is found in the many accounts of the plague. It is rare, however, to read the story of a plague *survivor.* We have such testimony in a letter from Erasmus of Rotterdam. Written in 1518, it relates

---

[11] Maarten 't Hart is an ethologist but also a writer. A long story in Dutch, published in 1978, tells of the treatment of rats, the conditions of the filming, and his withdrawal from the project. See Hart: Ongewenste zeereis.

[12] See Cronin: Werner Herzog, chapter 5.

[13] Sontag: Illness as Metaphor.

a journey from Basel to Leuven, during which the humanist contracts, or thinks he will contract the plague, in Cologne. Let us look at his testimony, recounted in an epistle written on 15 October to his friend Beatus Rhenanus.[14]

On September 11, 1518, Erasmus of Rotterdam was in Bonn. When he was about fifty years old, he was at the height of his glory; the humanist has just published the first edition of the Greek text and its Latin translation of the New Testament. Advisor to Emperor Charles V, he left his printer in Basel, Johann Froben, to go to Leuven. This journey is recounted in a letter written on October 15 to his friend Beatus Rhenanus. He takes the boat in Bonn early in the morning and docks in Cologne at 6, under an already noxious sky (l. 12: »cœlo iam pestilenti«). Everyone tries to avoid the city for fear of the plague. As the humanist is unable to rent a two-horse carriage, he decides to leave the city on his limping horse. He goes to Bedburg and the residence of Count Wilhelm II Von Neuenahr in Bedburg north of Cologne. He stays there for five days, in good health, in a delightful atmosphere, and reviews the proofs of the second edition of his New Testament. A terrible wind storm accompanies him next on a four-day Dantestic journey to the Southern Netherlands. Vomiting, shivering, fainting on his horse, nothing is spared him. Erasmus accurately describes his human misfortunes: his lower abdomen, black pus oozing from abscesses, the lack of hygiene. Arriving in Louvain on the evening of September 21, he does not dare to go to his home, the Collège du Lis, for fear that a rumor of plague might arise because of him (l. 194–195: »si pestis rumor ex me fuisset ortus.«). His printer friend, Dirk Martens, takes him in. A ballet of surgeons and doctors then begins. Erasmus questions his friend and asks him if they have diagnosed the plague? Dirk Martens answers positively. Erasmus, surprisingly, because he is generally afraid of the plague, starts laughing profusely, and »does not let any fantasy of the plague enter his mind« (l. 212–213: »Risi satis, nec ullam pestis imaginationem demitto in animum«). The humanist finally recovers, after 4 weeks of convalescence. After returning home, he wonders about the reality of the illness he has suffered. And concludes: »If there was a plague, I drove it away by effort and sorrow, as well as by fortitude; for very often, a large part of the illness lies in the imagination of this disease« (l. 250–252: »Si pestis fuit, pestem eam labore et incommoditate animique robore depuli: quando saepenumero magna morbi pars est morbi imaginatio.«).

Erasmus does not write »in the patient's imagination«, but, »in the patient's imagination of the illness.« In this sense, the humanist anticipates Susan Sontag's essay by five centuries. Illness is not only an affliction of the body but also of the

---

[14] Erasmus' correspondence was edited by Percy Stafford Allen with the help of his wife and his colleague H. W. Garrod from 1906 to 1947, cf. Allen (ed.): Opus Epistolarum Desiderii Erasmi Roterodami denuo recognitum et auctum. The letter relating to the trip is epistola 867. Cf. Gibaud: Les tribulations d'Érasme de Bâle à Louvain: 4–21 septembre 1518.

representations we make of the world. As these two authors see it, we must cure ourselves, but above all, we must strengthen what we believe in if we wish to be healed. Erasmus' reaction is exemplary. He protects his community (the Collège du Lis), isolates himself (he refuses to let friends come and visit him), but above all, he laughs. At the end of the letter, the humanist confides in his friend Beatus, telling him that he feared death in his youth, but that old age has made him serene. All the more so since the monument attesting that he lived is ready, his edition of the New Testament (l. 272–273: »iam nunc paratum est monimentum quo posteris tester me vixisse«). Erasmus drew strength from his laughter and thinking back to the core of his life, his work as a philologist on the holy text. The current virus is impressive today because it transforms the power and efficiency of our world and beliefs into factors of vulnerability. Count Dracula succumbs. He lets himself be touched, and the crowing of the cock surprises him. He's dying because he couldn't find the strength in him to laugh or be loved.

Werner Herzog goes even further because he changes the end of the story told by the novelist Bram Stoker and filmed by Murnau. No happy ending. Jonathan Harker succeeds the Count. New Nosferatu – he rides a horse and goes off to spread the disease elsewhere. The new vampire leaves town in broad daylight. His illness has become more robust, for he now withstands the light of day. He has mutated. »Now I know what I have to do« keeps repeating Lucy. Will we be able to hear her?

Fig. 1: The bat that heralds the disease, »Nosferatu – Phantom der Nacht« (movie by Werner Herzog 1979), screenshot.

References

Allen, Percy Stafford (ed.): Opus Epistolarum Desiderii Erasmi Roterodami denuo recognitum et auctum, Oxford 1906–1947.

Barnes, Julian E.: C.I.A. Hunts for Authentic Virus Totals in China, Dismissing Government Tallies, in: New York Times, 07.04.2020, https://www.nytimes.com/2020/04/02/us/politics/cia-coronavirus-china.html; last accessed 23.06.2020.

Center for Systems Science and Engineering (CSSE) at Johns Hopkins University: COVID-19 Dashboard, https://gisanddata.maps.arcgis.com/apps/opsdashboard/index.html#/bda7594740fd40299423467b48e9ecf6; last accessed 23.06.2020.

Cronin, Paul: Werner Herzog: A Guide for the Perplexed: Conversations with Paul Cronin, London 2014.

Diamond, Jared: Guns, Germs and Steel. The Fates of Human Societies, New York 1999.

Diamond, Jared / Nathan Wolfe: How We Can Stop the Next New Virus, in: Washington Post, 16.03.2020, https://www.washingtonpost.com/opinions/2020/03/16/how-we-can-stop-next-new-virus/; last accessed 23.06.2020.

Eldrige, Richard: Werner Herzog. Filmmaker and Philosopher, London 2019.

Ervig, Inga: Werner Herzog: Phantom der Nacht, München 2005.

Gibaud, Henri: Les tribulations d'Érasme de Bâle à Louvain: 4–21 septembre 1518, in : La correspondance d'Érasme et l'épistolographie humaniste, Bruxelles 1985, pp. 25–36.

Hart, Maarten 't: Ongewenste zeereis, Maatstaf, 26, 1978, pp. 77–97.

Herzog, Werner: Scenarios III. Stroszek. Nosferatu, Phantom of the Night. Where the Green Ants Dream. Cobra Verde, translated by Khrishna Winston, Minneapolis / London 2019.

Herzog, Werner: Stroszek-Nosferatu. Zwei Filmerzählungen, Munich 1979.

Lévy, Jacques: L'humanité habite le Covid-19, in: AOC (Analyse – Opinion – Critique), 26.03.2020, https://aoc.media/analyse/2020/03/25/lhumanite-habite-le-covid-19/; last accessed 23.06.2020.

Lussault, Michel: Le monde du virus, une performance géographique, in: AOC (Analyse – Opinion – Critique), 14.04.2020, https://aoc.media/analyse/2020/04/13/le-monde-du-virus-une-performance-geographique/; last accessed 23.06.2020.

Museo de las Momias de Guanajuato in Mexico, www.momiasdeguanajuato.gob.mx; last accessed 23.06.2020.

New York Times: Coronavirus-Maps: Tracking the Global Outbreak, https://www.nytimes.com/interactive/2020/world/coronavirus-maps.html; last accessed 23.06.2020.

Prawer, Siegbert Salomon: Nosferatu. Phantom der Nacht, London 2004.

Prodolliet, Ernest: Nosferatu. Die Entwicklung des Vampirfilms von Friedrich
    Wilhelm Murnau bis Werner Herzog, Freiburg 1980.
Sontag, Susan: Illness as Metaphor, New York 1978.

List of Figures

Fig. 1: The bat that heralds the disease, »Nosferatu – Phantom der Nacht« (movie by Werner Herzog 1979), screenshot. Reproduced with the permission of Werner Herzog Film, Wien, Austria.

Anne-Marie Bonnet

Aren't So-Called Conspiracy Theories the Most Influential Art of Our Time?

1. Art and Crisis

At the very beginning of the pandemic crisis when asked to write something[1] about art in this situation, I spontaneously agreed, but then quickly realized I was too overwhelmed by the new life conditions that had to be coped with. I was unwilling to sublimate and retire into an academic ivory tower and just go on thinking. There was insecurity and uncertainties; the confinement brought a great deal of physical, psychic, psychological and social frictions that had to be dealt with such that I could not produce a quick response to the call. Nevertheless, I was in the middle of it, following what was going on, acquainted with a great number of artists, receiving countless reviews, emails from institutions, galleries, museums, etc. Now, almost three months later, the world is not yet back as it was, and it will never be like before, but I/we are a little bit more trained to confront the new dystopic present »normality« and I feel more able and willing to exteriorize and share some thoughts and observations on the topic of art and the pandemic. In the meantime of course, there have been and still appear to be more and more contributions to the subject, not only online, but also in printed magazines.

So, as an embedded art historian, I will start with a few observations from the very beginning of the Covid-19 crisis. In a second step, comment and analyze the reactions in the art world over the last weeks (looking back) and finish with a few questions and/or theses.

2. »The Rabbit in the Air Moment«

Full awareness of all the uncertainties caused by the pandemic crept slowly into our consciousness until the shutdowns did not allow any further doubts. The so-generated deceleration provoked even a few positive feelings. All of a sudden, one had

---

[1] This text/essay may surprise with its mix of diagnosis and theses and it's meandering forward instead of a systematic argumentation: I decided to keep the trace of its genesis in an eventful time.

time to think, deadlines were postponed, allowing for a certain concentration and reflection on what is important, what matters and some moments in which to take pause. This, I describe as »the Rabbit in the Air« moment. The first reaction of most artists I know was to enjoy even more than usual time in the studio, concentration on their own work. How much of it was affected by the pandemic crisis, we will see later. Will there be any valuable artistic reaction to it? As with September 11? Have we seen any true/good artistic response to THAT paradigm shift in contemporaneity? We recall Stockhausen's reaction to the aesthetic of the attack on the WTC and the upset reactions to it. At that time, it was not yet viral ›shit storms‹, but indeed, an equivalent echo. I remember that a volume with images of September 11 by magnum photographers (who had a gathering in NYC at the time) with the title *Best of September 11* was displayed in the art section of a bookshop. Will we have a *Best of Corona Art* soon? A goldsmith in Munich has already designed a silver corona virus pendant with coral[2] and others have also created »Coronlinge«[3] earrings inspired by the shape of the virus. Is this momentous creativity an expression of a certain »acheiropoietic«[4] self defense? Irony? Or just a testimony to disbelief?

We all have seen, especially in Germany, that very quickly one thought about culture and the arts came to pervade. Copious online concerts, testimonies, initiatives of solidarity have been launched. The feuilletons – culture section in daily papers – have become more inter- and transcultural, inviting authors from other countries and continents to bear witness to the pandemic in their country. The feeling of international, global solidarity was aloof. And, as we know in Germany, even the state, willing to financially help art & culture, quite soon realized how many different forms of art and needs there were and the difficulty of providing adequate help in every case.

But most obvious was this: in pandemic times, art & culture were mainly addressed as a source of solace, soulfood, – a kind of red cross for the soul and sentiment. »On the one hand, culture has been elevated to a kind of secular universal religion that provides comfort in hard times like these. It is a therapeutic agent against loneliness, a weapon against populism and the humus of democracy«[5] as Jörg Häntzschel has diagnosed on May 19, 2020 in the feuilleton of the Süddeutsche Zeitung in reflections on »How the state should get culture going again«. The real importance of art and culture for society will become evident when the crisis lasts longer.[6] In a zoom conference with representatives of large museums on

---

[2] Nöllke: Ein Münchner Goldschmied hat das Virus zu einem Schmuckstück verarbeitet.
[3] Träupmann: Bornheimer Künstlerin stellt Corona-Ohrringe her.
[4] An »acheiropoieton« is an image in early christianism »not made by human hands« which had heavenly powers. An »acheiropoietical« behavior is nowadays more a kind of supertitious belief, like take an umbrella with you and will not rain.
[5] Häntzschel: Dem Publikum stehen keine leichten Zeiten bevor.
[6] Hübl: Fragen zur Zeit, p. 44; transl. by the author.

the topic of »Reimagining Museums« in and after the experience of the pandemic, it was repeatedly emphasized that »museums are not entertainment«, »they are psychological medicine« and »bridges between cultures«. The therapeutic as well as the cultural connecting role of art/culture was emphasized again and again. Nevertheless, only older white men spoke and it was very clear that they are the »managers of meaning«, they are the »custodians« of world culture and know best who can/should/may/could participate in art/culture, when and where. When the museum's leaders speak of »culture as part of our DNA or our identity«, of the »power of culture«, it is rather alarming since at the same time, they convey the conviction of being the custodians i.e. having control over the interpretation and meaning of all this art and cultural capital! How did they get »custody«? Where is the narrative on this part of the/our so called »cultural museological DNA«? Who is the »us« they speak of or intend to address? Or to educate?

3. Symbolic Capital vs. Economic Capital

In the pandemic crisis, arts were not recognized as first rate »system relevant«, but were at least spoken of, mainly to acknowledge the socially precariousness of most artists of all genres – and in Germany, at least a few economic support programs have been launched. There are lots of individual initiatives trying to combat the isolation or the lack of public via internet, digital museum-, studio- and gallery-tours. And of course, the art market and auction houses were very quick in creating online spaces where undisrupted occasions for sales could occur. It was an accepted fact that most artists are highly respected but economically disadvantaged, that their cultural capital is high but the material one, not and this seems to be an »accepted« »state of the arts«. Why?

Besides the perennial claim of the importance of culture in general, there were no serious debates about what art means for society nowadays, what its place is or function. Besides the most present and well known fueling of the/an art market/s. And listening to museum directors of big museums,[7] museums and cultures are meant to be bridges between cultures, place of interconnectedness, of course in the ways and modes they control, which is mainly top down. No one spoke about the extremely controversial, intended revision of the definition of museums at ICOM in which it was foreseen that museums would be places for debate[8] to dis-

---

[7] For instance, talk of Mohamed Khalif Al Mubarak, Chairman of Culture and Tourism Abu Dhabi, initiated by Abu Dhabi Louvre via Zoom

[8] Joseph Beuys already in the 1970's claimed the museum to be a place for »ständige Konferenz«, a place to debate about what culture is, means, should be.

cuss what art and culture is or should be! The revision of still mainly Eurocentric/Western categories and narratives was absent. The concept of entangled histories is something other than »interconnectedness« which translates as global interests in tourism aimed at fueling museum revenues. Of course, one speaks about accessibility for all and that in pandemic times, the local is more present and has to be rethought. But how? And for how long? And for whom?

That the virus did not make us all the same, was not a social equalizer, but sharpened social differences has been remarked in different spheres. In the art world, Covid-19 was also a litmus test or »reality check«. Since the big dealers, art fairs and galleries quickly organized online viewing rooms, sales etc. – the sales must go on –, but at the same time, the precarious survival conditions of most artists became even more precarious, once again enhancing how much Foucault's »conditions of/for the possibilities« are primordial, even when often ignored, pushed to the side or talked away. When art is not only a »psychological red cross«, then what is it or can it be?

4. »Science Is Looking for Answers, Art Is Looking for Questions« (Marc Quinn)

Science is usually associated with rationalism, logical thinking, systematic proving of theses. But we know (at least since Freud and the surrealists) that the human being is not only a rational being and history tells us that what was once science later sometimes was recognized as superstition or legend. One of the negative collateral damages of the relativism of postmodernism is certainly the actual blooming of total defiance in the form of knowledge and the politics of »alternative facts« or so called »fake news«. The recent regime of »thetic truth« has relativized the plausibility bonus of science(es).

As Marie Schmidt recently stated: »Paradoxes have a circular form, while common sense favors straightforwardness and a clear one-sidedness. This is why they are feared in politics and education, but create great moments of insight in art and philosophy«.[9] Is paradox really the response to the pandemic? Is it not much more the case that the many very different ways in which we deal with it reflect, as it were, the image of the respective socio-political state of affairs?

Has art not always been a special form of knowledge of the world, of communicating world understandings and ideas beyond purely linguistic or collective norms of understanding? The only place where the world can be encountered in ways other than through consumption? Art allows us to reflect upon, explore and experience

---

[9] Schmidt: Alice hinter den Masken; transl by the author.

the world beyond language. And just as Okwui Enwezor never tired of saying, art cannot improve the world, but helps us to look at things in a new or different way. The most important thing here is the impulse to think the world is a changeable one. Therefore, art makes you more alert and critical and less willing to accept it. It is not surprising that the first victims of all authoritarian regimes are the artists.

The recent success of so-called ›blue chip‹ art has also been revealing in that it clearly underlines the focus of neoliberal capitalist societies on the commercialization, distinction, investment etc. in and around the so-called »fine arts«. Due to the media's saturation of the few, the fact that art is and can be much more than only this has most recently also been brought to light by the pandemic: so many more voices are struggling to be heard. All these voices made evident, that all art forms have their own different ways to approach the world, offer other perspectives even modes of reinventing our »normality«. What helped us in the new »shut down normality«?

5. Art & Otherness/Alterity?

However, one wanted or could define it, art is, has always been, »other«. In the pandemic, everyone is confronted — nolens volens — with the question of »normality«, the »real«. Consensus is suspended and in the process of re-vision and redefinition, art will be looked to after contingency and politics have provided unsatisfactory answers. In crisis mode, the executive branch increasingly dictates everyday life and reactions are formed that apparently elude »common sense«. But after the pandemic has made the disadvantages of the so-called reasonable, i. e. mainly economically motivated politics (cutbacks in clinical care, outsourcing of primary production to Asia, precariousness of most of the professions relevant to the system) apparent, it is not entirely surprising that »alternative« models of explanation or solution are being sought. In times of uncontrollable so-called »social media« and their viral communication possibilities, completely new public spheres are emerging whose interactions are hardly controllable, thus far. Are these, primarily conspiracy-theoretically operating, world-illuminators to be seen as a new form of »situationist context art«, artivists or activists? As performative guerrillas? For example, the wildly proliferating alternatives of the ZPS (Zentrum für Politische Schönheit / Centre for Political Beauty), whose activism is known to be controversial.[10] They remind us of uneasy parts of our society and times, what

---

[10] By this I do not mean to put the artivists from the ZPS (Zentrum für Politische Schönheit) on one level with all the »conspirationists« but they use the tools of former avantgardes: provocation, guerilla tactic of disturbance of public order, pursue social and political goals with art or activism.

makes them different from the original Situationists from the late 1950ies and 1960ies is that they only use the old strategies of avant-gardes (provocation) but do not propose better more human orientated alternatives.

6. Why Art?

Why art? Why thinking? Thinking as self-defense against the unbearable present? Or to counteract it? In Western thinking, art is mostly thought to counteract nature, to be in competition with it, art is supposed to replace or continue it (»ars supera natura« since Aristotle) and it took a long time to separate itself from the so-called »imitation of nature«. In most non-European cultures (s. e. g. especially Japan) there is no dichotomy of art vs. nature, for example, and the focus on the individual and their subjective personal expression does not prevail. Nature is not thought/experienced as something »outside« or »other« and most of the parameters of Western art thinking do not apply. The topic of »art« (understanding) in a global perspective cannot be deepened at this point, even though it belongs to the resonance space of these considerations as an unsolved problem.

7. What Art?

»Art« as an »anthropological technique« is not considered on the same level as politics (ideological power), science (knowledge), economy (material power) or religion (faith). Art is just one distraction or leisure occupation, not a basic essential dimension of being human or living on earth. Perhaps the insecurities of the one-sided western thinking on art, thanks to the gradually arising assertion of so-called post-colonial consciousness, will lead to the diversification and expansion of ideas about what art is. The most spectacular symptom of the incipient relativization of previous hegemonic Western ideas about art can be seen in the new presentation of the MoMA's collections, whose wider reception has thus far been restricted by the pandemic. If art is no longer a purely aesthetic phenomenon, or a struggle to inscribe itself into a supposed art historical canon, what could it be? Who determined the so-called canon? What was its purpose?

Are we really living in »post-futurist times«, as the latest edition of KUNST-FORUM International claims? Has Covid-19 robbed us of the future and forced us into a radical presence, as Felwine Sarre puts it? Had we become accustomed to leaning on the future? To plan the future time is no longer conceivable in the way it once was. Nevertheless, the management of the present also has consequences for the future. (as in economy, debt, etc.). Have we not actually been denied the present? Denied a self-determined present, one we are less likely to suffer from or have to endure? Hasn't art always been a space of possibility? Art, not as escapism, not as a therapeutic agent, but as a medium for other forms of perception, of world view? I tend to agree with Hisham Matar who wrote: »the current circumstances have altered my attention. I think this is one of the ways that art works; it is there for our pleasure but also as a tool for thinking. It helps us consider the present and our place in it«.[11] How cold art become a tool for a more widely shared other mode of approaching the world?

8. The »Other« / Norm-Ality

Is »art« the other? What is its relation to so called norm-ality? What determines »norm-ality«? The socio-economic contingency in the so-called free market neo-liberal capitalism (not only in the western world) the democratic achievements of which have proven very vulnerable as the pandemic taught us? What did pre-pandemic norm-alitiy look like? Were not most of us dissatisfied with our so-called »normality«? Did we not complain that we were much too rushed ... had too little time? Were this not the most heard complaints? Why do we then long for it again? Before we slide again into a new »routine« we should take the chance to think about what was »actually« wrong before/at that time and how we could avoid it. How did we deal with art? What was it for us? what do we want from it? What do we want and can we do to change something? Was art a luxury we can not afford any more because there are more urgent needs? Or was art a need? Essential? Why? In what? This question raised by the pandemic are waiting for an answer and they will have to be answered and hopefully generated a new consciousness for the specific existential dimensions of art.

9. The Other Seeing? Seeing the Other? or the Changed Seeing?

How has life in the strange and uncertain pandemic times changed our looking, seeing, perceiving? Do pictures of people standing close to each other, street scenes or groups of people suddenly appear utopian? Antiquated? What was once normal now seems strange, no longer self-evident. Edward Hopper's pictures, whose

---

[11] Matarin: Something Happens When You Fall.

strange melancholic »je ne sais quoi« atmosphere may otherwise seem strange, suddenly seem familiar and highly topical. Watching even recent films from ante-Covid-19 times, we realize how far behind the times they already have become: all these people going about their business without social distancing. The expiration date of the documentary quality of images has become painfully evident, never before were the role of *Zeitgeist* and the multifaceted conditionings more evident. In the most current issue of a major German art review that reacted quickly with an issue on »Art in dystopic times«,[12] it is interesting to observe that most of the artistic perspectives mentioned relate in some way to the body now, it's osmotic relation to machines and digital devices (»Bodies in trouble«) and reflections on our stress response to the media and digital society, the state of permanent friction from all types of stimuli and images. The recently renewed interest in Haraway that can be observed, seems all the more prophetic; the theme of the post-futuristic body has become absolutely seminal due to the current pandemic and dystopian present in which our dependencies on digital interfaces are so obviously evident. The role of digital mediation vs that of physical presence affects the entire society and to a great degree, most art practices, the role of which often is to convey/represent other modes of dealing with reality via sensual, bodily, sensorial and sensual means (be it music, theater or visual arts). The vulnerability and questionability of our modus vivendi at the cost of nature (Anthropocene) and at the cost of the rest of the world, when we consider the Euro-North-American sphere which had become more and more evident lately (postcolonial paradigm shift), can't be looked at as academic fashion of thought anymore, but rather as a basic existential task/challenge for mankind. Numerous important artistic positions of the last years (s. for instance, recent Biennials in Istanbul or Manifesta) dealt with no less. Had we listened to artists earlier, like for instance to Joseph Beuys who advocated respect for nature and animal beings since the 1970ies maybe we would be in a less weak position.

10. Museum as Model

Artistic variety is too broad and multifaceted to be able to address all aspects, so allow me to take the »Museum« as symbol/metaphor for the role of arts in our society. The museum in its origins and functions is a very western institution, but in the last years, one could observe how much it became a central battlefield (as in »decolonizing museums«) for the revision of Eurocentric heteropatriarchal perspectives. For example, the newest presentation of the collections of the Museum

---

[12] Cf. Günzel: Post-futuristisch.

of Modern Art in NYC is a first sign of these changes. While museums depend on certain structures in the art world (which vary from country/continent to continent), they have the privilege to serve as the place in which to encounter arts and cultural documents. Since the beginning of digital modern/contemporary, they have to fight for and defend the role of real presence, for their importance as place of encounter and exchange with real art and people/audiences. The Covid-19 crisis has enhanced that situation. As I said at the beginning of my essay, it was most notably the art market that adapted quickly being less interested in mediating the real quality of a work than in its financial value. Like art itself, museums are catalysts of culture as Madeleine Grynsztejn (Director of the MCA Chicago) says. In her actual statement[13] about the experience of the pandemic in and for the museums, she reflects on the impact of Covid-19 and looks at solutions for the future. She concludes with three main strategies: »The Online Museum is here to stay, redefining museums as gathering places and goodbye blockbusters, hello collection.« Generalizing these considerations means that all art practices will have to deal with a mode of digital mediation, not as an »Ersatz«, but as a complemental quality. Art will have to be valued less for its aspects of social distinction and more as a privileged mode of communication. And, there will be new respect for immediacy and proximity, not as a refusal of the global or international, but for the primeval quality.

11. The Lens of Art and Culture

I want to quote and transfer Grynsztejn's conclusion for the role of museums to all forms of art: »We must be leaders in art *and* civic life. We will create opportunities for safe and engaging discourse both in and out of the museum, thus developing a wider outreach and building shared values and community through the lens of art and culture«.[14] During this time when the omnipresence of considerations on art by the international art market is distanced from our view, the pandemic crisis can bring us back and revitalize all that art is and can be. And to come back to my title and its initial question, which was of course provocative: the conspiracy theories[15] (if they can really by considered »theories«) have always existed, have mainly been ignored or ridiculed while they are also an expression of a certain

---

[13] Grynsztejn: In a Post-COVID World.
[14] Ibid.
[15] If it is adequate to speak of »theories« for those mindsets is not up for discussion here, but we may agree that ›conspiracy‹ makes an inscrutable word seem knowable, it seems to compensate the lack of concrete explanatory narratives or is in the contrary a reaction to complexity. They have always existed what is interesting is there present manifestations.

mode of response to the world. My question was inspired by an article from Ben Davies[16] whose thesis I do not agree with, but non the less, made me rethink my one sided first reaction to the so called »Hygiene Demonstrations« in Germany. A bunch of people of widely varying ideologies from far left to far right are standing up because they feel oppressed. Without wanting to comment on what they stand for, they made us realize how split and multifaceted humankind is and how difficult communication has turned, how vulnerable our »community« has become, to the point that the so called »ratio« (the Legacy of the Enlightenment) as a base for mutual understanding comes into question as well. These very special public actions are in fact an appeal, »Zeige deine Wunde« / »Show your Wound« to quote Joseph Beuys. In a disturbing way, those actions (»theories«) attest to the crisis of our civilization's ruthlessness towards nature and alterities. This is something art deals with in much more subtle ways; the time has come for it to receive increased and widespread attention. They express something uneasy we want to ignore although it is very real and active in the so-called parallel digital world. Nowadays it feels sometimes as if the analog world is a parallel world, because what really matters, moves people or is at stake (algorithms, so called social media, manipulation of facts and opinions) acts mainly digitally. These »conspiracy theories« and their manifestations are a sting in the flesh of democratic self-satisfaction, their means and goals are something that should not be ignored and we should think about and find powerful antidotes. Of course, they are not an art form or movement, they usurp strategies of former avant-garde actionisms but do not add any new insights or modes of reflection, as artistic movements did.

12. Is Less More?

What has each of us learned from the Covid-19 pandemic? In a very threatening way, each of us experienced how fragile we are, how dependent on others, both near and far. The individual experience can be transferred to the whole of society and the world. It became obvious that the destiny of mankind is no longer determined by mankind alone but by biology. A virus from the animal world threatened mankind world wide in a matter of weeks and even the seemingly most »civilized« cultures were quite helpless. We learned the effects of a globalized life ruthless to nature in the anthropocene. We have seen how the virus did not make us all the same, but how much it enhanced social differences and privileges. The pandemic highlighted, like a catalyst, all the critical points of the currently so-

---

[16] This question was inspired by the article by Davis: Why Conspiracy Theories Are the Most Influential Art of Our Time?

called civilization (cf. anthropocene): ruthless exploitation of nature, dictatorship of economy and industry. Each of us experienced the fragility of our lives and how dependent we are on others and the community. The New York Times even started a new column: *Take care of yourself and others*.[17] Perhaps, this could also be the motto for the future on a larger scale. Since art has always been an alternative – more seismographic – mode to respond to and approach the world, the art world could become a model for a revised way of handling, of »being in the world«. As Chris Martinez expressed: »What is attacked by Covid-19 is a certain blockbuster culture.«[18] The art business must return to financing that is concerned with the common good, back to a social pact that has as its horizon coexistence with nature and full equality. So, why not invest our energy directly and with full force in the intelligence of art and let it »contribute to better world technology and industrial development – including the art world?«[19]

Postscriptum …
or Some »Afterthoughts« on Art & »Systeme Relevance«

The pandemic generated a discussion on »systemic relevance« which produced surprising findings: At the same time, it became apparent that the so-called »systemic relevance« was only connected with precarious symbolic or little economic capital. The expiration date of this newly awarded »systemic relevance« is already foreseeable. Nevertheless, it was not even ascribed to art in the first place. The question of the criteria of »systemic relevance« has never been discussed, since they were obviously self-explanatory in that they guaranteed the necessary certainty of contingency in the pandemic. The concerns of art itself are apparently not located on this level of the basic guarantee of survival. As is well known, art enjoys a great freedom (in western democracies), which in Germany is even higher than that of freedom of opinion. The price of this freedom is high, because it also means socio-economic »freedom« (complete lack of rights and protection) i.e. »outlaw« status. The paradox or double bind of the freedom of art at the cost of socio-economic reinsurance is inscribed in the DNA of modern so-called free art. Art that sees itself as an »avant-garde« is always critical of the system or in a certain tension with the »system« (art world, society), and accordingly success also means that one operates the system. This dilemma (see above) is also part of

---

[17] This column is mainly focusing on cooking and food, nevertheless the impulse or momentum should be transmitted on larger concerns.
[18] Martinez: »Jetzt ist die Zeit für Veränderung«, p. 52; transl. by the author.
[19] Ibid.; transl. by the author.

modernist art folklore. In good times, the »system« (neoliberal capitalist western »democracies«) allow themselves the luxury to finance even its most fierce critics, but relevance is determined by its laws: »beware me of what I want«.[20] So in the pandemic, more than ever, the only thing that can be said is: system relevance no thanks!

References

Davis, Ben: Why Conspiracy Theories Are The Most Influential Art Of Our Time?, in: artnet news, 11.05.2020, https://news.artnet.com/opinion/why-conspiracy-theories-have-become-the-most-influential-art-form-of-our-time-part-i-1854738; last accessed 16.06.2020.

Günzel, Ann-Kathrin (ed.): Post-futuristisch. Kunst in dystopischen Zeiten, KUNSTFORUM International, Bd. 267, 2020.

Grynsztejn, Madeleine: In a Post-COVID World, What Museums Do outside Their Walls Will Become as Important as What They Put on Them, in: artnet news, 04.06.2020, https://news.artnet.com/opinion/madeleine-grynsztejn-mca-chicago-op-ed-1875996; last accessed 17.06.2020.

Häntzschel, Jörg: Dem Publikum stehen keine leichten Zeiten bevor, in: Süddeutsche Zeitung, 19.05.2020, https://www.sueddeutsche.de/kultur/kultur-hygieneregeln-gruetters-1.4911496; last accessed 17.06.2020.

Hübl, Michael: Fragen zur Zeit. Im Schatten der Stunde Null, Nach dem Ende der Covid-19 Krise wird sich zeigen, wie ernst es die Gesellschaft mit sich und der Kunst meint, in: Günzel, Ann-Kathrin (ed.): Post-futuristisch. Kunst in dystopischen Zeiten, KUNSTFORUM International, Bd. 267, 2020, pp. 42–45.

Martinez, Chris: »Jetzt ist die Zeit für Veränderung«. Die Kuratorin Chris Martinez über die Lehren der Pandemie, in: monopol, Magazin für Kunst und Leben, June 2020, p. 52.

Matarin, Hisham: Something Happens When You Fall. Two artworks that ask the question: What world will we find on the other side of this?, in: The New York Times Magazine, 22.05.2020, https://www.nytimes.com/interactive/2020/05/15/magazine/covid-quarantine-willi-ruge.html; last accessed 16.06.2020.

Nöllke, Paul: Ein Münchner Goldschmied hat das Virus zu einem Schmuckstück verarbeitet. Er will sich nicht von Covid-19 unterkriegen lassen, in: Abendzeitung, 08.05.2020, https://www.abendzeitung-muenchen.de/inhalt.goldschmied-entwirft-corona-schmuck-die-infektionskette.6436f55c-dbd0-430f-b9a5-40a2ab63ca5d.html; last accessed 16.06.2020.

---

[20] This is a quote of a truism by: Jenny Holzer.

Schmidt, Marie: Alice hinter den Masken, in: Süddeutsche Zeitung, 12.05.2020, https://www.sueddeutsche.de/kultur/coronavirus-masken-gesellschaft-1.4903903?reduced=true; last accessed 16.06.2020.

Träupmann, Susanne: Bornheimer Künstlerin stellt Corona-Ohrringe her, in: GeneralAnzeiger, 01.04.2020, https://www.general-anzeiger-bonn.de/region/voreifel-und-vorgebirge/bornheim/bornheimer-kuenstlerin-stellt-corona-ohrringe-her_aid-49847215; last accessed 16.06.2020.

Beatriz Barreiro Carril

Challenges to Coronavirus Crisis: A Cultural Rights Approach in the Spanish Context*

Coronavirus crisis poses important challenges for human rights. Cultural rights in particular – and in a specific way the right to take part in cultural life (RTPCL) as recognised in article 15.1.a) of the International Covenant on Economic, Social and Cultural Rights (ESCR) – are not an exception. Regarding the Spanish context, it is important to note that article 44 of the Spanish Constitution states that »public powers shall promote and protect access to culture, to which everyone is entitled«. Like Tomás de la Quadra-Salcedo pointed out, human rights can be object of limitations in the context of a state of alarm.[1] In the same way, from an international perspective, the United Nations Special Rapporteur on Cultural Rights, Karima Bennoune, recognises that if it is important to remember that »building [a new world after the pandemic] requires a cultural rights perspective both to the question of how we survive this difficult today, and how we imagine a better tomorrow,« it is as well important to have in mind that »some limitations to human rights [...] are foreseen in international law«.[2]

In any case, these limitation measures need to answer to the requirement of *proportionality*. This means that the selected measures need to be the less prejudicial in terms of human rights. In this sense the Committee on ESCR of United Nations which monitors the compliance of the aforementioned Covenant, has already shown its concern in relation with the measures adopted by the Spanish government as an answer to the economic crisis of 2008. The Committee made some considerations that still now remain relevant. In this sense, in 2012 it recommended the Sate to »review the reforms adopted in the context of the [...] economic and financial crisis to ensure that all the austerity measures introduced uphold the level of the protection attained in the realm of economic social and cultural rights and that, in all cases, such measures are temporary and propor-

---

* This is a translation of the text published in the blog of Fundación Alternativas in El País on 13.05.2020.
 1 Cf. de la Quadra-Salcedo: Límite y restricíon, no suspensión.
 2 Bennoune: Culture is the Heart of Our Response to Covid-19.

tionate and do not negatively impinge on economic, social and cultural rights«.³ In relation with the RTPCL, the Committee was »concerned that, in the context of the economic and financial crisis, budget cuts are a threat to the maintenance and development of creative and research capacity in the State party, as well as to opportunities for all individuals and communities to have effective access to take part in cultural life (art. 15)«. The Committee recommended »that the State party strengthened all currently existing measures and adopt any additional ones necessary to ensure the fullest possible enjoyment of the cultural rights enumerated in article 15 of the Covenant.« The 2018 revision by the Committee⁴ of the policies affecting ESCR were not much more positive, expressing the Committee its concern that »that five years after having introduced such measures, the State party has not carried out a full evaluation, in consultation with the persons affected, of the impact, proportionality, duration and possible withdrawal of those measures«. In relation to cultural rights, the Committee was concerned »about the negative impact that budget cuts, implemented in the context of the economic crisis, have had on the enjoyment of cultural rights, in particular on the promotion and dissemination of science and culture«.

Now, the Committee, in a Statement on the coronavirus disease (Covid-19)pandemic and economic, social and cultural rights⁵ of 17 April refers again to the requirement of *proportionality* stating that

»[w]here the measures adopted limit Covenant rights, the measures [...] must be necessary to combat the public health crisis posed by COVID-19, and be reasonable and proportionate. Emergency measures and powers adopted by States parties to address the pandemic should not be abused, and should be lifted as soon as they are no longer necessary for protecting public health«.

Therefore, the words of the Special Rapporteur on Cultural Rights, Karima Bennoune stating that she »oppose[s] to attempts to use human rights or cultural rights arguments to try to subvert these public health efforts inappropriately by for example organizing public religious gatherings or public protests against social distancing in ways that put others at risk« can be complemented with the insistence on the importance of the institutions of control and the notion of proportionality when limiting human rights, as the French magistrate and essayist Dennis Salas points out.⁶ In this sense, a recent decision of the German Constitutional

---

³ OHCHR: Consideration of Reports Submitted by States Parties under Articles 16 and 17 of the Covenant.
⁴ Cf. OHCHR: Concluding Observations on the Sixth Periodic Report of Spain.
⁵ Cf. OHCHR: Statement on the Coronavirus Disease (Covid-19) Pandemic and Economic, Social and Cultural Rights.
⁶ Cf. Sturm: Denis Salas: « La justice se trouve confrontée à un phénomène totalement inédit ».

Tribunal[7] is interesting. Following a case in which a Muslim association claimed the possibility of public prayers on the remaining Fridays of Ramadan, the Constitutional Tribunal notes that an exception can be made to the measure banning the holding of religious events if it can be ensured that there is no increased risk of infection. This, of course, will have to be established on a case-by-case basis, and not in a general way.

These issues have great relevance in the context of the current scenario in relation to the RTPCL, due to the great importance of holding face-to-face cultural events. In addition, the Committee on ESCR in the above-mentioned statement points out that States should take social protection measures that reach out to those who are most at risk of being affected by the crisis, and insist on

»the obligation to devote their maximum available resources to the full realization of all economic, social and cultural rights […] As this pandemic and the measures taken to combat it have had a disproportionately negative impact on the most marginalized groups, States must make every effort to mobilize the necessary resources to combat COVID-19 in the most equitable manner, in order to avoid imposing a further economic burden on these marginalized groups. Allocation of resources should prioritize the special needs of these groups«.

This attention to the groups who are especially vulnerable can be put in relation with the decree 17/2020 of 5 May, through which the government approved measures to support the cultural sector[8] in order to help cultural actors to face the economic and social impact derived from the coronavirus crisis. Among the measures included by the decree there is the possibility for public performance artists – subject to intermittence – to benefit from unemployment benefit.

It should be remembered as well that the RTPCL includes the right to be consulted and to participate in the design of policies that affect it, as the Special Rapporteur on Cultural Rights points out.[9] The meetings held in April between the Ministry of Culture and various organizations of the cultural sector can be read therefore in the light of the exercise of that right. The consideration by the sectorial committee on contemporary art of the inadequacy of the measures adopted through the aforementioned decree also deserves to be heard in the frame of the DPVC.[10] Adopting a human rights approach implies taking into account the opinion of the persons concerned in relation to the rights affected by the cultural

---

[7] Cf. Bundesverfassungsgericht: Beschluss vom 29. April 2020, 1 BvQ 44/20.
[8] Cf. Real Decreto-ley 17/2020, de 5 de mayo.
[9] Cf. Bennoune: Culture is the Heart of Our Response to Covid-19.
[10] The Minister of Culture sent a letter of reply to each of the 21 highly relevant contemporary artists who considered as insufficient the measures in the decree (cf. Hernando: Rodríguez Uribes responde a la cúpula del arte contemporáneo). Additional measures for the cultural sector were adopted at the end of May (cf. El Cultural: El Gobierno destina 7,3 millones de euros a la cultura).

policies at hand. As the Special Rapporteur of Cultural Rights states in her last annual report about defenders of cultural rights »many people may be cultural rights defenders, or function as such, without necessarily describing themselves in those terms.«[11] There is no doubt that all the groups that inside and outside Spain are promoting dignified conditions for workers in the cultural sector and public cultural policies that universalize participation and access to culture can be considered defenders of cultural rights. At the level of the European Union, several cultural organizations of different kinds have just launched a call for increased budgets for cultural policies, and at the international level,[12] the International Federation of Coalitions for Cultural Diversity calls on governments to take into account the specific needs of the cultural sector, particularly from the point of view of cultural diversity,[13] an issue that is deeply linked to the RPCL.

In fact, minority cultural expressions are those most in need of public support and that best guarantee the fabric of diversity. The publisher Antoine Gallimard points to the need for small bookshops in France to reopen as soon as possible – while respecting the necessary health measures, of course – as they are the guarantors of cultural diversity.[14] These considerations, from the point of view of the RTPCL, not only benefit artists, writers and publishers, but are also relevant from the point of view of access and participation. Access and participation require, as indicated by the Committee on ESCR in its 2009 General Comment on the RTPCL,[15] that States implement public policies so that the exercise of the RTPCL is within everyone's reach (including financially). If the recent the digital books' VAT alignment to that of the paper book is in line with this, the problem of the digital divide, which the Committee mentions in its statement in relation to the pandemic in the context of the right to education (and not in relation to the RTPCL in the strict sense), still needs to be addressed. This is an unsettled issue, since already in 2018 the Committee regretted »not having received specific information on the measures taken to ensure access to the benefits of scientific progress, including the Internet (art. 15).«[16] We see, therefore, that the current situation poses many challenges to the exercise of cultural rights, both from the point of view of the creation and the point of view of the access. International Human Rights Law offers an excellent framework to guide the undoubtedly difficult measures to be carried out in the field of cultural policies.

---

[11] OHCHR: Report of the Special Rapporteur in the field of cultural rights.
[12] Cf. ENCATC: Europe's Cultural and Creative Sectors Call for Ambitious EU Budgetary Measures to Get through the COVID-19 Crisis.
[13] Cf. FICDC: Message du Président de la FICDC.
[14] Cf. Bassets: Antoine Gallimard: »No creo que el mundo vaya a cambiar, sería demasiado bello«.
[15] Cf. OHCHR: Derecho de toda persona a participar en la vida cultural.
[16] OHCHR: Concluding Observations on the Sixth Periodic Report of Spain

References

Bassets, Marc: Antoine Gallimard: »No creo que el mundo vaya a cambiar, sería demasiado bello«, in: El Pais, 28.04.2020, https://elpais.com/cultura/2020-04-27/antoine-gallimard-no-creo-que-el-mundo-vaya-a-cambiar-seria-demasiado-bello.html; last accessed 16.06.2020.

Bennoune, Karima: Culture is the Heart of Our Response to Covid-19, https://www.ohchr.org/Documents/Issues/CulturalRights/BeyondTheOutbreak-online2020-KBspeech.pdf; last accessed 16.06.2020.

de la Quadra-Salcedo, Tomás: Límite y restricíon, no suspension, in: El Pais, 08.04.2020, https://elpais.com/elpais/2020/04/07/opinion/1586245220_558731.html; last accessed 16.06.2020.

El Cultural: El Gobierno destina 7,3 millones de euros a la cultura, 19.05.2020, https://elcultural.com/el-gobierno-destina-73-millones-de-euros-a-la-cultura; last accessed 16.06.2020.

European Network on Cultural Management and Policy (ENCATC): Europe's Cultural and Creative Sectors Call for Ambitious EU Budgetary Measures to Get through the COVID-19 Crisis, https://www.encatc.org/media/5387-ccs_covid19__statement_final.pdf; last accessed 16.06.2020.

Fédération Internationale des Coalitions pour la Diversité Culturelle (FICDC): Message du Président de la FICDC, 30.03.2020, https://ficdc.org/fr/publications/message-president-ficdc/; last accessed 16.06.2020.

Hernando, Silvia: Rodríguez Uribes responde a la cúpula del arte contemporáneo, in: El Pais, 18.05.2020, https://elpais.com/cultura/2020-05-18/rodriguez-uribes-responde-a-la-cupula-del-arte-contemporaneo.html; last accessed 16.06.2020.

Sturm, Florence: Denis Salas: « La justice se trouve confrontée à un phénomène totalement inédit », in : France culture, 24.03.2020, https://www.franceculture.fr/droit-justice/denis-salas-la-justice-se-trouve-confrontee-a-un-phenomene-totalement-inedit; last accessed 16.06.2020.

United Nations Committee on Economic, Social and Cultural Rights (OHCHR): Concluding Observations on the Sixth Periodic Report of Spain, 25.04.2018, https://tbinternet.ohchr.org/_layouts/15/treatybodyexternal/Download.aspx?symbolno=E%2fC.12%2fESP%2fCO%2f6&Lang=en; last accessed 16.06.2020.

United Nations Committee on Economic, Social and Cultural Rights (OHCHR): Consideration of Reports Submitted by States Parties under Articles 16 and 17 of the Covenant, 06.06.2012, https://tbinternet.ohchr.org/_layouts/15/treatybodyexternal/Download.aspx?symbolno=E%2fC.12%2fESP%2fCO%2f5&Lang=en; last accessed 16.06.2020.

United Nations Committee on Economic, Social and Cultural Rights (OHCHR): Derecho de toda persona a participar en la vida cultural (artículo 15, párrafo 1 a), del Pacto Internacional de Derechos Económicos, Sociales y Culturas), 17.05.

2010, https://tbinternet.ohchr.org/_layouts/15/treatybodyexternal/Download. aspx?symbolno=E%2fC.12%2fGC%2f21%2fREV.1&Lang=en; last accessed 16.06.2020.

United Nations Committee on Economic, Social and Cultural Rights (OHCHR): Statement on the Coronavirus Disease (Covid-19) Pandemic and Economic, Social and Cultural Rights, 17.04.2020, https://undocs.org/E/C.12/2020/1; last acessed 16.06.2020.

United Nations Cultural Rights Defenders: Report of the Special Rapporteur in the Field of Cultural Rights, https://undocs.org/en/A/HRC/43/50; last accessed 16.06.2020.

Grischka Petri

Masking the Invisible / Segments of Political Space

> »My *God*, my *God*, how large a *glasse*
> of the next *World* is *this*?«
> John Donne[1]

1. Classics, Crisis, Camouflage

In times of crisis, the classics have traditionally provided a source of solace.[2] Moreover, in times of intellectual crisis,[3] re-examining classical theses in light of current circumstances may prove beneficial. The current crisis scenario is both complex and simple: The simple fact is that a virus is currently spreading across the globe. It affects the human respiratory system, manifesting in some cases as a light cough and mild fever, and in other, more severe (and potentially fatal) cases affecting the kidneys, heart and blood circulation as well as other vital systems in the body. This virus is known as SARS-CoV-2 (Severe acute respiratory syndrome coronavirus 2); the illness has been named Coronavirus Disease 2019, or Covid-19. The complexities begin when we look to the fact that, at present, there is no vaccine against the virus, and effective treatments are but in the earliest stages of development. Severe cases of Covid-19 require intensive care, including the use of ventilators and support for other vital organs that may be affected by the body's efforts to battle the virus and to build antibodies. Hospitals with insufficient numbers of intensive care beds to care for Covid-19 patients may see a large number of deaths from the virus. Thus, preventative measures are needed to keep the number of cases under control.

Around the world, many – if not most – governments implemented a set of drastic measures designed to prevent the spread of the virus. These included self-isolation and distancing. Since older people are at greater risk of experiencing

---

[1] Donne: Devotions Upon Emergent Occasions, Expostulation XXI, p. 112.
[2] Cf. Findlen: Petrarch's Plague; and the starting point of the essay by Olson: Being in Uncertainty, in this volume.
[3] There has been talk of a lack of intellectual rigour in view of the Corona crisis; see e. g. Encke: Was Theorie noch kann, and Andina: »It's Just a Flu«, in this volume: »philosophy [...] has not been of much help«, p. 469.

more severe effects, visits to care homes were banned in a number of jurisdictions. Several countries imposed lockdown measures prohibiting people from leaving their homes except for specific purposes, such as shopping for essentials, seeking medical treatment, or going to work. Many industries, schools and nurseries closed, with home office work becoming the rule rather than the exception, even in sectors such as banking and academia. Indeed, this essay was written under the challenging but nonetheless happy conditions of intensified family life with three young girls aged between five and seven years, and a combination of home schooling, home kindergarten and home research. The distancing regime in force in my home state in Germany prohibited meeting more than one other person in public until 11 May 2020.[4] The countries that make up the United Kingdom also imposed Health Protection Regulations, based on the Public Health (Control of Disease) Act 1984. As of today (June 2020), there is no comprehensive overview of global legislation relating to the Covid-19 pandemic. The pertinent Wikipedia list could act as a starting point for a much-needed research project culminating in a fully searchable register.[5] As for the German legislation, the »LexCorona« initiative established by a Mainz-based law firm has set up a catalogue.[6] At present, the situation is continually changing. For these reasons, this essay will offer neither systematic nor definitive viewpoints, but instead aims to highlight a number of specific aspects. While the topic is of fundamental importance, the discussion must remain superficial for the time being.

1.1 The Political Animal

When considering the social distancing measures, perhaps one of the first classics that comes to mind is Aristotle, despite Thomas Hobbes's reservations about reading the ancient books of Policy.[7] As Aristotle famously wrote, »man is by nature a political animal [...] much more a political animal than any kind of bee or any herd animal [...].«[8] According to the Greek philosopher, mankind's distinguishing quality is his speech:

»speech serves to reveal [...] the just and the unjust. For it is peculiar to man as compared to the other animals that he alone has a perception of good and bad and just and unjust

---

[4] § 12 CoronaSchVO NW.
[5] Wikipedia: List of COVID-19 Pandemic Legislation.
[6] See the Lex Corona initiative.
[7] Hobbes: Leviathan, Ch. XXIX, Vol. 2, p. 506. Ginzburg: Fear Reverence Terror, p. 4, describes Aristotle as Hobbes's polemical target, the former basing his political theory on community, the latter basing it on fear.
[8] Aristotle: Politics, I.2, 1253a (9).

and the other things of this sort; and community in these things is what makes a household and a city.«[9]

Carnes Lord's explanation of the passage in his commentary on Aristotle states that the *logos* enables man to conduct himself morally in relation to others in a way that makes human community possible. Indeed, the relationship is much closer: because both the logos and community belong to the nature of mankind, moral conduct is vital to the survival of mankind as a species. If we view the law as the minimum standard for such morals, it becomes clear how it forms part of a kind of second nature: »For just as man is the best of the animals when completed, when separated from law and adjudication he is the worst of all.«[10]

Despite his rational explanation of the state as a human construct, there is a prominent, perhaps even prevalent biological factor in Aristotle's model.[11] This factor links the social entities of the family, the household and the city (*polis*). Aristotle revisits this idea when he explains that the political animals yearn to live together »even when they have no need of assistance from one another«.[12] This animal communicates face to face for the most part, with architecture providing the spatial framework within which this takes place: private buildings, possibly a farmhouse, a small village with its central meeting place, the spacious agora, a public forum – all serve communal and political communication in Aristotle's world. In that world, social interaction occurs between people sharing the same space. Many centuries later, Maurice Merleau-Ponty again explored the close structural connections and similarities between space, the body, and existence.[13] What may sound banal is nevertheless deeply rooted in our understanding of communication. Re-reading the *Politics*, it becomes clear that talk of »social distancing« demonstrates a kind of pre-digital fallacy, since what is actually meant is »physical distancing«. In the current age of digital communication, social interaction is no longer confined to the material meeting places of the polis. However, our terminology has in part failed to acknowledge this, while simultaneously revealing that, for all our technological progress, we continue to idealistically cling to concepts from Aristotle's time when it comes to defining our political and social essence.

---

[9] Ibid (12).
[10] Ibid (15).
[11] Cf. Kullmann: Man as a Political Animal in Aristotle, p. 102.
[12] Aristotle: Politics, III.6, 1257 8b (3).
[13] Cf. Merleau-Ponty: Phenomenology of Perception, pp. 149, 253 f. The body is a »subject of space«, ibid., p. 261.

1.2 The Kingdom of Sickness

In November 1623, the Dean of St Paul's Cathedral suddenly fell ill: »[T]his minute I was well, and am ill, this minute.«[14] While it is not entirely clear whether he was suffering from typhus or the so-called seven-day (or relapsing) fever, both diagnoses remain equally reasonable explanations for the epidemic fever that swept the city of London at the time.[15] It was a time during which epidemics came and went in waves, and the population lived – and died – with them. The Dean in question was none other than poet and scholar John Donne (1572–1631), who chronicled his symptoms and convalescence in daily meditations, expostulations, and prayers, which were published soon thereafter, in early 1624. Donne noted how his appetite became »dull and desirelesse«, and he prepared to die, realising how »in an instant, sleepe, which is the picture, the copy of death, is taken away, that the *Originall, Death* it selfe may succeed [...]«.[16] His reaction to his condition is reminiscent of our own recent thoughts during the ongoing Covid-19 pandemic. Across the world, society has put their confidence in the experts – Anthony Fauci in the USA, Christian Drosten in Germany, Anders Tegnell in Sweden, Massimo Galli in Italy, Ashley Bloomfield in New Zealand. John Donne too realised his dependency on the experts: »We *have* the Phisician, but *we are not* the Phisician«.[17] Donne also accepted that the disease necessitated certain official measures and that his own freedom of movement, and even his own authority over his body, were subject to regulation by others:

»The *disease* hath established a *Kingdome*, an *Empire* in mee, and will have certaine *Arcana Imperii, secrets of State*, by which it will proceed, & not be bound to *declare* them. But yet against those secret conspiracies in the State, the *Magistrate* hath the *rack*; and against these insensible diseases, *Phisicians* have their *examiners*; and those these imploy now«.[18]

This passage is interesting for several reasons. It describes a reversed hierarchy of power, where the disease is in charge, and it draws a comparison between the bodies of the individual and the state. Both body and state need to be maintained in good shape, and both may be exposed to states of emergency that demand swift action: »In States & matter of government it is so too; they are sometimes surprizd with such *accidents*, as that the *Magistrat* asks not what may be done by *law*, but does that, which must necessarily be done in that case.«[19] Donne also compares the invisible disease to a conspiracy. This metaphor is echoed in the conspiracy

---

14 Donne: Devotions Upon Emergent Occasions, Meditation I, p. 7.
15 Cf. Raspa: Introduction to Donne: Devotions Upon Emergent Occasions, pp. xiii–xvii.
16 Donne: Devotions Upon Emergent Occasions, Meditation II, p. 11.
17 Ibid.: Meditation IV, p. 20.
18 Ibid.: Meditation X, p. 52.
19 Ibid.: Meditation IX, p. 47.

theories prevalent in the face of the lack of knowledge about the new coronavirus. For the moment, however, I will comment further on the reversal of power. John Donne repeatedly returned to the idea that a serious illness deflates the powerful, »a fever can bring that head, which yesterday caried a *crown* of gold, five foot towards a *crown* of glory, as low as his own foot, today«.[20]

SARS-CoV-2, like all coronaviruses, is an apposite symbol of power in its apparent resemblance to the solar corona and, by extension, to a crown. Indeed, their »appearance, recalling the solar corona«[21] is the reason why this family of viruses were given their name. The connection between the sun and the crown was perhaps made most tightly and enduring closer to John Donne's time, when Louis XIV of France (King 1643–1715) chose the sun as his personal emblem for the celebrations of the birth of his son in 1662. He was not alone in his choice. Since the time of Charles V (the Wise), French monarchs had chosen the sun as their symbol,[22] while the Habsburg »empire on which the sun never sets« provided another impressive example. Nonetheless, it was Louis' XIV appropriation of the sun that proved the most successful. The sun was minted on several *jetons*, often combined with a more or less enigmatic motto, perhaps the most prominent being

Fig. 1: Jeton, Ordinaire des guerres, silver, 27 mm, 1658, Paris.

»nec pluribus impar« (fig. 1). Acting as a common symbolic denominator for both a virus and a monarch, the sun could be an example of those dangerous inherent meanings of legal images pointed out by Werner Gephart and Jure Leko.[23] By 1674,

---

[20] Ibid.: Meditation III, p. 15.
[21] Almeida: Coronaviruses, p. 650.
[22] Sabatier: La gloire du roi, p. 540; Ziegler: »Sonne«, pp. 358–365.
[23] Gephart/Leko: Law and the Arts, p. 12.

André Félibien, the official court historian, reported in his *Description sommaire du Chasteau du Versailles* that »Il est bon de remarquer d'abord que comme le Soleil est la Devise du Roy, & que les Poëtes confondent le Soleil & Apolon, Il n'y a rien dans cette superbe Maison qui n'ait raport à cette divinité«.[24] At this juncture it is neither necessary to repeat nor to summarise the numerous scholarly contributions since Ernst Kantorowicz's masterful study, the *King's Two Bodies* (1957). The mutual metaphor of the ruler's governmental and physical bodies proves its own unforgiving reality in the *Journal de la santé du roi Louis XIV*, as chronicled by the King's medical doctors.[25] While the French monarch's state is informed by the requirement of command and control, both over his own body and the country, John Donne's perspective is more personal, as he surrenders his body to the new king, the sickness that has taken hold of him. Donne reflects on his isolation as a social being; he calls out for compassion, and he suffers:

»As Sicknesse is the greatest misery, so the greatest misery of sicknes is *solitude*; when the infectuousnes of the disease deterrs them who should assist, from coming; Even the *Phisician* dares scarse some. [...] When I am dead, & my body might infect, they have a remedy, they may bury me; but when I am but sick, and might infect, they have no remedy, but their absence and my solitude. [...] [I]t is an *inhibition* to those who would truly come, because they may be made instruments, and pestiducts, to the infection of others, by their comming.«[26] Even God, in Donne's view, is a social being, since »all his externall actions testifie a love of *Societie*, and communion. In *Heaven* there are *Orders* of *Angels*, and *Armies of Martyrs*, & *in that house, many mansions*; in *Earth, Families, Cities, Churches, Colleges*, all *plurall things* [...]. [God] saw that it was not good, for man to bee *alone* [...].«[27]

God has made man a social animal, and the sickness stands in the way of this plan. However, to survive, it is necessary to isolate temporarily. The argument is all too familiar to us, and we have become familiar with a similar reasoning during the current pandemic. But this isolated state cannot continue indefinitely; in the words of Merleau-Ponty, »I can certainly turn away from the social world, but I cannot cease to be situated in relation to it«.[28] Again, it is Donne who introduces the idea of solidarity into the balance of arguments, in what is probably his best known meditation, the seventeenth. In it, Donne ponders how human fates are related and connected to one another and to God, how all individuals are part of mankind:

---

[24] Felibie: Description sommaire du chasteau de Versailles, pp. 11 f.

[25] D'Aquin / Vallot / Fagon: Journal de la santé du roi Louis XIV de l'année 1647 à l'année 1711. See also Bernard: Medicine at the Court of Louis XIV. The realities of the king's medical condition are in stark contrast to the widespread and longstanding belief in the power of his healing hands; see Bloch: Les Rois thaumaturges.

[26] Donne: Devotions Upon Emergent Occasions, Meditation V, pp. 24 f.

[27] Ibid.

[28] Merleau-Ponty: Phenomenology of Perception, p. 379.

»No Man is an *Iland*, intire of it selfe; every man is a peece of the *Continent*, a part of the *maine*; if a *Clod* bee washed away by the *Sea*, *Europe* is the lesse, as well as if a *Promontorie* were, as well as if a *Mannor* of thy *friends*, or of *thine own* were; Any Mans *death* diminishes *me*, because I am involved in *Mankinde*; And therefore never send to know for whom the *bell* tolls; It tolls for *thee*.«[29]

Phrased in more modern terms, John Donne desires a kind of emotionally based solidarity (perhaps »affective« in the sense described by Talcott Parsons[30]), and he is also prepared to offer it. My neighbour's fate is also mine.

1.3 Hobbes's Sick State and the Plague Doctors

Thomas Hobbes also reminded his readers of »this one Commandement of mutuall Charity, *Thou shalt love thy neighbour as thy selfe*«.[31] The mutual interdependencies of individual, state, and its monarch, and Hobbes's ideas about the »body politic«, which have been the subject of too many studies to mention,[32] are powerfully portrayed on the title page of Hobbes's *Leviathan* (1651), »perhaps the most famous visual image in the history of political philosophy«[33] and now commonly credited to the French master engraver, Abraham Bosse (fig. 2).[34] Bosse's workshop was within easy walking distance of Hobbes's lodgings in Paris where he wrote the Leviathan.[35] Bosse's etching positions both Donne's individual and the power of the monarch within a metaphorical figure of the state. Donne's metaphorical reflections on the correlating bodies of man and state are echoed in Thomas Hobbes's *Leviathan*, albeit from the opposite perspective. Hobbes observes that the »Infirmities [...] of a Common-wealth [...] resemble the diseases of a naturall body«,[36] a connection that Werner Gephart took as the starting point for the cover design of this volume.

---

[29] Donne: Devotions Upon Emergent Occasions, Meditation XVII, p. 87.
[30] Parsons: American Society, p. 149.
[31] Hobbes: Leviathan, Ch. XXX, Vol. 2, p. 530.
[32] See e. g. Crignon: Representation and the Person of the State; Sorgi: Hobbes on »Bodies Politic«. Agamben: Stasis, p. 45, even states that Hobbes' »entire philosophy is a meditation *de corpore*«.
[33] Malcolm: Editorial Introduction to the Leviathan, p. 128. Hobbes's book-title itself was conceived metaphorically and still elicits questions and debate; cf. Metzger: Die Bedeutung des Leviathan; Mintz: Leviathan as Metaphor; not to forget Schmitt: The Leviathan in the State Theory of Thomas Hobbes. Much of Schmitt's analysis of Hobbes stands the test of time, while his views on war and the state have unsurprisingly aged less well.
[34] For a thorough discussion of the authorship see Bredekamp: Thomas Hobbes. Der Leviathan, pp. 33–51.
[35] Malcolm: Editorial Introduction to the Leviathan, p. 134.
[36] Hobbes: Leviathan, Ch. XXIX, Vol. 2, p. 498.

Fig. 2: Abraham Bosse, Title engraving for Thomas Hobbes's Leviathan, London 1651.

Donne described the »vapour« of his sickness as being as weakening for his body as rumours were for the state:

»But extend this *vapour*, rarifie it; from so narow a roome, as our *Naturall bodies*, to any *Politike body*, to a *State*. That which is fume in us, is in a State, *Rumour*, and these *vapours* in us, which wee consider here pestilent, and infectious fumes, are in a State *infectious rumours*, detracting and dishonourable *Calumnies, Libels*.«[37]

Hobbes recommended the following remedy:

»I observe the *Diseases* of a Common-wealth, that proceed from the poyson of seditious doctrines; whereof one is, *That every private man is Judge of Good and Evill actions*. This is true in the condition of meer Nature, where there are no Civill Lawes; and also under Civill Government, in such cases as are not determined by the Law. [...] From this false doctrine, men are disposed to debate with themselves, and dispute the commands of the Common-wealth; and afterwards to obey, or disobey them, as in their private judgements they shall think fit. Whereby the Common-wealth is distracted and *Weakened*.«[38]

In Hobbes's state, the subjects ought to follow their leaders and not risk its stability by engaging in too many autonomous thoughts.[39] The political dream of the plague, as Foucault sees it, is a disciplined society,[40] and in this sense Hobbes's state would be well-equipped to deal with a pandemic. For Hobbes, a lack of obedience will undermine the concord of people and ultimately dissolve the commonwealth.[41] Individual conscience is too unreliable to obtain political stability; the »Law is the publique Conscience«.[42] Again, some of Hobbes's opinions appear to be written for our own times, such as his warning against »popular men«, or, to use our modern language, »celebrities«:

»Popularity of a potent Subject [...] is a dangerous Disease; because the people [...] by the flattery, and by the reputation of an ambitious man, are drawn away from their obedience to the Lawes, to follow a man, of whose vertues, and designes they have no knowledge.«[43]

Reading this, it is difficult not to think of the celebrities currently promulgating conspiracy propaganda and spreading misinformation about an invisible virus. Proponents include German vegan chef Attila Hildmann, German singer Xavier Naidoo, as well as international artists Whiz Khalifa and M.I.A. The issue appears to be an enduring one: In his *Journal of the Plague Year*, published in 1722,

---

[37] Donne: Devotions Upon Emergent Occasions, Meditation XII, p. 63.
[38] Hobbes: Leviathan, Ch. XXIX, Vol. 2, p. 502.
[39] Cf. May: Hobbes on Fidelity to Law.
[40] Foucault: Discipline and Punish, p. 198.
[41] Hobbes: Leviathan, Ch. XXX, Vol. 2, pp. 524 ff. Foucault comments on this passage; see Foucault: The Punitive Society, p. 27.
[42] Hobbes: Leviathan, Ch. XXIX, Vol. 2, p. 502.
[43] Ibid., p. 516.

Fig. 3a: Detail of Abraham Bosse, Title engraving for Thomas Hobbes's Leviathan, London 1651.

Fig. 3b: Detail of an engraving after Abraham Bosse for Thomas Hobbes, The Moral and Political Works, London 1750.

Daniel Defoe remarks on the thriving businesses of the fortune-tellers during the plague of 1665: »With what blind, absurd, and ridiculous Stuff, these Oracles of the Devil pleas'd and satisfy'd the People, I really know not; but certain it is, that innumerable Attendants crouded about their Doors every Day«.[44] Since great power commands great responsibility, for Hobbes, the sovereign (»be it a Monarch, or an Assembly«) is obliged to warrant »the safety of the people«, with the instruments of doctrine and example.[45] It is part of the sovereign's duties not »to let the people be ignorant, or mis-informed« of the reasons of the law.[46]

Against the background of the current Covid-19 pandemic, the obligation to provide clear, transparent and correct information can be inferred from Hobbes's stipulation. Against the backdrop of Hobbes's own time, one detail from the title etching has recently been thrown into stark relief: the two small figures in the foreground looking at the cityscape (fig. 3a). Francesca Falk was the first to af-

---

[44] Defoe: A Journal of the Plague Year, p. 28.
[45] Hobbes: Leviathan, Ch. XXX, Vol. 2, p. 520.
[46] Ibid.

ford these two minuscule silhouettes any more than minimal attention.⁴⁷ In line with Horst Bredekamp,⁴⁸ she reads the two figures as plague doctors, identifiable by their prominent beak shaped masks.⁴⁹ The invention of this distinctive plague doctor costume is commonly credited to Charles de Lorme (1584–1678), chief physician of three French kings, Henri IV., Louis XIII., and Louis XIV.⁵⁰ One of his medical examination »Quæstiones medicæ« at the Medical Faculty of Montpellier, assessed by professor meritissimus Jacques Pradilles, was »Daturne febris pestilens intermittens?« (Can pestilential fever be intermitted?). Delorme's theses, published in 1608, included the conclusion that pestilential fever could be transmitted by »Aër contagiosus« and could not be intermitted.⁵¹ Abbé Michel de Saint-Martin, a personal friend writing not long after Delorme's death in 1678, remembers how the plague doctor did his rounds and never forgot to put on his »habit de maroquin dont il étoit l'auteur« consisting of a long leather coat and a matching beak-shaped mask made from the same material, which he had invented during the Parisian plague of 1619.⁵² A watercolour by Luigi Sambon (1867–1931), an Italian-born physician who lectured at the Liverpool School of Tropical medicine, shows such a mask from the seventeenth century. It was part of an exhibition that Sambon organised for the International medical Congress of Rome, 1894 (fig. 4).⁵³ Similar masks are on display in the German Museum for the History of Medicine (Ingolstadt) and the German Historical Museum (Berlin), although some doubts as to their authenticity remain.⁵⁴

47 Falk: Hobbes' »Leviathan« und die aus dem Blick gefallenen Schnabelmasken.
48 Bredekamp: Thomas Hobbes visuelle Strategien, pp. 27, 108 (= 5th ed. as Thomas Hobbes. Der Leviathan, pp. 29, 110).
49 Falk: Hobbes' »Leviathan« und die aus dem Blick gefallenen Schnabelmasken, p. 250; her observation is shared by Agamben: Stasis, pp. 47 f., and Ginzburg: Fear Reverence Terror, p. 74, note 36.
50 See e.g. in Tybarenc: Encyclopedia of Infectious Diseases, p. 680. However, the sources indicated in the article are misleading. The correct reference to Saint-Martin, Moiens faciles et éprouvez (1683), who reports the invention by de Lorme, is cited by Blanchard: Notes historiques sur la peste, p. 591, and Mollaret/Brossollet: La peste, source méconnue d'inspiration artistique, pp. 43 f.
51 See Delorme: Pteleinodaphneiai, containing his examination theses in two instalments. The title of this dissertation is an amalgamation of the Greek versions of the names Laurier (laurel) and Orme (elm); see Julien: Quatre sujets médico-pharmaceutiques, p. 13. Delorme's main doctoral supervisor in Montpellier was André Dulaurens, which explains the playful combination of names. The exam questions are summarised in French translation in Bernardin: Hommes et mœurs au dix-septième siècle, pp. 4–7. Jacques Pradilles was a member of the examination board, together with François Ranchin, Richer de Belleval, and Pierre Dortoman. Traces of their professional lives at the faculty can be found in Astruc: Mémoires pour servir à l'histoire de la faculté de médicine de Montpellier.
52 Saint-Martin: Moiens faciles et éprouvez, pp. 33, 279. The first part of Saint-Martin's book, which contains the biography of Charles Delorme and other documents, remains unpaginated.
53 Blanchard: Notes historiques sur la peste, pp. 596 f. The reproduction of the watercolour is taken from this article.
54 Ruisinger: Die Pestarztmaske im Deutschen Medizinhistorischen Museum Ingolstadt, pp. 236 ff., 246 f.

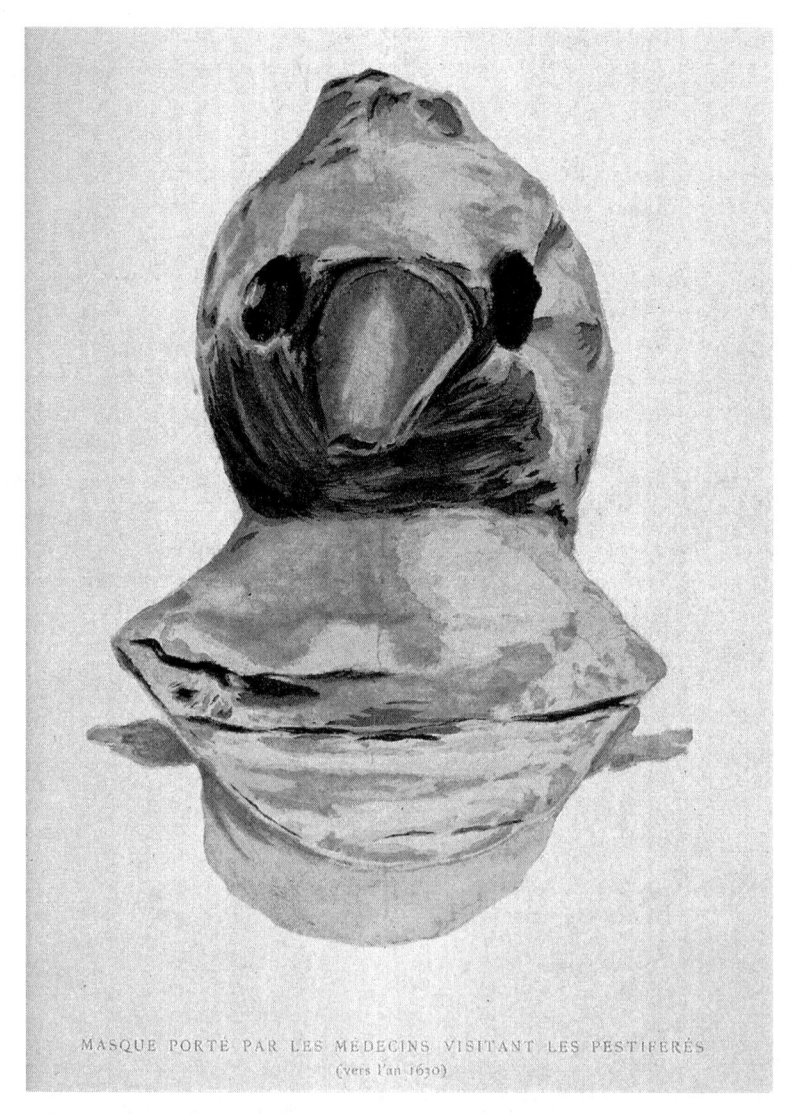

MASQUE PORTÉ PAR LES MÉDECINS VISITANT LES PESTIFÉRÉS
(vers l'an 1630)

Fig. 4: Luigi Sambon, A plague doctor's mask from the seventeenth century, watercolour, measurements unknown.

To be recognisable, the beaks of the mask are likely to be rendered in profile, and this is how the two tiny figures on the title etching for Hobbes's *Leviathan* have been interpreted. However, their presence is not easily explained. They fail as a reference to recent epidemics, being too early to comment on the great plague that tormented London in 1665–66 and killed a fifth of its population. The most recent and violent outbreak of the plague in Europe at the time was the Great

Plague of Seville, 1647–52, but while the disease remained present regionally in England, London and Paris were spared major plague epidemics during the 1640s and 1650s.⁵⁵ Francesca Falk, Giorgio Agamben, and Carlo Ginzburg concur in their association of the two figures with Hobbes's translation of Thucydides (1629): the Greek author describes the effects of the plague as a state of lawlessness, which corresponds with Hobbes's natural condition of mankind.⁵⁶ However, this contradicts the reading of the cityscape as a symbol of Hobbes's political model – we are shown the politically disciplined state under the rule of the sovereign,⁵⁷ possibly at war⁵⁸ but certainly not in a state of plague-ridden lawlessness, or, in Hobbes's translated words, »great licentiousnesse«.⁵⁹ Further doubts arise on closer inspection of the print. What are the figures looking at? Is it the façade of the church building? Why are they depicted together? Other depictions of plague doctors indicate that they usually worked alone. In addition, the distinctive low hats with wide brims, which were part of the typical plague doctor costume (fig. 5), would be absent from the two figures in question if the protruding lines were to be read as beaks.⁶⁰ Finally, plague doctors may have looked different in reality than the way they are typically represented. The iconography of the typical print showing plague doctors in their beak-mask and costume is not free from propaganda. Several were printed in Northern Europe and claimed to portray plague doctor costumes from Italy or France, with the not-so-hidden agenda of making a statement as to the superiority of the northern European health administrations. On these prints the plague is presented as a foreign problem.⁶¹ Writing in 1799, Jean-Pierre Papon even situates the plague doctor mask (»un masque à lunettes«) safely in Italy, ignoring the invention by the Ancien Régime doctor Delorme.⁶²

I would thus like to offer an alternative reading: taking into account all the foregoing observations, the two tiny profiles seen in Bosse's title-etching are ultimately unlikely to represent plague doctors. Quentin Skinner suggests that the figure on the left appears merely to be wearing a broad-brimmed hat,⁶³ and indeed

---

55   Cf. Harding: The Dead and the Living in Paris and London, 1500–1670, p. 25; Shrewsbury: History of Bubonic Plague in the British Isles, pp. 433–439.

56   Falk: Hobbes' »Leviathan« und die aus dem Blick gefallenen Schnabelmasken, p. 250; Agamben: Stasis, p. 49; Ginzburg: Fear Reverence Terror, p. 74, note 36. Ginzburg revised the text of his lecture for the book publication (in Italian in 2015, in English in 2017), which is why earlier versions of the text do not mention the two little figures.

57   Brandt: Das Titelblatt des Leviathan, p. 166.

58   Kristiansson/Tralau: Hobbes's hidden monster, pp. 304 ff., convincingly identify details of hostilities, such as smoking canons.

59   Thucydides: Eight Bookes of the Peloponnesian Warre, p. 109.

60   On the engraving by Gerhart Altzenbach see Townsend: The Plague Doctor. An excellent selection of prints showing plague doctor costumes can be found at the Public Domain Review.

61   Ruisinger: Die Pestarztmaske im Deutschen Medizinhistorischen Museum Ingolstadt, p. 248.

62   Papon: De la Peste, p. 52.

63   Skinner: From Humanism to Hobbes, p. 285, note 195.

Fig. 5: Gerhart Altzenbach, Kleidung widder den Todt: Anno 1656 (The Plague Doctor), engraving, 305 × 225 mm.

one of Abraham Bosse's numerous depictions of French noblemen (»Le Jardin de la Noblesse Française«) seen from behind (fig. 6) shows what else a curved form could signify: an ostrich feather in a hat. The figure on the left may be wearing a cape. Another group of silhouetted people cut off by a framing device, looking onto a scene in a city and wearing feathers, serves as a further comparison to the etching of the *Leviathan*: Bosse's frontispiece of *Les Amours d'Anaxandre*

Masking the Invisible / Segments of Political Space   389

Fig. 6: Abraham Bosse after Jean de Saint-Igny, French nobleman seem from behind, etching/engraving, 140 × 94 mm, 1629.

et d'Oraste (1629).⁶⁴ Alternatively, the two silhouettes on the title etching of the *Leviathan* could be identified as two monks, possibly Augustinians, Capuchins or Franciscans, whose monastic habit includes a hood. As the two figures belong to the religious half of the scene, this identification would make sense, just as the soldiers on the left are part of the representation of the secular organisation of power. The two monks observe the city beneath them. Perhaps because of the remaining ambiguities of identification, the figures were rendered without their headgear in later editions (fig. 3b). A comparative examination of the drawing for the title etching held at the British Library does not give rise to any alternative

---

⁶⁴ British Museum number 1895,1031.61.

conclusions: the two silhouettes are present here as well and could be wearing either hoods or feathers.⁶⁵

1.4 Carnival and Camouflage

As complicated as it can be to identify details of a print, it is even more complicated to identify a virus, which, after all, is invisible to the human eye. We must rely on laboratories and their testing capacities to prove its presence; it forms part of Merleau-Ponty's idea of a phenomenology of the »hidden«.⁶⁶ The first photographs of a human coronavirus were published in 1967 in an article by June D. Almeida (1930–2007), a Glaswegian medical laboratory technician with outstanding skills at the electron microscope, who at the time was working at St Thomas hospital in London, and David A. J. Tyrrell (1925–2005), a virologist at the Common Cold Unit in Wiltshire and later its director.⁶⁷ In everyday life we have to learn to read its symptoms. However, SARS-CoV-2 has been described as a particularly insidious virus, since it is most infectious just before symptoms become perceptible.⁶⁸ It virtually camouflages its presence to optimise further infections, a virus in disguise. Bearing in mind that two hotspots for the spread of Covid-19 were a carnival party in Heinsberg (Germany) and Mardi gras in New Orleans, this is an uncanny coincidence. SARS-CoV-2 is, of course, not the first disease to be activated invisibly. Before the French bacteriologist Alexandre Yersin (1863–1943) identified the bacterium responsible for the bubonic plague (later named after him *Yersinia pestis*) in 1894,⁶⁹ all that was known was that the disease could be transmitted by air. The plague doctor masks served both to keep a minimum distance and to filter the intake of air through aromatic substances that could be placed inside the mask. In a way, this costume mirrored the bacterium by rendering its bearer unidentifiable; yet, unlike the plague bacterium, it also sent a conspicuous signal. Present day Venetian carnival masks are a playful after-effect of the plague doctor's attire.⁷⁰ Foucault reminds us that a »whole literary fiction of the festival

---

⁶⁵ British Library, Egerton 1910 F1. Bredekamp: Thomas Hobbes. Der Leviathan, p. 113, understands the two forms to be part of a building.

⁶⁶ Merleau-Ponty: The Visible and the Invisible, p. 229.

⁶⁷ Almeida/Tyrrell: The Morphology of Three Previously Uncharacterized Human Respiratory Viruses.

⁶⁸ See for example He et al.: Temporal Dynamics in Viral Shedding and Transmissibility of COVID-19, speaking of a »probable substantial presymptomatic transmission«.

⁶⁹ On the discovery and its circumstances see Bibel/Chen: Diagnosis of Plague.

⁷⁰ Falk: Hobbes' »Leviathan« und die aus dem Blick gefallenen Schnabelmasken, pp. 251 f., mentions the example of an oil painting by Johannes Lingelbach, Carnival in Rome (Kunsthistorisches Museum, Vienna), dating from 1650/51, which shows a plague doctor on horseback during the carnival celebrations.

Fig. 7: Anonymous, Ah!/Le Cruchon/Le masque levé, etching and watercolour, 265 × 145 mm.

grew up around the plague«.[71] The virus, however, is not at play; it does not dress up in its asymptomatic invisibility. Whereas revellers remove their masks after carnival and kings can be unmasked to reveal their true character (fig. 7), the true character of a virus can only be researched. Carnival is a cultural technique; camouflage is a natural strategy.

The connection between contagiousness and invisibility is not exclusive to the plague or Covid-19. Returning to John Donne, he muses over the butterfly effect of infectious air:

---

[71] Foucault: Discipline and Punish, p. 197.

»What will not kill a man, if a *vapor* will? [...] If this were a violent shaking of the Ayre by *Thunder*, or by *Canon*, in that case the *Ayre* is condensed above the thicknesse of *water*, of water baked into *Ice*, almost *petrified*, almost made stone, and no wonder that that kills; but that that which is but a *vapor*, and a *vapor* not forced, but breathed, should kill, that our *Nourse* should overlay us, and *Ayre*, that nourishes us, should destroy us, [...], but *Fortune*, who is lesse then a *vapour*? But when our selves are the *Well*, that breaths out this exhalation, the *Oven* that spits out this fiery smoke, the *Myne* that spues out this suffocating, and strangling *dampe*, who can ever after this, aggravate his sorrow, by this *Circumstance*, That it was his *Neighbor*, his *familiar friend*, his *brother* that destroyed him, and destroyed him with a whispering, & calumniating breath, when wee our selves doe it to our selves by the same meanes, kill our selves with our owne *vapors*?«[72]

Indeed, this kind of anxious contemplation would not be out of place in the current pandemic. Breathing together in enclosed spaces is a dangerous activity.[73] Carnival celebrations, as well as other social and sociable events such as a choir rehearsal offer near ideal conditions for the transmission of SARS-CoV-2.[74] This means that the virus attacks by taking advantage of a deeply human quality, if we remember our Aristotelian status as social animals, and the disdain for social isolation evoked by John Donne. If we add Hobbes's natural state of fear to the equation, it is clear that we need well-defined norms that achieve at least two goals: keeping the numbers of SARS-CoV-2 infections effectively low, and facilitating a minimum of social interaction. While the assertion that the »plague doctors« on the title-etching of Hobbes's *Leviathan* indicate a concern for dedicated governmental health management[75] is untenable because it comes too early for »The Birth of Social Medicine«,[76] other, more general Hobbesian assessments are worthy of consideration. Beyond the claim that no law by the sovereign can be unjust, Hobbes also stipulates that a »good Law is that, which is *Needfull*, for the *Good of the People*, and withall *Perspicuous*.«[77]

---

[72] Donne, Devotions Upon Emergent Occasions, Meditation XII, pp. 62 f. The vapours that Donne describes were, at the time, not understood to be purely physiologically active but were considered a symptom of melancholia. The recommended treatment involved cutting a pigeon in half and applying it to the head; see ibid., p. 64, and Allen: Pigeon, p. 88.

[73] Prather/Wang/Chooley: Reducing Transmission of Sars-Cov-2.

[74] See for example Hamner et al.: High SARS-CoV-2 Attack Rate Following Exposure at a Choir Practice.

[75] Cf. Falk: Hobbes' »Leviathan« und die aus dem Blick gefallenen Schnabelmasken, p. 257. See also Biehl: Technologies of Invisibility, p. 249, who pairs Hobbes's Leviathan with Foucault's biopolitics to ask the question with a view to AIDS in Brazil, »Who is to be let die?«. It is tragic that his overall more positive assessment of the measures taken to prevent and control AIDS in Brazil forms such a stark contrast to the country's current mismanagement of the COVID-19 pandemic.

[76] Foucault: The Birth of Social Medicine, p. 134, dates the beginnings of »biohistory« to the eighteenth century.

[77] Hobbes: Leviathan, Ch. XXX, Vol. 2, p. 540.

2. The Mask in Its Social and Political Space

2.1 The Categorical Imperative of the Mask

Is a law making face masks obligatory such a good law?[78] During the so-called Spanish Flu pandemic of 1918–19, masks were compulsory in many places, including California. The city of San Francisco passed a mask order that was enforced between 22 October and 21 November 1918. Failure to comply carried a penalty of between $5 and $100 or imprisonment not to exceed 10 days (fig. 8).[79] When the pandemic hit Tucson, Arizona, public places such as schools, churches and theatres were shut down to curb transmission, despite the criticism of business owners and representatives of educational institutions. Patient numbers remained high and the city council decided to follow the example of San Francisco and implemented an order requiring the wearing of masks »in any place where people meet for the transaction of necessary business«, which was soon amended to in-

Fig. 8: Anonymous, Photograph of people wearing face masks in California, 1918.

---

[78] The question seems trivial in view of other problems such as the extent of the state of emergency (see e.g. the essay by Beaud/Guérin-Bargues: L'état d'urgence sanitaire, in this volume) but shall be discussed nevertheless.
[79] Dolan: Unmasking History, p. 4. More images can be found in Navarro: Influenza in 1918.

clude all public places and spaces.⁸⁰ After the lockdown was lifted, businesses and schools re-opened and meetings were permitted, but the mask order remained in force to prevent a second wave of infections. In his article on the Spanish Flu in Tucson, Luckingham cites the *Tucson Citizen*, a local newspaper, whose reporter acknowledged the local government's prerogative power. While sceptical, he conceded that the people had »delegated to certain authorities the power to make regulations on these matters and if they order us to mask, the only thing to do is submit gracefully«. The article also introduces a consideration for fellow citizens, a distant echo of Aristotle and John Donne, because »a fellow who does not believe in the mask should be willing to wear it for the peace of mind of the fellow who does«.⁸¹ In spite of this, masks never became popular in Tucson, and the order was more often than not ignored. The situation in San Francisco was comparable. When a second wave of influenza hit the city within weeks of the first, the mask ordinance was reinstated in January 1919 at the very same time a group of citizens founded the »Anti-Mask League«.⁸² Mask debates tend to create social conflict, as Brian Dolan reflects in his essay.⁸³ In the German state of North Rhine-Westphalia for example, as of 27 April 2020, employees and customers are obliged to wear a mask inside shops, when visiting farmers' markets or picking up food to go at restaurants and cafés, inside hospitals and medical practices, and when using public transport.⁸⁴ Masks have been made compulsory in public in a growing list of countries around the world.⁸⁵ Attitudes to the wearing of masks, however, continue to diverge noticeably.

Even before the current pandemic, commentators had remarked that it was common in Eastern Asia to wear masks in public.⁸⁶ The reasons are more complex than often acknowledged in popular Western understanding. In the case of Japan, they not only include individual health concerns in crowded spaces or past experience of pandemics and catastrophes such as the Fukushima nuclear disaster (2011), but also vanity (to cover a lack of make-up) as well as the proverbial societal politeness.⁸⁷ However, the general use of face masks in Japan is a relatively recent phenomenon observed since the early 2000s.⁸⁸ In the West, reservations

---

80 Luckingham/Bradford: To Mask or not to Mask, pp. 192 ff.
81 Ibid., p. 198. See also the essay by Suntrup: Corona, in this volume, and his comment on Helmuth Plessner's »hygiene of tact«.
82 Dolan: Unmasking History, pp. 3, 8–11.
83 Ibid., p. 22.
84 § 12a CoronaSchVO NW.
85 For an overview see Wikipedia: Face Masks During the COVID-19 Pandemic.
86 Yang: A Quick History of Why Asians Wear Surgical Masks in Public.
87 Burgess/Horii: Risk, Ritual and Health Responsibilisation. The authors conducted a survey amongst 120 passers-by in Tokyo; Hori: Why Do the Japanese Wear Masks?
88 Burgess/Horii: Risk, Ritual and Health Responsibilisation, p. 1187; Horii: Why Do the Japanese Wear Masks?

concerning covering the face are likely to have thwarted an earlier official recommendation to wear masks during the Covid-19 pandemic. In some countries, anti-mask laws apply to certain means of covering one's face. Both the German § 17a Versammlungsgesetz (Assembly Act) and Art. 5 of Italian law no. 152 of 22 May 1975 prohibit the wearing of face masks at larger public gatherings, such as demonstrations. These are examples of norms that aim to ensure that individuals can be identified (»Aufmachung, die geeignet und den Umständen nach darauf gerichtet ist, die Feststellung der Identität zu verhindern« and »caschi protettivi, o di qualunque altro mezzo atto a rendere difficoltoso riconoscimento della persona«, respectively). Though we may not have realised it before, this shows that the individual and their recognisable identity apparently play a fundamental role in the mechanisms of Western society. A mask de-individualises its wearer. Hans Belting notes that in certain African mask rituals, strong taboos protect the anonymity of the dancer wearing a mask.[89] In consequence, a mask can be perceived as disrespecting our values of individualism. These reservations have for a long time caused an ongoing, often polemically led[90] and ultimately unresolved debate about face coverings worn by Muslim women, such as the niqāb and the burqa.[91] They can be understood both as a liberating device and as one of oppression. Such vestments are compulsory in some jurisdictions[92] but have been banned in others.[93] The relevant European laws seem to have been driven by anxiety rather than any real prevalence of the wearing of face coverings[94]; in Islamism, meanwhile, veiling has become a politicised act.[95]

It can thus be concluded regarding Western societies that, in emotional terms, the mask is an embodied antonym of freedom, a symbol against the individual. As such. It is perhaps only natural that the people (»customers«) who have over many years been repeatedly told by corporate strategists that they need to self-optimise are likely to show resistance. Indeed, it seems that social distancing and compulsory masks have taken the fun out of shopping and transformed the event back into nothing more than an act of supply. The need to counterbalance individual freedom against a perceived collective (but ultimately similarly individual) protection of vulnerable groups has significantly shaped the public discourse and

[89] Belting: Face and Mask, p. 40.
[90] Boris Johnson's statement that »it is absolutely ridiculous that people should choose to go around looking like letter boxes« has become notorious. Nonetheless he argued against a ban in his article for The Telegraph, 5 August 2018.
[91] Cf. Grace: The Woman in the Muslim Mask, p. 1: »[…] remains a confusing and controversial topic«.
[92] If a hijab is not properly worn in Saudi Arabia and reveals the face or hair, the woman may be publicly beaten or jailed. The current sentence is up to 74 lashes; Grace: The Woman in the Muslim Mask, p. 21.
[93] See the instructive overview on Wikipedia: Islamic Dress in Europe.
[94] Cf. Cox: Behind the Veil, p. 249.
[95] Grace: The Woman in the Muslim Mask, p. 20.

commentary on the political measures taken.[96] The lockdown measures implemented to »flatten the curve« of the Covid-19 pandemic will have far-reaching and potentially long-lasting effects: nearly 39 million Americans lost their jobs in the space of just nine weeks. At the other end of the spectrum of interdependent developments, Sweden, where the lockdown measures were less strict than elsewhere in Europe, has seen a comparatively high Covid-19 death rate.[97] Defining in more detail what makes for »optimum solidarity« (Talcott Parsons) is a highly complex task, not least because it is unclear to which specific group or community such solidarity applies, and because solidarity is not always afforded the highest priority.[98]

In view of the overarching risks of national bankruptcy and death, wearing a mask seems but a small price to pay. What's more, protective masks appear to pass the Hobbesian necessity test. In a remarkably modern explanation of necessary laws, Hobbes writes that the law should not inhibit the people more than is necessary to achieve the aim, »as Hedges are set, not to stop Travellers, but to keep them in the way«.[99] The comparison is particularly salient for regulations that aim to safeguard the public by means of physical distancing; indeed, the aim here is by all means to keep people on the pathways that minimise the risk of viral transmission. Wearing a mask facilitates closer contact for the political animal, in particular for the political animal doing business.

Face masks have long been thought to protect the wearer. Charles Broquet, a French medical doctor at the time working in the colonies of South East Asia, remarked, with regard to Domenico Gargiulo's painting of the Piazza Mercatello in Naples during the plague of 1656, that Docteur Delorme's idea of a face mask protecting against infection was still pertinent.[100] However, the full equipment including the leather coat and the beak-shaped hood was deemed too scrupulous by Lodovico Moratori in 1714: »non è necessaria tanta scrupolosità«.[101] It is therefore important to differentiate between different protection levels of masks. This is not a new thought, either; a French manual of public hygiene dating from 1836 distinguishes numerous forms and constructions (fig. 9). The current pertinent technical report by the European Centre for Disease Prevention and Control defines three categories: [1] non-medical, so-called »community masks«, which are face covers made of cloth or other textiles, [2] medical face masks (also known as surgical or procedure masks), used by healthcare workers to prevent large respiratory drop-

---

[96] Angela Condello compares the situation to a »normative laboratory«, cf. Condello: Immersed in a Normative Laboratory, in this volume.

[97] See the charts on Our World in Data. The web page has been saved on archive.org as per 5 June 2020.

[98] Cf. Parsons: American Society, pp. 149 f.

[99] Hobbes: Leviathan, Ch. XXX, Vol. 2, p. 540.

[100] Broquet: Le masque dans la peste, p. 639.

[101] Muratori: Del governo della peste, p. 74.

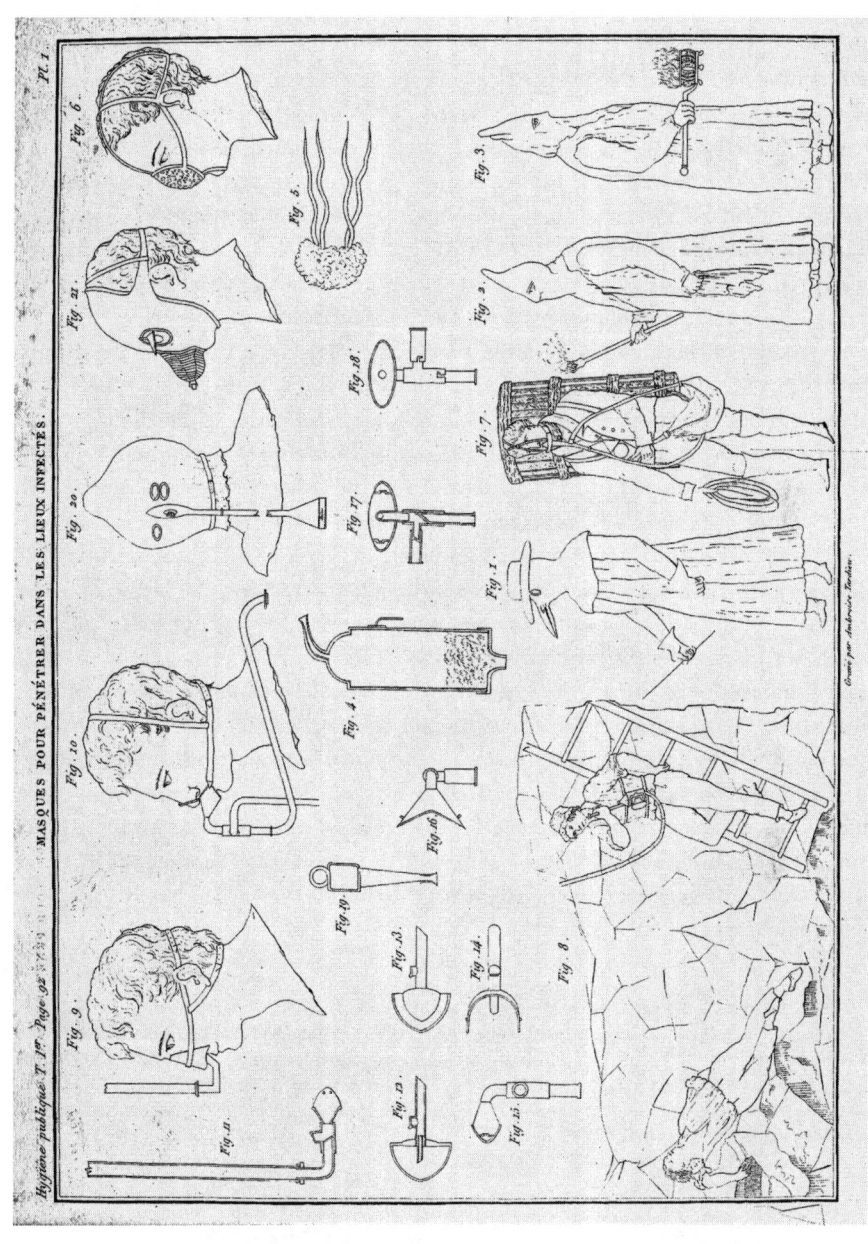

Fig. 9: Ambroise Tardieu, Masques pour pénétrer dans lieux infectés, Illustration from Alexandre Parent-Duchatelet, Hygiène publique, Paris 1836.

lets and splashes from reaching the mouth and the nose of the wearer and to help reduce and/or control at the source the spread of large respiratory droplets from the person wearing the face mask, and [3] filtering facepieces (FFP), designed to protect the wearer from exposure to airborne contaminants.[102] FFPs are classified according to the European EN 149 standard.[103] Perhaps the most relevant are the aerosol filtration percentage rates: FFP1 indicates a minimum of 80 %, FFP2 a minimum of 94 %, and FFP3 a minimum of 99 %. This means that FFPs protect the individual from contracting SARS-CoV-2 contaminated droplets and aerosols, whereas community masks do not. This might have been the reason why the use of the latter was not advocated from the beginning of the pandemic. Although masks »are providing the wearer with a sense of control over invisible threats and uncertainties, which would be otherwise experienced as uncontrollable and unsettling«,[104] their worth – in the absence of FFP2 or FFP3 filtration – lies not in their individual protection capabilities but in their collective dimension.

The Categorical Imperative as formulated by Immanuel Kant provides the theoretical framework within which these diverging aspects can be reconciled. In his *Critique of Practical Reason*, Kant stated: »So act that the maxim of your will could always hold at the same time as a principle in a giving of universal law.«[105] This elegantly strikes a balance between morals and the law, the individual and the state, with both parts acting as autonomous systems that mutually consider the other, or, to put it in Kant's own words, »reciprocally imply each other«.[106] If my individual will aims to maximise my personal freedom by taking off the mask, and I make this a universal principle, the community will suffer, because the virus will spread and some – more – people will die as a result. By contrast, if everybody wears a mask, the total virus load in the common good »air« is reduced and made safer for everyone. Clinical tests with face masks and hamsters seem to corroborate this.[107] The »community masks« thus protect the community. They are a means of strengthening the solidarity that is vital if we are to overcome the crisis.[108]

---

[102] European Centre for Disease Prevention and Control: Using face masks in the community.

[103] The normative framework for the standards is Regulation (EU) 2016/425 of the European Parliament and of the Council of 9 March 2016 on personal protective equipment (PPE). The EN 149 standard is instructively explained on Wikipedia: FFP Mask. It is usually offered for sale by the national standards bodies such as the BSI or the DIN. The publishers for the DIN offer the standard for free during the ongoing COVID-19 pandemic.

[104] Horii: Why Do the Japanese Wear Masks?

[105] Kant: Critique of Practical Reason, 5:30.

[106] Cf. Ibid., 5:29; Herbert: Kant Contra Hobbes, p. 17, speaks of »a system of mutual recognition of which there is no counterpart in political philosophy of either Hobbes or Locke.«

[107] Chan/Yuan/Zhang et al.: Surgical Mask Partition Reduces the Risk of Non-Contact Transmission in a Golden Syrian Hamster Model for Coronavirus Disease 2019.

[108] Though it is touched on repeatedly throughout this essay, this is not the place to discuss the concept of solidarity in any depth, however interesting it might be. Parsons dedicates a major part

2.2 Segmenting the Agora and Transparency Matters

The face of the individual as part of the community is masked appropriately. Recent developments rapidly overtook the »please smile instead of shaking hands« phase; now, a friendly smile has to be expressed in other ways. The mask is not the only visible change in public spaces. Space itself is undergoing a number of adaptions and transformations to minimise the risks of virus transmission. These incidental changes in appearance and restrictions on freedom of movement are considerable. Public space, the »natural« habitat of Aristotle's *zoon politikon*, is being converted into a non-place. Barriers, screens and shields have emerged in hitherto wide open spaces. While the »excess of space« or »spatial overabundance« diagnosed by Marc Augé in his analysis of the non-space is reversed,[109] his definition of the non-place as the opposite of an »anthropological place«, designed to a commercial end,[110] has always been true for supermarket checkouts.

With regard to the hygienic strategies described by Foucault, the current segmentation of public space does not come as a surprise. They conform to his observation, most prominently made at the outset of his chapter on »Panoticism« in *Discipline and Punish*, on the measures taken in a French town at the end of the seventeenth century in view of the plague: »First, a strict spatial partitioning [...], a prohibition to leave the town [...], everyone is ordered to stay indoors.«[111] In Western countries, the disciplinary mechanisms taken to contain the SARS-CoV-2 pandemic are less stringent and more transparent than in the historic examples described by Foucault, while the measures taken in China and other less democratic governmental systems seem closer to what Foucault observed in the French military regulations of the late seventeenth century.[112] Fortunately, nowadays infringements no longer carry the death penalty, although the fines are not insignificant. The ceaseless inspection and »permanent registration«[113] described by Foucault today forms part of the code for a warning and tracing app that can be installed on Android and iOS smartphones. Depending on the underlying architecture, this information is not even centralised for the sake of data protection.[114]

---

of his *American Society* to this task. See also the essays by Albrecht: Viral Coupling, commenting on Durkheim's »organic solidarity«, and Dreier: »Law as Culture« in Times of Corona, both in this volume, on solidarity and inequality during the current crisis.

[109] Cf. Augé: Non-Places, pp. 31, 40.

[110] Ibid., p. 94; on the supermarket pp. 99 f.

[111] Foucault: Discipline and Punish, p. 195.

[112] See also the essay on national habitus by Bucholc: The Corona Crisis as a Test of National Habitus, in this volume.

[113] Foucault: Discipline and Punish, p. 196.

[114] While the French app relies on a central server, circumventing the Apple/Google Bluetooth API, the German counterpart uses these but operates with datasets stored locally on the mobile devices. The code for the German app is documented on GutHub: Corona-Warn-App. An overview of the apps that are available internationally is available on Wikipedia: COVID-19 Apps, and a

Fig. 10: Distance markers in front of a museum entrance, Bonn, June 2020.

The strict »quadrillage«, the spatial partitioning and control imposed in French cities of the seventeenth century,[115] is translated into modern day measures in the form the minimum distance of 1.5–2 metres or comparable measurements, with marks and taped strips on the floor (fig. 10). Where space allows, this entails physical distancing and a »dilution« (if not dissolution) of crowds, groups, and queues. Where the available space is restricted, which is often the case indoors, that space is restructured. The glass panes that had all but disappeared from places of transaction such as ticket counters have returned in the form of transparent acrylic screens (»sneeze guards«). Queues at supermarket checkouts are separated by similar shields suspended from the ceiling, creating a kind of semi-transparent maze. Shops have dedicated staff whose job is to remind customers to keep a minimum distance (»two-metre marshals«).

If nothing else, the material iconography of the transparent protective shields promises a certain degree of consolation. Transparency has become an established symbol of the democratic state. This is why the material iconography of glass has

»COVID-19 Digital Rights Tracker« is maintained by top10VPN: COVID-19 Digital Rights Tracker. As per 18 June 2020, it listed 47 contact tracing apps available globally.
[115] Foucault: Abnormal, p. 44.

led to government buildings such as the old plenary chamber of the Bundestag in Bonn, designed by Günter Behnisch and completed in 1992, and the Reichstag dome designed by Norman Foster, completed in 1999.[116] The opposite may be a factor contributing to the draft executive order of the Trump administration titled »Make Federal Buildings Beautiful Again« – an initiative to re-establish the Neoclassical style for US government buildings.[117] A form of transparency was also a concern for Thomas Hobbes, when he counted perspicuity among the three prerequisites of a good law. The lawmaker ought to explain the reasons why the law was made.[118] Despite SARS-CoV-2 being invisible, our segmented space, though physically disrupted, remains visually perceptible.

Merleau-Ponty reaffirms the immersion of existence within space; »its modalities always express the total life of the subject, the energy with which he tends toward a future through his body and his world«.[119] This energy is being consumed by higher alert levels when moving in public. Arguably the »geometrical space« (Merleau-Ponty) and what could be termed psychological space are at odds. With space becoming a precious commodity, precautions of space travel have rubbed off to everyday experience. »Put your helmet on« (David Bowie, *Space Oddity*, 1969) has been turned into »Put your face mask on«, while »And all this science I don't understand« (Elton John, *Rocket Man*, 1972) has remained the same. The personal protection equipment of medical staff performing tests bears more than a passing resemblance to both the suits of astronauts and the police's »battle gear«, with bodies protected by helmets, shields, gloves and armour. The shared iconography and appearance of doctors, astronauts, soldiers and the police tell us that by putting on our masks, we follow a watered-down concept of military discipline. Whether we like it or not, our civic solidarity mandates an awareness of space. The invisibility of SARS-CoV-2 causes a paradoxical effect whereby individual compassion takes on the guise of a professional emergency response by an organised task force: the masks make us more uniform. Nonetheless, they enable us to access part of our spatial existence – the original political habitat of us social beings. For the time being, the protective face mask remains a powerful indicator of our categorical imperative, namely the imperative of our mutual solidarity as political individuals.

---

[116] Cf. Barnstone: The Transparent State. It is more than a footnote that the imagery of the parliamentary dome is reminiscent of the head of the sovereign of Hobbes's *Leviathan* etching, even more so with a view to the tourists visiting the building and climbing inside this »head«; see Bredekamp: Thomas Hobbes, pp. 155–159.
[117] Cf. the report in The Art Newspaper, March 2020: Ludel: Will US Architectural Body Have a Say on Trump's »Re-Beautification«.
[118] Hobbes: Leviathan, Ch. XXX, Vol. 2, p. 542.
[119] Merleau-Ponty: Phenomenology of Perception, p. 293, citation p. 296.

References

Agamben, Giorgio: Stasis. Civil War as a Political Paradigm (Homo Sacer II, 2), Stanford 2015.

Allen, Barbara: Pigeon, London 2009.

Almeida, June D. / David A. J. Tyrrell: The Morphology of Three Previously Uncharacterized Human Respiratory Viruses that Grow in Organ Culture, in: Journal of General Virology 1(2), 1967, pp. 175–180.

Almeida, June D. et al.: Coronaviruses, in: Nature 220, 1968, p. 650.

Aristotle, Politics, ed. Carnes Lord, 2nd ed., Chicago / London 2013.

Astruc, Jean: Mémoires pour servir à l'histoire de la faculté de médicine de Montpellier, Paris 1767.

Augé, Marc: Non-Places. Introduction to an Anthropology of Supermodernity, London / NewYork 1995.

Barnstone, Deborah Ascher: The Transparent State. Architecture and politics in postwar Germany, London / New York 2005.

Belting, Hans: Face and Mask: A Double History, Princeton / Oxford 2017.

Bernard, Léon: Medicine at the Court of Louis XIV., in: Medical History 6, 1962, pp. 201–213.

Bernardin, Napoléon Maurice: Hommes et mœurs au dix-septième siècle, Paris 1900.

Bibel, David J. / T. H. Chen: Diagnosis of Plague: An Analysis of the Yersin-Kitasato Controversy, in: Bacteriological Reviews 1976, pp. 633–651.

Biehl, João: Technologies of Invisibility: Politics of Life and Social Inequality, in: Jonathan Xavier India (ed.): Anthropologies of Modernity. Foucault, Governmentality, and Life Politics, Malden, Mass. / Oxford 2005, pp. 248–271.

Blanchard, Raphaël: Notes historiques sur la peste, in: Archives de parasitologie 3, 1900, pp. 589–643.

Bloch, Marc: Les Rois thaumaturges. Étude sur le caractère surnaturel attribué à la puissance royale particulièrement en France et en Angleterre, Strasbourg / Paris 1924.

Boeckl, Christine M.: Images of Plague and Pestilence: Iconography and Iconology, Kirksville, Mo., 2000.

Brandt, Reinhard: Das Titelblatt des Leviathan, in: Leviathan 15, 1987, pp. 165–186.

Bredekamp, Horst: Thomas Hobbes visuelle Strategien. Der Leviathan: Das Urbild des modernen Staates. Werkillustrationen und Portraits, Berlin 1999.

Bredekamp, Horst: Thomas Hobbes. Der Leviathan. Das Urbild des modernen Staates und seine Gegenbilder, 1651–2001, 5th ed., Berlin / Boston 2020.

Broquet, Charles: Le masque dans la peste. Présentation d'un modèle de masque antipesteux, in: Bulletin de la Société de pathologie exotique 4, 1911, pp. 636–645.

Burgess, Adam / Mitsutoshi Horii: Risk, Ritual and Health Responsibilisation: Japan's »safety blanket« of surgical face mask-wearing, in: Sociology of Health & Illness 34, 2012, pp. 1184–1198.

Chan, Jasper Fuk-Woo / Shuofeng Yuan / Anna Jinxia Zhang et al.: Surgical Mask Partition Reduces the Risk of Non-contact Transmission in a Golden Syrian Hamster Model for Coronavirus Disease 2019 (Covid-19), in: Clinical Infectious Diseases (pre-print, accepted manuscript), https://doi.org/10.1093/cid/ciaa644, 30.05.2020.

Cox, Neville: Behind the Veil: A Critical Analysis of European Veiling Laws, Cheltenham/Northampton, Mass., 2019.

Crignon, Philippe: Representation and the Person of the State, in: Hobbes Studies 31, 2018, pp. 48–74.

D'Aquin, Antoine / Antoine Vallot / Guy-Crescent Fagon: Journal de la santé du roi Louis XIV de l'année 1647 à l'année 1711, ed. Joseph Adrien Le Roi, Versailles 1862.

Defoe, Daniel: A Journal of the Plague Year, London 2003 [London 1722].

Delorme, Charles: Pteleinodaphneiai, hoc est Caroli Delorme Laureae Apollinares, a prima ad supremam, Paris 1608.

Dolan, Brian: Unmasking History: Who Was Behind the Anti-Mask League Protests During the 1918 Influenza Epidemic in San Francisco?, in: Perspectives in Medical Humanities, 2020, https://doi.org/10.34947/M7QP4M

Donne, John: Devotions Upon Emergent Occasions, ed. Anthony Raspa, 2nd ed., Oxford 1987 [London 1624].

European Centre for Disease Prevention and Control: Using face masks in the community, 08.04.2020, www.ecdc.europa.eu/sites/default/files/documents/COVID-19-use-face-masks-community.pdf; last accessed 03.07.2020.

Encke, Julia: Was Theorie noch kann, in: Frankfurter Allgemeine Sonntagszeitung, 26.04.2020, p. 33.

Falk, Francesca: Hobbes' »Leviathan« und die aus dem Blick gefallenen Schnabelmasken, in: Leviathan 39, 2011, pp. 247–266.

Félibien, André: Description sommaire du chasteau de Versailles, Paris 1674.

Findlen, Paula: Petrarch's Plague. Love, Death, and Friendship in a Time of Pandemic, in: The Public Domain Review, 11.06.2020, https://publicdomainreview.org/essay/petrarchs-plague; last accessed 17.06.2020.

Fleckner, Uwe / Martin Warnke / Hendrik Ziegler (eds.): Handbuch der politischen Ikonographie, 2 Bde., Munich 2011.

Foucault, Michel: Abnormal. Lectures at the Collège de France 1974–75, London / New York 2003.

Foucault, Michel: The Birth of Social Medicine, in: Power: Essential Works of Foucault, Vol. 3, ed. James D. Faubion, New York 2001, pp. 134–156.

Foucault, Michel: Discipline and Punish. The Birth of the Prison, 2nd ed., New York 1995 [Paris 1975].
Foucault, Michel: The Punitive Society. Lectures at the Collège de France 1972–73, Houndmills, Basingstoke 2015.
Gephart, Werner / Jure Leko: Introduction, in: Werner Gephart / Jure Leko (eds.): Law and the Arts. Elective Affinities and Relationships of Tension, Frankfurt am Main 2017, pp. 7–22.
Ginzburg, Carlo: Fear Reverence Terror. Reading Hobbes Today. Max Weber Lecture Series, European University Institute, San Domenico di Fiesole 2008.
Ginzburg, Carlo: Fear Reverence Terror. Five Essays in Political Iconography, Calcutta / London / New York 2015.
Grace, Daphne: The Woman in the Muslin Mask. Veiling and Identity in Postcolonial Literature, London / Sterling, Va., 2004.
GutHub: Corona-Warn-App, https://github.com/corona-warn-app/cwa-documentation, last accessed 25.06.2020.
Hamner, Lea / Polly Dubbel / Ian Capron et al.: High SARS-CoV-2 Attack Rate Following Exposure at a Choir Practice – Skagit County, Washington, March 2020, in: Morbidity and Mortality Weekly Report 69, 2020, pp. 606–610.
Harding, Vanessa: The Dead and the Living in Paris and London, 1500–1670, Cambridge 2002.
He, Xi / Eric H. Y. Lau / Peng Wu et al.: Temporal Dynamics in Viral Shedding and Transmissibility of COVID-19, in: Nature Medicine 26, 2020, 672–675.
Herbert, Gary B.: Kant Contra Hobbes, in: Hobbes Studies 17, 2005, pp. 3–7.
Hobbes, Thomas: Leviathan. The English and Latin Texts, ed. Noel Malcolm, 3 Vols., Oxford 2012.
Horii, Mitsutoshi: Why Do the Japanese Wear Masks? A Short Historical Review, in: Electronic Journal of Contemporary Japanese Studies, 2014, www.japanesestudies.org.uk/ejcjs/vol14/iss2/horii.html; last accessed 25.06.2020.
Julien, Pierre: Quatre sujets médico-pharmaceutiques dans l'œuvre de Callot, in: Revue d'histoire de la pharmacie 81, 1993, pp. 6–14.
Kant, Immanuel: Critique of Practical Reason, ed. Mary Gregor, 2nd ed., Cambridge 2015 [Riga 1788].
Kant, Immanuel: Groundwork of the Metaphysics of Morals, ed. Mary Gregor / Jens Timmermann, 2nd ed., Cambridge 2012 [Riga 1785].
Kantorowicz, Ernst H.: The King's Two Bodies. A Study in Medieval Political Theology, Princeton, N. J., 2016 [1957].
Kristiansson, Magnus / Johan Tralau: Hobbes's hidden monster: A new interpretation of the frontispiece of Leviathan, in: European Journal of Political Theory 13, 2014, pp. 299–320.
Kullmann, Wolfgang: Man as a political animal in Aristotle, in: David Keyt / Fred D. Miller Jr. (eds.): A Companion to Aristotle's Politics, Oxford 1991, pp. 94–117.

Lex Corona initiative: https://lexcorona.de/doku.php; last accessed, 03.07.2020.

Luckingham, Bradford: To Mask or not to Mask: A Note on the 1918 Spanish Influenza Epidemic in Tucson, in: The Journal of Arizona History 25, 1984, pp. 191–204.

Ludel, Wallace: Will US Architectural Body Have a Say on Trump's »Re-beautification«, in: The Art Newspaper, March 2020, p. 11.

Malcolm, Noel: Editorial Introduction to Thomas Hobbes's Leviathan, Oxford 2012.

May, Larry: Hobbes on Fidelity to Law, in: Hobbes Studies 5, 1992, pp. 77–89.

Merleau-Ponty, Maurice: Phenomenology of Perception, London / New York 2012 [Paris 1945].

Merleau-Ponty, Maurice: The Visible and the Invisible, ed. Claude Lefort, Evanston, Ill., 1968 [Paris 1964].

Metzger, Hans-Dieter: Die Bedeutung des Leviathan. Politischer Mythos oder politischer Begriff?, in: Hobbes Studies 5, 1992, pp. 23–52.

Mintz, Samuel I.: Leviathan as Metaphor, in: Hobbes Studies 2, 1989, pp. 3–9.

Mollaret, Henri H. / Jacqueline Brossollet: La peste, source méconnue d'inspiration artistique, in: Jaarboek Koninklijk Museum voor Schone Kunsten Antwerpen 1965, pp. 3–112.

Muratori, Lodovico Antonio: Del governo della peste, e delle maniere di guardarsene, Modena 1714.

Navarro, Julian A.: Influenza in 1918: An Epidemic in Images, in: Public Health Reports (Supplement) 125, 2010, pp. 9–14.

Our World in Data: Total confirmed COVID-19 deaths per million people, https://ourworldindata.org/grapher/total-covid-deaths-per-million?country=~SWE&region=Europe; last accessed 05.06.2020.

Papon, Jean-Pierre: De la Peste ou époques mémorables de ce fléau et les moyens de s'en préserver, 2 vols., Paris 1800.

Parent-Duchatelet, Alexandre: Hygiène publique, ou Mémoires sur les questions les plus importantes de l'hygiène, 2 vols., Paris 1836.

Parsons, Talcott: American Society. A Theory of the Societal Community, ed. Giuseppe Sciortino, London / New York 2016 [2007].

Prather, Kimberly A. / Chia C. Wang / Robert T. Schooley: Reducing Transmission of Sars-Cov-2, in: Science Vol. 368(6498), 2020, pp. 1422–1424.

Rousseau, Jean-Jacques: The Social Contract and Other Later Political Writings, ed. Victor Gourevitch, 2nd ed., Cambridge 2019.

Ruisinger, Marion Maria: Die Pestarztmaske im Deutschen Medizinhistorischen Museum Ingolstadt, in: NTM Zeitschrift für Geschichte der Wissenschaften, Technik und Medizin 28, 2020, pp. 235–252.

Sabatier, Gérard: La gloire du roi. Iconographie de Louis XIV de 1661 à 1672, in: Histoire, économie et société 19, 2000, pp. 527–560.

Saint-Martin, Michel de: Moiens faciles et éprouvez dont Monsieur de Lorme, premier Médecin & ordinaire de trois de nos Rois, & Ambassadeur à Cleves pour de Duc de Nevers, s'est servi pour vivre près de cent ans, 2nd ed., Caen 1683.

Schmitt, Carl: The Leviathan in the State Theory of Thomas Hobbes. Meaning and Failure of a Political Symbol, Westport, Conn./London 1996 [Hamburg 1938].

Shrewsbury, John F. D.: A History of Bubonic Plague in the British Isles, Cambridge 1970.

Skinner, Quentin: From Humanism to Hobbes: Studies in Rhetoric and Politics, Cambridge 2018.

Sorgi, Giuseppe: Hobbes on »Bodies Politic«, in: Hobbes Studies 9, 1996, pp. 71–87.

Thucydides: Eight Bookes of the Peloponnesian Warre, ed. Thomas Hobbes, London 1629.

Tibayrenc, Michel (ed.): Encyclopedia of Infectious Diseases. Modern Methodologies, Hoboken, N. J. 2007.

Top10VPN: COVID-19 Digital Rights Tracker, https://www.top10vpn.com/research/investigations/Covid-19-digital-rights-tracker/; last accessed 25.06.2020.

Townsend, G. L.: The Plague Doctor: An Engraving by Gerhart Altzenbach (17th century), in: Journal of the History of Medicine and Allied Sciences 22, 1965, pp. 276–277.

Wikipedia: COVID-19 Apps, https://en.wikipedia.org/wiki/COVID-19_apps; last accessed 25.06.2020.

Wikipedia: Face Masks During the COVID-19 Pandemic. https://en.wikipedia.org/wiki/Face_masks_during_the_COVID19_pandemic#Mask_use_and_policies_by_country_and_territory; last accessed 25.06.2020.

Wikipedia: FFP Mask, https://en.wikipedia.org/wiki/FFP_mask; last accessed 25.06.2020.

Wikipedia: Islamic Dress in Europe, https://en.wikipedia.org/wiki/Islamic_dress_in_Europe; last accessed 25.06.2020.

Wikipedia: List of COVID-19 Pandemic Legislation, https://en.wikipedia.org/wiki/List_of_COVID-19_pandemic_legislation; last accessed 25.06.2020.

Yang, Jeff: A Quick History of Why Asians Wear Surgical Masks in Public, Quartz, 19.11.2014, https://qz.com/299003/a-quick-history-of-why-asians-wear-surgical-masks-in-public (saved on archive.org); last accessed: 25.06.2020.

List of Figures

Fig. 1: Jeton, Ordinaire des guerres, silver, 27 mm, 1658, Paris, Bibliothèque nationale de France, département Monnaies, médailles et antiques, JEI-3837. Image: BnF, academic licence.

Fig. 2: Abraham Bosse, Title engraving for Thomas Hobbes's Leviathan, London 1651, private collection. Image: public domain.

Fig. 3a: Detail of Abraham Bosse, Title engraving for Thomas Hobbes's Leviathan, London 1651, private collection. Image: author.

Fig. 3b: Detail of an engraving after Abraham Bosse for Thomas Hobbes, The Moral and Political Works, London 1750, private collection. Image: author.

Fig. 4: Luigi Sambon, A plague doctor's mask from the seventeenth century, watercolour, measurements unknown, reproduced in Archives de parasitologie 3, 1900, pl. V. Image: archive.org.

Fig. 5: Gerhart Altzenbach, Kleidung widder den Todt: Anno 1656 (The Plague Doctor), engraving, 305 × 225 mm, Medical Historical Library, Harvey Cushing / John Hay Whitney Medical Library, Yale University. Image courtesy of Yale University.

Fig. 6: Abraham Bosse after Jean de Saint-Igny, French nobleman seem from behind, etching/engraving, 140 × 94 mm, 1629, Amsterdam, Rijksmuseum. Image: Rijksmuseum, public domain.

Fig. 7: Anonymous, Ah! / Le Cruchon / Le masque levé, etching and watercolour, 265 × 145 mm. Image courtesy of Paris Musées, open licence.

Fig. 8: Anonymous, Photograph of people wearing face masks in California, 1918, private collection. Image: public domain.

Fig. 9: Ambroise Tardieu, Masques pour pénétrer dans lieux infectés, illustration from Alexandre Parent-Duchatelet, Hygiène publique, Paris 1836, vol. 1, facing p. 92. Image: archive.org.

Fig. 10: Distance markers in front of a museum entrance, Bonn, June 2020. Image: author.

Frode Helmich Pedersen

A Pandemic of Narratives

What is a crisis? Is it a happening, an observation or perhaps more of an emotion? Regardless what one answers, it seems clear that a crisis is never simply a concrete and clear-cut phenomenon. In the current Corona-pandemic, the crisis is not limited to the fact that people get infected with a new kind of virus and thereby contract a potentially deadly disease. The crisis also includes our responses to the situation, how we choose to handle it and how we talk about it, both as individuals and as a community. There are no clear boundaries as to what properly belongs to the crisis and what should be regarded as separate from it. This means that what we refer to as *the crisis* will always be an unsettled phenomenon, too complex to be grasped in its entirety. Still, we cannot avoid trying to make some sense of the situation. How do we go about in our attempts to get an overview of the coronavirus pandemic?

In her 2014 book *Anti-Crisis* (which mainly deals with the financial crisis of 2007), Janet Roitman usefully comments that »a crisis is an observation that produces meaning«.[1] When a crisis occurs, there is always an immediate production of crisis-narratives. These narratives are typically in search for the *roots*, *origins*, and *causes* of the crisis. Here is Roitman elaborating on her point:

»[These narratives are all] concerned to unearth the history from which we have become alienated: they hope to reveal the *secret origin* (Lewis 2010, 1) the *deeper causes* (Skidelsky 2009, 4), the *underlying contradictions* (Harvey 2011, 89), the *hidden history* (McLean and Nocera 2010) – all of which have led to distortions or deviations from a proper or more correct historical progression. Moreover, these narrations, in their claim to reveal moments of alienation likewise claim to *reveal history* itself (Shiller 2008).«[2]

According to Roitman, crisis-narratives proceed from the question *what went wrong* and then go on to try and discover the moments where our recent history deviated from what we now, in retrospect, understand to have been the right path forward. The underlying premise of this kind of storytelling (which, I would add, is usually normative), is that it is always, at least in principle, possible to avoid a crisis by steering clear of the missteps that leads to the wrong kind of story – that

---

[1] Roitman: Anti-Crisis, p. 42.
[2] Ibid.; ins. by the author.

is, a story that inevitably ends up in the crisis-scenario. A further implication of the typical crisis-narrative is that there is always someone to blame for the crisis.

1. The Master Narrative and Its Spawn

We have seen many examples of such *unearthing* narratives during the current pandemic. These narratives are produced in a reversed chronological order, starting with the basic facts of crisis and then going back, step by step, to its original cause. In this case, the virus (SARS-CoV-2) was traced back to its genesis in the forests of China, where it likely resided in bats, civets or pangolins before it was transferred to humans. On the basis of the uncovering of the virus' zoonotic origins, a master narrative of the crisis was produced and then repeated in numerous variations in Western media. In this narrative, the main blame is put on the unsavory practices at Chinese wet-markets, where wild animals are being kept next to domestic ones and slaughtered in an unhygienic manner, before being consumed by unconcerned humans. The Huanan Seafood Market was here depicted as *the primal scene* of the crisis, *the scene of the crime*, as it were, with the clear implication that the Chinese are ultimately to blame for the global pandemic.

The accusatory implication was enhanced and made more or less explicit in many of the variations of the master narrative which spread across news media and other digital media during the early stages of the pandemic. In some variations of the narrative, the Chinese authorities are accused of having kept the scale of the outbreak hidden for too long, in others for having deliberately sent out its infected citizens to cause harm to its political rivals around the world, in still others it was suggested that the virus was manufactured by Chinese scientists. There was also a strain of narratives portraying the World Health Organization as a tool for Chinese manipulation, leading to the US withdrawing its support for the organization.

In addition to the many narratives that can be considered variations of the master narrative of the crisis, there was, in each of the affected nations, a rapid production of stories concerning the measures taken by governments in response to the outbreak, where multiple scenarios were being played out in narrative form – either ending up lambasting authorities for doing too little too late, or criticizing them for doing too much too early, depending on whether the central theme of the narrative centered on economic issues or health issues. There were also numerous legal narratives dealing, among other things, with juridical problems concerning the ›state of exception‹ that was temporarily introduced in many countries around the world in order to check the spread of the virus.

At the beginning of the lockdown-period in March 2020, representatives of almost every profession seemed compelled to tell the story about the crisis from their point of view. The rhetorical purpose of these narratives was, more often than not, to convince authorities and fellow citizens of the relative importance of their particular profession and its special need of economic protection. In addition, we got a profusion of *personal narratives* about life in quarantine, many of which were unmistakably normative with respect to how one ought to go about leading one's lives under the new circumstances. Indeed, most of the stories that were produced during the crisis were normative to some degree, not infrequently bordering on the accusatory. In Norway, where I live, there were frequent media stories about people who were not conducting themselves correctly during the lockdown, either by being too much out in the open, or not washing their hands properly, or walking in too close proximity to one another in the woods, or letting their children play with more than two friends at the all but abandoned playing fields. At the height of the crisis, the normative force of these narratives seemed to produce an almost hysterical sense of self-righteousness in parts of the population.

As a general media consumer, one could, as the crisis unfolded, easily get the feeling that the flood of narratives that were being offered through every conceivable channel every day could more properly be described as *an aspect of the crisis* than as a means of understanding it. The incessant production of new crisis-narratives seemed too chaotic to allow for thoughtful debate. The personal report of French philosopher Alain Badiou captures this experience. Initially, Badiou saw the crisis as a rather straightforward phenomenon: Beyond the »obvious protective measures and the time that the virus would take to disappear,« he didn't see why it was »necessary to climb on one's high horse«. There wasn't anything to be done, he thought, »other than try, like everyone else, to isolate himself at home«.[3] It wasn't until the generation of crisis-narratives reached a cacophonic pitch that he felt compelled to present his own analysis of the situation, in order to make some sense of where we stood.

Badiou's experience illustrates the point: The crisis is not simply identical with the spread of the disease but also includes the expressions, representations and new conceptions of normativity it produces, many of which come in narrative form. And like viruses, narratives have a way of spreading and mutating, potentially infecting its audience with all sorts of confused notions and skewed information. »An Epidemic of False Claims,« read a headline in the journal *The Scientific American* almost twenty years ago.[4] It would have been just as fitting today.

---

[3] Badiou: On the Epidemic Situation.
[4] Ioannidis: An Epidemic of False Claims.

2. Enjoy Your Narrative

It is a commonplace within post-classical narratology to view narrative as a cognitive tool used more or less instinctively by humans in order to make sense of their life-world. This is the notion behind the anthropology of the *homo narrans*, a term coined by the communication theorist Walter Fisher in the early eighties.[5] According to this view, humans actively construct their reality by creating (or internalizing) certain narratives, some of which concern fundamental questions of identity, providing answers to such questions as *where do I come from?*, *where do I belong?*, *what ought I to do?*, and so on. These identity narratives are frequently structured around various signifiers of inclusion and exclusion relative to the we-group to which the narrator belongs. As the literary scholar Albrecht Koschorke points out in his book *Wahrheit und Erfindung*, members of a we-group always have a positive view about themselves.[6] What can we learn about our current predicament from this line of thinking?

The first hypothesis I would suggest is that there is always a kind of enjoyment involved in accepting certain narratives about the crisis. When you accept one narrative over another, the accepted narrative is not chosen exclusively for its explanatory power but also for the (secret) pleasure it offers you. This enjoyment is connected, I would claim, to the positive picture the narrative paints of the implicit we-group of its intended audience. The we-group can either be stated outright or established through signifiers which are discernible by the adherents of the narrative. Even in times of uncertainty, or maybe I should rather say *especially* in such times, the narratives we subscribe to tend to be the ones that make us feel good about ourselves. The second hypothesis I should like to propose, is that this enjoyment is closely connected to the normative aspects of the narrative in question. The stories that we live by do not typically point the finger at ourselves, but tend instead to direct accusations elsewhere, leaving the we-group largely in the clear. To put it a little crudely: The narratives that we accept most readily are the one that ensures us that someone else is to blame.

These hypotheses can be illustrated by reviewing some of the dominant narratives in Norwegian news media during the crisis. One telling example is the narrative concerned with explaining why the crisis was so much worse in Italy (and Spain) than in countries like Germany and Norway. Variations of this narrative were quite frequent in the Norwegian press. I'll mention just one particular manifestation of it, appearing in an op-ed piece written by author and journalist Erik Martiniussen and published in Aftenposten, the leading centre-right news-

---

[5] Cf. Fischer: Narration as a Human Communication paradigm, p. 6.
[6] Koschorke: Wahrheit und Erfindung, p. 91.

paper in Norway. Martiniussen tells the story of the Italian overuse of antibiotics, both within the health care system and in the meat industry, which has resulted in a dramatic increase of antibiotic resistant bacteria. According to Martiniussen, this has led to a comparatively high likelihood that Italians who have contrated Covid-19 will experience a fatal outcome, since they run a high risk of being infected by resistant bacteria while their immune systems are weakened by the coronavirus. There is no treatment available to such patients. In the following passage, Martiniussen elaborates on his point:

»The high degree of antibiotic resistant bacteria is directly connected to overuse of antibiotics. In their primary health care, the Italians hand out more than double the amount of antibiotics than we do in Norway. In the meat production, the situation is even worse: Tons of our most important medicines are poured into an expanding pork-industry that produces 10 million pigs per year.«[7]

I am not here concerned with reviewing the validity of Martiniussen's claims, but rather with pointing out that the passage contains ideologically charged signifiers of inclusion and exclusion, making it evident that the we-group – i.e. *us Norwegians* – are behaving far more responsibly than the Italians, who are depicted as dangerously careless in their use of antibiotics. This ideological slant becomes even more evident in the closing paragraph. After mentioning that the problem is much the same in Spain as in Italy, Martiniussen concludes in this way:

»Here at home we should, at this moment, be very grateful that we have a health care system where antibiotics is only used when it is really needed and that we have farmers who barely use any antibiotics on their livestock at all. It is very likely that our restrictive practice with antibiotics will save the lives of many coronavirus patients.«[8]

The article's conclusion offers enjoyment to Norwegian readers in at least two respects: First, it promotes a positive view of our own high standards regarding the use of antibiotics, which are depicted as both rationally and morally superior to the practices in Italy and Spain. Second, it predicts a positive scenario regarding the unfolding of the pandemic in Norway in comparison with other countries. In this way, the narrative both boosts the Norwegian reader's positive feelings about his or her own identity, *and* it relieves his or her anxiety with respect to the ongoing outbreak. This makes this narrative decidedly more attractive than other narratives, which explain the same problem with reference to less ideologically charged factors, such as the fact that the Italian outbreak happened earlier than elsewhere, thereby excluding the possibility that Italian health authorities could

---

[7] Martiniussen: Derfor tar kornoaviruset så mange liv i Italia. [That is why the coronavirus claims so many Italian lives]; transl. by the author.
[8] Ibid.; transl. by the author.

learn from the experiences of other nations, or the fact that Italy both has a higher population density *and* a higher proportion of elderly than Norway. At least this was my impression as a reader of Norwegian newspapers during the crisis: Norwegians generally favored explanatory narratives that carried with them possibilities of enjoyment by confirming (implicitly or explicitly) the supposed advantages of Norwegian culture and attitudes.

3. The Narrative about the Swedish Response

This was nowhere more evident than in the case of the Swedish response to the outbreak. Sweden's response to the crisis was, as is well known, much more relaxed than that of most other European countries. Instead of locking the country down, the Swedes kept the schools and kindergartens open, while restaurants, ski-resorts, bars, nightclubs, hairdressers, trains etc. were allowed to operate more or less as usual. Instead of imposing restrictions on its public, Swedish authorities preferred to urge citizens to wash their hands and to restrict themselves according to their own judgement.

Norwegians and Danes reacted to the Swedish strategy with increasing disbelief. The Norwegian press ran story after story about the *Swedish mindset*, in order to explain how it could be possible that the Swedes could behave so irresponsibly during the worst pandemic to hit our shores since the black plague. The main story that arose out of these reports (in part informed by dissenting Swedes) focused on the supposed Swedish belief in reason, science and state authority, which was said to date back to (at least) 18th century Enlightenment, and which was reinforced during the period of strong social engineering in the postwar era. This historical development, so the story went, had made the Swedes put a much higher value on the opinions of experts than their European neighbors.[9]

But since the Scandinavian nations are all characterized by a high degree of societal trust, making its citizenry inclined to follow the instructions of their governments without much protest, the narrative about the Swedish response also had to be able to explain the unexpected behavior of Swedish epidemiologists. This was accomplished by highlighting the positivist notions of scientific rationality within the Swedish academic community, forbidding the experts from recommending measures that had not been scientifically proven to be effective.[10] If you combined this state of affairs with the alleged arrogance of Swedish academic elites, *plus* the systemic tendency in Sweden to leave these kinds of decisions to

---

[9] See for instance Werner: Annerledeslandet Sverige [The Special Country of Sweden].
[10] Tvedt: Svenske tilstander [On the Swedish Situation].

the experts rather than to the politicians, you had all the components of a *perfect storm* for a disastrous handling of the outbreak.[11] The ideologically charged conclusion of this narrative, as told from the Norwegian (and Danish) perspective, was that the Swedes were both culturally and politically deficient compared to us, who had proven our astuteness by reacting quickly and effectively as soon as it became apparent that we were dealing with a pandemic.

The dominant narrative about the Swedish response undoubtedly carried with it a significant opportunity for chauvinistic enjoyment and even *schadenfreude* for Norwegian readers. After all, the rivalry between the two nations goes back hundreds of years and includes an almost hundred-year long period where Norway was under the rule of the Swedish monarch (1814–1905). There was of course no express gloating over the Swedish plight in serious Norwegian newspapers, but the sheer number of Norwegian press reports about the high number of Swedish Covid-19 fatalities warrants, at least in my opinion, some suspicion with respect to the motives behind this reporting – especially when it is viewed in combination with the incessant readiness among Norwegians to moralize over the Swedish strategy of handling the crisis.[12] In light of this situation, I find it understandable that Swedish officials and commentators have become exasperated, claiming that the Swedes are now the victims of bullying from other European nations and that they feel treated as *persona non grata* in many countries, who deny Swedes access to their borders.[13]

4. Instead of a Conclusion

To the extent that I am permitted to present my own normative take on the situation, I would suggest that people would do well to actively resist the urge to look for (self-serving) cultural explanations for how the crisis has unfolded in other countries, and to fully acknowledge the fact that no one really knew how to respond when disaster struck. One cannot simply claim, as was often done in Norway, that serious health issues must outweigh economic issues, because economic issues can quickly turn into issues of public health, just as any health issue has an economic side. As we approach the summer of 2020, and many European borders are being partly reopened on behalf of the tourist industry, the budding optimism

---

[11] As of June 2020, the death rates resulting from Covid-19 are almost ten times as high in Sweden as in Norway.

[12] See for instance Meland: Dette ser verre og verre ut, Sverige [This is looking worse and worse, Sweden].

[13] Losnegård: Svensk ekspert: – Vi har blitt Europas mobbeoffer [Swedish Expert: – We have become the victims of Europan bullying].

is darkened by the shadow of a new master narrative about the crisis, whose outline is becoming clearer and more urgent by the day. This master narrative is not created retroactively and does not concern the question of what went wrong, but is instead a projection into the future, focusing on the likelihood of a coming massive global economic recession, resulting in widespread unemployment, increased poverty rates and the real possibility of violent social unrest in many countries – including the US, which is already in a state of upheaval in the wake of the murder of George Floyd at the hands of the Minneapolis police. Meanwhile, 22 US states are seeing jumps in new coronavirus cases, according to a recent CNN report, an ominous fact that can only work to increase our apprehensiveness.[14]

No one can predict how the crisis will evolve even in the near future, and it seems futile to try and sum up these brief reflections on crisis-narratives with an epigrammatic conclusion or a sage recommendation as to how we should proceed. Instead, I'll end by somewhat warily concurring with Slavoj Žižek's call to resist seeking a deeper, metaphysical meaning in the crisis[15] and instead try to deal as best we can with concrete problems as they arise. The reason for my wariness is simply this: Even as we *should* think twice before contributing to the persistent and increasing whirlwind of new crisis-narratives, that does not mean that we are free to desist from trying to make sense of the situation – and on the basis of this to prepare ourselves, as best we can, for what lies ahead.

References

Badiou, Alain: On the Epidemic Situation, in: Verso, 23.03.2020, https://www.versobooks.com/blogs/4608-on-the-epidemic-situation; last accessed 16.06.2020.

Fischer, Walter R.: Narration as a Human Communication paradigm: The Case of Public Moral Argument, in: Communication Monographs, 51, 1984, pp. 1–20.

Ioannidis, John P. A.: An Epidemic of False Claims, in: The Scientific American, 01.06.2011, https://www.scientificamerican.com/article/an-epidemic-of-false-claims/; last accessd 16.06.2020.

Koschorke, Albrecht: Wahrheit und Erfindung. Grundzüge einer allgemeinen Erzähltheorie, Frankfurt am Main 2013.

Losnegård, Aleksander: Svensk ekspert: – Vi har blitt Europas mobbeoffer, in: NRK, 25.05.2020, https://www.nrk.no/urix/svensk-ekspert_-_-vi-har-blitt-europas-mobbeoffer-1.15027988; last accessed 16.06.2020.

---

[14] Maxouris / Yan: As More Americans Head Out.
[15] Žižek: Pandemic! COVID-19 Shakes the World, p. 14.

Martiniussen, Erik: Derfor tar koronaviruset så mange liv i Italia, in: Aftenposten, 24.03.2020, https://www.aftenposten.no/meninger/kronikk/i/awEP27/derfor-tar-koronaviruset-saa-mange-liv-i-italia-erik-martiniussen; last accessed 16.06.2020.

Maxouris, Christina / Holly Yan: As More Americans Head Out, 22 States Are Seeing Jumps in New Coronavirus Cases, in: CNN, 08.06.2020, https://edition.cnn.com/2020/06/08/health/us-coronavirus-monday/index.html; last accessed 16.06.2020.

Meland, Astrid: Dette ser verre og verre ut, Sverige, in: Verdens Gang, 05.06.2020, https://www.vg.no/nyheter/meninger/i/g7obQ5/dette-ser-verre-og-verre-ut-sverige; last accessed 16.06.2020.

Roitman, Janet: Anti-Crisis, Durham / London 2014.

Tvedt, Oda Wiese: Svenske tilstander, in: Bergens Tidende, 15.03.2020, https://www.bt.no/; last accessed 16.06.2020.

Werner, Kjell: Annerledeslandet Sverige, in: Dagsavisen, 06.04.2020, https://www.dagsavisen.no/debatt/kommentar/annerledeslandet-sverige-1.1695376; last accessed 15.06.2020.

Žižek, Slavoj: Pandemic! COVID-19 Shakes the World, New York 2020.

V. No Lesson on the Lesson?
Or: »In the Name of Corona«?

Peter Goodrich
Zoonoses

The fear of bats in the belfry, attributed most often to the Victorians, has come to seem both prescient and strangely real. Patient zero was infected by a bat, meaning that Chiroptera produced the long fingers of Corona, of Covid-19. Zoonosis, animal borne disease, led to pandemic, to a world that suddenly realized that it too is blind and batty, but lacking echolocation in any grander sense. A sonically directed, nocturnal mammal, the microbat led to the microbe and to globally distributed infection. The etiology is important, figures fly and the zoonoses resulting from ecological and climatic blindness require recalibration of our cultural sonar and revivification of the quintessential art of justice, namely hearing the pleas of the excluded. Zoonoses are proboscatory, they offer the possibility of returning wit to the snoutfig of judgment. The philosopher Nagel's critique of consciousness via the interior life of bats takes on new forms.

A nocturnal avian mammal that flies by listening to sonic reverberations forms an unlikely yet protreptic figure, a return to what Coccia labels sensible life, an existence aware of the haptic, auditory, vegetal and material relations extant in *justissima tellus*, the phrase Vergil uses to depict the infinitely wise and supremely just matter of existence, purloined but not always put to good use by others. The *leges terrae* belong properly to that knowledge and material relationship, and the institution of socage, the various tenures were historically in and of the land, were aspects of legigraphic charting of meadows and fields, of what was suggestively called Reveland. Sir Edward Coke cites Cicero: »And amongst the Romans agriculture or tillage was of high estimation, insomuch as the senators themselves would put their hand to the plough; and it is said, that never prospered tillage better, than when the senators themselves plowed.«[1] They knew of what they spoke, the humus, moss and matter joined in body, revel, and legigraphy. Since the Industrial Revolution, however, there has been an increasingly one-way street between capital and reality, man fighting against the environment, the human overdetermining the natural, abstraction suppressing matter, temporality diminishing distance, history pitched against space. This unidirectionality is suddenly, visibly, in pandemic panic, reversed. Implicit in the chiasmus is also an annulment of the extant order of culture, a revenge even of the law of nature upon positive law. Zoonosis performs a volte face on anthroponosis, human borne disease, and in that swift

---

1 Coke: Institutes of the Laws of England, Second Book, Chapter 5, Sect. 117.

and global reversal lies a shattering of the crystal palace and, onward to my theme, a potentially radical, indeed tectonic rethinking of Western law.

The revenge of the spatial upon the temporal, of atmosphere upon rules, marks a greater turn around in the cultural affairs of law. Microbes are no respecters of either status or boundaries, their temporality is that of the double helix, transitional and transmissive, constantly becoming other, adapting, future oriented. The modern science of legality is predicated upon the temporal progress of law from past to present. The Code governs, *lex scripta*, the prior rule, and then in common law even more determined to project the priority of the past, the *dispositif* of precedent, the president is the past, the priority of antiquity, and *novum omne cave*. The theology of common law is based upon the triumph of antiquity over novelty and with the advent of a legal science of rule governed decisions, of the jural syllogism, the concretization of norms, the pure and abstract normativity of legal dispute resolution, or in the old language shared by common and civil law, *fugiendum ad montes, ad montes scripturarum,* or in the vernacular, flee to the mountains of text, to scriptures, the classics, the greats, and the past. The spatial and the material, the sonic and auditory aspects of *in vivo* encounters became ever more distant, mediated and remediated, derogated and derided dimensions of decision. Zoonoses were not to be understood and accommodated as facets of a shared and inter-relational cross species and transhuman environment but to be eliminated, denied juridical existence, as non-persons, as part of the non-being of the environment, the depredation of space, and the non-recognition of the seemingly, beautifully, aesthetically and necessarily inutilious.

The emergent question is whether law could be thought from the future, as a hauntology of the not yet. Precedent is dead. Thinking in the mode of melancholic and depressive retention of rules through the blinkers of a linear juridical temporality, *volksgeist* or *gemeinschaft* as an exclusively human space and community is not a solution. The progressive loss of the horizon of possibility, the slow cancellation of the future, is the result of capitalist realism, the absence of alternatives, the depression of the Left, now itself left to the imbrications of aesthetics and the dead weight of the past. The rearview mirror, the constricting logic of retrospect, the backward looking, are neither an answer to microbial pandemic nor to the spectre of the future. In juristic terms, but still in the materialist mode of the tellurian, what is to come, the not yet, is imaginary, oneiric, the subject of pataphysical reverie and the inventions of an aesthetics that won't look back. The question is directly that of how to address the unknown and the answer is to think through why you do not know it – be it earth, microbes, events, impersons, zoonoses, proboscations, the near and the far of the future. A hard task for jurists but one that is pataphysically impossible and hence exigent, ethical, and entirely desirable.

Precedent, the English *déformation professionelle* of lawyers, the Achilles heel of the oldest social science, is that of being bound to a project of mourning, the retention of ghosts that it cannot let go, a past that haunts and imposes upon the present because rational legal science, positivistic theories of the juridical are unable to listen to the dialogic and communal, common character of common law. The enclosures of land and property, the birth of the prison, the restraint of reason by enlightenment, the channeling of creativity by capital, all take on an acceleratingly unidirectional trajectory. Capital takes control of law at the level of legislatures first and then of courts and personnel. Little room is left for pataphysical jurisprudence and the science of imaginary solutions, space is contracted, the past is dominant, abstraction reigns and connections are lost. The commons drift, the multiverse of vegetal and organic life is subjected to the universe of linear rules and prescripted laws, the dull white regimen of a malleable legal realism where the policies of capital can anamorphically apply any norm to their own ends.

The reversal taking place involves the return of the spatial, and the expansion of the vegetal, organic and organismic. Matter has to matter and for that to be possible the expanse of the tellurian future, which in pre-modern law was a driving concern – the earth after all will exist long after humanity has ceased to be – has to be accorded legal being, a juristic entity that constitutes another sovereign and legislator, a voice in the multitude of heterotopic and transitional argots of expression. This is in essence the material call of wild jurisprudence, of earth law which seeks to move from the abstraction of positive law and the linear logic of calculus and decision, the econometrics of corporate policy, to the life of plants, the perspective of microbes, and overall recognition and attention to the essentially ineradicable, tellurian sources of human life. The future is fenestrated, a question of where you are looking, and it is cyclical, a question of *perpetuum mobile*, of organic life cycles, environmental exchanges, of species and places, vegetation and spirit, genius loci and inhabitation. The anterograde cultural character of capital has now to face the future and attend to the perspective of the tellurian environment upon which it has previously sought to act unilaterally supported by the closure of law hiding behind the barricade of the legal mind.

Wild jurisprudence treats earth, organisms, the vegetal, mineral and animal as mattering and having meaning in their own being. The perspective of crayfish, snails, iron ore, trees, as well as rivers and the sites and air surrounding religious and indigenous rites have value and could salvage juridical recognition. This forms an important development in pataphysical jurisprudence, where the definition of the science is »of the laws governing exceptions, and will explain the universe supplementary to this one; or, less ambitiously, will describe a universe which can be – and perhaps should be – envisaged in place of the traditional one«.[2] A science, recollect, of absences, spectres of the future now tied, such as it will be, to co-existence of all entities, the cohabitant character of a community of human

---

[2] Jarry: Exploits and Opinions of Doctor Faustroll, p. 22.

and natural, corporeal and material thought. The intellective web of law is a sieve to be used for moving in water. Audition, echolocation, legal hearing, introspects the resonances of concrete, the acoustics of glass, the breath of air, the patter of rain. Scent too, of oil, iron and freshly parked cars. Blood, sweat, tears, and in the old language of jurisprudence perspiration that falls during work on the earth, that is mingled with humus, is the arche-sign of belonging, of being in and of matter. A haptic sensibility and objective unconscious arrayed in the images external to subjectivity take us outside ourselves and into a questionable lawscape, an atmosphere, the matter of the imaginal and the scientific art of the pataphysical.

I am universal, I laugh. Muscle and bone jostle together, the diaphragm shakes, the face breaks up. The body changes state. *In ludo veritas*, wild utterance, with or without wine. The point is that laughter shatters the melancholic hold of the past. Cacchination catapults the subject out of their complacency, it lifts the body and thought to thinking again, seeing anew, a moment of epiphanic potential in which novel connections emerge. So, consider the new connectivity, the sudden expression of a minor genre in a major mode, the epistemically excluded zoonoses of Corona. An unexpected universal or at least one for which global culture was unprepared. A choice. Be universal, expand. Or be singular, contract. To laugh, the untainted laugh, *risus purus* is to open precisely to the bodily, the haptic and felt, to face an unknown without pretending to know, without precedent caging vision. Here is law and culture, a study of the those in robes faced by microbes. The gnosis of zoonosis.

References

Coke, Edward: The First Part of the Institutes of the Laws of England; or, a Commentary upon Littleton, London 1892.

Jarry, Alfred: Exploits and Opinions of Doctor Faustroll, Pataphysician, Boston 1996.

Greta Olson

Being in Uncertainty:
Thinking the Coronavirus Pandemic

In times of crisis and uncertainty, one looks to leaders, however defined, to provide strategies for dealing with everyday issues and for guidance concerning the operative future. One also looks to writers to provide images and narratives with which to understand the unknowns of the situation at hand. Those of us who are paid to take information in and to help to pass it on to others are called upon now to try to provide such images and narratives. What I find transpiring around my dining room table or in emails from students and in exchange with colleagues and friends is a circle of the same questions: What does this Covid-19 situation mean? When will this period of fearfulness and curtailment end? What will the future be? How will our lives be changed?

Yet much of the present is for me about not imposing a narrative on what is occurring. I refuse to offer any summative notion of what this period means but rather want to suggest the need to be in its uncertainty. Comparisons to other plagues and what happened after them seem ill-thought-out to me, even if they provide us with placating coordinates. This is a global pandemic that is occuring while many of us live in states of relative physical social isolation, while simultaneously being in a state of extraordinary connectedness to spatially distant others, as we hold virtual meetings, email, app, facetime, tweet, Instagram, and otherwise communicate from behind screens. Like many others, the Coronavirus pandemic has caused me to be in contact with friends with whom I have not spoken in years, from countries such as Mexico, Brazil, and Ghana.

Daniel Defoe describes the return to daily life as soon as the bubonic plague had run its course in London in 1665 as an instant return to the city's former »wickedness« or even »worse«:

»Some, indeed, said things were worse; that the morals of the people declined from this very time; that the people, hardened by the danger they had been in, like seamen after a storm is over, were more wicked and more stupid, more bold and hardened, in their vices and immoralities than they were before; but I will not carry it so far neither. It would take up a history of no small length to give a particular of all the gradations by which the course of things in this city came to be restored again, and to run in their own channel as they did before.«[1]

---

[1] Defoe: Journal of the Plague Year.

We genuinely do not know what will happen when this period of self-sequestering is over. Many ask if this pandemic will produce the next *Decameron* or other great plague artwork or a new invention for better living. I am wary of the normativity behind these expectations. One of the best pieces I have read about our current moment is by Aisha S. Ahmad. A survivor of war and food shortages, she writes about the importance of avoiding the »productivity porn« that was posted everywhere as the security measures began, for instance, about building lean muscle, keeping to writing schedules, and finding new ways to do everything better, including parenting. Rather, as she counsels, concentrate on the now, on keeping those around us as well as can be, attend to those who are alone, and adjust to an altered mental frame and way of being, a mental frame that will last even when this *crisis* has ended.[2]

Hence, mine is a situated reading of the present, an in medias res. Situatedness means an awareness of one's perceptual parameters and their limitations. I am a German-American, still legally a US American citizen, yet also a German civil servant as of many years. I am also the mother of three German children, and the grandmother to a German-Italian grandchild. My vision is therefore at least bifurcated, with family members living in Washington State and in California, in North Carolina, New York, Connecticut, and Boston as well as in Rome, the Netherlands, Sweden, Scotland, and in Germany.

1. Two Countries and Their Contrasting Affective and Legal-Cultural Responses to Covid-19

1.1 Germany: Earnestness, Calls for Extreme Caution, Collective Sacrifice, and Contingent and Calibrated Change

Angela Merkel's televised address on 18 March 2020 provided a model in communicatively effective calm leadership. The uniqueness of her choosing this televised forum spoke for the gravity of the situation. Speaking quietly and almost without facial expression, she asked her listeners to address the gravest crisis since the Second World War and was bitterly clear about the government's lack of precise knowledge of the future: »It is serious. Take this situation seriously.«[3] She spoke of the need for transparency in a democracy and rendering governmental actions comprehensible, and also the government's reliance on virologists and other sci-

---

[2] Ahmad: Why You Should Ignore All That.
[3] Die Bundesregierung: Fernsehansprache von Bundeskanzlerin Angela Merkel; transl. by the author.

entists in its evolving policies. In good social democratic fashion, she lauded not only the heroism of health care providers, but also of all those people working as cashiers or filling the shelves in supermarkets to keep daily life going. Most importantly, and with a great deal of quiet authenticity, she referred to her own experience of having grown up in the GDR to state that she understood the pain involved in a government requiring its citizens to not move or travel freely. There was an expectation in this address that her listeners would engage with the complexity of the situation and the many variables involved and that they would take her and scientists' recommendations seriously. I found myself wet-eyed at this address, happy to see an individual leading so well. Reassured.

One witnesses a general trust in government and legal-cultural policies in Germany. Everyone I know is deeply concerned about the economic recession that will follow after the Coronavirus pandemic has run its course. Young people in particular are worried about what they feel is a lack of their future and about their lives having been put on hold. The university where I work sends out weekly updates in German and English to the entire community of students, faculty, and administrative and maintenance staff. University workers are requested to attend carefully to what politicians are saying and to stay actively informed. We are asked frankly to be in the current, ever evolving state of uncertainty. This is to be, as Merkel said on 16 April, in the »fragile intermediate success« brought about by coherence with the previous health measures.[4] This means letting students know that we do not yet know exactly when we will see them face-to-face again, and nonetheless reassuring them that university life and their studies continue.

I chuckle about the groups of young men whom I pass by while running daily in the woods who are despite current social-distancing rules meeting to drink beer or smoke hash and listen to music. They have walked long distances to do so. I am encouraged by how carefully people around me accept and, yes, also enforce social distancing rules. This includes some better-than-thou finger pointing, for instance, about one's supposedly not walking correctly – that is one-by-one – on a country path. Yet there is also, as I see it, a rise in a sense of expressive solidarity, even as one complains about restrictions communally. Across the street from my apartment, people waiting to go into the sewing store exchange notes about how best to make masks. While standing in a stretched-out line for fresh morning bread, one makes friendly, masked remarks about the awkward dynamics of trying to maintain physical distance while nonetheless allowing pedestrians to pass by.

At the point of this writing, Germany is being lauded as the great exception due to its comparatively low rate of death as compared to the high numbers of people who have contracted the virus. Now an important debate has begun about relative costs. What is the calculus involved in terms not only of the population's

[4] Die Bundeskanzlerin: Ein zerbrechlicher Zwischenerfolg.

physical health and of other material costs, such as loss of income and an increase of material precarity, but also in terms of psychological strains? This is not a brutal utilitarianism. Rather, it is a general and genuine question about the extent of the negative impact of the measures taken and the insistence on moving slowly. One asks if in an ageing society of baby boomers, the decision to keep schools closed is a weighing of the interests of older people – and this includes myself – against the interests of younger ones.

1.2 The United States: Denial, Obfuscation, and Deflecting Blame – Polarization and the Desire for Good Governance

Remarking on President Donald Trump's daily antics in White House briefings since the outbreak of the virus has been a study in contrasts with Germany's leadership and political actions during the Coronavirus epidemic. First, according to the president, the virus and the disease it produces was a »hoax« or a product of those »Deep State« experts whom Trump has never trusted. Misinformation was spread by Trump about warm weather eliminating the virus, or the various drugs that would supposedly eliminate it. Second, Trump let politics get in the way of disseminating accurate information or moving to protect people. This, with the general fractionalization in the White House and in the United States, more widely, has caused individual states to have to compete for resources and protective equipment and ventilators. Trump's daily news briefings are platforms for a rehearsal of his favorite motifs. This includes xenophobia – »the Chinese virus,« »the foreign virus,« and the ban on European travelers entering the country in March – and a penchant for deflecting blame. The lack of medical supplies was the Obama administration's fault. The pandemic is the WHO's fault, or it is Dr. Anthony Fauci's fault. It is the Democrats' fault. It is the governors' fault. These are Trump's preferred, well-practiced, and previously also quite successful rhetorical moves. They have been noticeable since his early branding of himself during the 1980s, and, as an Americanist, I have been reluctantly analyzing them with students since Trump was elected president in 2016.

The real-life consequences of these moves have included a vast increase in hate crimes towards Asian Americans caused by such xenophobic rhetoric. Another effect is the still not insignificant group of Americans who, as my surgeon brother reports, when they visit his office tell him that they believe that Covid-19 is a fiction and an invention of what Trump calls »Fake News« media. This is distressing. More distressing still since the outbreak of the pandemic has been the daily and for me exceedingly painful revelation of the United States as a first- and third-world country. Regretfully, the people I know who have been infected with the virus are African Americans and Latinx individuals who mostly live in urban areas. Whereas the wealthier have retreated to home office in large spaces, often with access to the outdoors, this is anything but the case for those less well off. The stratification of access to health care and the quality with which it is given has never been more alarming than in the present when it is costing lives. It reflects »the unfairness of the economy – an unfairness measured not only in dollars but in deaths«.[5] The numbers of people who cannot afford not to work distresses further, with unemployment rates now surpassing those of the Depression. With Trump calling on supporters »to liberate« their Democratic-led states from their governors and to exercise Second Amendment rights, we witness a president who is actively encouraging his supporters to resist safety measures and to engage in violence. I was moved by a recent piece in *The Atlantic* about an expat German academic who was for the first time in his life regretting his move to the United States and feeling »*Heimweh*« for Germany's »boring, humorless, and far more competent political leaders«.[6] A row of new political science books discuss the failure of the US American project since the end of the cold war. I see my country of origin's failures now with pain.

In terms of my own ecology – the garden I am trying to cultivate with those around me – the virus has meant the following. The courses on presidential self-fashioning that I was planning to teach this summer term have needed to be altered to now dealing with understanding the Coronavirus pandemic trans-Atlantically. Two months ago, I was calling for Democrats Abroad to ignore Trump's tactics as the Diverter-in-Chief in order to concentrate on pressing political issues such as attacks on the independence of the judiciary, rollbacks of environmental protections, anti-immigration measures, and efforts to keep working-class people (Democrats) from voting. Trump's is a highly successful strategy of exhaustion, caused by the sheer volume of Twitter shouts in the night and the swath of erratic daily actions that need to be sorted out in terms of their political consequences. What I am now saying is that while we have to be canny about how this rhetoric functions, we also need to not allow ourselves to be diverted by it, or to be so exhausted by its volume and frequency that we inadvertently enlarge its compass and impact. Literally, it is dangerous to amplify it. This contributes to the branding and self-aggrandizing of Trump and the politics he stands for.

While recognizing the lesson of history that incumbent presidents have only very rarely not been granted a second term, I note that these are extraordinary times. One remarks on the discipline of the Democratic Party just before Super Tuesday in early March, with central contenders giving up the race in order to put their support behind Joseph Biden. Even good, if irascible, Bernie Sanders has conceded the need to act differently than he did in his primary competition with

---

[5] Gawande: The Blight: How Our Economy Has Created an Epidemic of Despair, p. 63.
[6] Mounk: For the First Time, I'm Doubting My Decision to Come to America.

Hillary Clinton four years ago and to try to unite Democratic voters. There is an affective sense of the import of restoring good governance to the country and, as I read the affective moment, a genuine desire for unity against the background of increasing social-economic and cultural stratification in a time of dire need.

2. Crisis and Post-Apocalyptic Fictions

»Crisis« is a powerful lexeme and metaphor. It suggests caesura, a before and after and the need for immediate action. Like a lot of words and images being used during this pandemic period such as »outbreak,« »spike,« »death toll,« and »killer illness,« »crisis« moves us affectively into a state of fear and a sense of the need for urgent action. It interrupts thinking and the admittance of uncertainty. Particularly when efforts to curb the spread of the coronavirus are coupled with war imagery, one needs to pause to consider their effects. This is a moment for media literacy and for consciously exercising sustainable media practices. Let's be careful to avoid an overexposure to fear news.

Instead, let's consider the genre of post-apocalyptic fictions. People of my students' ages have been readying themselves for the Coronavirus pandemic for years by participating in dystopic post-apocalyptic fictions and games. I mention the books and films *The Hunger Games*, the comic and television series *The Walking Dead*, and games like Dying Light, Fallout, and The Last of Us to channel readers' cultural markers. A theory of fictions says that they preconceive the current world and propose alternative ones. In the realm of imaginedness, more general truths can be explored and reflected on than non-fictional referentiality can allow for. The popularity of zombies and dead cityscapes during the last decade has not been an accidental occurrence. It has succeeded an era in which wealthy, aristocratic, and highly sexualized vampires added passion and drama to mortal humans' lives.

These post-apocalyptic scenarios have been readying us for Covid-19 in terms of the imaginaries they co-create. And the recent Twitter image of the anti-lockdown protest in Ohio from 16 April that so resembles the *Walking Dead* attests to the resemblance of life to fiction. Post-apocalypses ask participants to exercise new skills in altered worlds, where the memories of past life and ways of living are only vague. They reflect critically on current realities. And they provide avenues with which »to examine the resources [needed] for coping with real and imagined existential terror«.[7] As an admired former student tells me, post-apocalyptic games are emotionally satisfying because they are genuinely frightening and demon-

---

[7] Moya/Leal: ENGL 76: After the Apocalypse.

strate the best and worst of humankind when it is forced to go into survival mode. They ask us to dwell in the uncertainty of the now.

A reader of this text, a friend and colleague, wrote that she misses its central argument. On this 21st of April 2020, the message is to rest in the uncertainty of this time. I suggest that we resist the desire for narrative closure, and avoid making too early predictions about the future and continue to be in our current state of not knowing. Those sequestering in relative comfort like myself might want to avoid productivity porn as well a fear news and be choiceful about the narratives and images with which we engage and that we disseminate. This means avoiding propagating misinformation, like Trump's, and remaining painfully aware of how situated and contingent our relatively privileged experiences of this pandemic are. We really, really do not know.

References

Ahmad, Aisha S.: Why You Should Ignore All That Coronavirus-Inspired Productivity Pressure, in: The Chronicle of Higher Education, 27.03.2020, www.chronicle.com/article/Why-You-Should-Ignore-All-That/248366; last accessed 21.04.2020.

Defoe, Daniel: A Journal of the Plague Year [1722]. Gutenberg Project Online, 1995, https://www.gutenberg.org/files/376/376-h/376-h.htm; last accessed 21.04.2020.

Die Bundeskanzlerin: Ein zerbrechlicher Zwischenerfolg. Bund-Länder-Einigung zu Corona-Maßnahmen, https://www.bundeskanzlerin.de/bkin-de/aktuelles/-ein-zerbrechlicher-zwischenerfolg--1744242!mediathek; last accessed 25.06.2020.

Die Bundesregierung: Fernsehansprache von Bundeskanzlerin Angela Merkel, 18.03.2020, https://www.bundesregierung.de/breg-de/aktuelles/fernsehansprache-von-bundeskanzlerin-angela-merkel-1732134; last accessed 25.06.2020.

Gawande, Atul: The Blight: How Our Economy Has Created an Epidemic of Despair, in: The New Yorker, 23.03.2020, 63; last accessed 21.04.2020.

Mounk, Yascha: For the First Time, I'm Doubting My Decision to Come to America, in: The Atlantic, 28.03.2020, www.theatlantic.com/ideas/archive/2020/03/stayed-germany/608980/; last accessed 21.04.2020.

Moya, Paula / Jonathan Leal: ENGL 76: After the Apocalypse: Speculative Fictional Narratives at the Turn of the 21st Century. Course description, Stanford University, https://english.stanford.edu/sites/english/files/courses/syllabus/after_the_apocalypse_1.27.17.pdf; last accessed 21.04.2020.

Amel Grami

Trapped: Women and Domestic Violence in »Corona Time«

The intersection of culture and law at the dawn of the twenty-first century is still visible in many societies. Across different cultures; traditions, customs, religion and discriminatory legislation prevent women from accessing their rights, including the right to choose a partner, to abortion, hold a job, inherit property, pass their nationality to their husbands and children and obtain divorce or child custody. Often referred to as family law or Code of Personnel Status, these laws have affected women's everyday lives negatively, contributed to discrimination and to the justification of all forms of violence against women and girls.

However, since the *Arab revolution* we have witnessed a great women's mobilization and an increased demand for a more egalitarian society. The battle of women's rights activists in some countries (Tunisia, Morocco, Lebanon etc.) is to change discriminatory family laws that allowed the naturalization and concealment of domestic violence, as well as impunity for perpetrators. It should be noted that the question of protection came to the forefront through women who began breaking the silence around the issue of family violence. Feminists are engaged in efforts to establish new laws not only to provide gender equality at all levels, but also to protect women and girls as well as children from all forms of violence.

Believing that laws are deeply connected to political processes, Tunisian feminists were key actors in the expansion of women's rights since the beginning of the transition period. They have used various strategies to advocate for the change in discriminatory laws. On April 23, 2014, Tunisia withdrew all of its specific reservations to the Convention on the Elimination all Forms of Discrimination Against Women (CEDAW). This decision is considered by women's organizations that have struggled for the adoption of the Convention a major achievement towards equality.

Considering that a synergy exists between the national and international context, and that the path to change is through law, Tunisian women's rights activists succeeded to mobilize civil society in favor of a new law aiming to end violence against women and to make pressure on the members of the parliament and political leaders. After a long and heated debate the Tunisia's parliament approved a landmark bill on 26 July 2017 seeking to eliminate all forms of violence against women. This first national legislation dealing with violence against women is based on a human rights approach and entered into force in February 2018.¹ However, women continue to experience high levels of violence and discrimination in their everyday life. Violence against women is still underreported to police and authorities due to shame, stigma, and fear of repercussions, among other reasons. Since the outbreak of the Covid-19 pandemic, violence against women in Tunisia has increased five-fold during the period of confinement that began in early March 2020.

1. Women Alone Facing Their Abusers under the ›State of Emergency‹

Governments have decreed a state of emergency, and have announced a set of measures to prevent the expansion of Covid-19. Many of these measures have reduced constitutionally established individual rights and imposed limitations whose legality may be questioned under the rule of law. All over the world, millions of people have been placed under lockdown. All of them are excepted to obey and respect the rule of law. But what is happening to vulnerable people such as women, girls, children, people with disabilities, LGBT community, and immigrants in the time of a pandemic?

After few weeks of placing people under lockdown, Anita Bhatia, the Deputy Executive Director of the United Nations declared that »while we absolutely support the need to follow these measures of social distancing and isolation, we also recognize that it provides an opportunity for abusers to unleash more violence«.² Many women are being forced to *lockdown* at home with their abusers; at the same time, services to support survivors of domestic violence are being disrupted or made inaccessible.

In Tunisia, between March 23 and May 27 a hotline set up by the Ministry of Women for domestic violence witnessed a hike in reported abuse of women growing. A number of women callers say that their abusers are using the Covid-19 virus as a scare tactic to threaten or isolate them from their family and friends. Some perpetrators are threatening to throw their victims out on the street if they decide to report that a family member is sick. Others are taking advantage of the situation to oppress their partners, wives, daughters or mothers. In many cases, women struggle to make a call or to seek help online because judicial, police, health services and particularly women's associations that are the first responders are un-

---

1   Organic law n°2017-58 of 11 August 2017. The adopted text is the culmination of numerous drafts and a years-long struggle by a few civil society associations.
2   Bhatia, Anita cited by Godin: As Cities around the World Go on Lockdown.

able to help; they are often overwhelmed or have shifted priorities. We should acknowledge that civil society groups are affected by lockdown or reallocation of resources. In this sense it is clear that Corona virus have trapped women in their homes with their abusers, isolated them from the world and the resources that could help them. Unfortunately, they have few opportunities to distance themselves from their abusers.

Gender based violence has in fact serious consequences, including loss of self-esteem and self-worth, the harm of physical, mental, and psychological health, and loss of productivity. It can also cause unwanted pregnancies and infections, and burdens the victims with health care, legal, and judicial costs. With movement restrictions in place, offline violence is increasing online in chat rooms, gaming platforms and other such spaces; but no one is paying attention to this issue because domestic violence remains in Tunisia a hidden consequence of the Covid-19 pandemic. For this reason activists believe that women are now doubly vulnerable; they are facing two dangerous viruses: Corona and violence.[3]

Focusing on women's stories, we can detect the emergence of a new category of abusers in time of pandemic. Some men change in fact their behavior in this time of trouble, risk, uncertainty, anxiety, chronic stress and fear. They abuse women and girls verbally, sexually or physically as a way of denying their feelings and inability to solve their problems and new challenges.

Traditionally, employment has meant that a man would be out of the home for most of the day. From a cultural perspective, the public sphere is associated with men and masculinity where they construct their power and identities. Men are excepted to behave in a certain way, within established social forms of behavior and conduct. On the opposite side, the private space is associated with women and children, femininity, passivity, and domesticity. The fact that men are obliged to *stay at home* is perceived as an act of *feminizing Men*.

On the one hand, asked to do some domestic tasks and responsibilities is considered as a daily challenge for men and an act of crossing gender binaries; it is understood as doing women's work. On the other hand, being *out of work* or unemployed is related to self-image and often seen as a sign of weakness. Once they lose their jobs, men position themselves in relation to established discourses of power gender relation and normative masculinity where dominance is acceptable and considered as an aspect of doing masculinity. In this sense, confinement is perceived by men who are unable to deal with the psychological, financial and social consequences of the crisis as an opportunity to exercise gender-power. Hence, the shared idea that men seek respect by all the members of the family may involve the use of violence. This reality reveals that forms of masculinity are constructed

---

[3] Cf. Bajec: ›Violence is a Virus‹.

in relation to specific contexts and locations; it confirms the link between economic stress and intra-familial violence.

Generally speaking, home is the place we can rest, relax, enjoy time with friends, learn, grow etc. It is a safe space but in time of confinement and panic it becomes for men a prison as well as a space for the re-production of aggressive forms of masculinity and male violence. Social norms and gender order nurture the beliefs of male superiority, the social and cultural inferiority of women, leading to the casual acceptance of violence. Researches on violence against women and girls show that the most dangerous space for woman is her home. For women survivors of violence, home is a place where they are most likely to be battered and sexually assaulted by men. In this case, the lockdown on women, their obligation to *stay at home and be safe* is unrealistic and problematic in itself as the risk of being murdered may be higher than that of dying from the corona virus.

According to some women, another significant aspect responsible for this surge in domestic abuse is domestic labor. Gendered roles the world over have placed domestic work on women's shoulders, which is socially and culturally often demarcated as women's work and considered as a female *duty* and *responsibility*. Under lockdown, the care work at home has increased with children out of school. In some cases, elder care has also increased, and people who are sick and in need of assistance are now at home. All these responsibilities have fallen on the shoulders of women who, in many cases, while performing their domestic and care work they are victims of mistreatment, verbal, physical or psychological abuses.

If we look at the issue of gender roles from a different angle, we can say that home is one of many ways where women's contributions remain invisible, undervalued and unrecognized. Moreover, the educational curriculum is far from being gender-sensitive; rather, it contributes to sustaining the stereotypical image of women as mothers and caregivers. Many testimonies in the context of the Covid-19 lockdown shows that women are mainly or solely responsible for all housework during pandemic time. If it is not divided equitably, domestic work under lockdown can be especially taxing because physical activity affects well-being conditions.

For a long time, and since the Ebola pandemic experience, women's rights activists drew attention to the increasing rate of acts of violence against women in time of crisis. Recently, they warn the authority that in times of crisis such as the Covid-19 outbreak, women and girls may be at higher risk of intimate partner violence and other different forms of violence caused by other members of the family. It is the result of a prolonged period of confinement, restrictions of mobility, and heightened stress and tensions in the household.

It should be noted that for a long time, historical and social norms have supported male authority, control over women, and tolerated violence. Patriarchal societies have always considered aggressions against women at home a private affair that concerns no one but the family; it is a cultural and religious heritage. In this sense, marital rape for example is understood as a *marital right*. Feminists have denounced this naturalization of domestic violence affirming *the private as political.*

Despite the existence of Tunisian law aiming to end violence against women, women and girls are without effective protection. Violence against women, and particularly domestic violence, represent a vicious cycle that keeps women subordinated and disempowered. Moreover, in Corona time, no one pays attention to the psychological impact on single mothers, unemployed women, and students without income, migrants, refugee women and LGBT communities.

Stories of some women show that *stay at home and care for yourself* is not a message for all women. Because there is no clear measure for the needs of domestic and sexual workers, among other female workers, they are forced to work and take care of their families. We should acknowledge that those women are excluded from policies and even civil society.

2. Gender Politics and the Limits of Legal Reformism

Amending laws to eradicate patriarchal biases and to end violence against women has been a common goal for women's movements at the international and national levels. However, can we consider that laws are a guarantee for gender equality and protection of women's life? For feminists, the high number of women victims of violence under the lockdown time proves that the Tunisian government's reluctance to acknowledge and address violence against women reveals its patriarchal nature as well as the limitations of existing laws.

The new wave of violence has generated concerns since the beginning of the crisis. The team of activists, lawyers, consultants, social workers, and researchers are taking the responsibility of responding to their communities' needs and are adopting a holistic approach to provide protection and support services. Some women's associations have decided to be at the forefront of this pandemic. Aware that the policy of isolation and confinement leads to increased levels of domestic, sexual and gender-based violence – and therefore to a heightened need of protection, women's organizations launched many campaigns to raise awareness. They used CEDAW Convention to hold the government accountable to its treaty obligations. Also, organizations launched a campaign to raise awareness about domestic violence during the Covid-19 pandemic and are trying to take care of victims, namely women and children.

The Ministry of women's affair has decided to provide specific protection for women and girls inside the family, such as provisions on restraining orders, reporting violence, securing accommodation and/or medical expenses for victims. House shelter is one of essential service providers to survivors in response to gender-based violence, which are currently being implemented under a pilot program by the Ministry of Women's Affairs and some women's organizations. These facilities provide a safe space for women survivors, offering essential services, including health and physical care, psychosocial support, and legal aids.

A group of scholars have developed an online campaign with students about domestic violence and particularly rape. They provide a number of articles analyzing the reasons of this wave of violence and address the resulting social stigma. In some towns, when a member contracts the virus, they are labeled, stereotype and chased away from communities because of fear of infection. Moreover, families and friends of identified patients may also be stigmatized by extension. Although the health authorities decided that the body should be buried without religious rites and affirm that there is no risk of infection, some people have refused burial of Covid-19 victims in their local cemeteries. We should mention that there was no coordination between health authorities and the ministry of religious affairs. On many occasions, religious leaders failed to demonstrate that Islamic burial conventions can adapt to the Covid-19 reality. In the absence of guidance and communication from the beginning of the crisis through local imams, the media, and community leaders, discriminatory attitudes, misconceptions and rumors have been expected.

Women activists highlight factors, which impact the law effective applicability. They demonstrate the need for change in the police and judicial responses to domestic violence cases under quarantine. As expected, the Supreme Court suspended the operation of the courts in all instances until further notice so there is no access to legal aid. Consequently, trials scheduled are by default adjourned, causing further delays in the system and hampering to a great extent access to and the administration of justice. For this reasons, women activists drew attention to the dangers of lockdown to women. They argue that national authority should not see the pandemic as a period of inactivity; on the contrary, the criminal justice system and branches of government should remain high on alert and sustain individual rights and specifically women's rights.

According to women's organizations, the police failed to respond to cases of violence, leading to the rape or death of victims and impunity of the aggressors. Despite many training programs, some police officers who are not convinced about women's rights took the decision to leave issues of violence against women as a *personal* or *family* matter even outside of pandemic contexts. By taking this decision, they become part of the problem. We can say that they fail to consider the fact that the law has been originally designed to respond to women's particular protection needs. Other police officers have been hesitant to enter homes and conduct thorough investigations out of risk of exposure to the Corona virus. As a result of the system's malfunctions, limited access to formal legal services women are discouraged from reporting incidents of violence.

Although Tunisia is considered a ›progressive‹ country in comparison with its neighbors, a reform of the Code of Personal Status is needed. The delegation of personal status to religious jurisprudence complicates in fact the establishment of protection mechanisms, and often legitimizes violence against women. Since men are the heads of families according to religion, women will remain at the bottom of this hierarchy. Consequently, this implies that discrimination is legalized and remains protected by law. Feminists and women's organizations argue that the notion that men should be at the head of the family unit, preserves the inferiority of women under the law construing women as a legal category in need of protection, thus penetrating the essence of patriarchal relations. Inspired by religious texts, this legal structure infantilize women, treating them as minors in decisions related to governing their own lives and places them as second-class citizens. Suad Joseph points that:

»[m]ost constitutions of Arab states identify the basic unit of society as the family. This suggests the masculinization of citizenship in Arab states is tied to a culturally specific notion of the citizen as subject. The Arab citizen subject is seen as a patriarch, the head of a patriarchal family, legally constituted as the basic unit of the political community who accrues rights and responsibilities concomitant with that legal status.«[4]

Tunisia has been always perceived as a secular state. However, since *the revolution* (2011) it has become common to hear statements such as *no more rights for women. Men should be asking for their rights* expressed by men through a joke or by commenting a new law or a reform; such sentiments were made public by some political leaders, parliament members or artists or journalists. We should keep in mind that during the parliamentary session on the recent family violence law, many members opposed the bill. Such discourses, regardless of the level of their seriousness, imply that Tunisian women are currently enjoying a life free of violence and discrimination and insinuate that gender equality has been really achieved in Tunisia and is a question of the past. Tunisian women are seen as a model for all women in Islamic societies. Those perceptions, reactions, discourses and behaviors reveal that issuing a new law in favor of women cannot be seen in isolation but must be considered within the cultural, social, political, and economic contexts.

---

[4] Joseph: Gender and Citizenship in the Arab World, p. 13.

Conclusion

It is obvious that the crisis caused by the corona virus pandemic has led to exceptional measures and consequences in many countries. The pandemic time reveals that law can be affected, or suspended. However, the state of alert or state of emergency shall in no case affect the rights to life, personal integrity and dignity. All protective services for women and girls must be classified as *essential* and priorities during any disaster. For this reason, it is important for national responses to include specific communications to the public that justice and the rule of law is not suspended during periods of confinement or lockdown.

Lessons learned from pandemic time clearly illustrate the need to have a gender responsive, inclusive, and intersectional approach. The strategies for the prevention of gender-based violence need to be integrated into operational plans of the justice and security sectors for the crisis. Domestic violence hotlines, safe spaces, sexual and reproductive health services, referral pathways, and justice mechanisms are necessary in pre-pandemic times and even more important during times of crisis. Because the state is ostensibly here to protect all citizens from violence in its various forms any neglect should be read as a form of violence. In addition, it is important to stress that women and local civil society who mobilize to address the impact of domestic violence under lockdown need the resources, recognition, and support of their government.

Women's mobilization and efforts to reform laws that are carried out in isolation from social, or cultural contexts will rarely achieve their objectives; therefore, effective strategies require a different approach that includes influencing public discourse, gaining allies from among different stakeholders, and building coalitions. Sensitizing mass media, artists and the public discourse on matters related to law, women's human rights, and the state's obligations is very important. Influencing politicians, decision-makers, judges, as well as ordinary citizens, will contribute to rupturing of patriarchal culture.

By engaging in a public debate while advocating for legislative change, women's movements will stimulate a socio-cultural transformation alongside legal reform. Family law reform requires in fact a multi-faceted struggle, promoting a culture of human rights as well as understanding law as culture and a mode of life. It is simple to say that after the Corona crisis we will return to normality, but what is it? The meaning of normal is gendered; for the majority of women the normal has never existed.

Indeed, change is dialectical, requiring revisiting theories and modifying strategies, tools and policies for change. The global pandemic offers us the opportunity to reflect on and rethink our gender relations, roles and rights; and to re-evaluate our priorities as society. It seems that the journey to fulfill women's ambitions in enjoying a life free of violence and discrimination and to achieve an egalitarian society remains a distant future dream.

References

Bajec, Alessandra: ›Violence Is a Virus‹: Tunisia Opens New Women's Shelter as Domestic Abuse Surges During Lockdown, 30.04.2020, https://english.alaraby.co.uk/english/indepth/2020/4/30/tunisia-opens-new-womens-shelter-as-lockdown-violence-surgest; last accessed 22.05.2020.

Godin, Mélissa: As Cities around the World Go on Lockdown, Victims of Domestic Violence Look for a Way Out, 18.03.2020, https://time.com/5803887/coronavirus-domestic-violence-victims/; last accessed 12.05.2020.

Joseph, Suad: Gender and Citizenship in the Arab World, in: al-raida, No. 129–130, 2010, pp. 8–18 ff.

Pierre Brunet

Nous sommes la raison du virus

Qu'on me pardonne ce truisme : cette pandémie a bouleversé nos vies et continuera de les bouleverser longtemps ; il y aura un avant et un après. Mais quel monde serons-nous capables de construire ? En serons-nous seulement capables d'en construire un ? Dans un entretien accordé au Guardian le 25 mars 2020, la directrice exécutive du Programme des Nations Unies pour l'environnement a eu cette formule aussi étonnante que retentissante : « avec la pandémie du coronavirus et les crises climatique en cours, la nature nous envoie un message ».[1] Loin de moi l'idée de contester qu'il y ait un message mais la formule soulève plusieurs questions : est-ce vraiment « la nature » qui nous l'envoie ? N'y a-t-il qu'un message ? Est-ce si récent ? Si la nature nous « envoie des messages », il me semble qu'elle le fait depuis bien longtemps et, mieux encore, que certains humains ont eux aussi – eux surtout ! – envoyé des messages et continuent de le faire depuis plus longtemps encore ! Or, qui les a écoutés ? Qui les écoute encore ? D'autres observateurs considèrent qu'avec le confinement auquel le monde entier a été soumis, la nature « a repris ses droits ». Là encore, la formule, en apparence banale, donne à réfléchir : la nature avait donc des droits et on les lui aurait pris ? Mais qui ? Quels droits ? Quoi que l'on pense de ces deux formules, qui font de la nature un sujet grammatical actif, elles traduisent bien l'ambivalence de notre rapport à cette entité que nous nommons « nature » : utilisée comme une ressource quasiment inépuisable et devant satisfaire nos besoins, il suffit d'une catastrophe pour qu'elle devienne une personne dont on devrait respecter les « droits ».

1. Back to the Future

Il paraît à peine utile de citer une énième fois le fameux rapport Meadows de 1972, *The Limits of Growth* (et initialement traduit en français « Halte à la croissance ? », ce qui n'était en rien le message de fond du rapport)[2] qui, modélisations à l'appui, avertissaient que nous entrions dans un monde dont les ressources

---

[1] Carrington : Coronavirus ; trad. par l'auteur.
[2] Mais le titre a été revu lors d'une réédition : Meadows/Meadows/Randers : Les limites à la croissance.

étaient loin d'être infinies et que nos modes de vie ne pourraient pas perdurer, qu'il n'étaient pas *soutenables* pour employer un terme voué à devenir récurrent. Ce rapport est, encore aujourd'hui, souvent instrumentalisé par deux camps opposés. Les uns avancent qu'il contiendrait des prédictions qui se seraient avérées fausses – dont notamment celles de l'épuisement des ressources en pétrole ou la fin du monde – et il a été souvent critiqué au motif que les ressources sont toujours là. Les autres s'en servent pour justifier la promotion de la décroissance (c'est notamment le cas des francophones qui peuvent exploiter le titre français au demeurant trompeur). Or, la fonction du rapport n'est nullement de préconiser la décroissance ni de prédire la fin du pétrole pour l'année 2000 mais que le maintien d'un objectif de croissance risque de provoquer une diminution brutale de la population et une dégradation significative des conditions de vie de la fraction de la population survivante.

Très critiqué donc, ce rapport – par la suite actualisé – a, comme l'a dit J.-M. Jancovici, « une valeur prédictive »indicative« bien supérieure à celle des modèles purement économiques ».[3] Une des grandes ambiguïtés vient de ce que le terme *ressources* est souvent entendu dans un sens statique très trompeur. Si par ressources on entend des stocks auxquels on accorde de la valeur à un moment donné, on pourrait croire que tant que ces stocks existent, il est erroné d'en annoncer la fin voire de parler de leurs limites. Mais c'est oublier un peu vite que les stocks eux-mêmes dépendent des moyens qu'on a de les connaître et mieux encore d'y accéder. Si l'on prend en compte ces deux derniers éléments, on comprend en effet que des limites existent toujours mais que le propre de l'espèce humaine est de les faire reculer : les humains ont cette intelligence qui les conduit à élaborer des techniques susceptibles de leur permettre d'exploiter tout ce qu'ils jugent exploitables, comme ils savent transformer certaines matières inertes en ressources énergétiques pour satisfaire leurs besoins. Le pétrole de schiste en est un parfait exemple. Du jour où la technique d'extraction par fracturation hydraulique a été rendue possible, l'exploitation a commencé, sans égard pour les dommages écologiques locaux et globaux qu'ils provoquent. Mieux, on a parfois fait comme si ces dommages n'existaient pas ou étaient seulement temporaires. Autrement dit, tant que nous n'avons pas atteints nos limites, nous raisonnons comme si elles n'existaient pas.

Un autre rapport, lui aussi ancien conserve toute son actualité. Je pense ici au rapport Brundtland, *Notre avenir à tous* qui, en 1987, écrivait : « Le développement soutenable, c'est autre chose qu'une simple croissance. Il faut en effet modifier le contenu même de cette croissance, faire en sorte qu'elle engloutisse moins de matières premières et d'énergie et que ses fruits soient répartis plus équitablement ».[4]

---

[3] Jancovici : Rapport du Club de Rome.
[4] World Comission on Environment and Development : Our Common Future, p. 47 ; trad. par l'auteur.

Le même rapport faisait figurer « l'intégration des considérations relatives à l'économie et à l'environnement dans la prise de décisions » au titre des impératifs stratégiques.

Il serait également inutile de faire état des nombreux rapports du GIEC, pas plus qu'il n'est besoin de citer les divers articles, rapports et ouvrages d'écologues faisant état d'une baisse spectaculaire et spectaculairement rapide de la biodiversité ou encore de ceux des spécialistes de ressources énergétiques ou d'agronomes qui tous plaident pour que les politiques économiques et d'investissements – et donc les États et les entreprises qui déterminent les modes de production et de consommation – tiennent enfin compte des limites de la planète. Dans une tribune au Monde, Ibrahim Thiaw, le Secrétaire exécutif de la Convention des Nations unies sur la lutte contre la désertification, affirme : « Les animaux qui nous ont infectés ne sont pas venus à nous ; nous sommes allés les chercher ».[5] Qui peut lui donner tort ? Certainement pas cette étude, publiée en octobre 2007, et consacrée à la crise du SRAS de 2002–2003 qui se concluait sur cet avertissement : « la présence d'un grand réservoir de virus de type Sars-CoV chez les chauves-souris en fer à cheval, ainsi que la culture de mammifères exotiques dans le sud de la Chine, est une bombe à retardement ».[6] Pourquoi une bombe ? Parce que, comme l'indique le début de cette même étude, la croissance économique rapide du sud de la Chine a conduit à une augmentation de la demande pour des protéines animales y compris celles des animaux exotiques telles que les civettes et que la détention à l'intérieur des « marchés frais » (wet markets) de nombreux animaux sauvages, qui plus est au sein de cages surpeuplées, ne peut que favoriser la transmission de nouveaux virus des animaux à l'homme. Or, treize ans plus tard, nous apprenons qu'un pangolin – ou peut-être un civette ? – a très probablement servi d'hôte à un virus provenant, là aussi selon toute probabilité, d'une chauve-souris. Comme cela a été plusieurs fois souligné, cette pandémie n'était pas seulement prévisible, elle était même prévue et la question n'était pas de savoir *si* elle allait avoir lieu mais *quand*.

2. Money, Money

Il n'en demeure pas moins que si les chauves-souris et les pangolins sont sans doute des causes objectives de propagation du virus à l'homme, ils n'en sont pas la raison. La raison pour laquelle les humains ont été contaminés tient uniquement au commerce dont les pangolins font l'objet et ce d'ailleurs en violation du droit

---

[5] Thiaw : Coronavirus.
[6] Cheng et al. : Severe Acute Respiratory Syndrome ; trad. par l'auteur.

positif car, comme on le sait, toutes les espèces de pangolin – aussi bien asiatiques qu'africaines – sont inscrites à l'annexe 1 de la Convention sur le commerce international des espèces de faune et de flore sauvages menacés d'extinction (CITES) et sont donc à ce titre totalement interdites à la vente. Pourtant, elles font toujours l'objet d'un trafic commercial international.

Or ce trafic est très loin d'être négligeable. On estime qu'il constitue le troisième trafic illégal mondial, derrière le trafic de drogue et le trafic d'armes et qu'il rapporte, selon les estimations elles-mêmes assez difficiles à établir, de 15 à 160 milliards d'euros par an. Mieux encore, en pleine pandémie, ce trafic continue : on apprend que 9,5 tonnes d'écailles de pangolins ont été saisies au Nigeria le 19 janvier 2020 ou encore que 6 tonnes d'écailles ont été saisies en Malaisie à Port Kelang le 31 mars 2020. Auparavant, 820 kilos d'écailles avaient été récupérés en Chine (dans la région autonome zhuang du Guangxi et dans la province de l'Anhui) le 9 mars dernier. Ajoutons que sur les marchés clandestins chinois, un kilo d'écailles est estimé à 8000 dollars. Enfin, selon une étude chinoise officielle citée par le Los Angeles Times, l'élevage d'animaux sauvages est une industrie de près de 70 milliards d'euros, qui emploie 14 millions de personnes en particulier dans les zones les plus pauvres de la Chine. Dans un État qui exerce un contrôle sur sa population comme probablement aucun autre dans le monde, et qui de surcroît, travaille sans relâche à accroître ce contrôle, on ne peut pas ne pas penser que l'administration contribue à encourager cette industrie, sans aucun égard pour les règlementations internationales.

Ainsi la bombe à retardement a explosé en décembre 2019, elle a eu pour effet de plonger le monde entier dans une situation inédite, porteuse de dégâts économiques et sociaux, mais aussi politiques, considérables et pour certains difficilement réversibles. Mais cette bombe n'a nullement mis fin au trafic des animaux et donc au risque de propagation d'autres virus.

3. Business as Usual ?

Sans un réel effort de la part des gouvernements du monde entier, d'autres bombes continueront d'exploser. Cela étant, les trafics d'animaux ne sont pas non plus les seuls responsables des risques de pandémie et de crise sanitaire qui pèsent sur nous. Comme l'écrivent les auteurs d'un article paru le 27 avril 2020 sur le site de l'IPBES (situé à Bonn) les »conditions parfaites« pour la propagation des maladies de la faune aux humains résultent certes de l'exploitation des espèces sauvages mais aussi de la déforestation effrénée, de l'expansion incontrôlée de l'agriculture, de l'élevage intensif, de l'exploitation minière et du développement des infrastructures. Ils ajoutent : « cela se produit souvent dans les zones où vivent les communautés les plus vulnérables aux maladies infectieuses. Nos actions ont eu un impact négatif sur plus des trois quarts de la surface terrestre, détruit plus de 85 % des zones humides et utilisent plus d'un tiers de la surface terrestre et près des trois quarts de nos réserves en eau douce pour l'agriculture et l'élevage ». En un mot : « Une seule espèce est responsable de la pandémie de Covid-19 : la nôtre ».[7]

On comprend ainsi que si nous ne parvenons pas à tirer les leçons de cette pandémie, tout peut recommencer *comme avant*. La seule conclusion raisonnable est de ne surtout pas revenir au monde d'hier ! Malheureusement, la façon dont certaines autorités publiques ont réagi à l'arrivée du virus laisse penser que le déni de réalité et la dissonance cognitive sont des pratiques courantes et des réflexes difficiles à maîtriser. Je n'ose ici évoquer le cas du gouvernement français qui a brillé par son retard à réagir et l'administration française en général qui, depuis 2011, n'a eu de cesse d'adopter des mesures restrictives en matière de dépenses sanitaires au point de faire fondre le stock de masques de protection et de rendre la France dépendante de la Chine en matière d'approvisionnement. Le résultat est qu'il a fallu au gouvernement mettre en place un pont aérien dans l'urgence, extrêmement coûteux en lui-même afin d'aller acheter des masques en Chine à un prix trois fois supérieur à celui que pratiquaient auparavant des entreprises françaises lesquelles ont, à partir de 2011, fermé leurs portes. L'ironie est que c'est un gouvernement libéral qui leur a enjoint de reprendre la production en pleine crise.

Or, lorsqu'on entend les gouvernements actuels assurer les compagnies aériennes, les constructeurs automobiles et les grandes entreprises agroalimentaires de leur aide substantielle et inconditionnée, ou certains chefs d'État promouvoir un allègement voire la suppression des normes environnementales et garantir de leur soutien les entreprises du secteur de l'énergie, ou considérer que la déforestation est bénéfique à la production économique, on se surprend à penser que nous sommes revenus très loin en arrière !

4. Des droits pour la nature ?

En opposition radicale avec ces choix, il semble devenu urgent de promouvoir et de souligner l'interdépendance entre la santé des êtres humains, des animaux, des plantes et les écosystèmes qui nous sont communs. En un mot, il s'agit de consacrer l'idée que nous formons un seul monde et que l'espèce humaine doit cesser de se croire libre d'en disposer comme elle l'entend. Et si, dès lors, on se mettait à penser des droits non pas seulement pour les humains mais aussi pour les non

---

[7] Settele et al. : COVID-19 Stimulus Measures ; trad. par l'auteur.

humains – ce que l'on continue d'appeler « la nature » comme si elle existait en dehors de nous ?

On entend d'ici l'objection immédiate : ces droits seraient-ils dès lors naturels ? Reviendrions nous à des croyances d'un autre âge ? Il existe certes des juristes, des philosophes et des théologiens pour promouvoir l'idée d'une *Earth Jurisprudence*. C'est là une conception du droit explicitement jusnaturaliste, d'inspiration thomiste, selon laquelle on doit distinguer deux types de droit, hiérarchiquement organisés et reliés l'un à l'autre : au-dessus du droit positif humain, il existerait un *Great Law* qui se réfère au principe de la communauté biotique.

Pourtant, on peut aussi penser des droits de la nature qui ne seraient nullement au-dessus du droit positif et qui ne consisteraient pas non plus en principes moraux extérieurs au droit positif. Ces droits permettraient à des gardiens de plaider la cause des entités naturelles devant un juge – comme le proposait Christopher Stone en 1972 dans son article fondateur.[8] Cette proposition ne faisait aucune référence au droit naturel : Stone proposait de penser un cadre opératoire dans lequel des objet naturels pourraient plaider et obtenir réparation de leur propre préjudice en tant que bénéficiaires directs des décisions rendues. On sait que cette idée a connu des consécrations récentes et des succès mitigés en Equateur, Bolivie et plus récemment en Nouvelle-Zélande, en Colombie, en Inde etc. Le code civil français a introduit la réparation du « préjudice écologique ». Mais consacrés au plan constitutionnel, ces droits pourraient également limiter l'action du législateur et le contraindre à intégrer « des considérations relatives à l'économie et à l'environnement dans la prise de décisions » comme le recommandait le rapport Brundtland.[9]

Cette crise est notre fait car nous ne parvenons pas à prendre au sérieux la limitation des ressources et notre fragilité et continuons de penser pouvoir disposer du monde animal, végétal et terrestre comme autant de biens susceptibles d'être commercialisés et consommés. Ce sont les limites de notre liberté qu'il nous faut arriver non seulement à penser mais à poser. Cela suppose une profonde remise en cause mais ce n'est pas non plus la porte ouverte à toute forme d'irrationalisme. *Déclarer* des droits de la nature ne consiste pas à abaisser l'humain ou à *en finir avec l'humanisme*. Ou plutôt, il s'agit en effet d'en finir avec un humanisme anthropocentré qui s'exonère de toute responsabilité dans les maux qui affectent l'humanité en confondant les causes et les raisons : une chauve-souris et un pangolin sont en toute hypothèse les causes biologiques de la pandémie, ils n'en sont certainement pas la raison socio-économique. Attribuer des droits à la nature, peut être le moyen de nous contraindre à limiter notre liberté ou ce que nous prenons pour notre souveraineté – mais le mot ici n'a aucune signification juridique, il désigne plutôt l'affranchissement de toute contrainte et cette position de « maître et

---

[8] Stone : Should Trees Have Standing.
[9] World Comission on Environment and Development : Our Common Future ; trad. par l'auteur.

possesseur de la nature ». En définitive, les droits de la nature pourraient servir de concrétisation à un principe d'éco-proportionnalité que propose par exemple Gerd Winter et qui impose de mettre en balance l'exploitation de la nature (et des animaux) et sa protection en recherchant ainsi la soutenabilité de l'entreprise projetée. [10] Ce qui ne consiste pas encore en un préservationnisme qui aspirerait à laisser la nature « intacte ».

En dépit de ce que notre propre anthropomorphisme nous fait parfois penser, ce n'est pas la nature qui nous envoie des messages mais nous et nous seuls qui pouvons lui éviter de se mettre à brûler des forêts, à noyer des côtes, ou à souffler des terres habitées. Il ne suffit malheureusement pas de réclamer un droit à un environnement sain pour les humains, encore faut-il que les humains puissent se rappeler – et qu'on leur rappelle – qu'il ne sont pas seuls à avoir une *valeur intrinsèque*.

Ainsi, c'est précisément ce *renversement de la charge de la preuve* que la reconnaissance de la valeur intrinsèque de l'environnement peut apporter. Et avec elle, espère-t-on, un changement dans les modes de représentation mentale de la nature qui cesse d'être pensée comme un instrument. Bien évidemment, on ne peut pas exclure que la plupart des individus restent indifférents à ce changement de perception et s'en tiennent à une conception anthropocentrique reconnaissant une valeur instrumentale à la nature. Paradoxalement, c'est en s'appuyant sur un argument utilitariste et sur cette éthique anthropocentrique que l'on peut parvenir à convaincre les plus réticents d'adopter une éthique écocentrique : car s'il est vrai qu'à force d'utiliser et de modifier la nature comme ils le font, les humains risquent de disparaître, c'est finalement dans leur intérêt de lui reconnaître une valeur en elle-même.

Références

Carrington, Damian : Coronavirus: ›Nature is sending us a message‹, says UN environment chief, in : The Guardian, 25.03.2020, https://www.theguardian.com/world/2020/mar/25/coronavirus-nature-is-sending-us-a-message-says-un-environment-chief ; dernier accès 23.06.2020.

Cheng, Vincent C. C. / Susanna K. P. Lau / Patrick C. Y. Woo / Kwok Yung Yuen : Severe Acute Respiratory Syndrome Coronavirus as an Agent of Emerging and Reemerging Infection, in : Clinical Microbiology Reviews, 20(4), 2007, p. 660–694.

Jancovici, Jean-Marc : Rapport du Club de Rome – Donella Meadows, Dennis Meadows, Jørgen Randers et William W. Behrens III – 1972, https://janco

---

[10] Winter : Ecological Proportionality.

vici.com/recension-de-lectures/societes/rapport-du-club-de-rome-the-limits-of-growth-1972/; dernier accès 25.06.2020.

Meadows, Dennis / Donella Meadows / Jorgen Randers : Les limites à la croissance (dans un monde fini) : Le rapport Meadows, 30 ans après, Paris 2017.

Settele, Josef / Sandra Díaz / Eduardo Brondizio / Peter Daszak : COVID-19 Stimulus Measures Must Save Lives, Protect Livelihoods, and Safeguard Nature to Reduce the Risk of Future Pandemics, 27.04.2020, https://ipbes.net/covid19 stimulus; dernier accès 17.06.2020.

Stone, Christopher D.: Should Trees Have Standing – Toward Legal Rights for Natural Objects, in : Southern California Law Review 45, 1972, pp. 450–501.

Thiaw, Ibrahim : Coronavirus : « Les animaux qui nous ont infectés ne sont pas venus à nous ; nous sommes allés les chercher », in: Le Monde, 29.03.2020, https://www.lemonde.fr/idees/article/2020/03/29/coronavirus-la-pandemie-demande-que-nous-re-definissions-un-contrat-naturel-et-social-entre-l-homme-et-la-nature_6034804_3232.html; dernier accès 25.06.2020.

Winter, Gerd : Ecological Proportionality. An Emerging Principle of Law for Nature?, in : Christina Voigt (ed.) : A Rule of Law for Nature. New Dimensions and Ideas in Environmental Law, Cambridge, 2013, pp. 111–129.

World Comission on Environment and Development : Our Common Future, Oxford 1987.

Yousra Abourabi

A Global Warning on the Global Warming? The Effects of the Corona Crisis on the Perception of Environmental Norms

The Corona crisis had an immediate impact on the climate. As early as January 2020, there was a significant drop in air pollution in the Wuhan region of China, linked to the drop in human activity. After one month, between mid-February and mid-March, the rate of greenhouse gas emissions had already fallen by 25 %.[1] This first observation reinforced the anthropocenic thesis,[2] which postulates that humans are at the origin of the world's climate change. Although this thesis now seems to be widely accepted, it is nevertheless rejected by the climate sceptics – including the American President Donald Trump. Moreover, the recognition of human responsibility for the destruction of our environment does not act as a constraining factor for individuals in formulating a strong environmental response. Thus, part of international society, in the industrialized countries, is not ready to change its consumption habits, while the political class imperfectly juggles between the interests of citizens and those of multinational firms, without managing to put pressure on the latter. In the countries of the global South, the right to economic development and the responsibility of the industrialized states are claimed first and foremost, on the basis that these issues are incompatible with local environmental responsibility, despite the fact that several studies have now shown that sustainable development is largely based on the local valorization of the environment.[3]

The Covid crisis seems to have breathed new life into this debate, in a context of crisis in climate governance since the implementation failure of the Paris Agreement. Throughout the world, the lockdown imposed by the States has produced the same atmospheric effects as in Wuhan province. According to a study, CO_2 emissions declined by an average of 17 % every day during the global lockdown.[4] In the space of one spring season, nature has taken back its rights, and we have

---

[1] Carbon Brief: Analysis: Coronavirus Temporarily Reduced China's CO_2 Emissions by a Quarter.
[2] Cf. Bonneuil / Fressoz: L'événement anthropocène.
[3] Cf. Brunel: Le développement durable.
[4] Cf. Le Quéré et al.: Temporary Reduction in Daily Global CO_2 Emissions during the COVID-19.

been able to observe, with the naked eye – or with the naked ear – the return or the proliferation of several animal species near our homes.

Searching for the origins of the health crisis, biologists have also been able to identify an indirect correlation between the destruction of the natural habitat of the Pangolin and the emergence of the virus. The virus was first contracted in a wildlife market in Wuhan, where endangered species could be purchased. This event reopened the debate on viruses which, in the past, have also been created partly by a combination of environmental factors. All these studies have reminded us that »the human has forgotten his biological reality in favor of his technological superiority«.[5] They have also reinforced the emerging field of study on the ecology of health.

At the same time, confinement has imposed immobility, absolute silence, and a slowing down of activities, which has plunged many individuals into introspection leading to a redefinition of oneself and one's priorities. For some, time has lengthened, giving them the opportunity to take a moment to observe an insect, listen to a bird, or become aware of the freshness of the air they breathe. Time that some had lost in the era of careerism, industrialist productivism and, for some women, double work at home and at work. The relationship to work has been politically questioned: do we really need to travel for this or that activity? The question will be asked twice before a decision is taken. Obviously, this trend does not concern everyone, because a large part of international society, and not only the most precarious, has also been negatively affected by the lockdown, with sometimes radical consequences on mental health and domestic violence. Notwithstanding these disparities, the vulnerability of human life has been reconsidered by everyone in the context of fear fed daily by the media, which has had the effect of boosting individual practices of ›well-being‹ through attention to the physical body and solidarity as a means of strengthening self-esteem, at least for the wealthiest.

These two factors combined – the effects of Covid on the environment[6] and on psychologies[7] – are the subject of many studies, still in progress. Taken separately, they tend to show a greater involvement of State and non-State actors in the reduction of greenhouse gas emissions on the one hand, and a collective and global awareness of the value of the environment for individual and collective well-being on the other. Taken together, these two fields of study suggest the existence of a close correlation between social norms and legal norms in the field of the environment. This is what we will question in this article.

---

[5] »L'homme a oublié sa réalité biologique au profit de sa supériorité technologique«, in: Legendre: The Environment and Health, p. 291; transl. by the author.
[6] Cf. Rosenbloom/Markard: A COVID-19 Recovery for Climate.
[7] Cf. Sood: Psychological Effects of the Coronavirus Disease-2019 Pandemic.

1. The Return of Studies on the Zoonotic Origin of Infectious Diseases

Many infectious diseases are favored by the imbalance of ecosystems. For example, warmer winters mean longer periods of influenza, declining biodiversity and cleaner cities accelerate the spread of disease-carrying mosquitoes, while the loss of wildlife habitat can lead to the mutation of new forms of viruses. In general, as François-Xavier Weill of the Pasteur Institute notes, »it is clear that climate, by modifying human behavior, influences epidemics.«[8] Beyond climate, the impact of environmental destruction on health is no longer in doubt, as suggested by the attention paid to this correlation by the UN.

This new representation is the result of the scientific discoveries of the last century, after several scientists had been working, without success, on the identification of environmental factors of anthropocenic origin. In the 1990s, Rita Colwell defended the thesis of an »environmental origin« of cholera.[9] In the case of HIV AIDS, leads have long converged on transmission from chimpanzees (with the simian immunodeficiency virus SIV) to humans, combined with poor medical practice. However, it was not until 2014 that a large international study confirmed this hypothesis by identifying the causes of the first contaminations in the Congo Basin in the 1920s.[10] Similarly, it is now known that malaria is on the increase due to the degradation of tropical forests (logging, intensive agriculture, urbanization) and could be avoided through sustainable forest management.[11] The last infectious epidemic to date, that of Ebola, is due to contact with bats,[12] itself linked to the hunting of other infected wild animals and objects of trade such as bush meat.

Thus, epidemiological studies, which consist of observing human living conditions, have gradually shown that environmental factors can have direct effects (such as pollution peaks on chronic diseases) or indirect effects (such as land use changes and overexploitation of wild species on viruses). In the field of infectious diseases, zoonosis has been widely recognized. Already in 2001, a British study showed that 75 % of infectious diseases had a zoonotic origin.[13] Often several species are involved.[14]

In the same vein, Chinese researchers at the South China University of Agriculture[15] had identified, as early as September 2019, the Malaysian pangolin (a small

---

8   Rosier: Les relations complexes entre climat et maladies infectieuses.
9   Cf. Colwell: Global Climate and Infectious Disease: The Cholera Paradigm.
10 Cf. Faria et al.: The Early Spread and Epidemic Ignition of HIV-1 in Human Populations.
11 Cf. Dab: Health and Environment.
12 Cf. Marí Saéz et al.: Investigating the Zoonotic Origin of the West African Ebola Epidemic.
13 Cf. Taylor/Latham/Woolhouse: Risk Factors for Human Disease Emergence.
14 Cf. Rigaud/Perrot-Minnot/Brown: Parasite and Host Assemblages.
15 Cf. Liu/Chen/Chen: Viral Metagenomics Revealed Sendai Virus and Coronavirus Infection of Malayan Pangolins (Manis Javanica).

mammal classified as critically endangered, in particular because of poaching[16]) as a »possible intermediate host« that allowed the coronavirus to mutate and be transmitted from bats to humans. While the research community had some reservations about this hypothesis at the beginning of the crisis[17], pending more solid evidence, they nevertheless agree on the validity of an animal origin for the virus. Moreover, another study by Chinese researchers published in the journal Environmental Health in 2003 showed that the risk of SARS-CoV lethality in people breathing polluted air was 84 % higher than in people breathing relatively unpolluted air.[18] More recently, a group of 12 Italian researchers have hypothosized that the microparticles present in polluted air act as a carrier of the virus because they aggregate and remain in suspension for several hours.[19]

The link between health and the environment remains difficult to measure, however, as the latter is in most cases an indirect cause that requires not only in-depth research, but also strong advocacy in the face of powerful and well-armed communities of actors. Most of the lawsuits brought by individuals or associations against the use of toxic products in food, furniture or textiles for health reasons have failed. As for lawsuits for harm to endangered animals, they pose the problem of identifying the responsible actors. There is therefore not enough case law in environmental law, even in the most advanced countries in this field. This shortcoming is also due to the societal norms. A parallel can be drawn here with women's rights. In Morocco, for example, almost fifteen years after the reform of the Family Code, gender equality is struggling to make progress for three fundamental structural reasons. The first is the population's lack of information on its rights, due to a lack of state education and self-education. The second is the lack of awareness of what constitutes gender bias and its lack of political prioritization. The third lies in a defeatist representation of the outcome of a complaint or a trial because the authorities (police, judge) could consciously or unconsciously favor masculinist interests. In the field of the environment, these three reasons seem applicable: individuals are generally not informed or do not know enough about the impact of environmental degradation on health; consequently, our awareness of what constitutes an environmental health problem and its importance in relation to other political priorities is still low; finally, when this problem is identified, the chances of winning a lawsuit can be discouraging due to the lack of jurisprudence on the subject and the resistance of destructive actors. These three factors are interdependent.

---

[16] Cf. Le Monde: Le commerce illicite des pangolins est toujours en hausse.
[17] Morin: Coronavirus: le pangolin a-t-il pu servir d'hôte intermédiaire?
[18] Cf. Cui et al.: Air Pollution and Case Fatality of SARS in the People's Republic of China.
[19] SIMA: Relazione circa l'effetto dell'inquinamento da particolato atmosferico e la diffusione di virus nella popolazione.

Thus, health remains the main area that acts as a factor in confirming the place of the precautionary principle in environmental law,[20] while paradoxically being the area where the determinants are the most difficult to grasp.

2. The Normative Effects of a Large-Scale Immobility Experiment on Environmental Consciousness

The Covid-19 crisis has perhaps, more than other previous epidemics of zoonotic origin, reinforced global environmental awareness. The extent of the immobilization and distancing measures associated with the prevention of the Coronavirus pandemic will have escaped no one's notice. Mediatized throughout the world, those measures will have allowed the most reluctant to know that someone, on the other side of the world, is going through the same difficulties.[21] For many, this collective experience has certainly increased the sense of interdependence between citizens of different backgrounds and seems to have increased awareness of transnational links and the ›butterfly effect‹. This assumption can be partly verified by the increasing number of journalistic or academic publications devoted to this theme during the period of confinement,[22] in a more general context where the subject had already acquired more legitimacy in the field of Western, but also global, political ideas. Indeed, the recent tsunamis, hurricanes and heatwaves, simultaneously affecting several societies in different sectors, have served as reminders of the vulnerability of economic and health systems. The Covid crisis is part of this series of »total crises« defined by William Dab as a combination of »the physical factors of the environment, the organizational factors of the health care system, the social and economic factors, and a diplomatic dimension«.[23] On the other hand, it stands out because of its unprecedented impact on people's lifestyles.

Let's take the example of self-education. With containment, we witnessed to the explosion of distance learning as well as the multiplication of educational shows on television (in Morocco for example, the Marocopedia company has been hired by national television to set up a morning educational show for children). In addition, many publishers have offered their readers free digital access to some

---

[20] Cf. Legendre: The Environment and Health.
[21] Thelwall/Thelwall: Retweeting for COVID-19.
[22] Cf. Bonilla-Aldana/Dhama/Rodriguez-Morales: Revisiting the One Health Approach in the Context of COVID-19; Higgins-Desbiolles: Socialising tourism for social and ecological justice after COVID-19; and Klemeš et al.: Minimising the Present and Future Plastic Waste, Energy and Environmental Footprints Related to COVID-19.
[23] »On peut parler ici de ›crises totales‹. Elles conjuguent les facteurs physiques de l'environnement, les facteurs organisationnels du système de soins, les facteurs sociaux et économiques, une dimension diplomatique«, in: Dab: Health and Environment, p. 58; transl. by the author.

of their publications. At the same time, the reading of news, whether related to Coronavirus or related topics, also seemed to occupy an important part of people's daily activity, in a context where digital activism, especially in the field of ecology, is growing.[24] In addition, the decline in outdoor activities was also an opportunity for some to immerse themselves in pleasure reading. These factors combined suggest an increase in reading time. Although there is no overall statistical study yet to support our hypothesis, we can observe that eBook and E-pub sales platforms have announced an explosion, never seen before, in sales.[25]

In this context, Internet users have been more exposed to publications on environmental topics, which also increased. This can be observed thanks to new technologies for identifying hot topics among scientific or media publications. A first keyword search of the terms »Coronavirus and Climate Change« on Google gives almost 5 million results. The same result is obtained with the terms »Covid and Climate Change«. On Wikipedia, a page dedicated to the environmental impact of the pandemic[26] has already been filled in. In many academic and journalistic journals, the analysis of the link between the virus and global warming is dealt with daily. This trend is reinforced by the fact that many research teams have also taken advantage of lockdown as an opportunity to include citizens in nature observation experiments. In France, for example, the French League for the Protection of Birds has launched a large-scale observation experiment involving citizens volunteering to count the birds that live near their homes.[27] Other similar experiments have been carried out in other countries with other types of animals in different countries.

As a recent study shows, public opinion on environmental protection seems to be largely influenced by the amount of media coverage on this topic.[28] It can therefore be assumed that the more individuals are exposed to environmental information, the more they would develop an »environmental conscience«. However, if, as Edgar Morin said, »awareness is the fruit of evolution«,[29] the factors on which this evolution depends are controversial. For idealists like Hegel, it lies in the progress of ideas and science. For materialists like Marx, it depends above all

---

[24] Notaras: The Rise of Online Climate Activists.
[25] This is the case, for example, of the French-language Vivlio platform, which grew by 88 % from the first month of confinement. The same trend is observed in the English-speaking area, where reseller sites increased sales by 130 %. Cf. Infodujour: La lecture par temps de confinement; Robertson: How Reader Behavior Is Changing During the COVID-19 Crisis.
[26] Wikipedia: Impact of the COVID-19 Pandemic on the Environment.
[27] Solé: Biodiversité.
[28] Cf. Antilla: Self-Censorship and Science.
[29] Edgar Morin at the Budapest Club, Integral University Day: »How to respond in a positive, sustainable and integral way to the contemporary systemic crisis in its economic, social and ecological dimensions?«, 10 March 2009, quoted in Dartiguepeyrou: Where Are We in Terms of Our Ecological Awareness?, p. 17.

on the relations of production and the technical world. How then can we determine whether we are witnessing an »evolution« of consciousness towards a better consideration of the environment?

The oil crisis linked to the Covid crisis offers us a convincing field of reflection to try to answer the question because it puts into narrative both the productivist balance of power and the progress of science towards renewable energy. It should be remembered that oil crises have always raised awareness of the vulnerability of carbon economies and led to a questioning of production methods. The Corona-related oil crisis is not exempt from this trend. As early as March, the price of a barrel of oil in the United States fell below $0 (down to −37 $) for the first time in history, mainly due to the drop in global energy consumption combined with the reduction in storage capacity. The drop in oil prices could be seen as an incentive for more consumption. In reality, this drop has not had a significant impact on the price at the pump for consumers. In fact, from the beginning of the crisis, many producing countries such as Saudi Arabia and Kuwait have been committed to reducing production in order to recover prices. Thus, for many observers, this fall rather heralds a weakening of investments in this sector, even after an economic recovery. According to an IAEA report published in May 2020, the future decline in energy investment is expected in all sectors but will affect oil in the vast majority of cases.[30] Moreover, the zoonotic origin of the virus and the decrease in air pollution during containment are not the only factors affecting global environmental awareness. Experimentation with new forms of productive organization, in particular through teleworking, is a major argument in the debate on polluting transport. Nevertheless, here again, telework and the projected transition to »all-digital« poses many problems in terms of social disruption, work de-skilling, and also the energy and environmental costs associated with digital transition.

All this effervescence is thus visible in the attention paid to the environment in election campaigns and among decision-makers in various countries. According to studies conducted by the Pew Research Center, American interest in climate change has never been higher than in 2020.[31] It is highly likely that the environment will be an important issue in the next US elections. In France, President Macron declared in May that the »Green Deal should not be questioned but accelerated«. In China, although profound ecological reforms have been undertaken since well before Covid – China is aiming for a total ban on non-electric cars in 2030 – its environmental diplomacy has been resolutely strengthened recently. In Germany, Angela Merkel plans a »green recovery after the Coronavirus crisis«.[32] In South Korea, the Democratic Party is taking advantage of the crisis to

---

[30] Cf. IEA: World Energy Investment 2020 – Analysis.
[31] Cf. Kennedy: U.S. Concern about Climate Change Is Rising, but Mainly among Democrats.
[32] Cf. Nienaber/Wacket: Germany's Merkel Wants Green Recovery from Coronavirus Crisis.

announce, as early as March 2020, the launch of a ›Green New Deal‹ as the spearhead of the electoral campaign.[33] This party has justly won the elections. In addition, international organizations such as the OECD plead for a green recovery.[34] The most ambitious plan at this stage is certainly the European economic recovery plan, which projects a »green transition«. Finally, the Secretary General of the UN also recalled that climate change is a much greater threat than the Coronavirus.[35]

In developing countries, public debate on this issue is more timid. While some countries such as Malaysia are slowly considering a green economic recovery plan, others are not even asking the question. Nevertheless, in general, new development aid is encouraging the prioritization of renewable energies. Moreover, in the face of international pressure, many countries of the South will try to capitalize on their pre-crisis efforts to initiate new environmental policies through green financing. This may be the case of Morocco, which was already approaching 30 % renewable energies in its energy mix before the crisis, but which does not have a strong environmental policy in other sectors. In fact, we note that the environment, although very heterogeneous, is considered in the Post-Covid Recovery Commitment Plans of member states of the World Bank. The question that now arises is how these commitments should be reflected in the legislative field?

3. From Redefining Policy Priorities to Changing Environmental Standards

As Corinne Lepage rightly points out, when it comes to the environment, we must »change the imagination so that people will want to act«.[36] As Serge Morand notes, »The emergence of the AIDS virus, SARS (Severe Acute Respiratory Syndrome), avian flu (H5N7), swine flu (H1N1), West Nile virus and the recent outbreak of the Ebola virus in West Africa remind us that infectious diseases, while still posing a global health risk, speak to our imaginations«.[37] It would therefore seem that the current climate is a good vector for an imagination change and conducive to a

---

[33] Cf. Farand: South Korea to Implement Green New Deal after Ruling Party Election Win.
[34] Cf. OECD: Tackling the Coronavirus (COVID-19).
[35] Cf. BBC: Climate Change: World Mustn't forget ›Deeper Emergency‹.
[36] »Changer l'imaginaire pour que les gens aient envie d'agir«, in: Pineau/Lepage/Latour: Nous assistons à une revolution du droit international, p. 76; transl. by the author.
[37] »Les émergences des virus du sida, du SRAS (syndrome respiratoire aigu sévère), de la grippe aviaire (H5N7), de la grippe porcine (H1N1), du virus du Nil occidental (West Nile virus) et celle récente du virus Ébola en Afrique de l'Ouest nous rappellent que les maladies infectieuses, tout en présentant toujours un risque global pour la santé mondiale, parlent à nos imaginaires«, in: Morand: Biogéographie et écologie de l'émergence, p. 14; transl. by the author.

transition of consciousness, or even a »legal revolution«[38] in environmental matters. A certain number of recent events tend to support this idea.

Let's take China as an example. As early as January 2020, wildlife trafficking had been temporarily banned. Today, this ban is the subject of an article of law debated in parliament and has a good chance of passing. In order to preserve the culture of traditional medicine based on the use of wild animals, legislators have proposed laws obliging producers to use synthetic alternative ingredients.[39] More generally, the Chinese government has announced increased monitoring of air and water quality,[40] while the police have stepped up the fight against wildlife trafficking.[41] In comparison, this type of response had been weak following the outbreak of Ebola in West African countries.

This legislative trend can be observed in many other countries. In France, a collective of 100 lawyers launched a call during the containment period to strengthen environmental law.[42] In Europe, the debate on carbon tax at the borders has been relaunched. In the United States, Democrats in the House of Representatives are introducing a bill that would set new environmental standards for public transport. However, most of the bills are more focused on the fossil fuel and chemical sector. As regards the protection of forests against deforestation and poaching, the ecological transition seems more difficult. On the one hand, the problem lies in the difference, posed by German-Latin law, between the interest to act and the standing to act: who can or must defend a tree or an animal? On the other hand, this effervescence is limited by a counter-current, which we could describe as de-environmentalist, and which consists in the response or resistance to the advancement of environmental protection standards. This can be illustrated by the decision of the US Environmental Protection Agency (EPA) to suspend several environmental laws on March 26, 2020, or by the persistence of illegal trafficking in raw materials and wildlife facilitated by the complacency of local authorities in several countries around the world.

In both cases, the evolution of environmental legal standards is already a major issue within national and international political regimes. The epistemic communities that directly or indirectly support the actors in the negotiations are all the more armed by the immediate need to revive (or review) the economy and by the longer-term importance of protecting the health security of individuals. We will

---

[38] »Révolution légale«, in: Pineau/Lepage/Latour: Nous assistons à une revolution du droit international, p. 78.

[39] Cf. CNBC: China Legislators Take on Wildlife Trade, but Traditional Medicine Likely to Be Exempt.

[40] French.xinhuanet.com: (COVID-19) La Chine renforce la surveillance de l'environnement dans le contexte de l'épidémie.

[41] French.xinhuanet.com: La police chinoise renforce la lutte contre la criminalité liée aux animaux sauvages.

[42] Liberation.fr: Exigeons un droit à la hauteur de l'urgence climatique et environnementale.

undeniably witness a debate of ideas and concepts within this trend towards transition that seems irreversible, even for the polluting actors. The debate will focus both on the economic model to be favored in the context of the green transition and on its universal character in a context of North-South inequalities.

4. Conclusion

The Coronavirus crisis has resulted in large-scale lockdown, which made it possible to observe the effects of human activity on the degradation of the ecosystem (air pollution and destruction of wildlife habitats) and at the same time provided an opportunity for individuals to be exposed for longer periods to environmental information, including the zoonotic origin of pandemic viruses. These factors taken together seem to have sharpened transnational environmental awareness, so that the debate on this issue has become more lively both with regard to economic recovery plans and longer-term national policy orientations. The transition to more ecological development models still faces many obstacles (lack of information, lack of awareness, resistance from polluting actors). Nevertheless, the environmental bills and normative changes implied by the crisis are likely to become an important political and electoral issue in several countries.

In fact, the Covid crisis accompanies the transition of the field of health studies from a purely hygienic to a more environmentalist vision, and from a local to a global approach. In concrete terms, this would amount to treating the Coronavirus by requiring those around them to wash their hands regularly, but also by combating the environmental factors that cause its transmission in a faraway country. The concept of environmental health (or EcoHealth, according to the concept used by WHO) is gradually embracing the new emerging concept of »global health«.[43] Thus, to varying degrees, and depending on the country, the slow transition towards the greening of legal systems seems to be encouraged by the political effects of the Coronavirus crisis, suggesting on the one hand that there is indeed a transnational trend, and on the other a close correlation between the evolution of societal norms and that of legal norms.

---

[43] Bonilla-Aldana/Dhama/Rodriguez-Morales: Revisiting the One Health Approach in the Context of COVID-19.

References

Antilla, Liisa: Self-Censorship and Science: A Geographical Review of Media Coverage of Climate Tipping Points, in: Public Understanding of Science, 16.09.2008, https://doi.org/10.1177/0963662508094099; last accessed 26.06.2020.

British Broadcasting Corporation (BBC): Climate Change: World Mustn't Forget ›Deeper Emergency‹, in: BBC News, 22.04.2020, https://www.bbc.com/news/science-environment-52370221; last accessed 19.06.2020.

Bonilla-Aldana, D. Katterine / Kuldeep Dhama / Alfonso J. Rodriguez-Morales: Revisiting the One Health Approach in the Context of COVID-19: A Look into the Ecology of This Emerging Disease, in: Advances in Animal and Veterinary Sciences 8(3), 2020.

Bonneuil, Christophe / Jean-Baptiste Fressoz: L'Événement Anthropocène. La Terre, l'histoire et nous, Paris 2016.

Brunel, Sylvie: Le développement durable, Paris 2012.

Carbon Brief: Analysis: Coronavirus Temporarily Reduced China's CO_2 Emissions by a Quarter, 19.02.2020, https://www.carbonbrief.org/analysis-coronavirus-has-temporarily-reduced-chinas-co2-emissions-by-a-quarter; last accessed 23.06.2020.

Consumer News and Business Channel (CNBC): China Legislators Take on Wildlife Trade, but Traditional Medicine Likely to Be Exempt, 20.05.2020, https://www.cnbc.com/2020/05/21/china-legislators-tackle-wildlife-trade-traditional-medicine-likely-exempt.html; last accessed 19.06.2020.

Colwell, Rita R.: Global Climate and Infectious Disease: The Cholera Paradigm, in: Science 274(5295), 1996, pp. 2025–31.

Cui, Yan / Zuo-Feng Zhang / John Froines / Jinkou Zhao / Hua Wang / Shun-Zhang Yu / Roger Detels: Air Pollution and Case Fatality of SARS in the People's Republic of China: An Ecologic Study, in: Environmental Health, 2(15), 2003, pp. 2–15.

Dab, William: Health and Environment, Paris 2020.

Dartiguepeyrou, Carine: Where Do We Stand in Terms of Our Ecological Consciousness?, in: Truly Sustainable, 4(2), 2013, pp. 15–28.

Farand, Chloé: South Korea to Implement Green New Deal after Ruling Party Election Win, in: Climate Home News, 16.04.2020, https://www.climatechangenews.com/2020/04/16/south-korea-implement-green-new-deal-ruling-party-election-win/; last accessed 19.06.2020.

Faria, Nuno R. / Andrew Rambaut / Marc A. Suchard / Guy Baele / Trevor Bedford / Melissa J. Ward / Andrew J. Tatem / João D. Sousa / Nimalan Arinaminpathy / Jacques Pépin / David Posada / Martine Peeters / Oliver G. Pybus / Philippe Lemey: The Early Spread and Epidemic Ignition of HIV-1 in Human Populations, in: Science 346(6205), 2014, pp. 56–61.

French.xinhuanet.com: (COVID-19) La Chine renforce la surveillance de l'environnement dans le contexte de l'épidémie, 26.02.2020, http://french.xinhuanet.com/2020-02/26/c_138820025.htm?fbclid=IwAR3-xsXxovAIIaoQ9wObFKp69oc6ZXygrCMUXdOs8vRlPSxF7YmNgDHlLaQ; last accessed 19.06.2020.

French.xinhuanet.com: La police chinoise renforce la lutte contre la criminalité liée aux animaux sauvages, 02.03.2020, http://french.xinhuanet.com/2020-03/02/c_138835893.htm?fbclid=IwAR27gFBrpN2wAI4GXPUxAdL4xWLZBNCAiJq8mEQqCodRVE8TAReYXGtZu9M; last accessed 19.06.2020.

Higgins-Desbiolles, Freya: Socializing Tourism for Social and Ecological Justice after COVID-19, in: Tourism Geographies, https://doi.org/10.1080/14616688.2020.1757748.

International Energy Agency (IEA): World Energy Investment 2020 – Analysis, https://www.iea.org/reports/world-energy-investment-2020; last accessed 05.06.2020.

Infodujour: La lecture par temps de confinement, in: Infodujour.fr (blog), 06.05.2020, https://infodujour.fr/culture/litterature/34515-la-lecture-par-temps-de-confinement; last accessed 19.06.2020.

Kennedy, Brian: U.S. Concern about Climate Change Is Rising, but mainly among Democrats, in: Pew Research Center (blog), 16.04.2020, https://www.pewresearch.org/fact-tank/2020/04/16/u-s-concern-about-climate-change-is-rising-but-mainly-among-democrats/; last accessed 19.06.2020.

Klemeš, Jiří Jaromír / Yee Van Fan / Raymond R. Tan / Peng Jiang: Minimising the Present and Future Plastic Waste, Energy and Environmental Footprints Related to COVID-19, in: Renewable and Sustainable Energy Reviews, 127 (109883), 2020, https://doi.org/10.1016/j.rser.2020.109883.

Legendre, Myriam: The Environment and Health, in: Santé Publique, 15(3), 2003, pp. 291–302.

Le Monde: Le commerce illicite des pangolins est toujours en hausse, in: Le Monde.fr, 07.11.2019, https://www.lemonde.fr/afrique/article/2019/11/07/le-commerce-illicite-des-pangolins-est-toujours-en-hausse_6018338_3212.html; last accessed 19.06.2020.

Le Quéré, Corinne et al.: Temporary Reduction in Daily Global CO_2 Emissions during the COVID-19 Forced Confinement, in: Nature Climate Change, 2020, pp. 1–7.

Liberation.fr (Un collectif de cent spécialistes du droit, (Notre Affaire à tous)): Exigeons un droit à la hauteur de l'urgence climatique et environnementale, in: Libération.fr, 09.05.2020, https://www.liberation.fr/france/2020/05/09/exigeons-un-droit-a-la-hauteur-de-l-urgence_1787397; last accessed 19.06.2020.

Liu, Ping / Wu Chen / Jin-Ping Chen: Viral Metagenomics Revealed Sendai Virus and Coronavirus Infection of Malayan Pangolins (Manis Javanica), in: Viruses 11(11), 2019, p. 979.

Marí Saéz, Almudena et al.: Investigating the Zoonotic Origin of the West African Ebola Epidemic, in: EMBO Molecular Medicine, 7(1), 2015, pp. 17–23.

Morand, Serge: Biogéographie et écologie de l'émergence, in: Serge Morand / Muriel Figuié: Émergence de maladies infectieuses, 2016, pp. 13–36.

Morin, Hervé: Coronavirus: le pangolin a-t-il pu servir d'hôte intermédiaire?, in: Le Monde, 13.02.2020, https://www.lemonde.fr/planete/article/2020/02/07/le-pangolin-a-t-il-pu-servir-d-hote-intermediaire-au-coronavirus-2019-ncov_6028801_3244.html; last accessed 19.06.2020.

Nienaber, Michael / Markus Wacket: Germany's Merkel Wants Green Recovery from Coronavirus Crisis, in: Reuters, 28.04.2020, https://www.reuters.com/article/us-climate-change-accord-germany-idUSKCN22A28H; last accessed 19.06.2020.

Notaras, Mark: The Rise of Online Climate Activists, in: Our World.unu.edu, 10.02.2009, https://ourworld.unu.edu/en/the-rise-of-online-climate-activists; last accessed 23.06.2020.

Organisation for Economic Co-operation and Development (OECD): Tackling the Coronavirus (COVID-19): OECD Policy Contributions for Co-ordinated Action, https://www.oecd.org/coronavirus/en/; last accessed 19.06.2020.

Pineau, Jean-Yves / Corinne Lepage / Bruno Latour: Nous assistons à une revolution du droit international, in: DARD/DARD, 2(2), 2020, pp. 74–88.

Rigaud, Thierry / Marie-Jeanne Perrot-Minnot / Mark J. F. Brown: Parasite and Host Assemblages: Embracing the Reality Will Improve Our Knowledge of Parasite Transmission and Virulence, in: Proceedings of the Royal Society B: Biological Sciences, 277(1701), 2010, pp. 3693–3702.

Robertson, Carlyn: How Reader Behavior Is Changing During the COVID-19 Crisis, in: BookBub Partners Blog, 24.04.2020, https://insights.bookbub.com/reader-behavior-changing-covid19-crisis/; last accessed 19.06.2020.

Rosenbloom, Daniel / Jochen Markard: A COVID-19 Recovery for Climate, in: Science 368(6490), 2020, p. 447.

Rosier, Florence: Les relations complexes entre climat et maladies infectieuses, in: Le Monde.fr, 13.04.2019, https://www.lemonde.fr/planete/article/2019/04/13/les-relations-complexes-entre-climat-et-maladies-infectieuses_5449708_3244.html; last accessed 19.06.2020.

Società Italiana di Medicina Ambientale (SIMA): Relazione circa l'effetto dell'inquinamento da particolato atmosferico e la diffusione di virus nella popolazione (Position Paper), http://www.simaonlus.it/wpsima/wp-content/uploads/2020/03/COVID19_Position-Paper_Relazione-circa-l%E2%80%99effetto-dell%E2%80%99inquinamento-da-particolato-atmosferico-e-la-diffusione-di-virus-nella-popolazione.pdf; last accessed 23.06.2020.

Solé, Éléonore: Biodiversité: comptez les oiseaux pour la LPO!, in: Futura Planète,

19.04.2020, https://www.futura-sciences.com/planete/breves/oiseaux-biodiversite-comptez-oiseaux-lpo-2193/; last accessed 23.06.2020.

Sood, Sadhika: Psychological Effects of the Coronavirus Disease-2019 Pandemic, in: Research & Humanities in Medical Education, 7, 2020, pp. 23–26.

Taylor, Louise H. / Sophia M. Latham / Mark E. J. Woolhouse: Risk Factors for Human Disease Emergence, in: Philosophical Transactions of the Royal Society of London. Series B, Biological Sciences, 356(1411), 2001, pp. 983–89.

Thelwall, Mike / Saheeda Thelwall: Retweeting for COVID-19: Consensus Building, Information Sharing, Dissent, and Lockdown Life, in: *arXiv:2004.02793 [cs]*, 04.05.2020, http://arxiv.org/abs/2004.02793; last accessed 23.06.2020.

Wikipedia: Impact of the COVID-19 Pandemic on the Environment, https://en.wikipedia.org/w/index.php?title=Impact_of_the_COVID-19_pandemic_on_the_environment&oldid=961065508; last accessed 19.06.2020.

Clemens Albrecht

Viral Coupling – Society's Fight for Survival

A tiny virus has changed our society in ways we could not have imagined: empty streets, shut-down companies and runways of international airports packed with airplanes no longer taking passengers from one continent to another. The word *shutdown* is hanging over all of us and having an unparalleled real impact on worldwide activity – like the icy powers of a Disney princess who has frozen life around the globe with her spell. To grasp what is currently going on, we must understand how modern society works. Because it is not only the lives of thousands of individuals but society as a whole that is at danger here.

1. Organic Solidarity

Modern societies use functional differentiation, developing specific subsystems with respective functions: politics must make decisions that apply to everybody; science must make discoveries accepted as truths by others; the law must limit the abundance of possible actions to a lawful few. Functional systems are self-contained, with internal communication only referring to the system in which it is used. Information from outside the system is irritating and therefore translated into the system's own way of communication, following binary code: the government is ruling, the opposition is not; a scientific explanation is true, an older one is not; an action was lawful, another one was against the law.

A connection between these systems can only be made through »structural coupling« (Niklas Luhmann)[1], i.e. creating channels of information through which the systems can perceive their environment in a system-specific way and translate irritations into their internal means of communication. If economists, for example, find that political action must be taken, the political system will translate this finding into a question of power, used by the government to show its ability to act and by the opposition to attack the government. The paradox is that by egocentrically reproducing only itself, each system can best serve the greater good by

---

[1] Cf. Luhmann: Operational Closure and Structural Coupling; Die Gesellschaft der Gesellschaft, pp. 92 ff., 100 ff., 778 ff.

providing specific functions. Only by treating a scientific finding as a question of power, and not a question of truth, the political system can fulfill its specific function. The subsystems of society are like organs in a body: it is exactly by being different that they share a close collaborate connection with each other. For this phenomenon, sociologist Emile Durkheim has coined the term »organic solidarity«.[2]

2. Viral Disruption

At the moment, however, we are seeing another type of environmental communication: through viral coupling, information that cannot be translated internally to serve the system's survival is inserted. This begins with the bodies of those infected, paralyzing pulmonary functions. In the next step, the sheer quantity of patients is testing the limits of the medical system. The function of this system is to secure individual survival by distinguishing between sick and healthy and using state-of-the-art treatment methods.

Once clinics reach the point at which they do not have the capacities to treat everybody in need of treatment, they will have to decide whom to treat using parameters that are not medical as such. The infamous word is *triage* and derives from disaster medicine: age, chance of survival and value for society are criteria now taken into account when deciding whom to treat first. Professionally, physicians are hardly trained for making these kinds of decisions, and it is exactly because the list of criteria is open and not rooted in professional practice that underlying insecurities when making these decisions can lead to enormous individual stress: it is the physician as an individual who makes decisions on life or death, not an established social norm. While the economic system is practically made to handle shortages by adjusting prices, existential shortages in the medical system do not only affect individual organizations, such as hospitals or university clinics, but cause the very function of the medical system to collapse as sick people and their relatives expecting treatment are disappointed.

Such unmet social expectations have an endemic effect: the virus spreads to the next functional system. Outrage is immediately directed at the political system, accusing it of not having made the necessary decisions to secure the functionality of the medical system under stress: »You have destroyed the medical system in the name of saving money!« The political system loses credibility and legitimacy, its decisions no longer find acceptance – unless the opposition takes power, blaming the current situation on past decisions made by the old government and making different decisions.

[2] Cf. Durkheim: De la division du travail social.

If this is not the case, the virus will force its way through all functional systems, paralyzing them: the political system becomes a mere executive power, left only with enforcing existing norms; the economic system halts all payments; the legal system refers to emergency law and is brought into line by politics. Science loses its autonomy, too, as questions of truth are answered in the service of politics instead of irritating the political system with their inherent scientific logic, which is that of the ivory tower.

With the viral coupling of systems, it is hence not only individual parts of society that are undergoing a crisis but the entire system of functional differentiation. Viral coupling is causing functions to be mechanically interlinked, blocking each other like a screw in a gearbox. As a result, societies descend to »mechanical solidarity« (Emile Durkheim), to segmental forms of differentiation. It is not a coincidence that states are isolating themselves from others under current circumstances, cutting connections; that people are retreating to smaller or even tiny communities, in which fates are once more interlinked as a grandchild's party mood becomes a grandparent's lethal threat.

We have seen such situations in modern times, not caused by a pandemic but by wars. At the end of World War II, the major systems of social order had collapsed; the occupation law enforced by the victorious powers was considered arbitrary. In this time of social insecurity, in which everybody was a potential threat, it were small communities that rebuilt a more solid foundation for social order. It was the hour of families, neighborhoods and church communities, segmentally stabilizing everyday norms and thus gradually enabling functional differentiation.

We are facing a similar development today. It is not the hour of international organizations, of state unions and multinational agreements. Every political entity capable of acting, which usually is every national state, must first and foremost find a way of stabilizing itself by pushing back the spread of the virus through the isolation of segmental units. Only once this has been achieved, international collaboration can be gradually resumed. The shutdown is a controlled retrogression of society to segmental differentiation; a vaccine that is to protect the organism of society from a lethal disease by provoking a smaller, less severe one.

This, however, also shows that in crises, the functionally differentiated global society needs the segmental order of nations, states, neighborhoods and families latently underlying it. A social order that allows for nothing in between the individual and the global society – no communities and no intermediate institutions in their irrational historicity – and that has modernized and therefore abolished everything that seemed dysfunctional does not have anything to fall back on when trying to restabilize.

3. What Is the Consequence?

But what can we do in the meantime? As paradoxical as this may sound: return to the ivory tower of science. We can ask ourselves how to include the virus into research questions and use it as productive irritation of the scientific system. Because once companies start earning money with the crisis, once politicians start using the crisis as a resource in their struggle for power and once the medical system can show for successful treatments that can be built on – only then will this crisis be overcome. Does this mean we should simply return to the old system? In my opinion, we will need to rethink functional differentiation and consider how much global society we can actually afford. Is global mass tourism a good worth preserving? Do we really need a global market for basic foodstuffs? Shouldn't we be sacrificing some efficiency in the division of labor for the sake of limiting the mobility of capital, goods and people? On a more abstract level: do we need less society and more societies?

While differentiation may make modern society more stable on the inside, enabling it to process vast amounts of irritations, the construct as a whole becomes ever more vulnerable to changing environmental circumstances. In our common language, we call these changing circumstances *catastrophes*. Our modern global society is an artificial construct that is threatened by catastrophes more quickly and substantially than traditional societies, precisely because everything is interconnected through the division of labor.

Even if, going forward, the coronavirus becomes part of the equation of functional differentiation as an everyday risk – the next global catastrophe will come, be it an asteroid, an erupting volcano, a debt crisis, a climate surge or another pandemic destroying all the wealth we have built through globalization in one swoop. Precautions can only be made by taking a step back.

References

Durkheim, Émile: De la division du travail social, Paris 1893.
Luhmann, Niklas: Operational Closure and Structural Coupling: The Differentiation of the Legal System, in: Cardozo Law Review 13, 1992, pp. 1419–1441.
Luhmann, Niklas: Die Gesellschaft der Gesellschaft, Frankfurt 1997.

Tiziana Andina

»It's Just a Flu« —
What We Can Learn from Our Mistakes

1. The Scenario

We can learn a number of things from what's been happening these past few weeks, i.e. from the beginning of March 2020. I would like to try to articulate them starting from two sentences that we have all heard many times in recent weeks, when the course of the epidemic seemed more uncertain: »it's just a flu«, on the one hand, and its opposite »it's more serious than a simple flu«, on the other. The meaning of knowledge, common sense and decision-making has been measured around these two mutually exclusive ways of interpreting Covid-19. These are all issues that concern, in different ways, common sense, science, philosophy, and politics.

It may be a professional bias, but every time I heard these phrases I was reminded of a famous aphorism by Friedrich Nietzsche: »there are no facts, only interpretations«. Nietzsche's position, which was widely echoed among 20th-century philosophers, famously expressed skepticism towards the possibility of knowledge, i.e. towards the human ability to make true judgments: at best, he argued, we can make judgments that depend on the way we are made, perceive and reason. It is therefore very difficult to understand how things really are if, in the final analysis, all knowledge depends on us.

If you think about it, the fluctuations in interpreting Covid-19 seem to reflect the Nietzschean idea, all the more so because scientists, in expressing their views, have not shown the absolute harmony that people hoped for and politicians expected. In the early stages of the contagion, in fact, some virologists observed, data at hand, that the disease was not very different from the regular flu in terms of mortality and of the relationship between asymptomatic and serious cases. The most significant differences were likely to concern the higher number of patients admitted to intensive care, and the fact that Covid-19 had given signs of particular speed in terms of spread of contagion. Other virologists, instead, took an opposite view, namely that the flu was something entirely different, suggesting that the Covid-19 disease should be tackled through targeted strategies.

In this confusion, it should be noted that philosophy – especially the kind that still welcomes echoes of Nietzsche's reasoning – has not been of much help. The philosopher Giorgio Agamben, for example, in an article published in »Manifesto«,[1] an Italian newspaper, on 26 February, roughly supported the thesis of the scientists who interpreted Covid-19 as a variant of the flu, and reinforced it with the conspiracy component, which is always very appealing. The question Agamben posed is essentially this: if it is little more than a flu, as some scientists claim, why is the state taking such oppressive measures in terms of restricting personal freedoms? Perhaps someone is artfully building this narrative to exert a form of capillary control over people's lives? In short, does power want to make the state of exception permanent?

2. What We Can Learn

So let's see what we can learn from this situation. These are, indeed, things that concern at least four major areas of our life: common sense – that is, the ordinary way of conceptualizing reality –, science, politics, and philosophy.

Common sense and science. Agamben's thesis is evidently absurd and makes instrumental use of certain positions expressed by scientists. In this sense, it is useful to make a few observations. There is a common-sense objection that we can make to the proponents of the thesis of the flu variant. It is the same argument that Moore[2] opposed to Kant, who considered it an epistemological scandal that the existence of things outside of us – that is, outside our minds – should be accepted by faith. To prove the existence of my hands – Moore argued – I just need to raise them, move my right hand while saying »here is my hand« and pointing at it with my left hand. That's it. It is enough to exercise common sense to show that the flu and Covid-19 are not only not the same thing but probably not even similar things: what happened in China allowed one to draw these conclusions already at the beginning of 2020.

Science and politics. Then there's another point. Medicine is not an exact science, and neither is economics. This means, first of all, that the epistemological status of these sciences is different from that of mathematics or logic, but also of physics. Medicine and economics are empirical sciences that formulate hypotheses starting from reality. Now, reality is not infinitely interpretable, and fortunately imposes strong constraints. However, it does have a margin of interpretability, which

---

[1] Agamben: Lo stato d'eccezione provocato da un'emergenza immotivata. For further reflections by Agamben on these topics: Quodlibet.it: Una Voce Di Giorgio Agamben.
[2] Cf. Moore: Proof of an External World.

means that agreement among scientists is usually not absolute. A degree of disagreement, in fact, is part of the epistemological structure of science itself. Nonetheless, we are not allowed to conclude from this that the virus is a construction of the system or that climate change is not a real problem.[3] It is typical of science not to express completely unanimous opinions, because that is the way it is, but the role of politics remains fundamental. It is clear that, within this framework, the exercise of political decision-making cannot be substituted by science.

Science and values. Another point that I believe should be of interest to the scientific community is the relationship between science, reality, and the values to which scientists refer when formulating their opinions. What does it mean for empirical sciences such as medicine or economics to be confronted with reality, especially when models or statistics seem incapable of explaining what is happening despite being formally correct? For example, should the flu somehow cause more deaths in absolute terms than Covid-19, would this really indicate something significant when compared to the collapse of hospitals that are no longer able to treat the sick, cemeteries that can no longer welcome the dead, or entire communities in which children cannot stand by their dying parents? What values, in addition to objective data analysis, guide the formulation of scientific hypotheses?

Philosophy. Finally, let's come to philosophy. Great philosophers have never made fun of reality, simply because they generally regarded it as the most serious of all things. To explain its complexity they invented metaphysics, analyzed circumstances, reformulated problems, imagined possible worlds. They challenged it, like Nietzsche (who was defeated), but generally respected it. In my opinion, Agamben's position, in being unnecessarily radical, at this moment in history, has two faults, both of which are particularly serious: it is superficial and it is irresponsible. It is superficial because it tries to explain a very complex reality by means of a single idea, the conspiratorial exercise of political power, and it is irresponsible, in the double etymological sense of the word *respondeo* (*answer for* something and *answer to* someone), because it takes philosophy away from its main task, i.e. the commitment to provide non-dogmatic explanations through the exercise of critical thinking.

---

[3] Very often these questions intersect the so-called post-truth phenomenon. For an introductory discussion on this topic, cf. Condello / Andina: Post-Truth, Philosophy and Law.

3. Re-orienting the Future: What We Can Do

If this is the picture that has emerged in recent months, I believe that philosophy can and must commit itself – on the basis of the analysis of the state of affairs in which we find ourselves – to identifying strategies that could make it possible to shape social reality in different and, if possible, better ways than at present.

So let's start with the analysis of the situation. We already know that for some years now there have been signs pointing to a possible pandemic similar to the one caused by Covid-19. It would have been enough, after all, not to ignore them. To stick to the forecasts that have been around the Internet in recent weeks, it is useful to mention at least two statements: the first by former U.S. President Barack Obama, the second by the founder of Microsoft, Bill Gates. »We can't say we're lucky with Ebola because obviously it's having a devastating effect in West Africa but it is not airborne in its transmission. There may and likely will come a time in which we have an airborne disease that is deadly.«[4] This quote is taken from a conference given by Barack Obama in 2014, during his visit to the National Institutes of Health (NIH) in Bethesda, Maryland. The theme of his speech was Ebola, but what is more interesting to us today are Obama's considerations about the pandemic risks that globalization was likely to bring with it: »And in order for us to deal with that effectively, we have to put in place an infrastructure – not just here at home, but globally – that allows us to see it quickly, isolate it quickly, respond to it quickly.«[5] The same scenario was described a year later, in 2015, by Gates, in the TED conference entitled: *The Next Outbreak? We're Not Ready.*[6] The two speeches deserve some reflection, partly about the reasons for our surprise, partly about the meaning of some of the things said, which we can summarize in three words: future, responsibility, commitment. Three words that are the key to orienting the future to come.

Let's start with our surprise. We are usually so unaccustomed to the idea that one should pay serious attention to the future that we are surprised when we find out that someone has done it and quite well. In his lecture, Gates argued that, on the basis of the scientific evidence available to us (it was 2015), one of the greatest dangers for the survival of humankind is not the atomic risk – for which governments have, all in all, taken effective countermeasures – but the invisible threats, including, of course, viral pandemics. Therefore, he presented a possible scenario: an airborne viral contamination that spreads rather quickly. It is a sneaky contagion that leaves the sick in good condition for some time before they manifest the symptoms of the disease, so that it spreads and remains below the attention

---

[4] Obama: Remarks by the President on Research for Potential Ebola Vaccines.
[5] Ibid.
[6] Gates: The Next Outbreak? We're Not Ready.

threshold for an initial period, favoring contagion. If we add to all these circumstances the fact that the circulation of the virus could occur mainly in large urban centers, the health catastrophe is, unfortunately, assured, as about 55 % of the world population lives in urbanized areas.

Gates's reasoning starts from a series of empirical observations – the dynamics of the spread of Ebola and the critical issues that this epidemic has brought to light in our defense systems – to paint a picture that is even worse. The scenario is ominous, and therefore, concludes Gates, we must prepare ourselves, using the power of technology and relying on the results achieved in biology and medicine. More or less the same conclusion was drawn by Obama. Today we know that both were right: the scenario they painted was indeed highly probable, so much so that it became real and we were not ready precisely because we did not prepare for it. In other words, we failed to take on that responsibility.

Hans Jonas, a philosopher who has long reflected on the human condition and the central role of technology in our lives, published a book in 1979 that would prove very successful: *Das Prinzip Verantwortung*.[7] Jonas' thesis was that human beings had to assume a new attitude of responsibility towards themselves, their species, and the World, because the future would soon face dramatic challenges, as shown by the global issues related to climate, health, ecology – the so-called unstructured political problems. Therefore, the Kantian ethics of respect, which has been the fundamental reference for over two centuries, should be replaced by an ethics of individual and collective responsibility.

But what should we be responsible for, you might ask? The answer is quite simple in theory, while it is dramatically complex if it is translated into reality: we have to take responsibility – something we clearly do not like to do – for a commitment to orient the future. We systematically fail to respond to this task. This is clearly shown not only by the current Covid-19 affair, but also by a wealth of social aspects that many Western democracies have been neglecting for decades now: welfare,[8] pensions, global warming, climate change, public health. These are all aspects of our life that have to do with the future and the need to orient it: our tendency, for the most part, is instead to plunder the future, maximizing the profits we can make for the present and leaving the bill for the next generations to pay.

Except that, sooner or later, future generations will become present and, in this case, we already are that generation.[9] The long pause that a viral microorganism has imposed on the whole of humanity, at every latitude, is an unmissable opportunity to accept the challenge launched by Jonas: to rethink our actions in terms

---

7 Jonas: Das Prinzip Verantwortung.
8 On the topic of labor, cf. in particular Toracca / Condello: Law, Labour and the Humanities.
9 For an in-depth discussion of these issues, I refer the reader to my Transgenerazionalità. Una filosofia per le generazioni future.

of a responsibility extended to the future. This means questioning our values, changing the economy, re-educating adults and children, rethinking, finally, the happiness model that inspires our choices and actions. It is the only strategy to stop clumsily chasing after events instead of preventing them, so as to no longer be left at the mercy of what happens to us. And once we grow up, at last, we might be able to finally look at the moon instead of staring at the finger that is pointing at it.

4. Reorienting the Future: How We Can Act

What does all this mean, really? Arthur Danto, an American philosopher who dealt extensively with the philosophy of history,[10] taught us that history can only be written *from* the future: which means, roughly speaking, that there is a huge difference between the simple recording of events and facts – which is the task of chroniclers – and the weaving of the historical narrative. History requires a narrative that includes taking charge of the effects of the decisions we make, because there is no doubt that all decisions, whether made or not, as well as all actions, whether taken or not, come with consequences which are perhaps the most important part of the story. From our point of view today, we know that Barack Obama and Bill Gates, as well as all those who had feared the reality of the pandemic risk, were right.

Now, I believe that in the midst of the disaster in which we find ourselves, there is at least one thing that we really should not miss: the opportunity to understand how it happened that the world and its institutions could make such a global mistake. The analysis of what happened is obviously complex and will take some time, but for now I would like to try to suggest a few key words that might be useful to guide it: *analysis, imagination,* and *decision,* possibly applying *criteria of transgenerational justice*. I will try to show how all three of these words are related to the importance of not only mapping reality but also trying to peek in the direction of the future. The future has to be oriented, if we don't want to rush after it and eventually be overwhelmed by it.

Analysis. We now have more powerful and more sophisticated tools than ever before to perform analysis. And, in fact, the analyses we make are generally correct. Digital technologies and the infinite amount of data – which our behaviors produce and the giants of the web collect and punctually process – allow us to elaborate very precise analysis about behaviors, relationships, tastes, preferences, beliefs. In short, we have the ability to draw very precise maps of what we are like and of

---

[10] Cf. Danto: Analytical Philosophy of History; Danto: Narration and Knowledge.

our reality. And, in fact, both President Obama and Bill Gates did not look into the crystal ball – they simply saw a reality that already spoke volumes six years ago. This suggests that the problem is almost never the analysis itself, but rather lies in the next two stages – imagination and decision making. But what does it mean, exactly, to imagine, in this context?

Imagination, i.e. backcasting. Danto teaches us that to write about history you have to do it from the future, while the present, at best, can produce the chronicle of itself. Paradoxical as it may seem, however, if we want to establish an authentic and effective relationship with the future we must imagine it from the present. This is what social scientists call *backcasting*.[11] We could sum up this operation as follows: establishing where we want to go by building different desirable scenarios with our imagination, conceiving possible worlds and then walking things back from those worlds, engaging all the tools that are useful and appropriate to achieve our goal. In fact, the future dwells only in our imagination, literally speaking it does not exist, so we have to imagine it first and then build it; otherwise it will emerge from itself in disjointed ways that we often don't like at all.

Consider, for example, the Italian health system. It is an important piece of the country's welfare state. The analysis of what happened in northern Italy – in some of the richest and most developed regions of the country – offers an interesting case study, the results of which may be useful for a reflection looking towards a European perspective. As mentioned above, we now know from previous pandemics, as well as from the data available on people's behavior and the transformation of ecosystems, that we are and will continue to be particularly exposed to pandemic risks. The Italian Constitution (art. 32)[12] defines the framework within which the citizens, the parliament and the Italian government can design the health system, decide what it should become in, say, ten years' time, indicating, moreover, what values it should respect and embody. So how could it be imagined in the medium term? The pandemic has revealed many things: important weaknesses – especially in the Italian regions at the forefront – and strengths that have allowed the system not to buckle even under enormous pressure.

The analysis, therefore, will have to go into the detail of the tons of information that this tragedy has provided in order to focus on it and analyze it with precision. Technology can be of great help in this, as data collection can, in fact, be capillary and targeted. Once this operation has been completed, the public, through its political, territorial and national representations, should then ask what the health system should look like in the near future and in the medium term. Should it be more centralized or more localized? More specialized or more generalist? And

---

[11] For a preliminary analysis of backcasting, cf. Dreborg: Essence of Backcasting.
[12] For consultation, please refer to the website of the Senate of the Italian Republic.

how specialized and how generalist? Could it be fairer in the sense of becoming an effective instrument of wealth redistribution? What should be done to make it sustainable without leaving future generations with a huge debt linked to care systems? How should the relationship between young and old be thought about in terms of healthcare spending and access to care?

It is generally the elderly who need more care, as they often have co-morbidity problems, which means that it is this category of people who use most of the public resources allocated to this specific chapter of welfare. However, the Italian and Spanish cases have also shown that, faced with exceptional pressures, older people have suffered the most in terms of healthcare provision. Is this the healthcare system that it is useful and right to have? How will it be possible to minimize the risk of excluding older people from care – we know that managing the ageing population is an open challenge for Europe as a whole – and how will we rebalance spending in favor of the younger generations who generally make less use of health care?

All these issues do not only concern the health organization of a country, but also the values and the world view that that country expresses. If then, as in the case of Italy, that country is part of a larger community, like the European Union, it is obvious that one must also take into account the integration between the different visions expressed by all the countries that are part of that community. A shared backcasting will have to be put in place by all the countries in the community: in this sense the pandemic offers a unique opportunity to start a choral work in this direction, at least regarding specific chapters that make up the welfare of each European country.

Those I have listed are just some of the questions that should guide the backcasting work aimed at producing a series of desirable scenarios from which political decision-makers, through the mechanisms of representation, can finally choose. And in order to choose, it is obviously necessary to exercise the power of decision-making. Building scenarios involves and requires normativity, which we need to be aware of. The point, however, I think is this: is it possible to leave social action to self-regulation? We have had endless evidence that the system will not self-regulate: anything could come out, and more often than not chaos will emerge.

Decision, i.e. acting effectively and fairly. One of the most widespread problems with democratic systems, especially when they are governed by charismatic leaders or populist parties, is the lack of decision-making. Populism, after all, stands out for its tendency to devalue the forms and procedures of representative democracy, for the over-evaluation of charismatic leaders and, finally – as clearly seen in the weeks when the pandemic reached its peak – for the implementation of decision deferral techniques. Things are not much better for governments less affected by populism, because, in general, the daily measurement of consensus made possible by new technologies is a problem that afflicts all Western democracies, effectively undermining the concept of political representation.

In general, decisions are rarely made or not made at all, especially when they are likely to displease the electorate – whose moods are, by nature, rather unstable. In this framework, political action becomes a reflection of the will of the voters, and ceases to be a representative action. As is well known, the philosopher Thomas Hobbes spoke of a *persona ficta* to allude to the representative function of the sovereign as well as of assemblies.[13] Representing a community means exercising the power of decision-making resulting from the mediation and synthesis of the needs of those who are represented. The instrument of political representation makes it possible to exercise decision-making precisely because it legitimately detaches itself from the mere expression of individual wills. In this framework, the exercise of decision making is articulated in planning, synthesis, and choice.

It is useful to note that the exercise of representation can only allow decisions to be taken with justice in mind: sticking to Italy, the welfare system has been undermined, among other things, by political choices made in the 1980s that allowed many workers in the public sector to retire at just over forty years of age. The crisis provoked by Covid-19 will certainly aggravate the Italian public debt, which was already extremely high and was often contracted for patronage reasons. In this case, obviously, unlike in many circumstances in the past, there were dramatic and urgent reasons for the choice to aggravate the debt; however, it is good to bear in mind that this debt will have to be repaid over time, in large part by future generations.

Therefore, in my opinion, it is more urgent than ever that the medium and long term objectives become the focus of planning future scenarios. This implies an awareness of the specific reality in which we live, and a sense of responsibility, through planning and decision making, towards the world in which we would like to live. This is true for Italy, but not only: therein lies the meaning of the transition to the ethics of responsibility which Jonas has rightly urged us to. We must take responsibility not only for the material and immaterial resources we enjoy, but also in relation to time – the present we are going through and the future we will leave to those who will come after us.

---

[13] Cf. Hobbes: Leviathan, book I, § XVI.

References

Agamben, Giorgio: Lo stato d'eccezione provocato da un'emergenza immotivata, in: ilmanifesto.it, 26.02.2020, https://ilmanifesto.it/lo-stato-deccezione-provocato-da-unemergenza-immotivata/; last accessed 23.06.2020.
Andina, Tiziana: Transgenerazionalità. Una filosofia per le generazioni future, Rome 2020.
Condello, Angela / Tiziana Andina (eds.): Post-Truth, Philosophy and Law, London 2019.
Danto, Arthur C.: Analytical Philosophy of History, Cambridge 1967.
Danto, Arthur C.: Narration and Knowledge, New York 2007.
Dreborg, Karl H.: Essence of Backcasting, in: Futures, 28(9), 1996, pp. 813–828.
Gates, Bill: The Next Outbreak? We're Not Ready, in: TED, 2014, https://www.youtube.com/watch?v=6Af6b_wyiwI; last accessed 25.06.2020.
Jonas, Hans: Das Prinzip Verantwortung: Versuch einer Ethik für die technologische Zivilisation, Frankfurt am Main 1979.
Hobbes, Thomas: Leviathan [1651], Oxford 2012.
Moore, George Edward: Proof of an External World, in: Proceedings of the British Academy, 25, 1939, pp. 273–300.
Obama, Barack: Remarks by the President on Research for Potential Ebola Vaccines, 2 December 2014, https://obamawhitehouse.archives.gov/the-press-office/2014/12/02/remarks-president-research-potential-ebola-vaccines; last accessed 25.06.2020.
Quodlibet.it: Una Voce Di Giorgio Agamben, https://www.quodlibet.it/una-voce-giorgio-agamben; last accessed 10.05.2020.
Senate of the Italian Republic: Senato della Repubblica – La Costituzione (The Constitution), http://www.senato.it/1024; last accessed 14.05.2020.
Toracca, Tiziano / Angela Condello (eds.): Law, Labour and the Humanities: Contemporary European Perspectives, London 2019.

Gregor Albers

Personal Sacrifices for Public Health? Doubts on Interfering with Liberty to Protect Life*

Even those not afraid of death do fear suffering and dread the loss of their beloveds. We would be eager to pay a handsome price in order to protect our lives as well as those of our relatives and friends. But thankfully, we do not have to face the epidemic as isolated individuals, for we are all confronted with similar questions, and our community strives to protect everyone's lives and health. When, to that aim, the state restricts certain of our rights and liberties, this is usually justified by the mere claim that life and health outweighed those rights and liberties. It seems to me that the critical mistake of that argument does not consist in the assumption that life had absolute preponderance over any other legally protected interest.[1] In order to make that mistake, one already has to travel on the wrong road. The problem begins with a hasty readiness to set out with a pair of scales to put people's rights on it, instead of respecting them. It is not self-explanatory that the state should be allowed to balance lives and health of some – even of many – against rights and liberties of others. Even in favour of overwhelming interests of others, one is not obliged to sacrifice one's rights and liberties unless under extraordinary circumstances, and never without due compensation.

Even if it is to protect one's own health as well? Public debate tends to emphasise that the prohibitions are in everybody's interest. But put correctly, we are not restricted for our own sake, but for those of others. That is the only way it can be: The state cannot justify its order to a mature and responsible citizen by referring to her own interests. Everybody has a right to commit suicide. One may waste one's life for alcohol and cigarettes, and one may risk it using motorcycles or parachutes. Some people are always anxious, others foolhardy, and both kind of people may decide which risks they deem worthy to take in a life worth living. Take, for example, the duty to buckle your seatbelt when riding a car. Under Ger-

---

* An earlier version of this article has appeared in German as: Sonderopfer für die Volksgesundheit: Freiheitsbeschränkungen zum Lebensschutz in der Coronakrise, published May 11, 2020 on Verfassungsblog (https://verfassungsblog.de/sonderopfer-fuer-die-volksgesundheit/). I am indebted to Alex Bowen for raising valuable critical points and correcting the English version on very short notice.

[1] That assumption is indeed faulty, as pointed out by Schirmer: Kurven und Kosten.

man constitutional law, it is considered justified, but not because it protects the person who has to put on the belt. That duty is only lawful because it makes sure that the driver remains in control of her car, and because it prevents bodies from flying through the air in a way that might hurt others.[2] Where merely our own interests are concerned, the state may only inform about risks, also advise, maybe persuade or dissuade, but never command or proscribe. That holds true not only for the risk of dying from that virus, but also for the risk of dying from a heart attack because hospitals are overcrowded by Corona patients.

When we are ordered to rest our trade or profession, our academic or artistic vocation, our religious practices, not even to leave the house and to move around, this can only be right for the reason that it is useful to others. But under which circumstances may the state restrict one to support one other? The answer cannot be given by weighing costs and benefits: Even if I probably do not need my second kidney, without my consent, no one may transplant it to someone else who can make more use of it. The example shows how misleading it can be to frame a problem as distributional: No one is competent to assume the task of distributing two kidneys fairly between me and the other. It just happens that I have two kidneys and the other has none. Those who only look at the overall benefit miss the point of some positions being *a priori* attributed to every individual. It is crucial to make a difference between active intrusions into fundamental rights and a mere failure to protect constitutionally enshrined rights against dangers caused not by the state, but by third parties or by nature. Those who do not make that difference mistake the state as source of all good and evil. But the state did not provide us with our kidneys, nor with our fundamental liberties. That is why as a principle, one person's claim to be left alone by the state tends to be stronger than another person's claim for the state to help him. I do not share the impression that German lawyers are currently bearing a Kantian yoke that keeps them from offsetting interests against each other.[3] Such a yoke should not be shaken off, we should rather retrieve it and shoulder it proudly. By the way, this is not to be mistaken as a categorical argument against financial redistribution, as property and income are to a certain extent only made possible by society with others and therefor much less *a priori* assigned than kidneys or liberties.

If a police officer had to decide whether she should attend to a passer-by who has been dangerously hurt or rather prevent a marauding mob from destroying a deserted restaurant, it is obvious that she would have to save the injured person, not the restaurant. For life and health of that person outweigh the interests of the

---

[2] At least that was the opinion of the Constitutional Court in 1986; cf. Beschluss des Bundesverfassungsgerichts vom 24. 7. 1986, 1 BvR 331/85 and others, Neue Juristische Wochenschrift 1987, 180.

[3] As Christoph Winter puts it (»kantianische Fesseln der Aufrechnungsaversion«; loose translation by the author); cf. Winter: Die Krise der Rechtswissenschaften.

restaurant owner. Whether that police officer could instruct the owner to close his restaurant, if by some circumstance that became the means to save life and health of others, is a totally different question. If what I have argued so far is correct, an affirmative answer could not be based on the interests of such customers that are mature and wish to frequent the place well informed and at their own risks. However, I must admit at this point that the German constitutional court has taken a different direction on bans on smoking. It considered a statute banning smokers from restaurants and bars as being justified because it furthered the interests of non-smoking customers.[4] Thereby, the court essentially refused to acknowledge that non-smoking customers were capable to choose where they wanted to go.

When do I have to accept that my liberty is limited for the sake of someone's health? It is of course right that everyone's freedom is circumscribed by the freedom of everyone else. *Alterum non laedere*, not to harm another, was upheld as one of law's fundamental principles by the Roman jurist Ulpian.[5] Does this imply that there is »no freedom to be part of a chain of infection«[6]? *Intentionally*, one may no more infect others with a contagious disease than one may stab them with a knife. How much consideration one has to apply not to harm others *unintentionally*, can hardly be determined *a priori*. Accidents between cyclists and dogs are frequent. Is that enough reason for the dog not to be let off the lead, or for the cyclist not to use his bike? Do we impute the cyclist's head injury to himself if he did not wear a helmet? If my neighbour is afraid to catch my disease, does he have to stay at home or do I? Where the boundaries between our liberties lie is a matter of usage, social norm, or in the words of the German civil code: the level of care which is due when dealing with others.[7] The state is authorized to specify that boundary, also to adapt it to changed circumstances. The pandemic might have increased the personal space people may expect others to respect: Just as a cyclist can demand that an overtaking car observe a security distance, one can nowadays expect that no-one approaches closer than two metres without wearing a mask. As one can even allow another to touch him intimately or to tattoo his skin, that new norm does not hinder him from allowing others to approach closer than two metres.

Special rules apply when one creates a danger considered abnormal. If someone gets hurt by my pet or car, I am liable even if I was not negligent. If I dig a hole on

---

[4] Cf. Urteil vom 30.07.2008, 1 BvR 3262/07 and others, Entscheidungen des Bundesverfassungsgerichts (BVerfGE) 121, 317. The court wanted to entitle non-smokers to participate in that part of social life without having to jeopardize their health; cf. no. 127: »Nichtraucher sollen in diesem Bereich des gesellschaftlichen Lebens nicht nur um den Preis der Gefährdung ihrer Gesundheit teilnehmen können«.

[5] Cf. Digests 1,1,10,1 (Ulpian 1 *regularum*): Iuris praecepta sunt haec: honeste vivere, alterum non laedere, suum cuique tribuere; quoted from Mommsen/Krüger (ed.): Corpus Iuris Civilis.

[6] As argued by Bublitz: Es gibt keine Freiheit, Teil einer Infektionskette zu sein.

[7] Cf. section 276 (II) Civil Code: »Fahrlässig handelt, wer die im Verkehr erforderliche Sorgfalt außer Acht lässt«.

my ground, I have to prevent playing children from falling in. Other dangerous activities require a permit – hunting, for example – or are categorically forbidden (the use of certain chemicals). In lieu of private claims for damages or injunctions, a prohibition by public law is appropriate, if the group of endangered persons can hardly be identified, so that they cannot in advance negotiate protective measures with the endangerer. Following this principle, the state will be allowed to direct an infected person to avoid contact with other people, if those do not explicitly assume the risk of infection. At least in the cities, those directions might imply that the infected have to remain in domestic quarantine. Even against someone who is only highly suspected to be contagious, such an order can probably be issued for the period of time necessary to test him. But as long as I do not have reason to assume that I am infected, I do not create a peculiar danger for others and constitute merely what can be described as an integral part of the general risks of life, when I leave the house, go to work, go shopping, meet friends, do sports, go to a restaurant or the movies or to church. It is no more than the same danger as arouses from anyone else. My opinion is that even in our times, no more can be expected from me than to wear a mask or to keep a distance.

The need to specify the boundaries between liberties does not entitle the state to shift them abruptly and drastically or to draw them in a way that would hurt the core of any of those liberties. That way, the state would negate existing individual rights. This holds true – to give an example – for the freedom to run a restaurant. But can't this right of a restaurant owner be abrogated for a certain time on the grounds of democratic proceedings for the sake of the common good? Can't we expect him to sacrifice his business, so that the medical system won't be overstrained? To find an answer, it might help to consider sections 74 and 75 of the introduction of the General State Law for the Prussian States from 1794:

»§. 74. Singular rights and advantages of members of the state have to stand back behind rights and duties to further the common good, if a true contradiction (collision) should arise between them.

§. 75. In contrast, the state is held to indemnify him who has been urged to sacrifice his singular rights and advantages to the common good.«[8]

If such was already the position of absolutist Prussia, our democracies should not fall short of that standard of protection of private rights. And indeed, the same

---

[8] Quoted from Hans Hattenhauer (ed): Allgemeines Landrecht für die Preußischen Staaten von 1794: »§. 74. Einzelne Rechte und Vortheile der Mitglieder des Staats müssen den Rechten und Pflichten zur Beförderung des gemeinschaftlichen Wohls, wenn zwischen beyden ein wirklicher Widerspruch (Collision) eintritt, nachstehn. §. 75. Dagegen ist der Staat denjenigen, welcher seine besondern Rechte und Vortheile dem Wohle des gemeinen Wesens aufzuopfern genöthigt wird, zu entschädigen gehalten«.

assessment is today expressed in several provisions of German private,[9] constitutional[10] and administrative[11] law. Calling on someone to safeguard public interests against a danger which this person himself did not induce might under special circumstances be legalized by the need to »further the common good«. We can hardly reject this if we accept that even in the last decade, in the interest of a different common good, whole villages have been expropriated and destroyed to enable strip mining for brown coal.[12] Such expropriations could not be justified, were it not for the concept of solidarity.[13] The German Ethics Council was right to evoke that same concept as necessary grounds for state action in the Corona crisis.[14] But even if only taken under exceptional circumstances, all such measures do at least require that the addressee receives every possible compensation; otherwise they cannot be lawful.

I argue that such compensation must be paid to businesspeople ordered to suspend their activity to slow down the epidemic. Compared to people whose income is not affected by similar prohibitions – first of all compared to public servants like academics –, those self-employed are required to make a special sacrifice. It is not less peculiar because it is asked of so many; an infraction does not lose importance if it is bigger. The fact that compensation for so far-reaching measures would impose a heavy burden on public finance cannot be brought forward as an argument against such compensation. The funding of the public is a problem of the public, not of private individuals, and the costs of measures taken by the

---

[9] According to section 904 of the Civil Code, I may not prevent others from using and even destroying my things if they need them to avert a danger that outweighs the damage done to me, but they have to pay due compensation: »Der Eigentümer einer Sache ist nicht berechtigt, die Einwirkung eines anderen auf die Sache zu verbieten, wenn die Einwirkung zur Abwendung einer gegenwärtigen Gefahr notwendig und der drohende Schaden gegenüber dem aus der Einwirkung dem Eigentümer entstehenden Schaden unverhältnismäßig groß ist. Der Eigentümer kann Ersatz des ihm entstehenden Schadens verlangen«.

[10] Article 14 (III) of the Fundamental Law permits expropriation for the sake of the common good, if such expropriation is regulated by a statute that provides for fair and equitable compensation, the amount of which, if dispute arises, can only be determined by the ordinary courts (not by administrative courts): »Eine Enteignung ist nur zum Wohle der Allgemeinheit zulässig. Sie darf nur durch Gesetz oder auf Grund eines Gesetzes erfolgen, das Art und Ausmaß der Entschädigung regelt. Die Entschädigung ist unter gerechter Abwägung der Interessen der Allgemeinheit und der Beteiligten zu bestimmen. Wegen der Höhe der Entschädigung steht im Streitfalle der Rechtsweg vor den ordentlichen Gerichten offen«.

[11] To give an example on the federal level, section 51 (I) of the Law on the Federal Police provides that subjects compelled to prevent a danger they did not cause are entitled to compensation for their losses. Similar rules govern the actions of the police forces of the different German states.

[12] The destruction of the so-called Cathedral of Immerath provides the most recent image of that process. The relocation of Immerath was made possible by Bundesverfassungsgericht, Urteil vom 17.12.2013, 1 BvR 3139/08; 1 BvR 3386/08, BVerfGE 134, 242.

[13] On the sociological concept of solidarity and its relevance for the current crisis, cf. Gephart: Conclusion, in this volume.

[14] Cf. Deutscher Ethikrat: Solidarität und Verantwortung in der Corona-Krise.

public in the interest of the public must be borne by that same public, not by the individuals who had the bad luck to become that public's useful tool in its fight against a virus. This is where equality enters the picture, namely as a system to fairly distribute costs incurred in the public interest which is known as taxation. As master of that tool, the state is quite certainly more capable to carry the burden than the affected individuals, and it is obliged to do so as its orders caused the damage.[15] It is therefore unjust if payments made by the state to businesses it ordered closed are classified as public support, as those business owners are at least entitled to compensation.[16] In the case of such liberties that are difficult to counterbalance with money, it is even more questionable to meddle with them.

The Corona crisis presents the state with the problem of how to fulfil its functions while maintaining public health. How can it provide the services its citizens expect of it? Kindergartens and schools, care for the sick and the old, other governmental agencies – how are they possible under the conditions of an epidemic? Those are the questions the state has to answer. With the big question of how humans should live, it should not be concerned any more during the epidemic than at other times. The state cannot prescribe a way of life.

In the meantime, the hardest restrictions have been lifted in many countries. Those relaxations have often been motivated by the need to limit the economic damage to an extent that it might still be bearable. But as long as utility remains the only benchmark for public action, our liberties remain irrelevant in principle and precarious in practice. Now the first shock of facing a new and unexpected threat has worn off, and hope remains that general opinion will nourish doubts on that way of reasoning.

---

[15] Recent German theory of state liability argues the ordinary courts – which are in charge of compensation claims – shouldn't grant compensation for consequences of state actions considered as legal, if there is no statutory basis providing for such compensation. For state actions considered as illegal, compensation should be refused if the plaintiff could have obtained protection in advance from the administrative courts. But administrative courts tend to evaluate the lawfulness of state actions by weighing private and public interests without putting emphasis on the question whether or not the state pledges itself to compensate for its interference with the private interest. To me, it does not matter much whether one fancies to consider the public measures as unconstitutional insofar as they do not provide for compensation or whether one prefers to maintain them as lawful, but to grant compensation without a specific statutory basis. But one can not send the affected citizens on a wild-goose chase from ordinary courts to administrative courts and back; in the end, the measures can only be upheld if the addressees receive compensation.

[16] To clarify: I do not propose that the state had to compensate all damage suffered by individuals because of the pandemic. My argument does only refer to the damage caused by the state issuing orders to fight the pandemic.

References

Bublitz, Christoph: Es gibt keine Freiheit, Teil einer Infektionskette zu sein: Solidarität und Pflicht in der Pandemie, 09.04.2020, https://www.praefaktisch.de/covid-19/es-gibt-keine-freiheit-teil-einer-infektionskette-zu-sein-solidaritaet-und-pflicht-in-der-pandemie/; last accessed 22.06.2020.

Deutscher Ethikrat: Solidarität und Verantwortung in der Corona-Krise. Ad-Hoc-Empfehlung, Berlin 2020.

Hattenhauer, Hans (ed.): Allgemeines Landrecht für die Preußischen Staaten von 1794. Textausgabe, Frankfurt am Main / Berlin 1970.

Mommsen, Theodor / Paul Krüger (ed.): Corpus Iuris Civilis, Band 1, 21. Auflage Dublin / Zürich 1966.

Schirmer, Jan-Erik: Kurven und Kosten in Corona Times, 21.03.2020, https://verfassungsblog.de/kurven-und-kosten-in-corona-times/; last accessed 22.06.2020.

Winter, Christoph: Die Krise der Rechtswissenschaften vor dem Hintergrund von COVID-19, KI und Klimawandel, 06.05.2020, https://www.praefaktisch.de/002e/die-krise-der-rechtswissenschaften-vor-dem-hintergrund-von-covid-19-ki-und-klimawandel/; last accessed 22.06.2020.

Alexander F. Filippov

States, Bodies and Corona-Crisis: Sociological Notes to Pandemic

This article was conceived when the epidemic in Russia was just beginning, and a few hundred meters from the Kremlin I discussed with my colleagues the concept of dictatorship, which, it seemed, could again become relevant. At this time, Putin's speech was broadcast on television, introducing the first quarantine measures. Many considered them premature; subsequently, it was widely believed that these measures were introduced too late and were too mild or insufficiently consistent. After the interview, in the evening, I went to my university to pick up some books from the laboratory. The huge building looked strange without students; I did not expect that I would not return to it until the summer holidays. I would venture to say that I did not foresee anything, but I am not alone. We do not have, in the exact sense of the word, scientific knowledge about the social nature of what is happening, and much becomes clearer not thanks to research, but only over time, with the accumulation of experience. Now, when I am completing my short text, in Moscow, where the most stringent measures of isolation have recently been promised, many controls have already been canceled. No one could predict this. And today no one knows the result of this cancellation. True, the writer today has a significant advantage over those who spoke yesterday. This advantage is that for all the differences between the countries affected by the pandemic, most of the measures adopted in them turned out to be similar. The differences are only in the degree of their intensity. For individual decisions and for reactions to decisions, regularity is revealed. This at first does not seem surprising. Different countries produce weapons, but weapons of the same type cannot but have similar characteristics. Cars, computers, climate systems cannot but be built otherwise than relying on the same principles. One could say that treatment protocols, chemical formulas of medicines, and much more, also have high degrees of similarity. However, in this case the situation is different. We discuss not the decease itself, not the structure or contagiousness of the coronaviruses. What is at stage for us now can only be located at the edge of the social reality where it contacts an unforeseen and uncontrolled natural peril, a kind of evil indifferent to culture and progress. We discuss it from the social side analyzing responses, not the nature of challenge. Even if the nature would be seen as being in itself the realm of the substantial, necessary, not contingent on our decisions (albeit the artificial character of viruses is still under discussion), what matters is not so substantial: ranking of diseases by their degrees of danger (i.e. what should be estimated as the main danger here and now); the challenge for health systems (patients with what diseases should be treated first); *self-isolation* and *social distance* generally recognized and recommended measures – these are all questions for decisions, that is, they are all belonging to the sphere of the contingent. That the contingent looks like substantial, necessary, is the starting point for further reasoning.[1]

1. It is sociologically significant that the pandemic showed a widespread crisis of the legal system, and at the same time, changes in the concepts of normal and emergency situations. The system of international law was not ready for a pandemic, although what was happening was global.[2] Along with the crisis of international law, the universal criteria of legality disappeared. It is the legality of many measures in various countries that can be called into question, albeit some of them were nearer to the ideal of procedural purity than other. Their effectiveness does not change their legality in any sense. From various countries, there are reports, for example, that at the very beginning of the epidemic, when the ways of transmission of the virus were not well understood, patients (or those who were just suspected to be infected) were isolated in rooms without any or with very poor ventilation, creating a painful and often harmful oxygen deficiency. It is easy to imagine that more radical measures can be sometimes and somewhere recognized as criminal, for example, a complete destruction of the foci of infection along with people. Perhaps even now, in mid-2020, it is difficult to imagine a government that would do such a thing. However, there is no difference between the radical destruction of the carriers of the infection and the isolation that is potentially fatal. Are those measures justified? The term *justified* itself in relation to radical sanitary measures sounds very ambiguous. If a policeman who prevented a crime and used weapons would be tried, if a firefighter who extinguished property by extinguishing a fire would be tried, then those who introduced emergency isolation measures could possible also be tried. Where? Under whose jurisdiction? The peculiarity of the current situation is that there is no instance that could bring them to trial, consider the case and sentence or justify those who introduce emergency measures. There is no interested party who would stand on the point of view of law to challenge, for example, the prohibitions on passenger flights between countries. There is no world-wide international agreement on mutual isolation, although there are already reports that borders between several countries

---

[1] This uniformity is hardly broken by several examples of different kind of national policy (Sweden or Belarus). These counterexamples rather confirm the contingency of the policy.

[2] It was rather ready for international measures. Cf. in relation to the evolution of the concept of sovereignty: Jackson: Evolution of an Idea.

are reopening. Freedom of movement was limited, and legal justifications were found (if found) post factum.

To put again in other words. It is impossible to side with the law, because in an emergency, observing the law as a procedure can be dangerous. The maxim of natural law, the formula of which has been known at least since the time of Cicero, is the preservation of existence, a decision in favor of life, which is made even before the law is passed or the procedure takes time. The death of the body is irreversible both in case of crime and in case of illness, so you cannot wait. Salvation of body first – then the procedure. In an explicit form, it was precisely this maxim that was referred to by those who introduced emergency measures to combat the pandemic. It is from here, however, that the problem of the state of emergency arises as a normal situation of the application of emergency measures. A frequently encountered argument looks something like this: A disease is not equally fatal for everyone, however, if you do not limit its spread, there will be too many cases for the national health system. There is no cure for the disease, so the burden on hospitals must be reduced. Ultimately, infection cannot be avoided, but the process needs to be made smoother. It is for this that isolation measures are needed. Until now, we cannot talk about how effective these measures were – the main interest is how their modern state found itself in the introduction.

States in the context of globalization for a relatively short period of time and without internal and international resistance were able to regain the authority that they had during the pre-global order. Of course, world society[3] has not disappeared. The Internet and international supply chains, international finance, the news information systems, and even what can be called the international education system work. However, one of the main means (and possibly one of the main goals) of globalization has disappeared: free movement of people in such forms as tourism, scientific and educational visits, labor migration between countries and also world cities as nodes of globalization.

The concept of globalization, no matter how diverse and controversial it may be, implied peculiar combinations of two spatial forms of social life. On the one hand, the global literally has no place, it has no territory (every territory has borders, and the global is unlimited, without borders in any sense). That is why it is impossible to form a world-society adding together the territories of individual states. A state may border another state, but a state has no border with the global world. The *globalization elite* (Zygmunt Bauman) exists and matters, but the *crowd* or *mass* of globalization is no less important – the basis of tourism, labor migration, as well as an increasing number of refugees who come across tourists in *the same* places of tourism and recreation. On the other hand, the global needs its special places.

---

[3] In what follows I use the terms *global order* and *world-society* as pretty much interchangeable, however, they stem from different theoretical traditions.

Many of these places have become nodes of global networks that go beyond the jurisdiction of states, they can be seen as locals (as i. e. the offices of international organizations or transnational corporations), but functionally they belong to the borderless world. This world in its usual form almost disappeared and will be restored or reorganized now. One of the temporary results of the pandemic was the disintegration (or disaggregation, as Emile Durkheim would probably say) of the *one* global space into the world of separated political units. They have borders that are transparent for energy and information, for animals and viruses, but not for human bodies and their carriers. That is why a state of emergency could be introduced more or less formally in many of them. These are the unities where officials declare that they will control the movements of the humans and even their bodily contacts. Are these units always states? As a rule, they are in the sense that their borders coincide with the borders of the sovereign states officially recognizing each other in the frame of international law. It is possible however to introduce sanitary cordons and emergency regulations in territories that are de jure not those of sovereign states. There are states of emergency (even not officially declared) in large districts, cities etc. This tells about the specifics of the situation no less than the imposition of a state of emergency in the states without appropriate legal procedures. Even if the legal reasons and legal procedures would be provided, more or less suspicious are the speed of decision-making and human rights issues.

The mix of health surveillance and political decisionism is often criticized.[4] A state of emergency requires, of course, dictatorial or quasi-dictatorial competences somehow acquired by officials and authorities. In any case, the nature of the regulations that citizens had to face even in most democratic countries, was previously unimaginable and rather resembles disaster films.[5] Just to repeat: the similarity of at least several of these regulations in different countries can be explained by *objective necessity,* as if there was no other choice and politicians simply obey the *requirements of the moment.* In the end, with more or less decisiveness and consistency the measures of isolation, distancing and lockdowns are taken everywhere. However, this explanation would be incorrect. It was always a political decision. Could it be different? The condition for the success of sanitary-political measures is the degree of readiness of business, education and, more broadly, civil society, to accept the arguments epidemiologists provide us as sufficient reason for sub-

---

[4] One of the first world-known critics was Giorgio Agamben, who immediately saw the state of emergency here: »First and foremost, what is once again manifest is the tendency to use a state of exception as a normal paradigm for government«, Agamben: The Invention of an Epidemic. At the end of February, Agamben believed that infection was no more dangerous than normal flu. Jean-Luc Nancy immediately objected to him: »[...] [A]n entire civilization is in question, there is no doubt about it. There is a sort of viral exception – biological, computer-scientific, cultural – which is pandemic.«, Nancy: Viral Exception.

[5] See for example Contagion, 2011, a film directed by Steven Soderbergh.

mission to political decisions. This, on the one hand, requires political authorities to be able to turn input information into the basis for decisions, that is, transform information encoded as a *health/disease* distinction into the basis of a political decision. On the other hand, this political decision, as we see, goes beyond the normal. The state as the instance of violence threatens – for the sake of general security – with extreme, exceptional measure imposed on those who will not stay home or are about to do their business as usual.

2. Now we can ask, whether this violence is a simple threat to impose order even against the will of the people (a threat exercised by the state as a *union of domination – Herrschaftsverband* in the words of Max Weber) or we come nearer to the core of the things, if we follow here Emile Durkheim: »[…] individuals are no longer subject to any other collective control but the State's, since it is the sole organized collectivity. Individuals are made aware of society and of their dependence upon it only through the State.«[6] This is not the question of a normative integration; however, the dilemma must be formulated with all the possible stringency: whether the state is an imposed order of legitimate violence or – through measures of state coercion, – is it society that sees itself and regulates itself? If the state produces the legitimacy of coercion based on the tacitly assumed consensus on life and health, it is the only (or one of the rare) way(s) to make collectivity of individual lives visible and active. And vice versa: in this sense, the state exists only where such consensus exists or is produced and where, relying on it, emergency measures can be introduced, including neglecting the formalism of law. Using one expression of Carl Schmitt, we can say that this is not an exceptional situation, but a concrete order. Put together, these assumptions tell us something very substantial about the state: it is possible that state is coming back not through expropriation of rights and liberties but through reconquering its old territory of collective life. Probably, it will fail another time now. Let us take a look however at what it is doing.

By combining basic consensus and (the threats of) coercion, the state or similar agents separate the bodies in space, identify buildings as contagious, mark public transport and many places of communal life as dangerous, divide all the objects under their rule as clean and unclean (actually or potentially infectious) and restrict the movements of the bodies that could otherwise move without permission. It is necessary to understand the social logic of these measures. Its basis is not the fact of the disease, not even the fact of the pandemic as such. To identify diseases as contagious, with a typical course and threat of an epidemic, a special organ of social sensitivity is required: medical statistics. Unlike the plague, leprosy and deadly forms of influenza, the current disease is identified primarily by medical statistics long before it takes more easily visible forms. This explains the wide

---

[6] Durkheim: Suicide, p. 356.

spread of Covid-dissidents, especially in the first stage of infection in most countries. That is why protests against control measures arise even in the most acute periods of the epidemic. So, the state needs first to organize medical statistics and impose their data as the basis for its exceptional decisions. The immediate vision would be substituted by data spread around by the state official through the news systems. There are no other sources of information at hand. Statistics produces the sources for epidemiologists and, approved by the state, they decide what to do.

Our senses help us in the case of this infection no more than in the case of a radiation. A healthy-looking person may be terminally ill herself and would be a source of mortal threat to others. All the rules and habits of face-to-face interactions will fail, the state-produced order goes so far as to regulate the contacts between relatives and friends, it invades the sphere of the co-bodily presence, of culturally determined proxemics. It means that during the pandemic the states appear as acting collectivity there where, as it was believed, modernity no longer leaves chances for politics. Shortly after the Chernobyl disaster, Ulrich Beck wrote that human's lack of sensory organs for the perception of radiation leads to a rejection of everyday wisdom and, ultimately, to an increase in the importance of political decisions.[7] The same can be said now, it will hardly be the last time. States and other political institutions that were able to carry out emergency administration combined the sanitary and the political. They constitute the unity of power and reason, just as it was at the birth of the European police. From the very beginning, the police were more concerned with health than with crime prevention. Thus, the idea of quarantine is a revival of the idea of the sanitary-police reason of the state. This is a revival of a complex of archaic measures, which, however, are based on systems of modern production of trust, modern expert knowledge about danger, modern attitude to life and disease, as well as modern tracking and control apparatuses. Those who rebel today against the sanitary measures, the lockdowns *and* the police have good political instinct: to *defund the police* means to undermine the whole system of the health-carrying state with its reason and reasons.

3. It is this new normality that is called the state of exception. Exceptional is what is excepted from something normal. The question now arises whether the new normality is an exception or rather the previous, old normality will be seen as a rare exception, say, of peaceful openness between the normal future situations of lockdowns and closed borders. So far, we can say that this is something different from the state of emergency that they usually imagine. It is also not a dictatorship, and complete clarity is needed in this regard. Although some of the anti-epidemic measures suggest a dictatorship, we must understand that not every violation of the usual course of affairs is a dictatorship.

[7] Cf. Beck: Risk Society, pp. 72, 74.

A too widespread view of dictatorship and state of emergency as an opportunity to ignore law is, of course, completely wrong. Otherwise, there would be no laws regulating the introduction of the state of emergency, defining the ways it can be declared and its legal status, as well as, importantly, the procedure and terms for its cancellation. I referred to Giorgio Agamben above, however it is more important and appropriate to quote Carl Schmitt and his teachings on sovereignty now. According to Schmitt, it is the sovereign who can introduce a state of emergency. It is easy to flip this definition: the one who imposes a state of emergency actually turns out to be a sovereign. Schmitt's famous study of dictatorship (1921) shows that there are two kinds of dictatorship, respectively, two kinds of emergency.

In the *first* case, the *sovereign* says that, for example, it entrusts the defense of the besieged fortress to a general or gives a commissar extraordinary competences (commission) to act for a certain time at a certain place to establish quarantine. In the *second* case completely different version of the state of emergency arises during, say, a revolution, when the old sovereign no longer exists, or during a coup d'état, during the seizure of power, when the old law no longer applies.[8] It often happens that opponents would be called enemies *after* the revolution; it is impossible to get out of a state of emergency then (to come back to the old normality) because nobody would reduce the power of the new sovereign and defeat him. Enemies are killed, old rights warranties cancelled etc. One can only hope for the normalization of the new order.[9]

The usual fears of a state of emergency are also of two kinds. It would be objected in the first case that abuse is possible and that it will not be canceled on time, whereas they would say in the second case, that a sovereign dictatorship means the complete abolition of the rights and freedoms as such, and that all the obligations of the state would be cancelled. The sovereign dictatorship would be revealed and exposed as a will for power for the sake of power without any mixture of legal order. If the first type is an understandable legal regime that is established for the fulfillment of certain tasks, local and temporary, then the second does not have an external goal; it wants itself.

It is this understanding of the dictatorship regime that is the basis of modern criticism of emergency measures during a pandemic. Suppose that a state has no other goal than to maintain and increase its power. In this logic, the pandemic is a social construct. It is a product of the distinction between dangerous and safe, and the state monopolizes this distinction, referring to the opinion of virologists and epidemiologists. The statistics of diseases, medical criteria for the causes of death of patients, etc. should also be considered then a social construct. It can be pointed out that the very methods of producing knowledge about the viruses,

---

[8] Cf. Schmitt: Dictatorship, p. 119.
[9] Cf. Fusco: Normalising Sovereignty.

their dangers and the ways they would be spread around suggest, on their side, a normal situation, i.e. scientific discussions, independent control of the results, correcting errors etc. If there is no time for this, knowledge of what is happening would be formed through the too quick exclusion of alternatives. The very definition of a situation also occurs in abbreviated mode. The characteristics of the disease, the value and the compulsory nature of isolation measures – all these are the results of the examination, which neither in time nor in the procedure could be the same as in a normal situation in calm times. Measures to combat the epidemic are introduced not voluntary but in a situation of an acute lack of time; in juridical terms, they are not laws or measures according to laws but rather ad hoc measures. They would not have anything beyond them but a silent reference to a normal situation in which the values of scientific expertise were not questioned. Thus, the reason of the state and the scientific truth in the form of an emergency medicine build the core of a new order of decisions. It is difficult to expect that this will not be followed by the response of critics, not only ideological, but also political critics. Let us state this for the last time: if political decisions resemble those of an ad hoc temporary dictatorship, criticism will be directed against the way the situation is declared emergency, against the insufficient effectiveness of the measures, and against their introducing too late. However, if during the pandemic the political order would be transformed radically, in the direction of the so-called *sovereign dictatorship*, a more radical criticism would come immediately, denying any order of the state and its claims to reason. Those rebelling now against sanitary measures do not draw any distinctions between two kinds of dictatorship. By condemning their states for what is rather the first form, they blame it for being on the way to the second.

Let us now look at the matter from the other side. The epidemic has undermined the unity of wealth, health, comfort, enlightenment and security. In particular, at the first stage, an unexpectedly large number of those who were not protected from infection belonged to the highest strata of the world. That powerful people of the planet were forced to hide themselves from infection is a sociological fact of paramount importance. The epidemic calls into question the entire system of social distinctions. The fundamental difference between clean and unclean, dangerous and safe connected wealth, power, reason and purity. Places of residence of the rich and influential were places of guaranteed cleanliness, and all control systems were aimed at identifying the unclean, that which cannot be within the boundaries of guaranteed security. It can be assumed that over time, familiar distinctions will be restored, and places of poverty and dirt will again be places of greatest danger.

Nevertheless, it would be wrong to forget about the possibility of future epidemics in which privileged groups will be the sources, carriers, victims. Meanwhile, sanitary-police regulations are the highest power at the time of the epidemic, and thus the separation of territories can be accompanied by the separation of power and wealth, power and places of habitual security. The interaction of the upper layers can be physically dangerous, and this will entail consequences that are still difficult to list. Even now, we may suspect that part of the responsibility for the spread of the epidemic lies precisely with those who were still able to overcome closed borders and who continued their daily lives as if there were no prohibitions and isolation requirements in it. This contradiction between the universality of the requirements and the politically limited possibilities for their implementation will become increasingly significant.

This also brings us back to the problem of combining global and local. Local in the global era could be limited to the boundaries of small urban communities, campuses, business centers, technology parks, perfectly fit with the world cities. The possibility of instant electronic contact with those who are thousands of kilometers away involves the creation of places of increased comfort, security, that special freedom in which nothing threatens the open body. The demonstration of an open body itself turned into a sign of wealth and security, and the presence of bodies next to each other (which has always been in friendly circles, orders, families, communities) distinguished a new elite of globalization, able to travel great distances for the sake of a special experience of a presence inaccessible to the majority.

It is this state of affairs that undermines the new crisis. The main mottos of the present are self-isolation (in other words, voluntary imprisonment, on the model of the old ascetic practices) and social distance. Isolation combines voluntariness and coercion, spare time (a sign of freedom) and the inability to fill it with different forms of pleasant leisure. The distance is also arranged in a paradoxical way: places of normal proximity become places of distance after easing isolation: lines in shops, restaurants, sports, cinemas. This means that the whole world of social motives is losing importance. Everything that was the main motivator of behavior and a substitute for religious ways of constructing the meanings of life crumbles: the industry of entertainment, health, sports, tourism is not just ruined. It loses ground, because the body, elevated to the main value, was provided with health, longevity and the ability to experience the offered pleasures only in an environment of guaranteed security.

Understanding what is happening is just beginning. Perhaps the contours of the new world are now being seen to us completely wrong. Nothing could be worse than extrapolating what is unfolding in real time, beyond the limits of the closest possible experience. However, abandoning them is also unthinkable: this is our experience here and now.

References

Agamben, Giorgio: The Invention of an Epidemic, in: European Journal of Psychoanalysis, 26.02.2020, https://www.journal-psychoanalysis.eu/coronavirus-and-philosophers/; last accessed 19.06.2020.
Beck, Ulrich: Risk Society: Towards a New Modernity, London 1992.
Durkheim, Émile: Suicide: A Study in Sociology, London 2002.
Fusco, Gian Giacomo: Normalising Sovereignty: Reflections of Schmitt's Notions of Exception, Decision and Normality, in: Griffith Law Review, 26(1), 2017, pp. 128–146.
Jackson, Robert: Sovereignty: Evolution of an Idea. Cambridge/UK 2007.
Nancy, Jean-Luc: Viral Exception, in: European Journal of Psychoanalysis, 27.02.2020, https://www.journal-psychoanalysis.eu/coronavirus-and-philosophers/; last accessed 19.06.2020.
Schmitt, Carl: Dictatorship: From the Origin of the Modern Concept of Sovereignty to the Proletarian Class Struggle, Cambridge/UK 2014.

Martin Albrow

Has Covid-19 Brought Globalization to an End?*

Covid-19 is a human tragedy. There is no denying that. The latest figures for deaths worldwide from the virus at the time of writing (18/05/20) are 312,646 out of the total of recorded infections of 4,673,809. The repercussions for every sector of life are proving profound. Indeed, some commentators have announced that this is the end of globalization. Well, for a start, I would say that underestimates the impact of Covid-19. It is more than the end of something, it is a beginning, the beginning of a totalization, of which more later. The virus is even more total than global. After all, the global has long been synonymous with the future of human beings on this earth. But the virus looms over the very existence of the human species and all its imaginings of personal life, of empires and existence beyond the planet. The virus penetrates the recesses of individual reality and at the same time shakes the great powers of the world to their foundations. The child is not exempt. ›I want to go out to play with my friends‹ is a complaint repeated in every household, with no exceptions for class or culture. National leaders nervously check the figures of infections in their land and worry about their standing with their own citizens. China and the USA monitor ever more closely the resulting minutest shifts in their uneasy balance of power.

This is really total, when we learn that Chinese eating habits have to change and no longer will all be served from the same pot. The triple kiss on the Dutch cheeks, the Maori nose rubbing, even the cold handshake of the English, all physical contact greetings are forbidden under the ›social distancing‹ rules. Actually ›social distancing‹ is an inappropriate name for keeping physical space between people. What a government is limiting when it prohibits close personal contact should rightly be called ›physical distancing‹. It is demanding increasing space between human bodies. What might more properly be called ›social distancing‹, are those acts that sustain social relations over ever longer distances, currently conquering physical space as never before.

Ever increasing varieties of voice and video conversation and conferencing allow us to contact others over any distance. They are now familiar substitutes for presence in the office or even attendance at family events like weddings.

* All rights reserved. Copyright Martin Albrow 2020.

These relations at a distance are however still social, indeed come much closer to the true sense of the social. The social nature of human beings, celebrated over two millennia ago in Greece by Aristotle and in China by Confucius, now has achieved global recognition for being unlimited by presence or absence. This is true even as the virus emphasizes that also in our natures we are all made of the same physical stuff. The body is rooted to the spot, the social can roam free from such restrictions. We are reaching out to other human beings who could be anywhere in the world in the vivid and renewed recognition that we all belong to a single vulnerable biological species that ultimately has only science between itself and extinction.

This is the world society of the human species as it never has been before. It extends worldwide not simply through the overlapping linkages of neighbouring communities, which has always been a fact of life, but because each one of us has a real or potential link with someone else, no matter how far we are apart. The virus means we sustain our relations with our family and friends even as it forces us to keep our distance from them. By emphasizing absence it is a paradox that the virus illuminates with still greater clarity the nature of human society. Physical contact or proximity is not of its essence, even if it provides the necessary condition for human reproduction, (at least up until *in vitro* fertilization!).

Europeans in particular, with their past experience of incessant movement of people, have long recognised that social relations are not tied to time and place. They have a special history of restlessness, a desire to leave the familiar behind that has been a regular feature of their expansionism and empire building. This is what Michel de Montaigne, French originator of what has come to be known as the essay, observed over 400 years ago: ›I know that the arms of friendship are long enough to reach from one end of the world to the other, and especially this where there is a continual communication of offices.‹ And he goes on further to describe what is summed up in the old English saying ›absence makes the heart grow fonder.‹

Then it appears at first glance more than a little strange that many commentators have remarked that Covid-19 means the end of globalization. What actually they mainly have in mind is an idea of globalization that restricts it largely to the economic sphere, and in particular to free trade between nations. Ever since its foundation in 1843 *The Economist* has championed free trade between nations and has seen globalization in that light since the term became prominent in the 1980s. Hence it's cover title for March 22, ›Goodbye globalisation: The dangerous lure of self-sufficiency‹. But trade between countries is not everything in the world's economy. When the OECD published a special report on globalization in 1993 it emphasized transnational firms, jumping over tariff boundaries. People migrate to find jobs. They take their tastes with them. Culture and communication are even more global than trade.

›Self-sufficiency‹ in fact reinforces globalization. What it means is that a product made elsewhere should be made at home. That secures the spread of the product and methods of production. Montaigne pointed that out too when he said the Chinese had printing and artillery a thousand years before his time, so why the great fuss being made then about having them in Europe. Perhaps we should be talking about the globalization of confusion. *The Financial Times* only two months ago featured an article by Robert Armstrong, »Coronavirus is not a crisis of globalisation«. The *FT* and *The Economist* are two of the most influential publications in the world for business news. When they advance diametrically opposed judgments on the fallout from the virus and its consequences for globalization we can only conclude something is happening that is spooking global opinion leaders.

Staying cool, consider what could be more globalized than the daily figures of the worldwide spread of the virus that Johns Hopkins University publishes and that I have used at the start of this piece? What of the worldwide interest in what happens in a city in the middle of China? Wuhan is now a familiar place worldwide, when previously outside China most people would have been hard pressed to say which country it was in. That of course depends on global communication, as does the general knowledge that the Tokyo Olympics have had to be postponed for a year. The Olympics of course is a prime example of the long roots of globalization, an idea with antecedents in Ancient Greece, celebrated in Athens for the first time in the modern era in 1896, and now a movement that brings sports of all kinds together in one amazing festival every four years. The global becomes local in the Games itself but is already localized worldwide as they focus the efforts of aspiring athletes, players and participants all over the world for years ahead of them.

The currents that carry globalization forward are fundamentally cultural, the spread of ideas and knowledge in particular, especially in and through science and technology. National boundaries can do little to prevent the spread of knowledge and indeed today the quest for a vaccine for the virus is a shared effort across the globe, where the claims to ownership are insignificant compared with the vast fund of shared knowledge that is at the disposal of all medical scientists from every nation.

So what price these announcements of the end of globalization? What their authors have in mind primarily are the interruptions in supply chains as countries are forced to erect barriers to travel and the movement of goods during the Covid-19 crisis. They also are thinking of the accentuation of geo-political tensions as national leaderships come under more pressure from the impact of the virus on their citizens. Strengthening national borders, checking the flows of capital, goods and people certainly impedes the growth of international trade and the movement of people in search of work. Many have equated the rise of a single global market with globalization. Certainly there was a period when the drive towards worldwide freedom of trade, dubbed ›neo-liberalism‹ by its opponents was regarded as the core of globalization with its corresponding limitation on national governments' options to shape their own economic policies.

But that was a notion of globalization promoted by the interests that benefited most from it, above all by the most powerful nation-state. Complete free trade between countries may result in an overall increase in benefits, but they are distributed unevenly and it is the biggest national economy that gains the most. In the nineteenth century it was the British who championed free trade, in the twentieth the United States used to beat the drum for that kind of globalization, now it is more often China. In point of fact economic globalization should not be equated with tariff free trade. When a country imposes duties on imports it may also encourage foreign companies to locate production of those goods in it, thus creating new centres of local employment. What has been globalized is the product, something Coca-Cola understood early in the story of its world-wide expansion. That kind of corporate globalization has in turn prompted another complaint, that tastes are everywhere becoming standardized, or in the words of one critic, that the world has become ›flat‹. But corporate global strategy may adopt a different approach from Coca-Cola. If you go to a McDonalds in Budapest you can buy goulash, or in Beijing Sichuan double chicken burger. Certainly the World Trade Organization managed reduction of tariffs between countries has helped the growth of supply chains that extend across the world. In the case of sophisticated manufactured products the components themselves for the assembled item, for instance a motor vehicle, may come from any number of countries. The measures countries take to lessen the impact of Covid-19 may cause interruptions in those chains, but Toyotas will continue to be sold in the United States and Mercedes in China.

Globalization goes on all the time. What doesn't happen is a reduction in the diversity of life and differences between cultures. What doesn't happen is a march to the same destination. There is no single outcome, but there is the continuing experience of multiple cultures in the same place. Technologies of communication have brought the possibility of knowing what is happening to one's closest and dearest even when they are in another continent. They allow us to talk of events in far off places. One vivid example I used in my *The Global Age* in 1996 was of the ›milk drinking‹ Ganesh, the Indian god, that was seen in Delhi one day, and sightings were reported world-wide the next. *The Guardian* newspaper at the time called it ›the first example of global religious fervour propagated by mass telecommunications‹. The virus emphasizes the nature of social relationships as nothing before has done, even as it highlights the dangers of physical contact with relatives, friends and colleagues working in close proximity. The result has been worldwide transformation of the workplace, in factories, offices, shops, restaurants. In many cases these places of employment have been closed down altogether. Venues for sport and entertainment, stadiums and theatres have become echo chambers rather than echoing to applause. The underlying principles of many institutions have been brought into question. Justice and the law are not exempt.

The principle of trial by jury has for centuries occupied a central place in the English idea of the administration of justice. The standard way this has been put into practice in a criminal case is in a single court room, where a judge presides, faced by the accused person in the dock and lawyers for the prosecution and defence. A jury of 12 persons, chosen randomly from the general population, also sit together facing the accused. Normally members of the public will be admitted to a gallery above the court proceedings. The way the case proceeds in open court has of course made it a favourite dramatic setting for plays and films, though at times the court empties for the parties to consult each other. The culmination of the trial, beloved by the dramatist, celebrated in the classic film *Twelve Angry Men* starring Henry Fonda, is when the jury withdraws to a separate room in complete privacy to consider its collective verdict, often a protracted discussion that can take hours or even days. Covid-19 has caused the suspension of the whole process.

Only now, eight weeks after the lockdown in the UK, are tentative attempts being made to conduct trials that observe ›social distancing‹. Jury members have to sit 2 metres apart. Lawyers and officials argue about how they can be seated when the court room has not been designed for that kind of spacing. The jury room is now too small. Another court room has to be taken over for the jury's private consultations. The old saying ›justice delayed is justice denied‹ is taking on a new virus related meaning. It spans the world even as it penetrates the intimate spaces of personal life. It is total in its pervasiveness and extent, beyond anything the prophets of globalization could have imagined. This is something other than globalization, distinct in its origin and in its penetration, for each individual. Sometimes a person is affected directly, in their body. They die from catching the virus. You can't die from catching globalization. At other times they have to stay one or two metres away from other people. This is not globalization either, though it is the advice of the World Health Organization or their government.

This is pandemic. In its incidence it is helped by globalization in the sense of the ease with which people can travel these days and therefore multiply their contacts. But it also is quite different in its comprehensive impact. It penetrates every aspect of personal and institutional life. If one wants a term that suggests a process, like globalization does, then totalization would have to be more appropriate. What we experience now is the totalizing moment in human history. The past use of ›total‹ in writing about social and political affairs has of course been most prominent in the idea of totalitarianism. This cuts across regular thinking about types of government, because it has no direct relation to democracy. We can have open or total types of democracy in the sense that both depend on the will of the people, but in the total case, at its extreme, every institution and all aspects of personal life are subject to inspection and regulation.

The virus has brought the total moment to global society. To understand this we really have to be clear in our minds what the difference is between global and total. ›Global‹, since its rise in general use ever since the Second World War refers to the shared fate of our species on this earth. ›Total‹ means that every aspect of individual and collective life comes under scrutiny and control. You count, inspect and gather all the individual items together to get the total sum. You provide a cover that can accommodate everything when you go global. The total penetrates whatever there is, the global expands to ensure nothing is left out.

Covid-19 has brought the first *total-global* moment, unprecedented in human experience, so far as we know from recorded history. World wars have been approximations to it, but even they have not had the comprehensive impact that the virus is having on daily life everywhere on earth. It is common to say that nothing will ever be the same again. In this time of shock that may seem obvious. But world wars lasted very much longer than the virus has spread up to now and the world did recover enough to triple its population, double edged of course.

Many of the changes will come from the added impetus to the advance of communication technology precisely because it operates to intensify both the total and the global. Rivalry between states, competition between corporations, individual aspirations for contact and knowledge all add up to a comprehensive digitalization of life. Whether this relentless advance of technology will actually assist or imperil the future of humankind on this earth is a question that remains to be answered after the virus crisis has passed. Our best hope is that we learn lessons from the experience that can be put to good use in averting the worst consequences of climate change. The total may yet help the global.

Richard Münch

With the Corona Pandemic into the Governmentality of the Present?

The corona pandemic is perceived worldwide as an external threat to society. For this reason, precisely those mechanisms are taking effect which were already identified by Georg Simmel in his writing about the dispute.[1] The threat coming from outside enforces more internal cohesion. The interests of the individual take a back seat to the necessity of a common defence against the external threat. From one day to the next, the government, which previously had to watch powerlessly as its potential for citizens' votes dwindled, finds itself in the position of undisputed leadership behind which people gather to obtain protection from the external threat. Thus, governments enjoy previously unimaginable approval and popularity, while the opposition parties have to sit back and watch their approval ratings drop. The omnipresent voter polls regularly confirm this, so that the government and its voters know that they are on the right side. There is a state of emergency, and in this situation, it is easy for the government – even without having to make use of the emergency laws, which were highly controversial when they were introduced in 1968 – to apply the emergency procedure to push through laws with its parliamentary majority, without there being an extensive parliamentary debate. The opposition parties would even appear to be irresponsible troublemakers in such a debate. Constitutional law experts may see this as too far-reaching a restriction of parliamentary rights. But they can only say that with the utmost restraint if they do not want to appear as irresponsible dogmatists. Here the second mechanism identified by Georg Simmel comes to light. In the situation of external threat, critics become an internal danger that must be fought in order to be able to cope with the emergency with the unity that is perceived as necessary. This is the reason why critics and demonstrations against the restriction of civil liberties meet with little approval in the mass media, for which the threat scenario dominates the reporting. If they did not do so, they would very quickly be exposed to the suspicion that they themselves were endangering the health of the population in order to carry out critical reporting.

In a threat situation, there is only black and white. This is also evident in the role of science, in this case virology, in this event. It is forced to leave its own field

[1] Simmel: Soziologie, pp. 284–382.

and enter the field of government policy and form a symbiosis with the government. The usual dispute in science, and even more so the problem that about half of all medical studies cannot be replicated,[2] must be suppressed, because this would spread excessive uncertainty in a situation where safety is the order of the day. And unlike in science, this certainty can only arise in the field of politics by marginalizing doubts about the correctness of theoretical assumptions and empirical results and the measures derived from them. Critics, who must be heard in the field of medicine as a matter of principle, are found in the field of politics in the role of incorrigible grumblers who sacrifice the health of the population to their own image cultivation. As part of the government, virology cannot be conducted like science, but is itself subject to the constraints of politics, which must take decisive action in a situation that is perceived unreservedly as a threat from an external enemy, otherwise it will soon be suspected that it cannot be relied upon. Without the authority of virology, however, determined government action would stand on shaky ground and would run the risk of the mood changing and of the opposition parties, which have so far been marginalized, regaining support and being able to push the government out of office in the next election, because it did everything wrong in the crisis situation.

With the extent of the threat and the mass media images of its horror, the willingness of the citizens to accept extensive restrictions of their constitutionally guaranteed rights of freedom is growing. It is the hour of the government. At the same time, modern techniques of surveillance, as they are practiced in China and South Korea, are becoming a yardstick by which one can now orient oneself more easily than before.[3] There is a complete »tracking« respectively »tracing« of every slightest movement of the individual, in order to keep him/her under control and bring him/her on the right track for him/herself and the common good. The information technology of our time and the collection and analysis of Big Data provide the tools for this program.[4] What has so far appeared within Western civilization as a horror scenario in the sense of Huxley's *Brave New World* and Orwell's *Nineteen Eighty-Four*, acquires a new, undreamt-of legitimacy in the threatening situation.[5] The control of citizens by the government via WhatsApp seems necessary in view of the threatening situation and justified for the protection of the population. And since such threatening situations are no flash in the pan, but can occur again and again, and are best kept under control in such a way that they cannot develop their potential in the first place, the next, seemingly legitimate step is to make citizen control via WhatsApp permanent. China is demonstrat-

---

[2] Ioannidis: Why Most Published Research Findings Are False.
[3] Cf. Creemers: China's Social Credit System; Liang et al.: Constructing a Data-Driven Society.
[4] Cf. O'Neil: Weapons of Math Destruction.
[5] Huxley: Brave New World; Orwell: Nineteen Eighty-Four.

ing that this is possible, and as a leading economic power of the 21st century, it is now coming into play as a further threat, not so much as the nucleus of the global spread of Covid-19, but as an economic competitor whose success makes it a model for the world, including the Western world.

We also see this tendency to give more room to the control of people by caring governments and to restrict the rights of freedom for a higher goal in another threat scenario that arose long before Corona. This is the threat of climate change. There is no shortage of voices from climate experts and environmental politicians who consider this threat to be so serious that, in order to cope with it, the behavior of citizens must also be brought more under control and their freedom rights restricted, and even democracy must be replaced by a benevolent rule of experts.[6] Here, too, it can be observed that science no longer remains in its own field, in which dispute is part of everyday business, but enters into a symbiosis with government action. The *Intergovernmental Panel on Climate Change* (IPCC) is a body of experts from science, industry, governmental and non-governmental organizations under the umbrella of the United Nations that collects scientific findings and prepares them for global governance. Here, too, this processing no longer takes place in the scientific field, but in the political field, where different laws apply than in the scientific field. In this field, the IPCC has become the decisive authority that informs governments worldwide about the status of climate change on the basis of the knowledge it collects. The IPCC's credibility in the political arena depends – again, quite differently from that of science – on the panel speaking with one voice as far as possible. There is a certain compulsion to reach a consensus. No political guidelines for action could be derived from too many contradictions in its report. As a result, critics are not in the role of equal participants in the scientific discourse, but heretics who, due to their marginal position, cannot question the IPCC's credibility. This field structure of climate policy, however, inevitably has an impact on the scientific field, as a homologous power structure develops there, which acts as the scientific foundation of the IPCC. This applies completely independently of whether the truth is indeed on the side of the ruling scientists, both in the case of climate change and the corona pandemic. Either way, in both cases, in the wake of an external threat and in connection with the rise of China as a global model of economic success, a new form of rule emerges, one that sets limits to the rule of law and democracy and the Western civilization of individual freedom that was previously not considered legitimate, if the threat is not left to a one-off event but is instead made permanent.

If we follow Michel Foucault's studies on the history of governmentality, however, this would not be anything new in the West either, but rather the culmination of a creeping development towards a new paternalism in which the govern-

[6] Cf. Stehr: Climate Policy.

ment's concern for the welfare of the population takes precedence over the freedom rights of citizens, because by exercising these freedom rights they are only harming themselves.[7] Governing over a territory with the help of laws passed by parliament and thus democratically legitimized is increasingly overlaid by governing the population by means of scientific expertise, which appears to have no alternative and is thus removed from the democratic decision-making process.[8] This governmentality of the present is manifested in various forms, including science and education.[9] Recently, this also includes the use by governments of psycho-techniques of so-called nudging, which not long ago would have been regarded as a manipulation of the individual that penetrates the subconscious and is incompatible with the rule of law and rights to freedom as well as with democratic decision-making as public deliberation.[10] Tracking respectively tracing and nudging together form the appropriate instruments for a government of the population in unlimited spaces, in which one can in any case no longer rely on the validity of very specific law, because this law is bound by territorial boundaries. In Silicon Valley, psycho-technicians such as J. B. Fogg provide the necessary instruments of behavioral control through computers.[11] The outlines of a »psychological state« thus become visible.[12]

The corona pandemic thus reveals a basic conflict of our present about »old European« democratic versus current expertocratic governance, which points far beyond a one-time event and will occupy us for a long time to come. Giandomenico Majone has long ago stated that the legitimacy of European Union governance does not derive from democratic processes but is based on the knowledge of experts.[13] As we know, Niklas Luhmann liked to use the adjective »old European« to denote theoretical traditions that were no longer up to date, by which he also meant the theory of communicative action and with it the theory of deliberative democracy of his opponent Jürgen Habermas.[14] Accordingly, democracy and the rule of law in our present day would be nothing more than nostalgia, far removed from all reality. With the paradigm of »Law and Economics«, jurisprudence itself has already set out on the path of attaching economic thinking to legal discourse, which can be interpreted as part of the movement away from the rule of

[7] Foucault: Geschichte der Gouvernementalität.
[8] Bröckling/Krasmann/Lemke: Gouvernementalität der Gegenwart; Bröckling: Gute Hirten führen sanft.
[9] Münch: Academic Capitalism; Münch: Governing the School.
[10] See Yeung: ›Hypernudge‹.
[11] Cf. Fogg: Persuasive Technology.
[12] Jones/Pykett/Whitehead: Changing Behaviours.
[13] Majone: The Rise of the Regulatory State in Europe.
[14] Luhmann: Die Gesellschaft der Gesellschaft; Habermas: Theorie des kommunikativen Handelns; cf. Münch: Theorie des Handelns; Theory of Action; Stäheli: Luhmanns »Soziologische Aufklärung«.

law and towards the government of the people.[15] So, are we heading towards the end of »old European« governance? This is the sociological question that goes far beyond the unique phenomenon of a pandemic. In normative terms, the question is whether democracy, freedom rights and the rule of law should be sacrificed for higher purposes. In times of postmodern cultural relativism these are by no means rhetorical questions only.[16]

References

Bröckling, Ulrich / Susanne Krasmann / Thomas Lemke (eds.): Gouvernementalität der Gegenwart. Studien zur Ökonomisierung des Sozialen, Frankfurt am Main 2000.
Bröckling, Ulrich: Gute Hirten führen sanft. Über Menschenregierungskünste, Berlin 2017.
Creemers, Rogier: China's Social Credit System: An Evolving Practice of Control (09.05.2018), in: SSRN 3175792, 2018.
Fogg, Brian Jeffrey: Persuasive Technology: Using Computers to Change What We Think and Do, San Francisco/CA 2003.
Foucault, Michel: Geschichte der Gouvernementalität, 2 Bd., Frankfurt am Main 2006.
Frerichs, Sabine: False Promises? A Sociological Critique of the Behavioural Turn in Law and Economics, in: Journal of Consumer Policy 34(3), 2011, pp. 289–314.
Habermas, Jürgen: Theorie des kommunikativen Handelns, 2 Bd., Frankfurt am Main 1981.
Huxley, Aldous: Brave New World, New York 1932/1998.
Ioannidis, John P. A.: Why Most Published Research Findings Are False, in: PLoS Medicine 2(8), 2005, pp. 696–701.
Jones, Rhys / Jessica Pykett / Mark Whitehead: Changing Behaviours: On the Rise of the Psychological State, Cheltenham 2013.
Liang, Fan / Vishnupriya Das / Nadya Kostyuk / Muzammil M. Hussain: Constructing a Data-Driven Society: China's Social Credit System as a State Surveillance Infrastructure, in: Policy & Internet, 10(4), 2018, pp. 415–453.
Luhmann, Niklas: Die Gesellschaft der Gesellschaft, Frankfurt am Main 1997.
Majone, Giandomenico: The Rise of the Regulatory State in Europe, in: West European Politics, 17(3), 1994, pp. 77–101.

---

[15] Cf. Frerichs: False Promises?
[16] Cf. Münch: Die Kultur der Moderne; The Ethics of Modernity.

Münch, Richard: Academic Capitalism. Universities in the Global Struggle for Excellence, London/New York 2014.
Münch, Richard: Governing the School under Three Decades of Neoliberal Reform: From Educracy to the Education-Industrial Complex, London/New York 2020.
Münch, Richard: Die Kultur der Moderne, 2 Bd., Frankfurt am Main 1986/1993.
Münch, Richard: The Ethics of Modernity, Lanham/MD 2001.
Münch, Richard: Theorie des Handelns, Frankfurt am Main 1982/1988.
Münch, Richard: Theory of Action, London/New York 1988.
O'Neil, Cathy: Weapons of Math Destruction: How Big Data Increases Inequality and Threatens Democracy, New York 2016.
Orwell, George: Nineteen Eighty-Four, London 2012.
Simmel, Georg: Soziologie. Untersuchungen über die Formen der Vergesellschaftung. Frankfurt am Main 1992.
Stäheli, Urs: Luhmanns »Soziologische Aufklärung« – Kritik der Grenze?, in: Dietmar J. Wetzel (ed.): Perspektiven der Aufklärung. Mythos und Realität, Paderborn 2011, pp. 35–42.
Stehr, Nico: Climate Policy: Democracy Is Not an Inconvenience, in: Nature, 525(7570), 2015, pp. 449–450.
Yeung, Karen: ›Hypernudge‹: Big Data as a Mode of Regulation by Design, in: Information, Communication & Society 20(1), 2017, pp. 118–136.

Werner Gephart

Conclusion: »Communal« Dimensions of the Corona Crisis and the Rise of a New Validity Culture

Instead of relating the pandemic to ›metaphysics‹, as Markus Gabriel suggests,[1] most of the presentations viewed it more plainly as ›physics of customs and law‹ as Durkheim had entitled his »Leçons de sociologie: physique des moeurs et du droit«,[2] which could be resumed as ›corona normativities‹. First of all, the community-building effect is in striking proximity to examples of a *Schicksalsgemeinschaft* (community of fate), which is formed by the belief in a common fate borne by all in the face of an external or internal threat. The ›corona community‹ is an imagined community of those risking exposure to infection – many of whom will be viewed as ›lepers‹ as soon as they have been recognized and identified. Whether a community actually »generates, indeed produces« solidarity – as the well-meaning theory of community claims – is an open empirical question. The emergence of a new hot spot in Gütersloh, Germany, in a slaughterhouse has confirmed this: there have even been death threats to seasonal workers, mainly from Eastern Europe, who work under the most unworthy and infection-prone conditions (June 20, 2020). Questions also remain concerning how long solidarity trends will last, and whether we are dealing with an ›occasional community‹, as was observed after September 11, for example, following a hot and effervescent phase of flag waving.[3]

To generate ›community‹, politics – under the advisory authority of virologists and epidemiologists – again uses ›community techniques‹. They privilege dual forms of community, double monads, on the assumption that this reduces the risk of infection. One could call this technique ›dual archaization‹. The notoriously rumored herd immunity is also a ›communal‹ collective structure, a structural feature of the collective, the realization of which – as is common in the community of war and fate – requires individual victims. Following this logic, foreignness (*Fremdheit*) is defined as the *other*, who is in fact a potential vector. The *other* is not to be trusted. One must keep a distance from him/her, unmelodramatically, of course: a purely physical distance! This is why religious communities react so

---

[1] Cf. in this volume Gabriel: We Need a Metaphysical Pandemic.
[2] Cf. Durkheim: Leçons de sociologie.
[3] Cf. Gephart: On Law and Religion, esp. chapter IX: The Holy Community and the Flag.

sensitively when third parties, i. e. ›secular‹ people, mistrust ›fraternity‹ and thus deny the possibility of a ›universal brotherhood‹ as we learned with Benjamin Nelson.[4] At the same time, epidemiological logic promises that the exclusion of the *other* is precisely the including requirement for brotherly solidarity becoming a universal ›community of survival‹. Popular education has had to overcome this moral hiatus during the times of corona!

While on the one hand social ›cells‹ are being created that are neutral to infection (as long as they, in their monadic existence, stay in Hyde Park, along the Champs Élysées, or in the English Garden and do not interact with the outside world in any way), rules about distancing are subjected to social control. The forces of law and order are therefore called upon and authorized to question two people who are closer than the prescribed physical distance of 150 centimeters, ask them where they live, and, in turn, identify them as cohabitants who are legitimately following the social distancing rules. (This is just one example of how deeply the ›corona regime‹ had intervened in the most private corners of everyday life and may come back with a new shutdown even after deconfinement). Jan Suntrup's contribution is of interest in this respect.[5] The rules of a physical minimum distance thus have nothing to do with the Nietzschean ›pathos of distance‹,[6] ironically formulated by Suntrup as ›tact‹,[7] which according to Georg Simmel makes the virtues of the metropolitan city dweller, as an ideal type of modernist inhabitant, possible in the first place – no longer ›apartness‹ and ›capriciousness‹, ›anonymity‹ and ›blasé attitudes‹,[8] but protection against infection through the realism of social distancing and mask wearing against the Marxian metaphoric of the ›character mask‹.[9] In the emerging ›masked society‹, social interaction is reduced to eye contact, and physical touch is principally excluded and incriminated. Even speaking to one another becomes suspect at the thought of spreading droplets. Illocutionary binding effects, as imagined by speech act theory, are therefore impossible! An eerie silence thus hovered over our societies – a silence known to us only from sacred places and times and their derivatives, such as museums. But it wasn't long before this eerie silence was eclipsed by the recurring noise of the city and the outbreak of violence, not only in Minneapolis (May 2020),[10] but also in Stuttgart (June 2020).[11]

---

[4] Cf. Nelson: The Idea of Usury. For an interpretation of Nelson's concept in connection with the corona crisis, see in this volume Genovesi: »Support Your Local«.

[5] Cf. in this volume Suntrup: Corona.

[6] Cf. Nietzsche: Jenseits von Gut und Böse.

[7] Cf. in this volume Suntrup: Corona. In this context, see also in this volume Bojanić/Bojanić: The »Vocabulary« of Distance.

[8] Cf. Gephart: Georg Simmels Bild der Moderne.

[9] Cf. Marx: Das Kapital.

[10] In the wake of George Floyd's murder by a police officer on May 25, 2020, mass protests broke out worldwide (Black Lives Matter Movement) against racism and structural violence. Cf., e. g., Johnson: The George Floyd Uprising Has Brought Us Hope.

[11] Criminologist Christian Pfeiffer explicitly traces this connection in his interpretation of the

Conclusion

The global social experiment of lockdown according to the battle cry of old socialism? The idea that »all wheels stand still if your mighty arm wills it«[12] cannot be overlooked, especially in regard to social and sociological consequences.[13] What trauma are we inflicting on our grandkids when it becomes clear to them that if they want grandma and grandpa to live, they can no longer go to the sandbox or play with friends? How will we better control domestic (and mostly male) violence, which has exploded in a frightening way under the guise of lockdown, not only in Tunisia as Amel Grami impressively describes?[14] What type of damage does ›isolation torture‹ have on truly lonely people when they are denied minimal social contact? Isolation torture was a critical view of the ›contact ban‹ that led to Stammheim! It was given to ideological ringleaders and lawbreakers as the most severe punishment. This ›surveillance‹[15] is the universal ›punishment‹ of the purely coincidental contemporaneity of the corona crisis.

The reduction to communal forms of life, from the digital communication community to simpler structures; the reduction of economies to bartering in small corner shops; the systematic outsourcing of education from schools and universities to the family; the movement of gainful employment with a company into the ›home‹, whereby the modernization dynamics of separating ›household‹ from ›business‹ have been abandoned; the submission of a document to a state employee who is now sitting in his bedroom where he's placed his computer; the subjugation to ›conviviality‹ in private circles (the house party, the shared apartment, the mocked work gathering); the suspension of community rituals found in sports (the ›wave‹ in the stadium's south curve); the structuring of one's free time; the inevitable end to the aimless stroll through the city's streets – all of this shows us what makes a modern society, and why we maybe really are ›social beings‹ beyond institutions and formal relationships. Social beings who are in a web of countless interaction processes that must systematically intersect following the logic of ›corona socialization‹. George Simmel described this excellently in his *große Soziologie*:

---

events that were officially linked to a »party scene«! Quoted from Grimm: Kriminologe Pfeiffer: Krawalle sind Folge von Corona-Beschränkungen.

12 »Alle Räder stehen still, wenn dein starker Arm es will« (it's a line from the traditional ›hymn‹ of the German Workers' Association and a slogan of the German labour movement; transl. by the author).

13 For an interesting interpretation of the economic dimension, cf. in this volume Cattelan: Sacred Euro.

14 Cf. in this volume Grami: Trapped.

15 Corona apps, corona identity cards, etc. open a whole spectrum for surveillance mechanisms that may be regarded as legitimate the more the risk affection is internalized. Remember how the artist Ai Wei Wei protested against those surveillance techniques, especially in China, in a nearly prophetic way!

»Apart from phenomena that are visible from afar and impose their size and external importance everywhere, there is an unmeasurable number of smaller forms of relationships and types of interaction between people, which can be marginal in individual cases. However, the breadth of this in individual cases cannot be estimated at all, and, as they shift between the comprehensive, so to speak official, social formations, they bring about society as we know it.«[16]

It remains to be seen whether Peter Weibel[17] is right in saying that the crisis first reveals the true face of a new sociation (*Vergesellschaftung*) as distant society (*Ferngesellschaft*), or begins a nostalgic search for places of proximate community (*Gemeinschaft*) based on ›nation‹, ›family‹, or ›neighborhood‹ (actually meaning the search for the lost community of place, blood, and spirit as Tönnies called it); it is still unknown whether we are not tragically reminded of the secret pleasures of modernity as ways of life, such as the importance of fashion, the neurasthenic *Reiselust*, the diversity of life forms, and lifestyles and adventure. There is nothing natural about corona normativity. Instead, it seems to be the institutionalization of the naturalistic fallacy (*naturalistischer Fehlschluss*), which the philosophical critique of mingling should and has denounced for centuries. Richard Münch, in line with Foucault's analysis of governmentality, has brought to light the type of an »expertocratic governance« that rules the production of corona normativity![18] And it is not just a flu, as Tiziana Andina rightly remarks in her philosophical reflection![19]

The pace of the ›corona institution‹ stands in sharp contrast to the deceleration and eerie stillness of its life forms, which appear as the face of death, as Valérie Hayaert[20] and Alexandre Vanautgarden[21] analyzed. Insofar, I think it is more than appropriate for Jan Suntrup to begin his article by saying that »[t]he corona crisis reveals the ambivalence of the human condition in the 21st century.«[22] Where does the individual stand in this multilayered ›realm of normativity‹ that derives its deontic power from the force of *Gemeinschaft*?

---

[16] »Es bestehen außer jenen weithin sichtbaren, ihrem Umfang und ihrer äußeren Wichtigkeit allenthalben aufdrängenden Erscheinungen eine unermeßliche Zahl von kleineren, in den einzelnen Fällen geringfügig erscheinenden Beziehungsformen und Wechselwirkungsarten zwischen den Menschen, die aber von diesen einzelnen Fällen in gar nicht abzuschätzender Masse dargeboten werden, und, indem sie sich zwischen die umfassenden, sozusagen offiziellen sozialen Formungen schieben, doch erst die Gesellschaft, wie wir sie kennen, zustandebringen«, in: Simmel: Soziologie, pp. 14 f.; transl. by the author.
[17] Cf. Weibel: Virus, Viralität, Virtualität.
[18] Cf. in this volume Münch: With the Corona Pandemic into the Governamentality of the Present?, cit. p. 506.
[19] Cf. in this volume Andina: »It's Just a Flu«.
[20] Cf. in this volume Hayaert: Shallow Graves and Empty Tombs.
[21] Cf. in this volume Vanautgaerden: The Return of the Corpses.
[22] Cf. in this volume Suntrup: Corona, cit. p. 137.

Is there a conclusion to be drawn at this very moment? Certainly not about the situation's further development and its consequences for societal evolution under the threat of competing dynamics of climate change and increased digitalization. But some trends in the realm of normativity have become visible: first, a specific type of validity culture related to discourses of emergency that have been known to legal theorists for some time, and second, the difficult withdrawal of normative restrictions to re-install ›normality‹.

I. The Rise of a New Type of Pandemic Validity Culture

The validity culture of the ›state of emergency‹, that is of the ›corona emergency‹, is determined by the unlimited power to suspend the *entire* existing normative order and align it with the extraordinariness of a war, plague, or natural disaster. Symbols and rituals of validity, as well as the organizational validity of the commissioners, censors, and norm-bound agents of the state of emergency, are fixed on this one basis for validity, which superimposes traditional narratives of validity. Statistics define the normative scope. And – as belief in the constitution needs a kind of patriotism (*Verfassungspatriotismus*) – the current German Minister of Health, Jens Spahn, coined the term *Corona-Patriotismus*![23] As Marta Bucholc has convincingly shown,[24] the question remains why the ›corona code‹ has been followed in such an impressive way, creating an unusual state of conformity that might, however, embrace a different national habitus to obey the law.[25] In this realm of normativity, the main binary distinction is between health and disease – to be transformed in political decision, in the clear awareness that the mere pursuit of the law and its procedures would even be detrimental to health (such as the rules of presence in the traditions of parliamentary law, etc.), as Alexander F. Filippov rightly observes.[26]

The ideal-type of a ›pandemic validity culture‹ looks as sketched below. It allows, by the way, the transcendence of differences of legal cultures insofar as it produces a legitimate normative order by referencing the pandemic. In doing so, it is not claimed that a ›validity culture by procedure‹ became obsolete, or that the distinction between secular or sacred validity cultures lost their importance. But this type of creating a specific sphere of normativity has its own logic:

---

[23] Cf. Spahn: Interview by Südwest Presse.
[24] Cf. in this volume Bucholc: The Corona Crisis as a Test of National Habitus.
[25] … and the whole range of corona normativities until the very moment that divergent opinions became swiftly and uniformly legitimate again: from types of civil disobedience to the disobedience of a federal system that does not want to follow the leadership of a chancellor in all respects!
[26] Cf. in this volume Filippov: States, Bodies and Corona-Crisis.

Belief in Validity	Symbolic Validity	Normative Validity	Organizational Validity	Ritual Dynamics
Pathos of the ›exception‹ Pathos of the epidemiological argument	Symbolic power of the ›exception‹ against the banality of the ›normal‹	Power to suspend normative orders as legal, extra-juridical decision-making power	Institutions as decisions Quarantine, detention, fencing	Ritualistic vitalism of ›real‹ life Singing »Ode to Joy«
Scientism-based belief in validity »Corona-Patriotism«	Foundational statistics In the name of the pandemic	Illusion of a normative form Observance of rules as a health guarantee	Passing on normative state orders to private individuals or business as corona etiquette	Mask magic and ritual belief

Fig. 1: The ideal-type of a ›pandemic validity culture‹.

II. The Difficult Withdrawal from the Protective Regime of Exception

According to different strategies – reduced here to the avoidance of infection at any cost, be that through the logic of herd immunity, social distancing, mask wearing, or contact tracing – the re-entry into some kind of normal social life has followed different temporalities. In Germany, a sharp discrepancy between the opening of kindergartens on the one hand and the continued ban on gathering at universities on the other (and coupled with differences state to state), for example, elicits the impression that a giant normative pluralism exists, if not a patchwork in a tradition of legal culture that is so proud of its systematization and rationality![27] In Germany, the Green Party has taken over as a guardian of continental

---

[27] As a praise of this type of legal culture, see esp. Max Weber's so called ›sociology of law‹; cf. Weber: Wirtschaft und Gesellschaft. Recht; see also my interpretation in: Gephart: Law, Culture and Society.

legal traditions! Instead of a much expected unitarian, if not totalitarian, system, we are faced with exceptions from the exceptions of normalizing the normal, a kind of ›non-bindingness‹ that is contingency. It is the destiny of expertise-related normativites that claim that scientific justification is under the threat of opposing opinions, according to the logic of the sphere of science. But politics strive for collectively binding decisions, as Talcott Parsons rightly asserted, and do not withstand too much, a feature Niklas Luhmann identified as ›contingency‹. The more the formerly strict rules vanish, the less likely it is that a belief in their justification might be transferred to other phases of normative change. The orchestration of a normatively defined and guaranteed lockdown – combined with the smooth and variable reopening for spaces of liberty under the threat of the almighty value of statistics about infection rates – may leave citizens in a state of pure, if not poor, ›anomie‹, as Émile Durkheim called this dangerous state of societies[28] and the corresponding mental attitude, sensitive to the rise of anomic[29] suicide rates!

Insofar, we should have predicted the very moment when this unanimous, tacit consensus about obedience to the rules crumbled, when protestations and manifestations arose in plaints against corona-related restrictions. However, it is remarkable that this complex realm of corona normativities does not care at all about those concerns, with serious consequences for the likelihood of compliance with normativities in general. This fact manifests the greater deontic power of the state to impose changing rule-regimes, if necessary, against the will of the norm addressees with the help of an enforcement staff, which ultimately forces compliance with physical violence.

Crises ultimately have a tremendous effect on a society's *mode of differentiating* social systems, or social ›spheres‹ as I prefer to say. While one can speak of an ›implosion‹ of spheres during the financial crisis, metaphorically described as a ›deluge‹,[30] an enormous mixing and blending of politics, economics, law, and culture is taking place as if the epidemiological idea of ›contamination‹ has also torn down the boundaries of spheres. This interpretation must remain open for discussion: Clemens Albrecht[31] instead observes the shift to the sphere of science as the center of gravity! If we link the theory of social differentiation to one of its major sources in the history of ideas, namely to the theory of checks and balances (*Gewaltenteilung*), we might be more sensitive to the fact that de-differentiation might also affect the spheres of freedom!

The collection of the contributions in this volume, kindly offered by friends and supporters of the Käte Hamburger Center »Law as Culture«, began with a med-

---

[28] Cf. Durkheim: De la division du travail social.
[29] Cf. Durkheim: Le suicide.
[30] Cf. Gephart: Implosion von Wirtschaft, Politik und Religion.
[31] Cf. in this volume Albrecht: Viral Coupling. His observation of dominance is right, but does not exclude that the whole arrangement of sphere relations has become more porous!

ical contribution by Mariacarla Gadebusch-Bondio and Maria Marloth[32] for good reason: As cultural scientists, we ask ourselves, along with Richard Münch,[33] Alexander Filippov,[34] and Gregor Albers,[35] about the risks of freedom we take when we engage in a state of emergency as a form of legitimation of a »governmental« tendency in the sense of Michel Foucault. The fact that this does not have to degenerate into dictatorial delusion – but is precisely due to responsible ethical action (*Verantwortungsethik*) – may reassure the nervous observer. The inner-juridical discourse offers a wide range of consequential problems of positive law in all areas. Francesca Caroccia is convincing in identifying a ›cultural lag‹ in civil law compared to public law.[36] What interests legal analysis as cultural research – the internationalist and constitutional legal theorist Matthias Herdegen[37] is a wonderful example for this orientation – is the *Kulturbedeutung* of such a paradigm shift, which can only be contained by the fact that the voices for a free and constitutional normative order continue to assert themselves, without closing themselves off to the culture of the natural sciences and their respective discourses.

This collection cannot be anything more than a snapshot of a process in motion, where anxiety for our beloved reigns over our capacities to mock masks, contingent quantifications of physical distancing rules, and unintentional humor. The world is not only a »normative laboratory« as Angela Condello rightly calls it,[38] but also a laboratory about the sometimes lost insights into the social character of human beings, as numerous contributions have demonstrated. We remain irritated by the globality of the experience and its different local expressions at the same time, as nearly each essay proclaimed, from Tunis to Tokyo and London to Moscow, New York, Delhi, and Buenos Aires. But against all fallacies of misplaced naturalism, we observe how the social sphere and nature interferes, and the phantasma of a total mastering of nature as wilderness has come to an end. Further research is needed to compare systematically different regimes of the pandemic validity culture, the belief in the redemption of the world by way of rule obedience,[39] and balanced models for substantive social justice in times of pandemic crisis. There is still much to be explored in the uncanny realm of normativity!

---

[32] Cf. in this volume Gadebusch-Bondio / Marloth: Clinical Trials in Pandemic Settings.
[33] Cf. in this volume Münch: With the Corona Pandemic into the Governmentality of the Present?
[34] Cf. in this volume Filippov: States, Bodies and Corona-Crisis.
[35] Cf. in this volume Albers: Personal Sacrifices for Public Health?
[36] Cf. in this volume Caroccia: Searching for a Vaccine.
[37] Cf. in this volume Herdegen: The Corona Crisis.
[38] Cf. in this volume Condello: Immersed in a Normative Laboratory.
[39] In this sense, Francesca Caroccia sees »the rule itself as the condition for the survival of humanity«, in: Caroccia: Searching for a Vaccine, cit. p. 149, in this volume.

References

Durkheim, Émile: De la division du travail social, Paris 1893.
Durkheim, Émile: Leçons de sociologie: physique des moeurs et du droit, Paris 1950.
Durkheim, Émile: Le suicide, Paris 1897.
Gephart, Werner: Georg Simmels Bild der Moderne, in: Berliner Journal für Soziologie, Heft 2, 1993, pp. 183–192.
Gephart, Werner: Implosion von Wirtschaft, Politik und Religion. Krisenanalysen, in: Georg Pfleiderer / Alexander Heit (eds.): Sphärendynamik II. Religion in postsäkularen Gesellschaften, Baden-Baden 2012, pp. 75–101.
Gephart, Werner: Law, Culture and Society. Max Weber's Comparative Cultural Sociology of Law, Frankfurt am Main 2015.
Gephart, Werner: On Law and Religion: Durkheimian Theoretical Perspectives and Some Applications, Frankfurt am Main 2021 (forthcoming).
Grimm, Christian: Kriminologe Pfeiffer: Krawalle sind Folge von Corona-Beschränkungen, 22.06.2020, https://www.augsburger-allgemeine.de/politik/Kriminologe-Pfeiffer-Krawalle-sind-Folge-von-Corona-Beschraenkungen-id57597786.html; last accessed 25.06.2020.
Johnson, Derrick: The George Floyd Uprising Has Brought Us Hope. Now We Must Turn Protest to Policy, 30.06.2020, https://www.theguardian.com/commentisfree/2020/jun/30/black-lives-matter-protests-voting-policy-change; last accessed 01.07.2020.
Marx, Karl: Das Kapital. Kritik der politischen Ökonomie, Hamburg [1867] 2017.
Nelson, Benjamin: The Idea of Usury: From Tribal Brotherhood to Universal Otherhood, Chicago 1969.
Nietzsche, Friedrich: Jenseits von Gut und Böse: Vorspiel einer Philosophie der Zukunft, Stuttgart [1886] 1998.
Simmel, Georg: Soziologie. Untersuchungen über die Formen der Vergesellschaftung, Frankfurt am Main [1908] 1992.
Spahn, Jens: Interview by Südwest Presse, 22.06.2020, https://www.bundesgesundheitsministerium.de/presse/interviews/interviews/swp-220620.html; last accessed 23.06.2020.
Weber, Max: Wirtschaft und Gesellschaft. Recht (Max Weber-Gesamtausgabe: Volume I/22-3; edited by Werner Gephart / Siegried Hermes), Tübingen 2010.
Weibel, Peter: Virus, Viralität, Virtualität. Wie gerade die erste Ferngesellschaft der Menschheitsgeschichte entsteht, 20.03.2020, https://zkm.de/de/virus-viralitaet-virtualitaet; last accessed 01.06.2020.

About the Authors

Yousra Abourabi, Asst. Prof. Dr., is a political scientist. She is currently an assistant professor of Political Science and International Relations at SciencesPo Rabat – International University (Morocco). Furthermore, as a research associate at the Laboratoire d'Etudes Politiques et de Sciences Humaines et Sociales (LEPOSHS) at SciencesPo Rabat, she conducts research on African governance in the areas of climate change, gender, and migration. She is a visiting professor at SciencesPo Grenoble as well as a member of the Political Affairs cluster of the African Union's Economic, Social, and Cultural Council (ECOSOCC) and of the Global Campus on Human Rights' Academic Board. She was a Fellow at the Käte Hamburger Center »Law as Culture« from May to July 2020.

Gianmaria Ajani, Prof. Dr., is a legal scholar. He is Professor of Comparative Law at the University of Turin (Italy). He has done consulting work for national and international organizations, including public relations projects with the Chinese Ministry of Commerce on topics concerning private and commercial law legal reform. He has published extensively in both national and international journals on questions of codification, the transition from state to market economies, and law and language. He is co-editor (together with Tiziana Andina and Werner Gephart) of the journals *Brill Research Perspectives in Art and Law* and *Contratto e impresa/Europa*. He was awarded an honorary doctorate from the University of Savoie Mont Blanc. Moreover, he is an honorary professor at Shanghai Normal University and Zhonghan University of Economics and Law, Wuhan. He was a Fellow at the Käte Hamburger Center for Advanced Study in the Humanities »Law as Culture« from October 2019 to March 2020.

Gregor Albers, Dr., is a jurist and legal historian. He is a senior research assistant and lecturer at the University of Bonn's Institute of Roman Law and Comparative Legal History. His work focusses on contract law and its historical, comparative, and theoretical foundations. He is co-editor of *Wortgebunden. Zur Verbindlichkeit von Versprechen in Recht und Literatur* in the series »Law as Culture« (ed. by Werner Gephart, forthcoming).

Clemens Albrecht, Prof. Dr., has served as Chair of Cultural Sociology at the University of Bonn's Institute of Political Science and Sociology since April 2016. He has also served as a co-director of the Käte Hamburger Center for Advanced Study in the Humanities »Law as Culture« since October 2015. From 2005 to 2011,

Clemens Albrecht was the spokesperson for the section ›Kultursoziologie‹ of the German Sociological Association (DFG), and from 2011 to 2012, he was a member of the expert panel »How do we want to live together?«, which was part of the Federal Chancellor's »Future Dialogue« initiative. Furthermore, he is the director and editor-in-chief of *Sociologia Internationalis*.

Martin Albrow, Prof. Dr., is an eminent – and one of the first – globalization theorists and one of the most renowned English-language experts on Max Weber's writings. Since 1988 he has held many guest professorships and fellowships in Europe and the United States, including at the London School of Economics, the University of Munich, the State University of New York, and the Woodrow Wilson International Center for Scholars in Washington, D.C. Martin Albrow was a Fellow at the Käte Hamburger Center for Advanced Study in the Humanities »Law as Culture« from October 2012 to September 2013. Furthermore, he has been a Senior Fellow and a member of the Center's Scientific Advisory Board.

Tiziana Andina, Prof. Dr., is a philosopher. She is Professor of Philosophy at the University of Turin (Italy), where she is also Director of the Research Center LabOnt – Center for Ontology. She has published extensively on social ontology, the philosophy of art, cultural studies, and political philosophy. She is the co-editor (together with Gianmaria Ajani and Werner Gephart) of the journal *Brill Research Perspectives in Art and Law* and the editor of *Rivista di estetica*. Her recent publications include *Bridging the Analytical Continental Divide. A Companion to Contemporary Western Philosophy*, *Post-Truth. Philosophy and Law*, and *Institutions in Actions. The Nature and Rule of the Institutions in the Real World*. She was a Fellow at the Käte Hamburger Center for Advanced Study in the Humanities »Law as Culture« from March to September 2015.

Beatriz Barreiro Carril, Assoc. Prof. Dr., is a legal scholar and Associate Professor of International Law and International Relations at Rey Juan Carlos University (Madrid). She was a visiting researcher at the Max Planck Institute for Social Anthropology (Halle, Germany), the Institute for International and European Law at the University of Göttingen, the Centre for Ethics at the University of Toronto, and the Centre of Socio-Legal Studies at Oxford University. Furthermore, she is an observer of the UNESCO Committee for Cultural Diversity and a member of the Observatory for Diversity and Cultural Rights at the University of Fribourg. She was a Fellow at the Käte Hamburger Center for Advanced Study in the Humanities »Law as Culture« from June to August 2020.

Upendra Baxi, Prof. em. Dr. h.c. mult., is one of the most renowned contemporary Indian legal scholars. His academic career has led him to universities in Delhi,

Durham (Duke University), Sydney, Surat, New York, Toronto, and Warwick. He was a Fellow at the Käte Hamburger Center for Advanced Study in the Humanities »Law as Culture« from April to November 2011 and from July to December 2012.

Olivier Beaud, Prof. Dr., is a legal scholar. He is Professor of Constitutional Law at the University Panthéon-Assas (Paris II). From 2001 to 2006, he was Deputy Director of the Centre Marc Bloch in Berlin, and from 2007 to 2019, he served as Director of the Michel Villey Institute for Legal Culture and Philosophy of Law. In 2014 he was awarded the Reimar Lüst-Preis by the Alexander von Humboldt Foundation, and in 2019 he received the Prix du livre juridique for his book *La République injuriée*. He was a Fellow at the Käte Hamburger Center for Advanced Study in the Humanities »Law as Culture« from March to April 2020.

Petar Bojanić, Prof. Dr., is Director of the Centre for Ethics, Law and Applied Philosophy (CELAP) in Belgrade. Since 2010, he has also served as Director of the Institute for Philosophy and Social Theory (IFDT). Moreover, he has acted as Director of the Center for Advanced Studies – South East Europe (CAS SEE) at the University of Rijeka (Croatia) since its founding in 2013. He has held numerous fellowships and visiting professorships, including at the Society for Humanities at Cornell University (USA), the Centre for Modern Thought at the University of Aberdeen (Great Britain), the Institute of Advanced Studies at the University of Bologna (Italy), and the Essen Institute for Advanced Study in the Humanities (Germany). Following research stays at the Käte Hamburger Center for Advanced Study in the Humanities »Law as Culture« from June to September 2014 and from April to July 2016, he was once again a Fellow from August to November 2017.

Sanja Bojanić, Asst. Prof. Dr., is Executive Director of the Center for Advanced Studies for Southeast Europe (CAS SEE) at the University of Rijeka (Croatia). Her studies led her to interdisciplinary research based on experimental artistic practices, queer studies, and the particularities of affect theory. She worked, inter alia, at the Institut National d'Histoire de l'Art (Louvre, Paris), the Nouvel Observateur (Paris), and the Laboratory for Evaluation and Development of Digital Editing at the Maison des Sciences de l'Homme (Paris Nord, St. Denis). Following initial research stays from April to July 2016 and August to November 2017, she was once again a Fellow at the Käte Hamburger Center for Advanced Study in the Humanities »Law as Culture« from October to November 2019.

Anne-Marie Bonnet, Prof. Dr., is Professor of Medieval and Modern Art History at the University of Bonn's Department of Art History. Since 1999 she has also played an active role in various commissions, executive boards, and foundations, including the Kunstverein Bonn since 2005 and the Federal Commission on the Acquisition of Contemporary Art for the Art Collection of Germany from 2007 to 2011. She likewise served as a member on the advisory board for the jubilee exhibition *450 Jahre Kunstsammlungen Dresden* from 2009 to 2010. She was a Fellow at the Käte Hamburger Center for Advanced Study in the Humanities »Law as Culture« from October 2018 to March 2019.

Pierre Brunet, Prof. Dr., is a legal scholar. He is Professor at the University of Paris I (Panthéon Sorbonne), where he also previously served as Director of the LL.M. de droit français et droit európen and the Double LL.M. Sorbonne-Queen Mary programs. He is a co-editor and member of several editorial boards for French and foreign journals, such as *Droit et Société* (LGDJ). Moreover, he was a visiting professor at universities in Brazil, Italy, Japan, the United States, and Argentina. He was a Fellow at the Käte Hamburger Center for Advanced Study in the Humanities »Law as Culture« from May to September 2020.

Marta Bucholc, Prof. Dr., is a sociologist, legal scholar, and philosopher. She works at the Faculty of Sociology at the University of Warsaw. Until 2020 she was a research professor at the Käte Hamburger Center for Advanced Study in the Humanities »Law as Culture«. Her research focuses on historical sociology, the history of social theory, the sociology of law, the sociology of economy, and the sociology of knowledge. Her recent journal publications include *Law and Liberal Pedagogy in a Post-Socialist Society: The Case of Poland*, *Schengen and the Rosary. Catholic Religions and the Postcolonial Syndrome in Polish National Habitus*, and *Die PiS, das Virus und die Macht. Wahlen in Zeiten der Pandemie*.

Francesca Caroccia, Prof. Dr., is a legal scholar. She is Professor of Private Law at the University of L'Aquila (Italy) and coordinates the Conference of the Italian Rectors' Commission on Gender Questions. She has published extensively on questions of legal interpretation, contract, and tort, notably from the perspective of the intersection between private autonomy and judicial power. Among her main publications are *Ordine pubblico. La gestione dei conflitti culturali nel diritto privato*, *L'interpretazione del contratto*, *Il paradigma della condizione e le dinamiche negoziali*, and *Rethinking the Juridical System. Systematic Approach, Systemic Approach and Interpretation of Law*. She was a Fellow at the Käte Hamburger Center for Advanced Study in the Humanities »Law as Culture« from July to December 2013 and from May to September 2016.

Valentino Cattelan, Dr., works on the intersection of law, money, and culture by comparing Western capitalism and Islamic finance. He is the editor of *Islamic Social Finance: Entrepreneurship, Cooperation and the Sharing Economy* and *Islamic*

Finance in Europe: Towards a Plural Financial System. Valentino Cattelan is also the author of *Religion and Contract Law in Islam: From Medieval Trade to Global Finance* (in progress). He was a Fellow at the Käte Hamburger Center for Advanced Study in the Humanities »Law as Culture« from April to September 2018.

Jacques Commaille, Prof. Dr. Dr. h.c., is a sociologist. He is Professor emeritus at the École Normale Supérieure de Paris-Saclay and a senior researcher at the Institut des Sciences Sociales du Politique (ENS Paris-Saclay/Université Paris Nanterre/CNRS). His work is rooted in the political sociology of law as a contribution to a general theory of the social and political regulation of contemporary societies. His recent publications include *À quoi nous sert le droit?*, *After Legal Consciousness Studies: Transatlantic Dialogues* (ed. with Stephanie Lacour) and *Les métamorphoses de la régulation politique* (ed. with Bruno Jobert). He is a former member of the Center's Scientific Advisory Board.

Angela Condello, Ass. Prof. Dr. iur., PhD, is a legal scholar and philosopher. She is Assistant Professor of Legal Philosophy at the University of Messina (Italy) and Adjunct Professor at the University of Turin (Italy), where she holds a Jean Monnet module on human rights and critical legal thinking within European legal culture. She has published three monographs, including *Money, Social and Law* (with J.R. Searle and M. Ferraris), edited various journal issues (*Law and Literature, Law Text Culture, Rivista di Estetica, International Journal for the Semiotics of Law*), and both contributed to and edited numerous volumes (*Sensing the Nation's Law: Historical Inquiries into the Aesthetics of Democratic Legitimacy, Post-Truth, Philosophy and Law, Law, Labour and the Humanities. Contemporary European Perspectives, New Rhetorics for Contemporary Legal Discourse*). She was a Fellow at the Käte Hamburger Center for Advanced Study in the Humanities »Law as Culture« from January to December 2014.

Laurent de Sutter, Prof. Dr., is a legal scholar and legal theorist. He is Professor of Legal Theory at Vrije Universiteit Brussel, and the managing editor of the series *Perspectives Critiques* and *Theory Redux*. He is also a member of the editorial boards for *Décalages: An Althusser Studies Journal* and *Law & Literature*, and a member of the scientific council of the Collège International de Philosophie (Paris). He has authored numerous books, most recently *Poétique de la Police* in the series »Law as Culture« (ed. by Werner Gephart), *Postcritique*, and *Nach dem Gesetz*. He was a Fellow at the Käte Hamburger Center for Advanced Study in the Humanities »Law as Culture« from October 2014 to September 2015.

Thomas Dreier, Prof. Dr. iur., is a legal scholar. He is Professor of Private Law and Legal Issues of the Information Society at the Karlsruhe Institute of Technology

(KIT) and was awarded an honorary professorship and membership with the Faculty of Law at the University of Freiburg (Germany). He was a Fellow at the Käte Hamburger Center for Advanced Study in the Humanities »Law as Culture« from October 2014 to September 2015. Since October 2015, Thomas Dreier has been a Senior Fellow at the Center. He is the editor of *Concise European Copyright Law* and *Bild und Recht – Studien zur Regelung des Visuellen*.

Maurizio Ferraris, Prof. Dr. Dr. h. c., is a philosopher. He is Professor of Philosophy at the University of Turin (Italy), where he is also President of the LabOnt – Center for Ontology. He is Directeur de Recherche at the Collège d'Études Mondiales (Paris) and President of the editorial committee of *Rivista di Estetica*. He has worked in the fields of aesthetics, hermeneutics, and social ontology, attaching his name to the theory of documentality and contemporary new realism. He was a Fellow at the Käte Hamburger Center for Advanced Study in the Humanities »Law as Culture« from June 2013 to July 2014, and since September 2017 he has been member of the Center's Scientific Advisory Board. He is the author of *Manifest des Neuen Realismus* in the series »Law as Culture« (ed. by Werner Gephart).

Alexander F. Filippov, Prof. Dr. Sc., is a philosopher and sociologist. He is a tenured professor at the National Research University – Higher School of Economics (HSE) in Moscow. For several years, he chaired the HSE's Practical Philosophy division and now supervises a teaching and research group with the same title. Alexander F. Filippov is particularly interested in basic problems of social knowledge. He heads the Centre of Fundamental Sociology at the HSE and is the editor-in-chief of the *Russian Sociological Review*. Moreover, he has edited and translated into Russian a number of classical works in sociology and political philosophy. His own theoretical works include *Sociology of Space* and *Elements of Sociology: An Introduction to the History of the Discipline*.

Markus Gabriel, Prof. Dr., holds the Chair of Epistemology, Modern, and Contemporary Philosophy at the University of Bonn. He is Director of the International Center for Philosophy for the state of North Rhine-Westphalia, and of the Center for Science and Thought. He has come to be known as the founder of new realism through his works on *Why the World Does Not Exist*, *I Am Not Brain*, and *The Meaning of Thought*. His forthcoming book is entitled *Moral Progress in Dark Times*. He was Assistant Director of the Käte Hamburger Center for Advanced Study in the Humanities »Law as Culture« from April 2012 to September 2013.

Mariacarla Gadebusch-Bondio, Prof. Dr. phil. Dr. rer. med. habil., has headed the Institute of Medical Humanities at the University Hospital of Bonn since 2017. She is currently a guest professor at the University of Uppsala's Department of History of Science and Ideas, sponsored by awards from the Alexander von Humboldt Foundation and the Stiftelsen Riksbankens Jubileumsfond (29th Swedish Prize Award 2020). Her main research interests lie in the following areas: intersections between medicine and philosophy, norms and deviance in medical discourses, medical fallibility, ethical dimensions of predictive knowledge in medicine, patient narratives, and ethics and cancer.

Sergio Genovesi, M. A., has been a research associate at the Käte Hamburger Center for Advanced Study in the Humanities »Law as Culture« since 2019. His main research focuses include contemporary ontology, epistemology, aesthetics, and the ethics of technology. He has an international research profile and is now working on a dissertation that concerns the philosophy of events.

Werner Gephart, Prof. Dr. jur. Dr. h. c., is a legal scholar, sociologist, and artist. He is Founding Director of the Käte Hamburger Center for Advanced Study in the Humanities »Law as Culture« and has held numerous visiting professorships around the world. In 2019 he was appointed as President of the Jury Senior of the Institut Universitaire de France (IUF). He is the publisher of the series »Law as Culture« and co-editor of the volume *Recht*, which was part of the *Max Weber Gesamtausgabe (MWG I/22-3)*. His publications are centered on the cultural analysis of law, the sociology of religion, and aesthetics. He is co-editor of the international journal *Brill Research Perspectives in Art and Law* (together with Tiziana Andina and Gianmaria Ajani). In 2014, he was awarded an honorary doctorate in Philosophy by the University of Turin. Since 1988 he has held numerous exhibits in cities including Paris, Düsseldorf, Cologne, Bonn, St. Louis, Houston, Bloomington, Minneapolis, Tunis, New Delhi, and London.

Peter Goodrich, Prof. Dr., is a lawyer and cultural scientist. He was Founding Dean of Birkbeck College's Department of Law and is currently Professor and Director of the Program in Law and Humanities at Cardozo School of Law, New York. He is also a visiting professor of Law at New York University, Abu Dhabi. He is one of the leading representatives of the law and literature movement, as well as the founder and co-editor of *Law and Critique*. He has written numerous books in legal history and theory, law and literature, and semiotics. Among his recent publications are *Schreber's Law: Jurisprudence and Judgment in Transition* and *Imago Decidendi: On the Common Law of Images*. Goodrich is a member of the Center's Scientific Advisory Board.

Dieter Gosewinkel, Prof. Dr., is a historian and lawyer. He is Professor of History at the Freie Universität Berlin, Director of the Center for Global Constitutionalism at the Social Science Research Center Berlin (WZB), and a member of Academia

Europaea. His main fields of research are European constitutional history, history of citizenship, and civil society. Some of his major publications include *Die Verfassungen in Europa 1789–1949. Eine wissenschaftliche Textedition* (together with Johannes Masing) and *Schutz und Freiheit? Staatsbürgerschaft in Europa im 20. und 21. Jahrhundert*. Following his first fellowship from January to July 2016, he was a Fellow at the Käte Hamburger Center for Advanced Study in the Humanities »Law as Culture« again from October 2016 to February 2017.

Amel Grami, Prof. Dr., is Professor of Gender Studies at the University of Manouba (Tunisia), where she also coordinates a master's program in Gender, Culture, and Society. She was previously a member of the National Human Rights Council of Tunisia. Her research interests cover gender studies, cultural studies, religious studies, violent extremism, and women's writing. Among her most recent publications are *Introduction: Academia in Transformation – Testing the Paradigms of New Knowledge* and *Women and Terrorism: A Gender Perspective*. She was a Fellow at the Käte Hamburger Center for Advanced Study in the Humanities »Law as Culture« from May to August 2014.

Cécile Guérin-Bargues, Prof. Dr., is a legal scholar. She is Professor of Constitutional Law at the University Panthéon-Assas (Paris II). She was recognized with numerous awards for her doctorate in law, including the Prix de thèse 2008 of the National Assembly, of the Centre français de droit comparé, and of the University Panthéon-Assas (Paris II). She is a member of the editorial board for *Jus Politicum* and an elected member of the Standing Committee of the Conseil National de l'Enseignement Supérieur et de la Recherche (CNESER). Most recently, she published *L'Etat d'urgence. Etude constitutionnelle, historique et critique* (with Olivier Beaud).

Theresa Hanske, M. A., is a researcher at the Käte Hamburger Center for Advanced Study in the Humanities »Law as Culture«. She is a trained Vietnamese linguist and currently working on her dissertation on alterity in German conduct books between 1750 and 1850.

Valérie Hayaert, Dr., is a classicist, historian, and humanist researcher of the early modern European tradition. Her particular interest lies in images of justice, judicial rites, and symbolism and its role in contemporary courthouses. She received the EUI Alumni Prize for the best interdisciplinary thesis in 2006. Her first book, ›*Mens emblematica‹ et humanisme juridique*, was published in 2008. Her subsequent work looked at the aesthetics of justice in courthouses of the early modern period through today. Valérie Hayaert has taught in Cyprus, Tunisia, England, and France and held various positions and fellowships. She was a Fellow at the Käte

Hamburger Center for Advanced Study in the Humanities »Law as Culture« from April 2018 to March 2019. She is currently a research associate at the Institut des Hautes Études sur la Justice, Paris.

Matthias Herdegen, Dr. jur. utr. DDr. h. c., is Chair of Public Law and Director of the Institute for International Law at the University of Bonn. He was a visiting professor, inter alia, at New York University's Global Law School, the University of Paris I, Pontifical Javeriana University, and the University of St. Gallen. He was a member of the Parliamentary Commission on the Deployment of the Armed Forces. His recent publications include *Der Kampf um die Weltordung, The International Law of Biotechnology, Internationales Wirtschaftsrecht*, and *Völkerrecht*. He was a Fellow at the Käte Hamburger Center for Advanced Study in the Humanities »Law as Culture« from October 2012 to April 2013, October 2013 to March 2014, and October 2017 to March 2018.

Matthias Lehmann, Prof. Dr., is Chair of Civil Law, Private International Law, and International Business Law at the University of Bonn, where he is also Director of the Institute of Private International and Comparative Law. He has been awarded doctoral degrees both from the University of Jena and Columbia University. Matthias Lehmann is particularly interested in international and comparative aspects of banking and financial law. He is regularly a visiting professor at Sorbonne Université, the Université de Fribourg, and the Universidad Pablo de Olavide (Spain). He has been a visiting fellow at the London School of Economics and Political Science and a visiting academic at Oxford University. Furthermore, he was a Fellow at the Käte Hamburger Center »Law as Culture« from October 2018 to March 2019 as well as from October 2019 to March 2020.

Jure Leko, M. A., is a researcher at the Käte Hamburger Center for Advanced Study in the Humanities »Law as Culture«. Focused on the fields of cultural anthropology and sociology, his work pursues questions of cultural theory, examining comparative and legal anthropology, as well as political sociology, in the process. He is now working on his dissertation which concerns human rights and the legal struggles for recognition of Romani migrants. Furthermore, he is co-editor of the volume *Law and the Arts. Elective Affinities and Relationships of Tension* (with Werner Gephart).

Helga María Lell, Dr., is a legal philosopher. She is a researcher at CONICET (National Council of Scientific and Technological Research) as well as Research Postgrad Coordinator at the Economic and Legal Sciences Faculty of the National University of La Pampa (Argentina). She has published on questions of semantics in the legal field, citizenship, legal hermeneutics, and political institutions – all from philosophical, sociological, and historical perspectives. She was a Fellow at the Käte Hamburger Center for Advanced Study in the Humanities »Law as Culture« from April to June 2019.

Maria Marloth, Dr. med. M.Phil., is a research assistant and physician at the University of Cologne's Department of Psychiatry and Psychotherapy. After studying philosophy and human medicine at the Ludwig Maximilian University of Munich, the Technical University of Munich, and the University of Tor Vergata (Rome), she worked as a research assistant at the Technical University of Munich's Institute for History and Ethics of Medicine, where she obtained her doctorate degree in 2018.

Richard Münch, Prof. em. Dr., is a sociologist and a former member of the Center's Scientific Advisory Board. He is Professor emeritus of Sociology at the University of Bamberg. His primary research fields are sociological theory, in particular the work of Talcott Parsons, historical-comparative sociology, and contemporary sociological diagnosis. In 2018 Münch was awarded a prize for an outstanding scientific life's work by the German Sociological Association (DGS).

Caroline Okumdi Muoghalu, Dr., is a sociologist at the Department of Sociology and Anthropology at Obafemi Awolowo University (Nigeria). She was a Fellow at the Käte Hamburger Center »Law as Culture« from November to December 2018.

Masahiro Noguchi, Prof. Dr., is a political theorist and a professor at the Faculty of Law at Seikei University (Japan). He has published on Max Weber, Weber's reception in Japan, and the political theory of bureaucracy. His publications include *Kampf und Kultur: Max Webers Theorie der Politik aus der Sicht seiner Kultursoziologie* and *Makkusu Weba. Kindai to Kakutoshita Shisoka [Max Weber. A Sketcher of European Modernity]*. He received the Philipp Franz von Siebold Prize in 2019 for his contribution to Japanese-German cultural exchange. He was a Fellow at the Käte Hamburger Center for Advanced Study in the Humanities »Law as Culture« from April 2013 to March 2014.

Greta Olson, Prof. Dr., is a member of the Center's Scientific Advisory Board and Professor of English and American Literary and Cultural Studies at the University of Giessen. She works in the areas of cultural and narrative approaches to law, critical American studies, media, and feminism and sexuality studies. Her recent publications include *Beyond Gender: Futures of Feminist and Sexuality Studies – An Advanced Introduction* (co-edited), *How to Do Things with Narrative: Cognitive and Diachronic Perspectives* (with Jan Alber), and *The Politics of Form* (with Sarah Copland). The monograph that she began as a Fellow at the Käte Hamburger

Center for Advanced Study in the Humanities »Law as Culture«, *From Law and Literature to Legality and Affect*, will appear shortly.

Frode Helmich Pedersen, Dr., is Associate Professor of Nordic Literature at the University of Bergen's Department of Linguistic, Literary, and Aesthetic Studies. Frode Pedersen has served for many years as a literary critic with *Bergens Tidende* and *Morgenbladet*. He is a member of the Holberg Debate Advisory Group and a permanent member of the Kritisk kvartett literary criticism forum at Litteraturhuset in Bergen. He leads the research project »A Narratology of Criminal Cases«, funded by the Norwegian Research Council. He is a co-editor of *Narratives in the Criminal Process* (with Werner Gephart, forthcoming).

Grischka Petri, PD Dr. Dr., holds two doctoral degrees in Art History and Law, respectively, and has trained as a lawyer (German Bar Exam, 2005). Until 2020 he taught Art History at the University of Bonn, where he completed his habilitation in 2017. He is an honorary research fellow at the University of Glasgow. He is the author of *Künstlerethos – Kapital – Kontrolle. Eine Kunstgeschichte des Urheberrechts*, which will appear in the series »Law as Culture« (ed. by Werner Gephart). He was a Fellow at the Käte Hamburger Center for Advanced Study in the Humanities »Law as Culture« from April to October 2020.

Martin Przybilski, Prof. Dr., is a cultural and literary historian and holds a professorship for Medieval German Literature at Trier University, where he has also acted as Director of the Historical-Cultural Research Centre and as Vice President of teaching and student affairs. He specializes in the fields of Jewish-Christian relations in the Middle Ages and the Early Modern Period, as well as the cultural history of the body, spatial theory, and polemics as a means of cultural contact and demarcation. He was a Fellow at the Käte Hamburger Center for Advanced Study in the Humanities »Law as Culture« from October 2019 to March 2020.

Hamadi Redissi is a political scientist and President of the Observatoire Tunisien de la Transition Démocratique (OTTD). He is a founding member of the Centre Arabe de Recherches et d'Analyses Politiques et Sociales. He was a Fellow at the Käte Hamburger Center for Advanced Study in the Humanities »Law as Culture« from October to December 2010.

Raja Sakrani, Dr. jur., is a jurist and a cultural science scholar. Since 2010 she has been a scientific coordinator at the Käte Hamburger Center for Advanced Study »Law as Culture«. Currently, her research focuses on the reciprocal presence of Islamic traditions in Europe, enlarging the view of how the ›other‹ is treated in a complicated normative situation. She was the co-director of the international and interdisciplinary research project »Convivencia« with the Max Planck Institute for European Legal History in Frankfurt (2015–2018). She has conducted research and taught at the Universities of Paris (Sorbonne), Bonn, Basel, and Madrid.

Joachim J. Savelsberg, Prof. Dr., is a sociologist and a socio-legal scholar. He is Professor of Sociology and Law at the University of Minnesota, where he holds the Arsham and Charlotte Ohanessian Chairmanship. His recent work links human rights and collective violence issues with the sociology of knowledge and collective memory. His publications include *Representing Mass Violence: Conflicting Responses to Human Rights Violations in Darfur*, *American Memories: Atrocities and the Law* (with Ryan D. King), and *Knowing about Genocide: Armenian Suffering and Epistemic Struggles* (forthcoming). Joachim Savelsberg was a visiting professor in Graz, Berlin, and Munich in addition to completing fellowships at the Rockefeller Bellagio Center, the Johns Hopkins University, Harvard University's Center for European Studies, and various institutes for advanced study. From August 2013 to August 2014, he was also a Fellow at the Käte Hamburger Center for Advanced Study in the Humanities »Law as Culture«.

Martin Schermaier, Prof. Dr. iur., is a jurist and a legal historian. He is Professor at the University of Bonn's Institute for Roman Law and Comparative Legal History, a member of the state of North Rhine-Westphalia's Academy for Science and Art, and a principal investigator at the University of Bonn's Cluster of Excellence »Beyond Slavery and Freedom«. His main fields of interest are Roman law, medieval legal history, and modern private law. His recent publications include *Contemporary Use of Roman Rules. Prescription and Limitation in the Usus Modernus Pandectarum* and *Interpretatio triplex? Germanisten und Romanisten vor Savigny*. He is an affiliate researcher with the Käte Hamburger Center for Advanced Study in the Humanities »Law as Culture«. He was a Fellow at the Center from October 2011 to March 2012.

Theresa Strombach, M. A., works as a researcher at the University of Bonn's Department of German Linguistics. Her main research interests include linguistic cases of doubt, especially concerning case agreement, as well as morphosyntactic features of legal language. In her master thesis entitled *Ohne wenn und aber*, she examined both the usage and comprehensibility of (un-)introduced adverbial clauses in German legal texts. She was an assistant at the Käte Hamburger Center for Advanced Study in the Humanities »Law as Culture« from April 2016 to March 2020.

Jan Christoph Suntrup, PD Dr., is a visiting professor of Culture Theory at the University of the Bundeswehr, Munich. He was a visiting fellow at the École de droit de SciencesPo Paris and at the London School of Economics and Political Science (European Institute). Most recently, he published his habilitation *Umkämpftes Recht. Zur mehrdimensionalen Analyse rechtskultureller Konflikte durch die politische Kulturforschung* in the series »Law as Culture« (ed. by Werner Gephart). He worked as a researcher, research coordinator, and Fellow at the Käte Hamburger Center for Advanced Study in the Humanities »Law as Culture« from 2010 to March 2020.

Enrico Terrone, Assoc. Prof. Dr., is Juan de la Cierva Postdoctoral Fellow at the University of Barcelona's LOGOS Research Group. His main area of research is philosophy of film. He has published papers in international journals such as *British Journal of Aesthetics*, *Journal of Aesthetics and Art Criticism*, *Erkenntnis*, and *Ergo*. He was a Fellow at the Käte Hamburger Center for Advanced Study in the Humanities »Law as Culture« from October 2014 to January 2015.

Alexandre Vanautgaerden, Dr., is a historian and an art historian. He served as Director of the Erasmus House in Brussels from 1994 to 2012, as Director of the Geneva Library from 2012 to 2018, and as Editorial and Scientific Director of Exhibitions at the Musée Granet in Aix-en-Provence from 2018 to 2019. Alexandre Vanautgaerden is a specialist in the history of books, Erasmus, and new media. He has collaborated with numerous artists and has organized several exhibitions. His recent publications include *Fabienne Verdier, Sur les terres de Cézanne*, *Les labyrinthes de l'esprit. Renaissance libraries and collections in Renaissance*, and *L'intime du droit à la Renaissance*. He was a Fellow at the Käte Hamburger Center for Advanced Study in the Humanities »Law as Culture« from September 2019 to August 2020.

Diana Villegas, Dr., is a research fellow and lecturer (Maître de conférences) in Civil and Criminal Law at the University Panthéon-Assas (Paris II). Her thesis *Mafia Legal Order* (*L'ordre juridique mafieux*) uses legal pluralism theory to explain the social order of the Colombian mafia. In 2017 her work received the Choucri Cardahi Award from the Académie des sciences morales et politiques. She will be a Fellow at the Käte Hamburger Center for Advanced Study in the Humanities »Law as Culture« from May to October 2021.

Sam Whimster, Prof. Dr., is the Deputy Director of the Global Policy Institute (London) and editor of *Max Weber Studies*. Most recently, he edited *The Oxford Handbook of Max Weber* (with Edith Hanke and Lawrence Scaff). Besides Max Weber, his research interests lie in historical and comparative sociology, social theory, methods of empirical social research, and the sociology of the City of London. Sam Whimster was a Fellow at the Käte Hamburger Center for Advanced Study in the Humanities »Law as Culture« from October 2011 to January 2013.

Other Volumes in the Series of the
Käte Hamburger Center for Advanced Studies
in the Humanities »Law as Culture«
(edited by Werner Gephart)

Volume 00:
Gephart, Werner: Recht als Kultur. Für eine geisteswissenschaftliche Erforschung von Recht im Globalisierungsprozess, Klostermann, Frankfurt am Main 2010.

Volume 01:
Gephart, Werner (Ed.): Rechtsanalyse als Kulturforschung, Klostermann, Frankfurt am Main 2012.

Volume 02:
Jakobs, Günther: System der strafrechtlichen Zurechnung, Klostermann, Frankfurt am Main 2012.

Volume 03:
Zaczyk, Rainer: Selbstsein und Recht, Klostermann, Frankfurt am Main 2014.

Volume 04:
Gephart, Werner / Brokoff, Jürgen / Schütte, Andrea / Suntrup, Jan Christoph (Eds.): Tribunale. Literarische Darstellung und juridische Aufarbeitung von Kriegsverbrechen im globalen Kontext, Klostermann, Frankfurt am Main 2014.

Volume 05:
Albrow, Martin: Global Age Essays on Social and Cultural Change, Klostermann, Frankfurt am Main 2014.

Volume 06:
Ferraris, Maurizio: Manifest des Neuen Realismus, Klostermann, Frankfurt am Main 2014.

Volume 07:
Gephart, Werner: Law, Culture, and Society. Max Weber's Comparative Cultural Sociology of Law, Klostermann, Frankfurt am Main 2015.

Volume 08:
Bucholc, Marta: A Global Community of Self-Defense. Norbert Elias on Normativity, Culture and Involvement, Klostermann, Frankfurt am Main 2015.

Volume 09:
Gephart, Werner / Suntrup, Jan Christoph (Eds.): Rechtsanalyse als Kulturforschung II, Klostermann, Frankfurt am Main 2015.

Volume 10:
Gephart, Werner / Sakrani, Raja / Hellmann, Jenny (Eds.): Rechtskulturen im Übergang – Legal Cultures in Transition. Von Südafrika bis Spanien, vom Nachkriegsdeutschland zum Aufbruch der arabischen Welt, Klostermann, Frankfurt am Main 2015.

Volume 11:
Waldhoff, Christian (Ed.): Recht und Konfession – Konfessionalität im Recht?, Klostermann, Frankfurt am Main 2016.

Volume 12:
Gephart, Werner / Schermaier, Martin (Eds.): Rezeption und Rechtskulturwandel. Europäische Rechtstraditionen in Ostasien und Russland, Klostermann, Frankfurt am Main 2016.

Volume 13:
González Garcia, José: The Eyes of Justice. Blindfolds and Farsightedness, Vision and Blindness in the Aesthetics of Law, Klostermann, Frankfurt am Main 2017.

Volume 14:
Herdegen, Matthias: The Dynamics of International Law in a Globalised World. Cosmopolitan Values, Constructive Consent and Diversity of Legal Cultures, Klostermann, Frankfurt am Main 2016.

Volume 15:
Gephart, Werner / Suntrup, Jan Christoph (Eds.): The Normative Structure of Human Civilization. Readings in John Searle's Social Ontology, Klostermann, Frankfurt am Main 2017.

Volume 16:
Savelsberg, Joachim J.: Repräsentationen von Massengewalt – Strafrechtliche,

humanitäre, diplomatische und journalistische Perspektiven auf den Darfurkonflikt, Klostermann, Frankfurt am Main 2017.

Volume 17:
de Sutter, Laurent: Poétique de la police, Klostermann, Frankfurt am Main 2017.

Volume 18:
Gephart, Werner / Leko, Jure (Eds.): Law and the Arts. Elective Affinities and Relationships of Tension, Klostermann, Frankfurt am Main 2017.

Volume 19:
Gephart, Werner / Witte, Daniel (Eds.): Recht als Kultur? Beiträge zu Max Webers Soziologie des Rechts, Klostermann, Frankfurt am Main 2017.

Volume 20:
Gephart, Werner / Witte, Daniel (Eds.): The Sacred and the Law. The Durkheimian Legacy, Klostermann, Frankfurt am Main 2017.

Volume 21:
Gephart, Werner: Some Colours of the Law. Images and Interpretations, Klostermann, Frankfurt am Main 2017.

Volume 22:
Suntrup, Jan Christoph: Umkämpftes Recht. Zur mehrdimensionalen Analyse rechtskultureller Konflikte durch die politische Kulturforschung, Klostermann, Frankfurt am Main 2018.